Computer Architecture

Springer
Berlin
Heidelberg
New York
Barcelona
Hong Kong
London
Milan
Paris
Singapore
Tokyo

Silvia M. Mueller · Wolfgang J. Paul

Computer Architecture

Complexity and Correctness

With 214 Figures and 185 Tables

 Springer

Silvia Melitta Mueller
IBM Lab Böblingen – Dept. 3173
Schönaicherstr. 220
71032 Böblingen, Germany
E-mail: SMM@de.ibm.com

Wolfgang J. Paul
Fachbereich Informatik
Universität des Saarlandes
Im Stadtwald, Gebäude 45
66123 Saarbrücken, Germany
E-mail: wjp@cs.uni-sb.de

Cover picture by Jantje Janßen, Karlsruhe

Library of Congress Cataloging-in-Publication Data applied for

Die Deutsche Bibliothek – CIP-Einheitsaufnahme
Müller, Silvia Melitta:
Computer architecture: complexity and correctness; with 185 tables/
Silvia M. Müller; Wolfgang J. Paul. – Berlin; Heidelberg; New York;
Barcelona; Hong Kong; London; Milan; Paris; Singapore; Tokyo:
Springer, 2000
  ISBN 3-540-67481-0

ACM Subject Classification (1998): B, C

ISBN 3-540-67481-0 Springer-Verlag Berlin Heidelberg New York

Springer-Verlag is a company in the BertelsmannSpringer publishing group.
© Springer-Verlag Berlin Heidelberg 2000
Printed in Germany

Typesetting: Camera-ready by the authors
Design: design + production GmbH, Heidelberg
Printed on acid-free paper   SPIN 10769135   06/3142SR – 5 4 3 2 1 0

Preface

IN THIS BOOK we develop at the gate level the complete design of a pipelined RISC processor with delayed branch, forwarding, hardware interlock, precise maskable nested interrupts, caches, and a fully IEEE-compliant floating point unit. The design is completely modular. This permits us to give rigorous correctness proofs for almost every part of the design. Also, because we can compute gate counts and gate delays, we can formally analyze the cost effectiveness of all parts of the design.

Acknowledgments

This book owes much to the work of the following students and postdocs: P. Dell, G. Even, N. Gerteis, C. Jacobi, D. Knuth, D. Kroening, H. Leister, P.-M. Seidel.

March 2000
Silvia M. Mueller
Wolfgang J. Paul

Contents

Chapter

1

Introduction

Overview of the Content

In this book we develop at the gate level the complete design of a pipelined RISC processor with delayed branch, forwarding, hardware interlock, precise maskable nested interrupts, caches, and a fully IEEE-compliant floating point unit.

The educated reader should immediately ask "So what? Such designs obviously existed in industry several years back. What is the point of spreading out all kinds of details?"

The point is: the complete design presented here is *modular* and *clean*. It is certainly clean enough to be presented and explained to students. This opens the way to covering the following topics, both in this text and in the class room.

- To begin with the obvious: we determine cost and and cycle times of designs. Whenever a new technique is introduced, we can evaluate its effects *and side effects* on the cycle count, the hardware cost, and the cycle time of the whole machine. We can study tradeoffs between these very real complexity measures.

- As the design is modular, we can give for each module a clean and precise specification, of what the module is supposed to do.

- Following the design for a module, we give a complete explanation as to why the design meets the specification. By far the fastest way to give such an explanation is by a rigorous mathematical correctness proof.[1]

- From known modules, whose behavior is well defined, we hierarchically construct new modules, and we show that the new complicated modules constructed in this way meet their specifications by referring only to the specifications of the old modules and to the construction of the new modules. We follow this route up to the construction of entire machines, where we show that the hardware of the machines interprets the instruction set and that interrupts are serviced in a precise way.

Because at all stages of the design we use modules with well defined behavior, the process of putting them all together is in this text completely precise.

How to Use This Text
We see three ways to use this book:

- Again, we begin with the obvious: one can try to learn the material by reading the book alone. Because the book is completely self contained this works. A basic understanding of programming, knowledge of high school math, and some familiarity with proofs by induction suffices to understand and verify (or falsify!) each and every statement in this book.

- The material of this book can be covered in university classes during two semesters. For a class in "computer structures" followed by "computer architecture 1" the material is somewhat heavy. But our experience is, that students of the classes "computer architecture 1 and 2" deal well with the entire material. Many advanced topics like superscalar processors, out-of-order execution, paging, and parallel processing, that are not covered in this book, can be treated very well in a seminar parallel to the class "computer architecture 2". Students who have worked through the first part of this book usually present and discuss advanced material in seminars with remarkable maturity.

  Sections 2.1 to 2.5, chapter 7 and chapter 8 present a self-contained construction of the data paths of an IEEE-compliant floating point unit. This material can be covered during one semester in a class on computer arithmetic.

---

[1]Whether mathematical correctness proofs are to be trusted is a sore issue which we will address shortly.

- The book can be used as supplementary reading in more traditional architecture classes or as a reference for professionals.

To Believe or Not to Believe in Proofs

Computer architects tend not to like proofs. It is almost as if computer architects do not believe in mathematics. Even mathematical formulae are conspicuously rare in most textbooks on computer architecture, in contrast to most other engineering disciplines. The reason for this is simple:

- Correctness proofs are incredibly error prone. When it comes to the verification of computer systems, it is very difficult to tell a correct proof from a proof, which is almost but not quite correct. The proofs in this book are no exception.

- Shipping hardware which is believed to be correct and which turns out to be faulty later can cost a computer manufacturer a GREAT deal of money.

Thus, do we expect our readers to buy the correctness of all designs presented here based solely on the written proofs? Would we – the authors – be willing to gamble our fortune on the correctness of the designs? The only sane answer is: no. On the contrary, in spite of our best efforts and our considerable experience we consider it quite likely, that one or more proofs in the second half of the book will receive a nontrivial fix over the next two years or so.

Keeping the above stated limitations of written correctness proofs firmly in mind, we see nevertheless three very strong points *in favor* of using mathematics in a text book about computer architecture.

- The main foremost reason is speed. If one invests in the development of appropriate mathematical formalism, then one can express one's thoughts much more clearly and succinctly than without formalism. This in turn permits one to progress more rapidly.

  Think of the famous formula stating, that the square of the sum of a first number and a second number equals the sum of the square of the first number, two times the product of the first number with the second number, and the square of the second number. The line

  $$(a+b)^2 = a^2 + 2ab + b^2$$

  says the very same, but it is much easier to understand. Learning the formalism of algebra is an investment one makes in high school and which costs time. It pays off, if the time saved during calculations with the formalism exceeds the time spent learning the formalism.

In this book we use mathematical formalism in exactly this way. It is the very reason why we can cover so much material so quickly.

- We have already stated it above: at the very least the reader can take the correctness proofs in this book as a highly structured and formalized explanation as to why the authors think the designs work.

- But this is not all. Over the last years much effort has been invested in the development of computer systems which allow the formulation of theorems and proofs in such a precise way, that proofs can actually be verified by the computer. By now proofs like the ones in this book can be entered into computer-aided proof systems with almost reasonable effort.

  Indeed, at the time of this writing (February 2000) the correctness of a machine closely related to the machine from chapter 4 (with a slightly different more general forwarding mechanism) has been verified using the system PVS [CRSS94, KPM00]. This also includes the verification of all designs from chapter 2 used in chapter 4. Verification of more parts of the book including the floating point unit of chapter 8 is under way and progressing smoothly (so far).

Key Concepts

There are three key concepts, which permit us to develop the material of this book very quickly and at the same time in a completely precise way.

1. We distinguish rigorously between numbers and their representation. The simple formalism for this is summarized in chapter 2. This will immediately help to reduce the correctness proofs of many auxiliary circuits to easy exercises. More importantly, this formalism maintains order – and the sanity of the reader – in the construction of floating point units which happen to manipulate numbers in 7 different formats.[2]

2. The details of pipelining are very tricky. As a tool to better understanding them, we introduce in chapter 4 *prepared* sequential machines. This are machines which have the data path of a pipelined machine but which are operated sequentially. They are very easy to understand.

   Pipelined machines have to simulate prepared sequential machines in a fairly straightforward formal sense. In this way we can at least

---

[2]packed single and double precision, unpacked single and double precision, binary numbers, two's complement numbers, and biased integers

easily formulate what pipelined machines are *supposed* to do. Showing that they indeed do what they are supposed to do will occasionally involve some short but subtle arguments about the scheduling of instructions in pipelines.

3. In chapter 7 we describe the algebra of rounding from [EP97]. This permits us to formulate very concise assertions about the behavior of floating point circuits. It will allow us to develop the schematics of the floating point unit in a completely structured way.

Highlights

We conclude the introduction by highlighting some results from the chapters of this book. In chapter 2 we develop many auxiliary circuits for later use: various counters, shifters, decoders, adders including carry lookahead adders, and multipliers with Booth recoding. To a large extent we will specify the control of machines by finite state diagrams. We describe a simple translation of such state diagrams into hardware.

In chapter 3 we specify a sequential DLX machine much in the spirit of [PH94] and prove that it works. The proof is mainly bookkeeping. We have to go through the exercise because later we establish the correctness of pipelined machines by showing that they simulate sequential machines whose correctness is already established.

In section 4 we deal with pipelining, delayed branch, result forwarding, and hardware interlock. We show that the delayed branch mechanism can be replaced by a mechanism we call "delayed PC" and which delays *all* instruction fetches, not just branches.[3] We partition machines into data paths, control automaton, forwarding engine, and stall engine. Pipelined machines are obtained from the prepared machines mentioned above by an almost straightforward transformation.

Chapter 5 deals with a subject that is considered tricky and which has not been treated much in the literature: interrupts. Even formally specifying what an interrupt mechanism should do turns out to be not so easy. The reason is, that an interrupt is a kind of procedure call; procedure calls in turn are a high level language concept at an abstraction level way above the level of hardware specifications.

Achieving preciseness turns out to be not so bad. After all preciseness is trivial for sequential machines, and we generate pipelined machines by transformation of prepared sequential machines. But the interplay of interrupt hardware and forwarding circuits is nontrivial, in particular when it comes to the forwarding of special purpose registers like, e.g., the register, which contains the masks of the interrupts.

---

[3] We are much more comfortable with the proof since it has been verified in PVS.

Chapter 6 deals with caches. In particular we specify a bus protocol by which data are exchanged between CPU, caches, and main memory, and we specify automata, which (hopefully) realize the protocol. We explain the automata, but we do *not* prove that the automata realize the protocol. Model checking [HQR98] is much better suited to verify a statement of that nature.

Chapter 7 contains no designs at all. Only the IEEE floating point standard is rephrased in mathematical language and theorems about rounding are proven. The whole chapter is theory. It is an investment into chapter 8 where we design an entire fully IEEE-compatible floating point units with denormals, and exceptions, dual precision adder, multiplier, iterative division, format conversion, rounding. All this on only 120 pages.

In chapter 9 we integrate the pipelined floating point unit into the DLX machine. As one would expect, the control becomes more complicated, both because instructions have variable latency and because the iterative division is not fully pipelined. We invest much effort into a very comfortable forwarding mechanism. In particular, this mechanism will permit the rounding mode of floating point operations to be forwarded. This, in turn, permits interval arithmetic to be realized while maintaining pipelined operation of the machine.

Chapter 2

Basics

2.1 Hardware Model

STUDYING COMPUTER architecture without counting the cost of hardware and the length of critical paths is great fun. It is like going shopping without looking at price tags at all. In this book, we specify and analyze hardware in the model from [MP95]. This is a model at the gate level which gives at least rough price tags.

2.1.1 Components

In the model there are five types of basic components, namely: gates, flipflops, tristate drivers, RAMs and ROMs. Cost and delay of the basic components are listed in table 2.1. They are normalized relative to the cost and delay of a 1-bit inverter. For the basic components we use the symbols from figure 2.1.

Clock enable signals ce of flipflops and registers, output enable signals oe of tristate drivers and write signals w of RAMs are always active high. RAMs have separate data input and data output ports. All flipflops are assumed to be clocked in each cycle; thus there is no need to draw clock inputs.

A RAM with A addresses and d-bit data has cost

$$C_{ram}(A, d) = C_{RAMcell} \cdot (A + 3) \cdot (d + \log\log d)$$

BASICS

Table 2.1 Cost [g] (gate equivalents) and delay [d] of the basic components

	cost	delay			cost	delay
not	1	1		flipflop	8	4
nand, nor	2	1		3-state driver	5	2
and, or	2	1		RAM cell	2	–
xor, xnor	4	2		ROM cell	0.25	–
mux	3	2				

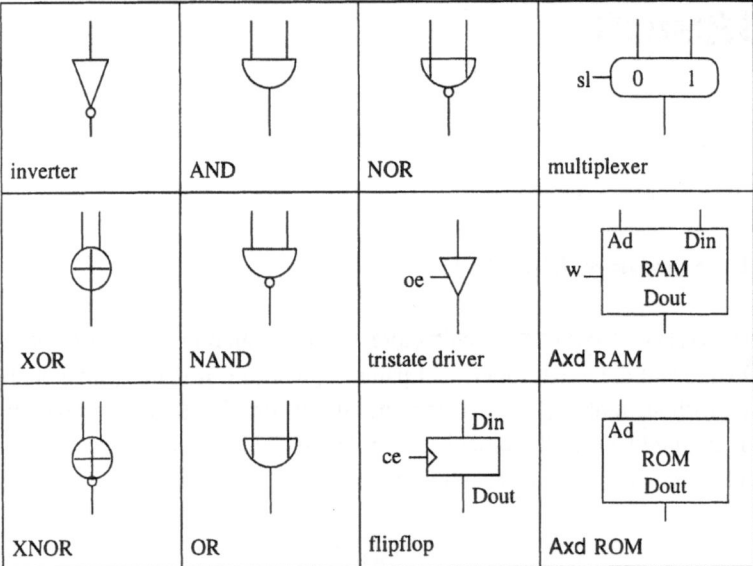

Figure 2.1 Symbols of the basic components

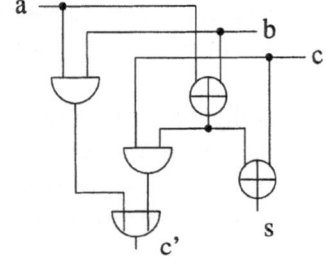

Figure 2.2 Circuit of a full adder FA

Table 2.2 Read and write times of registers and RAMs; d_{ram} denotes the access time of the RAM.

	register	RAM
read	0	d_{ram}
write	$\Delta = D_{ff} + \delta$	$d_{ram} + \delta$

and delay

$$D_{ram}(A, d) = \begin{cases} \log d + A/4 & ; A \leq 64 \\ 3 \cdot \log A + 10 & ; A > 64 \end{cases}$$

For the construction of register files, we use 3-port RAMs capable of performing two reads and one write in a single cycle. If in one cycle a read and a write to the same address are performed, then the output data of the read operation are left undefined.

Cost and delay of these multi-port RAMs are

$$\begin{aligned} C_{ram3}(A, d) &= 1.6 \cdot C_{ram}(A, d) \\ D_{ram3}(A, d) &= 1.5 \cdot D_{ram}(A, d). \end{aligned}$$

The circuit in figure 2.2 has cost C_{FA} and delay D_{FA}, with ◀ Example 2.1

$$\begin{aligned} C_{FA} &= 2 \cdot C_{xor} + 2 \cdot C_{and} + C_{or} \\ D_{FA} &= D_{xor} + \max\{D_{xor}, D_{and} + D_{or}\}. \end{aligned}$$

2.1.2 Cycle Times

In the computation of cycle times, we charge for reads and writes in registers and RAMs the times specified in table 2.2. Note that we start and end counting cycles at the point in time, when the outputs of registers have new values. The constant δ accounts for setup and hold times; we use $\delta = 1$.

Suppose circuit S has delay d_S and RAM R has access time d_{ram}. The four ◀ Example 2.2 schematics in figure 2.3 then have cycle times

$$\tau = \begin{cases} d_S + \Delta & \text{in case a)} \\ d_{ram} + d_S + \Delta & \text{in case b)} \\ d_S + d_{ram} + \delta & \text{in case c)} \\ d_S + 2 \cdot d_{ram} + \delta & \text{in case d)} \end{cases}$$

2.1.3 Hierarchical Designs

It is common practice to specify designs in a hierarchical or even recursive manner. It is also no problem to describe the cost or delay of hierarchical designs by systems of equations. For recursive designs one obtains recursive systems of difference equations. Section 2.3 of this chapter will contain numerous examples.

Solving such systems of equations in closed form is routine work in the analysis of algorithms *if* the systems are small. Designs of entire processors contain dozens of sheets of schematics. We will not even attempt to solve the associated systems of equations in closed form. Instead, we translate the equations in a straightforward way into C programs and let the computer do the work.

Running a computer program is a particular form of experiment. Scientific experiments should be reproducible as easily as possible. Therefore, all C programs associated with the designs in this book are accessible at our web site[1]. The reader can easily check the analysis of the designs, analyze modified designs, or reevaluate the designs with a new set of component costs and delays.

2.1.4 Notations for Delay Formulae

Let S be a circuit with inputs I and outputs O as shown in figure 2.4. It is often desirable to analyze the delay $D_S(I';O')$ from a certain subset I' of the inputs to a certain subset O' of the outputs. This is the maximum delay of a path p from an input in I' to an output in O'. We use the abbreviations

$$
\begin{aligned}
D_S(I';O) &= D_S(I') \\
D_S(I;O') &= D_S(O') \\
D_S &= D_S(I;O)
\end{aligned}
$$

Circuits S do not exist in isolation; their inputs and outputs are connected to registers or RAMs, possibly via long paths. We denote by $A_S(I';O')$ the maximum delay of a path which starts in a register or RAM, enters S via I' and leaves S via O'. We call $A_S(I';O')$ an *accumulated delay*. If all inputs I' are directly connected to registers, we have

$$
A_S(I';O') = D_S(I';O').
$$

---

[1]http://www-wjp.cs.uni-sb.de/info/papers/#books

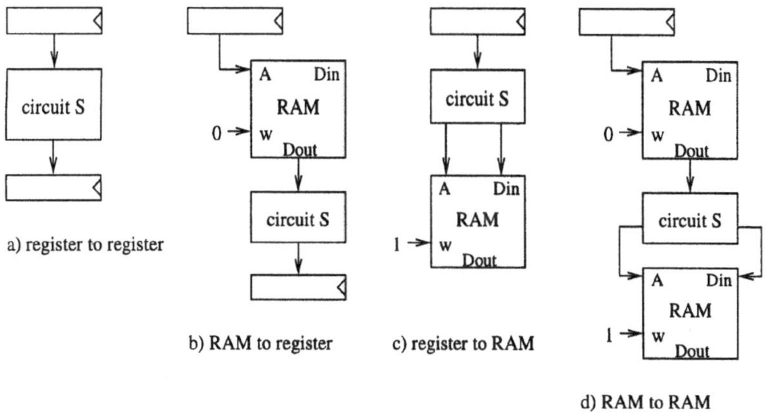

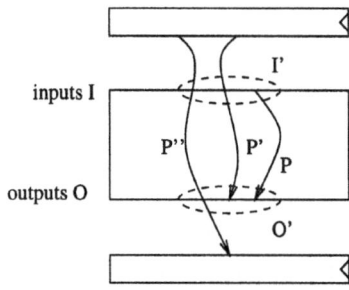

Figure 2.3 The four types of transfer between registers and RAMs

Figure 2.4 Paths through a circuit S. I' is a subset of its inputs I, and O' is a subset of its outputs O.

Similarly we denote by $T_S(I'; O')$ the maximum cycle time required by cycles through I' and O'. If $I' = I$ or $O' = O$ we abbreviate as defined above.

The schematic S_c of figure 2.5 comprises three cycles:　　　　◀ Example 2.3

- leaving circuit S_1 via output d_3,

- entering circuit S_2 via input d_1,

- entering circuit S_2 via input d_2.

Thus, the cycle time of S_c can be expressed as

$$T_{S_c} = \max\{T_{S_1}(d_3), T_{S_2}(d_1), T_{S_2}(d_2)\},$$

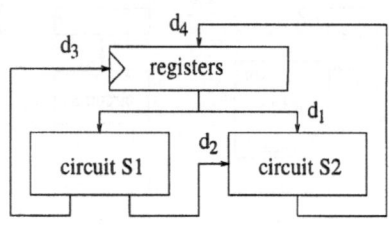

Figure 2.5 Schematic S_c

with

$$
\begin{aligned}
T_{S_1}(d_3) &= A_{S_1}(d_3) + \Delta &= D_{S_1}(d_3) + D_{ff} + \delta \\
T_{S_2}(d_1) &= A_{S_2}(d_1) + \Delta &= D_{S_2}(d_1) + D_{ff} + \delta \\
T_{S_2}(d_2) &= A_{S_2}(d_2) + \Delta &= A_{S_1}(d_2) + D_{S_2}(d_2) + D_{ff} + \delta.
\end{aligned}
$$

2.2 Number Representations and Basic Circuits

2.2.1 Natural Numbers

For bits $x \in \{0,1\}$ and natural numbers n, we denote by x^n the string consisting of n copies of x. For example, $0^3 = 000$ and $1^5 = 11111$. We usually index the bits of strings $a \in \{0,1\}^n$ from right to left with the numbers from 0 to $n-1$. Thus, we write

$$ a = a_{n-1} \ldots a_0 \qquad \text{or} \qquad a = a[n-1:0]. $$

For strings $a = a_{n-1} \ldots a_0 \in \{0,1\}^n$, we denote by

$$ \langle a \rangle = \sum_{i=0}^{n-1} a_i \cdot 2^i $$

the natural number with *binary representation* a. Obviously we have

$$ \langle a \rangle \in \{0, \ldots, 2^n - 1\}. $$

We denote by $B_n = \{0, \ldots, 2^n - 1\}$ the range of numbers which have a binary representation of length n. For $x \in B_n$ and $a \in \{0,1\}^n$ with $x = \langle a \rangle$, we denote by

$$ bin_n(x) = a $$

the n-bit binary representation of x. A *binary number* is a string which is interpreted as a binary representation of a number. We have for example

$$
\begin{aligned}
\langle 10^n \rangle &= 2^n \\
\langle 1^n \rangle &= 2^n - 1.
\end{aligned}
$$

Table 2.3 Computing the binary representation $\langle c's \rangle$ of the sum of the bits a, b, c.

a	b	c	c'	s
0	0	0	0	0
0	0	1	0	1
0	1	0	0	1
0	1	1	1	0
1	0	0	0	1
1	0	1	1	0
1	1	0	1	0
1	1	1	1	1

From the definition one immediately concludes for any $j \in \{0, \ldots, n-1\}$

$$\langle a[n-1:0]\rangle = \langle a[n-1:j]\rangle \cdot 2^j + \langle a[j-1:0]\rangle. \tag{2.1}$$

Addition The entries in table 2.3 obviously satisfy

$$\begin{aligned} s &= a \oplus b \oplus c \\ c' = 1 &\leftrightarrow a+b+c \geq 2 \\ \langle c's \rangle &= a+b+c. \end{aligned}$$

This is the standard algorithm for computing the binary representation of the sum of three bits. For the addition of two n-bit numbers $a[n-1:0]$ and $b[n-1:0]$, one first observes that

$$\langle a[n-1:0]\rangle + \langle b[n-1:0]\rangle \in \{0, \ldots, 2^{n+1}-2\}.$$

Thus, even the $sum + 1$ can be represented with $n+1$ bits. The standard algorithm for adding the binary numbers $a[n-1:0]$ and $b[n-1:0]$ as well as a carry in c_{in} is inductively defined by

$$\begin{aligned} c_{-1} &= c_{in} \\ \langle c_i s_i \rangle &= c_{i-1} + a_i + b_i \\ s_n &= c_{n-1} \end{aligned} \tag{2.2}$$

for $i \in \{0, \ldots, n-1\}$. Bit s_i is called the *sum bit* at position i, and c_i is called the *carry bit* from position i to position $i+1$. The following theorem asserts the correctness of the algorithm.

$$\langle a[n-1:0]\rangle + \langle b[n-1:0]\rangle + c_{in} = \langle c_{n-1}s[n-1:0]\rangle.$$

◀ Theorem 2.1

PROOF

by induction on n. For $n = 0$, this follows directly from the definition of the algorithm. From n to $n+1$ one concludes with equation (2.1) and the induction hypothesis:

$$
\begin{aligned}
\langle a[n:0]\rangle + \langle b[n:0]\rangle + c_{in} &= (a_n + b_n) \cdot 2^n + \langle a[n-1:0]\rangle \\
&\quad + \langle b[n-1:0]\rangle + c_{in} \\
&= (a_n + b_n) \cdot 2^n + \langle c_{n-1} s[n-1:0]\rangle \\
&= (a_n + b_n + c_{n-1}) \cdot 2^n + \langle s[n-1:0]\rangle \\
&= \langle c_n s_n \rangle \cdot 2^n + \langle s[n-1:0]\rangle \\
&= \langle c_n s[n:0]\rangle
\end{aligned}
$$

QED

2.2.2 Integers

For strings $a[n-1:0]$, we use the notation $\overline{a} = \overline{a_{n-1}} \ldots \overline{a_0}$, e.g., $\overline{10^4} = 01111$, and we denote by

$$
[a] = -a_{n-1} \cdot 2^{n-1} + \langle a[n-2:0]\rangle
$$

the integer with *two's complement representation a*. Obviously, we have

$$
[a] \in \{-2^{n-1}, \ldots, 2^{n-1} - 1\}.
$$

We denote by $T_n = \{-2^{n-1}, \ldots, 2^{n-1} - 1\}$ the range of numbers which have a two's complement representation of length n. For $x \in T_n$ and $a \in \{0,1\}^n$ with $x = [a]$, we denote by

$$
two_n(x) = a
$$

the n-bit two's complement representation of x. A *two's complement number* is a string which is interpreted as a two's complement representation of a number. Obviously,

$$
[a] < 0 \quad \leftrightarrow \quad a_{n-1} = 1.
$$

The leading bit of a two's complement number is therefore called its *sign bit*. The basic properties of two's complement numbers are summarized in

Lemma 2.2 ▶ *Let $a = a[n-1:0]$, then*

$$
\begin{aligned}
[0a] &= \langle a \rangle \\
[a] &\equiv \langle a[n-2:0] \rangle \bmod 2^{n-1} \\
[a] &= \langle a \rangle \bmod 2^{n} \\
[a_{n-1}a] &= [a] \quad (sign\ extension) \\
-[a] &= [\bar{a}] + 1
\end{aligned}
$$

The first two equations are obvious. An easy calculation shows, that   PROOF

$$
\langle a \rangle - [a] = a_{n-1} \cdot 2^{n};
$$

this shows the third equation.

$$
\begin{aligned}
[a_{n-1}a] &= -a_{n-1} \cdot 2^{n} + \langle a[n-1:0] \rangle \\
&= -a_{n-1} \cdot 2^{n} + a_{n-1} \cdot 2^{n-1} + \langle a[n-2:0] \rangle \\
&= [a]
\end{aligned}
$$

This proves the fourth equation.

$$
\begin{aligned}
[\overline{a_{n-1}}, \ldots, \overline{a_0}] &= -2^{n-1} \cdot \overline{a_{n-1}} + \sum_{i=0}^{n-2} \overline{a_i} \cdot 2^{i} \\
&= -2^{n-1} \cdot (1 - a_{n-1}) + \sum_{i=0}^{n-2} (1 - a_i) \cdot 2^{i} \\
&= -2^{n-1} + 2^{n-1} \cdot a_{n-1} + \sum_{i=0}^{n-2} 2^{i} - \sum_{i=0}^{n-2} a_i \cdot 2^{i} \\
&= -2^{n-1} + 2^{n-1} \cdot a_{n-1} + 2^{n-1} - 1 - \langle a[n-2:0] \rangle \\
&= -[a[n-1:0]] - 1
\end{aligned}
$$

This proves the last equation.   QED

Subtraction The basic subtraction algorithm for n bit *binary* numbers a
and b in the case where the result is nonnegative works as follows:

1. Add the binary numbers $a, \bar{b}$ and 1.

2. Throw away the leading bit of the result

We want to perform the subtraction $\langle 1100 \rangle - \langle 0101 \rangle = 12 - 5 = 7$. We compute   ◄ Example 2.4

1. $\langle 1100 \rangle - \langle 0101 \rangle = \langle 1100 \rangle + \langle 1010 \rangle + 1 = \langle 1100 \rangle + \langle 1011 \rangle = \langle 10111 \rangle$.

2. We discard the leading bit and state that the result is $\langle 0111 \rangle = 7$.

This is reassuring but it does not prove anything. In order to see why the algorithm works, observe that $\langle a \rangle - \langle b \rangle \geq 0$ implies $\langle a \rangle - \langle b \rangle \in \{0, \ldots, 2^n - 1\}$. Thus, it suffices to compute the result modulo 2^n, i.e., throwing away the leading bit does not hurt. The correctness of the algorithm now immediately follows from

Theorem 2.3 ▶ *Let $a = a[n-1:0]$ and $b = b[n-1:0]$, then*

$$\langle a \rangle - \langle b \rangle \equiv \langle a \rangle + \langle \bar{b} \rangle + 1 \bmod 2^n.$$

PROOF

$$
\begin{aligned}
\langle a \rangle - \langle b \rangle &= \langle a \rangle - [0b] \\
&= \langle a \rangle + [1\bar{b}] + 1 \\
&\equiv \langle a \rangle + \langle \bar{b} \rangle + 1 \bmod 2^n
\end{aligned}
$$

QED

The salient point about two's complement numbers is that addition algorithms for the addition of n-bit binary numbers work just fine for n-bit two's complement numbers as long as the result of the addition stays in the range T_n. This is not completely surprising, because the last $n-1$ bits of n-bit two's complement numbers are interpreted exactly as binary numbers. The following theorem makes this precise.

Theorem 2.4 ▶ *Let $a = a[n-1:0]$, $b = b[n-1:0]$ and let $c_{in} \in \{0,1\}$. Let $\langle s[n:0] \rangle = \langle a[n-1:0] \rangle + \langle b[n-1:0] \rangle + c_{in}$ and let the bits c_i and s_i be defined as in the basic addition algorithm for binary numbers. Then*

- $[a] + [b] + c_{in} \in T_n \quad \leftrightarrow \quad c_{n-1} = c_{n-2}.$

- *If $[a] + [b] + c_{in} \in T_n$, then $[a] + [b] + c_{in} = [s[n-1:0]]$.*

PROOF

$$
\begin{aligned}
[a] + [b] + c_{in} &= 2^{n-1}(-a_{n-1} - b_{n-1}) + \langle a[n-2:0] \rangle + \langle b[n-2:0] \rangle + c_{in} \\
&= -2^{n-1}(a_{n-1} + b_{n-1}) + \langle c_{n-2}s[n-2:0] \rangle \\
&= -2^{n-1}(a_{n-1} + b_{n-1} + c_{n-2} - 2 \cdot c_{n-2}) + \langle s[n-2:0] \rangle \\
&= -2^{n-1}(\langle c_{n-1}s_{n-1} \rangle - 2 \cdot c_{n-2}) + \langle s[n-2:0] \rangle \\
&= 2^n \cdot (-c_{n-1} + c_{n-2}) + [s[n-1:0]]
\end{aligned}
$$

One immediately verifies

$$2^n \cdot (-c_{n-1} + c_{n-2}) + [s[n-1:0]] \in T_n \quad \leftrightarrow \quad c_{n-1} = c_{n-2}$$

QED   and the theorem follows.

Observe that for $a = a[n-1:0]$ and $b = b[n-1:0]$ we have

$$[a] + [b] + c_{in} \in T_{n+1}.$$

Thus, if we perform the binary addition

$$\langle a_{n-1}a \rangle + \langle b_{n-1}b \rangle + c_{in} = \langle s[n+1:0] \rangle,$$

then we always get

$$[a] + [b] + c_{in} = [s[n:0]].$$

2.3 Basic Circuits

I N THIS section a number of basic building blocks for processors are constructed.

2.3.1 Trivial Constructions

One calls n multiplexers with a common select line sl an *n-bit multiplexer* or *n-bit mux*. Similarly, n flipflops with common clock enable line ce are called an *n-bit register*, and n tristate drivers with a common output enable line oe are called an *n-bit driver*.

For $x = x[n-1:0]$, we defined $\bar{x} = \overline{x_{n-1}} \ldots \overline{x_0}$. For $a = a[n-1:0]$, $b = b[n-1:0]$ and $\circ \in \{$AND, OR, NAND, NOR, XOR, XNOR$\}$, we define

$$a \circ b = (a_{n-1} \circ b_{n-1}, \ldots, a_0 \circ b_0).$$

The circuit in figure 2.6 (a) has inputs $a[n-1:0]$ and outputs $b[n-1:0] = \bar{a}$. It is called an *n-bit inverter*. The circuit in figure 2.6 (b) has inputs $a[n-1:0], b[n-1:0]$ and outputs $c[n-1:0] = a \circ b$. It is called an *n-bit $\circ$-gate*.

For $a \in \{0,1\}$, $b = b[n-1:0]$ and $\circ \in \{$AND, OR, NAND, NOR, XOR, XNOR$\}$, we define

$$a \circ b = a^n \circ b = (a \circ b_{n-1}, \ldots a \circ b_0).$$

The circuit in figure 2.6 (c) has inputs $a, b[n-1:0]$ and outputs $c = a \circ b$. The circuit consists of an n-bit $\circ$-gate where all inputs a_i are tied to the same bit a.

For $\circ \in \{$AND, OR$\}$, a balanced tree of $n-1$ many $\circ$-gates has inputs $a[n-1:0]$ and output $b = a_{n-1} \circ \ldots \circ a_0$. It is called an *n-input $\circ$-tree*.

The cost and the delay of the above trivial constructions are summarized in table 2.4. The symbols of these constructions are depicted in figure 2.7.

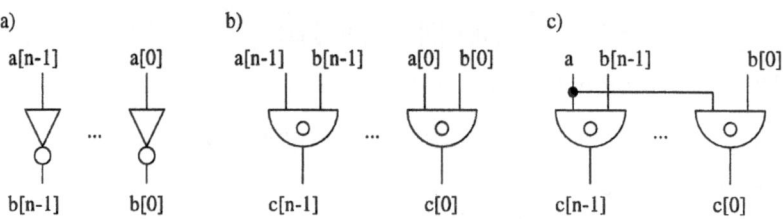

Figure 2.6 Circuits of an n-bit inverter (a) and of an n-bit ○-gate. The circuit (c) computes $a \circ b[n-1:0]$.

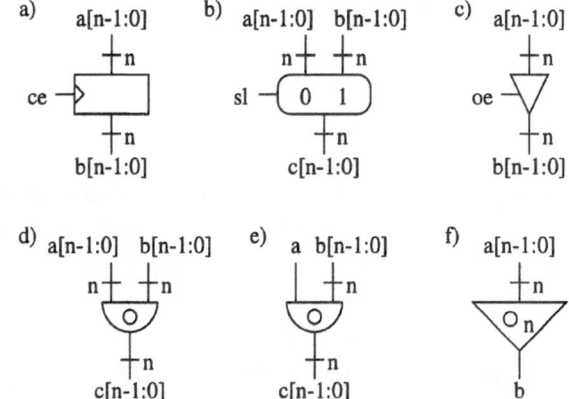

Figure 2.7 Symbols of an n-bit register (a), an n-bit mux (b), an n-bit tristate driver (c), an n-bit ○-gate (d, e), and an n-input ○-tree (f). In (e), all the inputs a_i are tied to one bit a.

Table 2.4 Cost and delay of the basic n-bit components listed in figure 2.7.

	n-bit				n-input
	register	mux	driver	○-gate	○-tree
cost	$n \cdot C_{ff}$	$n \cdot C_{mux}$	$n \cdot C_{driv}$	$n \cdot C_{\circ}$	$(n-1) \cdot C_{\circ}$
delay	D_{ff}	D_{mux}	D_{driv}	$D_{\circ}$	$\lceil \log n \rceil \cdot D_{\circ}$

2.3.2 Testing for Zero or Equality

An *n-zero tester* is a circuit with input $a[n-1:0]$ and output

$$b = \overline{a_{n-1} \vee \ldots \vee a_0}.$$

The obvious realization is an n-bit OR-tree, where the output gate is replaced by a NOR gate. Thus,

$$
\begin{aligned}
C_{zero}(n) &= (n-2) \cdot C_{or} + C_{nor} \\
D_{zero}(n) &= (\lceil \log n \rceil - 1) \cdot D_{or} + D_{nor}.
\end{aligned}
$$

An *n-equality tester* is a circuit with inputs $a[n-1:0]$ and $b[n-1:0]$ and output c such that

$$c = 1 \quad \leftrightarrow \quad a[n-1:0] = b[n-1:0].$$

Since $a[i] = b[i]$ is equivalent to $a[i] \oplus b[i] = 0$, the equality test can also be expressed as

$$c = 1 \quad \leftrightarrow \quad a[n-1:0] \oplus b[n-1:0] = 0^n.$$

Thus, the obvious realization is to combine the two operands bitwise by XOR and to pass the result through an n-zero tester:

$$
\begin{aligned}
C_{equal}(n) &= n \cdot C_{xor} + C_{zero}(n) \\
D_{equal}(n) &= D_{xor} + D_{zero}(n).
\end{aligned}
$$

2.3.3 Decoders

An *n-decoder* is a circuit with inputs $x[n-1:0]$ and outputs $Y[2^n-1:0]$ such that for all i

$$Y_i = 1 \quad \leftrightarrow \quad \langle x \rangle = i.$$

A recursive construction with delay logarithmic in n is depicted in figure 2.8. Let $k = \lceil n/2 \rceil$ and $l = \lfloor n/2 \rfloor$. The correctness of the construction is shown by induction on n. For the induction step one argues

$$
\begin{aligned}
Y[2^k \cdot i + j] = 1 \quad &\leftrightarrow \quad V[i] = 1 \wedge U[j] = 1 \\
&\leftrightarrow \quad \langle x[n-1:k] \rangle = i \wedge \langle x[k-1:0] \rangle = j \\
&\leftrightarrow \quad \langle x[n-1:k]x[k-1:0] \rangle = 2^k \cdot i + j
\end{aligned}
$$

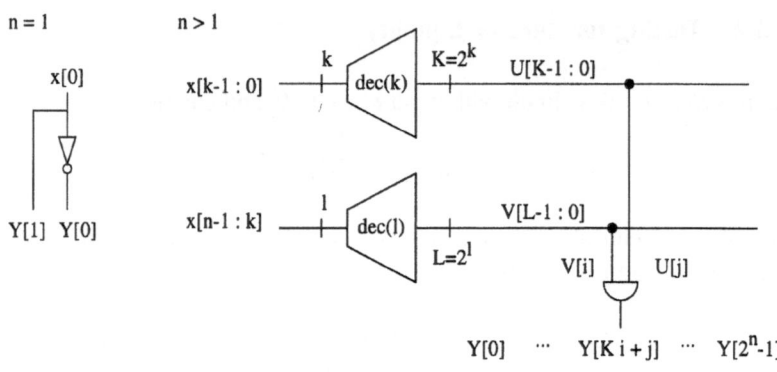

Figure 2.8 Recursive definition of an n-decoder circuit

The cost and delay of this decoder circuit run at

$$
\begin{aligned}
C_{dec}(1) &= C_{inv} \\
C_{dec}(n) &= C_{dec}(\lceil n/2 \rceil) + C_{dec}(\lfloor n/2 \rfloor) + 2^n \cdot C_{and} \\
D_{dec}(1) &= D_{inv} \\
D_{dec}(n) &= D_{dec}(\lceil n/2 \rceil) + D_{and}.
\end{aligned}
$$

Half Decoder An n-*half decoder* is a circuit with inputs $x[n-1:0]$ and outputs $Y[2^n - 1:0]$ such that

$$
Y[2^n - 1:0] = 0^{2^n - \langle x \rangle} 1^{\langle x \rangle}.
$$

Thus, input x turns on the $\langle x \rangle$ low order bits of the output of the half decoder.

Let L denote the lower half and H the upper half of the index range $[2^n - 1:0]$:

$$
L = [2^{n-1} - 1:0] \qquad , \qquad H = [2^n - 1:2^{n-1}].
$$

With these abbreviations, figure 2.9 shows a recursive construction of a half decoder. The cost and the delay are

$$
\begin{aligned}
C_{hdec}(1) &= 0 \\
C_{hdec}(n) &= C_{hdec}(n-1) + 2^{n-1} \cdot (C_{and} + C_{or}) \\
D_{hdec}(1) &= 0 \\
D_{hdec}(n) &= D_{hdec}(n-1) + \max\{D_{and}, D_{or}\}.
\end{aligned}
$$

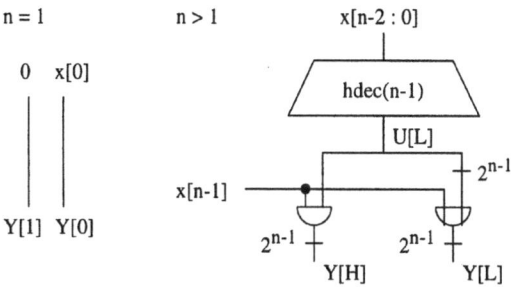

Figure 2.9 Recursive definition of an n-half decoder circuit

In the induction step of the correctness proof the last $\langle x[n-2:0]\rangle$ bits of U are set to one by induction hypothesis. If $x_{n-1} = 0$, then

$$
\begin{aligned}
\langle x \rangle &= \langle x[n-2:0]\rangle \\
y[H] &= 0^{2^{n-1}} \quad \text{and} \\
y[L] &= U.
\end{aligned}
$$

If $x_{n-1} = 1$, then

$$
\begin{aligned}
\langle x \rangle &= 2^{n-1} + \langle x[n-2:0]\rangle \\
y[H] &= U \quad \text{and} \\
y[L] &= 1^{2^{n-1}}.
\end{aligned}
$$

Thus, in both cases the last $\langle x \rangle$ bits of y are one.

2.3.4 Leading Zero Counter

For strings x, we denote by $lz(x)$ the number of leading zeros of x. Let $n = 2^m$ be a power of two. An n-leading zero counter is a circuit with inputs $x[n-1:0]$ and outputs $y[m:0]$ satisfying $\langle y \rangle = lz(x)$.

Figure 2.10 shows a recursive construction for n-leading zero counters. For the induction step of the correctness proof we use the abbreviations

$$
\begin{aligned}
H &= [n-1:n/2] \\
L &= [n/2-1:0] \\
\langle y_H \rangle &= lz(x[H]) \quad \text{and} \\
\langle y_L \rangle &= lz(x[L]).
\end{aligned}
$$

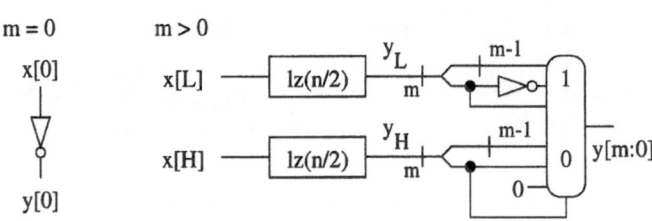

Figure 2.10 Recursive definition of an n-leading zero counter

Thus,

$$lz(x[H]x[L]) = \begin{cases} lz(x[H]) & \text{if } lz(x[H]) < 2^{m-1} \\ 2^{m-1} + lz(x[L]) & \text{if } lz(x[H]) \geq 2^{m-1} \end{cases}$$

$$= \begin{cases} \langle 0y_H[m-1:0] \rangle & \text{if } y_H[m-1] = 0 \\ z & \text{if } y_H[m-1] = 1 \end{cases}$$

where

$$z = \langle 10^{m-1} \rangle + \langle y_L[m-1:0] \rangle$$

$$= \begin{cases} 01y_L[m-2:0] & \text{if } y_L[m-1] = 0 \\ 10y_L[m-2:0] & \text{if } y_L[m-1] = 1 \end{cases}$$

$$= y_L[m-1]\overline{y_L[m-1]}y_L[m-2:0].$$

Cost and delay of this circuit are

$$C_{lz}(1) = C_{inv}$$
$$C_{lz}(n) = 2 \cdot C_{lz}(n/2) + C_{mux}(m+1) + C_{inv}$$
$$D_{lz}(1) = D_{inv}$$
$$D_{lz}(n) = D_{lz}(n/2) + D_{inv} + D_{mux}.$$

2.4 Arithmetic Circuits

WE USE three varieties of adders: carry chain adders, conditional sum adders, and carry look ahead adders.

2.4.1 Carry Chain Adders

A *full adder* is a circuit with inputs a, b, c and outputs c', s satisfying

$$\langle c' s \rangle = a + b + c.$$

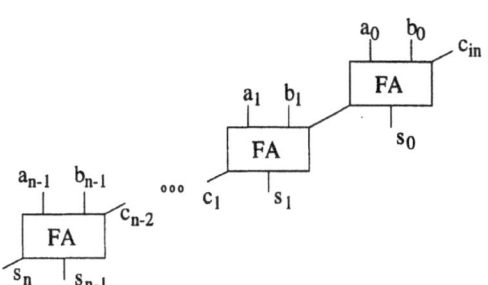

Figure 2.11 Circuit of the n-bit carry chain adder *CCA*

Table 2.5 Functionality of a half adder

a	c	c'	s
0	0	0	0
0	1	0	1
1	0	0	1
1	1	1	0

Full adders implement one step of the basic addition algorithm for binary numbers as illustrated in table 2.3 of section 2.2. The circuit in figure 2.2 of section 2.1 happens to be a full adder with the following cost and delay

$$C_{FA} = 2 \cdot C_{xor} + 2 \cdot C_{and} + C_{or}$$
$$D_{FA} = D_{xor} + \max\{D_{xor}, D_{and} + D_{or}\}.$$

An *n-adder* is a circuit with inputs $a[n-1:0]$, $b[n-1:0]$, c_{in} and outputs $s[n:0]$ satisfying

$$\langle a \rangle + \langle b \rangle + c_{in} = \langle s \rangle.$$

The most obvious adder construction implements directly the basic addition algorithm: by cascading n full adders as depicted in figure 2.11, one obtains a *carry chain adders*. Such adders are cheap but slow, and we therefore do not use them.

A *half adder* is a circuit with inputs a, c and outputs c', s satisfying

$$\langle c' s \rangle = a + c.$$

The behavior of half adders is illustrated in table 2.5. As we have

$$s = a \oplus c \quad \text{and} \quad c' = a \wedge c,$$

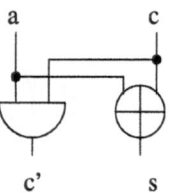

Figure 2.12 Circuit of a half adder *HA*

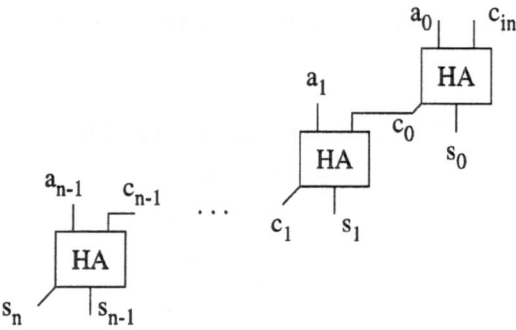

Figure 2.13 Circuit of an *n*-carry chain incrementer *CCI*

the obvious realization of half adders consists of one AND gate and one OR gate, as depicted in figure 2.12.

An *n-incrementer* is a circuit with inputs $a[n-1:0], c_{in}$ and outputs $s[n:0]$ satisfying

$$\langle a \rangle + c_{in} = \langle s \rangle.$$

By cascading *n* half adders as depicted in figure 2.13 (b), one obtains a *carry chain incrementer* with the following cost and delay:

$$
\begin{aligned}
C_{CCI}(n) &= n \cdot (C_{xor} + C_{and}) \\
D_{CCI}(n) &= (n-1) \cdot D_{and} + \max\{D_{xor}, D_{and}\}.
\end{aligned}
$$

The correctness proof for this construction follows exactly the lines of the correctness proof for the basic addition algorithm.

2.4.2 Conditional Sum Adders

The most simple construction for conditional sum adders is shown in figure 2.14. Let $m = \lceil n/2 \rceil$ and $k = \lfloor n/2 \rfloor$ and write

$$s[n:0] = s[n:m]\,s[m-1:0],$$

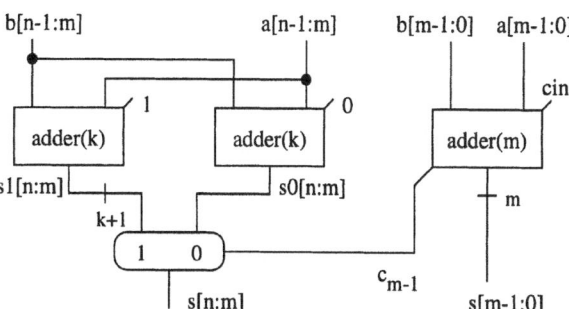

Figure 2.14 Simple version of an n-bit conditional sum adder; $m = \lceil n/2 \rceil$ and $k = \lfloor n/2 \rfloor$.

then

$$
\begin{aligned}
\langle s[n : m] \rangle &= \langle a[n-1 : m] \rangle + \langle b[n-1 : m] \rangle + c_{m-1} \\
&= \begin{cases} \langle a[n-1 : m] \rangle + \langle b[n-1 : m] \rangle & \text{if } c_{m-1} = 0 \\ \langle a[n-1 : m] \rangle + \langle b[n-1 : m] \rangle + 1 & \text{if } c_{m-1} = 1 \end{cases}
\end{aligned}
$$

Thus, the high order sum bits in figure 2.14 are computed twice: the sum bits $s^0[n : m]$ are for the case $c_{m-1} = 0$ and bits $s^1[n : m]$ are for the case $c_{m-1} = 1$. The final selection is done once c_{m-1} is known.

This construction should not be repeated recursively because halving the problem size requires 3 copies of hardware for the half sized problem and the muxes. Ignoring the muxes and assuming $n = 2^v$ is a power of two, one obtains for the cost $c(n)$ of an n-adder constructed in this manner the estimate

$$
\begin{aligned}
c(n) &> 3 \cdot c(n/2) \\
&> 3^v \cdot c(1) = 2^{v \cdot \log 3} \cdot c(1) \\
&= n^{\log 3} \cdot c(1) > n^{1.57} \cdot c(1)
\end{aligned}
$$

This is too expensive.

For incrementers things look better. The high order sum bits of incrementers are

$$
\begin{aligned}
\langle s[n : m] \rangle &= \langle a[n-1 : m] \rangle + c_{m-1} \\
&= \begin{cases} \langle a[n-1 : m] \rangle & \text{if } c_{m-1} = 0 \\ \langle a[n-1 : m] \rangle + 1 & \text{if } c_{m-1} = 1 \end{cases}
\end{aligned}
$$

This leads to the very simple construction of figure 2.15. Our incrementer of choice will be constructed in this way using carry chain incrementers

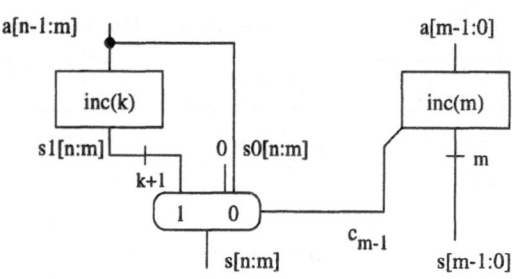

Figure 2.15 An n-bit conditional sum incrementer; $m = \lceil n/2 \rceil$ and $k = \lfloor n/2 \rfloor$.

for solving the subproblems of size k and m. Such an n-incrementer then has the following cost and delay

$$
\begin{aligned}
C_{inc}(n) &= C_{CCI}(m) + C_{CCI}(k) + C_{mux}(k+1) \\
D_{inc}(n) &= D_{CCI}(m) + D_{mux}.
\end{aligned}
$$

Note that in figure 2.15, the original problem is reduced to only two problems of half the size of the original problem. Thus, this construction could be applied recursively with reasonable cost (see exercise 2.1). One then obtains a very fast conditional sum incrementer *CSI*.

Indeed, a recursive construction of simple conditional sum adders turns out to be so expensive because disjoint circuits are used for the computation of the candidate high order sum bits $s^0[n:m]$ and $s^1[n:m]$. This flaw can be remedied if one constructs adders which compute both, the sum and the sum $+1$ of the operands a and b.

An *n-compound adder* is a circuit with inputs $a[n-1:0], b[n-1:0]$ and outputs $s^0[n:0], s^1[n:0]$ satisfying

$$
\begin{aligned}
\langle s^0 \rangle &= \langle a \rangle + \langle b \rangle \\
\langle s^1 \rangle &= \langle a \rangle + \langle b \rangle + 1.
\end{aligned}
$$

A recursive construction of the n-compound adders is shown in figure 2.16. It will turn out to be useful in the rounders of floating point units. Note that only two copies of hardware for the half sized problem are used. Cost and delay of the construction are

$$
\begin{aligned}
C_{add2}(1) &= C_{xor} + C_{xnor} + C_{and} + C_{or} \\
C_{add2}(n) &= C_{add2}(k) + C_{add2}(m) + 2 \cdot C_{mux}(k+1) \\
D_{add2}(1) &= \max\{D_{xor}, D_{xnor}, D_{and}, D_{or}\} \\
D_{add2}(n) &= D_{add2}(m) + D_{mux}(k+1).
\end{aligned}
$$

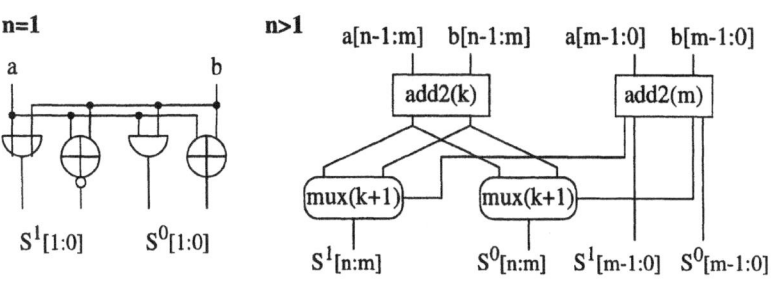

Figure 2.16 An n-compound adder $add2(n)$; $m = \lceil n/2 \rceil$, $k = \lfloor n/2 \rfloor$

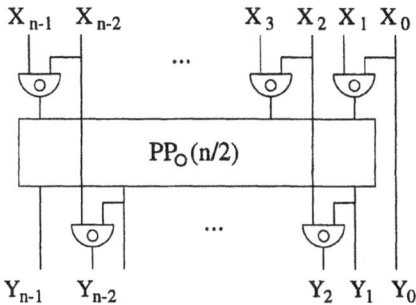

Figure 2.17 The recursive specification of an n-fold parallel prefix circuit of the function ∘ for an even n

2.4.3 Parallel Prefix Computation

Let $\circ : M \times M \to M$ be an associative, dyadic function. its n-fold *parallel prefix function* $PP_\circ(n) : M^n \to M^n$ maps n inputs $x_1, \cdots, x_n$ into n results $y_1, \cdots, y_n$ with $y_i = x_1 \circ \cdots \circ x_i$.

A recursive construction of efficient parallel prefix circuits based on ∘-gates is shown in figure 2.17 for the case that n is even. If n is odd, then one realizes $PP_\circ(n-1)$ by the construction in figure 2.17 and one computes $Y_{n-1} = X_{n-1} \circ Y_{n-2}$ in a straightforward way using one extra ∘-gate.

The correctness of the construction can be easily seen. From

$$X_i' = X_{2i+1} \circ X_{2i},$$

it follows

$$Y_i' = X_i' \circ \ldots \circ X_0' = X_{2i+1} \circ \ldots \circ X_0 = Y_{2i+1}.$$

The computation of the outputs

$$Y_{2i} = X_{2i} \circ Y_{2i-1}$$

is straightforward. For cost and delay, we get

$$
\begin{aligned}
C_{PP\circ}(1) &= 0 \\
C_{PP\circ}(n) &= C_{PP\circ}(\lfloor n/2 \rfloor) + (n-1) \cdot C_\circ \\
D_{PP\circ}(1) &= 0 \\
D_{PP\circ}(n) &\leq D_{PP\circ}(\lfloor n/2 \rfloor) + 2 \cdot D_\circ.
\end{aligned}
$$

2.4.4 Carry Lookahead Adders

For $a[n-1:0], b[n-1:0]$ and indices i,j with $i \leq j$ one defines

$$
p_{i,j}(a,b) = 1 \leftrightarrow \langle a[j:i] \rangle + \langle b[j:i] \rangle = \langle 1^{j-i+1} \rangle.
$$

This is the case if $c_j = c_{i-1}$, in other words if carry c_{i-1} is *propagated* by positions i to j of the operands to position j. Similarly, one defines for $0 < i \leq j$:

$$
g_{i,j}(a,b) = 1 \leftrightarrow \langle a[j:i] \rangle + \langle b[j:i] \rangle \geq \langle 10^{j-i+1} \rangle,
$$

i.e., if positions i to j of the operands *generate* a carry c_j independent of c_{i-1}. For $i = 0$ one has account for c_{in}, thus one defines

$$
g_{0,j}(a,b,c_{in}) = 1 \leftrightarrow \langle a[j:0] \rangle + \langle b[j:0] \rangle + c_{in} \geq \langle 10^{j-1+1} \rangle.
$$

In the following calculations, we simply write $g_{i,j}$ and $p_{i,j}$, respectively. Obviously, we have

$$
\begin{aligned}
p_{i,i} &= a_i \oplus b_i \\
g_{i,i} &= a_i \wedge b_i \qquad \text{for} \quad i > 0 \\
g_{0,0} &= ((a_0 \oplus b_0) \wedge c_{in}) \vee (a_0 \wedge b_0).
\end{aligned}
$$

Suppose one has already computed the generate and propagate signals for the adjacent intervals of indices $[i:j]$ and $[j+1:k]$, where $i \leq j < k$. The signals for the combined interval $[i:k]$ can then be computed as

$$
\begin{aligned}
p_{i,k} &= p_{i,j} \wedge p_{j+1,k} \\
g_{i,k} &= g_{j+1,k} \vee g_{i,j} \wedge p_{j+1,k}.
\end{aligned}
$$

This computation can obviously be performed by the circuit in figure 2.18 which takes inputs (g_1, p_1) and (g_2, p_2) from $M = \{0,1\}^2$ to output

$$
\begin{aligned}
(g,p) &= (g_2, p_2) \circ (g_1, p_1) \\
&= (g_2 \vee g_1 \wedge p_2, p_1 \wedge p_2) \quad \in M.
\end{aligned}
$$

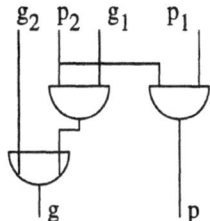

Figure 2.18 Circuit ∘, to be used in the carry lookahead adder

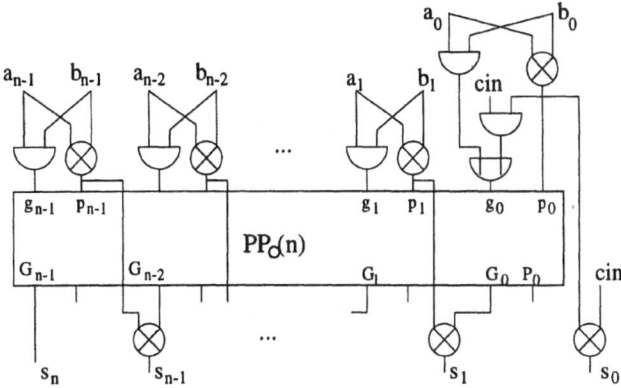

Figure 2.19 Circuit of an n-bit carry lookahead adder

A simple exercise shows that the operation ∘ defined in this way is associative (for details see, e.g., [KP95]).

Hence, figure 2.18 can be substituted as a ∘-gate in the parallel prefix circuits of the previous subsections. The point of this construction is that the i-th output of the parallel prefix circuit computes

$$(G_i, P_i) = (g_i, p_i) \circ \cdots \circ (g_0, p_0) = (g_{i,0}, p_{i,0}) = (c_i, p_{i,0}).$$

It follows that the circuit in figure 2.19 is an adder. It is called a *carry look ahead adder*.

The circuit in figure 2.18 has cost 6 and delay 4. We change the computation of output g using

$$g = \overline{\overline{g_2 \vee g_1 \wedge p_2}} = \overline{\overline{g_2} \wedge \overline{g_1 \vee p_2}}.$$

For the cost and the delay of operation ∘ this gives

$$C_\circ = C_{and} + C_{nand} + C_{nor} + C_{inv} = 7$$
$$D_\circ = \max\{D_{and}, D_{nand} + \max\{D_{nor}, D_{inv}\}\} = 2.$$

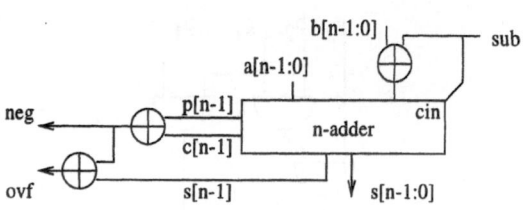

Figure 2.20 Circuit of an n-bit arithmetic unit AU

The cost and the delay of the whole CLA adder are

$$C_{CLA}(n) = C_{PP_0}(n) + 2n \cdot C_{xor} + (n+1) \cdot C_{and} + C_{or}$$
$$D_{CLA}(n) = D_{PP_0}(n) + 2 \cdot D_{xor} + D_{and} + D_{or}.$$

2.4.5 Arithmetic Units

An n bit arithmetic unit is a circuit with inputs $a[n-1:0]$, $b[n-1:0]$, sub and outputs $s[n:0], neg, ovf$. It performs operation

$$op = \begin{cases} + & \text{if} \quad sub = 0 \\ - & \text{if} \quad sub = 1 \end{cases}$$

The sum outputs s satisfy

$$[s] = [a] \, op \, [b] \quad \text{if} \quad [a] \, op \, [b] \in T_n.$$

The flag ovf indicates that $[a] \, op \, [b] \notin T_n$, whereas flag neg indicates that $[a] \, op \, [b] < 0$. This flag has to be correct even in the presence of an overflow. With the help of this flag one implements for instance instructions of the form "branch if $a < b$". In this case one wants to know the sign of $a - b$ even if $a - b$ is not representable with n bits.

Figure 2.20 shows an implementation of an n-bit arithmetic unit. The equation

$$-[b] = \bar{b} + 1$$

translates into

$$b' = b \oplus sub \quad \text{and} \quad c_{in} = sub.$$

The flag neg is the sign bit of the sum $[a] + [b] \in T_{n+1}$. By the argument at the end of section 2.2, the desired flag is the sum bit s_n of the addition

$$\langle a_{n-1}a \rangle + \langle b_{n-1}b \rangle + c_{in} = \langle s[n+1:0] \rangle.$$

It can be computed as

$$neg = s_n = c_{n-1} \oplus a_{n-1} \oplus b_{n-1} = c_{n-1} \oplus p_{n-1}.$$

By theorem 2.4, we have $ovf = c_{n-1} \oplus c_{n-2}$. In the carry lookahead adder, all the carry bits are available, whereas the conditional sum adder only provides the final carry bit c_{n-1}. Since the most significant sum bit equals $s_{n-1} = p_{n-1} \oplus c_{n-1}$, an overflow can be checked by

$$ovf = (c_{n-1} \oplus p_{n-1}) \oplus (c_{n-2} \oplus p_{n-1}) = s_{n-1} \oplus neg.$$

Let *add* denote the binary adder of choice; the cost and the delay of the arithmetic unit, then be expressed as

$$
\begin{aligned}
C_{AU}(n) &= (n+2) \cdot C_{xor} + C_{add}(n) \\
D_{AU}(n) &= 3 \cdot D_{xor} + D_{add}(n).
\end{aligned}
$$

2.4.6 Shifter

For strings $a[n-1:0]$ and natural numbers $i \in \{0, \ldots, n-1\}$ we consider the functions

$$
\begin{aligned}
cls(a,i) &= (a[n-i-1]\ldots a[0]a[n-1]\ldots a[n-i]) \\
crs(a,i) &= (a[i-1]\ldots a[0]a[n-1]\ldots a[i]) \\
lrs(a,i) &= (0^i a[n-1]\ldots a[i]).
\end{aligned}
$$

The function *cls* is called a *cyclic left shift*, the function *crs* is called a *cyclic right shift*, and the function *lrs* is called *logic right shift*. We obviously have

$$crs(a,i) = cls(a, n-i \bmod n).$$

Cyclic Left Shifter   An (n,i)-*cyclic left shifter* is a circuit with inputs $a[n-1:0]$, select input $s \in \{0,1\}$ and outputs $r[n-1:0]$ satisfying

$$
r = \begin{cases} cls(a,i) & \text{if } s = 1 \\ a & \text{otherwise} \end{cases}
$$

As shown in figure 2.21 such shifters can be built from n muxes.

Let $n = 2^m$ be a power of two. An n-*cyclic left shifter* is a circuit with inputs $a[n-1:0]$, select inputs $b[m-1:0]$ and outputs $r[n-1:0]$ satisfying

$$r = cls(a, \langle b \rangle).$$

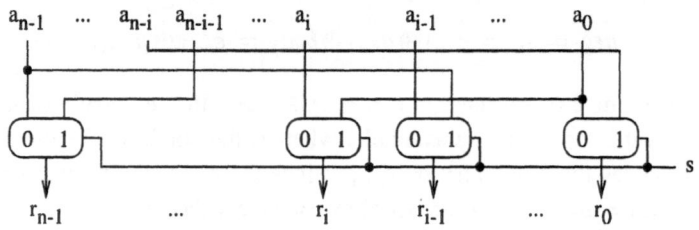

Figure 2.21 (n,i)-Cyclic left shifter

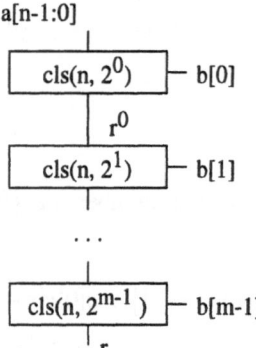

Figure 2.22 Circuit of an n-cyclic left shifter $CLS(n)$

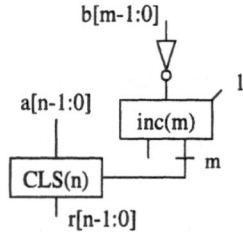

Figure 2.23 Circuit of an n-cyclic right shifter $CRS(n)$

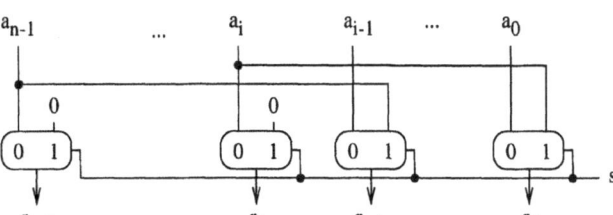

Figure 2.24 (n, i)-Logic right shifter

Such shifters can be built by cascading (n, i)-cyclic left shifters for $i \in \{ 0,$
$1, 2, 4, \ldots, 2^{m-1}\}$ as shown in figure 2.22.

By induction on i, one easily shows that the output $r^{(i)}$ of the $(n, 2^i)$-
cyclic left shifter in figure 2.22 satisfies

$$r^{(i)} = cls(a, \langle b[i : 0]\rangle).$$

Cyclic Right Shifter An *n-cyclic right shifter* is a circuit with inputs
$a[n - 1 : 0]$, select inputs $b[m - 1 : 0]$ and outputs $r[n - 1 : 0]$ satisfying

$$r = crs(a, \langle b \rangle).$$

It can be built from an *n*-cyclic left shifter by the construction shown in
figure 2.23. This works, because

$$
\begin{aligned}
n - \langle b \rangle &= n - [0b] = n + [1\bar{b}] + 1 \\
&\equiv \langle \bar{b} \rangle + 1 \bmod n.
\end{aligned}
$$

Logic Right Shifter An (n, i)-*logic right shifter* is a circuit with inputs
$a[n - 1 : 0]$, select input $s \in \{0, 1\}$ and outputs $r[n - 1 : 0]$ satisfying

$$
r = \begin{cases} lrs(a, i) & \text{if } s = 1 \\ a & \text{otherwise} \end{cases}
$$

It can be built from n muxes, as depicted in figure 2.24.

Let $n = 2^m$ be a power of two. An *n-logic right shifter* is a circuit with
inputs $a[n - 1 : 0]$, select inputs $b[m - 1 : 0]$ and outputs $r[n - 1 : 0]$ satisfying

$$r = lrs(a, \langle b \rangle).$$

In analogy to the cyclic left shifter, the *n*-logic right shifter can be built by
cascading the (n, i)-logic right shifters for $i \in \{ 0, 1, 2, 4, \ldots, 2^{m-1}\}$.

2.5 Multipliers

L ET $a = a[n-1:0]$ and $b = b[m-1:0]$, then

$$\langle a \rangle \cdot \langle b \rangle \leq (2^n - 1) \cdot (2^m - 1) < 2^{n+m} - 1. \tag{2.3}$$

Thus, the product can be represented with $n+m$ bits.

An (n,m)-*multiplier* is a circuit with an n-bit input $a = a[n-1:0]$, an m-bit input $b = b[m-1:0]$, and an $n+m$-bit output $p = p[n+m-1:0]$ such that $\langle a \rangle \cdot \langle b \rangle = \langle p \rangle$ holds.

2.5.1 School Method

Obviously, one can write the product $\langle a \rangle \cdot \langle b \rangle$ as a sum of *partial products*

$$\langle a \rangle \cdot \langle b \rangle = \sum_{t=0}^{m-1} \langle a \rangle \cdot b_t \cdot 2^t.$$

with

$$\langle a \rangle \cdot b_t \cdot 2^t = \langle a[n-1] \wedge b[t], \ldots a[0] \wedge b[t], 0^t \rangle.$$

Thus, all partial products can be computed with cost $n \cdot m \cdot C_{and}$ and delay D_{and}. We denote by

$$\begin{aligned} S_{j,k} &= \sum_{t=j}^{j+k-1} \langle a \rangle \cdot b[t] \cdot 2^t \\ &= \langle a \rangle \cdot \langle b[j+k-1:j] \rangle \cdot 2^j < 2^{n+k+j} \end{aligned} \tag{2.4}$$

the sum of the k partial products from position j to position $j+k-1$. Because $S_{j,k}$ is a multiple of 2^j it has a binary representation with j trailing zeros. Because $S_{j,k}$ is smaller than 2^{j+n+k} it has a binary representation of length $n+j+k$ (see figure 2.25). We have

$$\begin{aligned} S_{j,1} &= \langle a \rangle \cdot b[j] \cdot 2^j \\ \langle a \rangle \cdot \langle b \rangle &= S_{0,m} \\ S_{j,k+h} &= S_{j,k} + S_{j+k,h} \\ S_{0,t} &= S_{0,t-1} + S_{t-1,1}. \end{aligned}$$

The last line suggests an obvious construction of multipliers comprising $m-1$ many n-adders. This construction corresponds to the school method for the multiplication of natural numbers. If one realizes the adders as carry chain adders, then cost and delay of this multiplier construction can be shown (see exercise 2.2) to be bounded by

$$\begin{aligned} C_{mul}(n,m) &\leq m \cdot n \cdot (C_{and} + C_{FA}) \\ D_{mul}(n,m) &\leq D_{and} + (m+n) \cdot D_{FA}. \end{aligned}$$

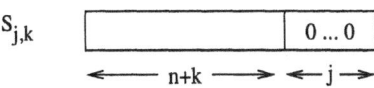

$S_{j,k}$

$\longleftarrow n+k \longrightarrow \longleftarrow j \longrightarrow$

Figure 2.25 $S_{j,k}$, the sum of the k partial products starting from position j.

2.5.2 Carry Save Adders

Let x be a natural number and suppose the two binary numbers $s[n-1:0]$ and $t[n-1:0]$ satisfy

$$\langle s \rangle + \langle t \rangle = x.$$

We then call s, t a *carry save representation* of x with length n.

A crucial building block for speeding up the summation of partial products are *n-carry save adders*. These are circuits with inputs $a[n-1:0]$, $b[n-1:0]$, $c[n-1:0]$ and outputs $s[n-1:0]$, $t[n:0]$ satisfying

$$\langle a \rangle + \langle b \rangle + \langle c \rangle = \langle s \rangle + \langle t \rangle,$$

i.e., the outputs s and t are a carry save representation of the sum of the numbers represented at the inputs. As carry save adders compress the sum of three numbers to two numbers, which have the same sum, they are also called *n-3/2-adders*. Such adders are realized, as shown in figure 2.26, simply by putting n full adders in parallel. This works, because

$$
\begin{aligned}
\langle a \rangle + \langle b \rangle + \langle c \rangle &= \sum_{i=0}^{n-1} (a_i + b_i + c_i) \cdot 2^i \\
&= \sum_{i=0}^{n-1} \langle t_{i+1} s_i \rangle \cdot 2^i \\
&= \sum_{i=0}^{n-1} (2 \cdot t_{i+1} + s_i) \cdot 2^i = \langle s \rangle + \langle t \rangle.
\end{aligned}
$$

The cost and the delay of such a carry save adder are

$$
\begin{aligned}
C_{3/2add}(n) &= n \cdot C_{FA} \\
D_{3/2add}(n) &= D_{FA}.
\end{aligned}
$$

The point of the construction is, of course, that the delay of carry save adders is independent of n.

35

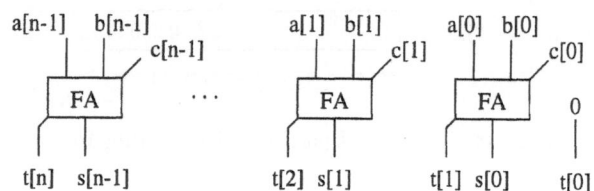

Figure 2.26 Circuit of an n-bit carry save adder, i.e., of an n-3/2-adder.

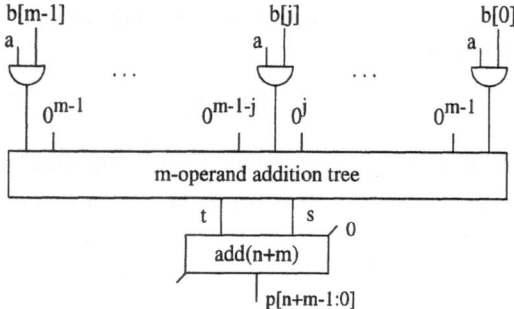

Figure 2.27 Circuit of an (n,m)-multiplier

2.5.3 Multiplication Arrays

An *addition tree with m operands* is a circuit which takes as inputs m binary numbers and which outputs a carry save representation of their sum. Using addition trees, one can construct (n,m)-multipliers as suggested in figure 2.27. First, one generates binary representations of the m partial products $S_{t,1}$. These are fed into an addition tree with m operands. The output of the tree is a carry save representation of the desired product. An ordinary adder then produces from the carry save representation the binary representation of the product.

We proceed to construct a particularly simple family of addition trees. In figure 2.28 (a) representations of the partial sums $S_{0,1}, S_{1,1}$ and $S_{2,1}$ are fed into an n-carry save adder. The result is a carry save representation of $S_{0,3}$ with length $n + 3$. In figure 2.28 (b) the representation of $S_{t-1,1}$ and a carry save representation of $S_{0,t-1}$ are fed into an n-carry save adder. The result is a carry save representation of $S_{0,t}$ with length $n + t$. By cascading $m - 2$ many n-carry save adders as suggested above, one obtains an addition tree which is also called a *multiplication array* because of its regular structure.

If the final addition is performed by an $(n + m)$-carry lookahead adder, one obtains an (n,m)-multiplier with the following cost and delay

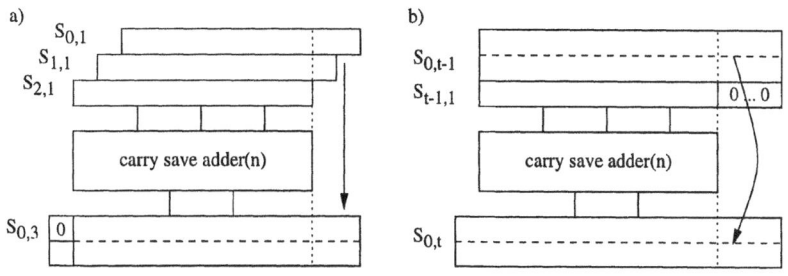

Figure 2.28 Generating a carry save representation of the partial sums $S_{0,3}$ (a) and $S_{0,t}$ (b).

$$C_{MULarray}(n,m) = n \cdot m \cdot C_{and} + (m-2) \cdot C_{3/2add}(n) + C_{CLA}(n+m)$$
$$D_{MULarray}(n,m) = D_{and} + (m-2) \cdot D_{3/2add}(n) + D_{CLA}(n+m).$$

2.5.4 4/2-Trees

The delay of multiplication arrays is proportional to m. The obvious next step is to balance the addition trees, hereby reducing the delay to $O(\log m)$. We use here a construction which is particularly regular and easy to analyze.

An *n-4/2-adder* is a circuit with inputs $a[n-1:0]$, $b[n-1:0]$, $c[n-1:0]$, $d[n-1:0]$ and outputs $s[n-1:0]$, $t[n-1:0]$ satisfying

$$\langle a \rangle + \langle b \rangle + \langle c \rangle + \langle d \rangle = \langle s \rangle + \langle t \rangle \bmod 2^n.$$

The obvious construction of n-4/2-adders from two n-3/2-adders is shown in figure 2.29. Its cost and delay are

$$C_{4/2add}(n) = 2 \cdot C_{3/2add}(n) = 2 \cdot n \cdot C_{FA}$$
$$D_{4/2add}(n) = 2 \cdot D_{3/2add}(n) = 2 \cdot D_{FA}.$$

Complete Addition Trees
With the help of 4/2-adders, one constructs complete balanced addition trees by the recursive construction suggested in figure 2.30. Note that we do *not* specify the width of the operands yet. Thus, figure 2.30 is not yet a complete definition. Let $K \geq 2$ be a power of two. By this construction,

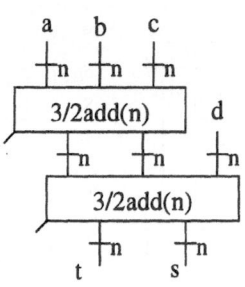

Figure 2.29 Circuit of an n-4/2-adder

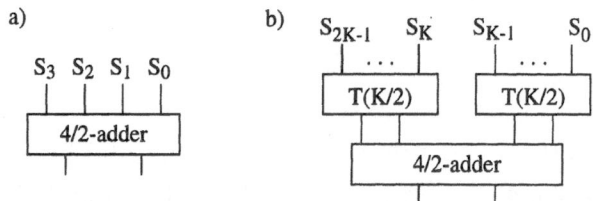

Figure 2.30 Complete balanced addition tree $T(K)$ with $2K$ operands $S_0, \ldots,$ S_{2K-1}, where K is a power of two; a) tree $T(2)$, b) tree $T(K)$.

one obtains addition trees $T(K)$ with $2K$ inputs. Such a 4/2-tree $T(K)$ has the delay

$$D_{T(K)} = \log K \cdot 2 \cdot D_{FA}.$$

Incomplete Addition Trees

For the construction of IEEE-compliant floating point units we will have to construct (n, m)-multipliers where m is not a power of two. Let

$$M = 2^{\lceil \log m \rceil} \quad \text{and} \quad \mu = \log(M/4).$$

Thus, M is the smallest power of two with $M \geq m$. As a consequence of the IEEE floating point standard [Ins85] and of the division algorithm used in the floating point unit, the length $m \in \{27, 58\}$ of the operand $b[m-1:0]$, and hence the number of operands of the addition tree, will satisfy the condition

$$3/4 \cdot M \leq m < M.$$

In this case, we construct an addition tree $T(m)$ with m operands as suggested in figure 2.31 [2]. The tree $T(m)$ has depth μ. The bottom portion

---

[2]For the complementary case see exercise 2.3

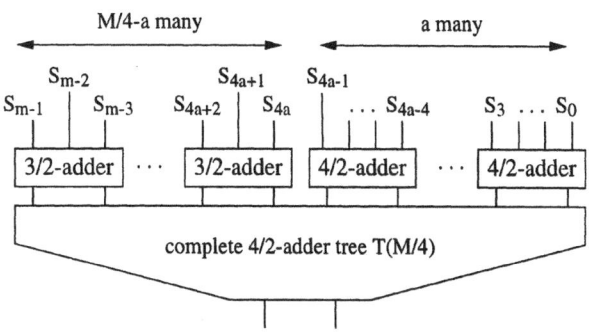

Figure 2.31 Construction of a 4/2-adder tree $\mathcal{T}(m)$ adding inputs $S_0, \ldots, S_{m-1}$

of the tree is a completely regular and balanced 4/2-tree $T(M/4)$ with $M/4$ many pairs of inputs and $M/8$ many 4/2-adders as leaves. In the top level, we have a many 4/2-adders and $M/4 - a$ many 3/2-adders. Here, a is the solution of the equation

$$4a + 3 \cdot (M/4 - a) = m,$$

hence

$$a = m - 3M/4.$$

Note that for $i = 0, 1, \ldots,$ the partial products $S_{i,1}$ are entered into the tree from right to left and that in the top level of the tree the 3/2-adders are arranged *left* of the 4/2-adders. For the delay of a multiplier constructed with such trees one immediately sees

$$D_{4/2mul}(n,m) = D_{and} + 2 \cdot (\mu + 1) \cdot D_{FA} + D_{CLA}(n+m).$$

Cost of the Addition Trees

Estimating the cost of the trees is more complicated. It requires to estimate the cost of all 3/2-adders and 4/2-adders of the construction. For this estimate, we view the addition trees as complete binary trees T in the graph theoretic sense. Each 3/2-adder or 4/2-adder of the construction is a node v of the tree. The 3/2-adders and 4/2-adders at the top level of the addition tree are then the leaves of T.

The cost of the leaves is easily determined. Carry save representations of the sums $S_{i,3}$ are computed by n-3/2-adders in a way completely analogous to figure 2.28 (a). The length of the representation is $n + 3$. Figure 2.32 shows that carry save representations of sums $S_{i,4}$ can be computed by two

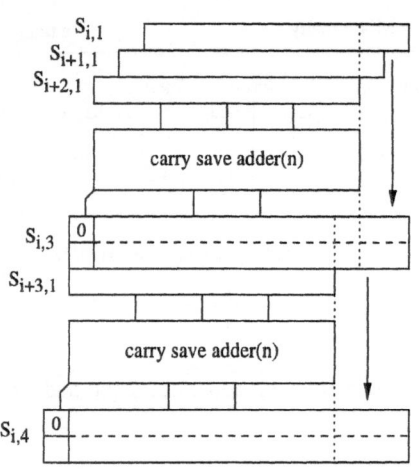

Figure 2.32 Partial compression of $S_{i,4}$

n-3/2 adders [3]. The length of the representation is $n+4$. Thus, we have

$$c(v) = 2 \cdot n \cdot C_{FA}$$

for all leaves v of T.

Let v be an interior node of the tree with left son $L(v)$ and right son $R(v)$. Node v then computes a carry save representation of the sum

$$S_{i,k+h} = S_{i,k} + S_{i+k,h},$$

where $R(v)$ provides a carry save representation of $S_{i,k}$ and $L(v)$ provides a carry save representation of $S_{i+k,h}$. If the length of the representations are $i+k$ and $i+k+h$, by Equation (2.4) we are then in the situation of figure 2.33. Hence node v consists of $2n+2h$ full adders.

If all 3/2-adders in the tree would have exactly n full adders, and if all 4/2-adders would have $2n$ full adders, the cost of the tree would be $n \cdot (m-2)$. Thus, it remains to estimate the number of *excess full adders* in the tree.

A Combinatorial Lemma

Let T be a complete binary tree with depth μ. We number the levels ℓ from the leaves to the root from 0 to μ. Each leaf u has weight $W(u)$. For some natural number k, we have $W(u) \in \{k, k+1\}$ for all leaves, and the weights are nondecreasing from left to right. Let m be the sum of the weights of

---

[3]Formally, figure 2.32 can be viewed as a simplified $(n+3)$-4/2-adder

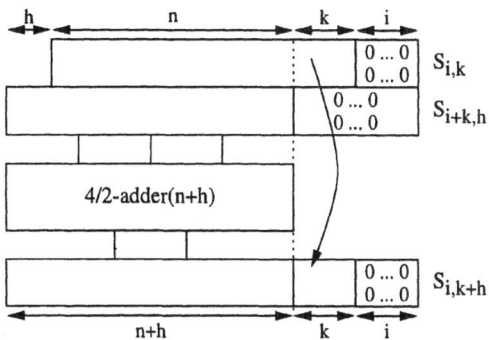

Figure 2.33 Partial compression of $S_{i,k+h}$

the leaves. For $\mu = 4$, $m = 53$, and $k = 3$, the leaves would, for example, have the weights 3333333333344444. For each subtree t of T, we define

$$W(t) = \sum_{u \text{ leaf of } t} W(u),$$

where u ranges over all leaves of t. For each interior node v of T we define $L(v)$ and $R(v)$ as the weight of the subtree rooted in the left or right son of v, respectively. We are interested in the sums

$$H_\ell = \sum_{level\ \ell} L(v) \qquad \text{and} \qquad H = \sum_{\ell=1}^{\mu} H_\ell,$$

where v ranges over all nodes of level ℓ. The cost H then obeys

◀ Lemma 2.5

$$(\mu \cdot m)/2 - 2^{\mu-1} < H \leq (\mu \cdot m)/2$$

By induction on the levels of T one shows that in each level weights are nondecreasing from left to right, and their sum is m. Hence,   PROOF

$$2H_\ell \leq \sum_{level\ \ell} L(v) + \sum_{level\ \ell} R(v) = \sum_{level\ \ell} W(v) = m.$$

This proves the upper bound.

In the proof of the upper bound we have replaced each weight $L(v)$ by the arithmetic mean of $L(v)$ and $R(v)$, overestimating $L(v)$ by

$$h(v) = (L(v) + R(v))/2 - L(v) = (R(v) - L(v))/2.$$

Observe that all nodes in level ℓ, except possibly one, have weights in $\{k \cdot 2^\ell, (k+1) \cdot 2^\ell\}$. Thus, in each level ℓ there is at most one node v_ℓ with $R(v_\ell) \neq L(v_\ell)$. For this node we have

$$h(v_\ell) \leq ((k+1) \cdot 2^{\ell-1} - k \cdot 2^{\ell-1})/2 = 2^{\ell-2}.$$

Hence, the error in the upper bound is at most

$$\sum_{\ell=1}^{\mu} 2^{\ell-2} < 2^{\mu-1}.$$

QED

We now use this lemma in order to estimate the number of excess full adders in the adder tree $\mathcal{T}(m)$ of figure 2.31. For that purpose, we label every leaf u of $\mathcal{T}(m)$ with the number $W(u)$ of partial products that it sums, i.e., in case of a 3/2-adder, u is labeled with $W(u) = 3$, and in case of a 4/2-adder it is labeled with $W(u) = 4$. In figure 2.31, we then have

$$h = W(L(u)),$$

and the number E of excess full adders can be estimated as

$$E = 2 \cdot H \leq \mu \cdot m.$$

The error in this bound is at most

$$2 \cdot 2^{\mu-1} = 2 \cdot 0.5 \cdot M/4 \leq m/3.$$

Thus, the upper bound is quite tight. A very good upper bound for the cost of 4/2-trees is therefore

$$\begin{aligned} C_{4/2tree}(n,m) &= (n \cdot (m-2) + E) \cdot C_{FA} \\ &\leq (n \cdot (m-2) + \mu \cdot m) \cdot C_{FA}. \end{aligned}$$

A good upper bound for the cost of multipliers built with 4/2-trees is

$$C_{4/2mul}(n,m) = n \cdot m \cdot C_{and} + C_{4/2tree}(n,m) + C_{CLA}(n+m).$$

2.5.5 Multipliers with Booth Recoding

Booth recoding is a method which reduces the number of partial products to be summed in the addition tree. This makes the addition tree smaller, cheaper and faster. On the other hand, the generation of partial products

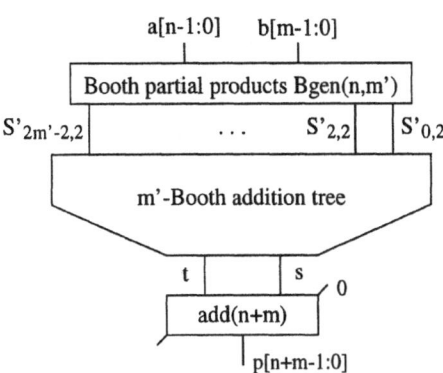

Figure 2.34 Structure of a (n,m)-Booth multiplier with addition tree

becomes more expensive and slower. One therefore has to show, that the savings in the addition tree outweigh the penalty in the partial product generation.

Figure 2.34 depicts the structure of a 4/2-tree multiplier with Booth recoding. Circuit *Bgen* generates the m' Booth recoded partial products $S'_{2j,2}$, which are then fed into a Booth addition tree. Finally, an ordinary adder produces from the carry save result of the tree the binary representation of the product. Thus, the cost and delay of an (n,m)-multiplier with 4/2-tree and Booth recoding can be expressed as

$$C_{4/2Bmul}(n,m) = C_{Bgen}(n,m') + C_{4/2Btree}(n',m') + C_{CLA}(n+m)$$
$$D_{4/2Bmul}(n,m) = D_{Bgen}(n,m') + D_{4/2Btree}(n',m') + D_{CLA}(n+m).$$

Booth-2 Recoding

In the simplest form (called Booth-2) the multiplier b is recoded as suggested in figure 2.35. With $b_{m+1} = b_m = b_{-1} = 0$ and $m' = \lceil (m+1)/2 \rceil$, one writes

$$\langle b \rangle = 2\langle b \rangle - \langle b \rangle = \sum_{j=0}^{m'-1} B_{2j} \cdot 4^j,$$

where

$$B_{2j} = 2b_{2j} + b_{2j-1} - 2b_{2j+1} - b_{2j} = -2b_{2j+1} + b_{2j} + b_{2j-1}.$$

The numbers $B_{2j} \in \{-2,-1,0,1,2\}$ are called *Booth digits*, and we define their sign bits s_{2j} by

$$s_{2j} = \begin{cases} 0 & \text{if} \quad B_{2j} \geq 0 \\ 1 & \text{if} \quad B_{2j} < 0. \end{cases}$$

43

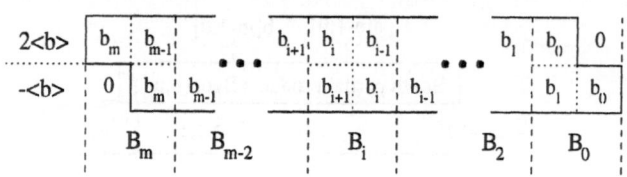

Figure 2.35 Booth digits B_{2j}

With

$$C_{2j} = \langle a \rangle \cdot B_{2j} \in \{-2^{n+1}-2, \ldots 2^{n+1}\}$$
$$D_{2j} = \langle a \rangle \cdot |B_{2j}| \in \{0, \ldots 2^{n+1}\}$$
$$d_{2j} = bin_{n+1}(D_{2j}),$$

the product can be computed from the sums

$$\langle a \rangle \cdot \langle b \rangle = \sum_{j=0}^{m'-1} \langle a \rangle B_{2j} 4^j = \sum_{j=0}^{m'-1} C_{2j} \cdot 4^j$$
$$= \sum_{j=0}^{m'-1} (-1)^{s_{2j}} \cdot D_{2j} \cdot 4^j.$$

In order to avoid negative numbers C_{2j}, one sums the positive E_{2j} instead:

$$E_{2j} = C_{2j} + 3 \cdot 2^{n+1}$$
$$E_0 = C_0 + 4 \cdot 2^{n+1}$$
$$e_{2j} = bin_{n+3}(E_{2j})$$
$$e_0 = bin_{n+4}(E_0).$$

This is illustrated in figure 2.36. The additional terms sum to

$$2^{n+1}\left(1 + 3 \cdot \sum_{j=0}^{m'-1} 4^j\right) = 2^{n+1}\left(1 + 3 \cdot \frac{4^{m'}-1}{3}\right) = 2^{n+1+2 \cdot m'}.$$

Because $2 \cdot m' > m$ these terms are congruent to zero modulo 2^{n+m}. Thus,

$$\langle a \rangle \cdot \langle b \rangle \equiv \left(\sum_{j=0}^{m'-1} E_{2j} \cdot 4^j\right) \bmod 2^{n+m}.$$

Lemma 2.6 ▶ *The binary representation e_{2j} of E_{2j} can be computed by*

$$\langle e_{2j} \rangle = \langle 1\overline{s_{2j}}, d_{2j} \oplus s_{2j} \rangle + s_{2j}$$
$$\langle e_0 \rangle = \langle \overline{s_0} s_0 s_0, d_0 \oplus s_0 \rangle + s_0.$$

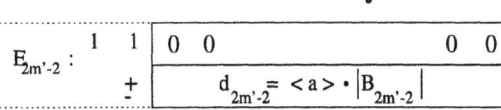

$$
\begin{array}{ll}
E_0 : & \quad 1 \quad 1 \;\big|\; 0 \quad 0 \qquad\qquad 0 \quad 0 \\
& \qquad\quad \pm \;\big|\; d_0 \;=\; <a> \cdot |B_0| \\[4pt]
E_2 : & \quad\;\; 1 \quad 1 \;\big|\; 0 \quad 0 \qquad\quad 0 \quad 0 \\
& \qquad\quad \pm \;\big|\; d_2 \;=\; <a> \cdot |B_2| \\[4pt]
E_4 : & \quad 1 \quad 1 \;\big|\; 0 \quad 0 \qquad 0 \quad 0 \\
& \quad\quad \pm \;\big|\; d_4 \;=\; <a> \cdot |B_4| \\
\end{array}
$$

$$
E_{2m'-2} : \quad 1 \quad 1 \;\big|\; 0 \quad 0 \qquad 0 \quad 0
$$
$$
\pm \;\big|\; d_{2m'-2} = <a> \cdot |B_{2m'-2}|
$$

Figure 2.36 Summation of the E_{2j}

For $j > 0$ and $s_{2j} = 0$, we have

$$
\begin{aligned}
\langle e_{2j} \rangle &= \langle 11, 0^{n+1} \rangle + \langle 00, d_{2j} \rangle = \langle 11, d_{2j} \rangle \\
&= \langle 1\overline{s_{2j}}, d_{2j} \oplus s_{2j} \rangle + s_{2j}.
\end{aligned}
$$

For $j > 0$ and $s_{2j} = 1$, we have

$$
\begin{aligned}
\langle e_{2j} \rangle &\equiv \langle 110^{n+1} \rangle + \langle 11\overline{d_{2j}} \rangle + 1 \bmod 2^{n+3} \\
&\equiv \langle 10, \overline{d_{2j}} \rangle + 1 \bmod 2^{n+3} \\
&= \langle 1\overline{s_{2j}}, d_{2j} \oplus s_{2j} \rangle + s_{2j}.
\end{aligned}
$$

For $j = 0$, one shows along the same lines that

$$
\langle e_0 \rangle = \langle \overline{s_0} s_0 s_0, d_0 \oplus s_0 \rangle + s_0
$$

By lemma 2.6, the computation of the numbers

$$
\begin{aligned}
F_{2j} &= E_{2j} - s_{2j} \\
f_{2j} &= bin_{n+3}(F_{2j}) \\
f_0 &= bin_{n+4}(F_0)
\end{aligned}
$$

is easy, namely

$$
\begin{aligned}
f_{2j} &= (1\overline{s_{2j}}, d_{2j} \oplus s_{2j}) \\
f_0 &= (\overline{s_0} s_0 s_0, d_0 \oplus s_0).
\end{aligned}
$$

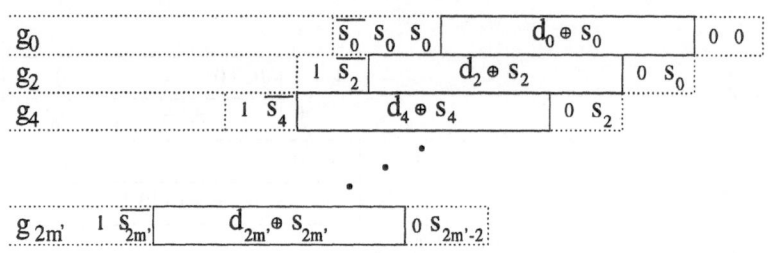

Figure 2.37 Construction of the partial products $S'_{2j,2}$

Instead of adding the sign bits s_{2j} to the numbers F_{2j}, one incorporates them at the proper position into the representation of F_{2j+2}, as suggested in figure 2.37. The last sign bit does not create a problem, because $B_{2m'-2}$ is always positive. Formally, let

$$g_{2j} = (f_{2j}0s_{2j-2}) \in \{0,1\}^{n+5}$$
$$g_0 = (f_000) \in \{0,1\}^{n+6},$$

then

$$\langle g_{2j} \rangle = 4 \cdot \langle f_{2j} \rangle + s_{2j-2} = 4 \cdot F_{2j} + s_{2j-2},$$

and with $s_{-2} = s_{2m'-2} = 0$, the product can also be written as

$$\langle a \rangle \cdot \langle b \rangle \equiv \left(\sum_{j=0}^{m'-1} E_{2j} \cdot 4^j \right) \bmod 2^{n+m}$$
$$= \sum_{j=0}^{m'-1} (4 \cdot (F_{2j} + s_{2j})) \cdot 4^{j-1}$$
$$= \sum_{j=0}^{m'-1} (4 \cdot F_{2j} + s_{2j-2}) \cdot 4^{j-1} = \sum_{j=0}^{m'-1} \langle g_{2j} \rangle \cdot 4^{j-1}.$$

We define

$$S'_{2j,2k} = \sum_{t=j}^{j+k-1} \langle g_{2j} \rangle \cdot 4^{j-1},$$

then

$$S'_{2j,2} = \langle g_{2j} \rangle \cdot 4^{j-1} = \langle f_{2j}, 0s_{2j-2} \rangle \cdot 4^{j-1}$$
$$S'_{2j,2(k+h)} = S'_{2j,2k} + S'_{2j+2k,2h}$$

and it holds:

Lemma 2.7 ▶ $S'_{2j,2k}$ *is a multiple of* 2^{2j-2} *bounded by* $S'_{2j,2k} \leq 2^{n+2j+2k+2}$. *Therefore, at most* $n+4+2k$ *non-zero positions are necessary to represent* $S'_{2j,2k}$ *in both carry-save or binary form.*

PROOF   by induction over k. For $k = 1$:

$$S'_{2j,2} < \langle 1^{n+6} \rangle \cdot 4^{j-1} < 2^{n+6} + 2^{2j-2} = 2^{n+2j+2 \cdot 1 + 2}.$$

For $k > 1$: It is known from the assumption that $S'_{2j,2k-2} < 2^{n+2j+2k}$. Thus,

$$
\begin{aligned}
S'_{2j,2k} &= S'_{2j,2(k-1)} + \langle g_{2(j+k-1)} \cdot 4^{j+k-2} \rangle \\
&< 2^{n+2j+2k} + 2^{n+5} \cdot 2^{2j+2k-2} \\
&= (1+2) \cdot 2^{n+2j+2k} < 2^{n+2j+2k+2}
\end{aligned}
$$

QED

2.5.6   Cost and Delay of the Booth Multiplier

Partial Product Generation   The binary representation of the numbers $S'_{2j,2}$ must be computed (see figure 2.37). These are

$$
\begin{aligned}
g_{2j} &= (1\overline{s_{2j}}, d_{2j} \oplus s_{2j}, 0 s_{2j-2}) \\
g_0 &= (\overline{s_0} s_0 s_0, d_0 \oplus s_0, 00)
\end{aligned}
$$

shifted by $2j - 2$ bit positions. The $d_{2j} = bin_{n+1}(\langle a \rangle \cdot |B_{2j}|)$ are easily determined from B_{2j} and a by

$$
d_{2j} = \begin{cases}
(0,\ldots,0) & \text{if} \quad B_{2j} = 0 \\
(0,a) & \text{if} \quad |B_{2j}| = 1 \\
(a,0) & \text{if} \quad |B_{2j}| = 2.
\end{cases}
$$

For this computation, two signals indicating $|B_{2j}| = 1$ and $|B_{2j}| = 2$ are necessary. We denote these signals by

$$
b1_{2j} = \begin{cases} 1 & \text{if } |B_{2j}| = 1 \\ 0 & \text{otherwise} \end{cases}
\qquad
b2_{2j} = \begin{cases} 1 & \text{if } |B_{2j}| = 2 \\ 0 & \text{otherwise} \end{cases}
$$

and calculate them by the Booth decoder logic BD of figure 2.38 (a). The decoder logic BD can be derived from table 2.6 in a straightforward way. It has the following cost and delay:

$$
\begin{aligned}
C_{BD} &= C_{xor} + C_{xnor} + C_{nor} + C_{inv} \\
D_{BD} &= \max\{D_{xor}, D_{xnor}\} + D_{nor}.
\end{aligned}
$$

The selection logic BSL of figure 2.38 (b) directs either bit $a[i]$, bit $a[i+1]$, or 0 to position $i+1$. The inversion depending on the sign bit s_{2j} then yields bit $g_{2j}[i+3]$. The select logic BSL has the following cost and delay:

$$
\begin{aligned}
C_{BSL} &= 3 \cdot C_{nand} + C_{xor} \\
D_{BSL} &= 2 \cdot D_{nand} + D_{xor}.
\end{aligned}
$$

Table 2.6 Representation of the Booth digits

$b[2j+1:2j-1]$	B_{2j}	$b[2j+1:2j-1]$	B_{2j}
000	0	100	-2
001	1	101	-1
010	1	110	-1
011	2	111	-0

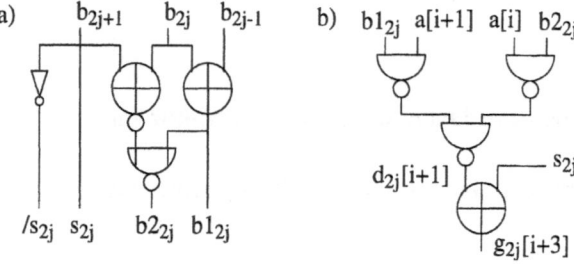

Figure 2.38 The Booth decoder BD (a) and the Booth selection logic BSL (b)

The select logic BSL is only used for selecting the bits $g_{2j}[n+2:2]$; the remaining bits $g_{2j}[1:0]$ and $g_{2j}[n+5:n+3]$ are fixed. For these bits, the selection logic is replaced by the simple signal of a sign bit, its inverse, a zero, or a one. Thus, for each of the m' partial products $n+1$ many select circuits BSL are required. Together with the m' Booth decoders, the cost of the Booth preprocessing runs at

$$C_{Bpre}(n,m') = m' \cdot (C_{BD} + (n+1) \cdot C_{BSL}).$$

Redundant Partial Product Addition Let $M' = 2^{\lceil \log m' \rceil}$ be the smallest power of two which is greater or equal $m' = \lceil (m+1)/2 \rceil$, and let $\mu' = \log(M/4)$. For $m \in \{27, 58\}$, it holds that

$$3/4 \cdot M' \leq m' < M'.$$

For the construction of the Booth 4/2-adder tree $T'(m')$, we proceed as in section 2.5.4, but we just focus on trees which satisfy the above condition.

The standard length of the 3/2-adders and the 4/2-adders is now $n' = n+5$ bits; longer operands require excess full adders. Let E' be the number of excess full adders. Considering the sums S' instead of the sums S, one shows that the top level of the tree has no excess full adders. Let H' be the sum of the labels of the left sons in the resulting tree. With Booth recoding, successive partial products are shifted by 2 positions. Thus, we now have

$$E' = 4 \cdot H'.$$

Since H' is bounded by $(\mu' \cdot m')/2$, we get

$$E' \leq 2 \cdot (\mu' \cdot m').$$

Thus, the delay and the cost of the 4/2-tree multiplier with Booth-2 recoding can be expressed as

$$
\begin{aligned}
C_{4/2Btree} &= (n' \cdot (m' - 2) + E') \cdot C_{FA} \\
&\leq (n' \cdot (m' - 2) + 2 \cdot \mu' \cdot m') \cdot C_{FA} \\
D_{4/2Btree} &= 2 \cdot (\mu' + 1) \cdot D_{FA}.
\end{aligned}
$$

Let C' and D' denote the cost and delay of the Booth multiplier but without the $(n+m)$-bit CLA adder, and let C and D denote the corresponding cost and delay of the multiplier without Booth recoding:

$$
\begin{aligned}
C' &= C_{4/2Bmul}(n,m) - C_{CLA}(n+m) \\
D' &= D_{4/2Bmul}(n,m) - D_{CLA}(n+m) \\
C &= C_{4/2mul}(n,m) - C_{CLA}(n+m) \\
D &= D_{4/2mul}(n,m) - D_{CLA}(n+m).
\end{aligned}
$$

For $n = m = 58$, we then get

$$
\begin{aligned}
C'/C &= 45246/55448 &= 81.6\% \\
D'/D &= 55/62 &= 88.7\%,
\end{aligned}
$$

and for $n = m = 27$, we get

$$
\begin{aligned}
C'/C &= 10234/12042 &= 84.9\% \\
D'/D &= 43/50 &= 86.0\%
\end{aligned}
$$

Asymptotically, C'/C tends to $12/16 = 0.75$. Unless m is a power of two, we have $\mu = \mu' + 1$ and $D - D' = 7$. Hence D'/D tends to one as n grows large.

When taking wire delays in a VLSI layout into account, it can be shown that Booth recoding also saves a constant fraction of time (independent of n) in multipliers built with 4/2-trees [PS98].

2.6 Control Automata

2.6.1 Finite State Transducers

Finite *state transducers* are finite automata which produce an output in every step. Formally, a finite state transducer is specified by a 6-tuple $(Z, In, Out, z_0, \delta, \eta)$, where Z is a finite set of states; $z_0 \in Z$ is called the *initial state*. *In* is a finite set of *input symbols*, *Out* is a finite set of *output symbols*,

$$\delta : Z \times In \to Z$$

is the *transition function*, and

$$\eta : Z \times In \to Out$$

is the *output function*.

Such an automaton works step by step according to the following rules:

- The automaton is started in state z_0.

- If the automaton is in state z and reads input symbol *in*, it then outputs symbol $\eta(z, in)$ and goes to state $\delta(z, in)$.

If the output function does not depend on the input *in*, i.e., if it can be written as

$$\eta : Z \to Out,$$

then the automaton is called a *Moore automaton*. Otherwise, it is called a *Mealy automaton*.

Obviously, the input of an automaton which controls parts of a computer will come from a certain number σ of input lines $in[\sigma - 1 : 0]$, and it will produce outputs on a certain number γ of output lines $out[\gamma - 1 : 0]$. Formally, we have

$$In = \{0, 1\}^{\sigma} \qquad \text{and} \qquad Out = \{0, 1\}^{\gamma}.$$

It is common practice to visualize automata as in figure 2.39 which shows a Moore automaton with 3 states z_0, z_1, and z_2, with the set of input symbols $In = \{0, 1\}^2$ and with the set of output symbols $Out = \{0, 1\}^2$. The automaton is represented as a directed graph (V, E) with labeled edges and nodes.

The set of nodes V of the graph are the states of the automaton. We draw them as rectangles, the initial state is marked by a double border. For any pair of states (z', z), there is an edge from z' to z in the set E of edges if $\delta(z', in) = z$ for some input symbol *in*, i.e., if a transition from state z' to

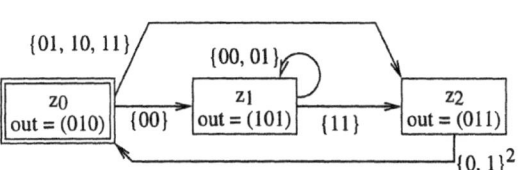

Figure 2.39 Representation of a Moore automaton with tree states, the set $In = \{0,1\}^2$ of input symbols and the set $Out = \{0,1\}^3$ of output symbols.

state z is possible. The edge $(z'z)$ is labeled with all input symbols in that take the automaton from state z' to state z. For Moore automata, we write into the rectangle depicting state z the outputs signals which are active in state z.

Transducers play an important role in the control of computers. Therefore, we specify two particular implementations; their cost and delay can easily be determined if the automaton is drawn as a graph. For a more general discussion see, e.g., [MP95].

2.6.2 Coding the State

Let $k = \#Z$ be the number of states of the automaton. Then the states can be numbered from 0 to $k-1$, and we can rename the states with the numbers from 0 to $k-1$:

$$Z = \{0,\dots,k-1\}.$$

We always code the current state z in a register with outputs $S[k-1:0]$ satisfying

$$S_i = \begin{cases} 1 & \text{if } z = i \\ 0 & \text{otherwise} \end{cases}$$

for all i. This means that, if the automaton is in state i, bit S_i is turned on and all other bits S_j with $j \neq i$ are turned off. The initial state always gets number 0. The cost of storing the state is obviously $k \cdot C_{ff}$.

2.6.3 Generating the Outputs

For each output signal $out_j \in Out$, we define the set of states

$$Z_j = \{z \in Z \mid out_j \text{ is active in state } z\}$$

in which it is active. Signal out_j can then obviously be computed as

$$out_j = \bigvee_{z \in Z_j} S_z.$$

We often refer to the cardinality

$$\nu_j = \#Z_j$$

as the frequency of the output signal out_j; ν_{max} and ν_{sum} denote the maximum and the sum of all cardinalities ν_j:

$$\nu_{max} = \max\{\nu_j \mid 0 \le j < \gamma\} \quad , \quad \nu_{sum} = \sum_{j=0}^{\gamma-1} \nu_j.$$

In the above example, the subsets are $Z_0 = \{z_1, z_2\}$, $Z_1 = \{z_0, z_2\}$, $Z_2 = \{z_1\}$, and the two parameters have the values $\nu_{max} = 2$ and $\nu_{sum} = 5$.

Each output signal out_j can be generated by a ν_j-input OR-tree at the cost of $(\nu_j - 1) \cdot C_{or}$ and the delay of $\lceil \log \nu_j \rceil \cdot D_{or}$. Thus, a circuit O generating all output signals has the following cost and delay:

$$C_O = \sum_{i=0}^{\gamma-1} (\nu_i - 1) \cdot C_{or} = (\nu_{sum} - \gamma) \cdot C_{or}$$

$$D_O = \max\{\lceil \log \nu_i \rceil \mid 1 \le i \le \gamma\} \cdot D_{or} = \lceil \log \nu_{max} \rceil \cdot D_{or}.$$

2.6.4 Computing the Next State

For each edge $(z, z') \in E$, we derive from the transition function δ the *boolean* function $\delta_{z,z'}$ specifying under which inputs the transition from state z to state z' is taken:

$$\delta_{z,z'}(in[\sigma - 1 : 0]) = 1 \quad \leftrightarrow \quad \delta(z, in[\sigma - 1 : 0]) = z'.$$

Let $D(z, z')$ be a disjunctive normal form of $\delta_{z,z'}$. If the transition from z to z' occurs for all inputs in, then $\delta_{z,z'} \equiv 1$, and the disjunctive normal form of $\delta_{z,z'}$ consists only of the trivial monomial $m = 1$. The automaton of figure 2.39 comprises the following disjunctive normal forms:

$$D(z_0, z_1) = \overline{in_1} \wedge \overline{in_0}, \quad D(z_0, z_2) = in_1 \vee in_0, \quad D(z_2, z_0) = 1,$$

$$D(z_1, z_1) = \overline{in_1}, \quad D(z_1, z_2) = in_1 \wedge in_0.$$

Let $M(z, z')$ be the set of monomials in $D(z, z')$ and let

$$M = \bigcup_{(z,z') \in E} M(z, z') \setminus \{1\}$$

be the set of all nontrivial monomials occurring in the disjunctive forms $D(z, z')$. The next state vector $N[k-1:1]$ can then be computed in three steps:

1. compute $\overline{in_j}$ for each input signal in_j,

2. compute all monomials $m \in M$,

3. and then compute for all z between 1 and $k-1$ the bit

$$
\begin{aligned}
N[z] &= \bigvee_{(z',z) \in E} S_{z'} \wedge \bigvee_{m \in M(z',z)} m \\
&= \bigvee_{(z',z) \in E} \bigvee_{m \in M(z',z)} (S_{z'} \wedge m).
\end{aligned}
\tag{2.5}
$$

Note that we do not compute $N[0]$ yet. For each monomial m, its length $l(m)$ denotes the number of literals in m; l_{max} and l_{sum} denote the maximum and the sum of all $l(m)$:

$$
l_{max} = \max\{l(m) \mid m \in M\} \quad , \quad l_{sum} = \sum_{m \in M} l(m).
$$

The computation of the monomials then adds the following cost and delay:

$$
\begin{aligned}
C_{CM} &= \sigma \cdot C_{inv} + (l_{sum} - \#M) \cdot C_{and} \\
D_{CM} &= D_{inv} + \lceil \log l_{max} \rceil \cdot D_{and}.
\end{aligned}
$$

For each node z, let

$$
\begin{aligned}
fanin(z) &= \sum_{(z',z) \in E} \#M(z',z) \\
fanin_{max} &= \max\{fanin(z) \mid 1 \le z \le k-1\} \\
fanin_{sum} &= \sum_{z=1}^{k-1} fanin(z),
\end{aligned}
$$

the next state signals $N[k-1:1]$ can then be generated at the following cost and delay:

$$
\begin{aligned}
C_{CN} &= fanin_{sum} \cdot (C_{and} + C_{or}) - (k-1) \cdot C_{or} \\
D_{CN} &= \lceil \log(fanin_{max}) \rceil \cdot D_{or} + D_{and}.
\end{aligned}
$$

Thus, a circuit NS computing these next state signals along these lines from the state bits $S[k-1:0]$ and the input $in[\sigma - 1:0]$ has cost and delay

$$
\begin{aligned}
C_{NS} &= C_{CM} + C_{CN} \\
D_{NS} &= D_{CM} + D_{CN}.
\end{aligned}
$$

Table 2.7 summarizes all the parameters which must be determined from the specification of the automaton in order to determine cost and delay of the two circuits O and NS.

Table 2.7 Parameters of a Moore control automaton

Parameter	Meaning
σ	# inputs in_j of the automaton
γ	# output signals out_j of the automaton
k	# states of the automaton
v_{max}, v_{sum}	maximal / accumulated frequency of all outputs
$\#M$	# monomials $m \in M$ (nontrivial)
l_{max}, l_{sum}	maximal / accumulated length of all $m \in M$
fan_{max}, fan_{sum}	maximal / accumulated fanin of states $z \neq z_0$

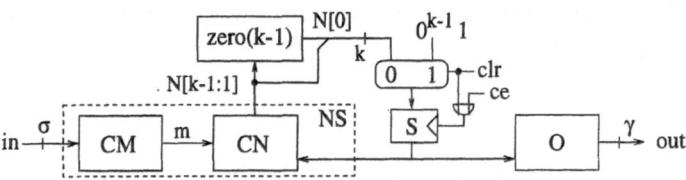

Figure 2.40 Realization of a Moore automaton

2.6.5 Moore Automata

Figure 2.40 shows a straightforward realization of Moore automata with clock enable signal ce and clear signal clr. The automaton is clocked when at least one of the signals ce and clr is active. At the start of the computation, the clear signal clr is active. This forces the pattern $0^{k-1}1$, i.e., the code of the initial state 0 into register S. As long as the clear signal is inactive, the next state N is computed by circuit NS and a zero tester. If none of the next state signals $N[k-1:1]$ is active, then the output of the zero tester becomes active and next state signal $N[0]$ is turned on.

This construction has the great advantage that it works even if the transition function is not completely specified, i.e., if $\delta(z, in)$ is undefined for some state z and input in. This happens, for instance, if the input in codes an instruction and a computer controlled by the automaton tries to execute an undefined (called illegal) instruction.

In the Moore automaton of figure 2.39, the transition function is not specified for z_1 and $in = (10)$. We now consider the case, that the automaton is in state z_1 and reads input (10). If all next state signals including signal $N[0]$ are computed according to equation (2.5) of the previous subsection, then the next state becomes 0^k. Thus, the automaton hangs and

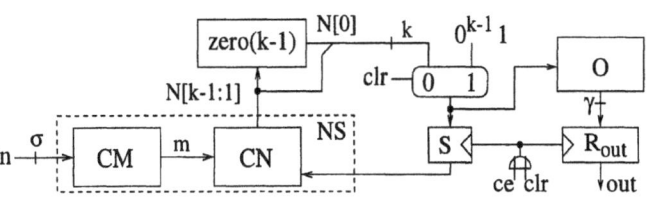

Figure 2.41 Realization of a Moore automaton with precomputed outputs

can only be re-started by activating the clear signal clr. However, in the construction presented here, the automaton falls gracefully back into its initial state. Thus, the transition $\delta(z_1, 10) = z_0$ is specified implicitly in this automaton.

Let $A(in)$ and $A(clr, ce)$ denote the accumulated delay of the input signals in and of the signals clr and ce. The cost, the delay and the cycle time of this realization can then be expressed as

$$
\begin{aligned}
C_{Moore} &= C_{ff}(k) + C_O + C_{NS} + C_{zero}(k-1) + C_{mux}(k) + C_{or} \\
A(out) &= D_O \\
T_{Moore} &= \max\{A(clr, ce) + D_{or}, A(in) + D_{NS} + D_{zero}(k-1)\} \\
&\quad + D_{mux} + \Delta.
\end{aligned}
$$

2.6.6 Precomputing the Control Signals

In the previous construction of the Moore automaton it takes time D_O from the time registers are clocked until the output signal are valid. In the construction of figure 2.41, the control signals are therefore precomputed and clocked into a separate register R_{out}. This increases the cycle time of the automaton by D_O, but the output signals $out[\gamma - 1 : 0]$ are valid without further delay. The cost, the delay, and the cycle time of the automaton then run at

$$
\begin{aligned}
C_{pMoore} &= C_{ff}(k) + C_O + C_{NS} + C_{zero}(k-1) + C_{mux}(k) + C_{ff}(\gamma) + C_{or} \\
A(out) &= 0 \\
T_{pMoore} &= \max\{A(clr, ce) + D_{or}, A(in) + D_{NS} + D_{zero}(k-1)\} \\
&\quad + D_{mux} + D_O + \Delta.
\end{aligned}
$$

This will be our construction of choice for Moore automata. The choice is not completely obvious. For a formal evaluation of various realizations of control automata see [MP95].

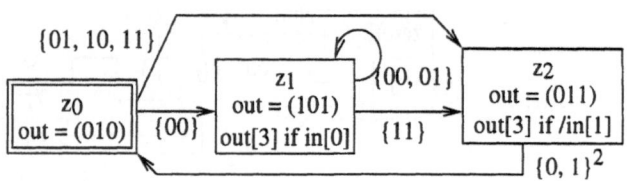

Figure 2.42 Representation of a Mealy automaton with tree states, inputs $in[1:0]$, and outputs $out[3:0]$; $out[3]$ is the only Mealy component of the output.

2.6.7 Mealy Automata

Consider a Mealy automaton with input signals $in[\sigma-1:0]$ and output signals $out[\gamma-1:0]$. In general, not all components $out[j]$ of the output will depend on both, the current state *and* the input signals $in[\sigma-1:0]$. We call $out[j]$ a *Mealy component* if it depends on the current state and the current input; otherwise we call $out[j]$ a *Moore component*.

Let out_j be a Mealy component of the output. For every state z in which out_j can be activated, there is a boolean function $f_{z,j}$ such that

$$out_j \text{ is active in state } z \quad \leftrightarrow \quad f_{z,j}(in) = 1.$$

If the Mealy output out_j is never activated in state z, then $f_{z,j} \equiv 0$. If the Mealy output out_j is always turned on in state z, then $f_{z,j} \equiv 1$. For any Mealy output out_j we define the set of states

$$Z'_j = \{z \mid f_{z,j} \not\equiv 0\}$$

where out_j can possibly be turned on.

Let $F(z,j)$ be a disjunctive normal form of $f_{z,j}$. With the help of $F(z,j)$ we can visualize Mealy outputs out_j in the following way. Let z be a state – visualized as a rectangle – in Z'_j; we then write inside the rectangle:

$$out_j \text{ if } F(z,i).$$

In figure 2.42, we have augmented the example automaton by a new Mealy output $out[3]$.

Let $MF(z,j)$ be the set of monomials in $F(z,j)$, and let

$$MF = \bigcup_{j=0}^{\gamma-1} \bigcup_{z\in Z'_j} MF(z,j) \setminus \{1\}$$

be the set of all nontrivial monomials occurring in the disjunctive normal forms $F(z,j)$. The Mealy outputs out_j can then be computed in two steps:

1. compute all monomials $m \in M \cup MF$ in a circuit CM (the monomials of M are used for the next state computation),

2. and for any Mealy output out_j, circuit O computes the bit

$$out_j = \bigvee_{z \in Z'_j} S[z] \wedge \bigvee_{m \in MF(z,j)} m = \bigvee_{z \in Z'_j} \bigvee_{m \in MF(z,j)} (S[z] \wedge m).$$

Circuit CM computes the monomials $m \in M \cup MF$ in the same way as the next state circuit of section 2.6.4, i.e., it first inverts all the inputs in_i and then computes each monomial m by a balanced tree of AND-gates. Let lf_{max} and l_{max} denote the maximal length of all monomials in MF and M, respectively, and let l_{sum} denote the accumulated length of all nontrivial monomials. Circuit CM can then generate the monomials of $M' = MF \cup M$ at the following cost and delay:

$$
\begin{aligned}
C_{CM} &= \sigma \cdot C_{inv} + (l_{sum} - \#M') \cdot C_{and} \\
D_{CM}(MF) &= D_{inv} + \lceil \log lf_{max} \rceil \cdot D_{and} \\
D_{CM}(M) &= D_{inv} + \lceil \log l_{max} \rceil \cdot D_{and}.
\end{aligned}
$$

Circuit CM is part of the circuit NS which implements the transition function of the automaton.

Since the Moore components of the output are still computed as in the Moore automaton, it holds

$$
out_j = \begin{cases}
\bigvee_{z \in Z_j} S[z] & \text{for a Moore component} \\
\bigvee_{z \in Z'_j} \bigvee_{m \in F(z,j)} (S[z] \wedge m) & \text{for a Mealy component.}
\end{cases}
$$

The number of monomials required for the computation of a Mealy output out_j equals

$$v_j = \sum_{z \in Z'_j} \#MF(z,j).$$

In analogy to the frequency of a Moore output, we often refer to v_j as the *frequency* of the Mealy output out_j. Let v_{max} and v_{sum} denote the maximal and the accumulated frequency of all outputs $out[\gamma - 1 : 0]$. The cost and the delay of circuit O which generates the outputs from the signals $m \in MF$ and $S[k-1:0]$ can be estimated as:

$$
\begin{aligned}
C_O &= v_{sum} \cdot (C_{and} + C_{or}) - \gamma \cdot C_{or} \\
D_O &= D_{and} + \lceil \log v_{max} \rceil \cdot D_{or}.
\end{aligned}
$$

A Mealy automaton computes the next state in the same way as a Moore automaton, i.e., as outlined in section 2.6.4. The only difference is that in

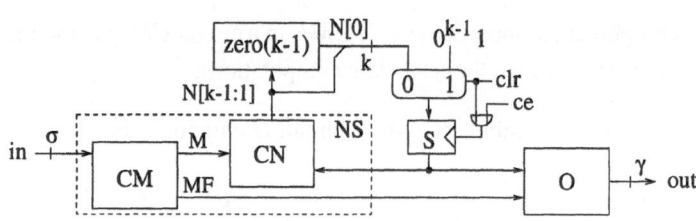

Figure 2.43 Realization of a Mealy automaton

the Mealy automaton, circuit CM generates the monomials required by the transition function as well as those required by the output function. Thus, the cost and delay of the next state circuit NS can now be expressed as

$$C_{NS} = C_{CM} + C_{CN}$$
$$D_{NS} = D_{CM}(M) + D_{CN}.$$

Let $A(in)$ and $A(clr, ce)$ denote the accumulated delay of the input signals in and of the signals clr and ce. A Mealy automaton (figure 2.43) can then be realized at the following cost and delay:

$$C_{Mealy} = C_{ff}(k) + C_O + C_{NS} + C_{zero}(k-1) + C_{mux}(k) + C_{or}$$
$$A(out) = A(in) + D_{CM}(MF) + D_O$$
$$T_{Mealy} = \max\{A(clr, ce) + D_{or}, A(in) + D_{NS} + D_{zero}(k-1)\}$$
$$+ D_{mux} + \Delta.$$

2.6.8 Interaction with the Data Paths

All the processor designs of this monograph consist of control automata and the so called *data paths* (i.e., the rest of the hardware). In such a scenario, the inputs *in* of an automaton usually code the operation to be executed; they are provided by the data paths DP. The outputs *out* of the automaton govern the data paths; these *control signals* at least comprise all clock enable signals, output enable signals, and write signals of the components in DP.

The interface between the control automaton and the data paths must be treated with care for the following two reasons:

1. Not all of the possible outputs $out \in \{0, 1\}^\gamma$ are admissible; for some values *out*, the functionality of the data paths and of the whole hardware may be undefined. For example, if several tristate drivers are

connected to the same bus, at most one these drivers should be enabled at a time in order to prevent bus contentions.

2. The signals *in* provided by the data paths usually depend on the current control signals *out*, and on the other hand, the output *out* of the automaton may depend on the current input *in*. Thus, after clocking, the hardware not necessarily gets into a stable state again, i.e., some control signals may not stabilize. However, stable control signals are crucial for the deterministic behavior of designs.

Admissible Control Signals

The functionality of combinatorial circuits is well defined [Weg87]. However, the structure of the processor hardware H is more complicated; its schematics also include flipflops, registers, RAMs, and tristate drivers. These components require control signals which are provided by a control automaton.

The control signals define for every value $out \in Out$ a *modified hardware* $H(out)$. In the modified hardware, a tristate driver with active enable signal $en = 1$ is treated like a gate which forwards its input data signals to its outputs. A tristate driver with inactive enable signal $en = 0$ is treated like there would be no connection between its inputs and its outputs. As a consequence, components and combinatorial circuits of $H(out)$ can have open inputs with an undefined input value.

A value $out \in Out$ of the control signals is called *admissible* if the following conditions hold:

- Tristate drivers are used in the data paths but not in the control automata.

- In the modified hardware $H(out)$, combinatorial circuits and basic components may have open inputs with an undefined value. Despite of these open inputs, each input of a register with active clock enable signal or of a RAM with active write signal has a value in $\{0,1\}$.

- In the modified hardware $H(out)$, any transfer between registers and RAMs is of one of the four types depicted in figure 2.3.

Note, for all of our processor designs, it must be checked that the control automata only generate admissible control signals.

Stable Control Signals

In order to keep the functionality of the whole hardware (control automaton and data paths DP) well defined, the data paths and the circuit O are partitioned into p parts each, $DP(1), \ldots, DP(p)$ and $O(1), \ldots, O(p)$, such that

- Circuit $O(i)$ gets the inputs $in(i) \subseteq \{in_0, \ldots, in_{\sigma-1}\}$; these inputs are directly taken from registers or they are provided by circuits of $DP(j)$, with $j < i$.

- Circuit $O(i)$ generates the output signals $out(i) \subseteq \{out_0, \ldots, out_{\gamma-1}\}$. These signals only govern the data paths $DP(i)$.

Circuit NS can receive inputs from any part of the data paths and from any output circuit $O(i)$.

The whole hardware which uses a common clock signal works in cycles. Let the control automaton only generate admissible control signals out. It then simply follows by induction over p that the control signals $out(i)$ stabilize again after clocking the hardware, and that the functionality of the hardware is well defined (for every clock cycle). The control signals $out(i)$ have an accumulated delay of

$$A_{O(i)} = D_{O(1)} + \sum_{j=2}^{i} (D_{DP(j)} + D_{O(j)}).$$

For Moore automata, such a partitioning of the data paths and of the automaton is unnecessary, since the control signals do not depend on the current state. However, in a Mealy automaton, the partitioning is essential. The signals $out(1)$ then form the Moore component of the output.

Parameters of the Mealy Automaton

The output signals of a Mealy automaton tend to be on the time critical path. Thus, it is essential for a good performance estimate, to provide the accumulated delay of every output circuit $O(i)$ respectively the accumulated delay of every subset $out(i)$ of output signals:

$$A_{O(i)} = A(out(i)).$$

Let $v_{max}(i)$ denote the maximal frequency of all output signals in $out(i)$, and let $lf_{max}(i)$ denote the maximal length of the monomials in the disjunctive normal forms $F(z, j)$, with $j \in out(i)$. Thus:

$$
\begin{aligned}
A(out(i)) &= A(in(i)) + D_{CM}(MF, i) + D_{O(i)} \\
D_{O(i)} &= D_{and} + \lceil \log v_{max}(i) \rceil \cdot D_{or} \\
D_{CM}(MF, i) &= D_{inv} + \lceil \log lf_{max}(i) \rceil \cdot D_{and}.
\end{aligned}
$$

Table 2.8 summarizes all the parameters which must be determined from the specification of the automaton in order to determine the cost and the delay of a Mealy automaton.

Table 2.8 Parameters of a Mealy control automaton with p output levels $O(1),\dots,O(p)$

Symbol	Meaning
σ	# input signals in_j of the automaton
γ	# output signals out_j of the automaton
k	# states of the automaton
fan_{sum}	accumulated fanin of all states $z \neq z_0$
fan_{max}	maximal fanin of all states $z \neq z_0$
$\#M'$	# monomials $m \in M' = MF \cup M$ of the automaton
l_{sum}	accumulated length of all monomials $m \in M'$
$lf_{max(i)},$ l_{max}	maximal length of the monomials of output level $O(i)$ and of the monomials $m \in M$ of the next state circuit
v_{sum}	accumulated frequency of all control signals
$v_{max(i)}$	maximal frequency of the signals $out(i)$ of level $O(i)$
$A_{clr,ce}$	accumulated delay of the clear and clock signals
$A_{in(i)},$ A_{in}	accumulated delay of the inputs $in(i)$ of circuit $O(i)$ and of the inputs in of the next state circuit

2.7 Selected References and Further Reading

THE FORMAL hardware model used in this book is from [MP95]. The extensive use of recursive definitions in the construction of switching circuits is very common in the field of Complexity of Boolean Functions; a standard textbook is [Weg87]. The description of Booth recoding at an appropriate level of detail is from [AT97], and the analysis of Booth recoding is from [PS98]. Standard textbooks on computer arithmetic are [Kor93, Omo94]. An early text on computer arithmetic with complete correctness proofs is [Spa76].

2.8 Exercises

Exercise 2.1 Let $m = \lceil n/2 \rceil$ for any $n > 1$. The high order sum bits of an n-bit incrementer with inputs $a[n-1:0]$, c_{in} and output $s[n:0]$ can be expressed as

$$
\begin{aligned}
\langle s[n:m] \rangle &= \langle a[n-1:m] \rangle + c_{m-1} \\
&= \begin{cases} \langle a[n-1:m] \rangle & \text{if} \quad c_{m-1} = 0 \\ \langle a[n-1:m] \rangle + 1 & \text{if} \quad c_{m-1} = 1, \end{cases}
\end{aligned}
$$

where c_{m-1} denotes the carry from position $m-1$ to position m. This suggests for the circuit of an incrementer the simple construction of figure 2.15 (page 26); the original problem is reduced to only two half-sized problems. Apply this construction recursively and derive formulae for the cost and the delay of the resulting incrementer circuit *CSI*.

Exercise 2.2 Derive formulae for the cost and the delay of an (n,m)-multiplier which is constructed according to the school method, using carry chain adders as building blocks.

Exercise 2.3 In section 2.5.4, we constructed and analyzed addition trees $\mathcal{T}(m)$ for (n,m)-multipliers without Booth recoding. The design was restricted to m satisfying the condition

$$3/4 \cdot M \leq m \leq M \quad \text{with} \quad M = 2^{\lceil \log m \rceil}.$$

This exercise deals with the construction of the tree $\mathcal{T}(m)$ for the remaining cases, i.e., for $M/2 < m < 3/4 \cdot M$. The bottom portion of the tree is still a completely regular and balanced 4/2-tree $T(M/4)$ with $M/4$ many pairs of inputs and $M/8$ many 4/2-adders as leaves. In the top level, we now have a many 3/2-adders and $M/4 - a$ many pairs of inputs which are directly fed to the 4/2-tree $T(M/4)$. Here, a is the solution of the equation

$$3a + 2 \cdot (M/4 - a) = m,$$

hence

$$a = m - M/2.$$

For $i = 0, 1, \ldots$, the partial products $S_{i,1}$ are entered into the tree from right to left and that in the top level of the tree the 3/2-adders are placed at the right-hand side.

1. Determine the number of excess adders in the tree $\mathcal{T}(m)$ and derive formulae for its cost and delay.

2. The Booth multiplier of section 2.5.5 used a modified addition tree $\mathcal{T}'(m)$ in order to sum the Booth recoded partial products. Extend the cost and delay formulae for the case that $M'/2 < m' < 3/4 \cdot M'$.

Chapter 3

A Sequential DLX Design

IN THE remainder of this book we develop a pipelined DLX machine with precise interrupts, caches and an IEEE-compliant floating point unit. Starting point of our designs is a sequential DLX machine without interrupt processing, caches and floating point unit. The cost effectiveness of later designs will be compared with the cost effectiveness of this basic machine.

We will be able to reuse almost all designs from this chapter. The design process will be – almost – strictly top down.

3.1 Instruction Set Architecture

WE SPECIFY the DLX instruction set without floating point instructions and without interrupt handling. DLX is a RISC architecture with only three instruction formats. It uses 32 general purpose registers $GPR[j][31:0]$ for $j \in \{0, \ldots 31\}$. Register $GPR[0]$ is always 0.

Load and store operations move data between the general purpose registers and the memory M. There is a single addressing mode: the effective address ea is the sum of a register and an immediate constant. Except for shifts, immediate constants are *always* sign extended.

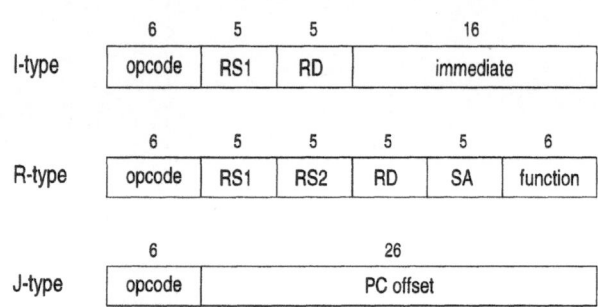

Figure 3.1 The three instruction formats of the DLX fixed point core. *RS*1 and *RS*2 are source registers; *RD* is the destination register. *SA* specifies a special purpose register or an immediate shift amount; *function* is an additional 6-bit opcode.

3.1.1 Instruction Formats

All three instruction formats (figure 3.1) have a 6-bit primary opcode and specify up to three explicit operands. The I-type (Immediate) format specifies two registers and a 16-bit constant. That is the standard layout for instructions with an immediate operand. The J-type (Jump) format is used for control instructions. They require no explicit register operand and profit from a larger 26-bit immediate operand. The third format, R-type (Register) format, provides an additional 6-bit opcode (*function*). The remaining 20 bits specify three general purpose registers and a field *SA* which specifies a 5-bit constant or a special purpose register. A 5-bit constant, for example, is sufficient for a shift amount.

3.1.2 Instruction Set Coding

Since the DLX description in [HP90] does not specify the coding of the instruction set, we adapt the coding of the MIPS R2000 machine ([PH94, KH92]) to the DLX instruction set. Tables 3.1 through 3.3 list for each DLX instruction its effect and its coding; the prefix "hx" indicates that the number is represented as hexadecimal. Taken alone, the tables are almost but not quite a mathematical definition of the semantics of the DLX machine language. Recall that mathematical definitions have to make sense if taken *literally*.

So, let us try to take the effect

$$RD = (RS1 > imm\,?\,1:0)$$

Table 3.1 I-type instruction layout. All instructions except the control instructions also increment the PC by four; $sxt(a)$ is the sign-extended version of a. The effective address of memory accesses equals $ea = \langle GPR[RS1] \rangle + \langle sxt(imm) \rangle$, where imm is the 16-bit intermediate. The width of the memory access in bytes is indicated by d. Thus, the memory operand equals $m = M[ea + d - 1], \cdots, M[ea]$.

IR[31 : 26]	Mnemonic	d	Effect
Data Transfer			
hx20	lb	1	RD = sxt(m)
hx21	lh	2	RD = sxt(m)
hx23	lw	4	RD = m
hx24	lbu	1	RD = 0^{24}m
hx25	lhu	2	RD = 0^{16}m
hx28	sb	1	m = RD[7 : 0]
hx29	sh	2	m = RD[15 : 0]
hx2b	sw	4	m = RD
Arithmetic, Logical Operation			
hx08	addi		RD = RS1 + imm
hx09	addi		RD = RS1 + imm
hx0a	subi		RD = RS1 - imm
hx0b	subi		RD = RS1 - imm
hx0c	andi		RD = RS1 $\wedge$ sxt(imm)
hx0d	ori		RD = RS1 $\vee$ sxt(imm)
hx0e	xori		RD = RS1 $\oplus$ sxt(imm)
hx0f	lhgi		RD = imm 0^{16}
Test Set Operation			
hx18	clri		RD = (false ? 1 : 0);
hx19	sgri		RD = (RS1 > imm ? 1 : 0);
hx1a	seqi		RD = (RS1 = imm ? 1 : 0);
hx1b	sgei		RD = (RS1 $\geq$ imm ? 1 : 0);
hx1c	slsi		RD = (RS1 < imm ? 1 : 0);
hx1d	snei		RD = (RS1 $\neq$ imm ? 1 : 0);
hx1e	slei		RD = (RS1 $\leq$ imm ? 1 : 0);
hx1f	seti		RD = (true ? 1 : 0);
Control Operation			
hx04	beqz		PC = PC + 4 + (RS1 = 0 ? imm: 0)
hx05	bnez		PC = PC + 4 + (RS1 $\neq$ 0 ? imm: 0)
hx16	jr		PC = RS1
hx17	jalr		R31 = PC + 4; PC = RS1

Table 3.2 R-type instruction layout. All instructions execute *PC += 4*. *SA* denotes the 5-bit immediate shift amount specified by the bits IR[10 : 6].

IR[31 : 26]	IR[5 : 0]	Mnemonic	Effect
Shift Operation			
hx00	hx00	slli	RD = sll(RS1, SA)
hx00	hx02	srli	RD = srl(RS1, SA)
hx00	hx03	srai	RD = sra(RS1, SA)
hx00	hx04	sll	RD = sll(RS1, RS2[4 : 0])
hx00	hx06	srl	RD = srl(RS1, RS2[4 : 0])
hx00	hx07	sra	RD = sra(RS1, RS2[4 : 0])
Arithmetic, Logical Operation			
hx00	hx20	add	RD = RS1 + RS2
hx00	hx21	add	RD = RS1 + RS2
hx00	hx22	sub	RD = RS1 - RS2
hx00	hx23	sub	RD = RS1 - RS2
hx00	hx24	and	RD = RS1 $\wedge$ RS2
hx00	hx25	or	RD = RS1 $\vee$ RS2
hx00	hx26	xor	RD = RS1 $\oplus$ RS2
hx00	hx27	lhg	RD = RS2[15:0] 0^{16}
Test Set Operation			
hx00	hx28	clr	RD = (false ? 1 : 0);
hx00	hx29	sgr	RD = (RS1 > RS2 ? 1 : 0);
hx00	hx2a	seq	RD = (RS1 = RS2 ? 1 : 0);
hx00	hx2b	sge	RD = (RS1 $\geq$ RS2 ? 1 : 0);
hx00	hx2c	sls	RD = (RS1 < RS2 ? 1 : 0);
hx00	hx2d	sne	RD = (RS1 $\neq$ RS2 ? 1 : 0);
hx00	hx2e	sle	RD = (RS1 $\leq$ RS2 ? 1 : 0);
hx00	hx2f	set	RD = (true ? 1 : 0);

Table 3.3 J-type instruction layout. *sxt(imm)* is the sign-extended version of the 26-bit immediate called PC offset.

IR[31 : 26]	Mnemonic	Effect
Control Operation		
hx02	j	PC = PC + 4 + sxt(imm)
hx03	jal	R31 = PC + 4; PC = PC + 4 + sxt(imm)

of instruction beqz in table 3.1 literally: the 5-bit string $RS1$ is compared with the 16-bit string imm using a comparison ">" which is not defined for such pairs of strings. The 1-bit result of the comparison is assigned to the 5-bit string RD.

This insanity can be fixed by providing five rules specifying the abbreviations and conventions which are used everywhere in the tables.

1. RD is a shorthand for $GPR[RD]$. Strictly speaking, it is actually a shorthand for $GPR[\langle RD \rangle]$. The same holds for $R1$ and $R2$.

2. Except in logical operations, immediate constants imm are always two's complement numbers.

3. In arithmetic operations and in test set operations, the equations refer to two's complement numbers.

4. All integer arithmetic is modulo 2^{32}. This includes all address calculations and, in particular, all computations involving the PC.

By lemma 2.2 we know that $[a] \equiv \langle a \rangle \bmod 2^{32}$ for 32-bit addresses a. Thus, the last convention implies that it does not matter whether we interpret addresses as two's complement numbers or as binary numbers.

The purpose of abbreviations and conventions is to turn long descriptions into short descriptions. In the tables 3.1 through 3.3, this has been done quite successfully. For three of the DLX instructions, we now list the almost unabbreviated semantics, where $sxt(imm)$ denotes the 32-bit sign extended version of imm.

1. Arithmetic instruction addi:

$$
\begin{aligned}
[GPR[RD]] &= [GPR[RS1]] + imm \bmod 2^{32} \\
&= [GPR[RS1]] + [sxt(imm)].
\end{aligned}
$$

2. Test set instruction sgri:

$$
[GPR[RD]] = [([GPR[RS1]] > [imm] ? 1 : 0)],
$$

or, equivalently

$$
GPR[RD] = 0^{31} ([GPR[RS1]] > [sxt(imm)] ? 1 : 0).
$$

3. Branch instruction beqz:

$$
\begin{aligned}
\langle PC \rangle &= \langle PC \rangle + 4 + ([GPR[RS1]] > 0 ? [imm] : 0) \bmod 2^{32} \\
&= \langle PC \rangle + 4 + ([GPR[RS1]] > 0 ? [sxt(imm)] : 0) \bmod 2^{32}.
\end{aligned}
$$

Observe that in the more detailed equations many hints for the implementation of the instructions become visible: immediate constants should be sign extended, and the 1-bit result of tests should be extended by 31 zeros.

3.1.3 Memory Organization

The memory is byte addressable, i.e., each memory address j specifies a memory location $M[j]$ capable of storing a single byte. The memory performs byte, half word, and word accesses. All instructions are coded in four bytes. In memory, data and instructions are *aligned* in the following way:

- half words must have even (byte) addresses. A half word h with address e is stored in memory such that

$$h[15:0] = M[e+1:e].$$

- words or instructions must have (byte) addresses divisible by four. These addresses are called *word boundaries*. A word or instruction w with address e is stored in memory such that

$$w[31:0] = M[e+3:e].$$

The crucial property of this storage scheme is, that half words, words and instructions stored in memory never cross word boundaries (see figure 3.2). For word boundaries e, we define the *memory word* with address e as

$$Mword[e] = M[e+3:e].$$

Moreover, we number the bytes of words $w[31:0]$ in little endian order (figure 3.3), i.e.:

$$
\begin{aligned}
byte_j(w) &= w[8j+7:8j] \\
byte_{[i:j]}(w) &= byte_i(w)\ldots byte_j(w)
\end{aligned}
$$

The definitions immediately imply the following lemma:

Lemma 3.1 ▶ *Let $\langle a[31:0]\rangle$ be a memory address, and let e be the word boundary $e = \langle a[31:2]\,00\rangle$. Then*

1. *the byte with address $\langle a \rangle$ is stored in byte $\langle a[1:0]\rangle$ of the memory word with address e:*

$$M(\langle a \rangle) = byte_{\langle a[1:0]\rangle}(Mword[\langle a[31:2]\,00\rangle]).$$

a) 1-bank desing

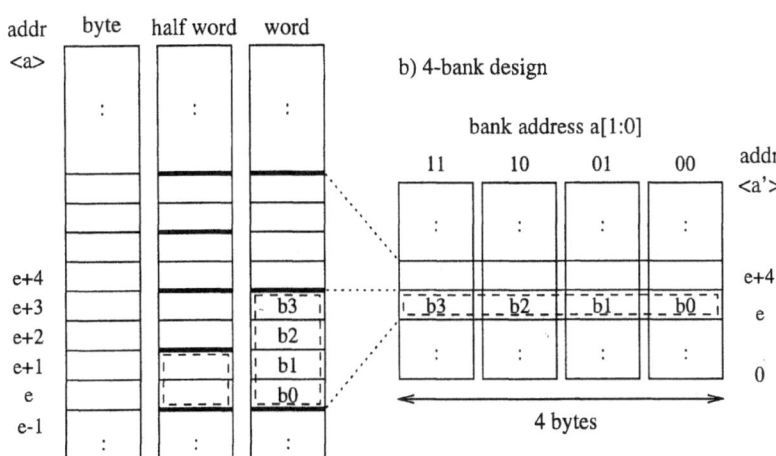

Figure 3.2 Storage scheme in an 1-bank memory system (a) and in a 4-bank memory system (b). A bank is always one byte wide. $a' = (a[31:2]00)$ and $e = \langle a' \rangle$.

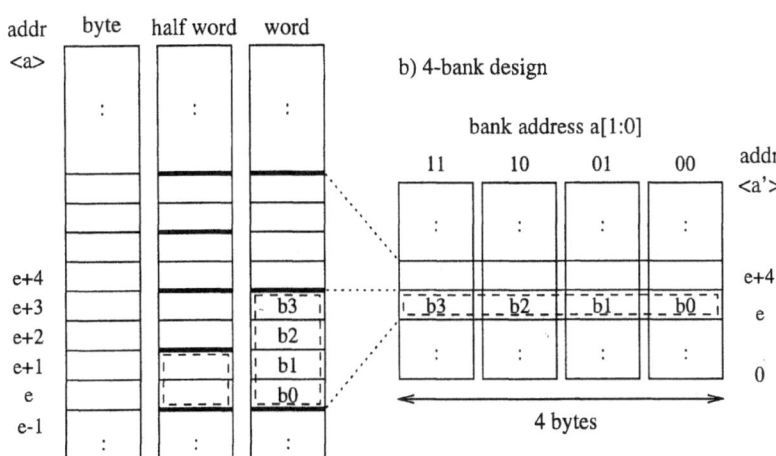

Figure 3.3 Ordering of the bytes within a word $w[31:0]$ – little endian order

2. *The piece of data which is d bytes wide and has address $\langle a \rangle$ is stored in the bytes $\langle a[1:0] \rangle$ to $\langle a[1:0] \rangle + d - 1$ of the memory word with address e:*

$$byte_{[\langle a[1:0] \rangle + d - 1 : \langle a[1:0] \rangle]}(Mword[\langle a[31:2]00 \rangle]).$$

3.2 High Level Data Paths

FIGURE 3.4 presents a high level view of the data paths of the machine. It shows busses, drivers, registers, a zero tester, a multiplexer, and the *environments*. Environments are named after some major unit or a register. They contain that unit or register plus some *glue logic* that is needed to adapt that unit or register to the coding of the instruction set. Table 3.4 gives a short description of the units used in figure 3.4. The reader should copy the table or better learn it by heart.

69

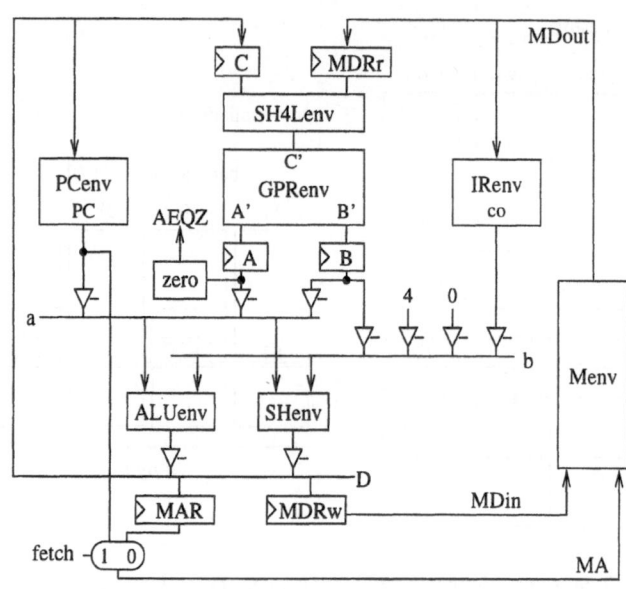

Figure 3.4 High level view of the sequential DLX data paths

We use the following naming conventions:

1. Clock enable signals for register R are called Rce. Thus, $IRce$ is the clock enable signal of the instruction register.

2. A driver from X to bus Y is called XYd, its output enable signal is called $XYdoe$. Thus, $SH4LDdoe$ is the output enable signal of the driver from the shifter for loads to the internal data bus.

3. A mux from anywhere to Y is called $Ymux$. Its select signal is called $Ymuxsel$.

We complete the design of the machine and we provide *a rigorous proof that it works* in a completely structured way. This involves the following three steps:

1. For each environment we specify its behavior and we then design it to meet the specifications.

2. We specify a Moore automaton which controls the data paths.

3. We show that the machine interprets the instruction set, i.e., that the hardware works correctly.

Table 3.4 Units and busses of the sequential DLX data paths

Large Units, Environments	
GPRenv	environment of the general purpose register file GPR
ALUenv	environment of the arithmetic logic unit ALU
SHenv	environment of the shifter SH
SH4Lenv	environment of the shifter for loads SH4L
PCenv	environment of the program counter PC
IRenv	environment of the instruction register IR
Menv	environment of the memory M
Registers	
A, B	output registers of GPR
MAR	memory address register
MDRw	memory data register for data to be written to M
MDRr	memory data register for data read from M
Busses	
A', B'	input of register A and register B
a, b	left/right source operand of the ALU and the SH
D	internal data bus of the CPU
MA	memory address
MDin	Input data of the memory M
MDout	Output data of the memory M
Inputs for the control	
AEQZ	indicates that the current content of register A equals zero
IR[31:26]	primary opcode
IR[5:0]	secondary opcode

Theoretically, we could postpone the design of the environments to the end. The design process would then be strictly top down – but the specification of seven environments in a row would be somewhat tedious to read.

3.3 Environments

3.3.1 General Purpose Register File

The general purpose register file environment contains a 32-word 3-port register file with registers $GPR_i[31:0]$ for $i = 0, \ldots, 31$. It is controlled by three control signals, namely

- the write signal *GPRw* of the register file GPR,

- signal *Rtype* indicating an R-type instruction, and

- signal *Jlink* indicating a jump and link instruction (jal, jalr)

In each cycle, the behavior of the environment is completely specified by very few equations. The first equations specify that the registers with addresses RS1 and RS2 are always read and provided as inputs to registers A and B. Reading from address 0, however, should force the output of the register file environment to zero.

$$A' = \begin{cases} GPR[RS1] & \text{if} \quad \langle RS1 \rangle \neq 0 \\ 0 & \text{if} \quad \langle RS1 \rangle = 0 \end{cases}$$

$$B' = \begin{cases} GPR[RS2] & \text{if} \quad \langle RS2 \rangle \neq 0 \\ 0 & \text{if} \quad \langle RS2 \rangle = 0 \end{cases}$$

Let *Cad* be the address to which register *C* is written. This address is usually specified by *RD*. In case of jump and link instructions (*Jlink* = 1), however, the PC must be saved into register 31. Writing should only occur if the signal *GPRw* is active:

$$Cad = \begin{cases} RD & \text{if} \quad Jlink = 0 \\ 31 & \text{if} \quad Jlink = 1 \end{cases}$$

$$GPR[Cad] := C \quad \text{if} \quad GPRw = 1$$

The remaining equations specify simply the positions of the fields *RS1*, *RS2* and *RD*; only the position of *RD* depends on the type of the instruction:

$$RS1 = IR[25 : 21]$$
$$RS2 = IR[20 : 16]$$
$$RD = \begin{cases} IR[20 : 16] & \text{if} \quad Rtype = 0 \\ IR[15 : 11] & \text{if} \quad Rtype = 1. \end{cases}$$

This completes the specification of the GPR environment.

Circuit *CAddr* of figure 3.5 generates the destination address at the following cost and delay:

$$C_{CAddr} = 2 \cdot C_{mux}(5)$$
$$D_{DAddr} = 2 \cdot D_{mux}(5).$$

The design in figure 3.5 is a straightforward implementation of the GPR environment with the cost:

$$C_{GPRenv} = C_{ram3}(32,32) + C_{CAddr} + 2 \cdot (C_{zero}(5) + C_{inv} + C_{and}(32)).$$

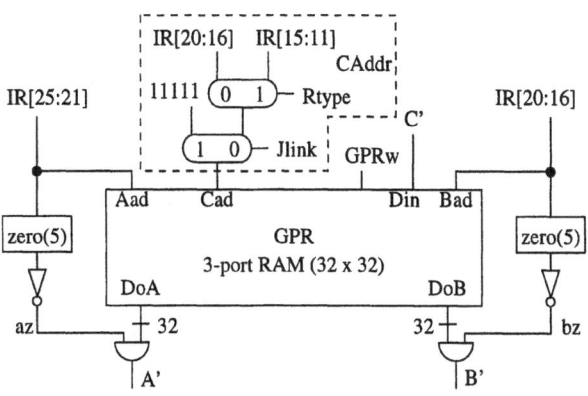

Figure 3.5 Implementation of the GPR environment

The register file performs two types of accesses; it provides data A' and B', or it writes data C' back. The read access accounts for the delay

$$
\begin{aligned}
D_{GPR,read} &= D_{GPRenv}(IR,GPRw;A',B') \\
&= \max\{D_{ram3}(32,32), D_{zero}(5) + D_{inv}\} + D_{and},
\end{aligned}
$$

whereas the write access takes time

$$
D_{GPR,write} = D_{CAddr} + D_{ram3}(32,32).
$$

3.3.2 Instruction Register Environment

This environment is controlled by the three control signals

- *Jjump* indicating an J-type jump instruction,

- *shiftI* indicating a shift instruction with an immediate operand, and

- the clock enable signal *IRce* of the instruction register IR.

The environment contains the instruction register, which is loaded from the bus *MDout*. Thus,

$$
IR := MDout \quad \text{if} \quad IRce = 1.
$$

The environment IRenv outputs the 32-bit constant

$$
co[31:0] = \begin{cases} *^{27}SA & \text{if} \quad shiftI = 1 \\ sxt(imm) & \text{if} \quad shiftI = 0, \end{cases}
$$

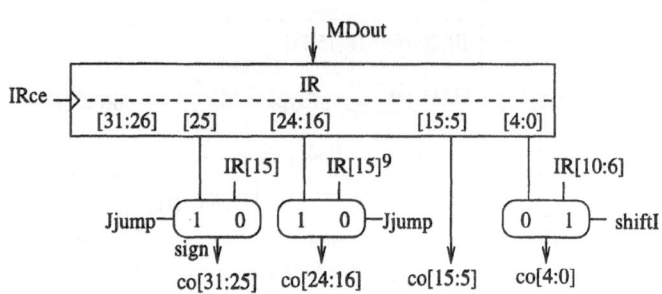

Figure 3.6 Implementation of the IR environment

where $sxt(a)$ denotes the 32-bit, sign extended representation of a. The position of the shift amount SA and of the immediate constant imm in the instruction word is specified by

$$SA = IR[10:6]$$
$$imm = \begin{cases} IR[15:0] & \text{if } Jjump = 0 \\ IR[25:0] & \text{if } Jjump = 1. \end{cases}$$

This completes the specification of the environment IRenv. The design in figure 3.6 is a straightforward implementation. Its cost and the delay of output co are:

$$C_{IRenv} = C_{ff}(32) + C_{mux}(15)$$
$$D_{IRenv}(co) = D_{mux}(15).$$

3.3.3 PC Environment

This environment is controlled by the *reset* signal and the clock enable signal $PCce$ of the PC. If the reset signal is active, then the start address 0^{32} of the boot routine is clocked into the PC register:

$$PC := \begin{cases} D & \text{if } PCce \wedge /reset \\ 0^{32} & \text{if } reset \end{cases}$$

This completes the specification of the PC environment. The design in figure 3.7 implements PCenv in a straightforward manner. Let $D_{PCenv}(In; PC)$ denote the delay which environment PCenv adds to the delay of the inputs of register PC. Thus:

$$C_{PCenv} = C_{ff}(32) + C_{mux}(32) + C_{or}$$
$$D_{PCenv}(In; PC) = \max\{D_{mux}(32), D_{or}\}.$$

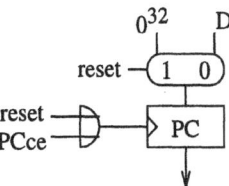

Figure 3.7 Implementation of the PC environment

3.3.4 ALU Environment

This environment is controlled by the three control signals

- *Rtype* indicating an R-type instruction,

- *add* forcing the ALU to add, and

- *test* forcing the ALU to perform a test and set operation.

The ALU is used for arithmetic/logic operations and for test operations. The type of the ALU operation is specified by three bits which we call $f[2:0]$. These bits are the last three bits of the primary or secondary opcode, depending on the type of instruction:

$$f[2:0] = \begin{cases} IR[28:26] & \text{if} \quad Rtype = 0 \\ IR[2:0] & \text{if} \quad Rtype = 1 \end{cases}$$

In case a test operation is performed, the result $t \in \{0,1\}$ is specified by table 3.5. In case of an arithmetic/logic operation, the result al is specified by table 3.6. Observe that in this table $al = a + b$ is a shorthand for $[al] = [a] + [b] \bmod 2^{32}$; the meaning of $a - b$ is defined similarly. For later use, we define the notation

$$al = a \, op \, b.$$

The flag ovf of the arithmetic unit AU indicates an overflow, i.e., it indicates that the value $[a] \, op \, [b]$ does not lie in the range T_{32} of a 32-bit two's complement number.

If signal *add* is activated, the ALU performs plain binary addition modulo 2^{32}. The final output alu of the ALU is selected under control of the signals *test* and *add* in an obvious way such that

$$alu = \begin{cases} 0^{31}t & \text{if} \quad test = 1 \\ al & \text{if} \quad test = 0 \text{ AND } add = 0 \end{cases}$$

$$\langle alu \rangle = \langle a \rangle + \langle b \rangle \bmod 2^{32} \quad \text{if} \quad test = 0 \text{ AND } add = 1$$

This completes the specification of the ALU.

Table 3.5 Specification of the test condition

cond.		false	$a > b$	$a = b$	$a \geq b$	$a < b$	$a \neq b$	$a \leq b$	true
f_2	$<$	0	0	0	0	1	1	1	1
f_1	$=$	0	0	1	1	0	0	1	1
f_0	$>$	0	1	0	1	0	1	0	1

Table 3.6 Coding of the arithmetic/logical ALU operations

	a+b	a-b	$a \wedge b$	$a \vee b$	$a \oplus b$	$b[15:0]0^{n-16}$
f_2	0	0	1	1	1	1
f_1	0	1	0	0	1	1
f_0	*	*	0	1	0	1

The Comparator

The coding of conditions from table 3.5 is frequently used. The obvious implementation proceeds in two steps. First, one computes the auxiliary signals l, e, g (less, equal, greater) with

$$
\begin{aligned}
l = 1 &\leftrightarrow a < b \leftrightarrow a - b < 0 \\
e = 1 &\leftrightarrow a = b \leftrightarrow a - b = 0 \\
g = 1 &\leftrightarrow a > b \leftrightarrow a - b > 0,
\end{aligned}
$$

and then, one generates

$$ t(a, b, f) = f_2 \wedge l \vee f_1 \wedge e \vee f_0 \wedge g. $$

Figure 3.8 depicts a realization along these lines using an arithmetic unit from section 2.4. Assuming that the subtraction signal *sub* is active, it holds

$$
\begin{aligned}
l &= neg \\
e = 1 &\leftrightarrow s[31:0] = 0^{32} \\
g &= \bar{e} \wedge \bar{l}.
\end{aligned}
$$

The cost and the delay of a 32-bit comparator are

$$
\begin{aligned}
C_{comp}(32) &= C_{zero}(32) + 2 \cdot C_{inv} + 4 \cdot C_{and} + 2 \cdot C_{or} \\
D_{comp}(32) &= \max\{D_{inv} + D_{and}, D_{zero}(32) + D_{or}, D_{zero}(32) + D_{inv}\} \\
&\quad + D_{and} + D_{or}.
\end{aligned}
$$

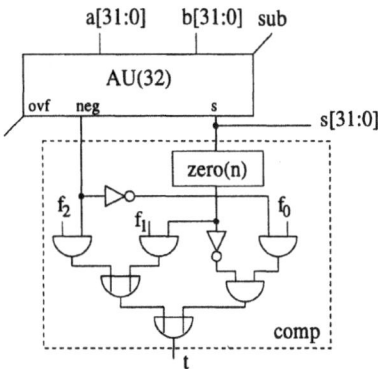

Figure 3.8 Arithmetic unit supplemented by the comparator circuit

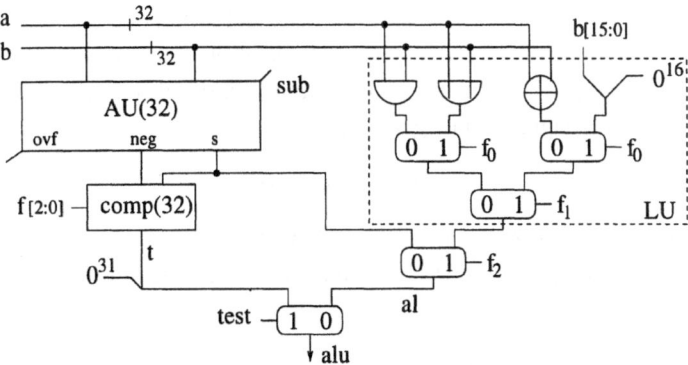

Figure 3.9 Implementation of the *ALU* comprising an arithmetic unit *AU*, a logic unit *LU* and a comparator

The Logic Unit

The coding of the arithmetic/logic functions in table 3.6 translates in a straightforward way into figure 3.9. Thus, the cost and the delay of the logic unit *LU* and of this ALU run at

$$C_{LU}(32) = C_{and}(32) + C_{or}(32) + C_{xor}(32) + 3 \cdot C_{mux}(32)$$
$$D_{LU}(32) = \max\{D_{and} + D_{or}, D_{xor}\} + 2 \cdot D_{mux}$$
$$C_{ALU} = C_{AU}(32) + C_{LU}(32) + C_{comp}(32) + 2 \cdot C_{mux}(32)$$
$$D_{ALU} = \max\{D_{AU}(32) + D_{comp}(32), D_{AU}(32) + D_{mux},$$
$$D_{LU}(32) + D_{mux}\} + D_{mux}.$$

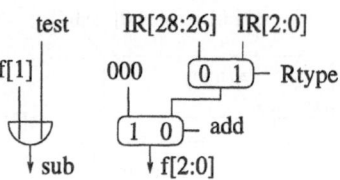

Figure 3.10 Glue logic of the ALU environment

The Glue Logic

Figure 3.10 suggests how to generate the signals *sub* and $f[2:0]$ from control signals *add* and *Rtype*. The mux controlled by signal *Rtype* selects between primary and secondary opcode. The mux controlled by *add* can force $f[2:0]$ to 000, that is the code for addition.

The arithmetic unit is only used for tests and arithmetic operations. In case of an arithmetic ALU operation, the operation of the AU is an addition (add or addi) if $f_1 = 0$ and it is a subtraction (sub or subi) if $f_1 = 1$. Hence, the subtraction signal can be generated as

$$sub = test \lor f_1.$$

The environment ALUenv consists of the ALU circuit and the ALU glue logic. Thus, for the entire ALU environment, we get the following cost and delay:

$$
\begin{aligned}
C_{ALUglue} &= C_{or} + 2 \cdot C_{mux}(3) \\
D_{ALUglue} &= 2 \cdot D_{mux}(3) + D_{or} \\
C_{ALUenv} &= C_{ALU} + C_{ALUglue} \\
D_{ALUenv} &= D_{ALUglue} + D_{ALU}.
\end{aligned}
$$

3.3.5 Memory Environment

The memory environment $Menv$ is controlled by three signals

- *mr* indicating a memory read access,

- *mw* indicating a memory write access, and

- *fetch* indicating an instruction fetch.

On instruction fetch (i.e., $fetch = 1$), the memory write signal must be inactive, i.e., $mw = 0$. The address of a memory access is always specified by the value on the memory address bus $MA[31:0]$.

Table 3.7 Coding the width of a memory write access

IR[27:26]	d	MAR[1:0]	mbw[3:0]
00	1	00	0001
		01	0010
		10	0100
		11	1000
01	2	00	0011
		10	1100
11	4	00	1111

Recall that the memory M is byte addressable. Half words are aligned at even (byte) addresses; instructions and words are aligned at word boundaries, i.e., at (byte) addresses divisible by 4. Due to the alignment, memory data never cross word boundaries. We therefore organize the memory in such a way that for every word boundary e the memory word

$$Mword[e] = M[e+3:e]$$

can be accessed in parallel. Thus, a single access suffices in order to load or store every byte, half word, word or instruction.

If $mr = 1$, the memory environment Menv performs a read operation, i.e., a load operation or an instruction fetch. Menv then provides on the bus $MDout$ the word

$$MDout[31:0] = Mword[\langle MA[31:2]00\rangle].$$

If the read operation accesses the d-byte data X, by lemma 3.1, X is then the subword

$$X = byte_{\langle MA[1:0]\rangle+d-1 : \langle MA[1:0]\rangle}(MDout)$$

of the memory bus $MDout$.

On $mw = 1$, the fetch signal is inactive ($fetch = 0$). Thus, a store operation is executed, and the memory environment performs a write operation. During a store operation, the bits $IR[27:26]$ of the primary opcode specify the number of bytes d to be stored in memory (table 3.7). The address of the store is specified by the memory address register MAR. If the d-byte data X are to be stored, then the memory environment expects them as the subword

$$X = byte_{\langle MAR[1:0]\rangle+d-1 : \langle MAR[1:0]\rangle}(MDin)$$

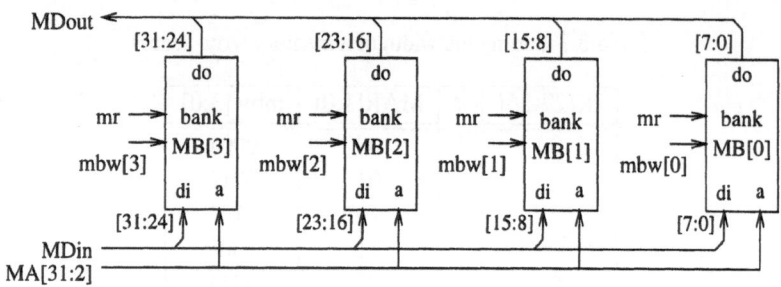

Figure 3.11 Connecting the memory banks to the data and address busses

of the memory bus *MDin* and performs the write operation

$$M[e+d-1:e] := X.$$

The data on the memory bus *MDin* are provided by register *MDRw*. For later use, we introduce for this the notation

$$m = bytes(MDRw).$$

Since memory accesses sometimes require multiple clock cycles, we need a signal *mbusy* indicating that the current memory access will *not* be completed during the current clock cycle. This signal is an input of the control unit; it can only be active on a memory access, i.e., if $mr = 1$ or $mw = 1$. We expect signal *mbusy* to be valid d_{mstat} time units after the start of each clock cycle.

This completes the specification of the memory environment Menv. Its realization is fairly straightforward. We use four memory banks $MB[j]$ with $j \in \{0, \ldots, 3\}$. Each bank $MB[j]$ is one byte wide and has its own write signal $mbw[j]$. Figure 3.11 depicts how the four banks are connected to the 32-bit data and address busses.

The Memory Control

The bank write signals $mbw[3:0]$ are generated as follows: Feeding the address bits $MAR[1:0]$ into a 2-decoder gives four signals $B[3:0]$ satisfying

$$B[j] = 1 \leftrightarrow \langle MAR[1:0] \rangle = j$$

for all j. From the last two bits of the opcode, we decode the width of the current access according to table 3.7 by

$$
\begin{aligned}
B &= \overline{IR[26]} \\
H &= \overline{IR[27]} \wedge IR[26] \\
W &= IR[27] \wedge IR[26].
\end{aligned}
$$

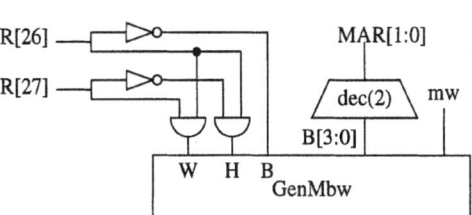

Figure 3.12 Memory control MC. Circuit *GenMbw* generates the bank write signals according to Equation 3.1

The bank write signals are then generated in a brute force way by

$$
\begin{aligned}
mbw[0] &= mw \wedge B[0] \\
mbw[1] &= mw \wedge (W \wedge B[0] \vee H \wedge B[0] \vee B \wedge B[1]) \\
mbw[2] &= mw \wedge ((W \wedge B[0] \vee H \wedge B[2]) \vee B \wedge B[2]) \\
mbw[3] &= mw \wedge ((W \wedge B[0] \vee H \wedge B[2]) \vee B \wedge B[3]).
\end{aligned}
\tag{3.1}
$$

When reusing common subexpressions, the cost and the delay of the memory control MC (figure 3.12) runs at

$$
\begin{aligned}
C_{MC} &= C_{dec}(2) + 2 \cdot C_{inv} + 12 \cdot C_{and} + 5 \cdot C_{or} \\
D_{MC} &= \max\{D_{dec}(2), D_{inv} + D_{and}\} + 2 \cdot D_{and} + 2 \cdot D_{or}.
\end{aligned}
$$

Let d_{mem} be the access time of the memory banks. The memory environment then delays the data MDout by

$$
D_{Menv}(MDout) = D_{MC} + d_{mem}.
$$

We do not elaborate on the generation of the *mbusy* signal. This will only be possible when we built cache controllers.

3.3.6 Shifter Environment SHenv

The shifter environment *SHenv* is used for two purposes: for the execution of the *explicit shift* operations sll (shift left logical), srl (shift right logical) and sra (shift right arithmetic), and second, for the execution of *implicit* shifts. An implicit shifted is only used during the store operations sb and sw in order to align the data to be stored in memory. The environment SHenv is controlled by a single control signal

- *shift4s*, denoting a shift for a store operation.

Table 3.8 Coding of the explicit shifts

IR[1:0]	00	10	11
type	sll	srl	sra

Explicit Shifts

We formally define the three explicit shifts. Obviously, left shifts and right shifts differ by the shift direction. Logic shifts and arithmetic shifts differ by the *fill bit*. This bit fills the positions which are not covered by the shifted operand any more. We define the explicit shifts of operand $a[n-1:0]$ by distance $b[m-1:0]$ in the following way:

$$sll(a,b) = (a_{n-\langle b \rangle-1}, \ldots, a_0, fill^{\langle b \rangle})$$
$$srl(a,b) = (fill^{\langle b \rangle}, a_{n-1}, \ldots, a_{\langle b \rangle})$$
$$sra(a,b) = (fill^{\langle b \rangle}, a_{n-1} \ldots, a_{\langle b \rangle})$$

where

$$fill = \begin{cases} 0 & \text{for logic shifts} \\ a_{n-1} & \text{for arithmetic shifts.} \end{cases}$$

Thus, arithmetic shifts extend the sign bit of the shifted operand. They probably have their name from the equality

$$[sra(a,b)] = \lfloor [a]/2^{\langle b \rangle} \rfloor,$$

which can be exploited in division algorithms for 2's complement numbers.

In case of an explicit shift operation, the last two bits $IR[1:0]$ of the secondary opcode select among the three explicit shifts according to table 3.8. By $shift(a,b,IR[1:0])$, we denote the result of the shift specified by $IR[1:0]$ with operands a and b.

Implicit Shifts

Implicit left shifts for store operation are necessary if a byte or half word – which is aligned at the right end of $a[31:0]$ – is to be stored at a byte address which is not divisible by 4. The byte address is provided by the memory address register MAR. Measured in bits, the shift distance (motivated by lemma 3.1) in this case equals

$$8 \cdot \langle MAR[1:0] \rangle = \langle MAR[1:0]000 \rangle.$$

The operand a is shifted cyclically by this distance. Thus, the output sh of the shifter environment SHenv is

$$sh = \begin{cases} shift(a,b,IR[1:0]) & \text{if } shift4s = 0 \\ cls(a,MAR[1:0]000) & \text{if } shift4s = 1. \end{cases}$$

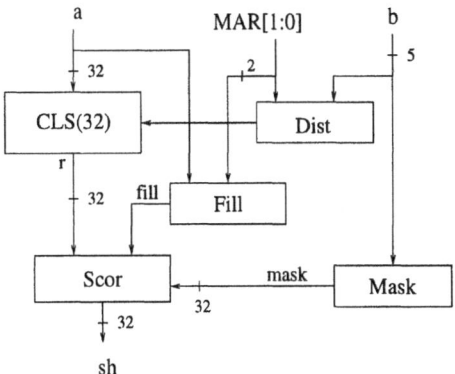

Figure 3.13 Top level of the shifter environment SHenv

This completes the specification of the shifter environment. Figure 3.13 depicts a very general design for shifters from [MP95]. A 32-bit cyclic left shifter *CLS* shifts operand $a[31:0]$ by a distance $dist[4:0]$ provided by the distance circuit *Dist*. The result $r[31:0]$ of the shift is corrected by circuit *Scor* as a function of the fill bit *fill* and a replacement mask $mask[31:0]$ which are provided by the corresponding subcircuits.

The Shift Correction

For every bit position i, circuit *Scor* replaces bit r_i of the intermediate result by the fill bit in case that the mask bit $mask_i$ is active. Thus,

$$sh_i = \begin{cases} fill & \text{if} \quad mask_i = 1 \\ r_i & \text{if} \quad mask_i = 0 \end{cases}$$

Figure 3.14 depicts a straightforward realization of the correction circuit. For the whole shifter environment SHenv, one obtains the following cost and delay:

$$
\begin{aligned}
C_{SHenv} &= C_{CLS}(32) + C_{Dist} + C_{Fill} + C_{Mask} + 32 \cdot C_{mux} \\
D_{SHenv} &= \max\{D_{Dist} + D_{CLS}(32), D_{Fill}, D_{Mask}\} + D_{mux}
\end{aligned}
$$

The Shift Distance

According to the shifters of section 2.4.6, an n-cyclic right shift can also be expressed as an n-cyclic left shift:

$$crs(a, \langle b \rangle) = cls(a, \langle \overline{b} \rangle + 1 \bmod n).$$

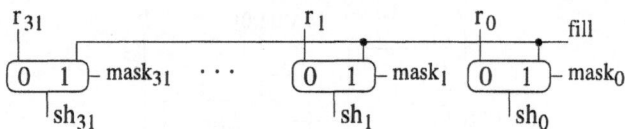

Figure 3.14 The shift-correction circuit Scor

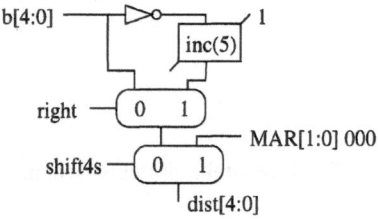

Figure 3.15 Circuit Dist selects the shift distance of shifter SH

Thus, in the distance circuit *Dist* of figure 3.15, the mux controlled by signal *right* selects the proper left shift distance of the explicit shift. According to table 3.8, bit $IR[1]$ can be used to distinguish between explicit left shifts and explicit right shifts. Thus, we can set

$$right \ = \ IR[1].$$

The additional mux controlled by signal *shift4s* can force the shift distance to $MAR[1:0]000$, i.e., the left shift distance specified for stores. The cost and the delay of the distance circuit *Dist* are

$$
\begin{aligned}
C_{Dist} &= C_{inv}(5) + C_{inc}(5) + 2 \cdot C_{mux}(5) \\
D_{Dist}(b) &= D_{inv}(5) + D_{inc}(5) + 2 \cdot D_{mux}(5) \\
D_{Dist}(MAR) &= D_{mux}(5).
\end{aligned}
$$

The Fill Bit
The fill bit is only different from 0 in case of an arithmetic shift, which is coded by $IR[1:0] = 11$ (table 3.8). In this case, the fill bit equals the sign bit a_{31} of operand a, and therefore

$$fill \ = \ IR[1] \wedge IR[0] \wedge a_{31}.$$

The cost and the delay of the fill bit computation run at

$$
\begin{aligned}
C_{Fill} &= 2 \cdot C_{and} \\
D_{Fill} &= 2 \cdot D_{and}.
\end{aligned}
$$

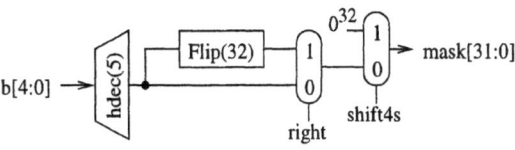

Figure 3.16 Circuit Mask generating the mask for the shifter SH.

The Replacement Mask

During an explicit left shift, the least significant $\langle b \rangle$ bits of the intermediate result r have to be replaced. In figure 3.16, a half decoder generates from b the corresponding mask $0^{32-\langle b \rangle}1^{\langle b \rangle}$. During an explicit right shift, the most significant $\langle b \rangle$ bits of the intermediate result r have to be replaced. The corresponding mask is simply obtained by flipping the left shift mask. Note that no gates are needed for this. Thus, in the gate model used here, flipping the mask does not contribute to the cost and the delay. On shifts for store, the mask is forced to 0^{32}, and the intermediate result r is not corrected at all. The cost and the delay of the mask circuit are

$$
\begin{aligned}
C_{Mask} &= C_{hdec}(5) + 2 \cdot C_{mux}(32) \\
D_{Mask} &= D_{hdec}(5) + 2 \cdot D_{mux}(32).
\end{aligned}
$$

For later use, we introduce the notation

$$
sh = shift(a, dist).
$$

Observe that in this shorthand, lots of parameters are hidden.

3.3.7 Shifter Environment SH4Lenv

This environment consists of the shifter for loads SH4L and a mux; it is controlled by a single control signal

$shift4l$ denoting a shift for load operation.

If signal $shift4l$ is active, the result R of the shifter SH4L is provided to the output C' of the environment, and otherwise, input C is passed to C':

$$
C' := \begin{cases} R & \text{if} \quad shift4l = 1 \\ C & \text{if} \quad shift4l = 0. \end{cases}
$$

Figure 3.17 depicts the top level schematics of the shifter environment SH4Lenv; its cost and delay can be expressed as

$$
\begin{aligned}
C_{SH4Lenv} &= C_{SH4L} + C_{mux}(32) \\
D_{SH4Lenv} &= D_{SH4L} + D_{mux}(32).
\end{aligned}
$$

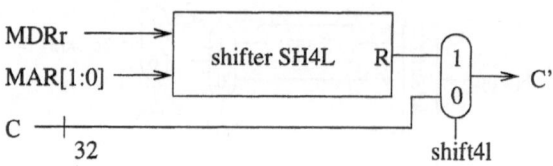

Figure 3.17 Top level schematics of the shifter environment SH4L

The shifter SH4L is only used in load operations. The last three bits $IR[28:26]$ of the primary opcode specify the type of the load operation (table 3.9). The byte address of the data, which is read from memory on a load operation, is stored in the memory address register MAR. If a byte or half word is loaded from a byte address which is not divisible by 4, the loaded data $MDRr$ has to be shifted to the right such that it is aligned at the right end of the data bus $D[31:0]$. A cyclic right shift by $\langle MAR[1:0]000 \rangle$ bits (the distance is motivated by lemma 3.1) will produce an intermediate result

$$r = crs(MDRr, MAR[1:0]000),$$

where the loaded data is already aligned at the right end. Note that this also covers the case of a load word operation, because words are stored at addresses with $MAR[1:0] = 00$. After the loaded data has been aligned, the portion of the output R not belonging to the loaded data are replaced with a fill bit:

$$R[31:0] = \begin{cases} fill^{24} r[7:0] & \text{for lb, lbu} \\ fill^{16} r[15:0] & \text{for lw, lwu} \\ r[31:0] & \text{for lw} \end{cases}$$

In an unsigned load operation, the fill bit equals 0, whereas in signed load operations, the fill bit is the sign bit of the shifted operand. This is summarized in table 3.9 which completes the specification of the shifter SH4L.

Figure 3.18 depicts a straightforward realization of the shifter SH4L. The shift distance is always a multiple of 8. Thus, the cyclic right shifter only comprises two stages for the shift distances 8 and 16. Recall that for 32 bit data, a cyclic right shift by 8 (16) bits equals a cyclic left shift by 24 (16) bits.

The first half word $r[31:16]$ of the intermediate result is replaced by the fill bit in case that a byte or half word is loaded. During loads, this is recognized by $IR[27]=0$. Byte $r[15:8]$ is only replaced when loading a single byte. During loads, this is recognized by $IR[27:26] = 00$. This explains the multiplexer construction of figure 3.18.

Table 3.9 Fill bit of the shifts for load

IR[28]	IR[27:26]	Type	MAR[1:0]	fill
0	00	byte, signed	00	MDRr[7]
			01	MDRr[15]
			10	MDRr[23]
			11	MDRr[31]
	01	halfword, signed	00	MDRr[15]
			10	MDRr[31]
	11	word		*
1	00	byte, unsigned		0
	01	halfword, unsigned		0

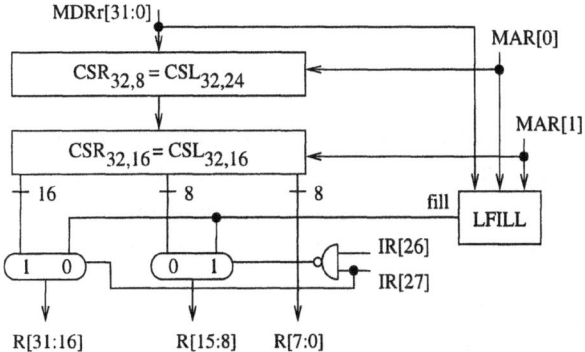

Figure 3.18 The shifter SH4L for load instructions

The circuit LFILL of figure 3.19 is a brute force realization of the fill bit function specified in table 3.9. The cost and the delay of the shifter SH4L and of circuit LFILL are

$$
\begin{aligned}
C_{SH4L} &= 2 \cdot C_{mux}(32) + C_{mux}(24) + C_{nand} + C_{LFILL} \\
D_{SH4L} &= \max\{2 \cdot D_{mux}(32), D_{nand}, D_{LFILL}\} + D_{mux}(24) \\
C_{LFILL} &= 5 \cdot C_{mux} + C_{and} + C_{inv} \\
D_{LFILL} &= \max\{3 \cdot D_{mux}, D_{inv}\} + D_{and}.
\end{aligned}
$$

For later use, we introduce the notation

$$
R = sh4l(MDRr, MAR[1:0]000).
$$

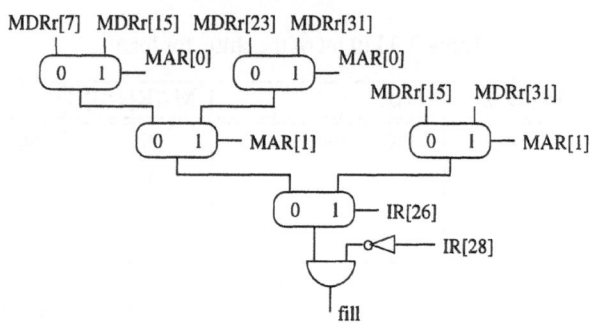

Figure 3.19 Circuit LFILL computes the fill bit for the shifter SH4L

3.4 Sequential Control

IT IS now amazingly easy to specify the control of the sequential machine *and* to show that the whole design is correct. In a first design, we will assume that memory accesses can be performed in a single cycle. Later on, this is easily corrected by a simple stalling mechanism.

3.4.1 Sequential Control without Stalling

Figure 3.20 depicts the graph of a finite state diagram. Only the names of the states and the edges between them are presently of interest. In order to complete the design, one has to specify the functions $\delta_{z,z'}$ for all states z with more than one successor state. Moreover, one has to specify for each state z the set of control signals active in state z.

We begin with an intermediate step and specify for each state z a set of register transfer language (RTL) instructions $rt(z)$ to be executed in that state (table 3.10). The abbreviations and the conventions are those of the tables 3.1 to 3.3. In addition, we use $M(PC)$ as a shorthand for $M(\langle PC \rangle)$. Also note that the functions op, $shift$, $sh4l$ and rel have hidden parameters.

We also specify for each type t of DLX instruction the intended path $path(t)$ through the diagram. All such paths begin with the states *fetch* and *decode*. The succeeding states on the path depend on the type t as indicated in table 3.11. One immediately obtains

Table 3.10 RTL instructions of the FSD of figure 3.20

State	RTL Instruction
fetch	$IR = M(\langle PC \rangle)$
decode	$A = RS1,$ $B = \begin{cases} RD & \text{if I-type instruction} \\ RS2 & \text{if R-type instruction} \end{cases}$ $co = \begin{cases} *^{27}SA & \text{if shift immediate slli, srli, srai} \\ sxt(imm) & \text{otherwise} \end{cases}$ $PC = PC + 4$
alu	$C = A \, op \, B$
test	$C = (A \, rel \, B ? 1 : 0)$
shift	$C = shift(A, B[4:0])$
aluI	$C = A \, op \, co$
testI	$C = (A \, rel \, co ? 1 : 0)$
shiftI	$C = shift(A, co[4:0])$
wbR	$RD = C$ (R-type)
wbI	$RD = C$ (I-type)
addr	$MAR = A + co$
load	$MDRr = Mword[\langle MAR[31:2]00 \rangle]$
sh4l	$RD = sh4l(MDRr, MAR[1:0]000)$
sh4s	$MDRw = cls(B, MAR[1:0]000)$
store	$m = bytes(MDRw)$
branch	
btaken	$PC = PC + co$
jimm	$PC = PC + co$
jreg	$PC = A$
savePC	$C = PC$
jalR	$PC = A$
jalI	$PC = PC + co$
wbL	$GPR[31] = C$

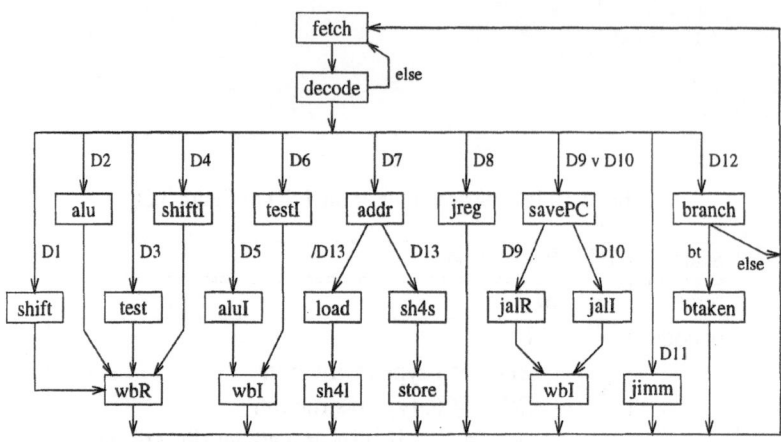

Figure 3.20 Finite state diagram (FSD) of the DLX machine

Lemma 3.2 ► *If the design is completed such that*

    1. for each type of instruction t, the path path(t) is taken, and that

    2. for each state s, the set of RTL instructions rtl(s) is executed,

then the machine is correct, i.e., it interprets the instruction set.

The proof is a simple exercise in bookkeeping. For each type of instruction t one executes the RTL instructions on the path $path(t)$. The effect of this on the visible DLX registers has to be as prescribed by the instruction set. We work out the details in some typical cases.

Arithmetic Instruction
Suppose $t = addi$. By table 3.11, the sequence of states executed is

$$path(t) \ = \ (fetch, decode, alui, wbi),$$

and by table 3.10, the sequence of RTL-instructions on this path is:

state s	rtl(s)
fetch	$IR = M(PC)$
decode	$A = GPR[RS1], B = GPR[RS2], \langle PC \rangle = \langle PC \rangle + 4 \bmod 2^{32}$
alui	$[C] = [A] + [imm]$ if this is in T_{32}
wbi	$GPR[RD] = C$

Table 3.11 Paths $path(t)$ through the FSD for each type t of DLX instruction

DLX instruction type	path through the FSD
arithmetic/logical, I-type: addi, subi, andi, ori, xori, lhgi	fetch, decode, aluI, wbI
arithmetic/logical, R-type: add, sub, and, or, xor, lhg	fetch, decode, alu, wbR
test set, I-type: clri, sgri, seqi, sgei, slsi, snei, slei, seti	fetch, decode, testI, wbI
test set, R-type: clr, sgr, seq, sge, sls, sne, sle, set	fetch, decode, test, wbR
shift immediate: slli, srli, srai	fetch, decode, shiftI, wbR
shift register: sll, srl, sra	fetch, decode, shift, wbR
load: lb, lh, lw, lbu, lhu	fetch, decode, addr, load, sh4l
store: sb, sh, sw	fetch, decode, addr, sh4s, store
jump register: jr	fetch, decode, jreg
jump immediate: j	fetch, decode, jimm
jump & link register: jalr	fetch, decode, savePC, jalR, wbL
jump & link immediate: jal	fetch, decode, savePC, jalI, wbL
taken branch beqz, bnez	fetch, decode, branch, btaken
untaken branch beqz, bnez	fetch, decode, branch

The combined effect of this on the visible registers is – as it should be

$$
\begin{aligned}
[GPR[RD]] \quad &= \quad C \ = \ [A] + [imm] \\
&= \quad [GPR[RS1]] + [imm] \quad \text{if this is in} T_{32}, \\
\langle PC \rangle \quad &= \quad \langle PC \rangle + 4
\end{aligned}
$$

It is that easy and boring. Keep in mind however, that with literal application of the abridged semantics, this simple exercise would end in complex and exciting insanity. Except for loads and stores, the proofs for all cases follow exactly the above pattern.

Store Instruction

Suppose instruction $M(PC)$ has type $t = store$ and the operand X to be stored is d bytes wide

$$X = byte_{d-1:0}(GPR[RD]),$$

then $path(t) = (fetch, decode, addr, sh4s, store)$. The effect of the RTL instructions of the last three states is

state s	rtl(s)
addr	$\langle MAR \rangle = \langle A \rangle + [imm] \bmod 2^{32}$
sh4s	$MRDw = cls(B, MAR[1:0]000)$
store	$M(\langle MAR \rangle + d - 1 : \langle MAR \rangle)$
	$= byte_{\langle MAR[1:0] \rangle + d - 1 : \langle MAR[1:0] \rangle}(MDRw)$

Thus, the combined effect of all states on MAR is

$$
\begin{aligned}
\langle MAR \rangle &= \langle A \rangle + [imm] \bmod 2^{32} \\
&= \langle GPR[RS1] \rangle + [imm] \bmod 2^{32} \\
&= ea,
\end{aligned}
$$

and the combined effect of all states on $MDRw$ is

$$
\begin{aligned}
MDRw &= cls(B, MAR[1:0]000) \\
&= cls(GPR[RD], MAR[1:0]000).
\end{aligned}
$$

Hence,

$$
X = byte_{\langle MAR[1:0] \rangle + d - 1 : \langle MAR[1:0] \rangle}(MDRw)
$$

and the effect of the store operation is

$$
M[ea + d - 1 : ea] = X.
$$

A Load Instruction

Suppose $M(PC)$ has type $t = load$, and the operand X to be loaded into register $GPR[RD]$ is d bytes wide. Thus, $path(t) = (fetch, decode, addr, load, sh4l)$, and the RTL instructions of the last three states are:

state s	rtl(s)
addr	$\langle MAR \rangle = \langle A \rangle + [imm] \bmod 2^{32}$
load	$MDRr = Mword(\langle MAR[31:2]00 \rangle)$
sh4l	$GPR[RD] = sh4l(MDRr, MAR[1:0]000)$

As in the previous case, $MAR = ea$. By lemma 3.1, it follows

$$
\begin{aligned}
X &= byte_{\langle MAR[1:0] \rangle + d - 1 : \langle MAR[1:0] \rangle} Mword(\langle MAR[31:2]00 \rangle) \\
&= byte_{\langle MAR[1:0] \rangle + d - 1 : \langle MAR[1:0] \rangle}(MDRr).
\end{aligned}
$$

With the fill bit *fill* defined as in table 3.9, one concludes

$$
\begin{aligned}
GPR[RD] &= sh4l(MDRr, MAR[1:0]000) \\
&= fill^{32-8d}X \\
&= \begin{cases} sxt(m) & \text{for load (signed)} \\ 0^{32-8d}m & \text{for load unsigned} \end{cases}
\end{aligned}
$$

The design is now easily completed. Table 3.12 is an extension of table 3.10. It lists for each state s not only the RTL instructions $rtl(s)$ but also the control signals activated in that state. One immediately obtains

For all states s, the RTL instructions rtl(s) are executed in state s. ◄ Lemma 3.3

For all states except *addr* and *btaken*, this follows immediately from the PROOF
specification of the environments. In state $s = addr$, the ALU environment performs the address computation

$$
\begin{aligned}
\langle MAR \rangle &= \langle A \rangle + \langle sxt(imm) \rangle \bmod 2^{32} \\
&= \langle A \rangle + [imm_{15}, sxt(imm)] \bmod 2^{32} \\
&= \langle A \rangle + [imm].
\end{aligned}
$$

The branch target computation of state $s = btaken$ is handled in a completely analogous way. QED

It only remains to specify the disjunctive normal forms D_i for figure 3.20 such that it holds:

For each instruction type t, the sequence path(t) of states specified by ◄ Lemma 3.4
table 3.11 is followed.

Each D_i has to test for certain patterns in the primary and secondary opcodes $IR[31:26, 5:0]$, and it possibly has to test signal $AEQZ$ as well. These patterns are listed in table 3.13. They have simply been copied from the tables 3.1 to 3.3. Disjunctive form D_8, for instance, tests if the actual instruction is a jump register instruction jr coded by

$$
IR[31:26] = hx16 = 010110.
$$

It can be realized by the single monomial

$$
D_8 = \overline{IR_{31}} \wedge IR_{30} \wedge \overline{IR_{29}} \wedge IR_{28} \wedge IR_{27} \wedge \overline{IR_{26}}.
$$

In general, testing for a single pattern with k zeros and ones can be done with a monomial of length k. This completes the specification of the whole machine. Lemmas 3.2 to 3.4 imply

The design correctly implements the instruction set. ◄ Theorem 3.5

Table 3.12 RTL instructions and their active control signals

state	RTL instruction	active control signals
fetch	$IR = M(\langle PC \rangle)$	fetch, mr, IRce
decode	$A = RS1,$ $B = \begin{cases} RD & \text{if I-type} \\ RS2 & \text{if R-type} \end{cases}$ $PC = PC + 4$ $co = \begin{cases} *^{27}SA & ; \text{shiftI} \\ sxt(imm) & ; \text{other.} \end{cases}$	Ace, Bce, Pce PCadoe, 4bdoe, add, ALUDdoe, shiftI,
alu	$C = A \text{ op } B$	Aadoe, Bbdoe, ALUDdoe, Cce, Rtype
test	$C = (A \text{ rel } B?1:0)$	*like alu*, test
shift	$C = shift(A, B[4:0])$	Aadoe, Bbdoe, SHDdoe, Cce, Rtype
aluI	$C = A \text{ op } co$	Aadoe, cobdoe, ALUDdoe, Cce
testI	$C = (A \text{ rel } co?1:0)$	*like aluI*, test
shiftI	$C = shift(A, co[4:0])$	Aadoe, cobdoe, SHDdoe, Cce, shiftI, Rtype
wbR	$RD = C$ (R-type)	GPRw, Rtype
wbI	$RD = C$ (I-type)	GPRw
addr	$MAR = A + co$	Aadoe, cobdoe, ALUDdoe, add, MARce
load	$MDRr = $ $Mword[\langle MAR[31:2]00 \rangle]$	mr, MDRrce
sh4l	$RD = sh4l(MDRr,$ $MAR[1:0]000)$	shift4l, GPRw
sh4s	$MDRw = $ $cls(B, MAR[1:0]000)$	Badoe, SHDdoe, shift4s, MDRwce
store	$m = bytes(MDRw)$	mw
branch		
btaken	$PC = PC + co$	PCadoe, cobdoe, add, ALUDdoe, PCce
jimm	$PC = PC + co$	*like btaken*, Jjump
jreg	$PC = A$	Aadoe, 0bdoe, add, ALUDdoe, PCce
savePC	$C = PC$	PCadoe, 0bdoe, add, ALUDdoe, Cce
jalR	$PC = A,$	*like jreg*
jalI	$PC = PC + co,$	*like jimm*
wbL	$GPR[31] = C$	GPRw, Jlink

Table 3.13 Nontrivial disjunctive normal forms (DNF) of the DLX finite state diagram and the corresponding monomials

Nontrivial DNF	Target State	Monomial $m \in M$		Length $l(m)$
		IR[31 : 26]	IR[5 : 0]	
D1	shift	000000	0001*0	11
		000000	00011*	11
D2	alu	000000	100***	9
D3	test	000000	101***	9
D4	shiftI	000000	0000*0	11
		000000	00001*	11
D5	aluI	001***	******	3
D6	testI	011***	******	3
D7	addr	100*0*	******	4
		10*0*1	******	4
		10*00*	******	4
D8	jreg	010110	******	6
D9	jalR	010111	******	6
D10	jalI	000011	******	6
D9 ∨ D10	savePC	like D9 and D10		
D11	jimm	000010	******	6
D12	branch	00010*	******	5
D13	sh4s	**1***	******	1
/D13	load	**0***	******	1
bt	btaken	AEQZ ·/IR[26]		2
		/AEQZ ·IR[26]		2
Accumulated length of $m \in M$: $\sum_{m \in M} l(m)$				115

3.4.2 Parameters of the Control Automaton

In the previous subsection, we have specified the control of the sequential DLX architecture without stalling. Its output function, i.e., the value of the control signals, depends on the current state of the control automaton but not on its current inputs. Thus, the sequential control can be implemented as a Moore automaton with precomputed control signals.

In this scenario, the automaton is clocked in every cycle, i.e., its clock signal is $ce = CONce = 1$. Signal *reset* serves as the clear signals *clr* of the Moore automaton in order to initialize the control on reset. Except for signal $AEQZ$, all the inputs of the control automaton are directly provided

Table 3.14 Parameters of the Moore control automaton

Parameter		Value
k	# states of the automaton	23
σ	# input signals in_j	13
γ	# output signals out_j	29
ν_{max}	maximal frequency of the outputs	12
ν_{sum}	accumulated frequency of the outputs	94
#M	# monomials $m \in M$ (nontrivial)	20
l_{max}	length of longest monomial $m \in M$	11
l_{sum}	accumulated length of all monomials $m \in M$	115
$fanin_{max}$	maximal fanin of nodes ($\neq$ fetch) in the FSD	4
$fanin_{sum}$	accumulated fanin	33

by the instruction register IR at zero delay. Thus, the input signals of the automaton have the accumulated delay:

$$A(in) = A(AEQZ) = D_{zero}(32)$$
$$A(clr, ce) = A(reset).$$

According to section 2.6, the cost and the delay of such a Moore automaton only depend on a few parameters (table 3.14). Except for the fanin of the states/nodes and the frequency of the control signals, these parameters can directly be read off the finite state diagram (figure 3.20) and table 3.13.

State $fetch$ serves as the initial state z_0 of the automaton. Recall that our realization of a Moore automaton has the following peculiarity: whenever the next state is not specified explicitly, a zero tester forces the automaton in its initial state. Thus, in the next state circuit NS, transitions to state $fetch$ can be ignored.

Fanin of the Nodes

For each edge $(z', z) \in E$ and $z \neq fetch$, we refer to the number $\#M(z', z)$ of monomials in $D(z', z)$ as the weight of the edge. For edges with nontrivial monomials, the weight can be read off table 3.13; all the other edges have weight 1. The fanin of a node z equals the sum of the weights of all edges ending in z. Thus, state wbR has the highest fanin of all states different from $fetch$, namely, $fanin_{max} = 4$, and all the states together have an accumulated fanin of $fanin_{sum} = 31$.

Table 3.15 Control signals of the DLX architecture and their frequency. Signals printed in italics are used in several environments.

	control signals		control signals
Top level	PCadoe, Aadoe, Badoe, Bbdoe, 0bdoe, SHDdoe, coBdoe, 4bdoe, ALUDdoe, Ace, Bce, Cce, MARce, MDRrce, MDRwce, *fetch*	GPRenv	GPRw, Jlink, *Rtype*
		PCenv	PCce
		ALUenv	add, test, *Rtype*
		Menv	mr, mw, *fetch*
		SHenv	shift4s
IRenv	Jjump, shiftI, IRce	SH4Lenv	shift4l

outputs out_j with a frequency $v_j > 1$							
Cce	7	PCce	6	GPRw	5	mr	2
PCadoe	5	Aadoe	9	Bbdoe	3	cobdoe	7
0bdoe	3	ALUDdoe	12	SHDdoe	3	Rtype	5
Jlink	2	Jjump	2	add	9	test	2

Frequency of the Control Signals

The first part of table 3.15 summarizes the control signals used in the top level schematics of the DLX architecture and in its environments. For each control signal out_j, its frequency can be derived from table 3.12 by simply counting the states in which out_j is active. These values are listed in the second part of table 3.15; signals with a frequency of 1 are omitted. Thus, the automaton generates $\gamma = 29$ control signals; the signals have a maximal frequency of $v_{max} = 12$ and an accumulated frequency of $v_{sum} = 93$.

3.4.3 A Simple Stall Engine

So far, we have assumed that a memory access can be performed in a single cycle, but that is not always the case. In order to account for those multi-cycle accesses, it is necessary to stall the DLX data paths and the main control, i.e., the update of registers and RAMs must be stopped. For that purpose, we introduce a *stall engine* which provides an *update enable* signal *ue* for each register or RAM.

Update Enable Signals

A register R is now controlled by two signals, the signal *Rce* which request the update and the *update enable signal Rue* which enables the requested update (figure 3.21). The register is only updated if both signals are active,

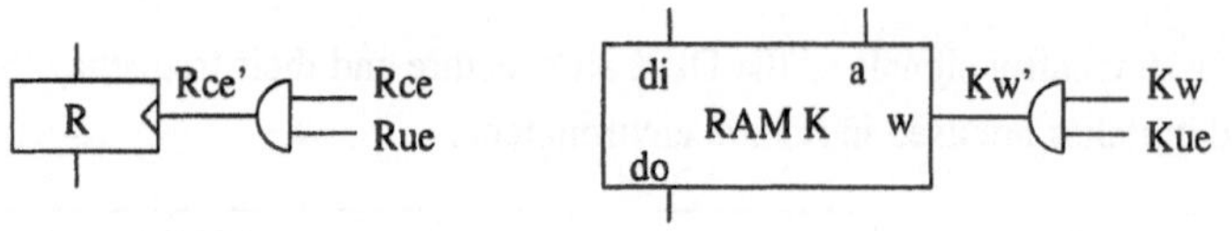

Figure 3.21 Controlling the update of registers and RAMs. The control automaton provides the request signals *Rce*, *Kw*; the stall engine provides the enable signals *Rue*, *Kue*.

i.e., $Rce = Rue = 1$. Thus, the actual *clock enable signal* of register R, which is denoted by Rce', equals

$$Rce' = Rce \wedge Rue.$$

The *clock request signal Rce* is usually provided by the control automaton, whereas signals *Rue* and *Rce'* are generated by a stall engine.

In analogy, the update of a RAM R is requested by signal *Rw* and enabled by signal *Rue*. Both signals are combined to the actual write signal

$$Rw' = Rw \wedge Rue.$$

Handling Multi-Cycle Memory Accesses

A memory access sometimes requires multiple clock cycles. The memory system M therefore provides a status signal *mbusy* indicating that the access will not be completed in the current cycle. Thus, on $mbusy = 1$, the DLX hardware is unable to run the RTL instructions of the current state to completion. In this situation, the correct interpretation of the instruction is achieved as follows:

- While *mbusy* is active, the memory system M proceeds its access, but the data paths and the control are stalled. This means that the Moore control automaton still requests the register and RAM updates according to the RTL instructions of its current state z, but the stall engine disables these updates. Thus, the hardware executes a NOP (no-operation), and the control automaton remains in its current state.

- In the cycle in which *mbusy* becomes inactive, the memory system completes its access, the stall engine enables the requested updates, and the data paths and the control execute the RTL instructions of the current state z.

Since the data paths and the control automaton are stalled simultaneously, the stall engine only provides a single update enable signal UE, which is inactive during an ongoing memory access ($mbusy = 1$). However, the update must be enabled during *reset* in order to ensure that the DLX machine can be restarted:

$$UE = \overline{mbusy} \vee reset.$$

This signal enables the update of all the registers and RAMs in the data paths and in the control automaton. Thus, the write signal of the general purpose register file GPR and the clock signal $CONce'$ of the Moore automaton, for instance, are then obtained as

$$
\begin{aligned}
GPRw' &= GPRw \wedge GPRue = GPRw \wedge UE \\
CONce' &= CONce \wedge CONue = CONce \wedge UE.
\end{aligned}
$$

Note that the read and write signals Mr and Mw of the memory M are *not* masked by signal UE.

According to table 3.15, the control automaton provides 8 clock request signals and 1 write request signal. Together with the clock of the Moore automaton, the stall engine has to manipulate 10 clock and write signals. Thus, the cost and the delay of this simple stall engine run at

$$
\begin{aligned}
C_{stall} &= C_{inv} + C_{or} + 10 \cdot C_{and} \\
D_{stall} &= D_{inv} + D_{or} + D_{and}.
\end{aligned}
$$

3.5 Hardware Cost and Cycle Time

IN THE previous sections, we derived formulae which estimate the cost and the delay of the data paths environments and of the control automaton. Based on these formulae, we now determine the cost and the cycle time of the whole DLX hardware. Note that all the adders in our DLX designs are carry lookahead adders, if not stated otherwise.

3.5.1 Hardware Cost

The hardware consists of the data paths and of the sequential control. If not stated otherwise, we do *not* consider the memory M itself to be part of the DLX hardware.

The data paths DP (figure 3.4) of the sequential DLX fixed-point core consist of six registers, nine tristate drivers, a multiplexer and six environments: the arithmetic logic unit ALUenv, the shifters SHenv and SH4Lenv,

Table 3.16 Cost of the DLX fixed-point core and of all its environments

	cost		cost		cost
ALUenv	1691	IRenv	301	DP	10846
SHenv	952	GPRenv	4096	CON	1105
SH4Lenv	380	PCenv	354	DLX	11951

and the environments of the instruction register IR, of the general purpose registers GPR and of the program counter PC. Thus, the cost of the 32-bit data paths equals

$$C_{DP} \; = \; 6 \cdot C_{ff}(32) + 9 \cdot C_{driv}(32) + C_{mux}(32) + C_{ALUenv} + C_{SHenv}$$
$$+ C_{SH4Lenv} + C_{IRenv} + C_{GPR} + C_{PCenv}.$$

The sequential control consists of a Moore automaton, of the memory control MC, and of the stall engine. The automaton precomputes its outputs and has the parameters of table 3.14. Thus, the control unit has cost

$$C_{CON} \; = \; C_{pMoore} + C_{MC} + C_{stall}.$$

Table 3.16 lists the cost of the sequential DLX hardware and of all its environments. The register file is the single most expensive environment; its cost account for 37% of the cost of the data paths. Of course, this fraction depends on the size of the register file. The control only accounts for 9% of the whole hardware cost.

3.5.2 Cycle Time

For the cycle time, we have to consider the four types of transfers illustrated in figure 2.3 (page 11). This requires to determine the delay of each paths which start in a register and end in a register, in a RAM, or in the memory. In this regard, the sequential DLX design comprises the following types of paths:

1. the paths which only pass through the data paths DP and the Moore control automaton,

2. the paths of a memory read or write access, and

3. the paths through the stall engine.

These paths are now discussed in detail. For the paths of type 1 and 2, the impact of the global update enable signal UE is ignored.

Paths through DP and the Moore Automaton

All these paths are governed exclusively by the output signals of the Moore automaton; these standard control signals, denoted by *Csig*, have zero delay:

$$A(Csig) = A_{pMoore}(out) = 0.$$

One type of paths is responsible for the update of the Moore automaton. A second type of paths is used for reading from or writing into the register file GPR. All the remaining paths pass through the ALU or the shifter SH.

Update of the Automaton

The time T_{pMoore} denotes the cycle time of the Moore control automaton, as far as the computation of the next state and of the outputs is concerned. According to section 2.6, this cycle time only depends on the parameters of table 3.14 and on the accumulated delay $A(in), A(clr, ce)$ of its input, clear and clock signals.

Register File Accesses

For the timing, we distinguish between read and write accesses. During a read access, the two addresses come directly from the instruction word IR. The data A' and B' are written into the registers A and B. The control signals *Csig* switch the register file into read mode and provide the clock signals *Ace* and *Bce*. The read cycle therefore requires time:

$$T_{GPRr} = A(Csig) + D_{GPRr} + \Delta.$$

During write back, the value C', which is provided by the shifter environment SH4Lenv, is written into the multiport RAM of the GPR register file. Both environments are governed by the standard control signals *Csig*. Since the register file has a write delay of D_{GPRw}, the write back cycle takes

$$T_{GPRw} = A(Csig) + D_{SH4Lenv} + D_{GPRw} + \delta.$$

This already includes the time overhead for clocking.

Paths through ALUenv and SHenv

The ALU and the shifter SH get their operands from the busses a and b. Except for value *co* which is provided by environment IRenv, the operands are either hardwired constants or register values. Thus, the data on the two operand busses are stable A_{BUSab} delays after the start of a cycle:

$$A_{BUSab} = A(Csig) + D_{IRenv}(co) + D_{driv}.$$

As soon as the operands become valid, they are processed in the ALU and the shifter SHenv. From the data bus D, the result is then clocked into a register (MAR, MDRw or C) or it passed through environment PCenv which adds delay $D_{PCenv}(IN; PC)$. Thus, the ALU and shift cycles require a cycle time of

$$T_{ALU/SH} = A_{BUSab} + \max\{D_{ALUenv}, D_{SHenv}\}$$
$$+ D_{driv} + D_{PCenv}(IN; PC) + \Delta.$$

Memory Read and Write Accesses

The memory environment performs read and write accesses. The memory M also provides a status flag *mbusy* which indicates whether the access can be completed in the current cycle or not. The actual data access has a delay of d_{mem}, whereas the status flag has a delay of d_{mstat}.

According to figure 3.4, bus MA provides the memory address, and register MDRw provides the data to be written into memory. Based on the address MA and some standard control signals, the memory control MC (section 3.3.5) generates the bank write signals $mbw[3:0]$. Thus,

$$A_{MC} = A(Csig) + D_{mux} + D_{MC}$$

delays after the start of each cycle, all the inputs of the memory system are valid, and the memory access can be started. The status flag *mbusy* therefore has an accumulated delay of

$$A_{Menv}(mbusy) = A_{MC} + d_{mstat},$$

and a write access requires a cycle time of

$$T_{Mwrite} = A_{MC} + d_{mem} + \delta.$$

On a read access, the memory data arrive on the bus MDout d_{mem} delays after the inputs of the memory are stable, and then, the data are clocked into the instruction register IR or into register MDRr. Thus, the read cycle time is

$$T_M = T_{Mread} = A_{MC} + d_{mem} + \Delta.$$

A read access takes slightly longer than a write access.

Paths through the Stall Engine

Based on the status flag *mbusy*, the stall engine generates the update enable signal UE which enables the update of all registers and RAMs in the DLX hardware. The stall engine then combines flag UE with the write and clock request signals provided by the Moore control automaton.

Table 3.17 Cycle time of the sequential DLX design

T_{DP}			T_{CON}		T_M
T_{GPRr}	T_{GPRw}	$T_{ALU/SH}$	T_{pMoore}	T_{stall}	
27	37	70	42	$37 + d_{mstat}$	$16 + d_{mem}$

Since *mbusy* has a much longer delay than the standard control signals of the Moore automaton, the stall engine provides the write and clock enable signals at an accumulated delay of

$$A_{stall} = A_{Menv}(mbusy) + D_{stall}.$$

Clocking a register adds delay $D_{ff} + \delta$, whereas the update of the 3-port RAM in environment GPRenv adds delay $D_{ram3}(32,32) + \delta$. Thus, the paths through the stall engine require a cycle time of

$$T_{stall} = A_{stall} + \max\{D_{ram3}(32,32), D_{ff}\} + \delta.$$

Evaluation of the Cycle Time

Table 3.17 lists the cycle times of the DLX data paths, of the control and of the memory system. In the data paths, the cycles through the functional units are most time critical; the register file itself could tolerate a clock which is twice as fast. The DLX data paths require a minimal cycle time of $T_{DP} = 70$ gate delays.

The control does not dominate the cycle time of the sequential DLX design, as long as the memory status time d_{mstat} stays under 44% of T_{DP}. The cycle time of the memory system only becomes time critical, if the actual access time d_{mem} is at least 74% of T_{DP}.

The cycle time τ_{DLX} of the sequential DLX design is usually the maximum of the cycle times required by the data paths and the control:

$$\tau_{DLX} = \max\{T_{DP}, T_{CON}\}.$$

The cycle time T_M of the memory environment only has an indirect impact on the cycle time τ_{DLX}. If the memory cycle time is less than τ_{DLX}, memory accesses can be performed in a single machine cycle. In the other case, $T_M \geq \tau_{DLX}$, the cycle time of the machine must be increased to T_M or memory accesses require $\lceil T_M / \tau_{DLX} \rceil$ cycles. Our designs use the second approach.

3.6 Selected References and Further Reading

THE DLX instruction set is from the classical textbook [HP90]. The design presented here is partly based on designs from [HP90, PH94, KP95, MP95]. A formal verification of a sequential processor is reported in [Win95].

Chapter

4

Basic Pipelining

IN THE CPU constructed in the previous chapter DLX instructions are processed *sequentially*; this means that the processing of an instruction starts only after the processing of the previous instruction is completed. The processing of an instruction takes between 3 and 5 cycles. Most of the hardware of the CPU is idle most of the time. One therefore tries to re-schedule the use of the hardware resources such that several instructions can be processed simultaneously. Obviously, the following conditions should be fulfilled:

1. No *structural hazards* exist, i.e., at no time, any hardware resource is used by two instructions simultaneously.

2. The machine is correct, i.e., the hardware interprets the instruction set.

The simplest such schedule is *basic pipelining*: the processing of each instructions is partitioned into the five *stages k* listed in table 4.1. Stages *IF* and *ID* correspond directly to the states *fetch* and *decode* of the FSD in figure 3.20. In stage *M*, the memory accesses of load and store instructions are performed. In stage *WB*, results are written back into the general purpose registers. Roughly speaking, everything else is done in stage *EX*. Figure 4.1 depicts a possible partition of the states of the FSD into these five stages.

We consider the execution of sequence $I = I_0, I_1, \ldots$ of DLX instructions, where instruction I_0 is preceded by a *reset*. For the cycles $T = 0, 1, \ldots$, the

Table 4.1 Stages of the pipelined instruction execution

k	shorthand	name
0	IF	instruction fetch
1	ID	instruction decode
2	EX	execute
3	M	memory
4	WB	write back

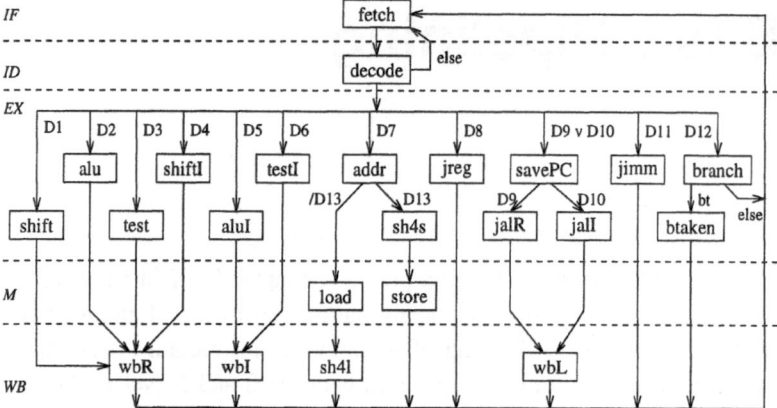

Figure 4.1 Partitioning of the FSD of the sequential DLX design into the five stages of table 4.1.

stages k and the instructions I_i, we use

$$I(k,T) = i$$

as a shorthand for the statement, that instruction I_i is in stage k during cycle T. The execution starts in cycle $T = 0$ with $I(0,0) = 0$.

Ideally, we would like to fetch a new instruction in every cycle, and each instruction should progress by one stage in every cycle, i.e.,

- if $I(0,T) = i$ then $I(0,T+1) = i+1$, and

- if $I(k,T) = i$ and $k < 4$ then $I(k+1,T+1) = i$.

For all stages k and cycles T we therefore have

$$I(k,T) = i \quad \leftrightarrow \quad T = k+i$$

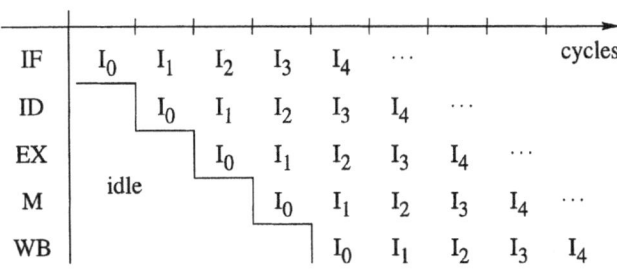

Figure 4.2 Pipelined execution of the instruction sequence I_0, I_1, I_2, I_3, I_4

This ideal schedule is illustrated in figure 4.2. Obviously, two instructions are never in the same stage simultaneously. If we can allocate each hardware resource to a stage k such that the resource is only used by instruction I_i while I_i is in stage k, then no hardware resource is ever used by two instructions simultaneously, and thus, structural hazards are avoided.

For the machine constructed so far this cannot be done for the following two reasons:

1. The adder is used in stage *decode* for incrementing the *PC*, and in stage *execute* it is either used for ALU operations or for branch target computations. The instructions jal and jalr use the adder even twice in the execute stage, namely for the target computation and for passing the PC to the register file. Thus, we at least have to provide an extra incrementer for incrementing the *PC* during *decode* and an ALU bypass path for saving the PC.

2. The memory is used in stages *fetch* and *memory*. Thus, an extra instruction memory *IM* has to be provided.

4.1 Delayed Branch and Delayed PC

IT IS still impossible to fetch an instruction in every cycle. Before we explain the simple reason, we introduce more notation.

For a register R and an instruction I_i, we denote by R_i the content of register R *after* the (sequential) execution of instruction I_i. Note that instruction I_i is fetched from instruction memory location PC_{i-1}. The notation can be extended to fields of registers. For instance, imm_i denotes the content of the immediate field of the instruction register IR_i. The notation can be extended further to expressions depending on registers.

107

Recall that the *control operations* are the DLX instructions beqz, bnez, jr, jalr, j and jal. The *branch target btarget$_i$* of a control operation I_i is defined in the obvious way by

$$btarget_i = \begin{cases} RS1_{i-1} & \text{for } jr, jalr \\ PC_{i-1} + 4 + imm_i & \text{for } beqz, bnez, j, jal \end{cases}$$

We say that a *branch or jump is taken* in I_i, (short $bjtaken_i = 1$), if

- I_i has the type j, jal, jr or jalr, or

- I_i is a branch beqz and $RS1_i = 0$, or

- I_i is a branch bnez and $RS1_i \neq 0$.

Now suppose that instruction I_i is a control operation which is fetched in cycle T, where

$$I_i = IM[PC_{i-1}].$$

The next instruction I_{i+1} then has to be fetched from location PC_i with

$$PC_i = \begin{cases} btarget_i & \text{if } bjtaken_i = 1 \\ PC_{i-1} + 4 & \text{otherwise,} \end{cases}$$

but instruction I_i is not in the instruction register before cycle $T + 1$. Thus, even if we provide an extra adder for the branch target computation in stage *decode*, PC_i cannot be computed before cycle $T + 1$. Hence, instruction I_{i+1} can only be fetched in cycle $T + 2$.

Semantics of the Delayed Branch

The way out of this difficulty is by very brute force: one *changes the semantics* of the branch instruction by two rules, which say:

1. A branch taken in instruction I_i affects only the PC computed in the following instruction, i.e., PC_{i+1}. This mechanism is called *delayed branch*.

2. If I_i is a control operation, then the instruction I_{i+1} following I_i is called the instruction in the *delay slot* of I_i. No control operations are allowed in delay slots.

A formal inductive definition of the delayed branch mechanism is

$$PC_{-1} = 0$$
$$bjtaken_{-1} = 0$$

$$PC_{i+1} = \begin{cases} btarget_i & \text{if } bjtaken_i = 1 \\ PC_i + 4 & \text{otherwise.} \end{cases}$$

Observe that the definition of branch targets $PC + 4 + imm$ instead of the much more obvious branch targets $PC + imm$ is motivated by the delayed branch mechanism. After a control operation I_i, one always executes the instruction $IM[PC_{i-1} + 4]$ in the delay slot of I_i (because I_i does not occupy a delay slot and hence, $bjtaken_{i-1} = 0$). With a branch target $PC + imm$, one would have to perform the computation

$$PC_{i+1} = PC_i + imm_{i+1} - 4$$

instead of

$$PC_{i+1} = PC_i + imm_{i+1}.$$

The delayed branch semantics is, for example, used in the MIPS [KH92], the SPARC [SPA92] and the PA-RISC [Hew94] instruction set.

Semantics of the Delayed PC

Instead of delaying the effect of taken branches, one could opt for delaying the effect of *all* PC calculations. A program counter PC' is updated according to the trivial sequential semantics

$$PC'_i = \begin{cases} PC'_{i-1} + imm_i & \text{if} \quad bjtaken_i = 1 \wedge I_i \in \{\text{beqz}, \text{bnez}, \text{j}, \text{jal}\} \\ RS1_{i-1} & \text{if} \quad bjtaken_i = 1 \wedge I_i \in \{\text{jr}, \text{jalr}\} \\ PC'_{i-1} + 4 & \text{otherwise} \end{cases}$$

The result is simply clocked into a delayed program counter DPC:

$$DPC_{i+1} = PC'_i.$$

The delayed program counter DPC is used for fetching instructions from IM, namely $I_i = IM[DPC_{i-1}]$. Computations are started with

$$PC'_{-1} = 4$$
$$DPC_{-1} = 0$$

We call this uniform and easy to implement mechanism *delayed PC*. The two mechanisms will later turn out to be completely equivalent.

Jump and Link Instructions

We continue our discussion with a subtle observation concerning the semantics of the jump and link instructions (jal, jalr) which are usually used for procedure calls. Their semantics changes by the delayed branch mechanism as well! Saving $PC + 4$ into $GPR[31]$ results in a return to the delay slot of the jump and link instruction. Of course, the return should be to the instruction *after* the delay slot (e.g., see the MIPS architecture manual [KH92]). Formally, if $I_i = IM(PC_{i-1})$ is a jump and link instruction, then

$$PC_i = PC_{i-1} + 4$$

because I_i is not in a delay slot, and instruction

$$I_{i+1} = IM(PC_i)$$

is the instruction in the delay slot of I_i. The jump and link instruction I_i should therefore save

$$GPR[31]_i = PC_i + 4 = PC_{i-1} + 8.$$

In the simpler delayed PC mechanism, one simply saves

$$GPR[31]_i = PC'_{i-1} + 4.$$

Equivalence of Delayed Branch and Delayed PC

Theorem 4.1 ▶ *Suppose a machine with delayed branch and a machine with delayed PC are started with the same program (without control operations in delay slots) and with the same input data. The two machines then perform exactly the same sequence $I_0, I_1, \ldots$ of instructions.*

PROOF   This is actually a simulation theorem. By induction on i, we will show two things, namely

1. $(PC_i, PC_{i+1}) = (DPC_i, PC'_i)$,

2. and if I_i is a jump and link instruction, then the value $GPR[31]_i$ saved into register 31 during instruction I_i is identical for both machines.

Since $bjtaken_{-1} = 0$, it follows that $PC_0 = 4$. Thus

$$(PC_{-1}, PC_0) = (0,4) = (DPC_{-1}, PC'_{-1}),$$

and part one of the induction hypothesis holds for $i = -1$.

In the induction step, we conclude from $i-1$ to i, based on the induction hypothesis $(PC_{i-1}, PC_i) = (DPC_{i-1}, PC'_{i-1})$. Since

$$
\begin{aligned}
DPC_i &= PC'_{i-1} &&\text{by the definition of } DPC \\
&= PC_i &&\text{by the induction hypothesis,}
\end{aligned}
$$

it only remains to show that

$$PC_{i+1} = PC'_i.$$

Since $DPC_{i-1} = PC_{i-1}$, the same instruction I_i is fetched with delayed branch and delayed PC, and in both cases, the variable $bjtaken_i$ has the same value.

If $bjtaken_i = 0$, it follows

$$
\begin{aligned}
PC_i' &= PC_{i-1}' + 4 \\
&= PC_i + 4 && \text{by the induction hypothesis} \\
&= PC_{i+1} && \text{by the definition of delayed branch.}
\end{aligned}
$$

If $bjtaken_i = 1$, then instruction I_i cannot occupy a delay slot, and therefore $bjtaken_{i-1} = 0$. If I_i is of type beqz, bnez, j or jal, then

$$
\begin{aligned}
PC_i' &= PC_{i-1}' + imm_i \\
&= PC_{i-2}' + 4 + imm_i && \text{because } bjtaken_{i-1} = 0 \\
&= PC_{i-1} + 4 + imm_i && \text{by the induction hypothesis for } i - 2 \\
&= btarget_i \\
&= PC_{i+1} && \text{because } bjtaken_i = 1.
\end{aligned}
$$

If I_i is of type jr or jalr, then

$$
\begin{aligned}
PC_i' &= RS1_{i-1} \\
&= btarget_i \\
&= PC_{i+1} && \text{because } bjtaken_i = 1,
\end{aligned}
$$

and part one of the induction hypothesis follows.

For the second part, suppose I_i is a jump and link instruction. With delayed branch, $PC_{i-1} + 8$ is then saved. Because I_i is not in a delay slot, we have

$$
\begin{aligned}
PC_{i-1} + 8 &= PC_i + 4 \\
&= DPC_i + 4 && \text{by induction hypothesis} \\
&= PC_{i-1}' + 4 && \text{by definition of delayed PC.}
\end{aligned}
$$

This is exactly the value saved in the delayed PC version.   QED

Table 4.2 illustrates for both mechanisms, delayed branch and delayed PC, how the PCs are updated in case of a jump and link instruction.

4.2 Prepared Sequential Machines

IN THIS section we construct a machine DLX_σ with the following properties:

1. The machine consists of data paths, a control as well as a stall engine for the clock generation.

Table 4.2 The impact of a jump and link instruction $I_i \in \{jal, jalr\}$ on the PCs under the delayed branch and the delayed PC regime

after	delayed branch		delayed PC		
	PC	GPR[31]	DPC	PC'	GPR[31]
I_{i-1}	PC_{i-1}		PC_{i-1}	$PC_i=PC_{i-1}+4$	
I_i	$PC_{i-1}+4$	$PC_{i-1}+8$	$PC'_{i-1}=PC_i$	$PC_{i+1}=btarget_i$	$PC'_{i-1}+4$
I_{i+1}	$btarget_i$		$PC'_i=btarget_i$	PC_{i+2}	

2. The data paths and the control of the machine are arranged in a 5-stage pipeline, but

3. Only one stage at a time is clocked in a round robin fashion. Thus, machine DLX_σ will be *sequential*; its correctness is easily proved using the techniques from the previous chapter.

4. The machine can be turned into a pipelined machine DLX_π by a very simple transformation concerning only the *PC* environment and the stall engine. Correctness is then shown by a simulation theorem stating – under certain hypotheses – that machine DLX_π simulates machine DLX_σ.

We call machine DLX_σ a *prepared sequential* machine. The overall structure of the data paths is depicted in figure 4.3. There are 5 stages of registers and RAM cells. Note, that we have arranged all registers and RAM cells at the bottom of the stage, where they are computed.

For each stage k – with the numbers or names of table 4.1 – we denote by $out(k)$ the set of registers and RAM cells computed in stage k. Similarly, we denote by $in(k)$ the set of registers and RAM cells which are inputs of stage k. These sets are listed in table 4.3 for all k. $R.k$ denotes that R is an output register of stage $k-1$, i.e., $R.k \in out(k-1)$.

The cost of the data paths is

$$C_{DP} = C_{PCenv} + C_{IMenv} + C_{IRenv} + C_{EXenv} + C_{DMenv}$$
$$+ \quad C_{SH4Lenv} + C_{GPRenv} + C_{CAddr} + 7 \cdot C_{ff}(32) + 3 \cdot C_{ff}(5+12).$$

Most of the environments can literally be taken from the sequential DLX designs. Only two environment undergo nontrivial changes: the PC environment and the execute environment *EXenv*. The PC environment has to be adapted for the delayed PC mechanism. For store instructions, the address calculation of state *addr* and the operand shift of state *sh4s* have now to be performed in a single cycle. This will not significantly slow down the

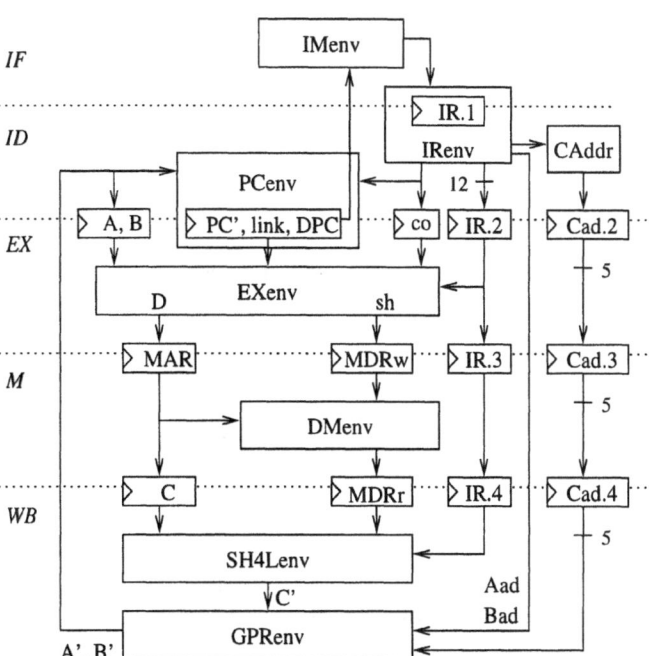

Figure 4.3 High level view of the prepared sequential DLX data paths

Table 4.3 Inputs and outputs of each stage k of the prepared DLX data paths

stage		$in(k)$	$out(k)$
0	IF	DPC, IM	IR
1	ID	GPR, PC', IR	A, B, PC', link, DPC, co, Cad.2
2	EX	A, B, link, co, Cad.2, IR	MAR, MDRw, Cad.3
3	M	MAR, MDRw, DM, Cad.3, IR	DM, C, MDRr, Cad.4
4	WB	C, MDRr, Cad.4, IR	GPR

cycle time, because only the last two bits of the address influence the shift distance, and these bits are known early in the cycle. Trivially, the memory M is split into an instruction memory IM and a data memory DM.

There is, however, a simple but fundamental change in which we clock the output registers of the stages. Instead of a single update enable signal UE (section 3.4.3), we introduce for every stage k a distinct update enable signal $ue.k$. An output register R of stage k is updated iff its clock request

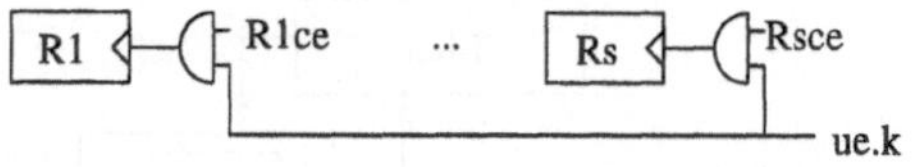

Figure 4.4 Controlling the update of the output registers of stage k

signal Rce and the update enable signal of stage k are both active (figure 4.4). Thus, the clock enable signal Rce' of such a register R is obtained as

$$Rce' = Rce \wedge ue.k.$$

As before, the read and write signals of the main memory M are not masked by the update enable signal $ue.3$ but by the full bit $full.3$ of the memory stage.

4.2.1 Prepared DLX Data Paths

Environment IRenv

of the instruction register is still controlled by the signals $Jjump$ (J-type jump), $shiftI$ and the clock signal $IRce$. The functionality is virtually the same as before. On $IRce = 1$, the output $IMout$ of the instruction memory is clocked into the instruction register

$$IR = IMout,$$

and the 32-bit constant co is generated as in the sequential design, namely as

$$co = constant(IR) = \begin{cases} PCoffset & \text{if} \quad Jjump = 1 \\ *^{27}SA & \text{if} \quad shiftI \\ imm & \text{otherwise.} \end{cases}$$

The cost and the delay of environment IRenv remain the same.

For the use in later pipeline stages, the two opcodes $IR[31:26]$ and $IR[5:0]$ are buffered in three registers $IR.k$, each of which is 12 bits wide.

Environment SH4Lenv

is controlled by signal $shift4l$ which requests a shift in case of a load instruction. The only modification in this environment is that the memory address is now provided by register C and not by register MAR. This has an impact on the functionality of environment SH4Lenv but not on its cost and delay.

Let $sh4l(a, dist)$ denote the function computed by the shifter $SH4L$ as it was defined in section 3.3.7. The modified SH4Lenv environment then provides the result

$$C' = \begin{cases} sh4l(MDRr, C[1:0]000) & \text{if } shift4l = 1 \\ C & \text{if } shift4l = 0. \end{cases}$$

Environments CAddr and GPRenv

As in the sequential design, circuit $CAddr$ generates the address Cad of the destination register based on the control signals $Jlink$ (jump and link) and $Itype$. However, the address Cad is now precomputed in stage ID and is then passed down stage by stage to the register file environment GPRenv. For later use, we introduce the notation

$$Cad = CAddr(IR).$$

Environment GPRenv (figure 4.5) itself has still the same functionality. It provides the two register operands

$$A' = \begin{cases} GPR[RS1] = GPR[\langle IR[25:21]\rangle)] & \text{if } \langle RS1 \rangle \neq 0 \\ 0 & \text{otherwise} \end{cases}$$

$$B' = \begin{cases} GPR[RS2] = GPR[\langle IR[20:16]\rangle)] & \text{if } \langle RS2 \rangle \neq 0 \\ 0 & \text{otherwise} \end{cases}$$

and updates the register file under the control of the write signal $GPRw$:

$$GPR[Cad.4] = C' \quad \text{if} \quad GPRw = 1.$$

Since circuit $CAddr$ is now an environment of its own, the cost of the register file environment GPRenv run at

$$C_{GPRenv} = C_{ram3}(32,32) + 2 \cdot (C_{zero}(5) + C_{inv} + C_{and}(32)).$$

Due to the precomputed destination address $Cad.4$, the update of the register file becomes faster. Environment GPRenv now only delays the write access by

$$D_{GPR,write} = D_{ram3}(32,32).$$

Let $A_{CON}(csWB)$ denote the accumulated delay of the control signals which govern stage WB; the cycle time of the write back stage then runs at

$$A_{SH4Lenv} = A_{CON}(csWB) + D_{SH4Lenv}$$
$$T_{WB} = T_{GPRw} = A_{SH4Lenv} + D_{GPR,write} + \Delta.$$

The delay $D_{GPR,read}$ of a read access, however, remains unchanged; it adds to the cycle time of stage IF and of the control unit.

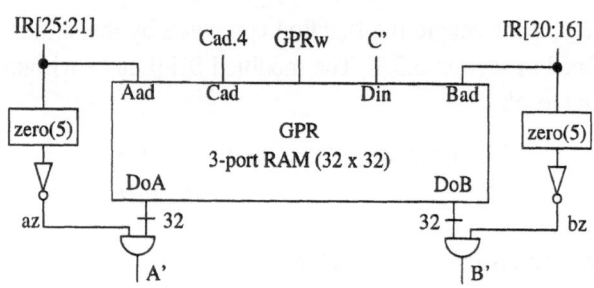

Figure 4.5 Environment GPRenv of the DLX_σ design

Memory Environments

The DLX design which is prepared for pipelined execution comprises two memories, one for instructions and one for the actual data accesses.

Environment IMenv   of the instruction memory is controlled by a single signal $fetch$ which activates the read signal Imr. The address of an instruction memory access is specified by register DPC. Thus, on $fetch = 1$, the environment IMenv performs a read operation providing the memory word

$$IMout = IMword[\langle DPC[31:2]\,00\rangle].$$

Since memory IM performs no write accesses, its write signal Imw is always inactive.[1] The control IMC of the instruction memory is trivial and has zero cost and delay. Let d_{Imem} denote the access time of the banks of memory IM. Since the address is directly taken from a register, environment IMenv delays the instruction fetch by

$$D_{IMenv}(IR) = D_{IMC} + d_{Imem} = d_{Imem}.$$

The instruction memory also provides a signal $ibusy$ indicating that the access cannot be finished in the current clock cycle. We expect this signal to be valid d_{Istat} time units after the start of an IM memory access.

Environment DMenv   of the data memory DM performs the memory accesses of load and store instructions. To a large extend, DMenv is identical to the memory environment of the sequential design, but the address is now always provided by register MAR.

Environment DMenv is controlled by the two signals Dmr and Dmw which request a memory read or write access, respectively. Since memory

---

[1]This is of course an abstraction. In chapter 6 we treat instruction caches which of course *can* be written.

DM is byte addressable, the control DMC generates four bank write signals $Dmbw[3:0]$ based on the address and the width of the write access as in the sequential design. The cost and delay of the memory control remain the same.

The data memory DM has an access time of d_{Dmem} and provides a flag $dbusy$ with a delay of d_{Dstat}. Signal $dbusy$ indicates that the current access cannot be finished in the current clock cycle. Let $A_{CON}(csM)$ denote the accumulated delay of the signals Dmr and Dmw, then

$$
\begin{aligned}
T_M &= T_{DMenv,read} = A_{CON}(csM) + D_{DMC} + d_{Dmem} + \Delta \\
A_{DMenv}(dbusy) &= A_{CON}(csM) + D_{DMC} + d_{Dstat}.
\end{aligned}
$$

PC Environment

The environment PCenv of figure 4.6 is governed by seven control signals, namely:

- *reset* which initializes the registers PC' and DPC,

- the clock signals *PCce* and *linkce*,

- *jump* which denotes one of the four jump instructions j, jal, jr and jalr,

- *jumpR* which denotes an absolute jump instruction (jr, jalr),

- *branch* which denotes a branch instruction beqz, bnez, and

- *bzero* which is active on beqz and inactive on bnez.

Based on these signals, its *glue logic PCglue* generates the clock signal of the registers PC' and DPC. They are clocked simultaneously when signal *PCce* is active or on reset, i.e., they are clocked by

$$PCce \lor reset.$$

In addition, *PCglue* tests operand A' for zero

$$AEQZ = 1 \quad \leftrightarrow \quad [A[31:0]] = 0$$

and generates signal *bjtaken* according to the specifications of section 4.1. Thus, *bjtaken* is set on any jump or on a taken branch:

$$bjtaken = jump \lor branch \land (bzero \text{ XNOR } AEQZ).$$

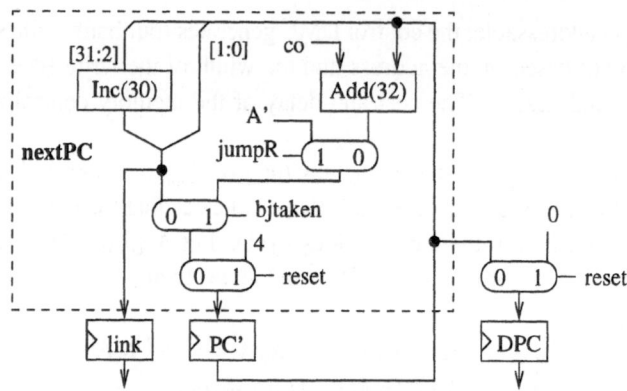

Figure 4.6 Environment PCenv implementing the delayed PC

Let $A_{CON}(csID)$ denote the accumulated delay of the control signals which govern stage ID. The cost of the glue logic and the delay of the signals $AEQZ$ and $bjtaken$ then run at

$$
\begin{aligned}
C_{PCglue} &= 2 \cdot C_{or} + C_{and} + C_{xnor} + C_{zero}(32) \\
D_{PCglue} &= D_{or} + D_{and} + D_{xnor} \\
A(AEQZ) &= A_{GPRenv}(A') + D_{zero}(32) \\
A(bjtaken) &= \max\{A_{CON}(csID), A(AEQZ)\} + D_{PCglue}.
\end{aligned}
$$

The environment PCenv implements the delayed PC mechanism of section 4.1 in a straightforward way. On an active clock signal, the two PCs are set to

$$
(DPC, PC') = \begin{cases} (0, 4) & \text{if } reset \\ (PC', pc') & \text{otherwise,} \end{cases}
$$

where the value $pc' = nextPC(PC', A', co)$ of the instruction I, which is held in register IR, is computed as

$$
pc' = \begin{cases} PC' + co & \text{if } bjtaken \wedge I \in \{\text{beqz}, \text{bnez}, \text{j}, \text{jal}\} \\ A' & \text{if } I \in \{\text{jr}, \text{jalr}\} \\ PC' + 4 & \text{otherwise.} \end{cases}
$$

PCenv also provides a register *link* which is updated under the control of signal *linkce*. On $linkce = 1$, it is set to

$$
link = PC' + 4,
$$

that is the PC to be saved in case of a jump and link instruction.

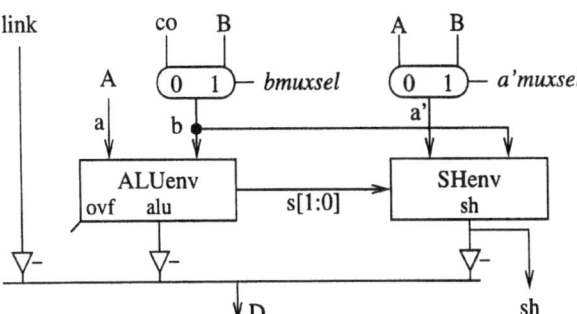

Figure 4.7 Execute environment of the prepared DLX

In order to update the two program counters, environment PCenv requires some operands from other parts of the data paths. The register operand A' is provided by the register file environment GPRenv, whereas the immediate operand co is provided by environment IRenv. The cost and the cycle time of environment PCenv can be estimated as

$$C_{PCenv} = 3 \cdot C_{ff}(32) + 4 \cdot C_{mux}(32) + C_{add}(32) + C_{inc}(30) + C_{PCglue}$$

$$T_{PCenv} = \max\{D_{inc}(30), A_{IRenv}(co) + D_{add}(32), A_{GPRenv}(A'),$$
$$A(bjtaken)\} + 3 \cdot D_{mux}(32) + \Delta.$$

Execute Environment

The execute environment $EXenv$ of figure 4.7 comprises the ALU environment and the shifter SHenv and connects them to the operand and result busses. Since on a store instruction, the address computation and the operand shift are performed in parallel, three operand and two result busses are needed.

Register A always provides the operand a. The control signals $bmuxsel$ and $a'muxsel$ select the data to be put on the busses b and a':

$$b = \begin{cases} B & \text{if } bmuxsel = 1 \\ co & \text{otherwise,} \end{cases} \qquad a' = \begin{cases} B & \text{if } a'muxsel = 1 \\ A & \text{otherwise.} \end{cases}$$

The data on the result bus D is selected among the register $link$ and the results of the ALU and the shifter. This selection is governed by three output enable signals

$$D = \begin{cases} link & \text{if } linkDdoe = 1 \\ alu & \text{if } ALUDdoe = 1 \\ sh & \text{if } SHDdoe = 1. \end{cases}$$

Note, that at most one of these signals should be active at a time.

ALU Environment   Environment ALUenv is governed by the same control signals as in the sequential design, and the specification of its results *alu* and *ovf* remains unchanged. However, it now provides two additional bits $s[1:0]$ which are fed directly to the shifter. These are the two least significant bits of the result of the arithmetic unit $AU(32)$. Depending on signal *sub*, which is provided by the ALU glue logic, the AU computes the sum or the difference of the operands a and b modulo 2^{32}:

$$[s] = ([a] + (-1)^{sub} \cdot [b]) \bmod 2^{32} = \begin{cases} [a] + [b] \bmod 2^{32} & \text{if } sub = 0 \\ [a] - [b] \bmod 2^{32} & \text{if } sub = 1. \end{cases}$$

The cost of the ALU environment and its total delay D_{ALUenv} remain the same, but the bits $s[1:0]$ have a much shorter delay. For all the adders introduced in chapter 2, the delay of these bits can be estimated based on the delay of a 2-bit AU

$$D_{ALUenv}(s[1:0]) = D_{ALUglue} + D_{AU}(2)$$

as it is shown in exercise 4.1.

Shifter Environment   The shifter environment SHenv is still controlled by signal *shift4s* which requests an implicit shift in case of a store operation, but its operands are different. On an explicit shift, the operands are provided by the busses a' and b, whereas on an implicit shift, they are provided by bus a' and by the result $s[1:0]$ of the ALU environment. Thus, the output *sh* of SHenv is now specified as

$$sh = \begin{cases} shift(a', b, IR[1:0]) & \text{if } shift4s = 0 \\ cls(a', s[1:0]000) & \text{if } shift4s = 1. \end{cases}$$

However, this modification has no impact on the cost and the delay of the environment. Assuming a delay of $A_{CON}(csEX)$ for the control signals of stage EX, the cost and the cycle time of the whole execute environment EXenv run at

$$\begin{aligned} C_{EXenv} &= C_{ALUenv} + C_{SHenv} + 2 \cdot C_{mux}(32) + 3 \cdot C_{driv}(32) \\ A_{EXenv} &= \max\{D_{ALUenv}, D_{ALUenv}(s[1:0]) + D_{SHenv}\} + D_{mux} + D_{driv} \\ T_{EX} &= T_{EXenv} = A_{EXenv} + \Delta. \end{aligned}$$

4.2.2   FSD for the Prepared Data Paths

Figure 4.8 depicts an FSD for the prepared data paths; the tables 4.4 to 4.6 list the corresponding RTL instructions and their active control signals.

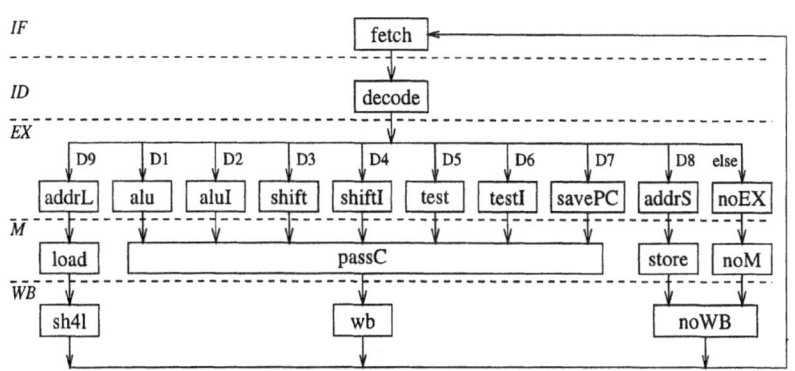

IF

ID

EX

M

WB

Figure 4.8 The FSD of the prepared sequential DLX design

Table 4.4 RTL instructions of stages IF and ID

	RTL instruction	type of I	control signals
IF	$IR = IM(DPC)$		fetch, IRce
ID	$A = A' = RS1,$		Ace,
	$AEQZ = zero(A'),$		
	$B = RS2, link = PC' + 4,$		Bce, linkce,
	$DPC = (reset\,?\,0\,:\,PC'),$		PCce,
	$PC' = (reset\,?\,4\,:\,pc'),$		PCce,
	$pc' = nextPC(PC', A', co)$	j, jal	jump
		jr, jalr	jumpR, jump
		beqz	branch, bzero
		bnez	branch
		otherwise	
	$co = constant(IR)$	j, jal	Jjump
		slli, srli, srai	shiftI
		otherwise	
	$Cad = CAddr(IR)$	jalr, jal	Jlink
		R-type	Rtype
		otherwise	

The nontrivial DNFs are listed in table 4.7. Except for the clocks Ace, Bce, $PCce$ and $linkce$, all the control signals used in the decode stage ID are Mealy signals. Following the pattern of section 3.4, one shows

Let the DLX design be completed such that   ◄ Theorem 4.2 ____

121

Table 4.5 RTL instructions of stage EX

state	RTL instruction	active control signals
alu	$MAR = A$ op B, $Cad.3 = Cad.2$	bmuxsel, ALUDdoe, MARce, Rtype, Cad3ce
test	$MAR = (A$ rel $B?1:0)$, $Cad.3 = Cad.2$	bmuxsel, ALUDdoe, MARce, test, Rtype, Cad3ce
shift	$MAR = \text{shift}(A, B[4:0])$, $Cad.3 = Cad.2$	bmuxsel, SHDdoe, MARce, Rtype, Cad3ce
aluI	$MAR = A$ op co, $Cad.3 = Cad.2$	ALUDdoe, MARce, Cad3ce
testI	$MAR = (A$ rel $co?1:0)$, $Cad.3 = Cad.2$	ALUDdoe, MARce, test, Cad3ce
shiftI	$MAR = \text{shift}(A, co[4:0])$, $Cad.3 = Cad.2$	SHDdoe, MARce, shiftI, Rtype, Cad3ce
savePC	$MAR = link$, $Cad.3 = Cad.2$	linkDdoe, MARce, Cad3ce
addrL	$MAR = A + co$, $Cad.3 = Cad.2$	ALUDdoe, add, MARce, Cad3ce
addrS	$MAR = A + co$, $MDRw =$ $\text{cls}(B, MAR[1:0]000)$	ALUDdoe, add, MARce, amuxsel, shift4s, MDRwce
noEX		

1. for each type of instruction, the path specified in table 4.8 is taken,

2. and for each state s, the set of RTL instructions rtl(s) is executed.

If every memory access takes only one cycle, then the machine interprets the DLX instruction set with delayed PC semantics.

The correctness of all pipelined machines in this chapter will follow from this theorem. Adding the stall engine from section 3.4.3 takes care of memory accesses which require more than one cycle.

4.2.3 Precomputed Control

We derive from the above FSD and the trivial stall engine a new control and stall engine with exactly the same behavior. This will complete the design of the prepared sequential machine DLX_σ.

Table 4.6 RTL instructions of the memory and write back stage

	state	RTL instruction	control signals
M	passC	$C = MAR$, $Cad.4 = Cad.3$	Cce, Cad4ce
	load	$MDRr = Mword[\langle MAR[31:2]00\rangle]$, $C = MAR$, $Cad.4 = Cad.3$	Dmr, MDRrce, Cce, Cad4ce
	store	$m = bytes(MDRw)$	Dmw
	noM		
WB	sh4l	$GPR[Cad.4] = sh4l(MDRr, MAR[1:0]000)$	shift4l, GPRw
	wb	$GPR[Cad.4] = C$	GPRw
	noWB	(no update)	

We begin with a stall engine which clocks all stages in a round robin fashion. It has a 5-bit register $full[4:0]$, where for all stages i, signal

$$ue_i = full_i \wedge /busy$$

enables the update of the registers in $out(i)$. Since memory accesses can take several cycles, the update of the data memory DM is enabled by $full_3$ and not by ue_3. Register $full$ is updated by

$$full[4:0] := \begin{cases} 00001 & \text{if} \quad reset \\ full[4:0] & \text{if} \quad busy \wedge /reset \\ cls(full) & \text{otherwise.} \end{cases}$$

Since the design comprises two memories, we compute the busy signal by

$$/busy = ibusy \text{ NOR } dbusy.$$

With signals $full$ defined in this way, we obviously can keep track of the stage which processes the instruction, namely: the instruction is in stage i iff $full_i = 1$. In particular, the instruction is in stage IF iff $full_0 = 1$, and it is in stage ID if $full_1 = 1$.

We proceed to transform the FSD by the following four changes:

1. The control signals activated in state IF are now *always* activated. In cycles with $full_0 = 1$, these signals then have the right value. In other cycles, they do not matter because IR is not clocked.

2. Moore signals activated in state ID are now always activated. They only matter in cycles with $full_1 = 1$.

BASIC PIPELINING

Table 4.7 Nontrivial disjunctive normal forms (DNF) of the FSD corresponding to the prepared data paths

Nontrivial DNF	Target State	Monomial $m \in M$		Length $l(m)$
		IR[31 : 26]	IR[5 : 0]	
D1	alu	000000	100***	9
D2	aluI	001***	******	3
D3	shift	000000	0001*0	11
		000000	00011*	11
D4	shiftI	000000	0000*0	11
		000000	00001*	11
D5	test	000000	101***	9
D6	testI	011***	******	3
D7	savePC	010111	******	6
		000011	******	6
D8	addrS	10100*	******	5
		1010*1	******	5
D9	addrL	100*0*	******	4
		1000*1	******	5
		10000*	******	5
DNF	Mealy Signals			
D10	Rtype	000000	******	6
D4	shiftI	000000	0000*0	(10)
		000000	00001*	(10)
D7	Jlink	010111	******	(6)
		000011	******	(6)
D11	jumpR	01011*	******	5
D12	Jjump	00001*	******	5
D13	jump	D11 OR D12		
D14	branch	00010*	******	5
D15	bzero	*****0	******	1
Accumulated length of $m \in M$: $\sum_{m \in M} l(m)$				126

Table 4.8 Paths $path(t)$ through the FSD for each type t of DLX instruction

DLX Instruction Type	Path through FSD
addi, subi, andi, ori, xori, lhgi	fetch, decode, aluI, passC, wb
add, sub, and, or, xor, lhg	fetch, decode, alu, passC, wb
clri, sgri, seqi, sgei, slsi, snei, slei, seti	fetch, decode, testI, passC, wb
clr, sgr, seq, sge, sls, sne, sle, set	fetch, decode, test, passC, wb
slli, srli, srai	fetch, decode, shiftI, passC, wb
sll, srl, sra	fetch, decode, shift, passC, wb
lb, lh, lw, lbu, lhu	fetch, decode, addrL, load, sh4l
sb, sh, sw	fetch, decode, addrS, store, noWB
jalr, jal	fetch, decode, savePC, passC, wb
others	fetch, decode, noEX, noM, noWB

3. Mealy signals activated in state ID are now activated in every cycle; they too matter only when $full_1 = 1$. Thus, the Mealy signals only depend on the inputs IR but not on the current state.

4. Finally observe that in figure 4.8 only state $decode$ has a fanout greater than one. In stage ID, we can therefore precompute the control signals of *all* stages that follow and clock them into a register $R.2 \in out(1)$. Table 4.9 lists for each state the signals to be clocked into that register. The inputs of register $R.2$ are computed in every cycle, but they are only clocked into register $R.2$ when

$$ue.1 = full.1 \wedge /busy = 1.$$

Register $R.2$ contains three classes of signals:

(a) signals x to be used in the next cycle only control stage EX,

(b) signals y to be used in the next two cycles control the stages EX and M, and

(c) signals z to be used in the next three cycles control the stages EX, M and WB.

The control signals y of stage M are delayed by one additional register $R.3 \in out(2)$, whereas the signals of stage WB are delayed by the registers $R.3$ and $R.4 \in out(3)$ as depicted in figure 4.9.

Table 4.9 Control signals to be precomputed during stage ID for each of the 10 execute states. The signals of the first table are all of type x, i.e., they only control stage EX.

EX	ALUDdoe	SHDdoe	linkDdoe	add	test	Rtype
M						
WB						
shift		1				1
shiftI		1				1
alu	1					1
aluI	1					
test	1				1	1
testI	1				1	
addrL	1			1		
addrS	1			1		
savePC			1			
noEX						

EX	MARce	bmuxsel	MDRwce amuxsel shift4s	Cad3ce	
M			Dmw	Cad4ce Cce	Dmr MDRrce
WB				GPRw	shift4l
Type	x	x	y	z	z
shift	1	1		1	
shiftI	1			1	
alu	1	1		1	
aluI	1			1	
test	1	1		1	
testI	1			1	
addrL	1			1	1
addrS	1		1		
savePC	1			1	
noEX					

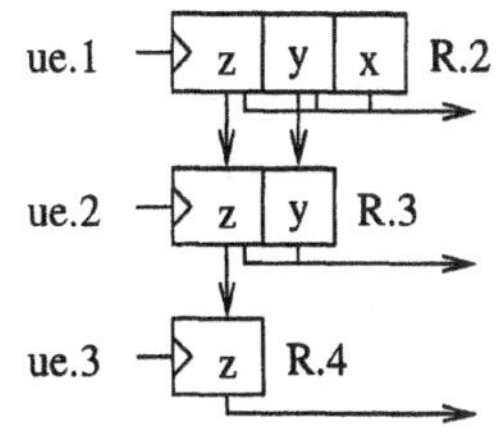

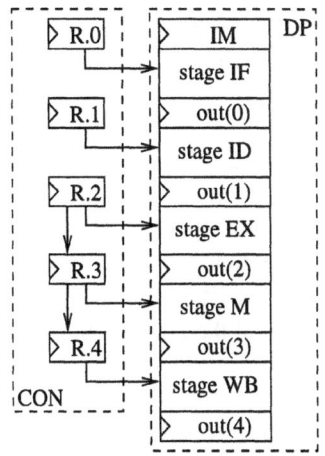

ue.1 → z y x R.2

ue.2 → z y R.3

ue.3 → z R.4

Figure 4.9 Buffering of the precomputed control signals

> R.0   > IM   DP
          stage IF
> R.1   > out(0)
          stage ID
> R.2   > out(1)
          stage EX
> R.3   > out(2)
          stage M
> R.4   > out(3)
CON   stage WB
          > out(4)

Figure 4.10 Structure of the data paths DP and the precomputed control CON of the DLX_σ machine

Table 4.10 Parameters of the two control automata; one precomputes the Moore signals (*ex*) and the other generate the Mealy signals (*id*).

	# states	# inputs	# and frequency of outputs		
	k	σ	γ	v_{sum}	v_{max}
ex	10	12	11	39	9
id	1	12	9	11	2

	fanin of the states		# and length of monomials		
	fan_{sum}	fan_{max}	#M	l_{sum}	l_{max}
ex	15	3	15	104	11
id	–	–	5	22	10

127

The new precomputed control generates the same control signals as the FSD, but the machine now has a very regular structure: Control signals coming from register $R.k \in out(k-1)$ control stage k of the data paths for all $k > 1$. Indeed, if we define $R.0$ and $R.1$ as dummy registers of length 0, the same claim holds for all k. The structure of the data paths and the precomputed control of machine DLX_σ is illustrated in figure 4.10.

The hardware generating the inputs of register $R.2$ is a Moore automaton with the 10 EX states, precomputed control signals and the parameters ex from table 4.10. The state $noEX$ serves as the initial state of the automaton. The next state only depends on the input IR but not on the current state. Including the registers $R.3$ and $R.4$, the control signals of the stages EX to WB can be precomputed at the following cost and cycle time:

$$
\begin{aligned}
C_{CON}(moore) &= C_{pMoore}(ex) + (3+2) \cdot C_{ff} \\
T_{CON}(moore) &= T_{pMoore}(ex).
\end{aligned}
$$

The Mealy signals which govern stage ID are generated by a Mealy automaton with a single state and the parameters id of table 4.10. All its inputs are provided by register IR at zero delay. According to section 2.6, the cost of this automaton and the delay of the Mealy signals can be estimated as

$$
\begin{aligned}
C_{CON}(mealy) &= C_{Mealy}(id) + (3+2) \cdot C_{ff} \\
A_{CON}(mealy) &= A_O(id).
\end{aligned}
$$

We do not bother to analyze cost and cycle time of the stall engine.

4.2.4 A Basic Observation

Later on, we will establish the correctness of pipelined machines by showing that they simulate machine DLX_σ. This will require an inductive proof on a cycle by cycle basis. We will always argue about a fixed but arbitrary sequence

$$I = I_0, I_1, \ldots$$

of instructions which is preceded by *reset* and which is itself not interrupted by *reset*.

If during a cycle the *busy* signal is active, then the state of the machine does not change at the end of that cycle. We therefore only number the cycles *during which the busy signal is inactive* with

$$T = 0, 1, \ldots$$

For such cycles T and signals R, we denote by R^T the value of R during cycle T; R can also be the output of a register. We abbreviate with

$$I_\sigma(k,T) = i$$

the fact that instruction I_i is in stage k of machine DLX_σ during cycle T. Formally, this can be defined as

- the execution starts in cycle $T = 0$, i.e., $I_\sigma(0,0) = 0$,

- if $I_\sigma(k,T) = i$ and $k < 4$, then $I_\sigma(k+1,T+1) = i$, and

- if $I_\sigma(4,T) = i$, then $I_\sigma(0,T+1) = i+1$.

For any other combination of T and k, the scheduling function $I_\sigma(k,T)$ is undefined. Hence,

$$I_\sigma(k,T) = i \quad \leftrightarrow \quad T = 5 \cdot i + k \quad \leftrightarrow \quad i = \lfloor T/5 \rfloor \quad \text{and} \quad k = T \bmod 5;$$

and for any cycle $T \geq 0$, stage k is full ($full^T[k] = 1$) iff $I_\sigma(k,T)$ is defined.

Recall that we denote by R_i the value of R after execution of instruction I_i. By R_{-1} we denote the initial value of R, i.e., the value of R just after reset. A basic observation about the cycle by cycle progress of machine DLX_σ is formulated in the following lemma.

Dateline Lemma. *Let* $I(k,T') = i$, *and let* $R \in out(t)$, *then*   ◄ Lemma 4.3

$$R^{T'} = \begin{cases} R_{i-1} & \text{if} \quad t \geq k \\ R_i & \text{if} \quad t < k \end{cases}$$

This is illustrated in figure 4.11. During cycle T', registers *above* stage k already have the new value R_i, whereas registers *below* stage k still have the old value R_{i-1}. In other words, *on downward arrows of figure 4.3 machine DLX_σ reads values R_i from the current instruction, whereas on upward arrows the machine reads values R_{i-1} from the previous instruction.*

This very intuitive formulation of the lemma is the reason why in figure 4.3 we have drawn the general purpose register file at the bottom of the pipeline and not – as is usual – in the middle of stage *ID*. A formal proof uses the fact that

$$R_{i-1} = R^{5i}$$

and proceeds for $T = 5i + k$ by induction on k. We leave the simple details as an exercise 4.2.

Another very intuitive way to state this lemma is in the following way. Imagine that wires between pipeline stages are so long, that we can wrap

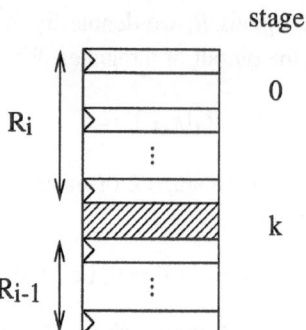

Figure 4.11 Illustration of lemma 4.3. In the current cycle, I_i is stage k.

the machine around the equator (with stage k east of stage $k + 1$ mod 5). Now imagine that we process one instruction per day and that we clock the pipeline stages at the dateline, i.e., the border between today and yesterday. Then the lemma states that east of the dateline we already have today's data whereas west of the dateline we still have yesterdays data.

Let $I(4, T) = i$, then $I(0, T + 1) = i + 1$, and the dateline lemma applies for all R

$$R^{T+1} = R_{(i+1)-1} = R_i.$$

4.3 Pipelining as a Transformation

WITH TWO very simple changes, we transform the prepared sequential machine DLX_σ from the previous section into a pipelined machine DLX_π:

1. Register DPC, i.e., the delayed PC is discarded. The instruction memory IM is now directly addressed by PC'. At reset, the instruction memory is addressed with address 0, and PC' is initialized with 4. This is illustrated in figure 4.12. Register PC' is still clocked by

$$PCce \vee reset.$$

2. The stall engine from figure 4.13 is used. For all i, signal ue_i enables the update of registers and RAM cells in $out(i)$. The update of the data memory DM is now enabled by

$$full_3 \wedge \overline{reset}.$$

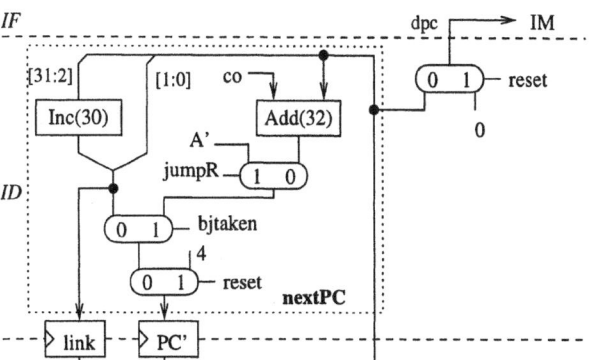

Figure 4.12 PC environment of the DLX_π design, implementing a delayed PC

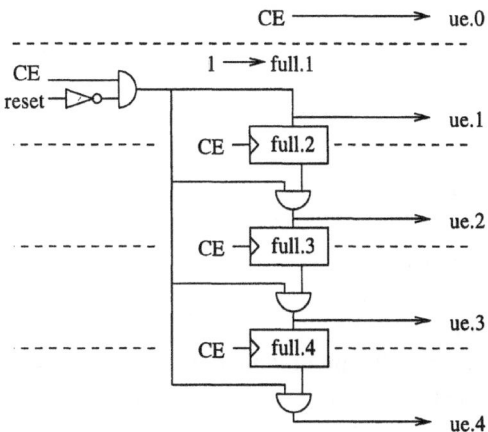

Figure 4.13 The stall engine of the DLX_π design

At reset, the signals $ue[4:0]$ are initialized with 00001. When only counting cycles T with an inactive *busy* signal, the update enable signals ue become active successively as indicated in table 4.11. Note that we now assume the reset signal to be active during cycle $T = 0$.

4.3.1 Correctness

We want to argue, that under certain hypotheses the pipelined machine DLX_π simulates the prepared sequential machine DLX_σ. We will have to

Table 4.11 Activation of the update enable signals $ue[4:0]$ after reset

T	reset	ue[0]	ue[1]	ue[2]	ue[3]	ue[4]	full[2]	full[3]	full[4]
0	1	1	0	0	0	0	*	*	*
1	0	1	1	0	0	0	0	0	0
2	0	1	1	1	0	0	1	0	0
3	0	1	1	1	1	0	1	1	0
4	0	1	1	1	1	1	1	1	1
...	0	1	1	1	1	1	1	1	1

argue simultaneously about registers R occurring in machine DLX_π and their counterpart in machine DLX_σ. Therefore, we introduce the notation R_π to denote a register in machine DLX_π; we denote by R_σ the corresponding register in machine DLX_σ. The notation R_i (the content of register R at the end of instruction I_i) will only be used for the sequential machine DLX_σ.

Duration of Reset

We generally assume that the reset signal is active long enough to permit an instruction memory access.

Initial Contents

The registers *visible* to the programmer are the general purpose registers *GPR*, the RAM cells in *IM* and *DM* and the program counters. The remaining registers are called *invisible*.

We assume, that during reset, the simulated machine (here DLX_σ) and the simulating machine (here DLX_π) have the same contents of the memories and the register file. In the sequential execution, reset is given in cycle $T' = -1$ whereas in the pipelined execution, reset is given in cycle $T = 0$. By construction, both machines do not update general purpose registers or memory cells during reset. Thus, in the two DLX designs any register $R \in \{GPR, PC', DPC\}$ and any memory cell M of DM and IM must satisfy

$$R_{-1} = R_\sigma^0 = R_\pi^1$$
$$M_{-1} = M_\sigma^0 = M_\pi^1.$$

Note that we make no such assumption for the remaining registers. This will be crucial when we treat interrupts. The mechanism realizing the jump to the interrupt service routine (*JISR*) will be almost identical to the present reset mechanism.

The schedule for the execution of instructions I_i by machine DLX_π is defined by

$$I_\pi(k, T) = i \quad \leftrightarrow \quad T = k + i.$$

The strategy of the correctness proof is now easily described. We consider cycle T for machine DLX_π and the *corresponding* cycle T' for machine DLX_σ, when the same instruction, say I_i is in the same stage, say k. Formally

$$I_\pi(k, T) = i = I_\sigma(k, T').$$

We then want to conclude by induction on T that stage k of the simulating machine has during cycle T the same inputs as stage k of the simulated machine during cycle T'. Since the stages are identical, we want to conclude for all signals S inside the stages

$$S_\pi^T = S_\sigma^{T'}. \tag{4.1}$$

This should hold in particular for the signals which are clocked into the output registers $R \in out(k)$ of stage k at the end of cycle T. This would permit us to conclude for these registers

$$R_\pi^{T+1} = R_\sigma^{T'+1} = R_i. \tag{4.2}$$

This almost works. Indeed it turns out that equations 4.1 and 4.2 hold after every invisible register has been updated at least once. Until this has happened, the invisible registers in the two machines can have different values because they can be initialized with different values.

Thus, we have to formulate a weaker version of equations 4.1 and 4.2. We exploit the fact, that invisible registers are only used to hold intermediate results (that is why they can be hidden from the programmer). Indeed, if the invisible register R is an input register of stage k, then the pipelined machine uses this register in cycle T only if it was updated at the end of the previous cycle. More formally, we have

Let $I_\pi(k, T) = i$, and let R be an invisible input register of stage k that was ◄ Lemma 4.4
not updated at the end of cycle $T - 1$, then:

1. *The set of output registers R' of stage k which are updated at the end of cycle T is independent of R^T.*

2. *Let R' be an output register of stage k that is updated at the end of cycle T, and let S be an input signal for R', then S^T is independent of R^T.*

This can be verified by inspection of the tables 4.4 to 4.6 and 4.8.

Therefore, it will suffice to prove equation 4.2 for all visible registers as well as for all invisible registers which are clocked at the end of cycle T. It will also suffice to prove equation 4.1 for the input signals S of all registers which are clocked at the end of cycle T.

Under the above assumptions and with a hypothesis about data dependencies in the program executed we are now able to prove that the machines DLX_π and DLX_σ produce the same sequence of memory accesses. Thus, the CPUs simulate each other in the sense that they have the same input/output behavior on the memory. The hypotheses about data dependencies will be removed later, when we introduce forwarding logic and a hardware interlock.

Theorem 4.5 ▶ *Suppose that for all $i \geq 0$ and for all $r \neq 0$, the instructions $I_{i-3}, \ldots, I_{i-1}$ do not write register $GPR[r]$, where $GPR[r]$ is a source operand of instruction I_i. The following two claims then hold for all cycles T and T', for all stages k, and for all instructions I_i with*

$$I_\pi(k, T) = i = I_\sigma(k, T') :$$

1. *For all signals S in stage k which are inputs to a register $R \in out(k)$ that is updated at the end of cycle T:*

$$S_\pi^T = S_\sigma^{T'}$$

2. *For all registers and $R \in out(k)$ which are visible or updated at the end of cycle T:*

$$R_\pi^{T+1} = R_i.$$

PROOF Proof by induction on the cycles T of the pipelined execution. Let $T = 0$. We have $I_\pi(0, 0) = 0 = I_\sigma(0, 0)$, i.e., instruction 0 is in stage 0 of machine DLX_π during cycle $T = 0$ and in stage 0 of machine DLX_σ during cycle $T' = 0$. The only input of stage 0 is the address for the instruction memory. This address is the output of register DPC for machine DLX_σ and signal dpc for machine DLX_π. By construction, both signals have in the corresponding cycles $T = 0$ and $T' = 0$ the same value, namely

$$DPC_\sigma^0 = dpc_\pi^0 = 0.$$

As stages 0 are for both machines identical, we have

$$S_\pi^0 = S_\sigma^0$$

for all internal signals S of stage 0 and claim 1 follows. In particular in both machines $IM(0)$ is clocked into the instruction register at the end of cycle $T = T' = 0$. Hence, claim 2 follows because of

$$IR_\pi^1 = IR_\sigma^1 = IR_0.$$

Table 4.12 Illustration of the scheduling function I_π for the stages $k-1$ and k.

stage s	$I_\pi(s,T)$	$I_\pi(s,T-1)$
k-1		i
k	i	i-1

In the induction step we conclude from $T-1$ to T. Thus, we have to show claim 1 for signals S in cycle T, and we have to show claim 2 for registers R in cycle $T+1$. According to figure 4.14, which illustrates the data flow between the stages of the DLX_σ design, there are the following four cases:

1. $k=2$ (execute) or $k=4$ (write back). This is the easy case. In figures 4.3 and 4.14, all edges into stage k come from output registers

$$R \in out(k-1)$$

of stage $k-1$. From the scheduling functions it can be concluded that

$$I_\pi(k-1,T-1) \;=\; I_\pi(k,T) \;=\; I_\sigma(k,T') \;=\; i.$$

This is illustrated in table 4.12. Let R be an input register of stage k which is visible or which was updated at the end of cycle $T-1$. Using lemma 4.3 with $t=1$ we conclude

$$
\begin{aligned}
R_\pi^T &= R_i && \text{by induction hypothesis} \\
&= R_\sigma^{T'} && \text{by lemma 4.3.}
\end{aligned}
$$

Hence, except for invisible input registers R which were not updated after cycle $T-1$, stage k of machine DLX_π has in cycle T the same inputs as stage k of machine DLX_σ in cycle T'. Stage k is identical in both machines (this is the point of the construction of the prepared machine !). By lemma 4.4, the set of output registers R' of stage k which are updated after cycle T or T', respectively, is identical for both machines, and the input signals S of such registers have the same value:

$$S_\pi^T \;=\; S_\sigma^{T'}.$$

If follows that at the end of these cycles T and T' identical values are clocked into R':

$$
\begin{aligned}
R_\pi'^{T+1} &= R_\sigma'^{T'+1} \\
&= R_i' \quad \text{by lemma 4.3.}
\end{aligned}
$$

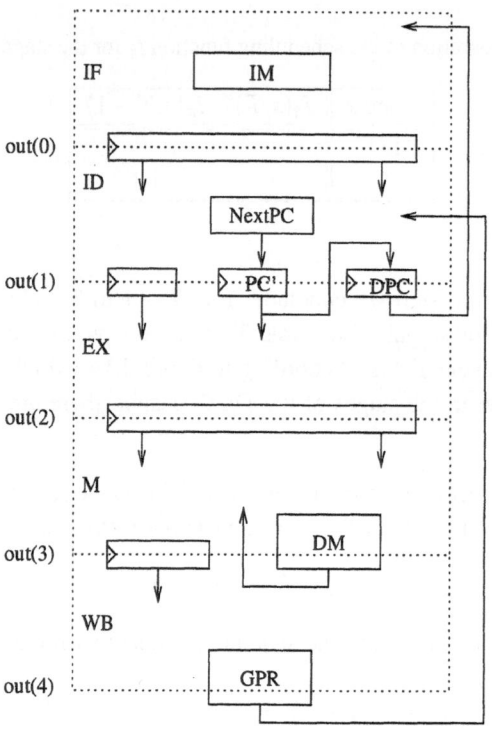

Figure 4.14 Data flow between the pipeline stages of the DLX_σ design

2. $k = 3$ (memory). The inputs of this stage comprise registers from $out(2)$ and the memory DM which belongs to $out(3)$. For input registers $R \in out(2)$, one concludes as above that

$$R_\pi^T \ = \ R_i \ = \ R^{T'}.$$

For $i > 0$, one concludes from the scheduling function (table 4.12)

$$I_\pi(3, T - 1) \ = \ i - 1.$$

We have $M \subset out(3)$, i.e., every memory cell is an output register of stage 3. Using lemma 4.3 with $t = k = 3$ and the induction hypothesis, we can conclude

$$M_\pi^T \ = \ M_{i-1} \ = \ M_\sigma^{T'}.$$

For $i = 0$, the scheduling function implies

$$I_\pi(3, T) \ = \ i \quad \leftrightarrow \quad T = 3.$$

Table 4.13 Illustration of the scheduling function I_π for the stages 0 and 1.

stage s	$I_\pi(s,T)$	$I_\pi(s,T-1)$
0	i	
1	i-1	i-2

In the DLX_π design, the data memory is only updated if

$$\overline{reset} \wedge full[3] = 1.$$

According to table 4.11, memory cell M is not updated during cycles $t \in \{1,2\}$, because the $full[3]_\pi^t = 0$. Since the DLX_π design is started with contents $M_\pi^1 = M_{-1}$, it follows

$$M_\pi^T = M_\pi^2 = M_\pi^1 = M_{-1}.$$

In the DLX_σ design, the update of the data memory DM is enabled by the flag $full[3]$. Thus, DM might be updated during reset, but then the update is disabled until I_0 reaches stage 3, since $full[3]_\sigma^t = 0$ for $t \in \{0,1,2\}$. Therefore,

$$M_{-1} = M_\sigma^0 = M_\sigma^{T'}.$$

Now the argument is completed as in the first case.

3. $k = 0$ (fetch). Here we have to justify that the delayed PC can be discarded. In the pipelined design, PC' is the only input register of stage IF, whereas in the sequential design, the input register is DPC. Both registers are outputs of stage $s = 1$.

For $i > 2$ one concludes from the scheduling functions (table 4.13)

$$I_\pi(1,T-1) = I_\pi(0,T-1)-1 = i-2.$$

The induction hypothesis implies (for $T > 1$)

$$PC_\pi'^T = PC_{i-2}'.$$

For $i = 1$ (and $T = 1$) we have by construction

$$PC_{-1}' = 4 = PC_\pi'^1.$$

Using lemma 4.3 with $t = 1$, we conclude for $T \geq 1$

$$PC_\pi'^T = PC_{i-2}' = DPC_{i-1} \quad \text{by construction}$$
$$= DPC_\sigma^{T'} \quad \text{by lemma 4.3.}$$

Now the argument is completed as in the first case.

Table 4.14 Illustration of the scheduling function I_π for the stages 1 to 4.

stage s	$I_\pi(s,T)$	$I_\pi(s,T-1)$
1	i	
2	i-1	
3	i-2	
4	i-3	i-4

4. $k = 1$ (decode). In either design, the decode stage has the input registers $IR \in out(0)$ and $GPR \in out(4)$. One shows $IR_\pi^T = IR^{T'}$ as above. If instruction I_i does not read a register $GPR[r]$ with $r \neq 0$, we are done, because the outputs of stage 4 are not used. In the other case, only the value $GPR[r]^T$ can be used. The scheduling function implies (table 4.14)

$$I_\pi(4, T-1) = i - 4.$$

For $i \geq 4$, we conclude using lemma 4.3 with $s = 4$ that

$$
\begin{aligned}
GPR[r]_\pi^T &= GPR[r]_{i-4} \qquad \text{by induction hypothesis} \\
&= GPR[r]_\sigma^{T'}.
\end{aligned}
$$

According to the hypothesis of the theorem, instructions I_{i-3} to I_{i-1} do not write register $GPR[r]$. Hence

$$GPR[r]_{i-1} = GPR[r]_{i-4}.$$

$i \leq 3$. The update of the register file GPR is enabled by signal $ue[4]$. The stall engine (table 4.11) therefore ensures that the register file is not updated during cycles $t \in \{1,2,3\}$. Thus,

$$GPR_{-1} = GPR_\pi^1 = \cdots = GPR_\pi^4.$$

The hypothesis of the theorem implies that instructions I_j with $0 \leq j < 3$ do not write register $GPR[r]$. Hence,

$$GPR[r]_{-1} = \cdots = GPR[r]_{i-1}.$$

By lemma 4.3 with $s = 4$, we conclude

$$GPR[r]_\pi^4 = GPR[r]_{i-1} = GPR[r]_\sigma^{T'}.$$

QED   The argument is completed as before.

4.3.2 Hardware Cost and Cycle Time

In the following, we determine the cost and the cycle time of the DLX_π design. Except for the PC environment and the stall engine, the pipelined design DLX_π and the prepared sequential design DLX_σ are the same. Since in section 4.2, the environments of the DLX_σ design are described in detail, we can focus on the PC environment and the stall engine.

The PC Environment

PCenv (figure 4.12) is governed by the same control signals as in the DLX_σ design, the glue logic *PCglue* also remains the same. The only modification in PCenv is that the register *DPC* of the delayed PC is discarded. The instruction memory *IM* is now addressed by

$$dpc = \begin{cases} PC' & \text{if } reset = 0 \\ 0 & \text{if } reset = 1. \end{cases}$$

Nevertheless, the PC environment still implements the delayed PC mechanism, where dpc takes the place of *DPC*.

Due to the modification, the PC environment becomes cheaper by one 32-bit register. The new cost is

$$C_{PCenv} = 2 \cdot C_{ff}(32) + 4 \cdot C_{mux}(32) + C_{add}(32) + C_{inc}(30) + C_{PCglue}.$$

The cycle time T_{PCenv} of the PC environment remains unchanged, but the address dpc of the instruction memory has now a longer delay. Assuming that signal *reset* has zero delay, the address is valid at

$$A_{PCenv}(dpc) = D_{mux}(32).$$

This delay adds to the cycle time of the stage IF and to the accumulated delay of signal *ibusy* of the instruction memory:

$$\begin{aligned} T_{IF} &= A_{PCenv}(dpc) + D_{IMenv}(IR) + \Delta \\ A_{IMenv}(ibusy) &= A_{PCenv}(dpc) + d_{Istat}. \end{aligned}$$

The Stall Engine

determines for each stage i the update enable signal $ue[i]$ according to figure 4.13. The registers $full[4:2]$ are clocked by *CE* when neither the instruction memory nor the data memory is busy or during *reset*:

$$\begin{aligned} CE &= /busy \lor (reset \land /ibusy) = /busy \lor (/reset \text{ NOR } ibusy) \\ /busy &= ibusy \text{ NOR } dbusy. \end{aligned}$$

During reset, the update is delayed until the instruction fetch is completed. Since signal *reset* has zero delay, the clock *CE* can be generated at an accumulated delay of

$$A_{stall}(CE) \;=\; \max\{A_{IMenv}(ibusy), A_{DMenv}(dbusy)\} + D_{nor} + D_{or}.$$

For each register $R \in out(i)$ and memory $M \in out(i)$, the stall engine then combines the clock/write request signal and the update signal and turns them into the clock/write signal:

$$Rce' \;=\; Rce \wedge ue[i], \qquad Mw' \;=\; Mw \wedge ue[i].$$

The update of the data memory DM is only enabled if stage 3 is full, and if there is no reset:

$$Dmw' \;=\; Dmw \wedge full[3] \wedge \overline{reset}.$$

The Moore control automaton provides 7 clock/write request signals and signal Dmw' (table 4.9). Together with two AND gates for the clocks of the stages IF and ID, the stall engine has cost

$$C_{stall} \;=\; 3 \cdot C_{ff} + 4 \cdot C_{and} + C_{inv} + 2 \cdot C_{nor} + C_{or} + (7 + 2 + 2) \cdot C_{and}.$$

As in the sequential design, the clocking of a register adds delay $D_{ff} + \delta$, whereas the update of the register file adds delay $D_{ram3}(32,32) + \delta$. Thus, the stall engine requires a cycle time of

$$T_{stall} \;=\; A_{stall}(CE) + 3 \cdot D_{and} + \max\{D_{ram3}(32,32), D_{ff}\} + \delta.$$

The write signal Dmw of the data memory has now a slightly larger accumulated delay. However, an inspection of the data memory control DMC (page 81) indicates that signal Dmw is still not time critical, and that the accumulated delay of DMC remains unchanged.

Hardware Cost

For the DLX_π design and the DLX_σ design, the top level schematics of the data paths DP are the same (figure 4.3), and so do the formula of the cost C_{DP}.

The control unit *CON* comprises the stall engine, the two memory controllers *IMC* and *DMC*, and the two control automata of section 4.2.3. The cost $C_{CON}(moore)$ already includes the cost for buffering the Moore signals up to the write back stage. The cost of the control and of the whole DLX_π core therefore sum up to

$$C_{CON} \;=\; C_{IMC} + C_{DMC} + C_{stall} + C_{CON}(moore) + C_{CON}(mealy)$$
$$C_{DLXp} \;=\; C_{DP} + C_{CON}.$$

Table 4.15 Cost of the DLX data paths and all its environments for the sequential DLX core (1) and for the pipelined design DLX_π (2). The last row lists the cost of the DLX_π relative to that of the sequential design.

	EX	SH4L	GPR	IR	PC	DP	CON	DLX
1	4083	380	4096	301	416	10846	1105	11951
2	3315	380	4066 / 30	301	1906	12198	756	12954
	0.81		1		4.58	1.12	0.68	1.08

Table 4.15 lists the cost of the DLX core and of its environments for the sequential design (chapter 3) and for the pipelined design. The execute environment of the sequential design consists of the environments ALUenv and SHenv and of the 9 drivers connecting them to the operand and result busses. In the DLX_π design, the busses are more specialized so that EXenv only requires three drivers and two muxes and therefore becomes 20% cheaper.

In order to resolve structural hazards, the DLX_π design requires an extended PC environment with adder and conditional sum incrementer. That accounts for the 358% cost increase of PCenv and of the 12% cost increase of the whole data paths.

Under the assumption that the data and control hazards are resolved in software, the control becomes significantly cheaper. Due to the precomputation and buffering of the control signals, the automata generate 19 instead of 29 signals. In addition, the execution scheme is optimized, cutting the total frequency v_{sum} of the control signals by half. The constant, for example, is only extracted once in stage ID, and not in every state of the execute stage.

Cycle Time

In order to determine the cycle time of the DLX design, we distinguish three types of paths, those through the control, through the memory system and through the data paths.

Control Unit CON The automata of the control unit generate Mealy and Moore control signals. The Mealy signals only govern the stage ID; they have an accumulated delay of 13 gate delays. The Moore signals are precomputed and therefore have zero delay:

$$A_{CON}(csID) = A_{CON}(mealy) = 13$$
$$A_{CON}(csEX) = A_{CON}(csM) = A_{CON}(csWB) = 0.$$

Table 4.16 Cycle time of the DLX fixed-point core for the sequential (1) and for the pipelined (2) design. In the pipelined design, d_{mem} denotes the maximum of the two access times d_{Imem} and d_{Dmem}; d_{mstat} denotes the maximum of the two status times d_{Istat} and d_{Dstat}.

	ID		EX	WB	IF, M	control CON	
	GPRr	PC	ALU/SH	GPRw	memory	auto	stall
1	27	70	70	37	$16 + d_{mem}$	42	$37 + d_{mstat}$
2	27	54	66	33	$16 + d_{mem}$	32	$41 + d_{mstat}$

The cycle time of the control unit is the maximum of the times required by the stall engine and by the automata

$$T_{CON} = \max\{T_{stall}, T_{auto}\}.$$

Compared to the sequential design, the automata are smaller. The maximal frequency of the control signals and the maximal fanin of the states are cut by 25% reducing time T_{auto} by 24% (table 4.16). The cycle time of the whole control unit, however, is slightly increased due to the stall engine.

Memory Environments   The cycle time T_M models the read and write time of the memory environments IMenv and DMenv. Pipelining has no impact on the time t_M which depends on the memory access times d_{Imem} and d_{Dmem}:

$$T_M = \max\{T_{IMenv}, T_{DMenv}\}.$$

Data Paths DP   The cycle time T_{DP} is the maximal time of all cycles in the data paths except those through the memories. This involves the stages decode, execute and write back:

$$T_{DP} = \max\{T_{ID}, T_{EX}, T_{WB}\}.$$

During decode, the DLX design updates the PC environment (T_{PCenv}), reads the register operands (T_{GPRr}), extracts the constant, and determines the destination address. Thus,

$$T_{ID} = \max\{T_{PCenv}, T_{GPRr}, A_{CON}(csID) + \max\{D_{IRenv}, D_{CAddr}\} + \Delta\}.$$

Table 4.16 lists all these cycle times for the sequential and the pipelined DLX design. The DLX_π design already determines the constant and the destination address during decode. That saves 4 gate delays in the execute and write back cycle and improves the total cycle time by 6%.

The cycle time of stage ID is dominated by the updating of the PC. In the sequential design, the ALU environment is used for incrementing the PC and for the branch target computation. Since environment PCenv has now its own adder and incrementer, the updating of the becomes 20% faster.

Pipelining has the following impact on the cost and the cycle time of the ◀ Result 4.6
DLX fixed-point core, assuming that the remaining data and control hazards can be resolved in software:

- *The data paths are about 12% more expensive, but the control becomes cheaper by roughly 30%. Since the control accounts for 5% of the total cost, pipelining increases the cost of the core by about 8%.*

- *The cycle time is reduced by 6%.*

In order to analyze the impact which pipelining has on the quality of the DLX fixed-point core, we have to quantify the performance of the two designs. For the sequential design, this was done in [MP95]. For the pipelined design, the performance strongly depends on how well the data and control hazards can be resolved. This is analyzed in section 4.6.

4.4 Result Forwarding

IN THIS section, we describe a rather simple extension of the hardware of machine DLX_π which permits to considerably weaken the hypothesis of theorem 4.5. For the new machine, we will indeed show theorem 4.5 but with the following hypothesis: If instruction I_i reads register $GPR[r]$, then the instructions I_{i-1}, I_{i-2} are not load operations with destination $GPR[r]$.

Suppose that for all $i \geq 0$ and $r \neq 0$, the instructions I_{i-1}, I_{i-2} are not load ◀ Theorem 4.7
operations with destination $GPR[r]$, where $GPR[r]$ is a source operand of instruction I_i. The following two claims then hold for all cycles T and T', for all stages k and for all instructions I_i with

$$I_\sigma(k, T') = I_\pi(k, T) = i.$$

1. *For all signals S in stage k which are inputs to a register $R \in out(k)$ that is updated at the end of cycle T:*

$$S_\pi^T = S_\sigma^{T'}$$

2. *For all registers and $R \in out(k)$ which are visible or updated at the end of cycle T:*

$$R_\pi^{T+1} = R_i.$$

4.4.1 Valid Flags

We first introduce three new precomputed control signals $v[4:2]$ for the prepared sequential machine DLX_σ. The valid signal $v[j]$ indicates that the data, which will be written into the register file at stage 4 (write back), is already available in the circuitry of stage j. For an instruction I_i, the valid signals are defined by

$$v[4] = 1; \qquad v[3] = v[2] = \begin{cases} 0 & \text{if instruction } I_i \text{ is a load} \\ 1 & \text{otherwise} \end{cases} = /Dmr_i,$$

where Dmr_i is the read signal of the data memory for I_i. Together with the write signal $GPRw$ of the register file and some other precomputed control signals, the signals $v[4:2]$ are pipelined in registers $R.2$, $R.3$ and $R.4$ as indicated in figure 4.15. For any stage $k \in \{2,3,4\}$, the signals $GPRw.k$ and $v[k].k$ are available in stage k. At the end of stage k, the following signals $C'.k$ are available as well:

- $C'.2$ which is the input of register MAR,

- $C'.3$ which is the input of register C, and

- $C'.4$ which is the data to be written into the register file GPR.

Observe that the signals $C'.k$ are inputs of output registers of stage k. Therefore, one can apply part 1 of the theorem to these signals in certain cycles. This is crucial for the correctness proof of the forwarding logic.

Obviously, the following statements hold:

Lemma 4.8 ▶ *For all i, for any stage $k \geq 2$, and for any cycle T with $I_\sigma(k,T) = i$, it holds:*

1. *I_i writes the register $GPR[r]$ iff after the sequential execution of I_i, the address r, which is different from 0, is kept in the registers $Cad.k$ and the write signals $GPRw.k$ are turned on, i.e.:*

   $$I_i \text{ writes } GPR[r] \quad \leftrightarrow \quad \langle Cad.k_i \rangle = r \wedge r \neq 0 \wedge GPRw.k_i = 1.$$

2. *If I_i writes a register $GPR[r]$, and if after its sequential execution, the valid flag $v[k]$ is turned on, then the value of signal $C'.k$ during cycle T equals the value written by I_i, i.e.:*

   $$I_i \text{ writes } GPR[r] \wedge v[k]_i = 1 \quad \rightarrow \quad C'.k^T = GPR[r]_i.$$

   Moreover, $C'.k$ is clocked into an output register of stage k at the end of cycle T.

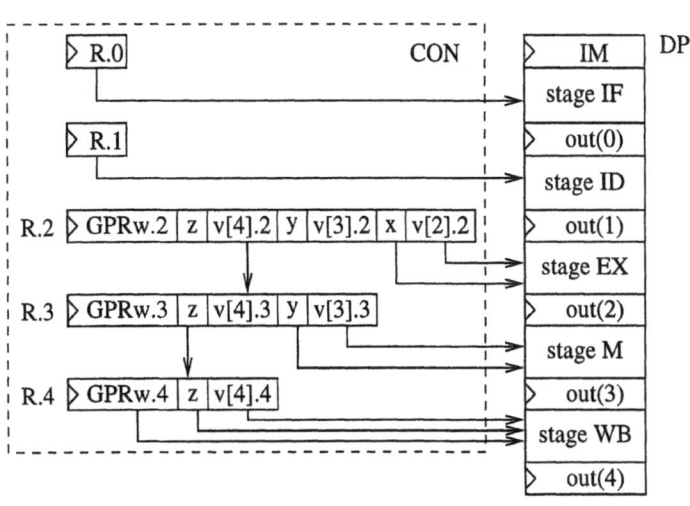

Figure 4.15 Structure of the data paths DP and of the precomputed control CON of the extended DLX_π machine

In the decode stage, the valid signals are derived from the memory read signal *Dmr*, which is precomputed by the control automata. The generation and buffering of the valid signals therefore requires the following cost and cycle time:

$$C_{VALID} = (3+2+1) \cdot C_{ff} + C_{inv}$$
$$T_{VALID} = T_{auto} + D_{inv}.$$

This extension effects the cost and cycle time of the precomputed control of the pipelined DLX design.

4.4.2 3-Stage Forwarding

We describe a circuit *Forw* capable of forwarding data from the three stages $j = 2, 3, 4$ into stage 1. It has the following inputs

1. $Cad.j, C'.j, GPRw.j$ as described above,

2. an address *ad* to be matched with *Cad*, and

3. a data *Din* from a data output port of the register file,

and it has an output *Dout* feeding data into stage 1. The data *Din* are fed into stage 1 whenever forwarding is impossible.

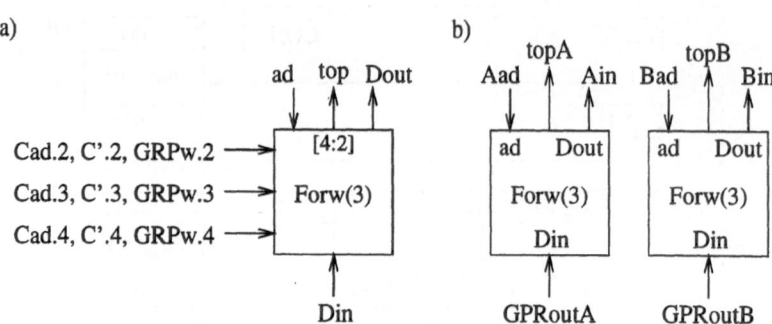

Figure 4.16 Block diagram of circuit $Forw(3)$ and the forwarding engine

The data paths of the pipelined machine DLX_π will be augmented by a *forwarding engine* consisting of two circuits $Forw(3)$, as depicted in figures 4.16. One of the circuits forwards data into register A, the other forwards data into register B. In general, forwarding engines will take care of *all* data transport from high stages to low stages, except for the instruction memory address. Thus, in the top level data path schematics (figure 4.17), there will be *no more upward edges* between the stages 1 to 4.

We proceed to specify circuit $Forw(3)$, give a simple realization and then prove the theorem 4.7.

Circuit Forw

For the stages $j \in \{2,3,4\}$, we specify the following signals:

$$hit[j] = (full.j \wedge GPRw.j) \wedge (ad \neq 0) \wedge (ad = Cad.j).$$

Signal $hit[j]$ is supposed to indicate that the register accessed by the instruction in stage 1 is modified by the instruction in stage j. Except for the first four clock cycles $T = 0, \ldots 3$ all pipeline stages are full (table 4.13), i.e., they process regular instructions. However, during the initial cycles, an empty stage is prevented from signaling a hit by its full flag. Signal

$$top.j = hit[j] \wedge \bigwedge_{x=2}^{j-1} /hit[x]$$

indicates moreover, that there occurs no hit in stages above stage j. The data output $Dout$ is then chosen as

$$Dout = \begin{cases} C'.j & \text{if } top.j = 1 \text{ for some } j \\ Din & \text{otherwise} \end{cases}$$

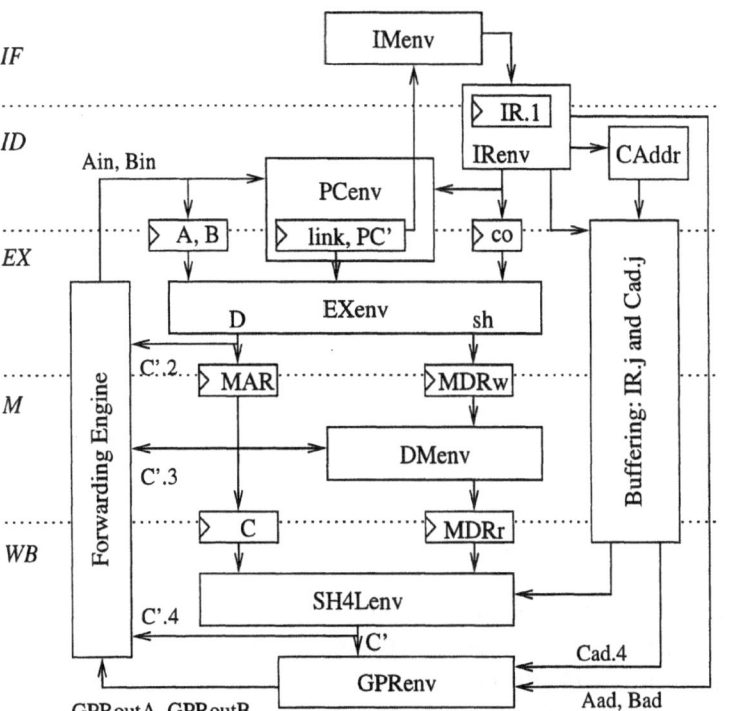

Figure 4.17 Top level schematics of the DLX_π data paths with forwarding. For clarity's sake, the address and control inputs of the stall engine are dropped.

Realization of Circuit Forw

An example realization is shown in figure 4.18. The circuitry to the left generates the three hit signals $hit[4:2]$, whereas the actual data selection is performed by the three multiplexers. The signals $top.j$ are implicit in the order of the multiplexers. The signals $top.j$, which will be needed by the stall engine, can be generated by two inverters and three AND gates. The cost of this realization of circuit $Forw$ then runs at

$$\begin{aligned} C_{Forw}(3) &= 3 \cdot (C_{equal}(5) + 3 \cdot C_{and} + C_{mux}(32)) \\ &\quad + C_{ortree}(5) + 2 \cdot C_{inv} + 3 \cdot C_{and}. \end{aligned}$$

This forwarding engine provides the output $Dout$ and the signals $top.j$ at the following delays

$$\begin{aligned} D_{Forw}(Dout;3) &= D_{equal}(5) + 2 \cdot D_{and} + 3 \cdot D_{mux} \\ D_{Forw}(top;3) &= D_{equal}(5) + 4 \cdot D_{and} + 3 \cdot D_{mux}; \end{aligned}$$

147

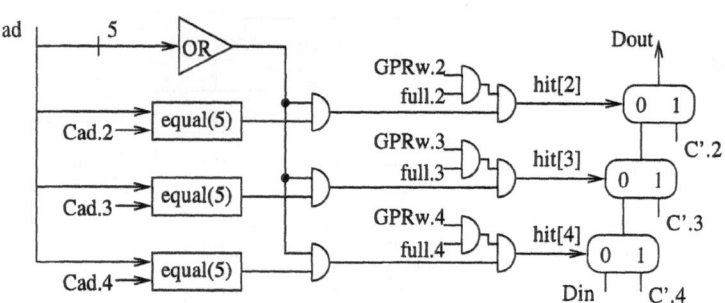

Figure 4.18 A realization of the 3-stage forwarding circuit $Forw(3)$

the delay is largely due to the address check. The actual data Din and $C'.j$ are delayed by no more than

$$D_{Forw}(Data;3) = 3 \cdot D_{mux}.$$

Let $A(C', Din)$ denote the accumulated delay of the data inputs $C'.i$ and Din. Since the addresses are directly taken from registers, the forwarding engine can provide the operands Ain and Bin at the accumulated delay $A(Ain, Bin)$; this delay only impacts the cycle time of stage ID.

$$A(C', Din) = \max\{A_{EXenv}, A_{SH4Lenv}, D_{GPR,read}\}$$
$$A(Ain, Bin) = \max\{A(C', Din) + A_{Forw}(Data, 3), D_{Forw}(Dout, 3)\}$$

The construction obviously generalizes to s-stage forwarding with $s > 3$, but then the delay is proportional to s. Based on parallel prefix circuits one can construct forwarding circuits $Forw(s)$ with delay $O(\log s)$ (see exercise 4.3).

4.4.3 Correctness

We now proceed to prove theorem 4.7. We start with a simple observation about valid bits in a situation where instruction I_i reads register $GPR[r]$ and one of the three preceding instructions $I_{i-\alpha}$ (with $\alpha \in \{1, 2, 3\}$) writes to register $GPR[r]$. In the pipelined machine, the read occurs in a cycle T when instruction I_i is in stage 1, i.e., when

$$I_\pi(k, T) = 1.$$

During this cycle, instruction $I_{i-\alpha}$ is in stage $1 + \alpha$:

$$I_\pi(1 + \alpha T) = i - \alpha.$$

We consider the time T', when instruction $I_{i-\alpha}$ is in stage $1+\alpha$ of the prepared sequential machine:

$$I_\sigma(1+\alpha T') = i - \alpha.$$

In cycle T', the prepared sequential machine has not yet updated register $GPR[r]$. The following lemma states, where we can find a precomputed version of $GPR[r]_{i-\alpha}$ in the sequential machine.

Suppose the hypothesis of theorem 4.5 holds, I_i reads $GPR[r]$, instruction $I_{i-\alpha}$ writes $GPR[r]$, and $I_\sigma(1+\alpha, T') = i - \alpha$, then   ◄ Lemma 4.9

$$C'.(1+\alpha)_\sigma^{T'} = GPR[r]_{i-\alpha}.$$

If $I_{i-\alpha}$ is a load instruction, then by the hypothesis of the theorem we have   PROOF
$\alpha = 3$. In this case, the valid bits are generated such that

$$v[4]_{i-\alpha} = v[1+\alpha]_{i-\alpha} = 1.$$

In any other case, the valid signals for any $j \geq 2$ equal

$$v[j]_{i-\alpha} = 1.$$

The claim now follows directly from lemma 4.8.   QED

Proof of Theorem 4.7 The proof proceeds along the same lines as the   PROOF
proof of theorem 4.5 by induction on T where T denotes a cycle in the pipelined execution with $I_\pi(k,T) = i$. Since only the inputs of stage 1 were changed, the proof for the case $T = 0$ and the induction step for $k \neq 1$ stay literally the same. Moreover, in the induction step, when we conclude from $T-1$ to T for $k = 1$, we can already assume the theorem for T and $k > 1$. We only need to show the claim for those input signals of stage 1, which depend on the results of later stages, i.e., the signals Ain and Bin. For all the other signals and output registers of stage 1, the claim can the be concluded as in the proof of theorem 4.5.

A read from $GPR[r]$ can be into register A or into register B. In the induction step, we only treat the case where instruction I_i reads $GPR[r]$ into register A. Reading into register B is treated in the same way with the obvious adjustments of notation.

There are two cases. In the interesting case, the hypothesis of theorem 4.5 does not hold for instruction I_i, i.e., there is an $\alpha \in \{1,2,3\}$ such that instruction $I_{i-\alpha}$ writes $GPR[r]$. By the hypothesis of the theorem, this instruction is not a load instruction. For the valid bits this implies

$$v[j]_{i-\alpha} = 1$$

for all stages j. Application of the induction hypothesis to the instruction register gives $IR_i = IR_\pi^T$. Since I_i reads $GPR[r]$, it follows for signal $Aadr$:

$$r = \langle Aad_i \rangle = \langle Aad_\pi^T \rangle.$$

Since $I_{i-\alpha}$ writes register $GPR[r]$, it follows by lemma 4.8 for any stage $j \geq 2$ that

$$GPRw.j_{i-\alpha} \wedge (\langle Cad.j_{i-\alpha} \rangle = r) \wedge (r \neq 0).$$

For stage $j = 1 + \alpha$, the pipelining schedule implies (table 4.14, page 138)

$$I_\pi(j, T) = I_\pi(1 + \alpha, T) = i - \alpha,$$

Note that none of the stages 0 to $i + \alpha$ is empty. By the induction hypothesis it therefore follows that

$$
\begin{aligned}
hit[1+\alpha]_\pi^T &= full.(1+\alpha)_\pi^T \wedge GPRw.(1+\alpha)_\pi^T \\
&\quad \wedge (r \neq 0) \wedge (\langle Cad.(1+\alpha)_\pi^T \rangle = r) \\
&= 1 \wedge GPRw.(1+\alpha)_{1-\alpha} \\
&\quad \wedge (r \neq 0) \wedge (\langle Cad.(1+\alpha)_{i-\alpha} \rangle = r) \\
&= 1.
\end{aligned}
$$

Let $I_{i-\alpha}$ be the last instruction before I_i which writes $GPR[r]$. Then no instruction between I_i and $I_{i-\alpha}$ writes $GPR[r]$, and we have

$$hit[l]_\pi^T = 0$$

for any stage l with $1 < l < 1 + \alpha$, and hence

$$top.(1+\alpha)_\pi^T = 1.$$

Let T' denote the cycle in the sequential execution with

$$I_\sigma(1+\alpha, T') = I_\pi(1+\alpha, T) = i - \alpha.$$

The forwarding logic delivers the output

$$
\begin{aligned}
Dout_\pi^T &= C'.(1+\alpha)_\pi^T \\
&= C'.(1+\alpha)_\sigma^{T'} \quad \text{by lemma 4.8 and by} \\
&\qquad\qquad\qquad\quad \text{the theorem for } T \text{ and } k = 1 + \alpha \\
&= GPR[r]_{i-\alpha} \quad \text{by lemma 4.9} \\
&= GPR[r]_{i-1}.
\end{aligned}
$$

In the simple second case, the stronger hypothesis of theorem 4.5 holds for I_i. For any $i \geq 4$, this means that none of the instructions $I_{i-1}, I_{i-2}, I_{i-3}$ writes $GPR[r]$. As above, one concludes that

$$hit[j]_\pi^T = 0,$$

for all j. Hence, the forwarding logic behaves like the old connection between the data output *GPRoutA* of the GPR environment and the input *Ain* of the decode stage delivering

$$Dout_\pi^T = Din_\pi^T = GPR[r]_{i-4} = GPR[r]_{i-1}.$$

For $i \leq 3$, the DLX_π pipeline is getting filled. During these initial cycles ($T \leq 3$), either stage $k > 1$ is empty or instruction I_j with $I_\pi(k, T) = j \leq 2$ does not update register GPR[r]. As above, one concludes that for any j

$$hit[j]_\pi^T = 0,$$

and that

$$Dout_\pi^T = Din_\pi^T = GPR[r]_{-1}$$

QED

4.5 Hardware Interlock

4.5.1 Stall Engine

In this section, we construct a nontrivial stall engine called *hardware interlock*. This engine stalls the upper two stages of the pipeline in a situation called a *data hazard* , i.e., when the forwarding engine cannot deliver valid data on time. Recall that this occurs if

1. an instruction I_i which reads from a register $r \neq 0$ is in stage 1,

2. one of the instructions $I_j with j \in \{i - 1, i - 2\}$ is a load with destination r,

3. and I_j is the last instruction before I_i with destination r.

This must be checked for both operands A and B. In the existing machine, we could characterize this situation by the activation of the signal *dhaz*:

$$
\begin{aligned}
dhaz &= dhazA \vee dhazB \\
dhazA &= topA.2 \wedge /v[2].2 \vee topA.3 \wedge /v[3].3 \\
dhazB &= topB.2 \wedge /v[2].2 \vee topB.3 \wedge /v[3].3.
\end{aligned}
$$

Based on this signal, we define the two clocks, the clock $CE1$ of the stages 0 and 1, and the clock $CE2$ of the stages 2 to 4:

$$
\begin{aligned}
CE2 &= /(ibusy \vee dbusy) \vee (reset \wedge /ibusy) \\
CE1 &= /(ibusy \vee dbusy \vee dhaz) \vee (reset \wedge /ibusy).
\end{aligned}
$$

Thus, $CE2$ corresponds to the old clock signal CE, whereas $CE1$ is also inactive in presence of a data hazard.

Whenever the lower stages of the pipeline are clocked while the upper stages are stalled, a *dummy instruction* (i.e., an instruction which should not be there) enters stage 2 and trickles down the pipe in subsequent cycles. We have to ensure that dummy instructions cannot update the machine. One method is to force a NOP instruction into stage 2 whenever $CE2 \wedge /CE1 = 1$. This method unfortunately depends on the particular instruction set and its encoding. When stalling a different pipeline, the corresponding part of the hardware has to be modified. A much more uniform method is the following:

1. Track true instructions and dummy instruction in stage k by a single bit $full.k$, where $full.k = 1$ signals a true instruction and $full.k = 0$ signals a dummy instruction.

2. In $CE2$ cycles with $full.k = 0$, do not update stage k and advance the dummy instruction to stage $k+1$ if $k+1 \leq 4$.

The following equations define a stall engine which uses this mechanism. It is clocked by $CE2$. A hardware realization is shown in figure 4.19. For $k \geq 2$,

$$
\begin{aligned}
ue.0 &= CE1 \\
full.1 &= 1 \\
ue.1 &= CE1 \wedge \overline{reset} \\
ue.k &= CE2 \wedge \overline{reset} \wedge full.k \\
full.k &:= ue.(k-1)
\end{aligned}
$$

This is an almost trivial set of equations. However, enabling the hit signals $hit[j]$ by the corresponding full flags is a subtle and crucial part of the mechanism. It ensures that dummy instructions cannot activate a hit signal $hit[j]$ nor the data hazard signal (exercise 4.4).

In order to prevent dummy instructions from generating a *dbusy* signal and from updating the data memory, the read and write signals Dmr' and Dmw' of the data memory DM are also enabled by the full flag:

$$
\begin{aligned}
Dmr' &= Dmr \wedge full.3 \\
Dmw' &= Dmw \wedge full.3 \wedge \overline{reset},
\end{aligned}
$$

where Dmr and Dmw are the read and write request signals provided by the precomputed control.

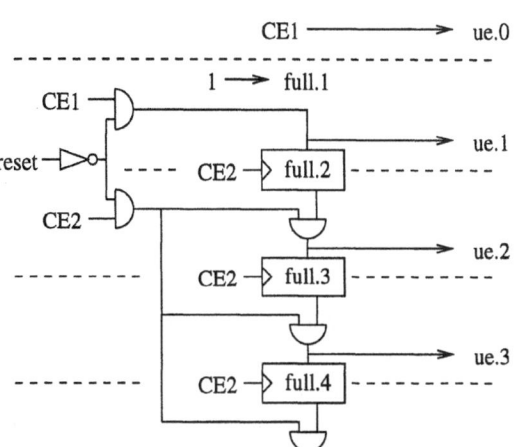

Figure 4.19 Hardware interlock engine of the DLX_π design

Hardware Cost and Delay

The modifications presented above only effect the stall engine. The Stall Engine of figure 4.19 determines the update enable signals $ue.i$ based on the clocks $CE1$ and $CE2$. These clock signals can be expressed as

$$CE2 = /busy \vee (/reset \text{ NOR } ibusy)$$
$$CE1 = (/busy \wedge /dhaz) \vee (/reset \text{ NOR } ibusy)$$
$$/busy = ibusy \text{ NOR } dbusy.$$

The clocks now also depend on the data hazard signal $dhaz$ which can be provided at the following cost and delay:

$$C_{dhaz} = 2 \cdot C_{inv} + 4 \cdot C_{and} + 3 \cdot C_{or}$$
$$A_{stall}(dhaz) = A_{Forw}(top; 3) + D_{and} + 2 \cdot D_{or}.$$

Since signal $reset$ has zero delay, the clocks can be generated at an accumulated delay of

$$A_{stall}(/busy) = \max\{A_{IMenv}(ibusy), A_{DMenv}(dbusy)\} + D_{nor}$$
$$A_{stall}(CE) = \max\{A_{stall}(/busy), A_{stall}(dhaz)\} + D_{and} + D_{or}.$$

For each register and memory, the stall engine turns the clock/write request signal into a clock/write signal. Due to the signal Dmr and Dmw, that now requires 11 AND gates. Altogether, the cost of the stall and interlock engine then runs at

$$C_{stall} = 3 \cdot C_{ff} + C_{inv} + (5 + 11 + 1) \cdot C_{and} + 2 \cdot C_{nor} + 2 \cdot C_{or} + C_{dhaz}.$$

Since the structure of the stall engine remains the same, its cycle time can be expressed as before:

$$T_{stall} = A_{stall}(CE) + 3 \cdot D_{and} + \max\{D_{ram3}(32,32), D_{ff}\} + \delta.$$

4.5.2 Scheduling Function

With the forwarding engine and the hardware interlock, it should be possible to prove a counterpart of theorem 4.7 with no hypothesis whatsoever about the sequence of instructions.

Before stating the theorem, we formalize the new scheduling function $I_\pi(k,T)$. The cycles T under consideration will be $CE2$ cycles. Intuitively, the definition says that a new instruction is inserted in every $CE1$ cycle into the pipe, and that subsequently it trickles down the pipe together with its $full.k$ signals. We assume that cycle 0 is the last cycle in which the reset signal is active.

The execution still starts in cycle 0 with $I_\pi(0,0) = 0$. The instructions are always fetched in program order, i.e.,

$$I_\pi(0,T) = i \quad \rightarrow \quad I_\pi(0,T+1) = \begin{cases} i & \text{if} \quad ue.0^T = 0 \\ i+1 & \text{if} \quad ue.0^T = 1. \end{cases} \quad (4.3)$$

Any instructions makes a progress of at most one stage per cycle, i.e., if $I_\pi(k,T) = i$, then

$$i = \begin{cases} I_\pi(k,T+1) & \text{if} \quad ue.k^T = 0 \\ I_\pi(k+1,T+1) & \text{if} \quad ue.k^T = 1 \quad \text{and} \quad k+1 \leq 4. \end{cases} \quad (4.4)$$

We assume that the reset signal is active long enough to permit an access with address 0 to the instruction memory. With this assumption, activation of the reset signal has the following effects:

$$\begin{aligned} CE2 &= 1 \\ ue.0 &= CE1 \\ ue.1 &= ue.2 = ue.3 = ue.4 = 0. \end{aligned}$$

After at most one cycle, the full flags are initialized to

$$full.1 = 1, \qquad full.2 = full.3 = full.4 = 0,$$

read accesses to the data memory are disabled ($DMr' = 0$), and thus,

$$busy = dhaz = 0.$$

When the first access to *IM* is completed, the instruction register holds

$$IR = IM[0].$$

This is the situation in cycle $T = 0$. From the next cycle on, the reset signal is turned off, and a new instruction is then fed into stage 0 in every $CE1$ cycle. Moreover, we have

$$ue.0^T = ue.1^T = CE1^T \qquad \text{for all} \quad T \geq 1,$$

i.e., after cycle $T = 0$, stages 0 and 1 are always clocked simultaneously, namely in every $CE1$ cycle. A simple induction on T gives for any $i \geq 1$

$$I_\pi(0,T) = i \quad \rightarrow \quad I_\pi(1,T) = i - 1 \qquad (4.5)$$

This means that the instructions wander in lockstep through the stages 0 and 1. For $T \geq 1$ and $1 \leq k \leq 3$, it holds that

$$ue.k^T = 1 \quad \rightarrow \quad ue.(k+1)^{T+1} = 1.$$

Once an instruction is clocked into stage 2, it passes one stage in each $CE2$ clock cycle. Thus, an instruction cannot be stalled after being clocked into stage 2, i.e., it holds for $k \in \{2,3\}$

$$I_\pi(k,T) = i \quad \rightarrow \quad I_\pi(k+1,T+1) = i. \qquad (4.6)$$

The stall engine ensures the following two features: ◀ Lemma 4.10

1. *An instruction I_i can never overtake the preceding instruction I_{i-1}.*

2. *For any stage $k \geq 1$ and any cycle $T \geq 1$, the value $I_\pi(k,T)$ of the scheduling function is defined iff the flag $full.k$ is active during cycle T, $full.k^T = 1$.*

1) Since the instructions are always fetched in-order (equation 4.3), instruction I_i enters stage 0 after instruction I_{i-1}. Due to the lockstep behavior of the first two stages (equation 4.5), there exists a cycle T with   PROOF

$$I_\pi(0,T) = i \wedge I_\pi(1,T) = i - 1.$$

Let $T' \geq T$ be the next cycle with an active $CE1$ clock. The stages 0 and 1 are both clocked at the end of cycle T'; by equation 4.4 it then follows that both instructions move to the next stage:

$$I_\pi(1,T'+1) = i \wedge I_\pi(2,T'+1) = i - 1.$$

Instruction I_{i-1} now proceeds at full speed (equation 4.6), i.e., it holds for $a \in \{1, 2\}$ that

$$I_\pi(2 + a, T' + 1 + a) = i - 1.$$

Instruction I_i can pass at most one stage per cycle (equation 4.4), and up to cycle $T + 1 + a$ it therefore did not move beyond stage $1 + a$. Thus, I_i cannot overtake I_{i-1}. This proves the first statement.

2) The second statement can be proven by a simple induction on T; we leave the details as an exercise (see exercise 4.5).

QED

Deadlock Free Execution

Finally, we have to argue that the stall mechanism cannot produce deadlocks. Let both clocks be active during cycle $T - 1$, i.e.,

$$CE1^{T-1} = CE2^{T-1} = 1,$$

let the instructions I, I' and I'' be in the stages 1 to 3 during cycle T. I', I'' are possibly dummy instructions. Furthermore, let $CE1^T = 0$. Thus, the hazard flag must be raised ($dhaz^T = 1$), and one of the instructions I' and I'' must be a load which updates a source register of I.

1. Assuming that instruction I' in stage 2 is such a load, then

$$v.2^T = v.3^{T+1} = 0 \quad \text{and} \quad v.4^{T+2} = 1.$$

   Instruction I' produces a data hazard during cycles T and $T + 1$. During these cycles, only dummy instructions which cannot activate the $dhaz$ signal enter the lower stages, and therefore

$$dhaz^{T+2} = 0 \quad \text{and} \quad CE1^{T+2} = 1.$$

2. Assuming that instruction I'' in stage 3 is the last load which updates a source register of I, then

$$v.2^T = v.3^{T+1} = 1, \quad v.3^T = 0 \quad \text{and} \quad v.4^{T+1} = 1.$$

   Instruction I'' produces a data hazard during cycle T, and a dummy instruction enters stage 2 at the end of the cycle. In the following $CE2$ cycle, there exists no data hazard, and the whole pipeline is clocked:

$$dhaz^{T+1} = 0 \quad \text{and} \quad CE1^{T+1} = 1.$$

Thus, the clock $CE1$ is disabled ($CE1 = 0$) during at most two consecutive $CE2$ cycles, and all instructions therefore reach all stages of the pipeline. Note that none of the above arguments hinges on the fact, that the pipelined machine simulates the prepared sequential machine.

We can now show the simulation theorem for arbitrary sequences of instructions:

For all i, k, T, T' such that $I_\pi(k,T) = I_\sigma(k,T') = i$ and $ue.k^T = 1$, the following two claims hold: ◀ Theorem 4.11

1. *for all signals S in stage k which are inputs to a register $R \in out(k)$ that is updated at the end of cycle T:*

$$S_\pi^T = S_\sigma^{T'}$$

2. *for all registers and $R \in out(k)$ which are visible or updated at the end of cycle T:*

$$R_\pi^{T+1} = R_i.$$

We have argued above that $IM[0]$ is clocked into register IR at the end of $CE2$ cycle 0, and that the PC is initialized properly. Thus, the theorem holds for $T = 0$. For the induction steps, we distinguish four cases: PROOF

1. $k = 0$. Stage 0 only gets inputs from the stages 0 and 1. Without reset, these two stages are clocked simultaneously. Thus, the inputs of stage 0 only change on an active $CE1$ clock. Arguing about $CE1$ cycles instead of $CE2$ cycles, one can repeat the argument from theorem 4.7.

2. $k \in \{2,4\}$. In the data paths, there exists only downward edges into stage k, and the instructions pass the stages 2 to 4 at full speed. The reasoning therefore remains unchanged.

3. $k = 3$. From $I_\pi(3,T) = i$ one cannot conclude $I_\pi(3,T-1) = i-1$ anymore. Instead, one can conclude

$$I_\pi(3,t) = i - 1$$

for the last cycle $t < T$ such that $I(3,t)$ is defined, i.e., such that a non-dummy instruction was in stage 3 during cycle t. Since dummy instructions do not update the data memory cell M, it then follows that

$$\begin{aligned} M_\pi^{t+1} &= M_{i-1} \quad \text{by induction hypothesis} \\ &= M_\pi^T. \end{aligned}$$

4. $k = 1$. For $I(1,T) = i$ and $ue.1^T = 1$ we necessarily have $dhaz^T = 0$. If I_i has no register operand GPR[r], then only downward edges are used, and the claim follows as before. Thus, let I_i read a register GPR[r] with $r \neq 0$. The read can be for operand A or B. We only treat the reading of operand A; the reading of B is treated in the same way with the obvious adjustments of notation.

If the instructions $I_0, \ldots I_{i-1}$ do not update register GPR[r], it follows for any $k > 1$ that

$$(GPRw.k_\pi^T = 0) \vee (\langle Cad.k_\pi^T \rangle \neq r),$$

or that stage k processes a dummy instruction, i.e., $full.k^T = 0$. Thus, hit signal $hit.k^T$ is inactive, and the reasoning of theorem 4.7 can be repeated.

If register GPR[r] is updated by an instruction preceding I_i, we define $last(i,r)$ as the index of the last instruction before I_i which updates register GPR[r], i.e.,

$$last(i,r) = \max\{j < i | I_j \text{ updates register } GPR[r]\}.$$

Instruction $I = I_{last(i,r)}$ is either still being processed, or it has already left the pipeline.

If instruction I is still in process, then there exists a stage $l \geq 2$ with

$$I_\pi(l,T) = last(i,r).$$

From lemma 4.10 and the definition of $last(i,r)$, it follows that

$$hitA.l_\pi^T = 1,$$

and that any stage between stage 1 and l is either empty or processes an instruction with a destination address different from r. By the construction of circuit $Forw$, it then follows that

$$topA.k_\pi^T = 1.$$

Since $dhaz_\pi^T = 0$, the hazard signal of operand A is also inactive, $dhazA_\pi^T = 0$. By the definition of this signal and by the simulation theorem for $l \geq 2$ it follows that

$$v.l_\pi^T = 1 = v.l_{last(i,r)}.$$

The decode stage $k = 1$ then reads the proper operand A of instruction I_i,

$$
\begin{aligned}
Ain_\pi^T &= C'.l_\pi^T & &\text{; design of the forwarding engine} \\
&= GPR[r]_{last(i,r)} & &\text{; theorem for stages 2 to 4} \\
&= GPR[r]_{i-1} & &\text{; definition of } last(i,r),
\end{aligned}
$$

Table 4.17 Cost of the sequential DLX core and of the pipelined DLX designs

Design	DP	CON	DLX
sequential	10846	1105	11951
basic pipeline	12198	756	12954
pipeline + forwarding	12998	805	13803
pipeline + interlock	13010	830	13840

and the claim follows for stage $k = 1$.

If instruction I already ran to completion, then there exists no stage $l \geq 2$ with

$$I_\pi(l, T) = last(i, r).$$

With reasoning similar to the one of the previous case it then follows that

$$Ain_\pi^T = GPR[r]_\pi^T = GPR[r]_{last(i,r)} = GPR[r]_{i-1},$$

and thus, I gets the proper operand A.   QED

4.6 Cost Performance Analysis

IN PREVIOUS sections we have described several variants of a pipelined DLX core and have derived formulae for their cost and cycle time. In the following, we will evaluate the pipelined and sequential DLX designs based on their cost, cycle time, and performance-cost ratio. The SPEC integer benchmark suite SPECint92 [Hil95, Sta] serves as workload.

4.6.1 Hardware Cost and Cycle Time

Table 4.17 lists the cost of the different DLX designs. Compared to the sequential design of chapter 3, the basic pipeline increases the total gate count by 8%, and result forwarding adds another 7%. The hardware interlock engine, however, has virtually no impact on the cost. Thus, the DLX_π design with hardware interlock just requires 16% more hardware than the sequential design.

Note that pipelining only increases the cost of the data paths; the control becomes even less expensive. This even holds for the pipelined design with forwarding and interlocking, despite the more complex stall engine.

Table 4.18 Cycle time of the DLX core for the sequential and the pipelined designs. The cycle time of CON is the maximum of the two listed times.

Design	A/B	PC	EX	IF, M		CON	
sequential	27	70	70	$18 + d_{mem}$	40	$39 + d_{mstat}$
basic pipe	27	54	66	$16 + d_{mem}$	32	$41 + d_{mstat}$
pipe + forwarding	72	93^a	66	$16 + d_{mem}$	34	$41 + d_{mstat}$
pipe + interlock	72	93^a	66	$16 + d_{mem}$	57	$43 + d_{mstat}$

[a]this time can be reduced to 89 by using a fast zero tester for AEQZ

According to table 4.18, the result forwarding slows down the PC environment and the register operand fetch dramatically, increasing the cycle time of the DLX core by 40%. The other cycle times stay virtually the same. The hardware interlocks make the stall engine more complicated and increase the cycle time of the control, but the time critical paths remains the same.

The significant slow down caused by result forwarding is not surprising. In the design with a basic pipeline, the computation of the ALU and the update of the PC are time critical. With forwarding, the result of the ALU is forwarded to stage ID and is clocked into the operand registers A1 and B1. That accounts for the slow operand fetch. The forwarded result is also tested for zero, and the signal AEQZ is then fed into the glue logic *PCglue* of the PC environment. *PCglue* provides the signal *bjtaken* which governs the selection of the new program counter. Thus, the time critical path is slowed down by the forwarding engine ($6d$), by the zero tester ($9d$), by circuit *PCglue* ($6d$), and by the selection of the PC ($6d$).

With the fast zero tester of exercise 4.6, the cycle time can be reduced by 4 gate delays at no additional cost. The cycle time ($89d$) is still 35% higher than the one of the basic pipeline. However, without forwarding and interlocking, all the data hazards must be resolved at compile time by rearranging the code or by insertion of NOP instructions. The following sections therefore analyze the impact of pipelining and forwarding on the instruction throughput and on the performance-cost ratio.

4.6.2 Performance Model

The performance is modeled by the reciprocal of the benchmark's execution time. For a given architecture A, this execution time is the product of the design's cycle time τ_A and its cycle count CC_A:

$$T_A = \tau_A \cdot CC_A.$$

Cycle Count of Sequential Designs

In a sequential design, the cycle count is usually expressed as the product of the total instruction count IC and the average number of cycles CPI which are required per instruction:

$$CC = IC \cdot CPI. \tag{4.7}$$

The CPI ratio depends on the workload and on the hardware design. The execution scheme of the instruction set Is defines how many cycles CPI_I an instruction I requires on average. On the other hand, the workload together with the compiler defines an instruction count IC_I for each machine instruction, and so the CPI value can be expressed by

$$CPI = \sum_{I \in \mathbf{Is}} \frac{IC_I}{IC} CPI_I = \sum_{I \in \mathbf{Is}} v_I \cdot CPI_I, \tag{4.8}$$

where v_I denotes the relative frequency of instruction I in the given workload.

Cycle Count of Pipelined Designs

Pipelining does not speed up the execution time of a single instruction, but it rather improves the instruction throughput, due to the interleaved execution. Thus, it is difficult to directly apply the formulae (4.7) and (4.8) to a pipelined design.

In case of perfect pipelining, it takes $(k-1)$ cycles to fill a k-stage pipeline. After that, an instruction is finished per cycle. In this case, the cycle count equals

$$CC = k - 1 + IC \approx IC.$$

For very long workloads, the cycle count virtually equals the instruction count. However, perfect pipelining is unrealistic; the pipeline must be stalled occasionally in order to resolve hazards. Note, that the stalling is either due to hardware interlocks or due to NOPs inserted by the compiler. Let v_h denote the relative frequency of a hazard h in the given workload, and let CPH_h denote the average number of stall cycles caused by this hazard. The cycle count of the pipelined design can then be expressed as

$$CC = IC + \sum_{\text{hazard } h} IC \cdot v_h \cdot CPH_h = IC \cdot \left(1 + \sum_h v_h \cdot CPH_h \right).$$

In analogy to formula (4.8), the following term is treated as the CPI ratio of the pipelined design:

$$CPI = 1 + \sum_{\text{hazard } h} \nu_h \cdot CPH_h. \tag{4.9}$$

4.6.3   Delay Slots of Branch/Jump Instructions

It is the matter of an optimizing compiler to make a good use of the branch/jump delay slots. In the most trivial case, the compiler just fills the delay slots with NOP instructions, but the compiler can do a much better job (table 4.19, [HP96]). It tries to fill the delay slots with useful instructions. There are basically three code blocks to choose the instructions from, namely:

1. The code block which immediately *precedes the branch/jump*. The delay slot can be filled with a non-branch instruction from this block, if the branch does not depend on the re-scheduled instruction, and if the data dependences to other instructions permit the re-scheduling. This always improves the performance over using a NOP.

2. The code from the *branch/jump target*. The re-scheduled instruction must not overwrite data which is still needed in the case that the branch is not taken. This optimization only improves the performance, if the branch is taken; the work of the delay slot is wasted otherwise.

3. The code from the *fall through of a conditional branch*. In analogy to the second case, the re-scheduled instruction must not overwrite data needed if the branch is taken. This optimization only improves the performance if the branch is not taken.

Strategy 1) is the first choice. The other two strategies are only used when the first one is not applicable. How well the delay slot can be filled also depends on the type of the branch/jump instruction:

- An unconditional, PC relative branch/jump is always taken and has a fixed target address. Thus, if the first strategy does not work, the target instruction can be used to fill the delay slot.

- An unconditional, absolute jump is always taken, but the target address may change. This type of jump usually occurs on procedure call or on return from procedure. In this case, there are plenty of independent instructions which can be scheduled in the delay slot, e.g., the instructions for passing a parameter/result.

Table 4.19 Percentage of conditional branches in the SPECint92 benchmarks and how well their delay slot (DS) can be filled. AV denotes the arithmetic mean over the five benchmarks.

	compress	eqntott	espresso	gcc	li	AV
% branch	17.4	24.0	15.2	11.6	14.8	16.6
empty DS	49%	74%	48%	49%	75%	59%

Table 4.20 Instruction mix [%] of the SPECint92 programs normalized to 100%.

instructions	compress	eqntott	espresso	gcc	li	AV
load	19.9	30.7	21.1	23.0	31.6	25.3
store	5.6	0.6	5.1	14.4	16.9	8.5
compute	55.4	42.8	57.2	47.1	28.3	46.2
call (jal, jalr)	0.1	0.5	0.4	1.1	3.1	1.0
jump	1.6	1.4	1.0	2.8	5.3	2.4
branch, taken	12.7	17.0	9.1	7.0	7.0	10.6
~, untaken	4.7	7.0	6.1	4.6	7.8	6.0

- A conditional branch. If the branch results from an if-then-else construct, it is very difficult to predict the branch behavior at compile time. Thus, if the first strategy does not work, the delay slot can hardly be filled with an useful instruction. For loops the branch prediction is much easier because the body of a loop is usually executed several times.

Thus, the delay slot of an unconditional branch/jump can always be filled; only conditional branches cause some problem. For these branches, the compiler can only fill about 40% of the delay slots (table 4.19).

4.6.4 CPI Ratio of the DLX Designs

For our analysis, we assume an average SPECint92 workload. Table 4.20 lists the frequencies of the DLX machine instructions on such a workload. The table is taken from [HP96], but we have normalized the number to 100%.

Table 4.21 Number of CPU cycles and memory accesses per DLX instruction.

instructions	CPU cycles	memory accesses	CPI_I
load, store	3	2	$5 + 2 \cdot WS$
compute	3	1	$4 + WS$
call (jal, jalr)	4	1	$5 + WS$
jump	2	1	$3 + WS$
branch, taken	3	1	$4 + WS$
branch, untaken	2	1	$3 + WS$

Sequential Design

For the sequential DLX design, table 4.21 specifies the number of CPU cycles and the number of memory accesses required by any machine instruction I. This table is derived from the finite state diagram of figure 3.20 (page 90). Let a memory access require WS wait states, on average. The CPI_I value of an instruction I then equals the number of its CPU cycles plus $(WS + 1)$ times the number of memory accesses. When combined with the instruction frequencies from table 4.20, that yields the following CPI ratio for the sequential DLX design:

$$CPI_{DLXs} = 4.26 + 1.34 \cdot WS.$$

Pipelined Design with Interlock

Even with result forwarding, the pipelined DLX design can be slowed down by three types of hazards, namely by empty branch delay slots, by hardware interlocks due to loads, and by slow memory accesses.

Branch Delay Slots   The compiler tries to fill the delay slot of a branch with useful instructions, but about 59% of the delay slots cannot be filled (table 4.19). In comparison to perfect pipelining, such an empty delay slot stalls the pipeline for $\text{CPH}_{NopB} = 1$ cycles. This hazard has the following frequency:

$$\nu_{NopB} = \nu_{branch} \cdot 0.59 = 0.166 \cdot 0.59 \approx 0.1.$$

Since these control hazards are resolved in software, every empty delay slot also causes an additional instruction fetch.

Hardware Interlock   Since the result of a load can only be forwarded from stage WB, the forwarding engine cannot always deliver the operands on time. On such a data hazard, the hardware interlock engine inserts up to two dummy instructions. The compiler reduces these data hazards by scheduling independent instructions after a load wherever that is possible.

According to [HP96], both interlocks can be avoided for 63% of the loads, and for another 11% at least one of the interlocks can be avoided. Thus, two interlocks occur only for 26% of all loads. Each interlock increases the cycle count by $CPH_{NopL} = 1$ cycle. On the workload under consideration, this hazard has a frequency of

$$\nu_{NopL} = \nu_{load} \cdot (2 \cdot 0.26 + 0.11) = 0.253 \cdot 0.63 \approx 0.16.$$

Slow Memory Accesses   In a hierarchical memory system, most of the accesses can be completed in a single cycle, but there are also slow accesses which require some wait states. Let every memory access require an average of $CPH_{slowM} = WS$ wait states. The frequency of a slow memory access then equals the number of loads, stores and instruction fetches:

$$\nu_{slowM} = \nu_{load} + \nu_{store} + \nu_{fetch}.$$

Since the branch hazards are resolved in software by inserting a NOP, they cause ν_{NopB} additional instruction fetches. Load hazards are resolved by a hardware interlock and cause no additional fetches. Thus, the frequency of instruction fetches equals

$$\nu_{fetch} = 1 + \nu_{NopB} = 1.1.$$

Summing up the stall cycles of all the hazards yields the following CPI ratio for the pipelined DLX design with forwarding:

$$\begin{aligned} CPI_{DLX_\pi} &= 1 + \nu_{NopB} \cdot 1 + \nu_{NopL} \cdot 1 + \nu_{slowM} \cdot CPH_{slowM} \\ &\approx 1.26 + 1.44 \cdot WS. \end{aligned}$$

Pipelined Design without Forwarding

The design $DLX_{\pi b}$ with the basic pipeline resolves the hazards in software; if necessary, the compiler must inserts NOPs. This design faces the same problems as the DLX_π design, but in addition, it must manage without result forwarding. Whenever the DLX_π pipeline would forward a result, the compiler must re-arrange the code or insert a NOP. According to simulations [Del97], these forwarding hazards stall the basic pipeline for $CPH_{forw} = 1$ cycles each, and they have a frequency of

$$\nu_{forw} = 0.39.$$

Table 4.22 Hardware cost, cycle time and CPI ratio of the DLX designs (sequential, basic pipeline, pipeline with interlock)

	Gate Count		Cycle Time		CPI Ratio		
	abs.	rel.	abs.	rel.	WS	0.3	1
DLX_s	11951	1.0	70	1.0	$4.26 + 1.34 \cdot WS$	4.66	5.60
$DLX_{\pi b}$	12949	1.08	66	0.94	$1.65 + 2.0 \cdot WS$	2.25	3.65
DLX_π	13833	1.16	89	1.27	$1.26 + 1.44 \cdot WS$	1.70	2.70

The simulation assumed that the additional hazards are resolved by inserting a NOP. Thus, every branch, load or forwarding hazard causes an additional instruction fetch. The frequency of fetches then runs at

$$
\begin{aligned}
\nu_{fetch} &= 1 + \nu_{NopB} + \nu_{NopL} + \nu_{forw} \\
&= 1 + 0.1 + 0.16 + 0.39 = 1.65,
\end{aligned}
$$

and slow memory accesses have a frequency of

$$
\nu_{slowM} = \nu_{load} + \nu_{store} + \nu_{fetch} = 0.253 + 0.085 + 1.65 \approx 2.0.
$$

Thus, the CPI ratio of the pipelined DLX design without forwarding is:

$$
\begin{aligned}
CPI_{DLX_{\pi b}} &= 1 + (\nu_{NopB} + \nu_{NopL} + \nu_{forw}) \cdot 1 + \nu_{slowM} \cdot CPH_{slowM} \\
&\approx 1.65 + 2.0 \cdot WS.
\end{aligned}
$$

4.6.5 Design Evaluation

Performance Study

According to table 4.22, pipelining and result forwarding improve the CPI ratio, but forwarding also increases the cycle time significantly. The CPI ratio of the three designs grows with the number of memory wait states. Thus, the speedup caused by pipelining and forwarding also depends on the speed of the memory system (figure 4.20).

Result forwarding and interlocking have only a minor impact (3%) on the performance of the pipelined DLX design, due to the slower cycle time. However, both concept disburden the compiler significantly because the hardware takes care of the data hazards itself.

The speedup due to pipelining increases dramatically with the speed of the memory system. In combination with an ideal memory system

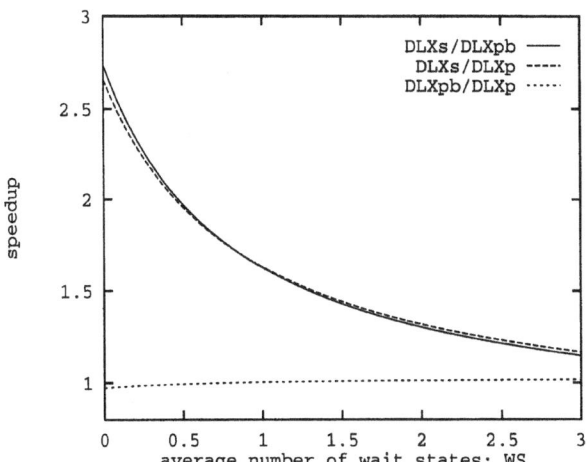

Figure 4.20 Speedup of pipelining and forwarding as a function of the memory latency (DLXs: sequential, DLXpb: basic pipeline, DLXp: pipeline with interlock)

($WS = 0$), pipelining yields a speedup of 2.7, whereas for $WS \geq 5.5$, the sequential DLX design becomes even faster than the pipelined designs. Thus, pipelining calls for a low-latency memory system.

Powerful, cache based memory systems, like that of the Dec Alpha 21064 [HP96], require about $WS = 0.25$ wait states per memory access, and even with a small 2KB on-chip cache, a memory speed of $WS = 0.5$ is still feasible (chapter 6). In the following, we therefore assume **WS = 0.3**. Under this assumption, pipelining speeds the DLX design up by a factor of 2.2.

Impact on the Quality of the DLX
Quality Metric The quality is the weighted geometric mean of the performance P and the reciprocal of the cost C:

$$Q = P^{1-q}/C^q. \tag{4.10}$$

The weighting parameter $q \in [0, 1]$ determines whether cost or performance has a greater impact on the quality. Therefore, we denote q as *quality parameter*. Commonly used values are:

- $q = 0$: Only performance counts, $Q = P$.

- $q = 0.5$: The resulting quality metric $Q = (P/C)^{0.5}$ models the cost-performance ratio.

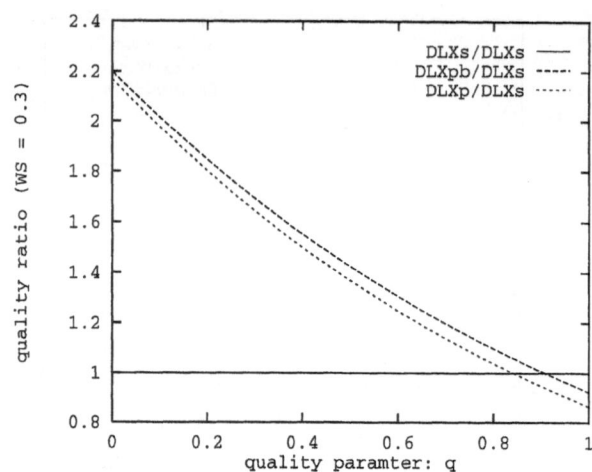

Figure 4.21 Quality ratio of the pipelined designs relative to the sequential design (DLXs: sequential, DLXpb: basic pipeline, DLXp: pipeline with interlock)

- $q = 1/3$: The resulting quality metric is $Q = (P^2/C)^{1/3}$. This means that a design A which is twice as fast as design B has the same quality as B if it is four times as expensive.

For a realistic quality metric, the quality parameter should be in the range $[0.2, 0.5]$: Usually, more emphasis is put on the performance than on the cost, thus $q \leq 0.5$. For $q = 0.2$, doubling the performance already allows for a cost ratio of 16; a higher cost ratio would rarely be accepted.

Evaluation Pipelining and result forwarding improve the performance of the DLX architecture significantly, but they also increase the cost of the fixed-point core. Figure 4.21 quantifies this tradeoff between cost and performance.

In combination with a fast memory system $(WS = 0.3)$, pipelining and result forwarding improve the quality of the DLX fixed-point core, at least under the realistic quality metric. In case that the cost is more emphasized than the performance, pipelining becomes unprofitable for $q > 0.8$.

4.7 Selected References and Further Reading

THE DESIGN presented here is partly based on designs from [PH94, HP96, Knu96]. The concept of delayed PC and pipelining as a transformation is from [KMP99a]. The formal verification of pipeline control without delayed branch is reported in [BS90, SGGH91, BD94, BM96, LO96, HQR98].

4.8 Exercises

Exercise 4.1 In chapter 2, we have introduced a conditional sum adder and a carry look-ahead adder, and extended them to an arithmetical unit AU. In addition to the n-bit sum/difference, the n-bit AU provides two flags indicating an overflow and a negative result. Let $D_{AU}(n)$ denote the maximal delay of the n-bit AU, and let $D_{AU}(s[1:0];n)$ denote the delay of the two least significant sum bits.

Show that for both AU designs and for any $n \geq 2$ the delay of these two sum bits can be estimated as

$$D_{AU}(s[1:0];n) \leq D_{AU}(2).$$

Exercise 4.2 Prove the dateline lemma 4.3 by induction on T.

Exercise 4.3 Fast s-stage Forwarding Engine. In section 4.4.2, we have presented a forwarding engine capable of forwarding data from 3 stages. The construction obviously generalizes to s-stage forwarding, with $s > 3$. The actual data selection (figure 4.18) is then performed by s cascaded multiplexers. Thus, the delay of this realization of an s-stage forwarding engine is proportional to s.

However, these s multiplexers can also be arranged as a balanced binary tree of depth $\lceil \log s \rceil$. Signal $top.j$ (as defined in section 4.4.2) indicates that stage j provides the current data of the requested operand. These signals $top.j$ can be used in order to govern the multiplexer tree.

1. Construct a circuit TOP which generates the signals $top.j$ using a parallel prefix circuit.

2. Construct an s-stage forwarding engine based on the multiplexer tree and circuit TOP. Show that this realization has a delay of $O(\log s)$.

3. How can the delay of the forwarding engine be improved even further?

Exercise 4.4 In case of a data hazard, the interlock engine of section 4.5 stalls the stages IF and ID. The forwarding circuit $Forw$ signals a hit of stage $j \in \{2,3,4\}$ by

$$hit[j] = (full.j \wedge GPRw.j) \wedge (ad \neq 0) \wedge (ad = Cad.j).$$

These hit signals are used in order to generate the data hazard signal *dhaz*. The check whether stage j is full (i.e., $full.j = 1$) is essential for the correctness of the interlock mechanism.

Show that, when simplifying the hit signals to

$$hit[j] = GPRw.j \wedge (ad \neq 0) \wedge (ad = Cad.j),$$

dummy instructions could also activate the hazard flag, and that the interlock engine could run into a deadlock.

Exercise 4.5 Prove for the interlock engine of section 4.5 and the corresponding scheduling function the claim 2 of lemma 4.10: for any stage k and any cycle $T > 0$, the value $I_\pi(k, T)$ is defined iff $full.k^T = 1$.

Exercise 4.6 Fast Zero Tester. The n-zero tester, introduced in section 2.3, uses an OR-tree as its core. In the technology of table 2.1, NAND/NOR gates are faster than OR gates. Based on the equality

$$\overline{\overline{a \vee b \vee c \vee d}} = \overline{\overline{a \vee b} \wedge \overline{c \vee d}} = (a \text{ NOR } b) \text{ NAND } (c \text{ NOR } d),$$

the delay of the zero tester can therefore roughly be halved.

Construct such a fast zero tester and provide formulae for its cost and delay.

Chapter

5

Interrupt Handling

5.1 Attempting a Rigorous Treatment of Interrupts

INTERRUPTS ARE events, which change the flow of control of a program by means other than a branch instruction. They are triggered by the activation of *event signals*, which we denote by $ev[j]$, $j = 0, 1, \ldots$. Here, we will consider the interrupts shown in table 5.1.

Loosely speaking, the activation of an event signal $ev[j]$ should result in a procedure call of a routine $H(j)$. This routine is called the *exception handler* for interrupt j and should take care of the problem signaled by

Table 5.1 Interrupts handled by our DLX design

index j	name	symbol
0	reset	reset
1	illegal instruction	ill
2	misaligned memory access	mal
3	page fault on fetch	pff
4	page fault on load/store	pfls
5	trap	trap
6	arithmetic overflow	ovf
$6 + i$	external I/O	ex_i

the activation of $ev[j]$. The exception handler for a page fault for instance should move the missing page from secondary memory into primary memory. Interrupts can be classified in various ways:

- They can be *internal*, i.e., generated by the CPU or the memory system, or *external*.

- They can be *maskable*, i.e., they can be ignored under software control, or *non maskable*.

- After an interrupt of instruction I the program execution can be resumed in three ways:

  - *repeat* instruction I,
  - *continue* with the instruction I^+ which would follow I in the uninterrupted execution of the program,
  - *abort* the program.

Table 5.2 classifies the interrupts considered here.

Finally, the interrupts have *priorities* defined by the indices j. Activation of $ev[j]$ can only interrupt handler $H(j')$ if $j < j'$. Moreover if $ev[j]$ and $ev[j']$ become active simultaneously and $j < j'$, then handler $H(j')$ should not be called. Thus, small indices correspond to high priorities.[1]

If we want to design an interrupt mechanism and prove that it works, we would like to do the usual three things:

1. define what an interrupt mechanism is supposed to do,

2. design the mechanism, and

3. show that it meets the specification.

The first step turns out to be not so easy. Recall that interrupts are a kind of procedure calls, and that procedure call is a high level language concept. On the other hand, our highest abstraction level so far is the assembler/machine language level. This is the right level for stating what the hardware is supposed to do. In particular, it permits to define the meaning of instructions like jal, which *support* procedure call. However, the *meaning* of the call and return of an entire procedure cannot be defined like the meaning of an assembler instruction.

There are various way to define the semantics of procedure call and return in high level languages [LMW86, Win93]. The most elementary way – called operational semantics – defines the meaning of a procedure by

---

[1]Priority 1 is urgent, priority 31 is not.

Table 5.2 Classifications of the interrupts

index j	symbol	external	maskable	resume
0	reset	yes	no	abort
1	ill	no	no	abort
2	mal	no	no	abort
3	pff	no	no	repeat
4	pfls	no	no	repeat
5	trap	no	no	continue
6	ovf	no	yes	continue/abort
$6+i$	ex_i	yes	yes	continue

prescribing how a certain abstract machine should interpret calls and returns. One uses a stack of procedure frames. A call pushes a new frame with parameters and return address on the stack and then jumps to the body of the procedure. A return pops a frame from the stack and jumps to the return address.

The obvious choice of the 'abstract machine' is the abstract DLX machine with delayed branch/delayed PC semantics defined by the DLX_σ instruction set and its semantics. The machine has, however, to be enriched. There must be a place where interrupt masks are stored, and there must be a mechanism capable of changing the PC as a reaction to event signals. We will also add mechanisms for collecting return addresses and parameters, that are visible at the assembler language level.

We will use a single interrupt service routine ISR which will branch under software control to the various exception handlers $H(j)$. We denote by $SISR$ the start address of the interrupt service routine.

We are finally able to map out the rest of the chapter. In section 5.2, we will define at the abstraction level of the assembler language

1. an extension of the DLX machine language,

2. a mechanism collecting return addresses and parameters, and

3. a mechanism capable of forcing the pair of addresses (SISR, SISR + 4) into (DPC, PC) as reaction to the activation of event signals.

In section 5.3, we define a software protocol for the interrupt service routine which closely parallels the usual definition of procedure call and return in operational semantics. This completes the *definition* of the interrupt mechanism.

In compiled programs, the body of procedures is generated by the compiler. Thus, the compiler can guarantee, that the body of the procedure is in a certain sense well behaved, for instance, that it does not overwrite the return address. In our situation, the compiled procedure body is replaced by the exception handler, which – among other things – obviously *can* overwrite return addresses on a procedure frame. They can also generate interrupts in many ways. Indeed, the attempt to execute an exception handler for page faults, which does not reside in memory will immediately generate another page fault interrupt, and so on.

In section 5.4, we therefore present a set of conditions for the exception handlers and show: if the exception handlers satisfy the conditions, then interrupts behave like kind of procedure calls. The proof turns out to be nontrivial mainly due to the fact, that instructions which change the interrupt masks can themselves be interrupted.

Given the machinery developed so far, the rest is straightforward. In section 5.5, we design the interrupt hardware for a prepared sequential machine according to the specifications of section 5.2. In section 5.6, we pipeline the machine and show that the pipelined machine simulates the prepared sequential machine in some sense. The main technical issue there will be a more powerful forwarding mechanism.

5.2 Extended Instruction Set Architecture

PAGE FAULT and misalignment interrupts are obviously generated by the memory system. Illegal interrupts are detected by the control automaton in the decode stage. Overflow interrupts can be generated by the two new R-type instructions addo, subo and the two new I-type instructions addio, subio specified in table 5.4. They generate the (maskable) overflow event signal $ev[5]$, if the result of the computation is not representable as a 32-bit 2's complement number. Trap interrupts are generated by the new J-type instruction trap (table 5.4). External interrupts are generated by external devices; for these interrupts we apply the following

Interrupt Convention:

The active event line $ev[j]$ of an external I/O interrupt j is only turned off, once interrupt j received service. Interrupt j *receives service* as soon as the ISR is started with interrupt level j' where $j' = j$, or where $j' < j$ and interrupt j' is of type abort. A formal definition of the concept of interrupt level will be given shortly.

Table 5.3 Special purpose registers used for exception handling

address	name	meaning
0	SR	status register
1	ESR	exception status register
2	ECA	exception cause register
3	EPC	the exception PC
4	EDPC	the exception delayed PC
5	Edata	exception data register

The DLX architecture is extend by 7 new registers, 6 of them are visible to the assembler programmer. They form the registers $SPR[0]$ to $SPR[5]$ of the new special purpose register file SPR. Names and addresses of the SPR registers are listed in table 5.3; their function is explained later.

Register's contents can be copied between the general purpose register file GPR and the special purpose register file SPR by means of the special move instructions movi2s (move integer to special) and movs2i (move special to integer). Both moves are R-type instructions (table 5.4). The binary representation of the special register address is specified in field SA.

The cause register CA is the new non visible register. It catches event signals $ev[j]$ which become active during the execution of instructions I_i in the following sense:

- If j is an internal interrupt, it is caught in the same instruction, i.e., $CA[j]_i = 1$.

- If j is external, it is caught in the current or in the next instruction; $CA[j]_i = 1$ or $CA[j]_{i+1} = 1$. Once the bit $CA[j]$ is active, it remains active till interrupt j receives service.

In any other situation, we have $CA[j]_i = 0$.

The interrupt masks are stored in the status register SR. For a maskable interrupt j, bit $SR[j]$ stores the mask of interrupt j. Masking means that interrupt j is disabled (masked) if $SR[j] = 0$, and it is unmasked otherwise. The masked cause MCA is derived from the the cause register and the status register. For instruction I_i, the masked cause equals

$$MCA[j]_i = \begin{cases} CA[j]_i & \text{; if interrupt } j \text{ is not maskable} \\ CA[j]_i \wedge SR[j]_{i-1} & \text{; if interrupt } j \text{ is maskable.} \end{cases}$$

Note that this is a nontrivial equation. It states that for instruction I_i, causes are masked with the masks valid after instruction I_{i-1}. Thus, if I_i happens to be a movi2s instruction with destination SR, the new masks have no affect on the MCA computation of I_i.

Jump to the ISR

From the masked cause MCA, the signal $JISR$ (jump to interrupt service routine) is derived by

$$JISR_i = \bigvee_{j=0}^{31} MCA[j].$$

Activation of signal $JISR$ triggers the jump to the interrupt service routine. Formally we can treat this jump either as a new instruction I_{i+1} or as a part of instruction I_i. We chose the second alternative because this reflects more closely how the hardware will work. However, for interrupted instructions I_i and registers or signals X, we have now to distinguish between

- X_i, which denotes the value of X after the (interrupted) execution of instruction I_i, i.e., after $JISR$, and

- X_i^u, which denotes the value of X after the uninterrupted execution of instruction I_i.

We proceed to specify the effect of $JISR$ for instruction I_i. The interrupt level il of the interrupt is

$$il_i = \min\{j \mid MCA[j]_i = 1\}.$$

Interrupt il has the highest priority among all those interrupts which were not masked during I_i and whose event signals $ev[j]$ were caught. Interrupt il can be of type continue, repeat or abort. If it is of type repeat, no register file and no memory location X should be updated, except for the special purpose registers. For any register or memory location X, we therefore define

$$X_i = \begin{cases} X_{i-1} & \text{if } il_i \text{ is of type repeat} \\ X_i^u & \text{otherwise} \end{cases}$$

By $SISR$, we denote the start address of the interrupt service routine. The jump to ISR is then realized by

$$(DPC, PC)_i = (SISR, SISR + 4).$$

The return addresses for the interrupt service routine are saved as

$$(EDPC, EPC)_i = \begin{cases} (DPC, PC')_{i-1} & \text{if } il_i \text{ is of type repeat} \\ (DPC, PC')_i^u & \text{if } il_i \text{ is of type continue} \\ (*, *) & \text{if } il_i \text{ is of type abort,} \end{cases}$$

i.e., on an interrupt of type abort, the return addresses do not matter. The exception data register stores a parameter for the exception handler. For traps this is the immediate constant of the trap instruction. For page fault and misalignment during load/store this is the memory address of the faulty access:

$$EDATA_i = \begin{cases} sext(imm)_i & \text{for } trap \text{ interrupts} \\ ea_i & \text{for } pf \text{ or } misa \text{ during load/store} \end{cases}$$

For page faults during fetch, the address of the faulty instruction memory access is DPC_{i-1}, which is saved already. Thus, there is no need to save it twice.

The exception cause register ECA stores the masked interrupt cause

$$ECA_i = MCA_i,$$

all maskable interrupts are masked by

$$SR = 0,$$

and the old masks are saved as

$$ESR_i = \begin{cases} SR_{i-1} & \text{if } il_i \text{ is of type repeat} \\ SR_i^u & \text{if } il_i \text{ is of type continue} \\ * & \text{if } il_i \text{ is of type abort.} \end{cases}$$

Thus, if the interrupt instruction sets new masks and it is interrupted by an interrupt of type continue, then the new masks are saved. This completes at the instruction level the description of the semantics of $JISR$.

The restoration of the saved parameters is achieved by a new J-type instruction rfe (return from exception) specified in table 5.4.

5.3 Interrupt Service Routines For Nested Interrupts

NESTED interrupts are handled by a software protocol. The protocol maintains an interrupt stack IS. The stack consists of frames. Each frame can hold copies of all general purpose registers and all special registers. Thus, with the present design we have a frame size of $32 + 6 = 38$ words.

We denote by $IS.TOP$ the top frame of the interrupt stack. Its base address is maintained in the interrupt stack pointer ISP. For this pointer, we reserve a special purpose register, namely

$$ISP = GPR[30].$$

Table 5.4 Extensions to the DLX instruction set. Except for rfe and trap, all instructions also increment the PC by four. *SA* is a shorthand for the special purpose register *SPR[SA]*; *sxt(imm)* is the sign-extended version of the immediate.

IR[31:26]	IR[5:0]			effect
Arithmetic Operation (I-type)				
hx08			addio	RD = RS1 + imm; ovf signaled
hx0a			subio	RD = RS1 - imm; ovf signaled
Arithmetic Operation (R-type)				
hx00	hx20		addo	RD = RS1 + RS2; ovf signaled
hx00	hx22		subo	RD = RS1 - RS2; ovf signaled
Special Move Instructions (R-type)				
hx00	hx10		movs2i	RD = SA
hx00	hx11		movi2s	SA = RS1
Control Instructions (J-type)				
hx3e			trap	trap = 1; Edata = sxt(imm)
hx3f			rfe	SR = ESR; PC = EPC; DPC = EDPC

We call the sequence of registers

$$EHR = (ESR, ECA, EDPC, EPC, EDATA)$$

the exception handling registers. For each frame F of the interrupt stack and for any register R, we denote by $F.R$ the portion of F reserved for register R. We denote by $F.EHR$ the portion of the frame reserved for copies of the exception handling registers. We denote by $IS.EHR$ the portions of *all* frames of the stack, reserved for copies of the exception handling registers.

The interrupt service routine, which is started after an *JISR*, has three phases:

1. SAVE (save status):

   (a) The current interrupt level

   $$il = min\{j \mid ECA[j] = 1\}$$

   is determined. For this computation, *ECA* has to be copied into some general purpose register *GPR[x]*. This register in turn has first to be saved to some reserved location in the memory. This write operation in turn does better not generate a page fault interrupt.

(b) If *il* is of type abort, an empty interrupt stack is initialized, and otherwise a new frame is pushed on the stack by the computation

$$ISP = ISP + frame\_size.$$

(c) The exception handling registers are saved:

$$IS.TOP.EHR = EHR.$$

(d) All maskable interrupts $j < il$ are unmasked:

$$SR = 0^{31-il}1^{il}.$$

This mask is precomputed and the assigned to *SR* in a single special move instruction. After this instruction, the interrupt service routine can be interrupted again by certain maskable interrupts.

2. Exception Handler $H(il)$: The interrupt service routine branches to the start of the proper routine for interrupt *il*. This routine will usually need some general purpose registers. It will save the corresponding registers to *IS.TOP*. After the proper work for interrupt *il* is done, the general purpose registers which were saved are restored. Observe that all this can be interrupted by (maskable) interrupts of higher priority. Finally the handler masks all maskable interrupts by a single special move instruction:

$$SR = GPR[0].$$

3. RESTORE (restore status): the following registers are restored from the stack:

$$EDPC = IS.TOP.EDPC$$
$$EPC = IS.TOP.EPC$$
$$ESR = IS.TOP.ESR$$

The top frame is popped from the stack:

$$ISP = ISP - frame\_size.$$

The interrupt service routine ends with an rfe instruction.

5.4 Admissible Interrupt Service Routines

WE INTEND interrupts to behave like procedure calls. The mechanism of the previous section defines the corresponding call and return mechanism. Handlers unfortunately are not generated by compilers and thus, the programmer has many possibilities for hacks which make the mechanism not at all behave like procedure calls. The obvious point of attack are the fields *IS.EHR*. Manipulation of *IS.TOP.EDPC* obviously allows to jump anywhere.

If the interrupt stack is not on a permanent memory page, each interrupt, including page fault interrupts, can lead to a page fault interrupt, and so on. One can list many more such pitfalls. The interesting question then obviously is: have we overlooked one?

In this section we therefore define an interrupt service routine to be admissible if it satisfies a certain set of conditions (i.e., if it does not make use of certain hacks). We then *prove* that with admissible interrupt service routines the mechanism behaves like a procedure call and return.

5.4.1 Set of Constraints

An interrupt service routine is called *admissible* if it complies with the following set of constraints:

1. The data structures of the interrupt mechanism must be used in a restricted manner:

    (a) The interrupt stack pointer *ISP* is only written by SAVE and RESTORE.

    (b) The segments of an IS frame which are reserved for the EHR registers are only updated by SAVE.

2. The ISR must be written according to the following constraints:

    (a) Instruction rfe is only used as the last instruction of the ISR.

    (b) The code segments SAVE and RESTORE avoid any non-maskable internal interrupt; in the current DLX architecture, that are the interrupts j with $0 < j < 6$.

    (c) Every handler $H(j)$ avoids any non-maskable internal interrupt i with a priority $i \geq j$.

    (d) If handler $H(j)$ uses a special move with source register R in order to update the status register SR, then the bit $R[i] = 0$ for any $i \geq j$.

Among other things, the conditions b) and c) require that page faults are avoided in certain handlers. That can only be ensured if the interrupt stack IS and the codes SAVE and RESTORE are held on permanent pages, i.e., on pages which cannot be swapped out of main memory. Let j_p denote the priority level of the page fault pff. For any $j \leq j_p$, the handler $H(j)$ and all the data accessed by $H(j)$ must also be held on permanent pages.

We will have to show that the interrupt mechanism can manage with a limited number of permanent pages, i.e., that the interrupt stack IS is of finite size.

3. The interrupt priorities are assigned such that

   (a) Non-maskable external interrupts are of type abort and have highest priority $j = 0$.

   (b) Maskable external interrupts are of type continue and have a lower priority than any internal interrupt.

   (c) If an instruction can cause several internal interrupts at the same time, the highest priorized of all the caused interrupts must then be of type repeat or abort.

The assignment of the interrupt priorities used by our DLX design (table 5.2) complies with these constraints.

The conditions 1 and 2 must hold whether the handler $H(j)$ is interrupted or not. This is hard to achieve because the ISR of another interrupt could corrupt the data structures and the registers used by $H(j)$. As a consequence, $H(j)$ could cause a misaligned memory access or overwrite an EHR field on the interrupt stack.

The following approach could, for instance, protect the stack IS against illegal updates. Besides the EHR registers, a frame of stack IS also backs data which are less critical, e.g., the general purpose registers. It is therefore suitable to use two stacks, one for the EHR registers and one for the remaining data. The EHR stack can then be placed on a special memory page which except for the code SAVE is *read-only*.

5.4.2 Bracket Structures

The code segments SAVE and RESTORE can be interpreted as left and right brackets, respectively. Before we can establish that admissible interrupt service routines behave in some sense like procedures we have to review some facts concerning bracket structures.

For sequences $S = S_1 \ldots S_t$ of brackets '(' and ')' we define

$$
\begin{aligned}
l(S) &= \text{the number of left brackets in } S \\
r(S) &= \text{the number of right brackets in } S.
\end{aligned}
$$

Sequence S is called a *bracket structure* if

$$
\begin{aligned}
l(S) &= r(S) \quad \text{and} \\
l(Q) &\geq r(Q) \quad \text{for all prefixes } Q \text{ of } S,
\end{aligned}
\tag{5.1}
$$

i.e., the number of left brackets equals the number of right brackets, and in prefixes of S there are never more right brackets than left brackets.

Obviously, if S and T are bracket structures, then (S) and ST are bracket structures as well. In bracket structures S one can pair brackets with the following algorithm:

> For all right brackets R from left to right do:
> { pair R with the left bracket L immediately left of R;
> cancel R and L from S;}

The above algorithm proceeds in rounds $k = 1, 2, \ldots$. Let $R(k)$ and $L(k)$ be the right and left bracket paired in round k, and let $S(k)$ be the string S before round k. We have $S(1) = S$. By induction on k one shows

Lemma 5.1 ▶   *1. $R(k)$ is the leftmost right bracket in $S(k)$,*

2. $L(k)$ exists, and

3. the portion Q of S from $L(k)$ to $R(k)$ is a bracket structure.

The proof is left as an exercise. Observe that up to round k, the above algorithm only works with the prefix $S_1 \ldots R(k)$ of S.

5.4.3 Properties of Admissible Interrupt Service Routines

We begin with some definitions. First, we define the interrupt level il in situations, where SAVE sequences are not interrupted:[2]

$$
il = \begin{cases}
\min\{j \mid MCA[j] = 1\} & \text{during SAVE} \\
\min\{j \mid IS.TOP.MCA[j] = 1\} & \text{outside of SAVE, if it exists} \\
32 & \text{otherwise}
\end{cases}
$$

---

[2]We show later that this is always the case

A sequence of instructions SAVE H RESTORE is called an *instance of* $ISR(j)$ if during H the interrupt level equals

$$il = j.$$

It is called a *non aborting execution of $ISR(j)$* if the interrupt level obeys

$$il = j \quad \text{during SAVE and RESTORE}$$
$$il \leq j \quad \text{during } H.$$

Thus, during executions of $ISR(j)$ the handler $H(j)$ can be interrupted. We do not consider infinite executions.

Assume that H does not end with a RESTORE sequence of interrupt level j, then

$$\text{SAVE}_1 \ H \ \text{SAVE}_2 \ H' \ \text{RESTORE}$$

is called an *aborting execution of ISR(j)* if

$$il = j \quad \text{during SAVE}_1$$
$$il \leq j \quad \text{during } H$$
$$il \leq 2 \quad \text{during SAVE}_2, H' \text{ and RESTORE.}$$

We call the execution of an interrupt service routine *properly nested* or simply *nested*, if

1. no code segment SAVE or RESTORE is interrupted,

2. the sequence of code segments SAVE and RESTORE forms an initial segment of a proper bracket structure, and if

3. paired brackets *belong to an instance* of some $ISR(j)$ in the following sense: Let L and R be paired SAVE and RESTORE sequences. Let H consist of the instructions between L and R

   (a) which do not belong to SAVE and RESTORE sequences, and

   (b) which are not included by paired brackets inside L and R.

   Then $L\,H\,R$ is an instance of some $ISR(j)$.

We call an execution *perfectly nested* if it is properly nested and the sequence of SAVEs and RESTOREs forms a proper bracket structure. In the following proofs we will establish among other things

Executions of admissible interrupt service routines are properly nested.   ◀ Theorem 5.2

We will first establish properties of perfectly nested executions of interrupt service routines in lemma 5.3. In lemma 5.4 we will prove by induction the existence of the bracket structure. In the induction step, we will apply lemma 5.3 to portions of the bracket structure, whose existence is already guaranteed by the induction hypothesis. In particular, we will need some effort to argue that RESTORES are never interrupted.

The theorem then follows directly from the lemmas 5.3 and 5.4.

Lemma 5.3 ▶ *Let the interrupt mechanism obey software constraints 1 to 3. Consider a perfectly nested execution of ISR(j). The sequence of instructions executed has the form*

$$\underbrace{I_a \dots I_b}_{\text{SAVE}} \quad \underbrace{\dots}_{H(j)} \quad \underbrace{I_c \dots I_d}_{\text{RESTORE}} \;,$$

we then have:

1. *If the execution of ISR(j) is not aborted, then the interrupt stack IS holds the same number of frames before and after ISR(j), and the segments of IS reserved for the EHR registers remain unchanged, i.e.,*

$$ISP_{a-1} = ISP_d \quad \text{and} \quad IS.EHR_{a-1} = IS.EHR_d.$$

2. *Preciseness. If ISR(j) is not aborted, the execution is resumed at*

$$(DPC_d, PC'_d) = \begin{cases} (DPC_{a-2}, PC'_{a-2}) & \text{if } j \text{ is a repeat interrupt} \\ (DPC^u_{a-1}, PC'^u_{a-1}) & \text{if } j \text{ is a continue interrupt} \end{cases}$$

with the masks

$$SR_d = \begin{cases} SR_{a-2} & \text{if } j \text{ is a repeat interrupt} \\ SR^u_{a-1} & \text{if } j \text{ is a continue interrupt.} \end{cases}$$

PROOF Proof by induction on the number n of interrupts which interrupt the execution of an $ISR(j)$.

$n = 0$. The execution of $ISR(j)$ is uninterrupted. Since interrupt j is not aborting, SAVE allocates a new frame on the stack IS, and RESTORE removes one frame. The handler $H(j)$ itself does not update the stack pointer (constraint 1), and thus

$$ISP_{a-1} = ISP_d.$$

According to constraint 1, the EHR fields on the interrupt stack IS are only written by SAVE. However SAVE just modifies the top frame of IS which is removed by RESTORE. Thus

$$IS.EHR_{a-1} = IS.EHR_d,$$

and claim 1 follows. With respect to claim 2, we only show the preciseness of the masks SR; the preciseness of the PCs can be shown in the same way.

$$
\begin{aligned}
SR_d &= ESR_{d-1} & \text{by definition of rfe} \\
&= IS.TOP.ESR_{c-1} & \text{by definition of RESTORE},
\end{aligned}
$$

where $IS.TOP$ denotes the top frame of the stack IS. Since the handler itself does not update the stack pointer ISP nor the EHR fields on the stack IS (constraint 1), it follows

$$
\begin{aligned}
IS.TOP.ESR_{c-1} &= IS.TOP.ESR_b \\
&= ESR_{a-1} & \text{by definition of SAVE},
\end{aligned}
$$

and by the definition of the impact of $JISR$ it then follows that

$$
SR_d = ESR_{a-1} = \begin{cases} SR_{a-2} & \text{if } j \text{ is a repeat interrupt} \\ SR_{a-1}^u & \text{if } j \text{ is a continue interrupt.} \end{cases}
$$

In the induction step, we conclude from n to $n+1$. The execution of $ISR(j)$ is interrupted by $n+1$ interrupts, and the codes SAVE and RESTORE of the corresponding instances of the ISR form a proper bracket structure. Since SAVE and RESTORE are uninterrupted, there are m top level pairs of brackets in the instruction stream of the handler $H(j)$; each pair corresponds to an instance $ISR(j_r)$:

$$
\underbrace{I_a \dots I_b}_{\text{SAVE}} \underbrace{\dots \overbrace{I_{a_1} \dots I_{d_1}}^{ISR(j_1)} \dots \overbrace{I_{a_2} \dots I_{d_2}}^{ISR(j_2)} \dots \overbrace{I_{a_m} \dots I_{d_m}}^{ISR(j_m)} \dots}_{H(j)} \underbrace{I_c \dots I_d}_{\text{RESTORE}}
$$

Each of the $ISR(j_r)$ is interrupted at most n times, and due to the induction hypothesis, they return the pointer ISP and the EHR fields on the stack unchanged:

$$
ISP_{a_r-1} = ISP_{d_r} \quad \text{and} \quad IS.EHR_{a_r-1} = IS.EHR_{d_r}.
$$

Since the instructions of the handler $H(j)$ do not update these data, it follows for the pointer ISP that

$$
ISP_b = ISP_{a_1-1} = ISP_{d_1} = \dots = ISP_{a_m-1} = ISP_{d_m} = ISP_{c-1}.
$$

The same holds for the EHR fields of the interrupt stack:

$$
IS.EHR_b = IS.EHR_{a_1-1} = \dots = IS.EHR_{d_m} = IS.EHR_{c-1}. \tag{5.2}
$$

Since RESTORE removes the frame added by SAVE, and since SAVE only updates the EHR fields of the top frame, the claim 1 follows for $n+1$. The preciseness of the $ISR(j)$ can be concluded like in the case $n = 0$, except for the equality

$$IS.TOP.EHR_b = IS.TOP.EHR_{c-1}.$$

QED   However, this equality holds because of equation 5.2.

Lemma 5.4 ▶ *Let the interrupt mechanism obey the software constraints. Then, non aborting executions of the interrupt service routine are properly nested.*

PROOF   We proceed in three steps:

1. SAVE is never interrupted: According to the software constraint 2, the codes SAVE and RESTORE avoid any non-maskable internal interrupt. Reset is the only non-maskable external interrupt, but we are only interested in a non aborted execution. Thus, SAVE and RESTORE can only be interrupted by a maskable interrupt.

If an instruction I_i causes an interrupt, all masks are cleared, i.e., $SR_i = 0$, and a jump to the ISR is initiated: $JISR_i = 1$. In the code SAVE, the masks are only updated by the last instruction. Since new masks apply to later instructions, SAVE cannot be interrupted by maskable interrupts either.

2. The code RESTORE avoids non-maskable interrupts, and only its last instruction updates the status register. Thus, RESTORE cannot be interrupted if it is started with $SR = 0$. The last instruction of any non-aborting interrupt handler is a special move

$$SR := GPR[0] = 0.$$

If this special move is not interrupted, then RESTORE is not interrupted either.

3. Let the code RESTORE comprise the instructions $R_1 \ldots R_s$. Note that by the construction of interrupt service routines every instance of ISR starts with a SAVE and – in case it is not aborted – it produces later exactly one first instruction R_1 of its RESTORE sequence. Therefore, in executions of the interrupt service routine the sequence of SAVEs (which are never interrupted) and instructions R_1 form an initial segment of a proper bracket structure.

In a non aborting execution, we denote by R_1^n the nth occurrence of R_1. We prove by induction on n that until R_1^n

- the code segment RESTORE is always started with $SR = 0$ (hence it is not interrupted),

- the code segments SAVE and RESTORE form a start sequence of a proper bracket structure, and

- paired brackets *belong to an execution* of some $ISR(j)$.

For $n = 1$ there must be a SAVE to the left of the first R_1. Consider the first such SAVE to the left of R_1^1. Then, this SAVE and R_1^1 belong to an uninterrupted instance of an $ISR(j)$. Thus, R_1^1 is started with $SR = 0$ and the first RESTORE is not interrupted.

For the induction step, consider R_1^{n+1}. There are n instructions R_1^i to its left. By induction hypothesis the code segments SAVE and RESTORE up to R_1^n form a start sequence of a proper bracket structure with paired brackets belonging to executions of some $ISR(j)$. By lemma 5.3, these executions are precise. Since the sequence of SAVEs and R_1s forms an initial segment of a bracket structure, we can pair R_1^{n+1} with a preceding SAVE code sequence L. Let H' be the sequence of instructions between L and R_1^{n+1}. Construct H from H' by canceling all executions of some $ISR(j)$. Because these executions are precise, we have during H a constant interrupt level

$$il = i,$$

thus, handler $H(i)$ is executed during H.

Let $ISR(j_n)$ denote the instance of the ISR which belongs to R_1^n. Instruction R_1^{n+1} is then either directly preceded

(a) by the special move I with $SR := 0$, or

(b) by the special move I followed by $ISR(j_n)$.

The first case is trivial (see $n = 1$). In the second case, $ISR(j_n)$ interrupts the special move, and interrupt j_n is of type continue. Due to the preciseness of $ISR(j_n)$, R_1^{n+1} is started with the masks $SR_m^u = 0$, and the $(n+1)$st RESTORE block is not interrupted.

QED

Priority Criterion. *For admissible interrupt service routines, it holds:*   ◀ Lemma 5.5

1. *During the execution of $ISR(j)$, maskable interrupts i with $i \geq j$ are masked all the time.*

2. *$ISR(j)$ can only be interrupted by an interrupt $i < j$ of higher priority.*

According to lemma 5.4, the codes SAVE and RESTORE can only be interrupted by reset. Thus, we focus on the interrupt handlers. For any *non-maskable* interrupt $j < 6$, claim two follows directly by constraint 2. For the *maskable interrupts* $j \geq 6$, we prove the claims by induction on the number n of interrupts which interrupt the handler $H(j)$.   PROOF

- $n = 0$: The ISR is always started with $SR = 0$, due to signal *JISR*. The ISR only updates the masks by a special move movi2s or by an rfe instruction. Since rfe is only used as the last instruction of an ISR (constraint 2), it has no impact on the masks used by the ISR itself. In case of a special move $SR := R$, the bit $R[i]$ must be zero for any $i \geq j$. Thus, the maskable interrupts are masked properly. Due to the definition of the masked interrupt cause of instruction I_l

$$MCA[j']_l = \begin{cases} CA[j']_l \wedge SR[j']_{l-1} & \text{; if interrupt } j' \text{ is maskable} \\ CA[j']_l & \text{; otherwise} \end{cases}$$

and the definition of the interrupt level

$$il_l = \min\{j' \mid MCA[j']_l = 1\},$$

$ISR(j)$ cannot be interrupted by a maskable interrupt $j' \geq j$, and the claim follows.

- $n > 0$: The handler $H(j)$ is interrupted n times, and the codes SAVE and RESTORE form a proper bracket structure. Thus, the instruction sequence of $ISR(j)$ has the following form

$$\text{Save} \ldots ISR(j_1) \ldots ISR(j_m) \ldots \text{Restore},$$

for an $m \leq n$. The instructions which belong to the code of the handler $H(j)$ do not unmask interrupts j' with $j' \leq j$. Due to the preciseness of the ISR, any $ISR(j_r)$ returns the masks SR delivered to it by register ESR. By induction on m it then follows that interrupt j_r has a higher priority than j, i.e., $j_r < j$.

Since any $ISR(j_r)$ is interrupted at most $n-1$ times, the induction hypothesis applies. $ISR(j_r)$ keeps all interrupts j' with $j' \geq j_r$ masked, and especially those with $j' \geq j$.

QED

Theorem 5.2 and lemma 5.5 imply:

Theorem 5.6 ▶ *Non aborting executions of admissible interrupt service routines are perfectly nested.*

PROOF Let LHR be a non aborting execution of $ISR(j)$, where L is a save sequence and R is a restore sequence. By theorem 5.2, the sequence of SAVEs and RESTOREs in LHR is an initial segment of a bracket structure. If the brackets L and R are paired, then the SAVE and RESTORE sequences in H form a bracket structure. Hence, the brackets in LHR form a bracket structure and LHR is perfectly nested.

Assume R is paired with a left bracket L' right of L:

$$L \ldots \underbrace{L' \ldots R}_{ISR(j)}.$$

Then by lemma 5.5, the interrupt level immediately before L' is greater than j, and LHR is not a non aborting execution.

QED

According to lemma 5.5, the ISR of an interrupt $j > 0$ can only be interrupted by an interrupt of higher priority. Thus, there can be at most one frame on the stack IS for each interrupt level $j > 0$. Reset can even interrupt $ISR(0)$. However, on reset, the ISR does not allocate a new frame, the stack IS is cleared instead. The size of the interrupt stack IS is therefore limited; the ISR uses at most 32 frames.

Like for many software protocols, fairness seems to be desirable for the interrupt mechanism. In this context, fairness means that every interrupt finally gets service. Due to the pure priority scheme, that cannot always be achieved. Consider the case that the event signals of two external interrupts $ev[15]$ and $ev[17]$ become active at the same time, that the external interrupt $ev[16]$ occurs whenever leaving $ISR(15)$ and vice versa. Under these conditions, interrupt 17 is starved by the interrupts 15 and 16. Thus fairness and a pure priority scheme do not go together. Nevertheless, one would at least like to guarantee that no internal interrupt gets lost.

Completeness *Let the interrupt mechanism obey the software constraints. Every internal interrupt j which occurs in instruction I_i and which is not masked receives service in instruction I_{i+1}, or instruction I_i is repeated after the ISR which starts with instruction I_{i+1}.*

◄ Lemma 5.7

Let instruction I_i trigger the internal interrupt j, i.e., $ev[j]_i = 1$. The cause bit $CA[j]_i$ is then activated as well. Under the assumption of the lemma, j is either non-maskable or it is unmasked ($SR[j]_{i-1} = 1$). In either case, the corresponding bit of MCA is raised, and an jump to the ISR is initiated. Thus, I_{i+1} is the first instruction of routine $ISR(k)$, where $k = il_i$ denotes the interrupt level after I_i. Due to the definition of the interrupt level, $k \leq j$. For $k = j$, the claim follows immediately. For $k < j$, interrupt k is either external or internal. In case of an external interrupt, k must be a reset (constraint 3) which aborts the execution servicing any pending interrupt. If k is an internal interrupt, it is of type abort or repeat due to constraint 3. Thus, $ISR(k)$ either services any pending interrupt by aborting the execution, or after $ISR(k)$, the execution is resumed at instruction I_i.

PROOF

QED

If the constraint 3 is relaxed, the completeness of the interrupt mechanism in the sense of lemma 5.7 cannot be guaranteed. Assume that instruction I_i causes two internal interrupts j and j', and that $j < j'$. If j is of type continue, $ISR(j)$ just services j and resumes the execution at the instruction which would follow I_i in case of $JISR_i = 0$. Thus, interrupt j' would get lost. If interrupt j is of type repeat, $ISR(j)$ does not service interrupt j' either. However, instruction I_i is repeated after the ISR, and the fault which corresponds to interrupt j' can occur again.

5.5 Interrupt Hardware

IN THIS section, we design the interrupt hardware of the prepared sequential architecture DLX_Σ according to the specifications of section 5.2. The instruction set architecture (ISA) is extended by

- the special purpose register file *SPR*,

- a register S which buffers data read from SPR,[3]

- the circuitry for collecting the interrupt events,

- the actual ISR call mechanism which in case of an active interrupt event forces the interrupt parameters into the SPR register file and the pair of addresses $(SISR, SISR + 4)$ into the registers *DPC* and PC', and by

- control realizing the instructions from table 5.4.

The enhanced ISA requires changes in the data paths and in the control (section 5.5.6). The data paths get an additional environment CAenv which collects the interrupt event signals and determines the interrupt cause (section 5.5.5). Except for the PC environment, the register file environment RFenv and circuit *Daddr*, the remaining data paths undergo only minor changes (section 5.5.4). Figure 5.1 depicts the top level schematics of the enhanced DLX data paths. Their cost can be expressed as

$$
\begin{aligned}
C_{DP} &= C_{PCenv} + C_{IMenv} + C_{IRenv} + C_{EXenv} + C_{DMenv} + C_{SH4Lenv} \\
&+ C_{RFenv} + C_{Daddr} + C_{CAenv} + C_{buffer} + 8 \cdot C_{ff}(32).
\end{aligned}
$$

Note that without interrupt hardware, reset basically performs two tasks, it brings the hardware in a well defined state (hardware initialization) and

---

[3]Registers A and B play this role for register file *GPR*

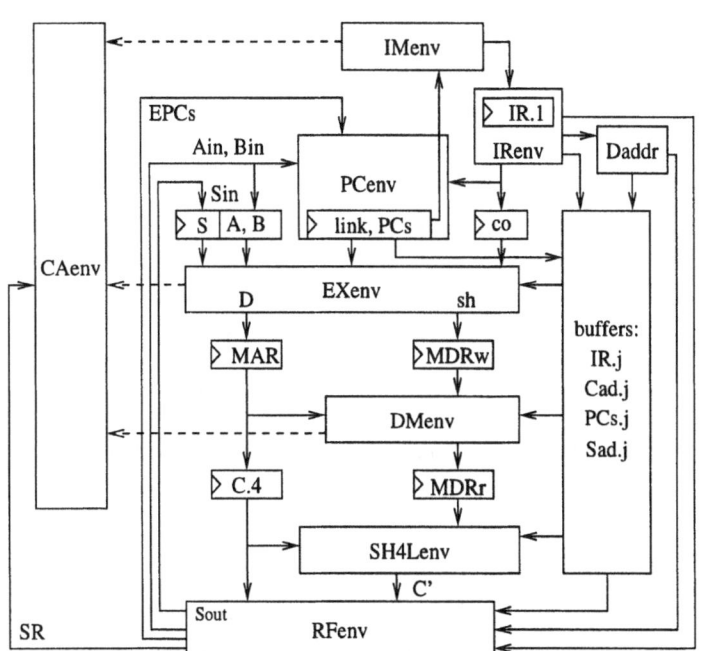

Figure 5.1 Data paths of the prepared sequential designs with interrupt support

restarts the instruction execution. In the DLX_Σ design with interrupt hardware, the reset signal itself initializes the control and triggers an interrupt. The interrupt mechanism then takes care of the restart, i.e., with respect to restart, signal *JISR* takes the place of signal *reset*.

5.5.1 Environment PCenv

The environment PCenv of figure 5.2 still implements the delayed PC mechanism, but it now provides an additional register *DDPC* (delayed delayed PC) which buffers the PC of the current instruction I_i:

$$DDPC_i = DPC_{i-1}.$$

The functionality of the environment also needs to be extended in order to account for the new control instruction rfe and to support a jump to the ISR. Without interrupt handling, the PCs are initialized on reset. Now, reset is treated like any other interrupt, and therefore, the PCs are initialized

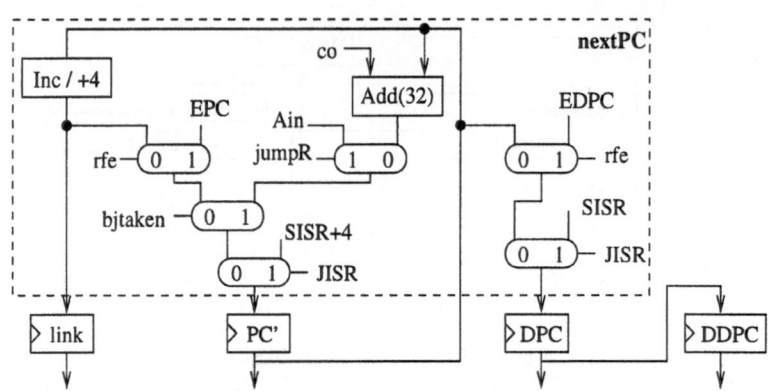

Figure 5.2 Environment PCenv with interrupt support

on *JISR*, instead:

$$(DPC_i, PC_i') = \begin{cases} (SISR, SISR + 4) & \text{if} \quad JISR_i = 1 \\ (DPC_i^u, PC_i'^u) & \text{otherwise.} \end{cases}$$

Except for an rfe instruction, the values $PC_i'^u$ and DPC_i^u are computed as before:

$$PC_i'^u = \begin{cases} EPC_{i-1} & \text{if} \quad I_i = \text{rfe} \\ PC_{i-1}' + imm_i & \text{if} \quad bjtaken_i = 1 \wedge I_i \in \{\text{beqz, bnez, j, jal}\} \\ RS1_{i-1} & \text{if} \quad bjtaken_i = 1 \wedge I_i \in \{\text{jr, jalr}\} \\ PC_{i-1}' + 4 & \text{otherwise} \end{cases}$$

$$DPC_i^u = \begin{cases} EDPC_{i-1} & \text{if} \quad I_i = \text{rfe} \\ PC_{i-1}' & \text{otherwise} \end{cases}$$

Thus, the new PC computation just requires two additional muxes controlled by signal rfe. The two registers *link* and *DDPC* are only updated on an active clock signal *PCce*, whereas PC' and *DPC* are also updated on a jump to the ISR:

$$DPCce = PC'ce = PCce \vee PCinit.$$

These modifications have no impact on register *link* nor on the glue logic *PCglue* which generates signal *bjtaken*. The cost of the environment now are

$$C_{PCenv} = 4 \cdot C_{ff}(32) + 6 \cdot C_{mux}(32) + C_{add}(32) + C_{inc}(30) + C_{PCglue}.$$

The two exception PCs are provided by environment RFenv. Let *csID* denote the control signals which govern stage ID, including signal *JISR*;

IR[20:11]   IR[10:6] 00001   IR[10:6] 00000

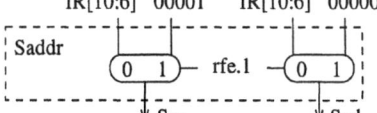

Figure 5.3 Circuit *Daddr*

and let $A_{CON}(csID)$ denote their accumulated delay. Environment PCenv then requires a cycle time of

$$
\begin{aligned}
T_{PCenv} \;=\; & \max\{D_{inc}(30), A_{IRenv}(co) + D_{add}(32), A_{GPRenv}(Ain),\\
& A_{RFenv}(EPCs), A(bjtaken), A_{CON}(csID)\}\\
& +3 \cdot D_{mux}(32) + \Delta.
\end{aligned}
$$

5.5.2 Circuit Daddr

Circuit *Daddr* consists of the two subcircuits *Caddr* and *Saddr*. As before, circuit *Caddr* generates the destination address *Cad* of the general purpose register file GPR. Circuit *Saddr* (figure 5.3) provides the source address *Sas* and the destination address *Sad* of the special purpose register file SPR.

The two addresses of the register file SPR are usually specified by the bits $SA = IR[10:6]$. However, on an rfe instruction, the exception status ESR is copied into the status register SR. According to table 5.3, the registers ESR and SR have address 1 and 0, respectively. Thus, circuit *Saddr* selects the source address and the destination address of the register file SPR as

$$
(Sas, Sad) \;=\; \begin{cases} (SA, SA) & \text{if } rfe = 0 \\ (00001, 00000) & \text{if } rfe = 1. \end{cases}
$$

Circuit *Daddr* provides the three addresses *Cad*, *Sas* and *Sad* at the following cost and delay:

$$
\begin{aligned}
C_{Daddr} \;&=\; C_{Caddr} + C_{Saddr}\\
C_{Saddr} \;&=\; 2 \cdot C_{mux}(5)\\
D_{Daddr} \;&=\; \max\{D_{Caddr}, D_{mux}(5)\} = D_{Caddr}.
\end{aligned}
$$

5.5.3 Register File Environment RFenv

The DLX architecture now comprises two register files, one for the general purpose registers GPR and one for the special purpose registers SPR. Both register files form the environment RFenv.

$$C_{RFenv} = C_{GPRenv} + C_{SPRenv}$$

The environment GPRenv of the general purpose register file has the same functionality as before. The additional SPR registers are held in a register file with an extended access mode. The special move instructions movi2s and movs2i access these registers as a regular register file which permits simultaneously one read and one write operation. However, on JISR all registers are read and updated in parallel. Before describing the environment SPRenv in detail, we first introduce a special register file with such an extended access mode.

A Special Register File

An $(K \times n)$ special register file SF comprises K registers, each of which is n bits wide. The file SF can be accessed like a regular two-port register file:

- the flag w specifies, whether a write operation should be performed

- the addresses adr and adw specify the read and write address of the register file, and

- Din and $Dout$ specify the data input and output of the register file.

In addition, the special register file SF provides a distinct write and read port for each of its registers. For any register $SF[r]$,

- $Do[r]$ specifies the output of its distinct read port, and

- $Di[r]$ specifies the data to be written into register $SF[r]$ on an active write flag $w[r]$.

In case of an address conflict, such a special write takes precedence over the regular write access specified by address adw. Thus, the data $d[r]$ to be written into $SF[r]$ equals

$$d[r] = \begin{cases} Di[r] & \text{if} \quad w[r] = 1 \\ Din & \text{otherwise.} \end{cases}$$

The register is updated in case of $w[r] = 1$ and in case of a regular write to address r:

$$ce[r] = w[r] \vee (w \wedge (\langle adw \rangle = r)). \tag{5.3}$$

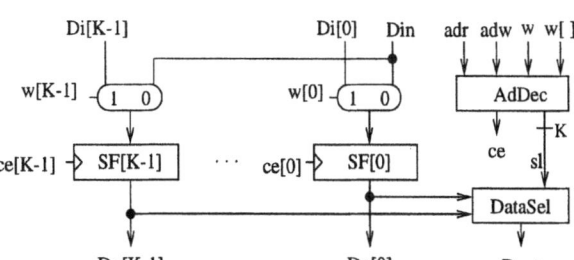

Figure 5.4 Special register file SF of size $(K \times n)$

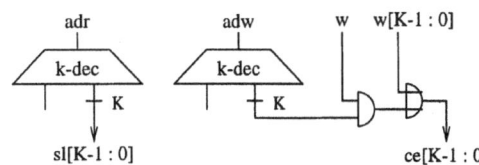

Figure 5.5 Address decoder AdDec of an SF register file

We do not specify the output *Dout* of the special purpose register file if a register is updated and read simultaneously.

Realization

Figure 5.4 depicts an example realization of a special register file SF of size $(K \times n)$. The multiplexer in front of register $SF[r]$ selects the proper input depending on the special write flag $w[r]$.

The address decoder circuit *AdDec* in figure 5.5 contains two k-bit decoders ($k = \lceil \log K \rceil$). The read address *adr* is decoded into the select bits $sl[K - 1 : 0]$. Based on this decoded address, the select circuit *DataSel* selects the proper value of the standard data output *Dout*. For that purpose, the data $Do[r]$ are masked by the select bit $sl[r]$. The masked data are then combined by n-OR-trees in a bit sliced manner:

$$Dout_j = \bigvee_{r=0}^{K-1} (Do[r]_j \wedge sl[r])$$

The write address *adw* is decoded into K select bits. The clock signals of the K registers are generated from these signals according to equation 5.3.

Thus, the cost of the whole register file SF runs at

$$
\begin{aligned}
C_{SF}(K,n) &= K \cdot (C_{ff}(n) + C_{mux}(n)) + C_{AdDec}(K) \\
&\quad + n \cdot C_{or} \cdot C_{tree}(K) + K \cdot C_{and}(n)
\end{aligned}
$$

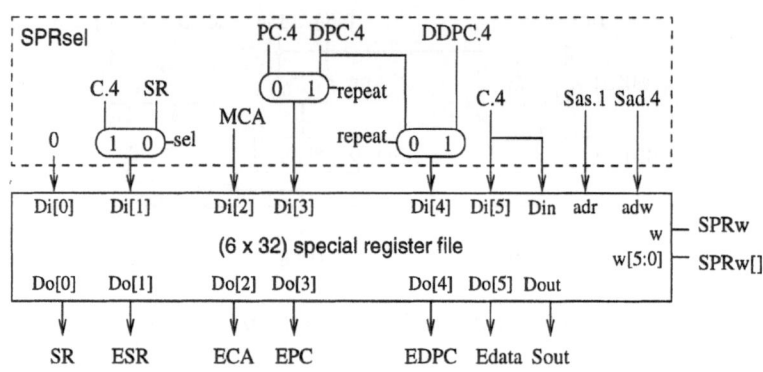

Figure 5.6 Environment SPRenv of the DLX_Σ design

$$C_{AdDec}(K) = 2 \cdot C_{dec}(\lceil \log K \rceil) + C_{and}(K) + C_{or}(K).$$

The distinct read ports have a zero delay, whereas the standard output $Dout$ is delayed by the address decoder and the select circuit:

$$D_{SF}(Do[r]) = 0;$$
$$D_{SF}(Dout) = D_{dec}(\lceil \log K \rceil) + D_{and} + D_{or} \cdot D_{tree}(K).$$

On a write access, the special register file has an access time of D_{SFw}, and the write signals w and $w[]$ delay the clock signals by $D_{SF}(w; ce)$:

$$D_{SFw} = \max\{D_{mux}(n), D_{dec}(\lceil \log K \rceil) + D_{and} + D_{or}\} + D_{ff}$$
$$D_{SF}(w; ce) = D_{and} + D_{or}.$$

Environment SPRenv

The core of the special purpose register environment SPRenv (figure 5.6) is a special register file of size 6×32. The names of these registers $SPR[5:0]$ are listed in table 5.3. The environment is controlled by the write signals $SPRw$ and $SPRw[5:0]$, and by the signals $JISR$, $repeat$, and sel.

The standard write and read ports are only used on the special move instructions movi2s and movs2i and on an rfe instruction. The standard data output of the register file equals

$$Sout_i = SPR[Sas]_{i-1},$$

and in case of a write request $SPRw = 1$, the register file is updated as

$$SPR[Sad]_i^u := C.4_i.$$

According to the specification of section 5.2, the SPR registers must also be updated on a trap instruction and on a jump to the ISR. These updates are performed via the six distinct write ports of the special register file.

Since a trap instruction always triggers an interrupt, i.e., $trap_i = 1$ implies $JISR_i = 1$, the SPR register only require a special write on $JISR$. The write signals are therefore set to

$$SPRw[r] = JISR.$$

On $JISR$, the status register SR is cleared. Register ECA buffers the masked cause MCA, and register Edata gets the content of $C.4$. On a trap, $C.4$ provides the trap constant, and on a load or store, it provides the effective memory address:

$$(Di[0], Di[2], Di[5]) = (0, MCA, C.4).$$

The selection of input $Di[1]$ is more complicated. If instruction I_i is interrupted, the new value of ESR depends on the type of the interrupt and on the type of I_i

$$Di[1]_i = \begin{cases} SR_{i-1} & \text{if } il_i \text{ is of type repeat} \\ SR_i^u & \text{if } il_i \text{ is of type continue} \\ * & \text{if } il_i \text{ is of type abort.} \end{cases}$$

where

$$SR_i^u = \begin{cases} C.4_i & \text{if } SPRw_i \wedge (\langle Sad_i \rangle = 0) \\ SR_{i-1} & \text{otherwise.} \end{cases}$$

The environment SPRenv selects the proper input

$$Di[1]_i = \begin{cases} C.4_i & \text{if } sel_i = 1 \\ SR_{i-1} & \text{otherwise,} \end{cases}$$

with

$$sel = \overline{repeat} \wedge SPRw \wedge (\langle Sad \rangle = 0).$$

According to the specification of $JISR$, if instruction I_i is interrupted, the two exception PCs have to be set to

$$(EPC, EDPC)_i = \begin{cases} (PC', DPC)_{i-1} & \text{if } il_i \text{ is of type repeat} \\ (PC', DPC)_i^u & \text{if } il_i \text{ is of type continue;} \end{cases}$$

whereas on an abort interrupt, the values of the exception PCs do not matter. Environment PCenv generates the values PC_i^u, DPC_i^u, and

$$DDPC_i^u = DPC_{i-1},$$

which are then passed down the pipeline together with instruction I_i. Except on an rfe instruction,

$$DPC_i^u = PC_{i-1},$$

but due to the software constraints, rfe can only be interrupted by reset which aborts the execution. Thus, the inputs of the two exception PCs can be selected as

$$(Di[3], Di[4]) = \begin{cases} (PC.4, DPC.4) & \text{if } repeat = 0 \\ (DPC.4, DDPC.4) & \text{if } repeat = 1 \end{cases}$$

Environment SPRenv consists of a special register file, of circuit SPRsel which selects the inputs of the distinct read ports, and of the glue logic which generates signal *sel*. Thus, the cost run at

$$\begin{aligned} C_{SPRenv} &= C_{SF}(6,32) + C_{SPRsel} + C_{SPRglue} \\ C_{SPRsel} &= 3 \cdot C_{mux}(32) \\ C_{SPRglue} &= C_{zero}(3) + 2 \cdot C_{and} + C_{inv}. \end{aligned}$$

All the data inputs are directly provided by registers at zero delay. Let its control inputs have a delay of $A_{CON}(csSPR)$. The output *Sin* and the inputs *Di* then have an accumulated delay of

$$\begin{aligned} A_{SPRenv}(Sin) &= D_{SF}(Dout) \\ A_{SPRenv}(Di) &= \max\{A_{CON}(csSPR), D_{zero}(3)\} + 2 \cdot D_{and} + D_{mux}, \end{aligned}$$

and the write access requires a cycle time of at most

$$T_{SPRenv} = A_{SPRenv}(Di) + D_{SFw} + \delta.$$

5.5.4 Modified Data Paths

The decode stage ID gets the new output register S. The two opcodes $IR[31:26]$ and $IR[5:0]$ and the destination address Cad of the general purpose register file are provided by stage ID, but they are also used by later stages. As before, these data are therefore passed down the pipeline, and they are buffered in each stage. Due to the interrupt handling, stage WB now also requires the three PCs and the address Sad of the register file SPR. Like the opcodes and the address Cad, these data wander down the pipeline together with the instruction. That requires additional buffering (figure 5.7); its cost runs at

$$C_{buffer} = C_{ff}(22) + 2 \cdot C_{ff}(22 + 3 \cdot 32).$$

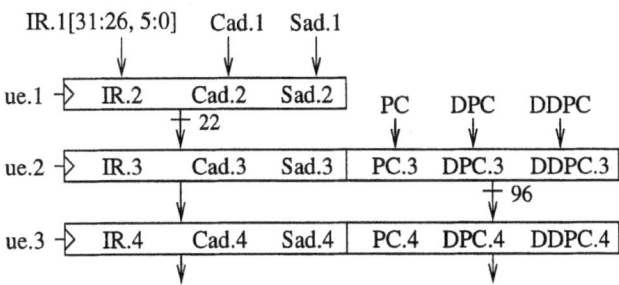

Figure 5.7 Buffering

The interrupt handling has no impact on the instruction register environment IRenv which extracts the immediate operand co and the shifter environment SH4Lenv.

Execute Environment

The execute environment $EXenv$ of figure 5.8 still comprises the ALU environment and the shifter SHenv and connects them to the operand and result busses. The three operand busses are controlled as before, and the outputs sh and ovf also remain the same.

The only modification is that the result D is now selected among six values. Besides the register value $link$ and the results of the ALU and the shifter, environment EXenv can also put the constant co or the operands S or A on the result bus:

$$D = \begin{cases} link & \text{if} & linkDdoe = 1 \\ alu & \text{if} & ALUDdoe = 1 \\ sh & \text{if} & SHDdoe = 1 \\ co & \text{if} & coDdoe = 1 \\ A & \text{if} & ADdoe = 1 \\ S & \text{if} & SDdoe = 1. \end{cases}$$

The result $D = co$ is used in order to pass the trap constant down the pipeline, whereas the result $D = A$ is used on the special move instruction movi2s. $D = S$ is used on rfe and movs2i.

The selection of D now requires two additional tristate drivers, but that has no impact on the delay of the environment. The cost of EXenv are

$$C_{EXenv} = C_{ALUenv} + C_{SHenv} + 2 \cdot C_{mux}(32) + 6 \cdot C_{driv}(32).$$

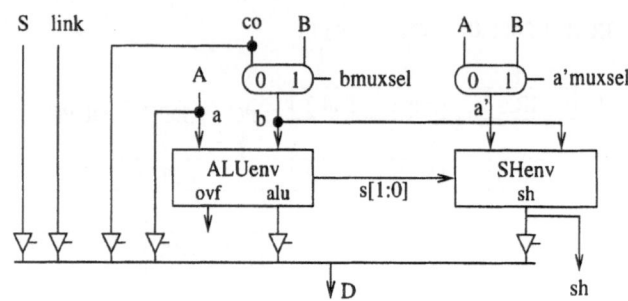

Figure 5.8 Execute environment EXenv with interrupt support

Instruction Memory Environment IMenv

The environment IMenv of the instruction memory is controlled by a single control signal Imr. The address is still specified by register DPC, but the memory IM has a slightly extended functionality. In addition to the data output $IMout$ and the busy flag $ibusy$, IM provides a second status flag ipf. The flag ipf indicates that the memory is unable to perform the requested access due to a page fault. The flag $ibusy$ indicates that the memory requires at least one more cycle in order to complete the requested access. Both flags are inactive if the memory IM does not perform an access. In case of a successful access ($ibusy = ipf = 0$), the instruction memory IM provides the requested memory word at the data output $IMout$ and otherwise, it provides an arbitrary but fixed binary value $IMdefault$:

$$IMout = \begin{cases} IMword[\langle DPC[31:2]00 \rangle] & \text{if } Imr \wedge /ibusy \wedge /ipf \\ IMdefault & \text{otherwise,} \end{cases}$$

The instruction memory control IMC checks for a misaligned access. The 4-byte instruction fetch is misaligned if the address is not a multiple of four:

$$imal = DPC[0] \vee DPC[1].$$

Let d_{Istat} denote the status time of the instruction memory. Since the address is directly taken from a register, the status flags $imal$, $ibusy$ and ipf are provided at the following cost and accumulated delay:

$$C_{IMC} = C_{or}$$
$$A_{IMenv}(flags) = \max\{D_{or}, d_{Istat}\}.$$

Data Memory Environment DMenv

The environment DMenv still consists of the data memory DM and the memory controller DMC. The memory DM performs the actual load or store access, whereas the controller DMC generates the four bank write signals $Dmbw[3:0]$ and checks for misalignment.

Except for the data output $DMout$ and an additional flag dpf, the functionality of the data memory DM itself remains the same. The flag dpf indicates that the memory is unable to perform the requested access due to a page fault. If the memory DM detects a page fault ($dpf = 1$), it cancels the ongoing access. Thus, the memory itself ensures that it is not updated by a store instruction which causes a page fault. The flags dpf and $dbusy$ are inactive if the memory performs no access ($Dmr.3 = Dmw.3 = 0$). On a successful read access, the data memory DM provides the requested memory word, and otherwise it provides a fixed value $DMdefault$:

$$DMout = \begin{cases} DMword[\langle MDRw[31:2]00\rangle] & \text{if } Dmr \wedge /dbusy \wedge /dpf \\ DMdefault & \text{otherwise,} \end{cases}$$

Memory Control DMC In addition to the bank write signals, the memory controller DMC now provides signal $dmal$ which indicates a misaligned access.

The bank write signals $Dmbw[3:0]$ are generated as before (page 81). In addition, this circuit $DMbw$ provides the signals B (byte), H (half word), and W (word) which indicate the width of the memory access, and the signals $B[3:0]$ satisfying

$$B[j] = 1 \quad \leftrightarrow \quad \langle s[1:0]\rangle = j.$$

A byte access is always properly aligned. A word access is only aligned, if it starts in byte 0, i.e., if $B[0] = 1$. A half word access is misaligned, if it starts in byte 1 or 3. Flag $dmal$ signals that an access to the data memory is requested, and that this access is misaligned ($malAc = 1$):

$$dmal = (Dmr.3 \vee Dmw.3) \wedge malAc$$
$$malAc = W \wedge \overline{B[0]} \vee H \wedge (B[1] \vee B[3])$$

The cost C_{DMC} of the memory controller is increased by some gates, but the delay D_{DMC} of the controller remains unchanged:

$$C_{DMC} = C_{DMbw} + C_{inv} + 3 \cdot C_{and} + 3 \cdot C_{or}$$
$$= C_{dec}(2) + 3 \cdot C_{inv} + 15 \cdot C_{and} + 8 \cdot C_{or}.$$

Let $A_{CON}(csM)$ denote the accumulated delay of the signals Dmr and Dmw, the cycle time of the data memory environment and the delay of its flags can then be expressed as

$$T_M = A_{CON}(csM) + D_{DMC} + d_{Dmem} + \Delta$$
$$A_{DMenv}(flags) = A_{CON}(csM) + D_{DMC} + d_{Dstat}.$$

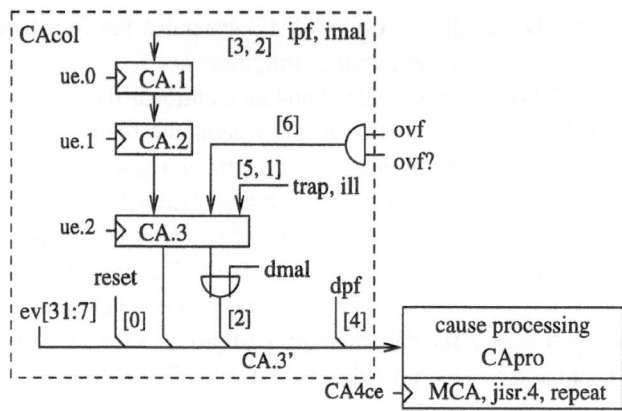

Figure 5.9 Schematics of the cause environment CAenv

5.5.5 Cause Environment CAenv

The cause environment CAenv (figure 5.9) performs two major tasks:

- Its circuit CAcol collects the interrupt events and clocks them into the cause register.

- It processes the caught interrupt events and initiates the jump to the ISR. This cause processing circuit CApro generates the flags *jisr* and *repeat*, and provides the masked interrupt cause MCA.

Cause Collection
The internal interrupt events are generated by the data paths and the control unit, but the stage in which a particular event is detected depends on the event itself (table 5.5).

The instruction memory and its controller IMC provide the flags *ipf* and *imal* which indicate a page fault or misaligned access on fetch. The flag *dmal*, generated by the controller DMC signals a misaligned data memory access. The flags *dmal* and *imal* are combined to the event flag *mal*. In the memory stage, the flag *dpf* of the data memory signals a page fault on load/store.

A trap and an illegal instruction *ill* are detected by the control unit. This will be done in stage EX in order to keep the automaton simple (see page 208). The ALU provides the overflow flag *ovf*, but an arithmetical overflow should only be reported in case of an instruction addo, subo, addio, or subio. Such an instruction is indicated by the control signal *ovf?* which activates the overflow check.

Table 5.5 Assignment of Internal Interrupt Events. It is listed in which stage an event signal is generated and by which unit.

event	signal	stage	unit
ill	ill	EX	control unit
mal	$imal$	IF	instruction memory control IMC
	$dmal$	M	data memory control DMC
pff	ipf	IF	instruction memory environment IMenv
pfls	dpf	M	data memory environment DMenv
trap	$trap$	EX	control unit
ovf	$ovf \wedge ovf?$	EX	ALU environment, control unit

Since the interrupt event signals are provided by several pipeline stages, the cause register CA cannot be assigned to a single stage. Register CA is therefore pipelined: $CA.i$ collects the events which an instruction triggers up to stage i. That takes care of internal events. External events could be caught at any stage, but for a shorter response time, they are assigned to the memory stage.

The control signals of the stage EX are precomputed. The cycle time of the cause collection $CAcol$, the accumulated delay of its output $CA.3'$, and its cost can be expressed as:

$$
\begin{aligned}
T_{CAcol} &= \max\{A_{IMenv}(flags), A_{ALUenv}(ovf) + D_{and}\} + \Delta \\
A_{CAcol}(CA.3') &= \max\{A_{DMenv}(flags), A_{DMC} + D_{or}\} \\
C_{CAcol} &= C_{and} + C_{or} + 9 \cdot C_{ff}.
\end{aligned}
$$

Cause Processing

(figure 5.10) The masked cause mca is obtained by masking the maskable interrupt events $CA.3'$ with the corresponding bits of the status register SR. The flag $jisr$ is raised if mca is different from zero, i.e., if at least one bit $mca[i]$ equals one.

$$
mca[i] = \begin{cases} CA.3'[i] \wedge SR[i] & \text{if } i \geq 6 \\ CA.3'[i] & \text{otherwise} \end{cases}
$$

$$
jisr = \bigvee_{i=0}^{31} mca[i]
$$

A repeat interrupt is signaled if one of the page faults is the event of highest priority among all the interrupt events j with $mca[j] = 1$:

$$
repeat = \overline{mca[0] \vee mca[1] \vee mca[2]} \wedge (mca[3] \vee mca[4])
$$

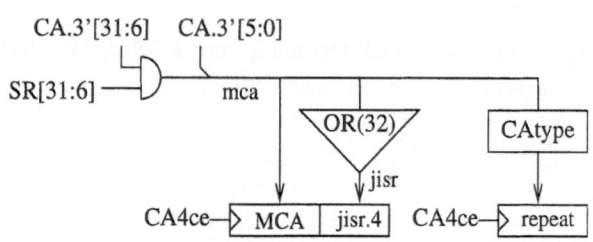

Figure 5.10 Cause processing circuit *CApro*.

Circuit *CAtype* generates flag *repeat* according to this equation. At the end of the cycle, the masked cause and the two flags *jisr* and *repeat* are clocked into registers. The cost and cycle time of the cause processing circuit CApro can be estimated as

$$
\begin{aligned}
C_{CApro} &= C_{and}(26) + C_{tree}(32) \cdot C_{or} + C_{ff}(34) + C_{CAtype} \\
C_{CAtype} &= 3 \cdot C_{or} + C_{and} + C_{inv} \\
D_{CApro} &= D_{and} + D_{tree}(32) \cdot D_{or} \\
T_{CApro} &= A_{CAcol}(CA.3') + D_{CApro} + \Delta.
\end{aligned}
$$

The cost and cycle time of the whole cause environment CAenv run at

$$
\begin{aligned}
C_{CAenv} &= C_{CAcol} + C_{CApro} \\
T_{CAenv} &= \max\{T_{CAcol}, T_{CApro}\}.
\end{aligned}
$$

5.5.6   Control Unit

As in the previous designs, the control unit basically comprises two circuits:

- The control automaton generates the control signals of the data paths based on an FSD. These signals include the clock and write request signals of the registers and RAMs.

- The stall engine schedules the instruction execution. It determines the stage which currently executes the instruction and enables the update of its registers and RAMs.

The control automaton must be adapted to the extended instruction set, but the new instructions have no impact on the stall engine. Nevertheless, the DLX_Σ design requires a new stall engine, due to the ISR call mechanism.

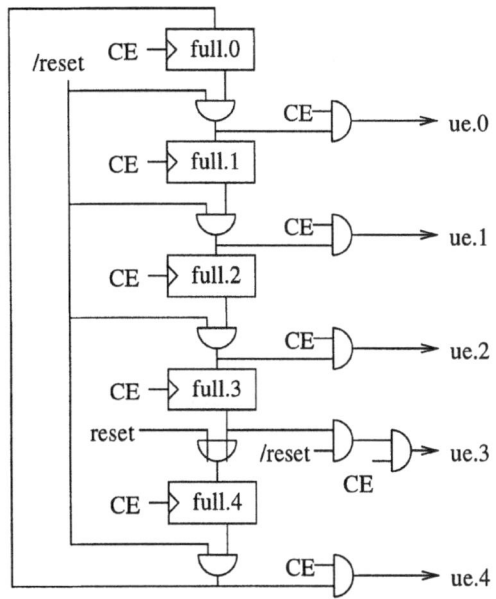

Figure 5.11 Stall engine of the sequential DLX design with interrupt hardware

Stall Engine of the DLX_Σ Design

There is still one central clock CE for the whole DLX_Σ design. The stall engine (figure 5.11) clocks the stages in a round robin fashion based on the vector $full[4:0]$. This vector is initialized on reset and shifted cyclically on every clock CE. However, in the first cycle after reset, the execution is now started in stage WB:

$$full[4:0] := \begin{cases} 10000 & \text{if } reset \\ cls(full) & \text{if } CE \wedge /reset \\ full & \text{otherwise.} \end{cases}$$

The update enable bit $ue.i$ enables the update of the of the output registers of stage i. During reset, all the update enable flags are inactive

$$ue[4:0] = full[4:0] \wedge CE \wedge \overline{reset}.$$

A jump to the interrupt service routine is only initiated, if the flag $jisr.4$ is raised and if the write back stage is full:

$$JISR = jisr.4 \wedge full[4].$$

Thus, a dummy instruction can never initiate a jump to the ISR.

On reset, the flags $CA.3'[0]$ and *jisr* are raised. However, a jump to the ISR can only be initiated in the following cycle, if the global clock CE and the clock CA4ce of the cause processing circuit are also active on reset

$$CE = (Ibusy \text{ NOR } Dbusy) \vee reset$$
$$CA4ce = ue.3 \vee reset.$$

As before, the clock CE is stalled if one of the memories is busy. In order to avoid unnecessary stalls, the busy flags are only considered in case of a successful memory access. Since the memories never raise their flags when they are idle, the flags *Ibusy* and *Dbusy* can be generated as

$$Ibusy = ibusy \wedge full.0 \wedge (imal \text{ NOR } ipf)$$
$$Dbusy = dbusy \wedge full.3 \wedge (dmal \text{ NOR } dpf).$$

The interrupt mechanism requires that the standard write to a register file or to the memory is canceled on a repeat interrupt. Since the register files GPR and SPR belong to stage WB, their protection is easy. Thus, the write signals of the two register files are set to

$$GPRw' = GPRw \wedge ue.4 \wedge (JISR \text{ NAND } repeat)$$
$$SPRw' = SPRw \wedge ue.4 \wedge (JISR \text{ NAND } repeat).$$

For the data memory, the protection is more complicated because the memory DM is accessed prior to the cause processing. There are only two kinds of repeat interrupts, namely the two page faults pff and $pfls$; both interrupts are non-maskable. Since the interrupt event $pfls$ is provided by the memory DM, the memory system DM itself must cancel the update if it detects a page fault. The other type of page fault $(ev[2] = pff)$ is already detected during fetch. We therefore redefine the write signal *Dmw* as

$$Dmw.3 := Dmw.2 \wedge \overline{CA.2[2]}.$$

As before, the memory update is disabled if the memory stage is empty

$$Dmw'.3 = Dmw.3 \wedge full.3.$$

Signal $Dmw'.3$ is used by the memory controller DMC in order to generate the bank write signals.

The remaining clock and write signals are enabled as before. With this stall engine, a reset brings up the DLX_Σ design no matter in which state the hardware has been before:

Let T be the last machine cycle in which the reset signal is active. In the next machine cycle, the DLX_Σ design then signals a reset interrupt and performs a jump to the ISR: ◄ Lemma 5.8

$$reset^T = 1 \wedge reset^{T+1} = 0 \quad \rightarrow \quad JISR^{T+1} = 1 \ and \ MCA[0]^{T+1} = 1.$$

Since the global clock is generated as PROOF

$$CE = (Ibusy \ \text{NOR} \ Dbusy) \vee reset,$$

the DLX_Σ design is clocked whenever the reset signal is active, and especially in cycle T. Due to reset, the flags $full[4:0]$ get initialized

$$full[4:0]^{T+1} = 10000,$$

and the clock enable signal for the output registers of $CApro$ is

$$CA4ce^T = ue.3^T \vee reset^T = 1.$$

Hence, the output registers of the cause processing circuit are updated at the end of cycle T with the values

$$MCA[0]^{T+1} = mca[0]^T = reset^T$$
$$jisr.4^{T+1} = \bigvee_{j=0}^{31} mca[j]^T = 1.$$

Consequently,

$$JISR^{T+1} = jisr.4^{T+1} \wedge full.4^{T+1} = 1,$$

and ISR(0) is invoked in cycle $T + 1$. QED

Control Automaton

The control automaton is constructed as for the DLX_σ design without interrupt handling (section 4.2.3). The automaton is modeled by a sequential FSD which is then transformed into precomputed control:

- The control signals of stage IF and the Moore signals of ID are always active, whereas the Mealy signals of stage ID are computed in every cycle.

- The control signals of the remaining stages are precomputed during ID. This is possible because all their states have an outdegree of one. There are three types of signals: signals x are only used in stage EX, signals y are used in stage EX and M, and signals z are used in all three stages.

However, there are three modifications. The automaton must account for the 8 new instructions (table 5.4). It must check for an illegal opcode, i.e., whether the instruction word codes a DLX instruction or not. Unlike the DLX_σ design, all the data paths registers invisible to the assembler programmer (i.e., all the registers except for PC', DPC, and the two register files) are now updated by every instruction. For all these registers, the automaton just provides the trivial clock request signal 1.

The invisible registers of the execute stage comprise the data registers MAR and MDRw and the buffers IR.3, Cad.3, Sad.3, PC.3, DPC.3, and DDPC.3. By default, these registers are updated as

$$(IR.3, Cad.3, Sad.3) \quad := \quad (IR.2, Cad.2, Sad.2)$$
$$(PC.3, DPC.3, DDPC.3) \quad := \quad (PC.2, DPC.2, DDPC.2)$$
$$(MAR, MDRw) \quad := \quad (A, shift(A, co[4:0]))$$

Besides the buffers, the invisible registers of the memory stage comprise the data registers C.4 and MDRr. Their default update is the following:

$$(IR.4, Cad.4, Sad.4) \quad := \quad (IR.3, Cad.3, Sad.3)$$
$$(PC.4, DPC.4, DDPC.4) \quad := \quad (PC.3, DPC.3, DDPC.3)$$
$$(C.4, MDRr) \quad := \quad (MAR, DMdefault).$$

The automaton is modeled by the FSD of figure 5.12. The tables 5.6 and 5.7 list the RTL instruction; the update of the invisible registers is only listed if it differs from the default. Note that in the stages M and WB, an rfe is processed like a special move movi2s. Table 5.8 lists the nontrivial disjunctive normal forms, and table 5.10 lists the parameters of the automaton.

In stage ID, only the selection of the program counters and of the constant got extended. This computation requires two additional Mealy signals $rfe.1$ and $Jimm$. In stage EX, the automaton now also has to check for illegal instructions; in case of an undefined opcode, the automaton gets into state Ill. Since this state has the largest indegree, Ill serves as the new initial state. State noEX is used for all legal instructions which already finish their actual execution in stage ID, i.e., the branches beqz and bnez and the two jumps jr and j.

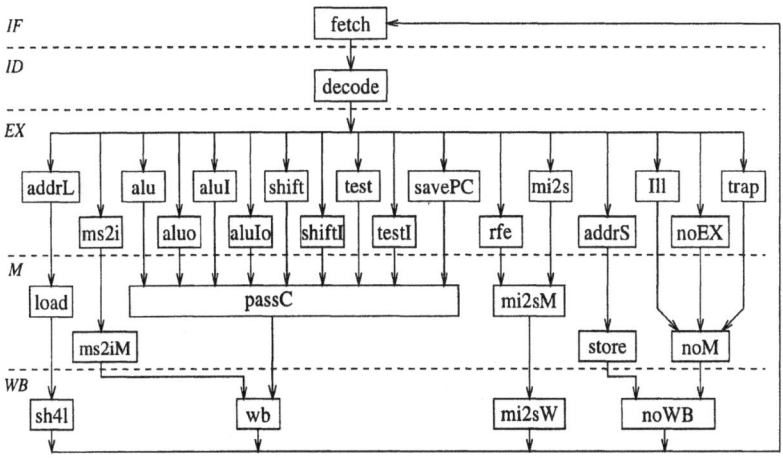

Figure 5.12 FSD of the *DLX*$_\Sigma$ design with interrupt handling

Table 5.6 RTL instructions of the stages IF and ID

	RTL instruction	type of I	signals
IF	$IR.1 = IM(DPC)$		fetch, IRce
ID	$A = A' = RS1, AEQZ = zero(A'),$ $B = RS2, PC' = (reset\ ?\ 4\ :\ pc'),$ $DPC = (reset\ ?\ 0\ :\ dpc),$ $S = SPR[Sas],$ $link = PC' + 4, DDPC = DPC,$ $IR.2 = IR.1, Sad.2 = Sad,$		Ace, Bce, PC'ce, DPCcee Sce PCce,
	$co = constant(IR.1)$	j, jal, trap	Jimm
		slli, srli, srai	shiftI
		otherwise	
	$(pc', dpc) =$ $nextPC(PC', A', co, EPCs)$	rfe	rfe.1
		j, jal	jump
		jr, jalr	jumpR, jump
		beqz	branch, bzero
		bnez	branch
		otherwise	
	$Cad = Caddr(IR.1)$	jalr, jal	Jlink
		R-type	Rtype
		otherwise	
	$(Sas, Sad) = Saddr(IR.1)$	rfe	rfe.1
		otherwise	

Table 5.7 RTL instructions of the stages EX, M, and WB. The update of the invisible registers is only listed if it differs from the default.

	state	RTL instruction	control signals
EX	alu	$MAR = A$ op B, $MDRw = \text{shift}(A, B[4:0])$	ALUDdoe, Rtype, bmuxsel
	aluo	$MAR = A$ op B, *overflow?* $MDRw = \text{shift}(A, B[4:0])$	ALUDdoe, Rtype, ovf? bmuxsel
	test	$MAR = (A \text{ rel } B?1:0)$, $MDRw = \text{shift}(A, B[4:0])$	ALUDdoe, test, Rtype, bmuxsel
	shift	$MAR = MDRw =$ $\text{shift}(A, B[4:0])$,	SHDdoe, Rtype, bmuxsel
	aluI	$MAR = A$ op co,	ALUDdoe,
	aluIo	$MAR = A$ op co, *overflow?*	ALUDdoe, ovf?
	testI	$MAR = (A \text{ rel } co?1:0)$	ALUDdoe, test
	shiftI	$MAR = \text{shift}(A, co[4:0])$	SHDdoe, shiftI, Rtype
	savePC	$MAR = link$	linkDdoe,
	addrL	$MAR = A + co$,	ALUDdoe, add,
	addrS	$MAR = A + co$, $MDRw =$ $\text{cls}(B, MAR[1:0]000)$	ALUDdoe, add, amuxsel, shift4s
	trap	$MAR = co$, $trap = 1$	coDdoe, trap
	Ill	$MAR = A$, $ill = 1$	ADdoe, ill
	rfe	$MAR = S$	SDdoe
	ms2i	$MAR = S$	SDdoe
	mi2s noEX	default updates	ADdoe
M	load	$MDRr =$ $Mword[\langle MAR[31:2]00\rangle]$	Dmr
	store	$m = bytes(MDRw)$	Dmw
	others	default updates	
WB	sh4l	$GPR[Cad.4] =$ $sh4l(MDRr, MAR[1:0]000)$	shift4l, GPRw
	wb	$GPR[Cad.4] = C.4$	GPRw
	mi2sW	$SPR[Sad.4] = C.4$	SPRw
	noWB	no update	

Table 5.8 Nontrivial disjunctive normal forms of the DLX_Σ control automaton

stage	DNF	state/signal	IR[31 : 26]	IR[5 : 0]	length
EX	D1	alu	000000	1001**	10
			000000	100**1	10
	D2	aluo	000000	1000*0	11
	D3	aluI	0011**	******	4
			001**1	******	4
	D4	aluIo	0010*0	******	5
	D5	shift	000000	0001*0	11
			000000	00011*	11
	D6	shiftI	000000	0000*0	11
			000000	00001*	11
	D7	test	000000	101***	9
	D8	testI	011***	******	3
	D9	savePC	010111	******	6
			000011	******	6
	D10	addrS	10100*	******	5
			1010*1	******	5
	D11	addrL	100*0*	******	4
			1000*1	******	5
			10000*	******	5
	D12	mi2s	000000	010001	12
	D13	ms2i	000000	010000	12
	D14	trap	111110	******	6
	D15	rfe	111111	******	6
	D16	noEX	00010*	******	5
			000010	******	6
			010110	******	6
ID	D17	Rtype	000000	******	6
	D6	shiftI	000000	0000*0	(10)
			000000	00001*	(10)
	D9	Jlink	010111	******	(6)
			000011	******	(6)
	D18	jumpR	01011*	******	5
	D19	jump	00001*	******	5
			01011*	******	(5)
	D20	branch	00010*	******	(5)
	D21	bzero	*****0	******	1
	D15	rfe.1	111111	******	(6)
	D22	Jimm	00001*	******	(5)
			111110	******	(6)
Accumulated length of all nontrivial monomials					206

Table 5.9 Control signals to be precomputed during stage ID

	EX	M	WB
y	shift4s, amuxsel	Dmw	
z		Dmr	shift4l
			SPRw
			GPRw

type x signals (stage EX only)		
trap, coDdoe	ADdoe	ovf?
	SDdoe	add?
linkDdoe	Rtype	ill
ALUDdoe	bmuxsel	test
SHDdoe		

	ill	add	test	Rtype	ovf?	bmuxsel	Dmw	Dmr	SHDdoe
shift				1		1			1
shiftI				1					1
alu				1		1			
aluo				1	1	1			
aluIo					1				
test		1	1			1			
testI		1							
addrL		1						1	
addrS		1					1		
Ill	1								
inactive in states: aluI, savePC, trap, mi2s, rfe ms2i, noEX									

	ALUDdoe	linkDdoe	trap	ADdoe	SDdoe	SPRw	GPRw
shift							1
shiftI							1
alu	1						1
aluo	1						1
aluI	1						1
aluIo	1						1
test	1						1
testI	1						1
addrL	1						1
addrS	1						
savePC		1					1
trap			1				
mi2s				1		1	
ms2i					1		1
rfe					1	1	
Ill				1			
noEX				1			

Table 5.10 Parameters of the two control automata; one precomputes the Moore signals (*ex*) and the other generate the Mealy signals (*id*).

	# states	# inputs	# and frequency of outputs		
	k	σ	γ	ν_{sum}	ν_{max}
ex	17	12	16	48	11
id	1	12	9	13	2

	fanin of the states		# and length of monomials		
	fan_{sum}	fan_{max}	#M	l_{sum}	l_{max}
ex	26	3	26	189	12
id	–	–	4	17	10

The stage EX, M and WB are only controlled by Moore signals, which are precomputed during decode. All their states have an outdegree of one. It therefore suffices to consider the states of stage EX in order to generate all these control signals. For any of these signals, the table 5.9 list its type (i.e., x, y, or z) and the EX states in which it becomes active.

Correctness of the Design

Along the lines of section 3.4 it can be show that the DLX_Σ design interprets the extended DLX instruction set of section 5.2 with delayed PC semantics.

In the sequential DLX design without interrupt handling, any instruction which has passed a stage k only updates output registers of stages $k' > k$ (lemma 4.3). In the DLX_Σ design, this dateline criterion only applies for the uninterrupted execution. If an instruction I_i gets interrupted, the two program counters PC' and DPC get also updated when I_i is in the write back stage. Furthermore, in case of a repeat interrupt, the update of the data memory is suppressed. Thus, for the DLX_Σ design, we can just formulate a weak version of the dateline criterion:

Let $I_\Sigma(k, T') = i$. For any memory cell or register $R \in out(t)$ different from   ◀ Lemma 5.9
PC' and DPC, we have

$$R^{T'} = \begin{cases} R_{i-1} & \text{if } t \geq k \\ R_i & \text{if } t < k. \end{cases}$$

If $R \in \{PC', DPC\}$, then R is an output register of stage $t = 1$ and

$$R^{T'} = \begin{cases} R_{i-1} & \text{if } k \in \{0,1\} \\ R_i^u & \text{if } k \geq 2. \end{cases}$$

If the execution of instruction I_i is not interrupted, i.e., if $JISR^{T'} = 0$ with $I_\Sigma(4, T') = i$, then $R_i = R_i^u$ for any register R.

If $I_\Sigma(4, T') = i$, then $I_\Sigma(0, T' + 1) = i + 1$ and lemma 5.9 implies for all R

$$R^{T'+1} = R_i.$$

5.6 Pipelined Interrupt Hardware

AS IN the basic DLX design (chapter 4), the same three modifications are sufficient in order to transform the prepared sequential design DLX_Σ into the pipelined design DLX_Π. Except for

- a modified PC environment,

- extensive hardware for result forwarding and hazard detection, and

- a different stall engine,

the DLX_Σ hardware can be used without changes. Figure 5.13 depicts the top-level schematics of the DLX_Π data paths. The modified environments are now described in detail.

5.6.1 PC Environment

Figure 5.14 depicts the PC environment of the DLX_Π design. The only modification over the DLX_Σ design is the address provided to the instruction memory IM. As for the transformation of chapter 4, memory IM is now addressed by the input dpc of register DPC and not by its output.

$$dpc = \begin{cases} SISR & \text{if} \quad JISR = 1 \\ EDPC & \text{if} \quad JISR = 0 \land rfe.1 = 1 \\ PC' & \text{otherwise} \end{cases}$$

However, the delayed program counter must be buffered for later use, and thus, register DPC cannot be discarded.

The cost of environment PCenv and most of its delays remain the same. The two exception PCs are now provided by the forwarding circuit $FORW$. Thus,

$$\begin{aligned} A_{PCenv}(dpc) &= \max\{A_{JISR}, A_{FORW}(EDPC)\} + 2 \cdot D_{mux}(32) \\ T_{PCenv} &= \max\{D_{inc}(30), A_{IRenv}(co) + D_{add}(32), A_{GPRenv}(Ain), \\ &\qquad A_{FORW}(EPCs), A(bjtaken), A_{CON}(csID)\} \\ &\quad + 3 \cdot D_{mux}(32) + \Delta. \end{aligned}$$

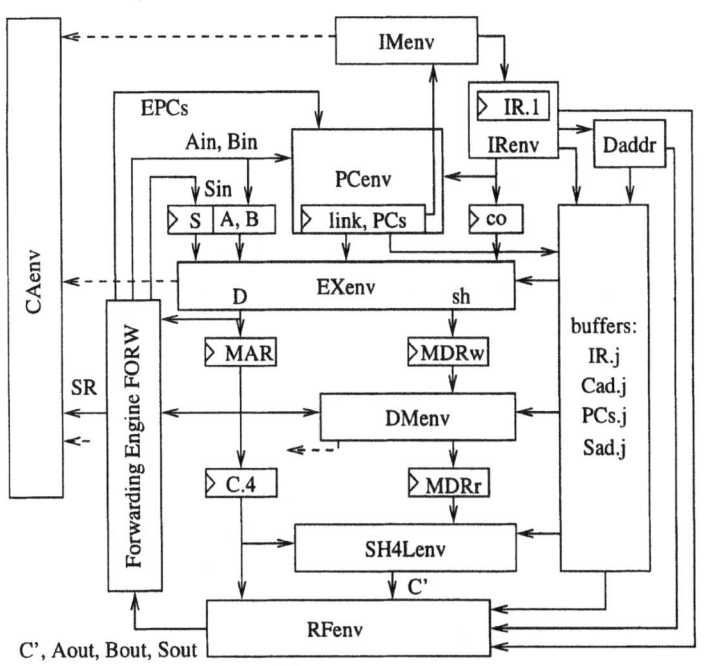

Figure 5.13 Data paths of the pipelined design DLX_Π with interrupt support

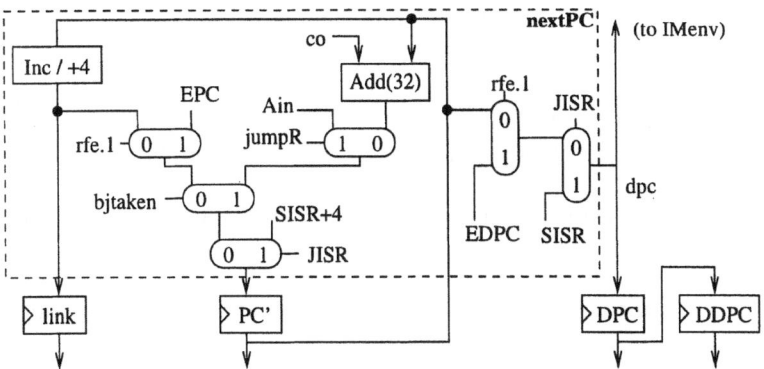

Figure 5.14 Environment PCenv of the DLX_Π design

The modified PC environment also impacts the functionality and delay of the instruction memory environment. On a successful read access, the instruction memory now provides the memory word

$$IMout = IMword[\langle dpc[31:2]00\rangle].$$

The cycle time of IMenv and the accumulated delay of its flags are

$$T_{IMenv} = A_{PCenv}(dpc) + d_{Imem} + \Delta$$
$$A_{IMenv}(flags) = A_{PCenv}(dpc) + max\{D_{or}, d_{Istat}\}.$$

5.6.2 Forwarding and Interlocking

The data paths comprise two register files, GPR and SPR. Both are updated during write back. Since their data are read by earlier stages, result forwarding and interlocking is required. The two register files are treated separately.

General Purpose Registers
During movs2i instructions, data are copied from register file SPR via register S and the $C.k$ registers into the register file GPR. The forwarding circuits to S have to guarantee that the uninterrupted execution of I_i, i.e.,

$$I_\Pi(2,T) = I_\Pi(3,T+1) = I_\Pi(4,T+2) = i,$$

implies $S^T = S_{i-1}$. During stages EX, M and WB the data then wander down the $C.k$ registers like the result of an ordinary fixed point operation. Thus we do not modify the forwarding circuits for registers A and B at all.

Special Purpose Registers
Data from the special purpose registers are used in three places, namely

- on a movs2i instruction, $SPR[Sas]$ is read into register S during decode,

- the cause environment reads the interrupt masks SR in the memory stage, and

- on an rfe instruction, the two exception PCs are read during decode.

Updates of the SPR registers are performed in three situations:

- On a movi2s instruction, value $C.4$ is written into register $SPR[Sad]$.

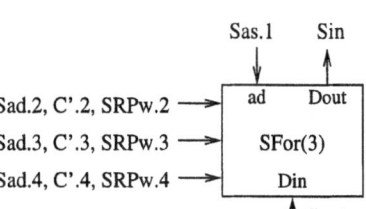

Figure 5.15 Forwarding of SPR into register S

- Register SR is updated by rfe. Recall that in stages 2 to 4, we have implemented this update like a regular write into SPR with write address $Sad = 0$.

- All special purpose registers are updated by *JISR*. Forwarding the effect of this looks like a nightmare. Fortunately, all instructions which could use forwarded versions of values forced into SPR by *JISR* get evicted from the pipe by the very same occurrence of *JISR*.

Therefore, one only needs to forward data from the inputs of the $C.k$ registers with destinations in SPR specified by Sad.

Forwarding of S Forwarding data with destination SPR into register S is exactly like forwarding data with destination GPR into A or B, except that for address $ad = 0$ the data are now forwarded as well. Thus, connecting the three stage forwarding circuit $SFor(3)$ as depicted in figure 5.15 handles the forwarding into register S. Note that no data hazards are introduced.

Circuit SFor Figure 5.16 depicts a realization of the 3-stage forwarding circuit $SFor$. It is derived from the circuit $Forw$ of figure 4.18 in the obvious way. Let $D_{SFor}(Data; 3)$ denote the delay, the data inputs require to pass circuit SFor(3). For an n-bit address ad, the cost and delay of SFor(3) can be modeled as

$$
\begin{aligned}
C_{SFor}(3) &= 3 \cdot C_{mux}(32) + 6 \cdot C_{and} + 3 \cdot C_{equal}(n) \\
D_{SFor}(hit) &= D_{equal}(n) + D_{and} \\
D_{SFor}(Dout; 3) &= D_{SFor}(hit) + 3 \cdot D_{mux}(32) \\
D_{SFor}(Data; 3) &= 3 \cdot D_{mux}(32).
\end{aligned}
$$

Circuit *SFor* is slightly faster than the forwarding circuit *Forw* for the GPR operands.

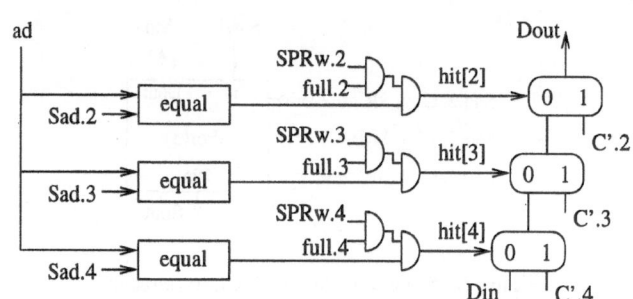

Figure 5.16 3-stage forwarding circuit $SFor(3)$ for an SPR register

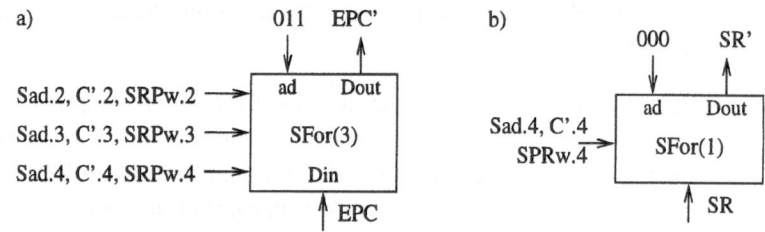

Figure 5.17 Forwarding of EPC into register PC' (a) and of register SR into the memory stage (b)

Forwarding of EPC The forwarding of EPC into the program counter PC' during rfe instructions is done by a circuit $SFor(3)$ which is connected as depicted in figure 5.17 (a). Note that the address input ad of the forwarding circuit has now been tied to the fixed address 3 of the register EPC. No data hazards are introduced.

Forwarding of SR The forwarding of register SR into the memory environment requires forwarding over a single stage with a circuit $SFor(1)$ connected as depicted in figure 5.17 (b). This circuit is obtained from circuit $SFor(3)$ by the obvious simplifications. It has cost and delay

$$
\begin{aligned}
C_{SFor}(1) &= C_{mux}(32) + 2 \cdot C_{and} + C_{equal}(3) \\
D_{SFor}(Dout;1) &= D_{SFor}(hit) + D_{mux}(32) \\
D_{SFor}(Data;1) &= D_{mux}(32).
\end{aligned}
$$

Again, no data hazards were introduced.

Forwarding of EDPC The forwarding of EDPC during rfe instructions to signal dpc in the PC environment would work along the same lines,

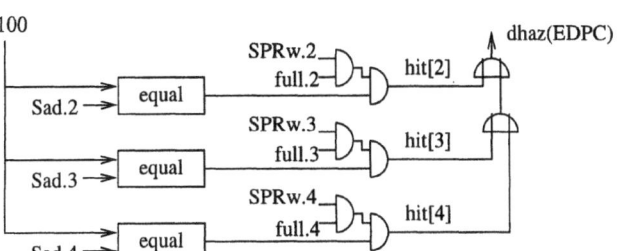

Figure 5.18 Data hazard detection for EDPC

but this would increase the instruction fetch time. Therefore, forwarding of EDPC to dpc is omitted. The data hazards caused by this can always be avoided if we update in the RESTORE sequence of the interrupt service routine register EDPC before register EPC.

If this precaution is not taken by the programmer, then a data hazard signal

$$dhaz(EDPC) \ = \ hit.2 \ \vee \ hit.3 \ \vee \ hit.4$$

is generated by the circuit in figure 5.18. Note that this circuit is obtained from circuit $SFor(3)$ by the obvious simplifications. Such a data hazard is only of interest, if the decode stage processes an rfe instruction. That is the only case in which a SPR register requests an interlock:

$$dhazS \ = \ dhaz(EDPC) \ \wedge \ rfe.1.$$

Cost and Delay The hazard signal $dhazS$ is generated at the following cost and delay

$$C_{dhazS} \ = \ 3 \cdot C_{equal}(3) + 7 \cdot C_{and} + 2 \cdot C_{or}$$
$$A_{dhazS} \ = \ D_{equal}(3) + 2 \cdot D_{and} + 2 \cdot D_{or}.$$

The address and control inputs of the forwarding circuits $SFor$ are directly taken from registers. The input data are provided by the environment EX-env, by register C.4 and by the special read ports of the SPR register file. Thus,

$$A_{FORW}(S, EPC) \ = \ \max\{D_{SFor}(Dout; 3), D_{SFor}(Data; 3) + A_{EXenv}\}$$
$$A_{FORW}(SR) \ = \ \max\{D_{SFor}(Dout; 1), D_{SFor}(Data; 1) + A_{SH4Lenv}\}$$
$$A_{FORW}(EDPC) \ = \ 0.$$

The forwarding of the SPR operands is performed by an 1-stage and two 3-stage forwarding circuits:

$$C_{SFORW} = C_{SFor}(1) + 2 \cdot C_{SFor}(3).$$

5.6.3 Stall Engine

The stall engine of the DLX_Π design is very similar to the interlock engine of section 4.5 except for two aspects: the initialization is different and there are additional data hazards to be checked for. On a data hazard, the upper two stages of the pipeline are stalled, whereas the remaining three stages proceed. The upper two stages are clocked by signal $CE1$, the other stages are clocked by signal $CE2$.

A data hazard can now be caused by one of the general purpose operands A and B or by a special purpose register operand. Such a hazard is signaled by the activation of the flag

$$dhaz = dhazA \lor dhazB \lor dhazS.$$

Updating of the Full Vector

The full vector is initialized on reset and on every jump to the ISR. As in the DLX_Σ design, a jump to the ISR is only initiated if the write back stage is not empty

$$JISR = jisr.4 \land full.4.$$

On JISR, the write back stage is updated and stage IF already fetches the first instruction of the ISR. The update enable signals $ue.4$ and $ue.0$ must therefore be active. The instructions processed in stages 1 to 3 are canceled on a jump to the ISR; signal $JISR$ disables the update enable signals $ue[3 : 1]$. In the cycle after JISR, only stages 0 and 1 hold a valid instruction, the other stages are empty, i.e., they process dummy instructions.

Like in the DLX_Σ design, an active reset signal is caught immediately and is clocked into register MCA even if the memory stage is empty. In order to ensure that in the next cycle a jump to the ISR is initiated, the reset signal forces the full bit $full.4$ of the write back stage to one.

The following equations define such a stall engine. A hardware realization is depicted in figure 5.19.

$$
\begin{aligned}
ue.0 &= CE1 \\
ue.1 &= CE1 \land /JISR & full.1 &= 1 \\
ue.2 &= CE2 \land /JISR \land full.2 & full.2 &:= ue.1 \\
ue.3 &= CE2 \land /JISR \land full.3 & full.3 &:= ue.2 \\
ue.4 &= CE2 \land full.4 & full.4 &:= ue.3 \lor reset
\end{aligned}
$$

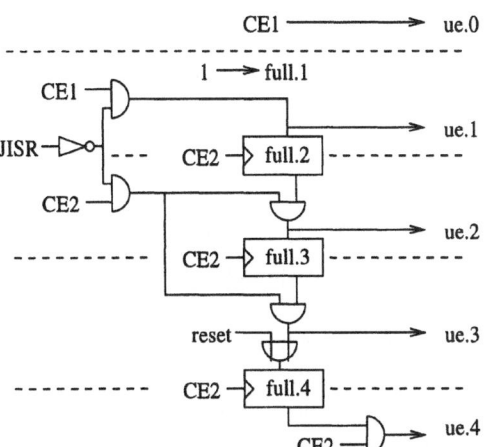

Figure 5.19 Stall engine of the DLX_Π design with interrupt support

Clock Signals

Like in the pipelined design DLX_π without interrupt handling, there are two clock signals. Signal $CE1$ governs the upper two stages of the pipeline, and signal $CE2$ governs the remaining stages.

$$
\begin{aligned}
CE1 &= (/busy \land /dhaz) \lor (JISR \land /Ibusy) \\
&= (/busy \land /dhaz) \lor (/JISR \text{ NOR } Ibusy) \\
CE2 &= /busy \lor (/JISR \text{ NOR } Ibusy) \lor reset.
\end{aligned}
$$

Both clocks are inactive if one of the memories is busy; CE1 is also inactive on a data hazard. However, on JISR both clocks become active once the instruction memory is not busy. In order to catch an active reset signal immediately, the clock CE2 and the clock $CA4ce$ of the cause processing circuit must be active on reset

$$CA4ce = ue.3 \lor reset.$$

In order to avoid unnecessary stalls, the busy flags are only considered in case of a successful memory access. Since the memories never raise their flags when they are idle, the busy flags are generated as

$$
\begin{aligned}
Ibusy &= ibusy \land (imal \text{ NOR } ipf) \\
Dbusy &= dbusy \land (dmal \text{ NOR } dpf) \\
/busy &= Ibusy \text{ NOR } Dbusy.
\end{aligned}
$$

The interrupt mechanism requires that the standard write to a register file or memory is canceled on a repeat interrupt. The register files GPR and SPR are protected as in the sequential design. A special write to the SPR register file is enabled by signal $ue.4$. The write signals of the register files are therefore generated as

$$
\begin{aligned}
GPRw' &= GPRw \wedge ue.4 \wedge (JISR \text{ NAND } repeat) \\
SPRw' &= SPRw \wedge ue.4 \wedge (JISR \text{ NAND } repeat) \\
SPRw'[5:0] &= SPRw[5:0] \wedge ue.4.
\end{aligned}
$$

For the data memory, the protection becomes more complicated. Like in the sequential design DLX_Σ, the memory system DM itself cancels the update if it detects a page fault, and in case of a page fault on fetch, the write request signal is disabled during execute

$$
Dmw.3 := Dmw.2 \wedge \overline{CA.2[2]}.
$$

However, the access must also be disabled on JISR and on reset. Thus, signal $Dmw3$ which is used by the memory controller DMC in order to generate the bank write signals is set to

$$
Dmw'.3 = Dmw.3 \wedge full.3 \wedge (JISR \text{ NOR } reset).
$$

The remaining clock and write signals are enabled as in the pipelined design DLX_π without interrupt handling: the data memory read request is granted if stage M is full

$$
Dmr'.3 = Dmr.3 \wedge full.3,
$$

and the update of an register $R \in out(i)$ is enabled by $ue.i$

$$
Rce' = Rce \wedge ue.i.
$$

Like for the DLX_Σ design (lemma 5.8), it follows immediately that with this stall engine, an active reset signal brings up the DLX_Π design, no matter in which state the hardware has been before:

Lemma 5.10 ▶ *Let T be the last machine cycle in which the reset signal is active. In the next machine cycle, the DLX_Π design then signals a reset interrupt and performs a jump to the ISR:*

$$
reset^T = 1 \wedge reset^{T+1} = 0 \quad \rightarrow \quad JISR^{T+1} = 1 \text{ and } MCA[0]^{T+1} = 1.
$$

Table 5.11 Start of the execution after reset under the assumption that no data hazards occur. A blank entry indicates that the value is undefined.

T	reset	JISR	$ue[0, 1, 2, 3, 4]$					$full[2, 3, 4]$			IF
-1	1		1								
0	0	1	1	0	0	0	1			1	I_0
1	0	0	1	1	0	0	0	0	0	0	I_1
2	0	0	1	1	1	0	0	1	0	0	I_2
3	0	0	1	1	1	1	0	1	1	0	I_3
4	0	0	1	1	1	1	1	1	1	1	I_4

Scheduling Function

The scheduling functions of the pipelined DLX designs with and without interrupt handling are very much alike. The execution starts in cycle $T = 0$, which is the first cycle after reset (table 5.11). According to lemma 5.10, the first instruction I_0 of the ISR is fetched in cycle $T = 0$, and

$$I_\Pi(0,0) = 0.$$

The instructions are still fetched in program order and wander in lock-step through the stages 0 and 1:

$$I_\Pi(0,T) = i \;\rightarrow\; I_\Pi(0,T+1) = \begin{cases} i & \text{if} \quad ue.0^T = 0 \\ i+1 & \text{if} \quad ue.0^T = 1 \end{cases}$$

$$I_\Pi(1,T) = i \;\rightarrow\; I_\Pi(0,T) = i+1$$

Any instruction makes a progress of at most one stage per cycle, and it cannot be stalled once it is clocked into stage 2. However, on an active *JISR* signal, the instructions processed in stages 1 to 3 are evicted from the pipeline. Thus, $I_\Pi(k,T) = i \wedge (JISR^T = 0 \vee k = 0)$ implies

$$i = \begin{cases} I_\Pi(k,T+1) & \text{if} \quad ue.k^T = 0 \\ I_\Pi(k+1,T+1) & \text{if} \quad ue.k^T = 1 \quad \text{and} \quad k+1 \leq 4 \end{cases}$$

and for $k \geq 2$, the instructions proceed at full speed:

$$I_\Pi(k,T) = i \wedge JISR^T = 0 \;\rightarrow\; I_\Pi(k+1,T+1) = i.$$

Note that on $JISR = 1$, the update enable signals of the stages 0 and 4 are active whereas the ones of the remaining stages are inactive.

Cost and Delay

The computation of the inverted hazard signal $/dhaz$ requires the data hazard signals of the two GPR operands A and B and the data hazard signal $dhazS$ of the SPR operands.

$$/dhaz = (dhazA \lor dhazB) \text{ NOR } dhazS.$$

Since for the two GPR operands, the hazard detection is virtually the same, the cost and delay of signal $/dhaz$ can be modeled as

$$
\begin{aligned}
C_{dhaz} &= 2 \cdot C_{dhazA} + C_{dhazS} + C_{or} + C_{nor} \\
A_{dhaz} &= \max\{A_{dhazA} + D_{or}, A_{dhazS}\} + D_{nor}.
\end{aligned}
$$

The inverted flag $/busy$, which combines the two signals $Dbusy$ and $Ibusy$, depends on the flags of the memory environments. Its cost and delay can be modeled as

$$
\begin{aligned}
C_{busy} &= 2 \cdot C_{and} + 3 \cdot C_{nor} \\
A_{busy} &= \max\{A_{IMenv}(flags), A_{DMenv}(flags)\} + D_{and} + 2 \cdot D_{nor}.
\end{aligned}
$$

The two clock signals CE1 and CE2 depend on the busy flag, the data hazard flag $/dhaz$, and the JISR flags.

$$JISR = jisr.4 \land full.4 \qquad /JISR = jisr.4 \text{ NAND } full.4.$$

We assume that the reset signal has zero delay. The two clocks can then be generated at the following cost and delay

$$
\begin{aligned}
C_{CE} &= 3 \cdot C_{or} + C_{nor} + C_{and} + C_{dhaz} + C_{busy} + C_{and} + C_{nand} \\
A_{JISR} &= \max\{D_{and}, D_{nand}\} \\
A_{CE} &= \max\{A_{dhaz}, A_{JISR}, A_{busy}\} + D_{and} + D_{or}.
\end{aligned}
$$

The core of the stall engine is the circuit of figure 5.19. In addition, the stall engine generates the clock signals and enables the update of the registers and memories. Only the data memory, the two register files, the output registers of environment CApro, and the registers PC' and DPC have non-trivial update request signals. All the other data paths registers $R \in out(i)$ are clocked by $ue.i$. The cost and the cycle time of the whole stall engine can therefore be modeled as

$$
\begin{aligned}
C_{stall} &= 3 \cdot C_{ff} + C_{or} + 5 \cdot C_{and} \\
&\quad + C_{CE} + C_{nand} + C_{nor} + C_{or} + C_{inv} + 9 \cdot C_{and} \\
T_{stall} &= A_{CE} + 3 \cdot D_{and} + \delta \\
&\quad + \max\{D_{SF}(w, ce; 6, 32) + D_{ff}, D_{ram3}(32, 32)\}
\end{aligned}
$$

Table 5.12 Cost of the data paths of the pipelined DLX designs with/without interrupt hardware

environment	EX	RF	PC	CA	buffer	FORW	DP
DLX_π	3315	4066	1906	–	408	812	13010
DLX_Π	3795	7257	2610	471	2064	1624	20610
increase	14%	78%	37%	–	406%	100%	58%

5.6.4 Cost and Delay of the DLX_Π Hardware

In following, we determine the cost and the cycle time of the DLX_Π design and compare these values to those of pipelined design DLX_π without interrupt handling.

Cost of the Data Paths

Except for the forwarding circuit FORW, the top level schematics of the data paths of the two DLX design with interrupt support are the same. The cost of the DLX_Π data paths DP (figure 5.13) can therefore be expressed as

$$
\begin{aligned}
C_{DP} = \ & C_{IMenv} + C_{IRenv} + C_{PCenv} + C_{Daddr} \\
& + C_{EXenv} + C_{DMenv} + C_{SH4Lenv} + C_{RFenv} \\
& + C_{buffer} + C_{CAenv} + C_{FORW} + 8 \cdot C_{ff}(32).
\end{aligned}
$$

Table 5.12 lists the cost of the data paths and its environments for the two pipelined DLX designs. Environments which are not effected by the interrupt mechanism are omitted. The interrupt mechanism increases the cost of the data paths by 58%. This increase is largely caused by the register files, the forwarding hardware, and by the buffering. The other data paths environments become about 20% more expensive.

Without interrupt hardware, each of the stages ID, EX and M requires 17 buffers for the two opcodes and one destination address. In the DLX_Π design, each of these stages buffers now two addresses and three 32-bit PCs. Thus, the amount of buffering is increased by a factor of 4.

The environment RFenv now consists of two register files GPR and SPR. Although there are only 6 SPR registers, they almost double the cost of environment RFenv. That is because the GPR is implemented by a RAM, whereas the SPR is implemented by single registers. Note that an 1-bit register is four times more expensive than a RAM cell. The register implementation is necessary in order to support the extended access mode – all 6 SPR registers can be accessed in parallel.

Table 5.13 Cost of the control of the two pipelined DLX designs

environment	stall	MC	automata	buffer	CON	DLX
DLX_π	77	48	609	89	830	13840
DLX_Π	165	61	952	105	1283	21893
increase	114%	27%	56%	18%	44%	58%

Cost of the Control

According to the schematics of the precomputed control (figure 4.15), the control unit CON buffers the valid flags and the precomputed control signals. For the GPR result, 6 valid flags are needed, i.e., $v[4:2].2$, $v[4:3].3$ and $v[4].4$. Due to the extended ISA, there is also an SPR result. Since this result always becomes valid in the execute stage, there is no need for additional valid flags.

Since the control automata already provide one stage of buffering, precomputed control signals of type x need no explicit buffering. Type y signals require one additional stage of buffers, whereas type z signals require two stages of buffers. According to table 5.9, there are three control signals of type z and one of type y. Thus, the control requires

$$6+2\cdot3+1\cdot1=13$$

flipflops instead of 11. One inverter is used in order to generate the valid signal of the GPR result. In addition, the control unit CON comprises the stall engine, the two memory controllers IMC and DMC, and two control automata (table 5.10). Thus, the cost of unit CON can be modeled as

$$\begin{aligned} C_{CON} &= C_{IMC}+C_{DMC}+C_{stall}+C_{CON}(moore)+C_{CON}(mealy) \\ &\quad +13\cdot C_{ff}+C_{inv}. \end{aligned}$$

Table 5.13 lists the cost of the control unit, of all its environments, and of the whole DLX hardware. The interrupt mechanism increases the cost of the pipelined control by 44%. The cost of the stall engine is increased above-average (+114%).

Cycle Time

According to table 5.14, the interrupt support has virtually no impact on the cycle time of the pipelined DLX design. The cycle times of the data paths environments remain unchanged, only the control becomes slightly slower. However, as long as the memory status time stays below 43 gate delays, the cycle time of the DLX_Π design is dominated by the PC environment.

Table 5.14 Cycle times of the two pipelined DLX designs; d_{mem} denotes the maximum of the two access times d_{Imem} and d_{Dmem} and d_{mstat} denotes the maximum of the two status times d_{Istat} and d_{Dstat}.

| | ID | | EX | WB | DP | IF, M | CON / stall | |
	A/B	PC						max(,)
DLX_π	72	89	66	33	89	$16 + d_{mem}$	57	$43 + d_{mstat}$
DLX_Π	72	89	66	33	89	$16 + d_{mem}$	57	$46 + d_{mstat}$

5.7 Correctness of the Interrupt Hardware

IN THIS section, we will prove that the pipelined hardware DLX_Π together with an admissible ISR processes nested interrupts in a precise manner. For a sequential design, the preciseness of the interrupt processing is well understood. We therefore reduce the preciseness of the pipelined interrupt mechanism to the one of the sequential mechanism by showing that the DLX_Π design simulates the DLX_Σ design on any non-aborted instruction sequence.

In a first step, we consider an uninterrupted instruction sequence $I_0, \ldots, I_p$, where I_0 is preceded by JISR, and where I_p initiates a JISR. In a second step, it is shown that the simulation still works when concatenating several of these sequences. With respect to these simulations, canceled instructions and external interrupt events are a problem.

Canceled Instructions
Between the fetching of instruction I_p which initiates a jump to the ISR and the actual JISR, the DLX_Π design starts further instructions $I_{p+1}, \ldots, I_{p+\delta}$. However, these instructions are canceled by JISR before they reach the write back stage. Thus, with respect to the simulation, we consider sequence $P = I_0, \ldots, I_p, \ldots, I_{p+\delta}$ for the pipelined design, and sequence $P' = I_0, \ldots, I_p$ for the sequential design.

External Interrupt Events
are asynchronous to the instruction execution and can occur at any time. Due to the pipelined execution, an instruction sequence P is usually processed faster on the DLX_Π design than on the DLX_Σ design. For the simulation, it is therefore insufficient to assign a given external event to a fixed cycle. Instead, the instruction sequences P and P' are extended by a sequence of external events. For any external interrupt $ev[j]$, we use the following assignment, which is illustrated in table 5.15:

Table 5.15 Assignment of external interrupt events for an uninterrupted instruction sequence P

cycle	ev[j]	JISR	full.3	full.4	M	WB
$T-1$	0	0				
T	1	0	0		–	
$T+1$	1	0	0	0	–	–
...	1	0	0	0	–	–
$t-1$	1	0	1	0	I_i	–
t	1	0		1		I_i

Let the external interrupt event $ev[j]$ be raised during cycle T of the pipelined execution of P

$$ev[j]_\Pi^{T-1} = 0 \quad \text{and} \quad ev[j]_\Pi^{T} = 1,$$

let t be the first cycle after T for which the write back stage is full, and let $T'+1$ be the cycle in the sequential execution of P' corresponding to cycle t, i.e.,

$$I_\Pi(4,t) \;=\; i \;=\; I_\Sigma(4,T'+1).$$

In the sequential execution of P, event $ev[j]$ is then assigned to cycle T'

$$ev[j]_\Sigma^{T'} = 1.$$

Since the external events are collected in stage 3, it is tempting to argue about the first cycle $\hat{t} \geq T$ in which stage 3 is full, i.e., $i = I_\Pi(3,\hat{t})$. For a single uninterrupted instruction sequence P that makes no difference because the instruction processed in stage 3 is always passed to stage 4 at the end of the cycle. Thus,

$$I_\Pi(3,\hat{t}) \;=\; I_\Pi(4,\hat{t}+1) \;=\; I_\Pi(4,t).$$

However, when concatenating two sequences $P = I_0, \ldots I_{p+\delta}$ and $Q = J_0$, $J_1, \ldots$, the instruction processed in stage 3 can be canceled by JISR. Therefore, it is essential to argue about the instruction executed in stage 4. In the example of table 5.16, the external event $ev[j]$ is signaled while the DLX_Π design performs a jump to the ISR. When arguing about stage 3, the external event is assigned to instruction I_{p+1} which has no counterpart in the sequential execution, whereas when arguing about stage 4, the event is assigned to the first instruction of sequence Q.

Table 5.16 Assignment of external interrupt events when concatenating two instruction sequences P and Q

cycle	ev[j]	JISR	full.3	full.4	M	WB
$T-1$	0	0	1		I_p	
$T = \hat{t}$	1	1	1	1	I_{p+1}	I_p
$T+1$	1	0	0	0	$-$	$-$
...	1	0	0	0	$-$	$-$
$t-1$	1	0	1	0	J_0	$-$
t	1	0		1		J_0

The proofs dealing with the admissibility of the ISR (section 5.4) only argue about signal *JISR* and the values of the registers and memories visible to the assembler programmer, i.e., the general and special purpose register files, the two PCs and the two memories IM and DM:

$$C = \{GPR[0], \ldots GPR[31], SPR[0], \ldots, SPR[5], PC', DPC, DM, IM\}.$$

For the simulation, signal *JISR* and the contents of storage C are therefore of special interest.

Let $P = I_0, \ldots, I_p, \ldots, I_{p+\delta}$ and $P' = I_0, \ldots, I_p$ be two instruction sequences ◄ Theorem 5.11
extended by a sequence of external events, as defined above. Sequence P is processed by the pipelined design DLX_Π and P' by the sequential design DLX_Σ. Let instruction I_0 be preceded by JISR

$$JISR_\Sigma^{-1} = 1 \quad and \quad JISR_\Pi^0 = 1,$$

and let both designs start in the same configuration, i.e.,

$$\forall R \in C \quad R_\Sigma^0 = R_\Pi^1.$$

Let T_p and T_p' denote the cycles in which I_p is processed in the write back stage

$$I_\Pi(4, T_p) = I_\Sigma(4, T_p') = p \wedge ue.4_\Pi^{T_p} = 1.$$

The initial PCs then have values $PC'^0_\Sigma = SISR + 4$ and $DPC_\Sigma^0 = SISR$. For any instruction $I_i \in P'$, any stage k, and any two cycles T, T' with

$$I_\Pi(k, T) = I_\Sigma(k, T') = i \wedge ue.k_\Pi^T = 1$$

the following two claims hold:

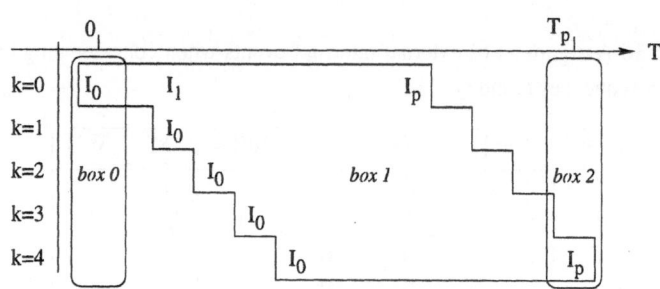

Figure 5.20 Pairs (k, T) of the pipelined execution. Box 0 is covered by the hypothesis of the simulation theorem, the boxes 1 and 2 correspond to the claims 1 and 2.

1. (a) *for all signals S in stage k which are inputs to a register $R \in$ out(k) that is updated at the end of cycle T:*

$$S_\Pi^T = S_\Sigma^{T'},$$

(b) *for all registers $R \in$ out(k) which are visible or updated at the end of cycle T:*

$$R_\Pi^{T+1} = R_\Sigma^{T'+1} = \begin{cases} R_i^u & if \quad T < T_p \\ R_i & if \quad T = T_p, \end{cases}$$

(c) *for any cell M of the data memory DM and $k = 3$:*

$$M_\Pi^{T+1} = M_\Sigma^{T'+1} = M_i,$$

2. *and for any $R \in C$ and $T = T_p$*

$$R_\Pi^{T+1} = R_\Sigma^{T'+1} = R_p.$$

With respect to the pipelined execution, there are three types of pairs (k, T) for which the values S^T and R^{T+1} of the signals S and output registers R of stage k are of interest (figure 5.20):

- For the first cycle, the theorem makes an assumption about the contents of all registers and memories $R \in C$ independent of the stage they belong to (box 0).

- Claim 1 covers all the pairs (k, T) for which $I_\Pi(k, T)$ is defined and lies between 0 and p (box 1).

Table 5.17 Start of the execution after reset or JISR respectively

T'	DLX$_\sigma$			DLX$_\Sigma$			
	reset	ue[0:4]	full[0:4]	reset	JISR	ue[0:4]	full[0:4]
-2				1	*	*	*
-1	1	*	*	0	1	00001	00001
0	0	10000	10000	0	0	10000	10000
1	0	01000	01000	0	0	01000	01000
2	0	00100	00100	0	0	00100	00100
3	0	00010	00010	0	0	00010	00010
4	0	00001	00001	0	0	00001	00001
5	0	10000	10000	0	0	10000	10000

T	DLX$_\pi$			DLX$_\Pi$			
	reset	ue[0:4]	full[2:4]	reset	JISR	ue[0:4]	full[2:4]
-1				1	*	*	*
0	1	10000	*	0	1	10001	**1
1	0	11000	000	0	0	11000	000
2	0	11100	100	0	0	11100	100
3	0	11110	110	0	0	11110	110
4	0	11111	111	0	0	11111	111

- For the final cycle T_p, claim 2 covers all the registers and memories $R \in C$ independent of the stage they belong to (box 2).

The above theorem and the simulation theorem 4.11 of the DLX design without interrupt handling are very similar. Thus, it should be possible to largely reuse the proof of theorem 4.11. Signal *JISR* of the designs DLX_Σ and DLX_Π is the counterpart of signal *reset* in the designs DLX_σ and DLX_π. This pair of signals is used to initialize the PC environment and they mark the start of the execution. In the sequential designs, the execution is started in cycle -1, whereas in the pipelined designs, it is started in cycle 0:

$$reset_\sigma^{-1} = JISR_\Sigma^{-1} = JISR_\Pi^0 = reset_\pi^0 = 1.$$

Proof of Theorem 5.11   PROOF

Claim 1 is proven by induction on the cycles T of the pipelined execution, but we only present the arguments which are different from those used in the proof of theorem 4.11. The original proof strongly relies on the dateline lemma 4.3 and on the stall engines (the scheduling functions).

Except for the initial cycle, the stall engines of the two sequential designs produce identical outputs (table 5.17). The same is true for the stall engines of the two pipelined designs. For the initial cycle $T = 0$, the pipelined scheduling function is only defined for stage $k = 0$:

$$I_\Pi(0,0) = I_\Sigma(0,1) = 0.$$

Stage 0 has the instruction memory and its address as inputs. In the pipelined design, IM is addressed by dpc, whereas in the sequential design it is addressed by register DPC. Since

$$DPCce = PCce \wedge ue.1 \vee JISR,$$

it follows from the hypothesis of the theorem and the update enable flags that

$$dpc_\Pi^0 = DPC_\Pi^1 = DPC_\Sigma^0 = DPC_\Sigma^1.$$

The memory IM is read-only and therefore keeps its initial contents. Thus, on design DLX_Π in cycle $T = 0$ stage 0 has the same inputs as on design DLX_Σ in cycle $T' = 1$.

Note that the stages k of the designs DLX_Σ and DLX_Π generate the same signals S and update their output registers in the same way, given that they get identical inputs. This also applies to the data memory DM and its write request signal $Dmw'.3$ which in either design is disabled if the instruction encounters a page fault on fetch. Thus, with the new dateline lemma 5.9, the induction proof of claim 1 can be completed as before.

Claim 2 is new and therefore requires a full proof. For the output registers of stage 4, claim 1 already implies claim 2. Furthermore, in the designs DLX_Σ and DLX_Π, the instruction memory is never updated. Thus, claim 2 only needs to be proven for the two program counters PC' and DPC, and for the data memory DM.

The instruction sequence P' of the sequential design was constructed such that instruction I_p causes an interrupt. Since signal $JISR$ is generated in stage 4, claim 1 implies

$$JISR_\Sigma^{T'_p} = JISR_\Pi^{T_p} = 1.$$

In either design, the two PCs are initialized on an active $JISR$ signal, and therefore

$$DPC_\Sigma^{T'_p+1} = SISR = DPC_\Pi^{T_p+1}$$
$$PC'^{T'_p+1}_\Sigma = SISR+4 = PC'^{T_p+1}_\Pi.$$

The data memory DM belongs to the set $out(3)$. For stage 3, the two scheduling functions imply

$$I_\Pi(3, T_p - 1) = I_\Sigma(3, T'_p - 1) = p.$$

In the sequential design, the data memory is only updated when the instruction is in stage 3, i.e., when $full.3 = 1$. Claim 1 then implies that

$$DM_{\Pi}^{T_p} = DM_{\Sigma}^{T'_p} = DM_p.$$

JISR is only signaled if $full.4 = 1$. For cycle T'_p, the sequential stall engine then implies that

$$full.3_{\Sigma}^{T'_p} = 1 \quad \text{and} \quad Dmw_{\Sigma}^{T'_p} = 0.$$

Thus, the data memory is not updated during JISR, and therefore

$$DM_{\Sigma}^{T'_p} = DM_{\Sigma}^{T'_p+1}.$$

In the pipelined design, the write enable signal of the data memory is generated as

$$Dmw.3 = Dmw'.3 \wedge full.3 \wedge (JISR \text{ NOR } reset).$$

Since signal $Dmw.3$ is disabled on an active $JISR$ signal, the data memory is not updated during cycle T_p, and therefore,

$$DM_{\Pi}^{T_p+1} = DM_{\Pi}^{T_p}.$$

That completes the proof of claim 2.   QED

We will now consider an arbitrary instruction sequence Q, which is processed by the pipelined DLX design, and which is interrupted by several non-aborting interrupts. Such a sequence Q can be broken down into several uninterrupted subsequences

$$P_i = I_{(i,0)}, \ldots, I_{(i,p_i)}, \ldots, I_{(i,p_i+\delta_i)}.$$

This means that for any sequence P_i, instruction $I_{(i,0)}$ is preceded by JISR, $I_{(i,p_i)}$ is the only instruction of P_i which causes an interrupt, and instruction $I_{(i,p_i+\delta_i)}$ is the last instruction fetched before the jump to the ISR. For the sequential execution, we consider the instruction sequence $Q' = P'_1, P'_2, \ldots$ which is derived from sequence Q by dropping the instructions evicted by JISR, i.e.,

$$P'_i = I_{(i,0)}, \ldots, I_{(i,p_i)}.$$

The external interrupt events are assigned as before. The scheduling functions are extended in an obvious way. For the designs DLX_Σ and DLX_Π,

$$I_\Sigma(k,T) = (i,j) \quad \text{and} \quad I_\Pi(k,T) = (i,j)$$

denote that in cycle T pipeline stage k processes instruction $I_{(i,j)}$.

Like the two DLX designs without interrupt hardware, the designs DLX_Σ and DLX_Π are started by reset and not by JISR. Lemmas 5.8 and 5.10 imply that after reset, both designs come up gracefully; one cycle after reset $JISR = 1$ and the designs initiate a jump to ISR(0). Thus, we can now formulate the general simulation theorem for the designs DLX_Σ and DLX_Π:

Theorem 5.12 ▶ *Let $Q = P_1, P_2, \ldots$ and $Q' = P'_1, P'_2, \ldots$ be two instruction sequences extended by a sequence of external events, as defined above. Sequence Q is processed by the pipelined design DLX_Π and Q' by the sequential design DLX_Σ. In the sequential execution, reset is given in cycle -2, whereas in the pipelined execution, reset is given in cycle -1:*

$$reset_\Sigma^{-2} = 1 = reset_\Pi^{-1}.$$

Let both designs be started with identical contents, i.e., any *register and memory R of the data paths satisfies*

$$R_\Sigma^{-1} = R_\Pi^0, \qquad (5.4)$$

and let the first instruction $I_{(1,0)}$ be preceded by JISR

$$JISR_\Sigma^{-1} = 1 = JISR_\Pi^0.$$

For every pair (P_i, P'_i) of subsequences, the DLX_Π design processing P_i then simulates the DLX_Σ design on P'_i in the sense of theorem 5.11.

PROOF   As shown in the proof of theorem 5.11 claim 2, both designs initialize the PCs on JISR in the same way, thus

$$(PC', DPC)_\Sigma^0 = (PC', DPC)_\Pi^1.$$

The instruction memory is ready-only, and the update of the data memory is disabled on $ue.3 = 0$. Table 5.17 and equation 5.4 therefore imply

$$(IM, DM)_\Sigma^0 = (IM, DM)_\Pi^1.$$

In either design, the output registers of stage 4 are updated during JISR. Since stage 4 gets identical inputs it also produces identical outputs. Thus,

$$\forall R \in C \quad R_\Sigma^0 = R_\Pi^1,$$

and for the subsequences P_1 and P'_1 simulation theorem 5.11 is applicable. Since instruction $I_{(1,p_1)}$ causes an interrupt, claim 2 of theorem 5.11 implies that during the cycles T_1 and T'_1 with

$$I_\Pi(4, T_1) = (1, p_1) \quad \text{and} \quad I_\Sigma(4, T'_1) = (1, p_1)$$

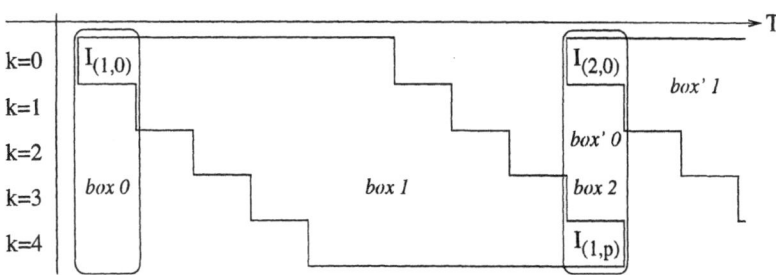

Figure 5.21 Scheduling of the first two subsequences P_1, P_2 for the pipelined execution of sequence Q

the two designs are in the same configuration, i.e.,

$$\forall R \in C \quad R_\Sigma^{T_1'+1} = R_\Pi^{T_1+1}. \qquad (5.5)$$

In the sequential execution, the next subsequence is stared one cycle after JISR, i.e.,

$$I_\Sigma(4, T_i') = (i, p_i) \quad \rightarrow \quad JISR_\Sigma^{T_i'} = 1 \wedge I_\Sigma(0, T_i' + 1) = (i+1, 0),$$

whereas in the pipelined execution, the next subsequence is already started during JISR, i.e.,

$$I_\Pi(4, T_i) = (i, p_i) \quad \rightarrow \quad JISR_\Pi^{T_i} = 1 \wedge I_\Pi(0, T_i) = (i+1, 0).$$

For the first two subsequences, figure 5.21 illustrates this scheduling behavior.

Thus, cycle $T_1' + 1$ corresponds to the cycle 0 of the sequential execution of P_2', and that cycle $T_1 + 1$ corresponds to the cycle 1 of the pipelined execution of P_2. Equation 5.5 then implies that the subsequences P_2 and P_2' are started in the same configuration, and that theorem 5.11 can be applied.

With the same arguments, the theorem follows by induction on the subsequences of Q and Q'. QED

5.8 Selected References and Further Reading

INTERRUPT SERVICE routines which are not nested are, for example, described in [PH94]. Mechanisms for nested interrupts are treated in [MP95] for sequential machines and in [Knu96] for pipelined machines.

5.9 Exercises

Exercise 5.1 Let t_1 and t_2 be cycles of machine DLX_Π, and let $t_1 < t_2$. Suppose external interrupts i and j are both enabled, interrupt i becomes active in cycle t_1, interrupt j becomes active in cycle t_2, and no other interrupts are serviced or pending in cycle t_2.

1. Show that it is possible that interrupt j is serviced before interrupt i.

2. Why does this not constitute a counterexample for the correctness proof?

Exercise 5.2 **Invalid address exception**. Two addresses are stored in special purpose registers UP and LOW. A maskable exception of type abort has to be signalled, if a memory location below LOW or above UP is accessed.

1. Design the hardware for this exception.

2. Design the forwarding mechanism for the registers UP and LOW.

3. Determine the effect on the cost and the cycle time.

Exercise 5.3 **Protected mode**. We want to run the machine in two modes, namely protected mode and user mode. Only the operating system should run in protected mode.

1. Design an interrupt mechanism for a mode exception which is activated if a change of the following values is attempted in user mode: $mode$, UP, LOW, the mask bits for the mode exception and the invalid address exception.

2. Is it possible to merge the invalid address exception and the mode exception into a single exception?

3. What should be the priorities of the new exception(s)?

4. How is the correctness proof affected?

Exercise 5.4 **Protection of the interrupt stack.**

1. Design an interrupt mechanism, where the interrupt stack can only be accessed by the operating system; the code segments SAVE and RESTORE are part of the operating system.

2. What requirements for the interrupt service routine from the correctness proof can be guaranteed by the operating system?

3. What requirements for the interrupt service routine cannot be guaranteed by the operating system alone?

Exercise 5.5 Suppose we want to make the misaligned exception of type repeat.

1. Sketch an exception handler which fetches the required data.
2. What should be the priority of such an exception?
3. How is the correctness proof affected?

Chapter 6

Memory System Design

ONE WAY to improve the performance of an architecture, is trying to increase the instruction throughput, for example by pipelining, but that calls for a fast memory system, as the analysis of section 4.6.5 has turned out.

Thus, users would like to have a very large (or even unlimited) amount of fast and cheap memory, but that is unrealistic. In general, only small RAM is fast, and fast RAMs are more expensive than slower ones. In this chapter we therefore study the key concept for designing a memory system with high bandwidth, low latency, high capacity, and reasonable cost.

The pipelined DLX design requires two memory ports, one port for instruction fetch and the second port for data accesses. Since the sequential DLX design can manage with just one memory port, we first develop a fast memory system based on the sequential DLX architecture. In section 6.5, we then integrate the memory system into the pipelined DLX design.

6.1   A Monolithic Memory Design

IN THE simplest case, the memory system is monolithic, i.e., it just comprises a single level. This memory block can be realized on-chip or off-chip, in static RAM (SRAM) or in dynamic RAM (DRAM). DRAM is about 4 to 10 times cheaper and slower than SRAM and can have a 2 to 4 times higher storage capacity [Ng92]. We therefore model the cost and delay of DRAM as

$$C_{DRAM}(A,d) = C_{SRAM}(A,d)/\alpha$$
$$D_{DRAM}(A,d) = \alpha \cdot D_{SRAM}(A,d),$$

with $\alpha \in \{4, 8, 16\}$. Thus, on-chip SRAM yields the fastest memory system, but that solution has special drawbacks, as will be shown now.

6.1.1 The Limits of On-chip RAM

Chapter 3 describes the sequential design of a DLX fixed point core. The main memory is treated as a black box which has basically the functionality of a RAM; its temporal behavior is modeled by two parameters, the (minimal) memory access time d_{mem} and the memory status time d_{mstat}.

All CPU internal actions of this DLX design require a cycle time of $\tau_{CPU} = 70$ gate delays, whereas the memory access takes $T_M = 18 + d_{mem}$ delays. If a memory access is performed in $1 + W$ cycles, then the whole DLX fixed point unit can run at a cycle time of

$$\tau_{DLX} = \max\left\{\tau_{CPU}, \left\lceil \frac{T_M}{W+1} \right\rceil\right\}. \tag{6.1}$$

The parameter W denotes the number of wait states. From a performance point of view, it is desirable to run the memory without wait states and at the speed of the CPU, i.e.,

$$T_M = 18 + d_{mem} \leq \tau_{CPU} = 70. \tag{6.2}$$

Under these constraints, the memory access time d_{mem} can be at most 52 gate delays. On-chip SRAM is the fastest memory available. According to our hardware model, such an SRAM with A entries of d bits each has the following cost and access time

$$C_{SRAM}(A,d) = 2 \cdot (A+3) \cdot (d + \log\log d)$$
$$D_{SRAM}(A,d) = 3 \cdot \log A + 10, \quad \text{if } A > 64.$$

The main memory of the DLX is organized in four banks, each of which is one byte wide. If each bank is realized as an SRAM, then equation (6.2) limits the size of the memory to

$$4 \cdot A = 4 \cdot 2^{\lfloor (52-10)/3 \rfloor} = 2^{16} \text{ bytes.}$$

That is much to small for main memory. Nevertheless, these 64 kilo bytes of memory already require 1.3 million gates. That is roughly 110 times the

Table 6.1 Signals of the bus protocol

signal			type	CPU	memory
MDat	data of the memory access		bidirectional	write read	read write
MAd	memory address		unidirectional	write	read
burst	burst transfer	status flag	unidirectional	write	read
w/r	write/read flag				
BE	byte enable flags				
req	request access	hand-shake	unidirectional	write	read
reqp	request pending			read	write
Brdy	bus ready				

cost of the whole DLX fixed point core ($C_{DLX} = 11951$). Thus, a large, monolithic memory system must be implemented *off-chip*, and a memory access then definitely takes several CPU cycles. The access time of the main memory depends on many factors, like the memory address and the preceding requests. In case of DRAMs, the memory also requires some time for internal administration, the so called *refresh cycles*. Thus, the main memory has a non-uniform access time, and in general, the processor cannot foresee how many cycles a particular access will take. Processor and main memory therefore communicate via a bus.

6.1.2 A Synchronous Bus Protocol

There exist plenty of bus protocols; some are synchronous, the others are asynchronous. In a synchronous protocol, memory and processor have a common clock. That simplifies matters considerably. Our memory designs therefore uses a synchronous bus protocol similar to the pipelined protocol of the INTEL Pentium processor [Int95].

The bus signals comprise the address *MAd* and the data *MDat* of the memory access, the status flags specifying the type of the access, and the handshake signals coordinating the transfer. The data lines *MDat* are bidirectional, i.e., they can be read and written by both devices, the processor and the memory system. The remaining bus lines are unidirectional; they are written by one device and read by the other (table 6.1). The protocol uses the three handshake signals request (*req*), request pending (*reqp*), and bus ready (*Brdy*) with the following meaning:

- *Request* is generated by the processor. This signal indicates that a new transfer should be started. The type of the access is specified by some status flags.

- *Request Pending reqp* is generated by the main memory. An active signal $reqp = 1$ indicates that the main memory is currently busy performing an access and cannot accept a new request.

- *Bus Ready* is also generated by the main memory. On a read access, an active bus ready signal $(Brdy = 1)$ indicates that there are valid data on the bus MDat. On a write access, an active bus ready signal indicates that the main memory no longer needs the data MDat.

The main memory provides its handshake signals *reqp* and *Brdy* one cycle ahead. That leaves the processor more time for the administration of the bus. During the refresh cycles, the main memory does not need the bus. Thus, the processor can already start a new request but the main memory will not respond $(reqp = 1, Brdy = 0)$ until the refresh is finished.

Bus Convention
The data unit to be transferred on the bus is called *bus word*. In our memory design, the bus word corresponds to the amount of data which the processor can handle in a single cycle. In this monograph, the bus width is either 32 bits or 64 bits. The memory system should be able to update subwords (e.g., a single byte) and not just a whole bus word. On a write access, each byte i of the bus word is therefore accompanied by an enable bit BE_i.

On a burst transfer, which is indicated by an active *burst* flag, MAd specifies the address of the first bus word. The following bus words are referenced at consecutive addresses. The bus word count *bwc* specifies the number of bus words to be transferred. Our protocol supports burst reads and burst writes. All the bursts have a fixed length, i.e., they all transfer the same amount of data. Thus, the *bwc* bits can be omitted; the *status flags* of the bus protocol comprise the write/read flag w/r, the *burst* flag, and the byte enable flags BE.

Read Bus Transfers
Figure 6.1 depicts the idealized timing of the bus protocol on a single-word read transfer $(burst = 0)$ followed by a fast burst read $(burst = 1)$. The two transfers are overlapped by one cycle.

In order to initiate a read access, the processor raises the request signal *req* for one cycle and pulls the write/read signal to zero, $w/r = 0$. In the same cycle, the processor provides the address MAd and the burst flag to the memory. The width *bwc* of the access can be derived from the burst

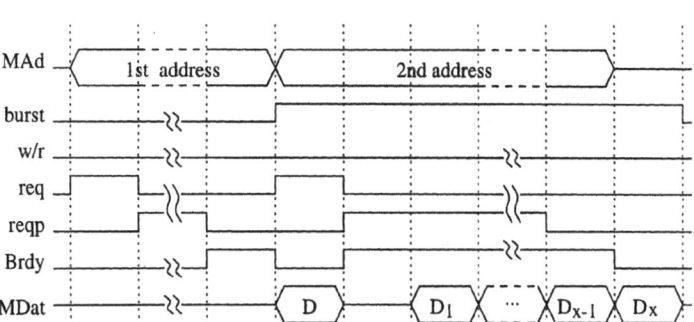

Figure 6.1 A single-word read transfer followed by a fast x-word burst read. On a fast read transfer, the cycle marked with * is omitted.

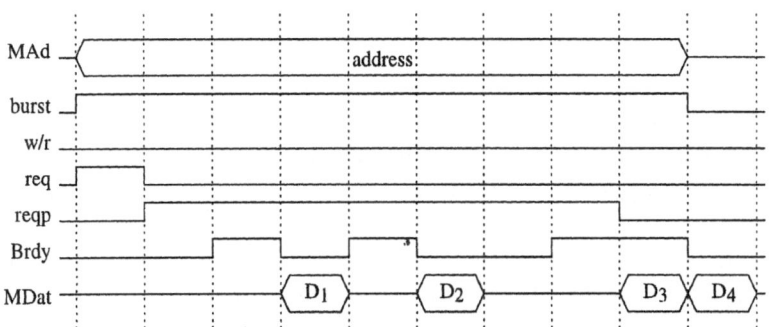

Figure 6.2 A 4-2-3-1 read burst transfer

flag. The memory announces the data by an active bus ready signal $Brdy = 1$, one cycle ahead of time. After a request, it can take several cycles till the data is put on the bus. During this time, the memory signals with $repq = 1$ that it is performing an access. This signal is raised one cycle after the request and stays active ($repq = 1$) till one cycle before a new request is allowed. The processor turns the address and the status signals off one cycle after $req = 0$. A new read access can be started one cycle after $req = 0$ and $reqp = 0$.

On a burst read any of the bus words can be delayed by some cycles, not just the first one. In this case, the Brdy line toggles between 0 and 1. The burst transfer of figure 6.2 has a 4-2-3-1 access pattern; the first bus word arrives in the fourth cycle, the second word arrives two cycles later, and so on. The fastest read access supported by this protocol takes $2 + bwc$ bus cycles. The first word already arrives two cycles after the request.

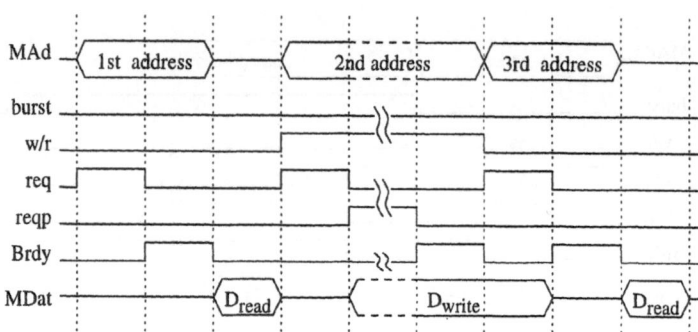

Figure 6.3 Fast read transfer followed by a write transfer and another read.

Write Bus Transfers

Figure 6.3 depicts the idealized timing of the bus protocol on a fast read followed by a write and another fast read. The write transfer starts in the fourth cycle.

In order to initiate a write transfer, the processor raises the request line *req* for one cycle, it raises the write/read line and puts the address *MAd*, the burst flag *burst* and the byte enable flags *BE* on the bus. In the second cycle, the (first) bus word is transferred. The memory signals with $Brdy = 1$ that it needs the current data MDat for just one more cycle.

Like on a read access, signal *reqp* is turned on one cycle after the request if the transfer takes more than 3 cycles. One cycle before the memory can accept a new access, it turns signal *reqp* off. One cycle later, the processor turns the address and the status signals off.

On a write burst transfer, each of the bus words can be delayed by some cycles. The burst write of figure 6.4 performs a 4-2-1-1 transfer. The fastest write transfer supported by this protocol takes $bwc + 2$ bus cycles.

Back to Back Transfers

The bus protocol supports that two succeeding transfers can be overlapped by one cycle. However, when switching between reads and writes, the data bus MDat must be disabled for at least one cycle in order to prevent bus contention. On a write transfer, the processor uses the MDat bus from the second to the last cycle, whereas on a read transfer, the bus MDat is used in the third cycle at the earliest. Thus, a read transfer can be overlapped with any preceding transfer, but a write transfer can only be overlapped with a preceding write. At best, the processor can start a new read transfer one cycle after

$$req = 0 \land reqp = 0,$$

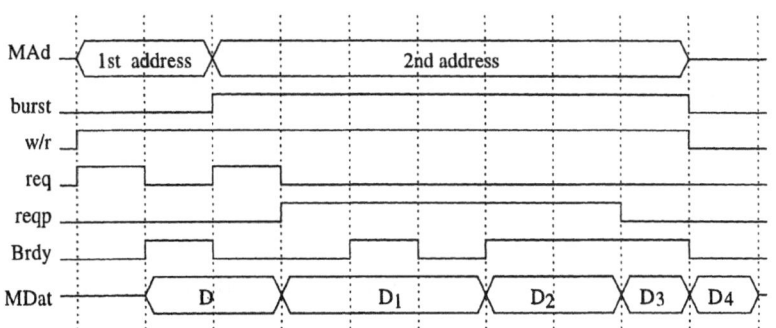

Figure 6.4 Fast single-word write transfer followed by a 4-2-1-1 burst write.

and it can start a new write transfer one cycle after

$$req = 0 \land reqp = 0 \land (w/r = 0 \lor Brdy = 0).$$

6.1.3 Sequential DLX with Off-Chip Main Memory

In this section, we connect the sequential DLX design of chapter 3 to a 64 MB (Mega Byte) off-chip memory, using the bus protocol of section 6.1.2. This modification of the memory system only impacts the implementation of the memory environment and its control. The other environments of the DLX design remain unchanged.

Moreover, the global functionality of the memory system and its interaction with the data paths and main control of the design also remains the same. The memory system is still controlled by the read and write signals mr and mw, and by the opcode bits $IR[27:26]$ which specify the width of the access. On a read, the memory system provides the memory word

$$MDout[31:0] \; = \; Mword[\langle MA[31:2]00 \rangle],$$

whereas on a d-byte write access with address $e = \langle MA[31:0] \rangle$ and offset $o = \langle MA[1:0] \rangle$, the memory system performs the update

$$M[e+d-1:e] \; := \; byte_{[o+d-1:o]}(MDin).$$

With $mbusy = 1$, the memory systems signals the DLX core that it cannot complete the access in the current cycle.

Implementation of the Memory System
So far, the memory environment, i.e., the data paths of the memory system, consists of four memory banks, each of which is a RAM of one byte width

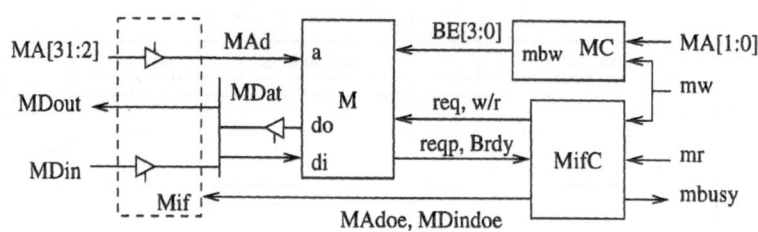

Figure 6.5 Memory system of the DLX with off-chip memory

(figure 3.11). Based on the control signals and the offset, the memory control MC generates the bank write signals mbw[3:0] which enable the update of the memory (figure 3.12).

Now the memory system (figure 6.5) consists of the off-chip main memory M, the memory interface Mif, the memory interface control $MifC$, and the original memory control MC. The memory interface connects the memory M to the data paths.

The memory of the 32-bit DLX architecture is byte addressable, but all reads and the majority of the writes are four bytes (one word) wide. Thus, the data bus $MDat$ between the processor and the main memory can be made one to four bytes wide. On a one-byte bus, half word and word accesses require a burst access and take at least one to three cycles longer than on a four-byte bus. In order to make the common case fast, we use a four-byte data bus. On a write transfer, the 32-bit data are accompanied by four byte enable flags $BE[3:0]$. Since bursts are not needed, we restrict the bus protocol to single-word transfers.

Memory Interface The memory interface Mif which connects the data paths to the memory bus and the external memory uses 32-bit address and data lines. Interface Mif forwards the data from the memory bus MDat to the data output MDout. On $MAdoe = 1$, the interface puts the address MA on the address bus MAd, and on $MDindoe = 1$ it puts the data MDin on the bus MDat.

Except for the memory interface Mif, the data paths of environment Menv are off-chip and are therefore not captured in the cost model. Thus,

$$C_{Menv} = C_{Mif} = 2 \cdot C_{driv}(32).$$

Off-Chip Memory The off-chip memory M obeys the protocol of section 6.1.2. On a read access requested by $req = 1$ and $w/r = 0$, it provides the data

$$MDat[31:0] = Mword[\langle MAd[31:2]00 \rangle].$$

On a write access ($w/r = 1$), the memory performs the update

$$Mword[\langle MAd[31:2]00\rangle] := X_3, X_2, X_1, X_0,$$

where for $i \in \{0, \ldots, 3\}$ the byte X_i is obtained as

$$X_i = \begin{cases} M[\langle MAd[31:2]00\rangle + i] & \text{if} \quad BE[i] = 0 \\ byte_i(MDat) & \text{if} \quad BE[i] = 1. \end{cases}$$

Memory Interface Control The memory interface control MifC controls the tristate drivers of the memory interface and generates the handshake signal *req* and the signals w/r and *mbusy* according to the bus protocol of section 6.1.2. In the sequential DLX design, transfers are never overlapped, and the address on bus MAd is always provided by the same source MA. The bus protocol can therefore be simplified; the address MA and signal w/r are put on the bus during the *whole* transfer.

In the FSD of the main control (figure 3.20) there are three states performing a memory access, namely fetch, load and store. The only combination of accesses which are performed directly one after another is store - fetch. In the first two cycles of a read access, bus MDat is not used. Thus, the memory interface can already put the data on the bus MDat during the first cycle of the write transfer without risking any bus contention. The control MifC can therefore generate the enable signals and the write/read signal as

$$\begin{aligned} w/r &= mw \\ MAdoe &= mem = mr \lor mw \\ MDindoe &= mw. \end{aligned}$$

The handshake signals are more complicated. Signal *req* is only active during the first cycle of the access, and signal *mbusy* is always active except during the last cycle of the transfer. Thus, for the control MifC a single transfer is performed in three steps. In the first step, MifC starts the off-chip transfer as soon as $reqp = 0$. In the second step, which usually takes several cycles, MifC waits till the memory signals $Brdy = 1$. In the third step, the transfer is terminated. In addition, MifC has to ensure that a new request is only started if in the previous cycle the signals *reqp* and *Brdy* were inactive. Since the accesses are not overlapped, this condition is satisfied even without special precautions.

The signals *req* and *mbusy* are generated by a Mealy automaton which is modeled by the FSD of figure 6.6 and table 6.2. According to section 2.6, cost and delay of the automaton depend on the parameters listed in

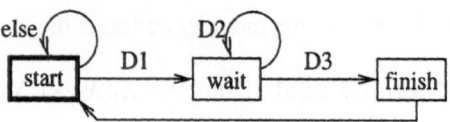

Figure 6.6 FSD underlying the Mealy automaton MifC; the initial state is *start*.

Table 6.2 Disjunctive normal forms DNF of the Mealy automaton of MifC

DNF	source state	target state	monomial $m \in M$	length $l(m)$
D1	start	wait	mem	1
D2	wait	wait	/Brdy	1
D3	wait	finish	Brdy	1

DNF	mealy signal	state	$m \in M$	$l(m)$
D1	req	start	mem	(1)
D4	mbusy	start	mem	(1)
		wait	1	0

table 6.3 and on the accumulated delay of its inputs *Brdy* and *mem*. Let $C_{Mealy}(MifC)$ denote the cost of the automaton, then

$$C_{MifC} = C_{Mealy}(MifC) + C_{or}.$$

The input *Brdy* only affects the next state of the automaton, but input *mem* also affects the computation of the Mealy outputs. Let the main memory provide the handshake signals with an accumulated delay of $A_M(Brdy)$, and let the bus have a delay of d_{bus}. The inputs and outputs of the automaton then have the following delays:

$$A_{in}(MifC) = A_M(Brdy) + d_{bus} \quad \text{(next state)}$$
$$A_{in(1)}(MifC) = A_{CON}(mw, mr) + D_{or} \quad \text{(outputs only)}$$
$$A_{MifC} = A_{Mealy}(out).$$

Cost and Delay

Table 6.4 lists the cost of the DLX design and of the environments affected by the change of the memory interface. The new memory interface is fairly cheap and therefore has only a minor impact on the cost of the whole DLX design.

Table 6.3 Parameters of the Mealy automaton used in the control MifC

# states	# inputs	# and frequency of outputs		
k	σ	γ	v_{sum}	v_{max}
3	2	2	3	2
fanin of the states		# and length of monomials		
fan_{max}	fan_{sum}	#M	l_{sum}	l_{max}
2	3	3	3	1

Table 6.4 Cost of the memory interface Mif, of the data paths DP, of the control CON and of the whole DLX for the two memory interfaces.

	Mif	DP	CON	DLX
old memory interface	–	10846	1105	11951
new memory interface	320	11166	1170	12336
increase [%]		+3	+6	+3

Cycle Time The cycle time τ_{DLX} of the DLX design is the maximum of three times, namely: the cycle time T_{CON} required by the control unit, the time T_M of a memory access, and the time T_{DP} for all CPU internal cycles.

$$\tau_{DLX} = \max\{T_{CON}, T_M, T_{DP}\}$$

The connection of the DLX to an off-chip memory system only affects the memory environment and the memory control. Thus, the formula of T_{CON} and T_M need to be adapted, whereas the formula of T_{DP} remains unchanged.

So far, time T_{CON} accounted for the update of the main control automaton (T_{auto}) and for the cycle time T_{stall} of the stall engine. The handling of the bus protocol requires a Mealy automaton, which needs to be updated as well; that takes $T_{Mealy}(MifC)$ delays. In addition, the new automaton provides signal $mbusy$ to the stall engine. Therefore,

$$T_{stall} = A_{MifC} + D_{stall} + \max\{D_{ram3}(32,32), D_{ff}\} + \delta$$

and the control unit now requires a minimal cycle time of

$$T_{CON} \doteq \max\{T_{auto}, T_{stall}, T_{Mealy}(MifC)\}.$$

Timing of Memory Accesses The delay formula of a memory access changes in a major way. For the timing, we assume that the off-chip memory is controlled by an automaton which precomputes its outputs. We further assume that the control inputs which the off-chip memory receives through the memory bus add d_{Mhsh} (memory handshake) delays to the cycle time of its automaton.

The memory interface starts the transfer by sending the address and the request signal *req* to the off-chip memory. The handshake signals of the DLX processor are valid A_{MifC} delays after the start of the cycle. Forwarding signal *req* and address *MA* to the memory bus and off-chip takes another $D_{driv} + d_{bus}$ delays, and the processing of the handshake signals adds d_{Mhsh} delays. Thus, the transfer request takes

$$T_{Mreq} = A_{MifC} + D_{driv} + d_{bus} + d_{Mhsh} + \Delta.$$

After the request, the memory performs the actual access. On a read access, the memory reads the memory word, which on a 64 MB memory takes $D_{MM}(64MB)$ gate delays. The memory then puts the data on the bus through a tristate driver. The memory interface receives the data and forwards them to the data paths where they are clocked into registers. The read cycle therefore takes at least

$$T_{Mread} \quad = \quad D_{MM}(64MB) + D_{driv} + d_{bus} + \Delta.$$

In case of a write access, the memory interface first requests a transfer. In the following cycles, the memory interface sends the data MDin and the byte enable bits. Once the off-chip memory receives these data, it performs the access. The cycle time of the actual write access (without the memory request) can be estimated as

$$T_{Mwrite} \quad = \quad \max\{A_{MC}, A_{MifC} + D_{driv}\} + d_{bus} + D_{MM}(64MB) + \delta$$
$$T_{Maccess} \quad = \quad \max\{T_{Mwrite}, T_{Mread}\} \ = \ T_{Mwrite}.$$

Table 6.5 lists the cycle times of the data paths and control, as well as the access and request time of the memory system, assuming a bus delay of $d_{bus} = 15$ and $d_{Mhsh} = 10$. The access time of the memory depends on the version of the DRAM used.

The control and the memory transfer time are less time critical. They can tolerate a bus delay and handshake delay of $d_{bus} + d_{Mhsh} = 56$ before they slow down the DLX processor. However, the actual memory access takes much longer than the other cycles, even with the fastest DRAM ($\alpha = 4$). In order to achieve a reasonable processor cycle time, the actual memory access is performed in W cycles; the whole transfer takes $W + 1$ cycles.

Table 6.5 Cycle time of the DLX design and of its main parts, which are the data paths DP, the control unit CON and the memory system MM.

T_{DP}	T_{CON}		T_{Mreq}	$T_{Maccess}$		
	$\max\{A,$	$B\}$		$\alpha = 4$	$\alpha = 8$	$\alpha = 16$
70	$13 + d_{bus}$ $= 28$	42	$14 + d_{bus} + d_{Mhsh}$ $= 39$	355	683	1339

The DLX design with a direct connection to the off-chip memory can then be operated at a cycle time of

$$\tau_{DLX}(W) = \max\{T_{DP}, T_{CON}, T_M(W)\}$$

$$T_M(W) = \max\{T_{Mreq}, \lceil T_{Maccess}/W \rceil\}.$$

Increasing the number W of wait states improves the cycle time of the DLX design, at least till $W = \lceil T_{Maccess}/T_{DP} \rceil$. For larger W, the main memory is no longer time critical, and a further increase of the wait states has no impact on the cycle time.

According to section 4.6, the performance is modeled by the reciprocal of a benchmark's execution time, and on a sequential DLX design, the run time of a benchmark Be is the product of the instruction count $IC(Be)$ of the benchmark, of the average cycles per instruction CPI, and of the cycle time τ_{DLX}:

$$T_{DLX}(Be) = IC(Be) \cdot CPI(Be, W) \cdot \tau_{DLX}(W).$$

Increasing the number of wait states improves the cycle time, but is also increases the CPI ratio. Thus, there is a trade-off between cycle time and cycle count which we now quantify based on SPECint92 benchmark workloads. Table 6.6 lists the DLX instruction mix of these workloads and the number of cycles required per instruction. According to formula (4.8) from section 4.6, the benchmarks compress and li and the average SPECint92 workload, for example, achieve the following CPI ratios:

$$CPI(\text{compress}) = 4.19 + 1.25 \cdot W$$

$$CPI(\text{li}) = 4.38 + 1.49 \cdot W$$

$$CPI(\text{SPECint}) = 4.26 + 1.34 \cdot W.$$

We increase the number of wait states W from 1 to $\lceil T_{Maccess}/T_{DP} \rceil$ and study the impact on the cycle time, on the CPI ratio and on the run time of

Table 6.6 DLX instruction mix for the SPECint92 programs and for the average workload. CPI_I denotes the average number of cycles required by instruction I.

	CPI_I	instruction mix					
		compress	eqntott	espresso	gcc	li	AV
load	5 + 2 W	19.9	30.7	21.1	23.0	31.6	25.3
store	5 + 2 W	5.6	0.6	5.1	14.4	16.9	8.5
compute	4 + 1 W	55.4	42.8	57.2	47.1	28.3	46.2
call	5 + 1 W	0.1	0.5	0.4	1.1	3.1	1.0
jump	3 + 1 W	1.6	1.4	1.0	2.8	5.3	2.4
taken	4 + 1 W	12.7	17.0	9.1	7.0	7.0	10.6
untaken	3 + 1 W	4.7	7.0	6.1	4.6	7.8	6.0

Table 6.7 Performance of the DLX core on the compress and li benchmarks and on the average SPECint92 workload. Parameter α denotes the factor by which off-chip DRAM is slower than standard SRAM.

DRAM α	W	τ_{DLX}	compress		li		SPEC aver.	
			CPI	TPI	CPI	TPI	CPI	TPI
4	1	355	5.4	1934.0	5.9	2083.8	5.6	1988.7
	2	178	6.7	1193.1	7.4	1309.2	6.9	1235.3
	3	119	8.0	947.0	8.8	1052.0	8.3	985.1
	4	89	9.2	820.0	10.3	918.9	9.6	855.8
	5	71	10.5	743.2	11.8	838.5	11.0	777.7
	6	70	11.7	820.6	13.3	930.6	12.3	860.4
8	9	76	15.5	1177.1	17.8	1349.0	16.3	1239.3
	10	70	16.7	1172.0	19.2	1346.5	17.6	1235.1
16	19	71	28.0	1990.7	32.6	2314.6	29.7	2107.7
	20	70	29.3	2050.5	34.1	2386.0	31.0	2171.7

the benchmarks. Since the instruction count IC of the benchmarks remains the same, table 6.7 lists the average time required per instruction

$$TPI \;=\; \frac{T}{IC} \;=\; CPI \cdot \tau_{DLX}.$$

instead of the run time. The CPI ratio and the TPI ratio vary with the workload, but the optimal number of wait states is the same for all the benchmarks of the SPECint92 suite.

On fast DRAM ($\alpha = 4$), the best performance is achieved on a memory

Table 6.8 Typical memory hierarchy of a large workstation in 1995

level	size	location	technology	access time
register	< 1 KB	on-chip	custom memory CMOS / BiCMOS	2–5 ns
L1 cache	< 64 KB	on-chip	CMOS SRAM	3–10 ns
L2 cache	< 4 MB	off-chip	CMOS SRAM	3–10 ns
main memory	< 4 GB	off-chip	CMOS DRAM	80–400 ns
disk storage	> 1 GB	off-chip	Magnetic disk	5 ms

system with five wait states. The DLX system then spends about 61% $(1.34 \cdot 5/11.0)$ of the run time waiting for the off-chip memory. On the slower DRAM with $\alpha = 8$ (16), the memory is operated with 10 (19) wait states, and the DLX even waits 76% (86%) of the time.

Thus a large, monolithic memory has got to be slow, and even in a sequential processor design, it causes the processor to wait most of the time. Pipelining can increase the performance of a processor significantly, but only if the average latency of the memory system is short $(W < 2)$. Thus, the monolithic memory is too slow to make pipelining worthwhile, and the restriction to a single memory port makes things even worse. In the next section, we therefore analyze whether a hierarchical memory system is better suited.

6.2 The Memory Hierarchy

PRESENTLY (2000) a low to mid range desktop machine has about 64 to 128 MB of main memory. In order to provide that much memory at reasonable cost and high speed, all commercial designs use a memory hierarchy. Between the on-chip register files and the off-chip main memory, there are placed several levels of memory (table 6.8, taken from [HP96]). The levels close to the CPU are called *cache*.

As one goes down the hierarchy, the cost per bit decreases and the storage capacity and the access time increase. This is achieved by changing the type of memory and the technology. With respect to the memory type, one switches from fast on-chip SRAM (static random access memory) to off-chip SRAM, to DRAM (dynamic RAM) and then to disks and tapes.

On a memory access, the processor first accesses the first level (L1) cache. When the requested data is in the L1 cache, a *hit* occurs and the data is accessed at the speed of the L1 cache. When the data is not in this memory level, a *miss* occurs and the hardware itself forwards the request to the next level in the memory hierarchy till the data is finally found.

A well designed multi-level memory system gives the user the illusion that the whole main memory runs roughly at the speed of the L1 cache. The key to this temporal behavior is the *locality of memory references* (section 6.2.1). In addition, the levels of the memory hierarchy are transparent, i.e., invisible to the user. For the levels between the CPU and the main memory, this is achieved by caching (section 6.2.2).

In a hierarchical memory system, special attention has to be payed to the following aspects:

- The *identification* of a memory reference, i.e., how can a memory reference be found in the memory hierarchy.

- The *placement policy* determines where the data is placed in a particular memory level.

- If a particular level of the memory hierarchy is full, new data can only be brought into this level, if another entry is evicted. The *replacement policy* determines which one to replace.

- The *allocation policy* determines under which circumstances data is transfered to the next higher level of the hierarchy.

- The *write policy* determines which levels of the memory hierarchy are updated on a write access.

- The *initialization* of the cache after power-up.

The transfer between two neighboring levels of RAM memory goes always along the same lines.[1] For simplicity, we therefore focus on a two-level memory system, i.e., an L1 cache backed by the main memory.

6.2.1   The Principle of Locality

The key for the nice temporal behavior of multi-level memory is a principle known as *locality of reference* [Den68]. This principle states that the memory references, both for instructions and data, tend to cluster. These clusters change over time, but over a short time period, the processor primarily works on a few clusters of references. Locality in references comes in two flavors:

---

[1] Additional considerations come into play, when one level is no random access memory, like disks or tapes.

- **Temporal Locality** After referencing a sequence S of memory locations, it is very likely that the following memory accesses will also reference locations of sequence S.

- **Spatial Locality** After an access to a particular memory location s, it is very likely that within the next several references an access is made to location s or a neighboring location.

For the instruction fetches, the clustering of the references is plausible for the following two reasons: First, the flow of control is only changed by control instructions (e.g., branch, trap, and call) and interrupts, but these instructions are only a small fraction of all executed instructions. In the SPEC benchmarks, for example, the control instructions account for 15% of all instructions, on average [HP96]. Second, most iterative constructs, like loops and recursive procedures, consist of a relatively small number of instructions which are repeated may times. Thus, in the SPEC benchmarks, 90% of the execution time is spent in 10 to 15% of the code [HP96].

For the data accesses, the clustering is harder to understand, but has for example been observed in [Den80, CO76]. The clustering occurs because much of the computation involves data structures, such as arrays or sequences of records. In many cases, successive references to these data structures will be to closely located data items.

Hierarchical memory designs benefit from the locality of references in the following two ways: Starting a memory transfer requires more time than the actual transfer itself. Thus, fetching larger blocks from the next level of the memory hierarchy saves time, if the additional data is also used later on. Due to spatial locality, this will often be the case. Temporal locality states, that once a memory item is brought into the fast memory, this item is likely to be used several times before it is evicted. Thus, the initial slow access is amortized by the fast accesses which follow.

6.2.2 The Principles of Caches

All our designs use byte addressable memory. Let the main memory size be 2^m bytes, and let the cache size be 2^c bytes. The cache is much smaller than the main memory; $2^c \ll 2^m$. The unit of data (bytes) transferred between the cache and the main memory is called *block* or *cache line*. In order to make use of spatial locality, the cache line usually comprises several memory data; the line sizes specifies how many. The cache size therefore equals

$$2^c = \# \text{ lines} \times \text{ line size.}$$

The cache lines are organized in one of three ways, namely: direct mapped, set associative, or fully associative.

A Direct Mapped Cache

For every memory address $a = \langle a[m-1:0] \rangle$, the placement policy specifies a *set* of cache locations. When the data with memory address a is brought into the cache, it is stored at one of these locations. In the simplest case, all the sets have cardinality one, and the memory address a is mapped to cache address

$$
\begin{aligned}
ca = \langle ca[c-1:0] \rangle &= a \bmod 2^c \\
&= \langle a[m-1:0] \rangle \bmod 2^c = \langle a[c-1:0] \rangle.
\end{aligned}
$$

i.e., the memory address is taken modulo the cache size.

A cache which implements this placement policy is called *direct mapped cache*. The replacement policy of such a cache is trivial, because there is only one possible cache location per memory address. Thus, the requested cache line is either empty, or the old entry must be evicted.

Since the cache is much smaller than the main memory, several memory locations are mapped to the same cache entry. At any given time, one needs to know whether a cache entry with address ca holds valid memory data, but that is not enough. If the entry is valid ($valid(ca) = 1$), one also needs to know the corresponding memory address $madr(ca)$. The cache data C with address ca then stores the following memory data

$$
C[ca] = M[\langle madr(ca) \rangle].
$$

Since the cache is direct mapped, the c least significant bits of the two addresses ca and $a = \langle madr(ca) \rangle$ are the same, and one only needs to store the leading $m - c$ bits of the memory address as tag:

$$
\begin{aligned}
tag(ca) &= a[m-1:c] \\
madr(ca) &= a[m-1:0] = tag(ca), ca[c-1:0].
\end{aligned}
$$

A cache line therefore comprises three fields, the valid flag, the address tag, and the data (figure 6.7). Valid flag and tag are also called the directory information of the cache line. Note that each of the 2^l cache lines holds line-size many memory data, but the cache only provides a *single* tag and valid bit per line. Let the cache address ca be a line boundary, i.e., ca is divisible by the line size 2°, then

$$
\begin{aligned}
valid(ca) &= valid(ca+1) &= \ldots = &\ valid(ca+2^o-1) \\
tag(ca) &= tag(ca+1) &= \ldots = &\ tag(ca+2^o-1).
\end{aligned}
$$

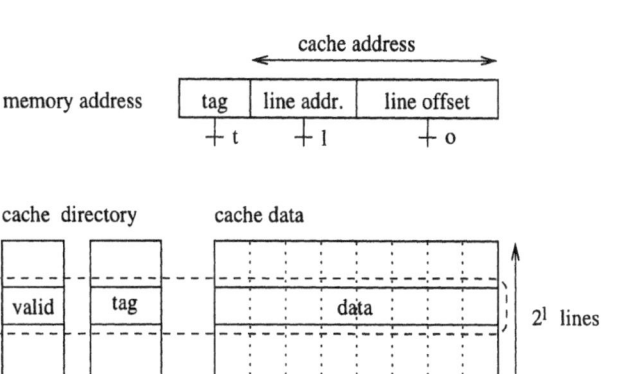

Figure 6.7 Organization of a byte addressable, direct mapped cache. The cache comprises 2^l lines, each of which is 2° bytes wide.

Thus, all the bytes of a cache line must belong to consecutive memory addresses.

$$Cline(ca) = C[ca + 2^o - 1 : ca] = M[\langle madr(ca)\rangle + 2^o - 1 : \langle madr(ca)\rangle].$$

Such a data structure makes it straightforward to detect whether the memory data with address a is in the cache or not. If the data is in the direct mapped cache, it must be stored at cache address $ca = \langle a[c-1:0]\rangle$. The cache access is a hit, if the entry is valid and if the tag matches the high-order bits of the memory address, i.e.,

$$hit = (valid(ca) \wedge (tag(ca) = a[m-1:c])).$$

On a read access with address ca, the cache provides the valid flag $v = valid(ca)$, the tag $t = tag(ca)$ and the data

$$d = Cline(\langle ca[c-1:o]0^o\rangle).$$

Each field of the cache line, i.e., valid flag, tag and data, can be updated separately. A write access to the cache data can update as little as a single byte but no more than the whole line.

Sectored Cache

The cache line can be very wide, because it holds several memory data. In order to reduce the width of the cache data RAM, the line is broken into several (2^s) *sectors* which are stored in consecutive cells of the cache data

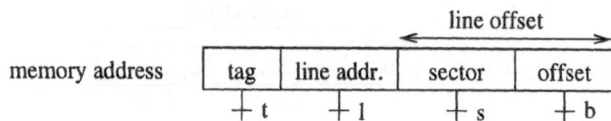

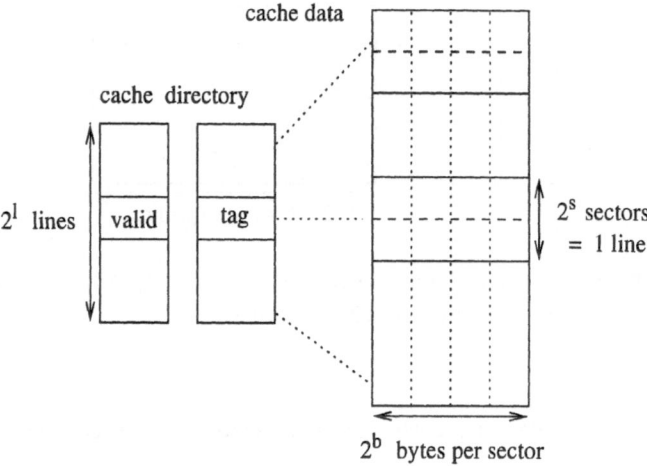

Figure 6.8 Organization of a byte addressable, direct mapped cache with sectors. Each cache line comprises 2^s sectors, each of which is 2^b bytes wide.

RAM. However, all the sectors of a cache line still have the same tag and valid flag[2]. The line-offset in the memory address is split accordingly in an s-bit sector address and in a b-bit sector offset, where $o = s + b$. Figure 6.8 depicts the organization of such a direct mapped cache.

With sectoring, the largest amount of cache data to be accessed in parallel is a sector not a whole line. Thus, on read access with address ca the sectored cache provides the data

$$
\begin{aligned}
d \;&=\; Csector[\langle ca[c-1:b]\,0^b\rangle] \\
&=\; C[\langle ca[c-1:b]\,0^b\rangle + 2^b - 1 : \langle ca[c-1:b]\,0^b\rangle].
\end{aligned}
$$

A k-Way Set Associative Cache

A k-way set associative cache provides a *set* of k possible cache locations for a memory address. Such an associative cache comprises k *ways* (figure 6.9), which are referenced with the same cache address. Each way is a direct mapped cache with directory and cache data providing exactly one

---

[2]Some cache designs allow that each sector has its own valid flag, in order to fetch only some sectors of a line.

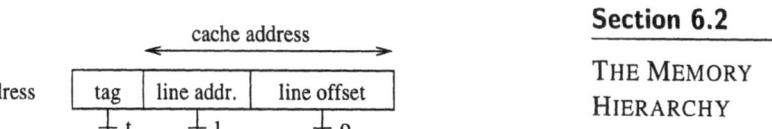

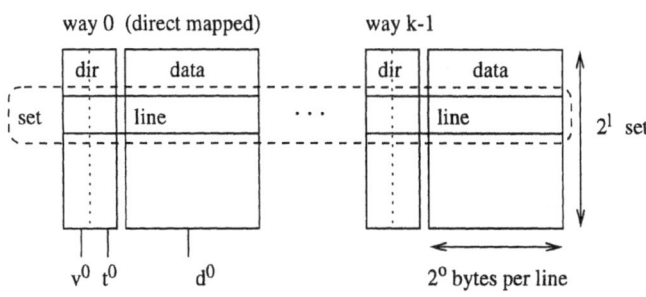

Figure 6.9 Organization of a byte addressable, k-way set associative cache. The cache comprises k ways (direct mapped caches). Each way holds 2^l lines which are 2^0 bytes wide; v^i, t^i and d^i denote the valid flag, the tag and the data of way i.

cache position per cache address ca. These k positions form the set of ca. There are two special cases of k-way set associative caches:

- For $k = 1$, the cache comprises exactly one way; the cache is direct mapped.

- If there is only one set, i.e., each way holds a single line, then each cache entry is held in a separate way. Such a cache is called *fully associative*.

The associativity of a set associative, first level cache is typically 2 or 4. Occasionally a higher associativity is used. For example, the PowerPC uses an 8-way cache [WS94] and the SuperSPARC uses a 5-way instruction cache [Sun92]. Of course, the cache line of a set associative cache can be sectored like a line in a direct mapped cache. For simplicity's sake, we describe a non-sectored, set associative cache. We leave the extension of the specification to sectored caches as an exercise (see exercise 6.1).

Cache Size

Let l denote the width of the line address, and let o denote the width of the line offset. Each way then comprises 2^l lines, and the whole cache comprises 2^l sets. Since in a byte addressable cache, the lines are still 2° bytes wide, each way has a storage capacity of

$$\text{size}(way) = 2^{c'} = 2^l \cdot 2^o$$

bytes. The size (in byte) of the whole k-way set associative cache equals

$$k \cdot \text{size}(way) = k \cdot 2^l \cdot 2^o.$$

Since in a k-way set associative cache there are several possible cache positions for a memory address a, it becomes more complicated to find the proper entry, and the placement and replacement policies are no longer trivial. However, the placement is such that *at any given time, a memory address is mapped to at most one cache position.*

Identification of a Cache Entry

The set of a set associative cache corresponds to the line of a direct mapped cache (way). Thus, the cache address ca is computed as the memory address a modulo the size $2^{c'}$ of a cache way

$$ca[c' - 1 : 0] = a[c' - 1 : 0].$$

For this address ca, every way provides data d^i, a valid flag v^i, and a tag t^i:

$$v^i = valid^i(ca), \qquad t^i = tag^i(ca), \qquad d^i = Cline^i(\langle ca[c' - 1 : o]0^o\rangle).$$

A local hit signal h^i indicates whether the requested data is held in way i or not. This local hit signal can be generated as

$$h^i = v^i \wedge (t^i = a[m - 1 : m - t]).$$

In a set associative cache, a hit occurs if one of the k ways encounters a hit, i.e.,

$$hit = h^0 \vee h^1 \vee \ldots \vee h^{k-1}.$$

On a cache hit, exactly one local hit signal h^j is active, and the corresponding way j holds the requested data d. On a miss, the cache provides an arbitrary value, e.g., $d = 0$. Thus,

$$d = \begin{cases} d^j & \text{if} \quad hit = 1 \text{ and } h^j = 1 \\ 0 & \text{if} \quad hit = 0 \end{cases} = \bigvee_{i=0}^{k-1}(d^i \wedge h^i).$$

Line Replacement

In case of a miss, the requested data is not in the cache, and a new line must be brought in. The replacement policy specifies which way gets the new line. The selection is usually done as follows:

1. As long as there are vacant lines in the set, the replacement circuit picks one of them, for example, the way with the smallest address.

2. If the set is full, a line must be evicted; the replacement policy suggests which one. The two most common policies are the following:

- *LRU* replacement picks the line which was *least recently used*. For each set, additional history flags are required which store the current ordering of the k ways. This *cache history* must be updated on every cache access, i.e., on a cache hit and on a line replacement.

- *Random* replacement picks a random line of the set and therefore manages without cache history.

Allocation and Write Policies

The allocation policy distinguishes between read and write accesses. New data is only brought into the cache on a miss, i.e., if the referenced data is not in the cache. Besides the requested data, the whole line which corresponds to that data is fetched from the next level of the memory hierarchy. The cache allocation operation can either be combined with the actual cache access (*forwarding*), or the cache access must be re-started after the allocation.

In case the miss occurs on a read access, i.e., on an instruction fetch or on a load operation, the requested data is always brought into the cache. For write accesses, three different types of allocation policies are possible:

1. *Read Allocate:* A write hit always updates the data RAM of the cache. On a write miss, the requested data and the corresponding line will not be transferred into the cache. Thus, new data is only brought in on a read miss.

2. *Write Allocate:* A write always updates the data RAM of the cache. In case of a write miss, the referenced line is first transferred from the memory into the cache, and then the cache line is updated. This policy allocates new lines on *every* cache miss.

3. *Write Invalidate:* A write never updates the data RAM of the cache. On the contrary, in case of a write hit, the write even invalidates the cache line. This allocation policy is less frequently used.

A particular piece of data can be stored in several levels of the hierarchical memory system. In order to keep the memories consistent, a write access must update all the instances of the data. For our two-level memory system, this means that on a write hit, cache and main memory are updated. However, the main memory is rather slow. From a performance point of view, it is therefore desirable to hide the main memory updates or

Table 6.9 Combinations of write and allocation policies for caches.

	Write Allocate	Read Allocate	Write Invalidate
Write Through	+	+	+
Write Back	+	+	−

even avoid some of them. The latter results in a *weak memory consistency*. The write policy specifies which of the two consistency models should be used:

1. *Write Through* supports the strong consistency model. A write always updates the main memory. Write buffers between cache and main memory allow the processor to go on, while the main memory performs the update. Thus, the slow memory updates can largely be hidden. The update of the cache depends on the allocation policy. Write through can be combined with any of the three allocation policies.

2. *Write Back* applies the weak consistency model. A write hit only updates the cache. A dirty flag indicates that a particular line has been updated in the cache but not in the main memory. The main memory keeps the old data till the whole line is copied back. This either occurs when a dirty cache line is evicted or on a special update request. This write policy can be combined with read allocate and write allocate but not with write invalidate (exercises in section 6.7).

Table 6.9 lists the possible combinations of the allocation and write policies.

Initialization and Invalidation

After power-up, all the cache RAMs hold binary but arbitrary values, and the information stored in a cache line is invalid even if the corresponding valid flag is raised. Thus, the valid flags must be cleared under hardware control, before starting the actual program execution. In case that the replacement policy relies on a cache history, the history RAM must be initialized as well. This initialization depends on the type of the history information.

Besides reads and writes, the cache usually supports a third type of access, namely the *line invalidation*. In case that the line invalidation access is a hit, the corresponding cache line is evicted, i.e., its valid flag is cleared,

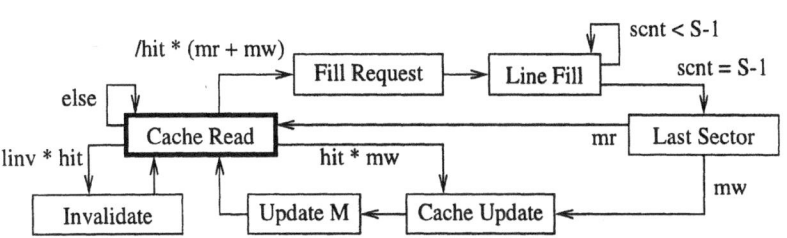

Figure 6.10 Cache accesses of the memory transactions read, write and line invalidate on a sectored, write through cache with write allocation.

and the history is updated as well. In case of a miss, the invalidation access
has no impact on the cache. Line invalidation is necessary, if a particular
level of the memory system comprises more than one cache, as it will be
the case in our pipelined DLX design (section 6.5). In that situation, line
invalidation is used in order to ensure that a particular memory word is
stored in at most one of those parallel caches.

6.2.3 Execution of Memory Transactions

The cache as part of the memory hierarchy has to support four types of
memory transactions which are reading ($rw = 1$) or writing ($mw = 1$) a
memory data, invalidating a cache line ($linv = 1$), and initializing the whole
cache. Except for the initialization, any of the memory transactions is
performed as a sequence of the following basic cache accesses:

- reading a cache sector including cache data, tag and valid flag,

- updating the cache directory, and

- updating a sector of the cache data.

The sequences of the memory transactions depend on the allocation and
write policies. The flow chart of figure 6.10 depicts the sequences for a
sectored, write through cache with write allocation and read forwarding.
Each transaction starts in state Cache Read. A cache line is S sectors wide.
Let the sector boundary a denote the memory address of the transaction,
and let ca denote the corresponding cache address.

Read Transaction
The read transaction starts with a Cache Read access. The cache generates
the hit signal $hit(ca)$ and updates the cache history. On a hit ($hit(ca) = 1$),

the cache determines the address *way* of the cache way which holds the requested data, and it provides these data

$$d = Csector^{way}(ca) = Msector(a).$$

That already completes the read transfer.

In case of a miss, address *way* specifies the cache way chosen by the replacement policy. In subsequent cycles, the cache performs a *line fill*, i.e., it fetches the memory line $Mline(a')$ with $a' = \langle a[m-1:o]0^o\rangle]$ sector by sector and writes it at cache line address $ca' = \langle ca[c-1:o]0^o\rangle$.

This line fill starts with a Fill Request. The cache line is invalidated, i.e., $valid^{way}(ca) = 0$. This ensures that a valid cache line always holds consistent data, even if the line fill is interrupted in between. The cache also requests the line from memory and clears a sector counter *scnt*.

In each of the next $S-1$ Line Fill cycles, one sector of the line is written into the cache and the sector counter is incremented:

$$
\begin{aligned}
Csector^{way}(ca' + scnt) &:= Msector(a' + scnt) \\
scnt &:= scnt + 1.
\end{aligned}
$$

In the cycle Last Sector, the cache fetches the last sector of the line. Due to forwarding, the requested data are provided at the data output of the cache. In addition, the directory is updated, i.e., the new tag is stored in the tag RAM and the valid flag is turned back on:

$$tag^{way}(ca) := a[m-1:m-t], \qquad valid^{way} := 1.$$

This is the last cycle of a read transaction which does not hit the cache.

Write Transaction

Like a read transaction, the write transaction starts with a Cache Read access, which in case of a miss is followed by a line fill. The write transaction then proceeds with a Cache Update cycle, in which a memory update is requested and the cache sector is updated as

$$Csector^{way}(ca) := X_{B-1}, \ldots, X_0,$$

with

$$X_i = \begin{cases} byte_i(Csector^{way}(ca)) & \text{if} \quad CDw[i] = 0 \\ byte_i(Din) & \text{if} \quad CDw[i] = 1. \end{cases}$$

The transaction ends with an Update M cycle, in which the memory performs the requested write update.

Line Invalidation Transaction

This transaction also starts with a Cache Read access, in order to check whether the requested line is in the cache. In case of a miss, the line is not in the cache, and the transaction ends after the Cache Read access. In case of a hit, the line is invalidated in the next cycle (Invalidate):

$$valid^{way} := 0.$$

6.3 A Cache Design

A K-WAY set associative cache comprises k cache ways, each of which is identical with a direct mapped cache. In a first step, we therefore design a byte addressable, sectored, direct mapped cache. We then extend the design to a k-way associative cache (section 6.3.2). Finally, the cache is integrated into a cache interface which implements the write allocation, write through policy.

The cache design must support all the cache accesses which according to section 6.2.3 are required to perform the standard memory transactions. In order to split the update of the directory and of the cache data, the tags, valid flags and cache data are stored in separate RAMs. The cache is controlled by the following signals:

- the rd flag which indicates a cache read access,

- the *clear* flag which clears the whole cache,

- the write signals Vw and Tw which enable the update of the cache directory (valid and tag), and

- the $B = 2^b$ bank write signals $CDw[B-1:0]$ which specify the bytes of the cache sector to be updated.

The cache gets a memory address $a = \langle a[m-1:0] \rangle$, a valid flag, and a B-byte data Di and provides a flag *hit* and data Do. The flag *hit* indicates whether the requested memory data are held in the cache or not. As depicted in figure 6.8 (page 258), the memory address a is interpreted as tag a_tag, line address a_line, sector address a_sector, and sector offset a_byte:

$$
\begin{aligned}
a\_tag &= a[m-1:l+s+b] \\
a\_line &= a[l+s+b-1:s+b] \\
a\_sector &= a[s+b-1:b] \\
a\_byte &= a[b-1:0].
\end{aligned}
$$

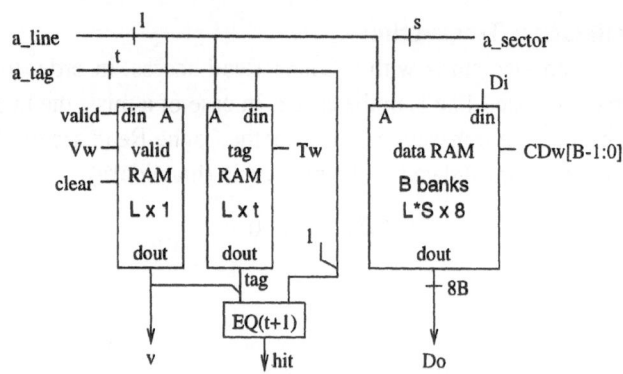

Figure 6.11 Byte addressable, direct mapped cache with $L = 2^l$ lines. The cache line is organized in $S = 2^s$ sectors, each of which is $B = 2^b$ bytes wide.

According to the FSD of figure 6.10, all the memory transactions start with a cache read access ($\$rd = 1$); updates of the directory and of the cache data only occur in later cycles. The design of the k-way set associative cache will rely on this feature.

6.3.1 Design of a Direct Mapped Cache

Figure 6.11 depicts the data paths of a sectored, byte addressable, direct mapped cache with $L = 2^l$ cache lines. The cache consists of valid, tag and data RAMs and an equality tester. The valid RAM V and the t bits wide tag RAM T form the cache directory.

Since all sectors of a line share the same tag and valid flag, they are only stored once; the valid and tag RAM are of size $L \times 1$ and $L \times t$. Both RAMs are referenced with the line address a_line. The write signals Vw and Tw control the update of the directory. On $Tw = 0$ the tag RAM provides the tag

$$tag = T[\langle a\_line \rangle],$$

and on $Tw = 1$, the tag a_tag is written into the tag RAM

$$T[\langle a\_line \rangle] := a\_tag.$$

The valid RAM V is a special type of RAM which can be cleared in just a few cycles[3]. That allows for a fast initialization on reset. The RAM V is

---

[3]The IDT71B74 RAM, which is used in the cache system of the Intel i486 [Han93], can be cleared in two to three cycles [Int96].

cleared by activating signal *clear*. On $Vw = clear = 0$, it provides the flag

$$v = V[\langle a\_line \rangle],$$

whereas on a write access, requested by $Vw = 1$ and $clear = 0$, the RAM V performs the update

$$V[\langle a\_line \rangle] := valid.$$

On every cache access, the equality tester EQ checks whether the line entry is valid and whether the tag provided by the tag RAM matches the tag a_tag. If that is the case, a hit is signaled:

$$hit = 1 \quad \leftrightarrow \quad (v \wedge (tag = a\_tag)) \quad \leftrightarrow \quad ((v, tag) = (1, a\_tag)).$$

The data portion of the cache line is organized in $S = 2^s$ sectors, each of which is $B = 2^b$ bytes wide. The *data* RAM of the cache therefore holds a total of 2^{l+s} sectors and is addressed with the line and sector addresses a_line and a_sector. The cache is byte addressable, i.e., a single write can update as little as a single byte but no more than a whole sector. In order to account for the different widths of the writes, the data RAM is organized in B banks. Each bank is a RAM of size $L \cdot S \times 8$, and is controlled by a bank write signal $CDw[i]$.

On a read access, the B bank write signals are zero. In case of a hit, the cache then provides the whole sector to the output Do:

$$Do = data[\langle a\_line, a\_sector \rangle + B - 1 : \langle a\_line, a\_sector \rangle].$$

If $CDw[B-1:0] \neq 0^B$ and if the access is a hit, the data RAMs are updated. For every i with $CDw[i] = 1$, bank i performs the update

$$data[\langle a\_line, a\_sector \rangle + i] := byte_i(Di).$$

The cost of this direct mapped cache (1-way cache, $1) run at:

$$
\begin{aligned}
C_{\$1}(t, l, s, b) &= C_{SRAM}(2^l, 1) + C_{SRAM}(2^l, t) \\
&\quad + C_{EQ}(t+1) + 2^b \cdot C_{SRAM}(2^{l+s}, 8).
\end{aligned}
$$

The cache itself delays the read/write access to its data RAMs and directory and the detection of a hit by the following amount:

$$
\begin{aligned}
D_{\$1}(data) &= D_{SRAM}(L \cdot S, 8) \\
D_{\$1}(dir) &= \max\{D_{SRAM}(L, 1), D_{SRAM}(L, t)\} \\
D_{\$1}(hit) &= D_{\$1}(dir) + D_{EQ}(t+1).
\end{aligned}
$$

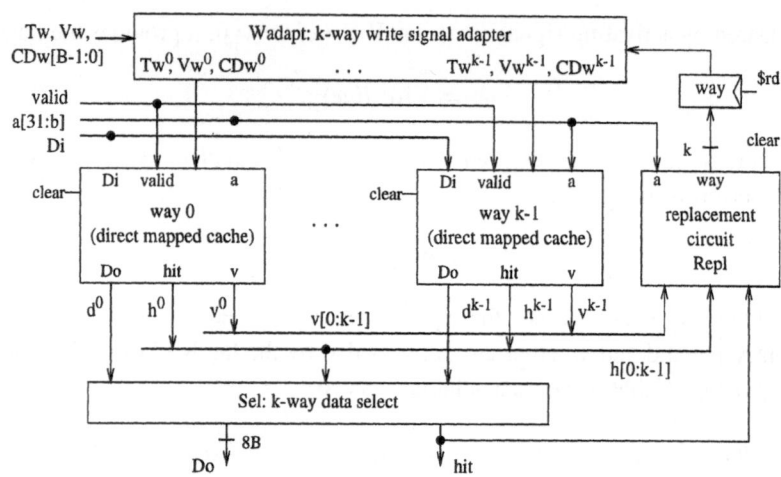

Figure 6.12 Byte addressable, k-way set associative cache. The sectors of a cache line are $B = 2^b$ bytes wide.

6.3.2 Design of a Set Associative Cache

The core of a set associative cache (figure 6.12) are k sectored, direct mapped caches with L lines each. The k cache ways provide the local hit signals h^i, the valid flags v^i, and the local data d^i. Based on these signals, the select circuit *Sel* generates the global hit signal and selects the data output *Do*. An access only updates a single way. The write signal adapter *Wadapt* therefore forwards the write signals Tw, Vw, and CDw to this active cache way.

The replacement circuit *Repl* determines the address *way* of the active cache way; the address is coded in unary. Since the active cache way remains the same during the whole memory transaction, address *way* is only computed during the first cycle of the transaction and is then buffered in a register. This first cycle is always a cache read ($\$rd$). Altogether, the cost of the k way cache is:

$$C_{\$k}(t,l,s,b) = k \cdot C_{\$1}(t,l,s,b) + C_{Sel} + C_{Wadapt}$$
$$+ C_{Repl} + C_{ff}(k).$$

Data Select Circuit
Each cache way provides a local hit signal h^i, a valid flag v^i, and the local data d^i. An access is a cache hit, if one of the k-ways encounters a hit:

$$hit = h^0 \vee h^1 \vee \cdots \vee h^{k-1}.$$

On a cache hit, exactly one local hit signal h^i is active, and the corresponding way i holds the requested data Do. Thus,

$$Do = \bigvee_{j=0,\ldots,k-1} (d^j \wedge h^j)$$

When arranging these OR gates as a binary tree, the output Do and the *hit* signal can be selected at the following cost and delay:

$$C_{Sel} = C_{tree}(k) \cdot C_{or} + 8B \cdot (C_{and}(k) + C_{tree}(k) \cdot C_{or})$$
$$D_{Sel} = D_{and} + D_{tree}(k) \cdot D_{or}.$$

Write Signal Adapter

Circuit *Wadapt* gets the write signals Tw, Vw and $CDw[B-1:0]$ which request the update of the tag RAM, the valid RAM and the B data RAMs. However, in a set associative cache, an access only updates the active cache way. Therefore, the write signal adapter forwards the write signals to the active way, and for the remaining $k-1$ ways, it disables the write signals.

Register *way* provides the address of the active cache way coded in unary. Thus, the write signals of way i are obtained by masking the signals Tw, Vw and $CDw[B-1:0]$ with signal bit $way[i]$, e.g.,

$$Vw^i = \begin{cases} Vw & \text{if } way[i] = 1 \\ 0 & \text{if } way[i] = 0 \end{cases} = Vw \wedge way[i].$$

The original $B+2$ write signals can then be adapted to the needs of the set associative cache at the following cost and delay

$$C_{Wadapt} = k \cdot C_{and}(B+2)$$
$$D_{Wadapt} = D_{and}.$$

LRU Replacement Circuit

The replacement circuit *Repl* performs two major tasks. On every cache read access, it determines the address *way* of the active cache way and updates the cache history. On a cache miss, circuit *Repl* determines the eviction address ev; this is the address of the way which gets the new data.

The circuit *Repl* of figure 6.13 keeps a K-bit history vector for each set, where $K = k \cdot \log k$. The history is stored in an $L \times K$ RAM which is updated on a cache read access ($\$rd = 1$) and by an active clear signal:

$$Hw = \$rd \vee clear.$$

On $clear = 1$, all the history vectors are initialized with the value Hid. Since the same value is written to all the RAM words, we assume that

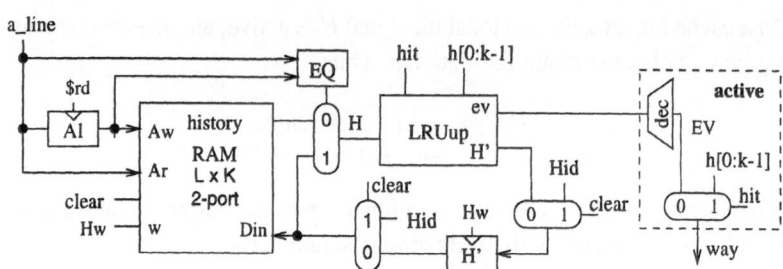

Figure 6.13 Circuit *Repl* of a k-way set associative cache with LRU replacement

this initialization can be done in just a few cycles, as it is the case for the valid RAM. Circuit *LRU up* determines the new history vector H' and the eviction address ev; circuit *active* selects the address *way*.

Updating the cache history involves two consecutive RAM accesses, a read of the cache history followed by a write to the history RAM. In order to reduce the cycle time, the new history vector H' and the address are buffered in registers. The cache history is updated during the next cache read access. Since the cache history is read and written in parallel, the history RAM is dual ported, and a multiplexer forwards the new history vector H_l', if necessary. On *clear* = 1, register H' is initialized as well. The cost of circuit *Repl* can be expressed as:

$$C_{Repl} = C_{SRAM2}(L,K) + C_{ff}(K) + 3 \cdot C_{mux}(K)$$
$$+ C_{ff}(l) + C_{EQ}(l) + C_{or} + C_{LRUup} + C_{active}.$$

We now describe the circuits *active* and *LRU up* in detail.

Detection of the Active Way

On a cache hit, the active cache way is the way which holds the requested data; this is also the cache way which provides an active hit signal h^i. On a miss, the active way is specified by the eviction address ev which is provided by the cache history. Since ev is coded in binary, it is first decoded providing value EV. Thus,

$$way = \begin{cases} EV & \text{if} \quad hit = 0 \\ h[k-1:0] = (h^{k-1}, \ldots, h^0) & \text{if} \quad hit = 1 \end{cases}$$

is the address of the active way coded in unary. The circuit *active* (figure 6.13) determines the address of the active way at the following cost and delay:

$$C_{active} = C_{dec}(\log k) + C_{mux}(k)$$

$$D_{active}(ev) = D_{dec}(\log k) + D_{mux}(k)$$
$$D_{active}(hit) = D_{mux}(k).$$

Cache History

For each set l, circuit $Repl$ keeps a history vector

$$H_l = (H_l^0,\ldots,H_l^{k-1}), \quad \langle H_l^i \rangle \in \{0,\ldots,k-1\}.$$

H_l is a permutation of the addresses $0,\ldots,k-1$ of the cache ways, it provides an ordering of the k ways of set l. The elements of the vector H_l are arranged such that the data of way H_l^i was used more recently than the data of way H_l^{i+1}. Thus, H_l^0 (H_l^{k-1}) points to the data of set l which was most (least) recently used. In case of a miss, the cache history suggests the candidate for the line replacement. Due to LRU replacement, the least recently used entry is replaced; the eviction address ev equals H_l^{k-1}.

On power-up, the whole cache is invalidated, i.e., all the valid flags in the k direct mapped caches are cleared. The cache history holds binary but arbitrary values, and the history vectors H_l are usually not a permutation of the addresses $0,\ldots,k-1$. In order to ensure that the cache comes up properly, all the history vectors must be initialized, e.g., by storing the identity permutation. Thus,

$$Hid = (H^0,\ldots,H^{k-1}), \quad \langle H^i \rangle = i.$$

Update of the Cache History

The cache history must be updated on every cache read access, whether the access is a hit or a miss. The update of the history also depends on the type of memory transaction. Read and write accesses are treated alike; line invalidation is treated differently.

Let a read or write access hit the way H_l^i. This way is at position i in vector H_l. In the updated vector R, the way H_l^i is at the first position, the elements $H_l^0,\ldots,H_l^{i-1}$ are shifted one position to the right, and all the other elements remain the same:

$$H = (\; H_l^0, \; \ldots \;, H_l^{i-1}, H_l^i, H_l^{i+1}, \; \ldots \;, H_l^{k-1} \;)$$

$$R = (\; H_l^i, H_l^0, \; \ldots \;, H_l^{i-1}, H_l^{i+1}, \; \ldots \;, H_l^{k-1} \;)$$
$$x = (\; 0 \quad \ldots \quad 0 \;\; 1 \;\; 0 \quad \ldots \quad 0 \;)$$
$$y = (\; * \;\; 0 \; \ldots \; 0 \;\; 0 \;\; 1 \quad \ldots \quad 1 \;)$$

The meaning of the vectors x and y will be described shortly.

In case of a read/write miss, the line of way $ev = H_l^{k-1}$ is replaced. Thus, all the elements of the history vector H_l are shifted one position to the right and ev is added at the first position:

$$R = (ev, H_l^0, H_l^1, \ldots, H_l^{k-2}) = (H_l^{k-1}, H_l^0, H_l^1, \ldots, H_l^{k-2}).$$

In case that an invalidation access hits the way H_l^i, the cache line corresponding to way H_l^i is evicted and should be used at the next line fill. In the updated vector I, the way H_l^i is therefore placed at the last position, the elements $H_l^{i+1}, \ldots, H_l^{k-1}$ are shifted one position to the left, and the other elements remain the same:

$$H = (H_l^0, \ldots, H_l^{i-1}, H_l^i, H_l^{i+1}, \ldots, H_l^{k-1})$$

$$I = (H_l^0, \ldots, H_l^{i-1}, H_l^{i+1}, \ldots, H_l^{k-1}, H_l^i)$$

If the invalidation access causes a cache miss, the requested line is not in the cache, and the history remains unchanged: $I = H_l$. Note that the vector I can be obtained by shifting cyclically vector R one position to the left

$$I = (R^1, \ldots, R^{k-1}, R^0). \tag{6.3}$$

Realization of the History Update

Circuit *LRUup* (figure 6.14) performs the update of the history vector. On a cache hit, the binary address J of the cache way with $h^{(J)} = 1$ is obtained by passing the local hit signals $h[k-1:0]$ through an encoder. The flag

$$x_i = 1 \quad \leftrightarrow \quad (H_l^i = J \wedge hit = 1),$$

indicates whether the active cache way is at position $(i+1)$ of the history vector H_l. Circuit *LRUup* obtains these flags in the obvious way. A parallel prefix OR circuit then computes the signals

$$y_i = \bigvee_{n=0}^{i-1} x_n \quad , i = 1 \ldots k-1,$$

where $y_i = 0$ indicates that the active cache way is not among the first i positions of the history vector H_l. Thus, the first element of the updated history vector R can be expressed as

$$R^0 = \begin{cases} J & \text{if} \quad hit = 1 \\ H_l^{k-1} & \text{if} \quad hit = 0, \end{cases}$$

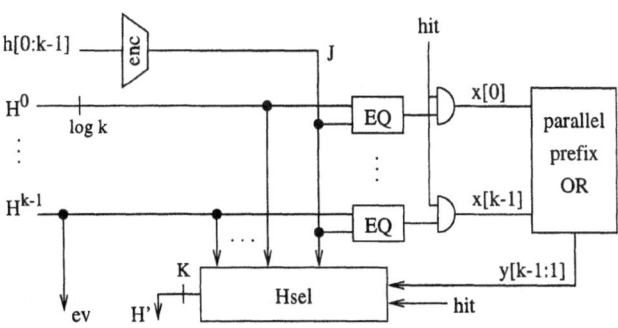

Figure 6.14 Circuit *LRUup* which updates the cache history

and for any $i \geq 1$

$$R^i = \begin{cases} H_l^{i-1} & \text{if} \quad y_i = 0 \\ H_l^i & \text{if} \quad y_i = 1. \end{cases}$$

According to equation 6.3, the new history vector H' can be obtained as

$$H' = \begin{cases} R & \text{if} \quad linv = 0 \\ I & \text{if} \quad linv = 1 \end{cases} = \begin{cases} (R^0, R^1, \ldots, R^{k-1}) & \text{if} \quad linv = 0 \\ (R^1, \ldots, R^{k-1}, R^0) & \text{if} \quad linv = 1. \end{cases}$$

Circuit *Hsel* implements these selections in a straightforward manner at the following cost and delay

$$C_{Hsel} = 2k \cdot C_{mux}(\log k)$$
$$D_{Hsel} = 2 \cdot D_{mux}(\log k).$$

The cost of the whole history update circuit *LRUup* run at:

$$\begin{aligned} C_{LRUup} &= C_{enc}(\log k) + k \cdot (C_{EQ}(\log k) + C_{and}) \\ &\quad + C_{PP}(k) \cdot C_{or} + C_{Hsel}. \end{aligned}$$

Delay of the Replacement Circuit

The circuit *Repl* gets the address a and the hit signals h^i and *hit*. Based on these inputs, it updates the history RAM and the registers H' and *way*. The update of the RAM is obviously much faster than the update of the registers. We therefore focus on the amount of time by which circuit *Repl* itself delays the update of its registers. For any particular input signal, the propagation delay from the input to the registers of *Repl* can be expressed as:

$$D_{Repl}(hit) = D_{and} + D_{PP}(k) \cdot D_{or} + D_{Hsel} + D_{mux} + D_{ff}$$

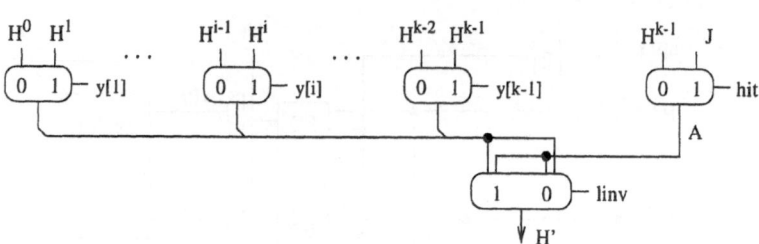

Figure 6.15 Circuit *Hsel* selects the history vector H'. Flag *linv* signals a line invalidation access.

Table 6.10 Updating the LRU history of set l in a 2-way cache.

inputs			read/write				line invalidation			
$H_l^1 H_l^0$		$h^1 h^0$	$H_l'^1 H_l'^0$		way^1 way^0		$H_l'^1 H_l'^0$		way^1 way^0	
0	*	0 0	1	0	0	1	0	1	*	*
1	*	0 0	0	1	1	0	1	0	*	*
*	*	0 1	1	0	0	1	0	1	0	1
*	*	1 0	0	1	1	0	1	0	1	0

$$D_{Repl}(h^i) = D_{enc}(\log k) + D_{EQ}(\log k) + D_{Repl}(hit)$$
$$D_{Repl}(a) = \max\{D_{SRAM2}(L,K), D_{EQ}(l)\} + D_{mux}(K)$$
$$+ \max\{D_{EQ}(\log k) + D_{Repl}(hit), D_{active}(ev) + D_{ff}\},$$

where $K = k \cdot \log k$. Note that these delays already include the propagation delay of the register. Thus, clocking just adds the setup time δ.

LRU Replacement in a 2-Way Cache

When accessing a set l in a 2-way cache, one of the two ways is the active cache way and the other way becomes least recently used. In case of a line invalidation (*linv* $= 1$), the active way becomes least recently used. According to table 6.10, the elements of the new history vector H_l' and the address of the active way obey

$$way^1 = \begin{cases} H_l^1 & ; \text{ on a miss} \\ h^1 & ; \text{ on a hit} \end{cases} \qquad way^0 = /way^1$$

$$H_l'^1 = way^1 \text{ XNOR } linv \qquad H_l'^0 = /H_l'^1.$$

Thus, it suffices to keep one history bit per set, e.g., H_l^1. That simplifies the LRU replacement circuit significantly (figure 6.16), and the initializa-

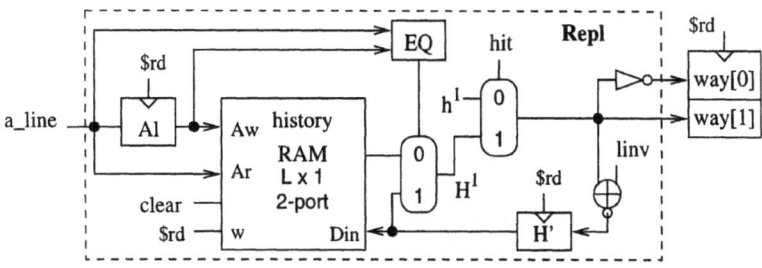

Figure 6.16 LRU replacement circuit *Repl* of a 2-way set associative cache.

tion after power-up can be dropped. Since an inverter is not slower than an XNOR gate, the cost and delay of circuit *Repl* can then be estimated as

$$C_{Repl} = C_{SRAM2}(L, 1) + C_{ff}(l) + C_{EQ}(l) + 2 \cdot C_{mux} + C_{inv} + C_{xnor} + C_{ff}$$

$$
\begin{aligned}
D_{Repl}(h^i) &= D_{Repl}(hit) = D_{mux} + D_{xnor} + D_{ff} \\
D_{Repl}(a) &= \max\{D_{SRAM2}(L, 1), D_{EQ}(l)\} + 2 \cdot D_{mux} + D_{xnor} + D_{ff}.
\end{aligned}
$$

Delay of a Set Associative Cache

The k-way set associative cache receives the address a, the data Di and the control signals *clear*, rd, Vw, Tw and $CDw[B-1:0]$. In the delay formula, we usually distinguish between these three types of inputs; by cs we denote all the control inputs of the cache design.

The cache design of figure 6.12 delays its data Do and its hit signal by the following amount:

$$
\begin{aligned}
D_{\$k}(Do) &= D_{\$1}(Do) + D_{Sel} \\
D_{\$k}(hit) &= D_{\$1}(hit) + D_{Sel}.
\end{aligned}
$$

The cache also updates the directory, the data RAMs and the cache history. The update of the cache history H is delayed by

$$D_{\$k}(; H) = \max\{D_{\$1}(hit) + D_{Repl}(h^i), D_{\$k}(hit) + D_{Repl}(hit), D_{Repl}(a)\}.$$

Thus, the propagation delay from a particular input to the storage of the k-way cache can be expressed as:

$$
\begin{aligned}
D_{\$k}(a; \$k) &= \max\{D_{\$k}(; H), D_{\$1}(; data, dir)\} \\
D_{\$k}(cs\$; \$k) &= \max\{D_{\$k}(; H), D_{Wadapt} + D_{\$1}(; data, dir)\} \\
D_{\$k}(Di; \$k) &= D_{\$1}(; data).
\end{aligned}
$$

Table 6.11 Active cache interface control signals for each state of the standard memory transactions, i.e., for each state of the FSD of figure 6.10.

state	cache control signals	CDw[B:0]
Cache Read	$rd, (linv)	0^B
Fill Request	scntclr, scntce, Vw, lfill	
Line Fill	scntce, lfill, Sw	1^B
Last Sector	scntce, valid, Vw, Tw, lfill,Sw	
Cache Update	$w	MBW[B-1:0]
Update M	—	0^B
Invalidate	Vw	

6.3.3 Design of a Cache Interface

In the following, a sectored cache is integrated into a cache interface $if which implements the write allocate and write through policies. The cache interface also supports forwarding, i.e., while a cache line is fetched from main memory, the requested sector is directly taken from the memory bus and is forwarded to the data output of $if.

Section 6.2.3 describes how such a cache interface performs the standard memory transactions as a sequence of basic cache accesses. That already specifies the functionality of $if. Those sequences, which are depicted in the FSD of figure 6.10, consist of four types of cache accesses, namely a read access ($rd), a write hit access ($w), a line invalidation (linv) and a line fill (lfill). The line fill requires several cycles.

The cache interface is controlled by the following signals:

- the signals $rd, $w, linv and lfill specifying the type of the cache access,

- the write signals Vw and Tw of the valid and tag RAM,

- the memory bank write signals $MBW[B-1:0]$,

- the write signal Sw (sector write) requesting the update of a whole cache sector, and

- the clock and clear signal of the sector counter scnt.

Table 6.11 lists the active control signals for each state of the standard memory transactions.

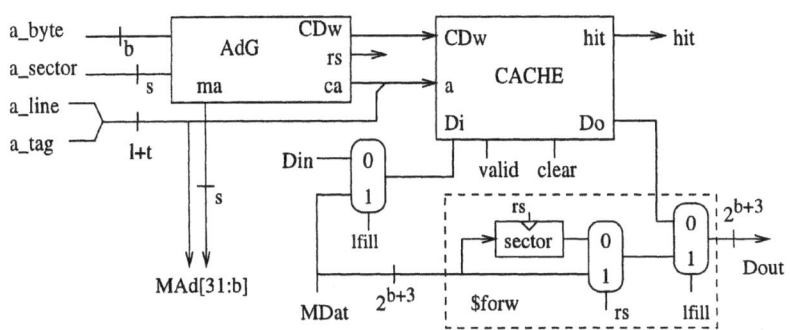

Figure 6.17 Cache interface $if with forwarding capability

The cache interface receives the address a and the data Din and $MDat$. Since all cache and memory accesses affect a whole sector, address a is a sector boundary:

$$\langle a\_byte \rangle = 0,$$

and the cache and memory ignore the offset bits a_byte of the address. The interface $if provides a hit signal, the data $Dout$, the memory address MAd, a cache address, and the input data Di of the cache. On a line fill, Di is taken from the memory data bus MDat, whereas on a write hit access, the data is taken from Din

$$Di = \begin{cases} MDat & \text{if} \quad lfill = 1 \\ Din & \text{if} \quad lfill = 0. \end{cases} \tag{6.4}$$

Figure 6.17 depicts an implementation of such a cache interface. The core of the interface is a sectored k-way cache, where k may be one. The width of a sector ($B = 2^b$ bytes) equals the width of the data bus between the main memory and the cache. Each line comprises $S = 2^s$ sectors. A multiplexer selects the input data Di of the cache according to equation 6.4. The address generator circuit AdG generates the addresses and bank write signals CDw for the accesses. Circuit $\$forw$ forwards the memory data in case of a read miss. The cost of the cache interface runs at

$$\begin{aligned} C_{\$if}(t,l,s,b) &= C_{\$k}(t,l,s,b) + C_{mux}(B \cdot 8) + C_{AdG} + C_{\$forw} \\ C_{\$forw} &= 2 \cdot C_{mux}(B \cdot 8) + C_{ff}(B \cdot 8). \end{aligned}$$

The Cache Address Generator

The address generator (figure 6.18) generates the write signals CDw and the low order address bits of the cache and main memory address.

According to section 6.2.3, a standard access ($lfill = 0$) affects a single sector of a cache line. On such an access, the low order bits of the main

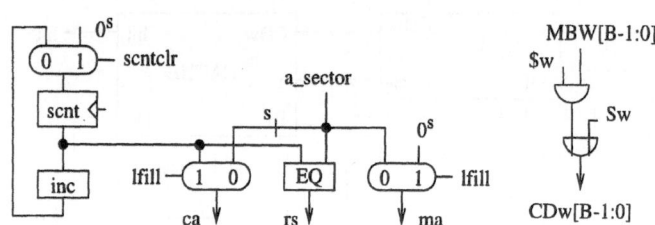

Figure 6.18 Address generation for the line fill of a sectored cache. The outputs *ca* and *ma* are the low order bits of the cache and memory address. Signal *rs* indicates that the current sector equals the requested sector.

memory and of the cache address equal the sector address *a_sector*. On a line fill ($lfill = 1$), the whole line must be fetched from main memory. The memory requires the start address of the cache line:

$$MAd[31:b] = (a\_tag, a\_line, ma)$$

with

$$ma = \begin{cases} a\_sector & \text{if} \quad lfill = 0 \\ 0^s & \text{if} \quad lfill = 1. \end{cases}$$

Thus, the address generator clears *ma* on a line fill.

On a line fill, the cache line is updated sector by sector. The address generator therefore generates all the sector addresses $0, \ldots, 2^s - 1$ for the cache, using an s-bit counter *scnt*. The counter is cleared on $scntclr = 1$. The sector bits of the cache address equal

$$ca = \begin{cases} a\_sector & \text{if} \quad lfill = 0 \\ scnt & \text{if} \quad lfill = 1. \end{cases}$$

In addition, circuit AdG provides a signal *rs* (requested sector) which indicates that the current sector with address *scnt* equals the requested sector

$$rs = 1 \quad \leftrightarrow \quad a\_sector = scnt.$$

This flag is obtained by an s-bit equality tester.

The address generator also generates the bank write signal $CDw[B - 1 : 0]$ for the data RAM of the cache. Because of write allocate, the data RAM is updated on a line fill and on a write hit (table 6.11). On a line fill, signal *Sw* requests the update of the whole cache sector ($CDw[B - 1 : 0] = 1$), whereas on a write hit ($\$w = 1$), the bank write signals of the memory determine which cache banks have to be updated. Thus, for $0 \le i < B$, the bank write signal $CDw[i]$ is generated as

$$CDw[i] = Sw \lor MBW[i] \land \$w.$$

By $cs\$if$, we denote all the control inputs of the cache interface. These signals are provided by the control unit CON. The data paths provide the address a. Let $A_{CON}(cs\$if)$ and $A_{DP}(a)$ denote the accumulated delay of these inputs. The cost and the cycle time of circuit AdG and the delay of its outputs can then be expressed as

$$
\begin{aligned}
C_{AdG} &= C_{ff}(s) + C_{inc}(s) + C_{EQ}(s) + 3 \cdot C_{mux}(s) \\
&\quad + C_{and}(B) + C_{or}(B)
\end{aligned}
$$

$$
\begin{aligned}
A_{AdG}(ma) &= A_{AdG}(ca) = \max\{A_{DP}(a), A_{CON}(cs\$if)\} + D_{mux} \\
A_{AdG}(rs) &= A_{DP}(a) + D_{EQ}(s) \\
A_{AdG}(CDw) &= A_{CON}(cs\$if) + D_{and} + D_{or} \\
T_{AdG} &= \max\{A_{CON}(cs\$if), D_{inc}(s)\} + D_{mux} + D_{ff} + \delta.
\end{aligned}
$$

Forwarding of the Requested Cache Sector

Circuit $\$forw$ of figure 6.17 performs the read forwarding. On a read hit, the output data $Dout$ are provided directly by the cache. On a cache miss, the line is fetched from main memory. During the line fill access, the requested sector, i.e., the sector with address $ca = a\_sector$, is clocked into a register as soon as it is provided on the MDat bus. This event is signaled by $rs = 1$. In the last line fill cycle, circuit $forw provides the requested sector to the output $Dout$, bypassing the cache. If $\langle a\_sector \rangle = S - 1$, the requested sector lies on the bus MDat during the last fill cycle and has not yet been clocked into the register. Thus, the forwarding circuit selects the data output as

$$
Dout = \begin{cases} Do & \text{if} \quad lfill = 0 \\ sector & \text{if} \quad lfill = 1 \wedge rs = 0 \\ MDat & \text{if} \quad lfill = 1 \wedge rs = 1 \end{cases}
$$

at the following delay

$$
D_{\$forw} = 2 \cdot D_{mux}(8B).
$$

Delays of the Cache Interface

Based on the cache address ca, the cache itself provides the hit signal and the data Do. These two outputs therefore have an accumulated delay of:

$$
\begin{aligned}
A_{\$if}(hit) &= A_{AdG}(ca) + D_{\$k}(hit) \\
A_{\$if}(Do) &= A_{AdG}(ca) + D_{\$k}(Do).
\end{aligned}
$$

As for the whole DLX design, we distinguish between cycles which involve the off-chip memory and those which are only processed on-chip.

The memory address MAd and the data MDat are used in the first kind of cycles. The cache interface provides address MAd at an accumulated delay of

$$A_{\$if}(MAd) = A_{AdG}(ma).$$

The propagation of the data *MDat* to the output *Dout* and to the registers and RAMs of the interface adds the following delays:

$$
\begin{aligned}
D_{\$if}(MDat;Dout) &= D_{\$forw} \\
D_{\$if}(MDat;\$if) &= D_{mux}(8B) + D_{\$k}(Di;\$k).
\end{aligned}
$$

With respect to the on-chip cycles, the output *Dout* and the input data *Di* of the cache have the following accumulated delays:

$$
\begin{aligned}
A_{\$if}(Dout) &= \max\{A_{\$if}(Do), A_{AdG}(rs)\} + D_{\$forw} \\
A_{\$if}(Di) &= \max\{A_{CON}(cs\$if), A_{DP}(Din)\} + D_{mux}(8B).
\end{aligned}
$$

The k-way cache comprises RAMs and registers, which have to be updated. The actual updating of a register includes the delay D_{ff} of the register and the setup time δ, whereas the updating of a RAM only includes the setup time. The additional delay D_{ff} for the registers is already incorporated in the delay of the k-way cache. In addition to the cache address *ca*, the cache also needs the input data *Di* and the write signals in order to update its directory and cache data. The minimal cycle time of the cache interface can therefore be expressed as:

$$
\begin{aligned}
T_{\$if} = \; &\max\{T_{AdG}, A_{AdG}(CDw) + D_{\$k}(cs\$;\$k) + \delta, \\
&A_{AdG}(ca) + D_{\$k}(a;\$k) + \delta, A_{\$if}(Di) + D_{\$k}(Di;\$k) + \delta\}.
\end{aligned}
$$

6.4 Sequential DLX with Cache Memory

6.4.1 Changes in the DLX Design

IN SECTION 6.1.3, it has turned out that the sequential DLX core which is directly connected to the slow external memory spends most of its run time waiting for the memory system. We now analyze whether a fast cache between the processor core and the external memory can reduce this waiting time. Adding the cache only affects the memory environment Menv and the memory control. As before, the global functionality of the memory system and its interaction with the data paths and main control of the DLX design remain the same.

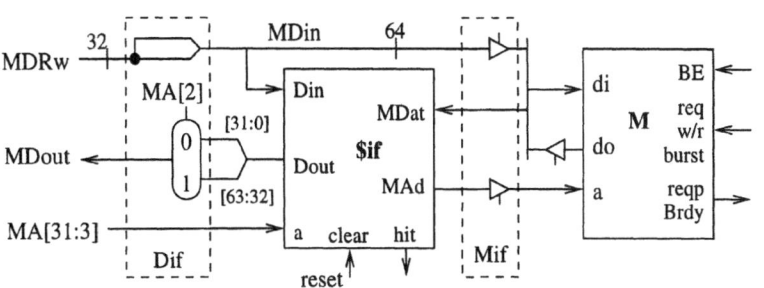

Figure 6.19 Memory environment of the sequential DLX with cache memory

Memory Environment

Figure 6.19 depicts the memory environment *Menv*. The cache interface $if of section 6.3 is placed between the memory interface *Mif* and the data paths interface *Dif*. The cache interface implements the write through, write allocate policy. Since there is only a single cache in the DLX design, line invalidation will not be supported. The cache is initialized/cleared on reset. The off-chip data bus MDat and the cache sectors are $B = 2^b = 8$ bytes wide.

Memory Interface Mif   The memory interface still forwards data and addresses between the off-chip memory and the memory environment. However, the memory address MAd is now provided by the cache interface, and the data from the memory data bus are forwarded to the data input MDat of the cache interface.

Interface Dif   The cache interface is connected to the data paths through a 32-bit address port MA and two data ports MDin and MDout. In the memory environment, the data busses are 64 bits wide, whereas in the data paths they are only 32 bit wide. Thus, the data ports must be patched together. On the input port MDin, circuit *Dif* duplicates the data MDRw

$$MDin[63:32] = MDin[31:0] = MDRw[31:0].$$

On the output port Dout, a multiplexer selects the requested 32-bit word within the double-word based on the address bit MA[2]:

$$MDout = \begin{cases} Dout[31:0] & \text{if } MA[2] = 0 \\ Dout[63:32] & \text{if } MA[2] = 1. \end{cases}$$

Let the sectored cache comprise 2^l lines, each of which is split in $S = 2^s$ sectors. The cost of the memory environment and of the interfaces Mif and

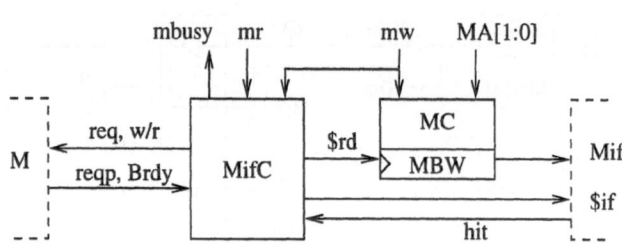

Figure 6.20 Block diagram of the memory control

Dif then run at

$$C_{Mif} = C_{driv}(32) + C_{driv}(64)$$
$$C_{Dif} = C_{mux}(32)$$
$$C_{Menv} = C_{Mif} + C_{Dif} + C_{\$if}(29 - l - s, l, s, 3).$$

The Memory Control
As in the sequential DLX design which is directly connected to the off-chip memory (section 6.1.3), the memory system is governed by the memory control circuit MC and the memory interface control $MifC$ (figure 6.20).

Memory Controller MC   The memory controller generates the memory bank write signals. Since the memory system now operates on double-words, twice as many write signals Mbw[7:0] are required. The original four signals mbw[3:0] still select within a word, and the leading offset bit of the write address MA[2] selects the word within the sector. Thus, the new bank write signals can be obtained as

$$Mbw[4 \cdot i + j] = \begin{cases} mbw[j] \wedge MA[2] & ; i = 1 \\ mbw[j] \wedge /MA[2] & ; i = 0 \end{cases} \quad j = 0, \ldots 3.$$

Stores always take several cycles, and the bank write signals are used in the second cycle, at the earliest. The memory control therefore buffers the signals Mbw in a register before feeding them to the cache interface and to the byte enable lines BE of the memory bus. Register MBW is clocked during the first cycle of a memory transaction, i.e., on $\$rd = 1$:

$$MBW[7:0] := \begin{cases} Mbw[7:0] & \text{if } \$rd = 1 \\ MBW[7:0] & \text{if } \$rd = 0. \end{cases}$$

Thus, circuit MC provides the signal MBW at zero delay

$$A_{MC}(MBW) = 0.$$

The cost and cycle time of the memory control MC run at

$$C_{MC} = C_{MC}(mbw) + C_{and}(8) + C_{inv} + C_{ff}(8)$$
$$T_{MC} = A_{MC}(mbw) + D_{and}(8) + \Delta.$$

Memory Interface Control As in the DLX of section 6.1.3, the memory interface control MifC controls the tristate drivers of the memory interface and generates the handshake signal *req* and the bust status signals *burst*, w/r and *mbusy* according to the bus protocol. In addition, control MifC provides the control signals of the cache interface.

The FSD of figure 6.10 together with table 6.11 specify the cache operations for the different memory transactions. However, the line fill and the write hit also access the off-chip memory. On such a memory access, the bus protocol of section 6.1.2 must be obeyed. Thus, the FSD must be extended by the bus operations. Figure 6.21 depicts the extended FSD. Note that on a burst read (line fill), the memory turns signal *reqp* off two cycles before sending the last sector. Thus, signal *reqp* = 0 can be used in order to detect the end of the line fill. Table 6.12 lists the active control signals for each state of the FSD.

Circuit MifC uses a Mealy automaton which generates the control signals as modeled by the FSD. Table 6.13 lists the parameters of the automaton. There are only two Mealy signals, namely *mbusy* and *$rd*. Both signals are just used for clocking. According to section 2.6.8, their accumulated delay can be expressed as

$$A_{CON}(mbusy, \$rd) = A_{MifC}(Mealy) = A_{out(2)}(MifC).$$

The remaining MifC control signals are Moore signals. Since the automaton precomputes its Moore outputs, these control signals are provided at zero delay

$$A_{MifC} = A_{MifC}(Moore) = 0.$$

The MifC automaton receives the inputs *mw* and *mr* from the main control, the hit signal from the cache interface, and the handshake signals *Brdy* and *reqp* from the memory. These inputs have an accumulated delay of

$$A_{in}(MifC) = \max\{A_{CON}(mw, mr), A_{\$if}(hit), A_M(Brdy, reqp) + d_{bus}\}.$$

Timing of Memory Accesses

As in the DLX design without cache, we assume that the off-chip memory is controlled by an automaton which precomputes its outputs and that the control inputs which the off-chip memory receives through the memory bus add d_{Mhsh} delays to the cycle time of its automaton. With a cache, the

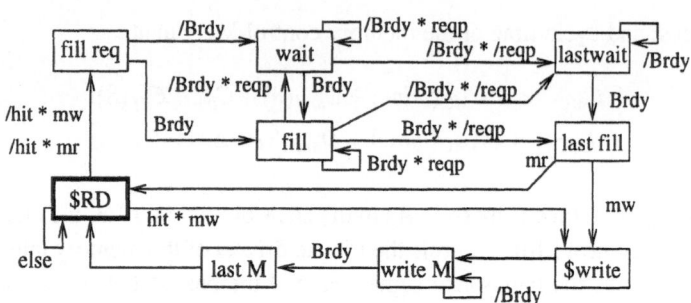

Figure 6.21 FSD of the MifC control automaton; $RD is the initial state.

Table 6.12 Active control signals for the FSD modeling the MifC control. Signals
$rd and /mbusy are Mealy signals, the remaining signals are Moore signals.

state	signals for $if	additional signals
$RD	$rd = mr ∨ mw	/mbusy = (hit ∧ mr) ∨ (/mr ∧ /mw)
fill req	scntclr, scntce, Vw, lfill	req, burst, MAddoe
fill	scntce, lfill, Sw	burst, MAddoe
wait	lfill	burst, MAddoe
last wait	lfill	burst, MAddoe
last fill	scntce, valid, Vw, Tw, lfill, Sw	MAddoe /mbusy = mr
$ write	$w	w/r, req, MAddoe, MDindoe
write M		w/r, MAddoe, MDindoe
last M		MDindoe, /mbusy

off-chip memory only performs a burst read access or a single write access.
Both accesses start with a request cycle.

The memory interface starts the memory access by sending the address
and the request signal *req* to the off-chip memory, but the address is now
provided by the cache interface. That is the only change. Forwarding
signal *req* and address *MAd* to the memory bus and off-chip still takes
$D_{driv} + d_{bus}$ delays, and the processing of the handshake signals adds d_{Mhsh}
delays. Thus, the memory request takes

$$T_{Mreq} = \max\{A_{MifC}, A_{\$if}(MAd)\} + D_{driv} + d_{bus} + d_{Mhsh} + \Delta.$$

After the request, the memory performs the actual access. The timing
of the single write access is modeled as in the design without cache. The

Table 6.13 Parameters of the MifC Mealy automaton; index (1) corresponds to the Moore signals and index (2) to the Mealy signals.

# states	# inputs	# and frequency of the outputs			
k	σ	γ	v_{sum}	$v_{max(1)}$	$v_{max(2)}$
9	5	15	40	7	4
fanin of the states		#, length, frequency of the monomials			
fan_{sum}	fan_{max}	#M	l_{sum}	l_{max}	$l_{max(2)}$
18	3	14	24	2	2

memory interface sends the data MDin and the byte enable bits. Once the off-chip memory receives these data, it performs the access:

$$T_{Mwrite} = \max\{A_{MC}(MBW), A_{MifC} + D_{driv}\} + d_{bus} + D_{MM}(64MB) + \delta.$$

On a burst read transfer, we distinguish between the access of the first sector and the access of the later sectors. A 64 MB memory provides the first sector with a delay of $D_{MM}(64MB)$. Sending them to the memory interface adds another $D_{driv} + d_{bus}$ delays. The sector is then written into the cache. Thus, reading the first sector takes at least

$$T_{Mread} = D_{MM}(64MB) + D_{driv} + d_{bus} + D_{\$if}(MDat;\$if) + \delta.$$

We assume, that for the remaining sectors, the actual memory access time can be hidden. Thus, the cache interface receives the next sector with a delay of $D_{driv} + d_{bus}$. Circuit $if writes the sector into the cache and forwards the sector to the data paths where the data are multiplexed and clocked into a register:

$$T_{Mrburst} = D_{driv} + d_{bus} + \delta \\ + \max\{D_{\$if}(MDat;\$if), D_{\$if}(MDat;Dout) + D_{mux} + D_{ff}\}.$$

Due to the memory access time, the write access and the reading of the first sector take much longer than the CPU internal cycles. Therefore, they are performed in W CPU cycles.

If a read access hits the cache, the off-chip memory is not accessed at all. The cache interface provides the requested data with an delay of $A_{\$if}(Dout)$. After selecting the appropriate word, data MDout is clocked into a register:

$$T_{\$read} = A_{\$if}(Dout) + D_{mux} + D_{ff}.$$

Table 6.14 Cost of the DLX design which is connected to the off-chip DRAM, either directly or through a 16 KB, direct mapped cache.

L1 cache	Menv	DP	CON	DLX
no	320	11166	1170	12336
16KB	375178	386024	1534	387558
increase factor	1170	35	1.3	31

Updating the cache interface on a read or write access takes $T_\$$. Thus, the memory environment of the DLX design requires a CPU cycle time of at least

$$T_M(W) = \max\{T_{\$read}, T_{\$if}, T_{Mreq}, T_{Mrburst}, \lceil T_{Maccess}/W \rceil\}$$
$$T_{Maccess} = \max\{T_{Mwrite}, T_{Mread}\}.$$

Cost and Cycle Time

Presently (2000) large workstations have a first level cache of 32KB to 64KB (table 6.8), but the early RISC processors (e.g. MIPS R2000/3000) started out with as little as 4KB to 8KB of cache. We consider a cache size of 16KB for our DLX design. This sectored, direct mapped cache is organized in 1024 lines. A cache line comprises $S = 2$ sectors, each of which is $B = 8$ bytes wide. The cache size and other parameters will be optimized later on.

According to table 6.14, the 16KB cache increases dramatically the cost of the memory environment Menv (factor 1200) and of the DLX processor (factor 31), but the cost of the control stays roughly the same. Adding a first level cache makes the memory controller MC more complicated; its automaton requires 9 instead of 3 states. However, this automaton is still fairly small, and thus, the whole DLX control is only 30% more expensive.

Table 6.15 lists the cycle times of the data paths, the control, and the memory system. The stall engine generates the clock and write signals based on signal *mbusy*. Due to the slow hit signal, signal *mbusy* has a much longer delay. That more then doubles the cycle time of the control, which now becomes time critical. The cycle time τ_{DLX} of the DLX core is increased by a factor of 1.27.

A memory request, a cache update, and a cache read hit can be performed in a single processor cycle. The time $T_{Mrburst}$ is also not time critical. Reading the first word from the off-chip memory requires several processor cycles; the same is true for the write access ($T_{Maccess}$). Since the memory data is written into a register and into the cache, such a read

Table 6.15 Cycle time of the DLX design which and without cache memory

cache	A_{hit}	A_{mbusy}	T_{MifC}	T_{stall}	T_{CON}	T_{DP}
no	–	7	28	33	42	70
16KB	55	64	79	89	89	70

cache	$T_{\$if}$	$T_{\$read}$	T_{Mreq}	$T_{Mrburst}$	$T_{Maccess}$		
					$\alpha = 4$	$\alpha = 8$	$\alpha = 16$
no	–	–	39	–	355	683	1339
16KB	48	57	36	63	391	719	1375

access takes even 36 delays longer.

The DLX design with first level cache can be operated at a cycle time of

$$\tau_{DLX}(W) \;=\; \max\{T_{DP}, T_{CON}, T_M(W)\}.$$

Increasing the number W of wait states improves the cycle time, but it also increases the CPI ratio. There is a trade-off between cycle time and cycle count.

Performance and Quality of the Design

In order to make the cache worthwhile, the cache better improves the performance of the DLX quite a bit. The memory system has no impact on the instruction count. However, the cache can improve the CPI ratio and the TPI ratio by speeding up the average memory accesses.

$$TPI \;=\; \frac{T}{IC} = CPI \cdot \tau_{DLX}.$$

Number of Memory Cycles In the DLX design without cache, a memory access takes always $1 + W$ cycles. After adding the cache, the time of a read or write access is no longer fixed. The access can be a cache hit or miss. In case of a miss, the whole cache line ($S = 2$ sectors) must be fetched from the external memory. Such a line fill takes $W + S$ cycles. Thus, the read access can be performed in a single cycle, if the requested data is in the cache, and otherwise, the read access takes $1 + W + S$ cycles due to the line fill.

A store first checks the cache before it performs the write access. Due to the write through, write allocate policy, the write always updates the cache and the external memory. Like in the system without cache, the update of the memory takes $1 + W$ cycles, and together with the checking of the

Table 6.16 Number of processor cycles required for a memory access.

	read hit	read miss	write hit	write miss
with cache	1	$1+S+W$	$2+W$	$2+W+S+W$
without cache	$1+W$		$1+W$	

cache, a write hit takes $2+W$ cycles. A cache miss adds another $W+S$ cycles (table 6.16).

CPI Ratio For a given benchmark, the *hit ratio* p_h measures the fraction of all the memory accesses which are cache hits, and the *miss ratio* ($p_m = 1 - p_h$) measures the fraction of the accesses which are cache misses. This means that the fraction p_m of the memory accesses is a cache miss and requires a line fill.

Let CPI_{ideal} denote the CPI ratio of the DLX design with an ideal memory, i.e., with a memory which performs every access in a single cycle. In analogy to the CPI ratio of a pipelined design (section 4.6), the cache misses and memory updates can be treated as hazards. Thus, the CPI ratio of the DLX design with L1 cache can be expressed as:

$$CPI_{L1} = CPI_{ideal} + v_{store} \cdot (1+W) + v_{miss} \cdot (W+S)$$
$$v_{miss} = p_m \cdot (1 + v_{load} + v_{store}).$$

The CPI ratio of the DLX design with ideal memory can be derived from the instruction mix of table 6.6 in the same manner as the CPI ratio of the DLX without cache. That table also provides the frequency of the loads and stores. According to cache simulations [Kro97, GHPS93], the 16KB direct mapped cache of the DLX achieves a miss ratio of 3.3% on the SPECint92 workload. On the compress benchmark, the cache performs slightly better ($p_m = 3.1\%$). Thus, the DLX with 16KB cache yields on these two workloads a CPI ratio of

$$CPI_{L1}(compr) = 4.19 + 0.056 \cdot (1+W) + 0.031 \cdot 1.255 \cdot (S+W)$$
$$= 4.32 + 0.09 \cdot W$$

$$CPI_{L1}(SPEC) = 4.26 + 0.085 \cdot (1+W) + 0.033 \cdot 1.338 \cdot (S+W)$$
$$= 4.43 + 0.13 \cdot W.$$

Based on these formulae, the optimal cycle time and optimal number of wait states can be determined as before. Although the CPI and TPI ratios vary with the workload, the optimal cycle time is the same for all the

Table 6.17 Optimal cycle time and number W of wait states

L1	$\alpha = 4$		$\alpha = 8$		$\alpha = 16$	
cache	W	τ	W	τ	W	τ
no	5	71	10	70	19	71
16KB	5	89	8	90	16	89

Table 6.18 CPI and TPI ratios of the two DLX designs on the compress benchmark and on the average SPECint92 workload.

	compress ($p_m = 3.1\%$)			SPECint ($p_m = 3.3\%$)		
DRAM: α	4	8	16	4	8	16
CPI_{noL1}	10.5	16.7	28.0	11.0	17.6	29.7
CPI_{L1}	4.8	5.0	5.8	5.1	5.5	6.5
CPI_{noL1}/CPI_{L1}	2.2	3.3	4.8	2.1	3.2	4.6
TPI_{noL1}	753.7	1172.0	1990.7	788.7	1235.1	2107.7
TPI_{L1}	424.5	453.6	512.6	452.1	492.3	579.4
TPI_{noL1}/TPI_{L1}	1.8	2.6	3.9	1.7	2.5	3.6
Break even: eq	0.14	0.21	0.28	0,14	0.21	0.28

SPECint92 benchmarks; it only depends on the speed of the main memory (table 6.17). Depending on the speed of the main memory, the cache increases the optimal cycle time by 25% or 30%, but for slow memories it reduces the number of wait states.

According to table 6.18, the cache improves the CPI ratio roughly by a factor of 2 to 5. Due to the slower cycle time, the TPI ratio and the performance of the DLX processor is only improved by a factor of about 2 to 4. Especially in combination with a very slow external memory ($\alpha = 16$), the cache achieves a good speedup. Thus, there is a trade-off between cost and performance.

Cost Performance Trade-Off　For any two variants A and B of the DLX design, the parameter eq specifies the quality parameter q for which both variants are of the same quality:

$$\frac{1}{C_A^q \cdot TPI_A^{1-q}} = \frac{1}{C_B^q \cdot TPI_B^{1-q}}.$$

For quality parameters $q < eq$, the faster of the two variants is better, and for $q > eq$, the cheaper one is better. For a realistic quality metric, the quality parameter q lies in the range of $[0.2, 0.5]$.

Depending on the speed of the off-chip memory, the break even point lies between 0.14 and 0.28 (table 6.18). The DLX with cache is the faster of the two designs. Thus, the 16KB cache improves the quality of the sequential DLX design, as long as the performance is much more important than the cost.

Altogether, it is worthwhile to add a 16KB, direct mapped cache to the DLX fixed point core, especially in combination with a very slow external memory. The cache increases the cost of the design by a factor of 31, but it also improves the performance by a factor of 1.8 to 3.7. However, the DLX still spends 13% to 30% of its run time waiting for the main memory, due to cache misses and write through accesses.

6.4.2   Variations of the Cache Design

Every cache design has many parameters, like the cache size, the line size, the associativity, and the cache policies. This section studies the impact of these parameters on the performance and cost/performance ratio of the cache design.

Impact of the Line Size

As already pointed out in section 6.2.1, the memory accesses tend to cluster, i.e., at least over a short period of time, the processor only works on a few clusters of references. Caches profit from the temporal and spatial locality.

Temporal Locality   Once a memory data is brought into the cache, it is likely to be used several times before it is evicted. Thus, the slow initial access is amortized by the fast accesses which follow. If the cache is to small, it cannot accommodate all the clusters required, and data will be evicted although they are needed shortly thereafter. Large caches can reduces these evictions, but cache misses cannot vanish completely, because the addressed clusters change over time, and the first access to a new cluster is *always* a miss. According to table 6.19 ([Kro97]), doubling the cache size cuts the miss ratio by about one third.

Spatial Locality   The cache also makes use of the spatial locality, i.e., whenever the processor accesses a data, it is very likely that it soon ac-

Table 6.19 Miss ratio of a direct mapped cache depending on the cache size [K byte] and the line size [byte] for the average SPECint92 workload; [Kro97].

cache size	line size [byte]				
	8	16	32	64	128
1 KB	0.227616	0.164298	0.135689	0.132518	0.150158
2 KB	0.162032	0.112752	0.088494	0.081526	0.088244
4 KB	0.109876	0.077141	0.061725	0.057109	0.059580
8 KB	0.075198	0.052612	0.039738	0.034763	0.034685
16 KB	0.047911	0.032600	0.024378	0.020493	0.020643
32 KB	0.030686	0.020297	0.015234	0.012713	0.012962
64 KB	0.020660	0.012493	0.008174	0.005989	0.005461

cesses a data which is stored close by. Starting a memory transfer requires W cycles, and then the actual transfer delivers 8 bytes per cycle. Thus fetching larger cache lines saves time, but only if most of the fetched data are used later on. However, there is only limited amount of spatial locality in the programs.

According to table 6.19, the larger line sizes reduces the miss ratio significantly up to a line size of 32 bytes. Beyond 64 bytes, there is virtually no improvement, and in some cases the miss ratio even increases. When analyzing the CPI ratio (table 6.20), it becomes even more obvious that 32-byte lines are optimal. Thus, it is not a pure coincidence that commercial processors like the Pentium [AA93] or the DEC Alpha [ERP95] use L1 caches with 32-byte cache lines.

However, 32 bytes is not a random number. In the SPECint92 integer workload, about 15% of all the instructions change the flow of control (e.g., branch, jump, and call). On average, the instruction stream switches to another cluster of references after every sixth instruction. Thus, fetching more than 8 instructions (32 bytes) rarely pays off, especially since the instructions account for 75% of the memory references.

Impact on Cost and Cycle Time   Doubling the cache size cuts the miss ratio by about one third and improves the cycle count, but it also impacts the cost and cycle time of the DLX design (table 6.21). If a cache of 8KB or more is used, the fixed point core with its 12 kilo gates accounts for less than 10% of the total cost, and doubling the cache size roughly doubles the cost of the design.

For a fixed cache size, doubling the line size implies that the number of cache lines in cut by half. Therefore, the cache directory only requires half

Table 6.20 CPI ratio of the DLX with direct mapped cache on the SPECint92 workload. Taken from [Kro97].

DRAM	cache	line size [byte]				
α	size	8	16	32	64	128
	1 KB	6.60	6.31	6.40	7.08	8.99
	2 KB	6.07	5.83	5.84	6.19	7.25
	4 KB	5.65	5.49	5.51	5.76	6.44
4	8 KB	5.37	5.26	5.25	5.37	5.74
	16 KB	5.15	5.08	5.06	5.13	5.35
	32 KB	5.02	4.96	4.95	4.99	5.13
	64 KB	4.94	4.89	4.87	4.87	4.92
	1 KB	7.77	7.22	7.20	7.86	9.85
	2 KB	6.98	6.53	6.45	6.77	7.86
	4 KB	6.35	6.06	6.02	6.25	6.94
8	8 KB	5.93	5.73	5.66	5.77	6.14
	16 KB	5.60	5.46	5.42	5.46	5.69
	32 KB	5.39	5.30	5.27	5.30	5.44
	64 KB	5.27	5.19	5.16	5.15	5.20

as many entries as before, and the directory shrinks by half. Thus, doubling the line size reduces the cost of the cache and the cost of the whole DLX design. Increasing the line size from 8 to 16 bytes reduces the cost of the DLX design by 7-10%. Doubling the line size to 32 bytes saves another 5% of the cost. Beyond 32 bytes, an increase of the line size has virtually no impact on the cost.

Table 6.21 also lists the cycle time imposed by the data paths, the control and the cache interface:

$$T_{DLX} = \max\{T_{DP}, T_{CON}, T_{\$if}, T_{\$read}\}.$$

The cache influences this cycle time in three ways: $T_{\$if}$ and $T_{\$read}$ account for the actual update of the cache and the time of a cache read hit. The cache directory also provides the hit signal, which is used by the control in order to generate the clock and write enable signals (T_{CON}). This usually takes longer than the cache update itself and for large caches it becomes even time critical. Doubling the line size then reduces the cycle time by 3 gate delays due to the smaller directory.

Table 6.21 Cost and cycle time of the DLX design with a direct mapped cache

cache size [KB]	cost C_{DLX} [kilo gates]					cycle time T_{DLX}				
	line size [B]									
	8	16	32	64	128	8	16	32	64	128
1	42	39	37	36	36	80	70	70	70	70
2	69	62	59	57	57	83	80	70	70	70
4	121	109	103	100	98	86	83	80	70	70
8	226	202	190	185	182	89	86	83	80	70
16	433	388	365	354	348	92	89	86	83	80
32	842	756	713	692	681	95	92	89	86	83
64	1637	1481	1403	1364	1345	98	95	92	89	86

Increasing the Associativity

Caches are much smaller than the main memory, and thus, many memory addresses must be mapped to the same set of cache locations. In the direct mapped cache, there is exactly *one* possible cache location per memory address. Thus, when fetching a new memory data, the cache line is either empty, or the old entry must be evicted. That can cause severe *thrashing*:

Two or more clusters of references (e.g., instruction and data) share the same cache line. When accessing these clusters by turns, all the accesses are cache misses and the line must be replaced every time. Thus, the slow line fills cannot be amortized by fast cache hits, and the cache can even deteriorate the performance of the memory system.

Using a larger cache would help, but that is very expensive. A standard way out is to increase the associativity of the cache. The associativity of a first level cache is typically two or four. In the following, we analyze the impact of associativity on the cost and performance of the cache and DLX design.

Impact on the Miss Ratio   Table 6.22 lists the miss ratio of an associative cache with random or LRU replacement policy on a SPECint92 workload. This table is taken from [Kro97], but similar results are given in [GHPS93]. LRU replacement is more complicated than random replacement because it requires a cache history, but it also results in a significantly better miss ratio. Even with twice the degree of associativity, a cache with random replacement performs worse than a cache with LRU replacement. Thus, we only consider the LRU replacement.

In combination with LRU replacement, 2-way and 4-way associativity improve the miss ratio of the cache. For moderate cache sizes, a 2-way

Table 6.22 Miss ratio [%] of the SPECint92 workload on a DLX cache system with 32-byte lines and write allocation; [Kro97].

cache	direct	2-way		4-way	
size	mapped	LRU	random	LRU	random
1 KB	13.57	10.72	19.65	9.41	12.30
2 KB	8.85	7.02	13.34	6.53	8.40
4 KB	6.17	4.54	8.82	4.09	5.41
8 KB	3.97	2.52	6.16	2.04	3.05
16 KB	2.44	1.39	3.97	1.00	1.52
32 KB	1.52	0.73	2.44	0.58	0.83
64 KB	0.82	0.52	1.52	0.44	0.56

Table 6.23 Cost and CPU cycle time of the DLX design with a k-way set associative cache (32-byte lines).

cache	cost C_{DXL} [kilo gates]					T_{DLX}		
size	absolute			increase				
[KB]	k = 1	2	4	$1 \to 2$	$2 \to 4$	1	2	4
1	37	38	41	3.9 %	7.2 %	70	70	70
2	59	61	62	2.6 %	5.0 %	70	70	70
4	103	105	108	1.7 %	3.4 %	80	74	70
8	190	193	197	1.2 %	2.4 %	83	84	76
16	365	368	375	0.9 %	1.8 %	86	87	86
32	713	718	729	0.7 %	1.5 %	89	90	89
64	1403	1416	1436	0.8 %	1.4 %	92	93	92

cache achieves roughly the same miss ratio as a direct mapped cache of twice the size.

Impact on the Cost   Like for a direct mapped cache, the cost of the cache interface with a set associative cache roughly doubles when doubling the cache size. The cache interface accounts for over 90% of the cost, if the cache size is 8KB or larger (table 6.23). 2-way and 4-way associativity increase the total cost by at most 4% and 11%, respectively. The relative cost overhead of associative caches gets smaller for larger cache sizes.

When switching from 2-way to 4-way associativity, the cost overhead is about twice the overhead of the 2-way cache. That is for the following reasons: In addition to the cache directory and the cache data RAMs, a set associative cache with LRU replacement also requires a cache history and some selection circuits. In a 2-way cache, the history holds one bit per sector, and in a 4-way cache, it holds 8 bits per sector; that is less than 0.5% of the total storage capacity of the cache. The significant cost increase results from the selection circuits which are the same for all cache sizes. In the 2-way cache, those circuits account for about 900 gate equivalents. The overhead of the 4-way cache is about three times as large, due to the more complicated replacement circuit.

Impact on the Cycle Time   The cache provides the hit signal which is used by the control in order to generate the clock signals. Except for small caches (1KB and 2KB), the control even dominates the cycle time T_{DLX} which covers all CPU internal cycles (table 6.23). Doubling the cache size then increases the cycle time by 3 gate delays due to the larger RAM.

In a 32-bit design, the tags of a direct mapped cache of size X KB are

$$t_1 \; = \; 32 - \log X$$

bits wide according to figure 6.7. Thus, doubling the cache size reduces the tag width by one. In a set associative cache, the cache lines are distributed equally over the k cache ways, and each way only holds a fraction $(1/k)$ of the lines. For a line size of 32 bytes, we have

$$
\begin{aligned}
L_k &= L_1/k = X/(32 \cdot k) \\
t_k &= 32 - \log X + \log k = t_1 + \log k
\end{aligned}
$$

The cache tags are therefore $\log k$ bits wider than the tags of an equally sized direct mapped cache.

In each cache way, the local hit signal $h[i]$ is generated by an equality tester which checks the t_k-bit tag and the valid flag:

$$D_{\$k}(h[i]) \; = \; D_{RAM}(L_k, t_k) + D_{EQ}(t_k + 1).$$

The core of the tester is a $(t_k + 1)$-bit OR-tree. For a cache size of of 1KB to 64KB and an associativity of $k \leq 4$, we have

$$
\begin{aligned}
32 - \log(64K) + \log 1 \; &\leq \; t_k \; \leq \; 32 - \log(1K) + \log 4 \\
17 \; &\leq \; t_k + 1 \; \leq \; 25
\end{aligned}
$$

and the equality tester in the hit check circuit of the k-way cache has a fixed depths. However, the access of the cache data and the directory is $3 \log k$ delays faster due to the smaller RAMs

$$D_{\$k}(h[i]) \; = \; D_{\$1}(h[i]) - 3 \log k.$$

Table 6.24 Optimal cycle time τ_{DLX} and number of wait states for the DLX design with caches and two types of main memory ($\alpha \in \{4,8\}$).

cache	$\alpha = 4$						$\alpha = 8$					
size	1		2		4		1		2		4	
C	W	τ	W	τ	W	τ	W	τ	W	τ	W	τ
1 KB	6	70	6	70	5	72	10	71	10	70	10	70
2 KB	6	70	6	70	6	70	10	71	10	71	10	70
4 KB	5	80	6	74	6	70	9	80	10	74	10	71
8 KB	5	83	5	84	5	77	9	83	9	84	10	76
16 KB	5	86	5	87	5	86	9	86	9	87	9	86
32 KB	5	89	5	90	5	89	9	89	8	90	8	90
64 KB	5	92	5	93	5	92	8	92	8	93	8	92

The local hit signals of the k cache ways are combined to a global hit signal using an AND gate and an k-bit OR-tree. For $k \geq 2$, we have

$$
\begin{aligned}
D_{\$k}(hit) &= D_{\$k}(h[i]) + D_{and} + D_{ORtree}(k) \\
&= D_{\$1}(h[i]) - 3\log k + 2 + 2\log k.
\end{aligned}
$$

Thus, for a moderate cache size, the 2-way cache is one gate delay slower than the other two cache designs.

Impact on the Performance Table 6.24 lists the optimal cycle time of the DLX design using an off-chip memory with parameter $\alpha \in \{4,8\}$, and table 6.25 lists the CPI and TPI ratio of these designs. In comparison to a direct mapped cache, associative caches improve the miss ratio, and they also improve the CPI ratio of the DLX design. For small caches, 2-way associativity improves the TPI ratio by $4 - 11\%$, and 4-way associativity improves it by $5 - 17\%$. However, beyond a cache size of 4KB, the slower cycle time of the associative caches reduces the advantage of the improved miss ratio. The 64KB associative caches even perform worse than the direct mapped cache of the same size.

Doubling the cache size improves the miss ratio and the CPI, but it also increases the cycle time. Thus, beyond a cache size of 4KB, the 4-way cache dominates the cycle time T_{DLX}, and the larger cycle time even out-weights the profit of the better miss ratio. Thus, the 4KB, 4-way cache yields the best performance, at least within our model. Since larger caches increase cost and TPI ratio, they cannot compete with the 4KB cache.

In combination with a fast off-chip memory ($\alpha = 4$), this cache speeds the DLX design up by a factor of 2.09 at 8.8 times the cost. For a memory

Table 6.25 CPI and TPI ratio of the DLX design with cache. The third table lists the CPI and TPI reduction of the set associative cache over the direct mapped cache (32-byte lines).

CPI ratio						
cache	$\alpha = 4$			$\alpha = 8$		
size	1	2	4	1	2	4
1 KB	6.67	6.29	5.90	7.74	7.20	6.96
2 KB	6.04	5.79	5.73	6.85	6.51	6.42
4 KB	5.51	5.46	5.40	6.18	6.05	5.96
8 KB	5.25	5.07	5.02	5.80	5.55	5.58
16 KB	5.06	4.94	4.89	5.53	5.35	5.28
32 KB	4.95	4.86	4.84	5.37	5.14	5.12
64 KB	4.87	4.83	4.82	5.16	5.11	5.10

TPI ratio						
cache	$\alpha = 4$			$\alpha = 8$		
size	1	2	4	1	2	4
1 KB	466.9	440.3	425.0	549.3	504.2	487.0
2 KB	422.7	405.6	401.1	486.5	462.2	449.3
4 KB	441.1	404.2	378.2	494.7	447.4	423.2
8 KB	435.6	426.2	386.2	481.5	466.1	423.9
16 KB	435.5	429.6	420.6	475.9	465.7	454.5
32 KB	440.9	437.2	430.7	478.4	462.8	460.6
64 KB	447.9	449.4	443.7	474.4	475.0	468.8

	CPI reduction				TPI reduction			
cache	$\alpha = 4$		$\alpha = 8$		$\alpha = 4$		$\alpha = 8$	
size	2	4	2	4	2	4	2	4
1 KB	6.1	13.0	7.4	11.2	6.1	9.9	8.9	12.8
2 KB	4.2	5.4	5.3	6.8	4.2	5.4	5.3	8.3
4 KB	0.9	2.1	2.3	3.7	9.1	16.6	10.6	16.9
8 KB	3.4	4.6	4.5	4.0	2.2	12.8	3.3	13.6
16 KB	2.5	3.5	3.4	4.7	1.4	3.5	2.2	4.7
32 KB	2.0	2.4	4.5	5.0	0.8	2.4	3.4	3.9
64 KB	0.7	0.9	0.9	1.2	-0.3	0.9	-0.1	1.2

Table 6.26 Speedup and cost increase of the DLX with 4-way cache over the design without cache

cache size		1KB	2KB	4KB
speedup:	$\alpha = 4$	1.86	1.97	2.09
	$\alpha = 8$	2.54	2.75	2.92
relative cost increase		3.34	5.16	8.78

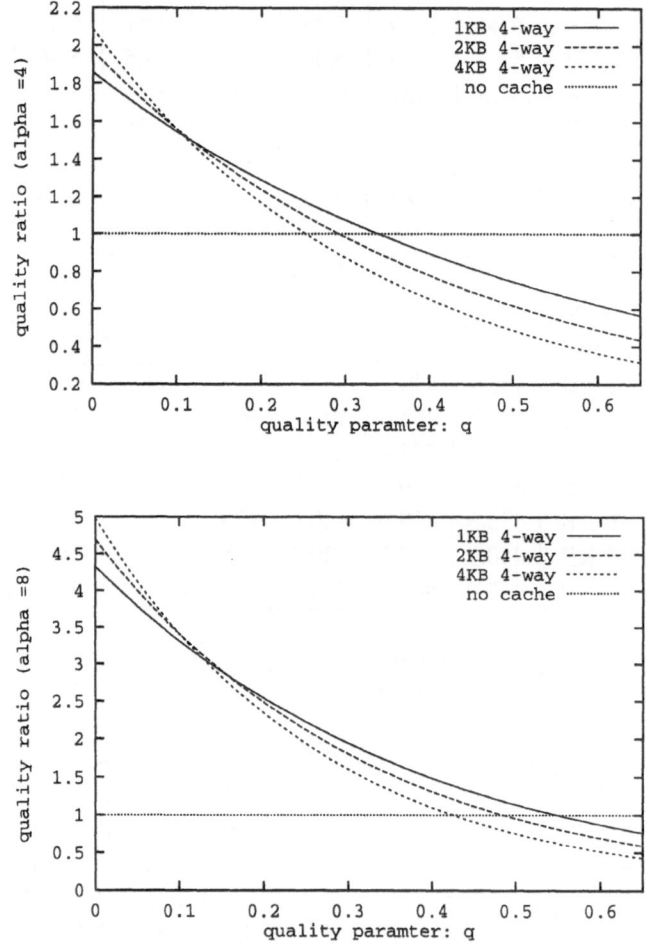

Figure 6.22 Quality ratio of the designs with 4-way cache relative to the design without cache for two types of off-chip memory.

system with $\alpha = 8$, the cache even yields a speedup of 2.9. According to table 6.26, the speedup of the 1KB and 2KB caches are at most 6% to 15% worse than that of the 4KB cache at a significantly better cost ratio. Thus, there is a trade-off between cost and performance, and the best cache size is not so obvious. Figure 6.22 depicts the quality of the DLX designs with a 4-way cache of size 1KB to 4KB relative to the quality of the design without cache. The quality is the weighted geometric mean of cost and TPI ratio: $Q = C^{-q} \cdot TPI^{q-1}$.

As long as more emphasis is put on the performance than on the cost, the caches are worthwhile. In combination with fast off-chip memory ($\alpha = 4$), the design with an 1KB cache is best over the quality range of $q \in [0.1, 0.34]$. For slower memory, the 1KB cache even wins up to a quality parameter of $p = 0.55$ (at $q = 0.5$ cost and performance are equally important). Only for $q < 0.13$, the 4KB cache wins over the 1KB cache, but these quality parameters are not realistic (page 167). Thus, when optimizing the DLX design for a reasonable performance and quality, a cache size of 1 KB is most appropriate.

Artifact The performance optimization suggests a 4 times larger cache than the quality metric. This is due to the very inexpensive DLX core which so far only comprises a simple fixed point core without multiplier and divider. Adding a floating point unit (chapter 9) will increase the cost of the DLX core dramatically, and then optimizing the DLX design for a good performance or for a good quality will result in roughly the same cache size.

6.5 Pipelined DLX with Cache Memory

IN ORDER to avoid structural hazards, the pipelined DLX core of the sections 4 and 5 requires an instruction memory *IM* and a data memory *DM*. The cache system described in this section implements this *split* memory by a separate instruction and data cache. Both caches are backed by the *unified* main memory, which holds data and instructions.

The split cache system causes two additional problems:

- *The arbitration of the memory bus.* Our main memory can only handle one access at a time. However, an instruction cache miss can occur together with a write through access or a data cache miss. In such a case, the data cache will be granted access, and the instruction cache must wait until the main memory allows for a new access.

- *The data consistency of the two caches.* As long as a memory word is placed in the instruction cache, the instruction cache must be aware of the changes done to that memory word. Since in our DLX design, all the memory writes go through the data cache, it is only the instruction cache which must be protected against data inconsistency.

Although we do not allow for self modifying code, data consistency is still a problem for the following reason. During compile time, the program code generated by the compiler is treated as data and is therefore held in the data cache. When running the program, the code is treated as instructions and must be placed in the instruction cache. After re-compiling a program, the instruction cache may still hold some lines of the old, obsolete code. Thus, it must be ensured that the processor fetches the new code from the main memory instead of the obsolete code held in the instruction cache.

As usual, one can leave the consistency to the user and the operating system or can support it in hardware. In case of a software solution, the instruction cache must be *flushed* (i.e., all entries are invalidated) whenever changing existing code or adding new code. It is also feasible to flush the instruction cache whenever starting a new program.

In our design, we will go for a hardware solution. The two caches snoop on the memory bus. On a data cache miss, the requested line is loaded into the data cache, as usual. If the instruction cache holds this line, its corresponding cache entry is invalidated. In analogy, a line of the data cache which holds the instructions requested by the instruction cache is also invalidated on an instruction cache miss. At any time a particular memory line is in at most *one* cache.

6.5.1   Changes in the DLX Data Paths

As in the sequential DLX design (section 6.4), the caches only impact the memory environments and the memory control circuits. This section describes how to fit the instruction and data cache into the memory environments *IMenv* and *DMenv* of the pipelined design DLX_Π supporting interrupts, and how the memory interface *Mif* connects these two environments to the external main memory. The new memory control is described in section 6.5.2.

Environment of the Data Memory

The core of the data environment *DMenv* (figure 6.23) is the cache interface $D\$if$ as it was introduced in section 6.3. The data cache (Dcache) is a sectored, write through, write allocate cache with a 64-bit word size. In

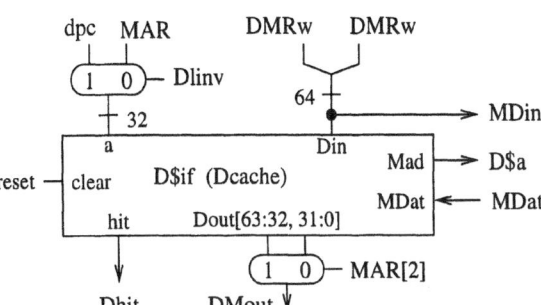

Figure 6.23 Data memory environment DMenv with cache

addition to the standard control signals of a cache interface, the memory environment is governed by the reset signal and by signal *Dlinv* which requests a line invalidation access due to an instruction cache miss.

As in the sequential design (section 6.4), the cache interface D$if is connected to the data paths through a 32-bit address port and two data ports MDin and DMout. Due to the 64-bit cache word size, the data ports must be patched together. On the input port MDin, data MDRw is still duplicated

$$MDin[63:32] = MDin[31:0] = MDRw[31:0].$$

On the output port Dout, a multiplexer selects the requested 32-bit word within the double-word based on the address bit MAR[2]:

$$DMout = \begin{cases} Dout[31:0] & \text{if} \quad MAR[2] = 0 \\ Dout[63:32] & \text{if} \quad MAR[2] = 1. \end{cases}$$

On an instruction cache miss the data cache is checked for the requested line (*Dlinv* = 1). In case of a snoop hit, the corresponding Dcache entry is invalidated. For the snoop access and the line invalidation, the Dcache interface uses the address *dpc* of the instruction memory instead of address MAR:

$$a = \begin{cases} MAR & \text{if} \quad Dlinv = 0 \\ dpc & \text{if} \quad Dlinv = 1. \end{cases}$$

A multiplexer selects between these two addresses. Since the Dcache is only flushed on reset, the clear input of the Dcache interface D$if is connected to the reset signal. The hit signal *Dhit* is provided to the memory control.

The data memory environment communicates with the memory interface *Mif* and the external memory via the address port D$a and the data ports

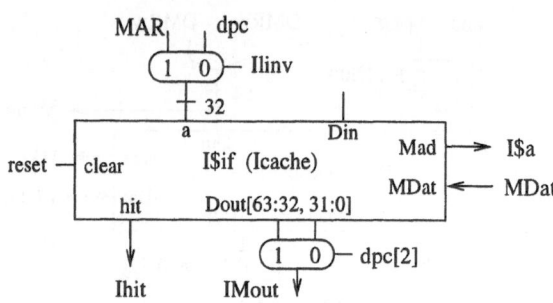

Figure 6.24 Instruction memory environment IMenv with cache

MDin and MDat. The Dcache interface provides the memory address

$$D\$a = Mad.$$

Let the sectored cache comprise 2^{ld} lines, each of which is split in $S = 2^{sd}$ sectors. The data memory environment then has cost

$$C_{DMenv} = C_{\$if}(29 - ld - sd, ld, sd, 3) + 2 \cdot C_{mux}(32).$$

Assuming that control signal $Dlinv$ is precomputed, address a and data Din have the following accumulated delay:

$$A_{D\$if}(a) = A_{PCenv}(dpc) + D_{mux}$$
$$A_{D\$if}(Din) = 0.$$

Environment of the Instruction Memory

Figure 6.24 depicts how to fit a first level instruction cache (Icache) into the instruction memory environment *IMenv*. The instructions in the Icache are only read by the DLX core but never written. Thus, the Icache interface *I\$if* could actually be simplified. Nevertheless, we use the standard cache interface. However, the input data port *Din* is not connected.

The address port *a* and the data port *Dout* of the cache interface I\$if are connected to the data paths like in the environment DMenv. However, the program counter *dpc* now serves as standard cache address, whereas address *MAR* is only used in case of a snoop access or a line invalidation. Flag *Ilinv* signals such an access:

$$IDout = \begin{cases} Dout[31:0] & \text{if } dpc[2] = 0 \\ Dout[63:32] & \text{if } dpc[2] = 1 \end{cases}$$

$$a = \begin{cases} MAR & \text{if } Ilinv = 1 \\ dpc & \text{if } Ilinv = 0. \end{cases}$$

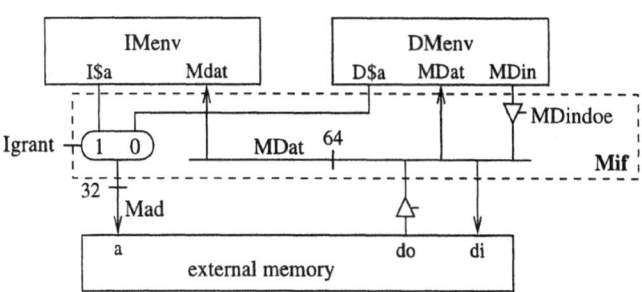

Figure 6.25 Interface Mif connecting *IMenv* and *DMenv* to the external memory

The Icache is, like the Dcache, flushed on reset; its hit signal *Ihit* is provided to the memory control. The environment IMenv communicates with memory interface *Mif* and the external memory via the address port I$a and the data port MDat. The Icache interface provides the memory address $I\$a = Mad$.

Let the instruction cache comprise 2^{li} lines with 2^{si} sectors per line and $2^b = 8$ bytes per sector; the cost of environment IMenv can be expressed as

$$C_{IMenv} = C_{\$if}(29 - li - si, li, si, 3) + 2 \cdot C_{mux}(32).$$

The Icache address a has the same accumulated delay as the Dcache address.

Interface of the Main Memory

The memory interface *Mif* (figure 6.25) connects the two memory environments of the pipelined DLX design to the external memory. The environments DMenv and IMenv communicate with the external memory via the 32-bit address bus MAd and the 64-bit data bus MDat. The memory interface is controlled by the signals *MDindoe* and *Igrant*.

On $Igrant = 1$, the Icache interface is granted access to the external memory; the memory interface forwards address I$a to the address bus. On $Igrant = 0$, the Dcache interface can access the external memory and circuit Mif forwards address D$a:

$$MAd = \begin{cases} I\$a & \text{if} \quad Igrant = 1 \\ D\$a & \text{if} \quad Igrant = 0. \end{cases}$$

On $MDindoe = 1$, the memory interface forwards the data MDin of the data memory environment to the data bus MDat.

303

6.5.2 Memory Control

In analogy to the sequential DLX design with cache, the memory system is governed by the memory control circuits *DMC* and *IMC* and by the memory interface control *MifC*.

Instruction Memory Control IMC

The control IMC of the instruction memory is exactly the same as the one used in the pipelined design DLX_Π of chapter 5. Circuit IMC signals a misaligned instruction fetch by $imal = 1$. Since the DLX core never writes to the instruction memory, the bank write signals are always inactive and can be tied to zero:

$$Imbw[7:0] = 0^8.$$

Data Memory Control DMC

As in the pipelined design DLX_Π without caches, the data memory control DMC generates the bank write signals of the data memory and checks for a misaligned access. However, twice as many write signals DMbw[7:0] are required because the memory system now operates on double-words. The original four signals Dmbw[3:0] select within a word, and the address bit MAR[2] selects the word within the sector. Thus, the new bank write signals are obtained as

$$
\begin{aligned}
DMbw[3:0] &= Dmbw[3:0] \wedge /MAR[2] \\
DMbw[7:4] &= Dmbw[3:0] \wedge MAR[2].
\end{aligned}
$$

As in the sequential design with cache, the control DMC buffers these bank write signals in a register before feeding them to the Dcache interface and to the byte enable lines BE of the memory bus. Register DMBw is clocked during the first cycle of a data memory transaction, signaled by $D\$rd = 1$:

$$DMBw[7:0] := DMbw[7:0] \quad \text{if} \quad D\$rd = 1.$$

Circuit DMC detects a misaligned access like in the DLX_Π design. Flag $dmal = 1$ signals that an access to the data memory is requested, and that this access is misaligned (i.e., $malAc = 1$):

$$dmal = (Dmr.3 \vee Dmw.3) \wedge malAc.$$

In addition, it now also masks the memory read and write signals *Dmr* and *Dmw* with the flag *dmal*:

$$
\begin{aligned}
Dmra &= Dmr.3 \wedge /dmal = /Dmr.3 \text{ NOR } malAc \\
Dmwa &= Dmw.3 \wedge /dmal = /Dmw.3 \text{ NOR } malAc.
\end{aligned}
$$

Let *dmc* denote the data memory control of the pipelined design without cache. The cost, delay and cycle time of the extended memory control DMC can then be expressed as

$$C_{DMC} = C_{dmc} + C_{and}(8) + 3 \cdot C_{inv} + C_{ff}(8) + 2 \cdot C_{nor}$$
$$A_{DMC}(DMBw) = 0$$
$$A_{DMC}(dmal) = A_{DMC}(Dmra, Dmwa) = A_{dmc}$$
$$T_{DMC} = A_{dmc} + D_{and} + \Delta.$$

Memory Interface Control

Like in the sequential design, the memory interface control MifC controls the cache interface and the access to the external memory bus. Since there are two caches in the pipelined DLX design, the control MifC consists of two automata $I\$ifC$ and $D\$ifC$. Each automaton generates a busy flag (ibusy, dbusy), a set of cache control signals, a set of handshake and control signals for the memory bus, and some signals for the synchronization. The cache control signals (i.e.: $\$rd$, Vw, Tw, Sw, lfill, valid, scntce, scntclr, linv, $\$w$) are forwarded to the corresponding cache interface I$if and D$if.

The D$ifC control provides the following synchronization signals

- *Dinit* indicating that D$ifC is in its initial state,

- *Igrant* granting the Icache access to the memory bus, and

- *isnoop* requesting the Icache to perform a snoop access.

The I$ifC signal *iaccess* indicates an ongoing transaction between Icache and memory.

For the memory bus, control D$ifC provides the request signal *Dreq*, the flags Dw/r, *Dburst* and the enable signal *MDindoe*. Since the Icache interface only uses the bus for fetching a new cache line, its burst and r/w flag have a fixed value. Based on flag *Igrant*, control MifC selects the bus signals as

$$(req, w/r, burst) = \begin{cases} (Dreq, Dw/r, Dburst) & \text{if} \quad Igrant = 0 \\ (Ireq, 0, 1) & \text{if} \quad Igrant = 1 \end{cases}$$

using a 3-bit multiplexer. Thus, the cost of circuit MifC can be expressed as

$$C_{MifC} = C_{mux}(3) + C_{I\$ifC} + C_{D\$ifC}.$$

The two automata I$ifC and D$ifC are very much like the Mealy automaton of the sequential MifC control, except that they provide some new signals, and that they need two additional states for the snoop access. In

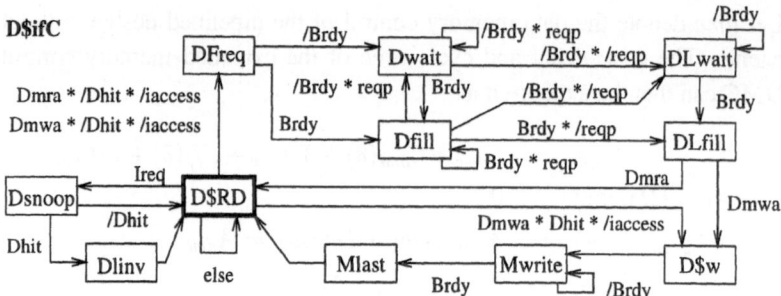

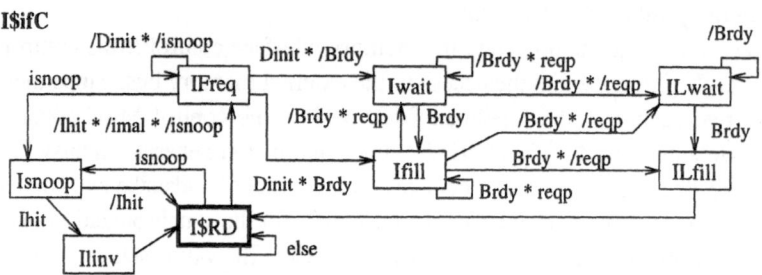

Figure 6.26 FSDs modeling the Mealy automata of the controls D\$if and I\$if

the I\$ifC automaton, the states for the memory write access are dropped. Figure 6.26 depicts the FSDs modeling the Mealy automata of the D\$ifC and I\$ifC control. Table 6.27 lists the active control signals for each state; table 6.28 lists the parameters of the two automata, assuming that the automata share the monomials.

The inputs of the two automata have the following accumulated delay:

$$A_{in}(I\$ifC) = \max\{A_{IMC}, A_{IMenv}(Ihit), A_M(reqp, Brdy) + d_{bus}\}$$
$$A_{in}(D\$ifC) = \max\{A_{dmc}, A_{DMenv}(Dhit), A_M(reqp, Brdy) + d_{bus}\}.$$

The two busy signals and the signals *D\$rd* and *I\$rd* are the only Mealy control signals. As in the sequential design, these signals are just used for clocking. The remaining cache control signals (cs\$if) and the bus control signals are of type Moore and can be precomputed. They have delay

$$A_{MifC}(cs\$if) = 0$$
$$A_{MifC}(req, w/r, burst) = D_{mux}.$$

Since the automata only raise the flags *ibusy* and *dbusy* in case of a non-faulty memory access, the clock circuit of the stall engine can now simply

Table 6.27 Active control signals for the FSDs modeling the MifC control; X denotes the data (D) or the instruction (I) cache.

state	$if control	D$ifC only	I$ifC only
XFreq	scntclr, scntce, Vw, lfill	Dreq, Dburst, isnoop	Ireq, iaccess
Xfill	scntce, lfill, Sw	Dburst	iaccess
Xwait	lfill	Dburst	iaccess
XLwait	lfill	Dburst	iaccess
XLFill	scntce, valid, Vw, Tw, lfill, Sw	/dbusy = Dmra	/ibusy, iaccess
Xsnoop		D$rd, Dlinv, Igrant	I$rd, Ilinv
Xlinv	Vw	Dlinv, Igrant	Ilinv
I$RD	I$rd = /imal, /ibusy = (imal ∧ /isnoop) ∨ (Ihit ∧ /isnoop)		
D$w	$w, Dw/r, Dreq, MDindoe		
Mwrite	Dw/r, MDindoe		
Mlast	MDindoe, /mbusy		
D$RD	Igrant, Dinit, D$rd = Dmra ∨ Dmwa /dbusy = (dmal ∧ /Ireq) ∨ (Dhit ∧ /Ireq)		

Table 6.28 Parameters of the Mealy automata used in the memory interface control MifC

	# states	# inputs	# and frequency of outputs			
	k	σ	γ	v_{sum}	$v_{max(1)}$	$v_{max(2)}$
D$ifC	11	8	18	42	5	3
I$ifC	8	6	11	29	5	3

	fanin of the states		# and length of nontrivial monomials			
	fan_{sum}	fan_{max}	#M	l_{sum}	l_{max}	$l_{max(2)}$
D$ifC	20	3	18	35	3	2
I$ifC	16	3	10	17	3	2

obtain the busy signal as

$$busy = ibusy \lor dbusy$$

at an accumulated delay of

$$A_{ce}(busy) = \max\{A_{out(2)}(I\$ifC), A_{out(2)}(D\$ifC)\} + D_{or}.$$

Bus Arbitration

This is the tricky part. Let us call $D\$ifC$ the *D-automaton*, and let us call $I\$ifC$ the *I-automaton*. We would like to show the following properties:

Lemma 6.1 ▶

1. *Memory accesses of the D-automaton and of the I-automaton do not overlap,*

2. *memory accesses run to completion once they are started, and*

3. *a cache miss in DM (IM) always generates a snoop access in IM (DM).*

Before we can prove the lemma, we first have to formally define, in what cycles a memory access takes place. We refer to the bus protocol and count an access from the first cycle, when the first address is on the bus until the last cycle, when the last data are on the bus.

PROOF

Proof of the lemma:
After power up, the automata are in their initial state and no access is taking place.

The *D*-automaton controls the bus via signal *Igrant*. It grants the bus to the *I*-automaton ($Igrant = 1$) only during states D\$RD, Dsnoop and Dlinv, and it owns the bus ($Igrant = 1$) during the remaining states. Therefore, accesses of the *D*-automaton can only last from state DFreq to DLfill or from state D\$w to Mlast. During these states, the *I*-automaton does not have the bus. Thus, accesses do not overlap, and accesses of the *D*-automaton run to completion once they are started.

The *I*-automaton attempts to start accesses in state *IFreq*, but it may not have the bus. Thus, accesses of the *I*–automaton can only last from state IFreq with $Igrant = 1$ until state ILfill. In each of these states we have $iaccess = 1$.

Suppose state IFreq is entered with $Igrant = 0$. Then, the access starts in the cycle when the *D*-automaton is back in its initial state D\$RD. In this cycle we have

$$Igrant = Dinit = iaccess = 1.$$

Thus, the access of the *I*-automaton starts, the *I*-automaton leaves state IFreq, and the active signal *iaccess* prevents the *D*-automaton from entering states DFreq or D$w before the access of the *I*-automaton runs to completion.

If state IFreq is entered with $Igrant = 1$, the access starts immediately, and the *D*-automaton returns to its initial state within 0, 1 or 2 cycles. From then on, things proceed as in the previous case.

In state DFreq signal *isnoop* is active which sends the *I*-automaton from its initial state into state Isnoop. Similarly, in state IFreq signal *Ireq* is active which sends the *D*-automaton from its initial state into state Dsnoop.   QED

6.5.3   Design Evaluation

For the sequential DLX design (section 6.4) which is connected to a 64 MB main memory, it has turned out that a 4 KB cache with 32 byte lines yields a reasonable performance and cost performance ratio. Thus, our pipelined DLX design will also implement 4 KB of first level cache; the data and the instruction cache comprise 2 KB each.

Timing of the Memory Accesses
As for the sequential DLX design with cache, the temporal behavior of the memory system is modeled by the request cycle time T_{Mreq}, the burst read time $T_{Mrburst}$, the read/write access time $T_{Maccess}$ to off-chip memory, the cache read access time $T_{\$read}$, and the cycle time $T_{\$if}$ of the caches (see page 283).

In the pipelined DLX design, the Icache and the Dcache have the same size, and their inputs have the same accumulated delay, thus

$$T_{\$if} = T_{I\$if} = T_{D\$if} \quad \text{and} \quad T_{\$read} = T_{I\$read} = T_{D\$read}.$$

The formulae of the other three memory cycle times remain unchanged. The cycle time T_{DLX} of all internal cycles and the cycle time τ_{DLX} of the whole system are still modeled as

$$T_{DLX} = \max\{T_{DP}, T_{CON}, T_{\$read}, T_{\$if}, T_{Mreq}, T_{Mrburst}\}$$
$$\tau_{DLX} = \max\{T_{DLX}, \lceil T_{Maccess}/W \rceil\}.$$

Impact on Cost and Cycle Time
According to table 6.29, the 4KB cache memory increases the cost of the pipelined design by a factor of 5.4. In the sequential design this increase factor is significantly larger (8.8) due to the cheaper data paths.

Table 6.29 Cost of the DLX_Π design without cache and with 2KB, 2-way Icache and Dcache

	Menv	DP	CON	DLX
no cache	–	20610	1283	21893
with caches	96088	116698	2165	118863

Table 6.30 Cycle time of the design DLX_Π with 2KB, 2-way Icache and Dcache

MifC	stall	DP	$read	$if	Mreq	Mrburst	Maccess	
							$\alpha = 4$	$\alpha = 8$
65	79	89	55	47	42	51	379	707

The two caches and the connection to the external memory account for 81% of the total cost of the pipelined design. The memory interface control now comprises two Mealy automata, one for each cache. It therefore increases the cost of the control by 69%, which is about twice the increase encountered in the sequential design.

Table 6.30 lists the cycle time of the DLX_Π design and of its memory system, assuming a bus and handshake delay of $d_{bus} = 15$ and $d_{Mhsh} = 10$. The data paths dominate the cycle time T_{DLX} of the processor core. The caches themselves and the control are not time critical. The memory request and the burst read can be performed in a single cycle; they can tolerate a bus delay of $d_{bus} = 53$.

Impact of the Cache Size

The pipelined DLX design implements a split cache system, i.e., it uses a separate instruction cache and data cache. The cost of this cache system is roughly linear in the total cache size (table 6.31). Compared to the unified cache system of the sequential DLXs design, the split system implements the cache interface twice, and it therefore encounters a bigger overhead. Using 2-way set associative caches, the split system with a total cache size of 1KB is 15% more expensive than the unified cache system. For a larger cache size of 4KB (32 KB), the overhead drops to 4% (1%).

The split cache can also be seen as a special associative cache, where half the cache ways are reserved for instructions or data, respectively. The cost of the split and unified cache system are then virtually the same; the difference is at most 2%.

Like in the sequential design, the cycle time of the control increases with

Table 6.31 Cost of the memory environments and the cycle time of the pipelined DLX design depending on the total cache size and the associativity. $C_{Menv,\Sigma}$ denotes the cost of the unified cache in the sequential DLX design. The cost is given in kilo gates.

	$C_{Menv,\Sigma}$		C_{Menv}		T_{CON}		T_{DP}
# way	2	4	1	2	1	2	1,2
1 KB	26	29	27	30	71	73	89
2 KB	48	51	49	52	75	75	89
4 KB	92	96	93	96	83	79	89
8 KB	178	185	181	184	93	87	89
16 KB	353	363	356	360	96	97	89
32 KB	701	717	705	711	99	100	89

the cache size, due to the computation of the hit signal. However, if the size of a single cache way is at most 2KB, the control is not time critical. In spite of the more complex cache system, this is the same cache size bound as in the sequential DLX design. That is because the stall engine and main control of the pipelined design are also more complicated than those used in the sequential design.

Impact on the Performance and the Quality

CPI Ratio In section 4.6.4, we have derived the CPI ratio of the pipelined design DLX_Π on a SPECint92 workload as

$$CPI_{DLX_\Pi} = 1.26 + (\nu_{fetch} + \nu_{load} + \nu_{store}) \cdot CPH_{slowM}.$$

The workload comprises 25.3% loads and 8.5% stores. Due to some empty delay slots of branches, the pipelined DLX design must fetch 10% additional instructions, so that $\nu_{fetch} = 1.1$.

As in the sequential DLX design with cache interface, the memory access time is not uniform (table 6.16, page 288). A read hit can be performed in just a single cycle. A standard read/write access to the external memory ($T_{Maccess}$) requires W processor cycles. Due to the write through policy, a write hit then takes $2 + W$ cycles. For a cache line with S sectors, a cache miss adds another $S + W$ cycles. Let p_{Im} and p_{Dm} denote the miss ratio of the instruction and data cache. Since on a cache miss, the whole pipeline is usually stalled, the CPI ratio of the pipelined design with cache

Table 6.32 Miss ratios of a split and a unified cache system on the SPECint92 workload depending on the total cache size and the associativity.

# way	Icache 1	Icache 2	Dcache 1	Dcache 2	Effective 1	Effective 2	Unified Cache 1	Unified Cache 2	Unified Cache 4
1 KB	8.9	8.2	22.8	15.2	12.4	9.9	13.6	10.8	9.4
2 KB	6.6	5.9	14.1	9.4	8.5	6.8	8.9	7.0	6.5
4 KB	4.7	4.4	9.4	5.5	5.9	4.7	6.2	4.5	4.1
8 KB	3.0	2.4	6.8	3.5	4.0	2.7	4.0	2.5	2.0
16 KB	2.0	1.1	3.5	2.6	2.4	1.5	2.4	1.5	1.0
32 KB	1.1	0.4	2.6	1.8	1.5	0.8	1.5	0.7	0.6

interface can be expressed as

$$
\begin{aligned}
CPI_{L1p} &= 1.26 + \nu_{store} \cdot (1+W) \\
&\quad + (\nu_{fetch} \cdot p_{Im} + \nu_{load/store} \cdot p_{Dm}) \cdot (W+S) \\
&= 1.35 + 0.085 \cdot W \\
&\quad + (1.1 \cdot p_{Im} + 0.34 \cdot p_{Dm}) \cdot (W+S).
\end{aligned}
\tag{6.5}
$$

Effective Miss Ratio   According to table 6.32, the instruction cache has a much better miss ratio than the data cache of the same size. That is not surprising, because instruction accesses are more regular than data accesses. For both caches, the miss ratio improves significantly with the cache size.

The pipelined DLX design strongly relies on the split first level cache, whereas the first level cache of the sequential DLX design and any higher level cache can either be split or unified. We have already seen that a split cache system is more expensive, but it maybe achieves a better performance.

For an easy comparison of the two cache designs, we introduce the effective miss ratio of the split cache as:

$$
\begin{aligned}
p_{miss\,eff} &= \frac{\#\text{miss on fetch} + \#\text{miss on load/store}}{\#\text{fetch} + \#\text{load/store}} \\
&= \frac{\nu_{fetch} \cdot p_{Im} + \nu_{load/store} \cdot p_{Dm}}{\nu_{fetch} + \nu_{load/store}}.
\end{aligned}
$$

This effective miss ratio directly corresponds to the miss ratio of a unified cache. According to table 6.32, a split direct mapped cache has a smaller miss ratio than a unified direct mapped cache; that is because instructions and data will not thrash each other. For associative caches, the advantage

Table 6.33 Optimal cycle time τ, number of wait states W, CPI and TPI ratio of the pipelined DLX design with split 2-way cache.

total cache size	memory: $\alpha = 4$				memory: $\alpha = 8$			
	W	τ	CPI	TPI	W	τ	CPI	TPI
1 KB	4	90	2.82	253.5	8	89	3.72	331.2
2 KB	4	92	2.46	226.3	8	89	3.19	283.7
4 KB	4	95	2.22	211.1	8	89	2.83	251.9
8 KB	5	89	2.12	188.4	8	89	2.49	221.4
16 KB	4	97	1.85	179.2	8	97	2.27	220.1
32 KB	4	100	1.77	177.3	7	103	2.06	212.3

of a split system is not so clear, because two cache ways already avoid most of the thrashing. In addition, the unified cache space can be used more freely, e.g., more than 50% of the space can be used for data. Thus, for a 2-way cache, the split approach only wins for small caches ($< 4KB$).

On the other hand, the split cache can also be seen as a special associative cache, where half the cache ways are reserved for instructions or data, respectively. Since the unified cache space can be used more freely, the unified 2-way (4-way) cache has a better miss ratio than the split direct mapped (2-way) cache. Commercial computer systems use large, set associative second and third level caches, and these caches are usually unified, as the above results suggest.

Performance Impact   Table 6.33 lists the optimal number of wait states and cycle time of the pipelined DLX design as well as the CPI and TPI ratios for two versions of main memory. The CPI ratio improves significantly with the cache size, due to the better miss ratio. Despite the higher cycle time, increasing the cache size also improves the performance of the pipelined design by 30 to 36%. In the sequential DLX design, the cache size improved the performance by at most 12% (table 6.25). Thus, the speedup of the pipelined design over the sequential design increases with the cache size.

Compared to the sequential design with 4-way cache, the pipelined design with a split 2-way cache yields a 1.5 to 2.5 higher performance (table 6.34). The cache is by far the most expensive part of the design; a small 1KB cache already accounts for 60% of the total cost. Since the pipelined and sequential cache interfaces have roughly the same cost, the overhead of pipelining decreases with the cache size. The pipelined DLX design is at most 27% more expensive, and the cost increase is smaller than the perfor-

Table 6.34 Speedup and cost increase of the pipelined design with split 2-way cache relative to the sequential design with unified 4-way cache.

total cache size	cost [kilo gates]			speedup	
	DLX_Σ	DLX_Π	increase	$\alpha = 4$	$\alpha = 8$
1 KB	41	52	27%	1.68	1.47
2 KB	62	74	19%	1.77	1.58
4 KB	108	118	9%	1.79	1.68
8 KB	197	207	5%	2.05	1.91
16 KB	375	383	2%	2.35	2.06
32 KB	729	734	1%	2.43	2.17

mance improvement. In combination with caches, pipelining is definitely worthwhile.

6.6 Selected References and Further Reading

TWO TEXTBOOKS on cache design are [Prz90, Han93]. A detailed analysis of cache designs can also be found in Hill's Thesis [Hil87].

6.7 Exercises

Exercise 6.1 In section 6.2.2, we specified a sectored, direct mapped cache and a non-sectored, set associative cache. Extend these specifications to a sectored, set associative cache. As before, a cache line comprises S sectors.

Exercise 6.2 This and the following exercises deal with the design of a *write back* cache and its integration into the sequential DLX design. Such a cache applies the weak consistency model. A write hit only updates the cache but not the external memory. A dirty flag for each line indicates that the particular line has been updated in the cache but not in the main memory. If such a dirty line is evicted from the cache, the whole line must be copied back before starting the line fill. Figure 6.27 depicts the operations of a write back cache for the memory transactions read and write.

Modify the design of the k-way cache and of the cache interface in order to support the write back policy and update the cost and delay formulae. Special attention has to be payed to the following aspects:

- A cache line is only considered to be dirty, if the dirty flag is raised and if the line holds valid data.

- The memory environment now performs two types of burst accesses, the line fill and the write back of a dirty cache line. The data RAMs of the cache are updated on a line fill but not on the write back.

Exercise 6.3 Integrate the write back cache interface into the sequential DLX design and modify the cost and delay formulae of the memory system. The memory environment and the memory interface control have to be changed. Note that the FSD of figure 6.27 must be extended by the bus operations.

Exercise 6.4 A write back cache basically performs four types of accesses, namely a cache read access (read hit), a cache update (write hit), a line fill, and a write back of a dirty line. Let a cache line comprise S sectors. The read hit then takes one cycle, the write hit two cycles, and the line fill and the write back take $W + S$ cycles each.

Show that the write back cache achieves a better CPI ratio than the write through cache if the number of dirty misses and the number of writes (stores) obey:

$$\frac{W - 1}{W + S} > \frac{\text{\# dirty misses}}{\text{\# writes}}.$$

Exercise 6.5 Analyze the impact of the write back policy on the cost, performance, and quality of the sequential DLX design. Table 6.35 lists the ratio of dirty misses to writes for a SPECint92 workload [Kro97].

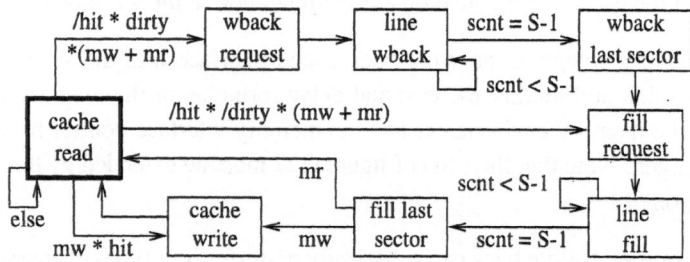

Figure 6.27 Cache operations of the memory transactions read and write

Table 6.35 Ratio of dirty misses to write accesses on the SPECint92 workload.

cache	line size [byte]				
size	8	16	32	64	128
1 KB	0.414	0.347	0.328	0.337	0.402
2 KB	0.315	0.243	0.224	0.223	0.262
4 KB	0.256	0.190	0.174	0.169	0.183
8 KB	0.197	0.141	0.107	0.093	0.098
16 KB	0.140	0.097	0.073	0.061	0.060
32 KB	0.107	0.072	0.053	0.044	0.042

Chapter 7

IEEE Floating Point Standard and Theory of Rounding

IN THIS chapter, we introduce the algebra needed to talk concisely about floating point circuits and to argue about their correctness. In this formalism, we specify parts of the IEEE floating point standard [Ins85], and we derive basic properties of IEEE-compliant floating point algorithms. Two issues will be of central interest: the number representation and the rounding.

7.1 Number Formats

7.1.1 Binary Fractions

Let $a = a[n-1:0] \in \{0,1\}^n$ and $f = f[1:p-1] \in \{0,1\}^{p-1}$ be strings. We then call the string $a[n-1:0].f[1:p-1]$ a *binary fraction*. An example is 110.01. The value of the fraction is defined in the obvious way

$$\langle a[n-1:0].f[1:p-1] \rangle \;=\; \sum_{i=0}^{n-1} a_i \cdot 2^i + \sum_{i=1}^{p-1} f_i \cdot 2^{-i}.$$

In the above example, we have $\langle 110.01 \rangle = 6 + .25 = 6.25$. We permit the cases $p = 0$ and $n = -1$ by defining

$$\langle a. \rangle \;=\; \langle a.0 \rangle = \langle a \rangle$$
$$\langle .f \rangle \;=\; \langle 0.f \rangle.$$

Thus, binary fractions generalize in a natural way the concept of binary numbers, and we can use the same notation to denote their values. Some obvious identities are

$$\langle 0a.f \rangle = \langle a.f \rangle = \langle a.f0 \rangle$$
$$\langle a.f \rangle = \langle af \rangle \cdot 2^{-(p-1)}$$

As in the decimal system, this permits to use fixed point algorithms to perform arithmetic on binary fractions. Suppose, for instance, we want to add the binary fractions $a[n-1:0].f[1:p-1]$ and $b[m-1:0].g[1:q-1]$, where $m > n$ and $p > q$. For some result $s[m:0].t[1:p-1]$ of an ordinary binary addition we then have

$$\langle a.f \rangle + \langle b.g \rangle = \langle 0^{m-n}a.f \rangle + \langle b.g0^{p-q} \rangle$$
$$= (\langle 0^{m-n}af \rangle + \langle bg0^{p-q} \rangle) \cdot 2^{-(p-1)}$$
$$= \langle s[m:0]t[1:p-1] \rangle \cdot 2^{-(p-1)}$$
$$= \langle s.t \rangle$$

7.1.2 Two's Complement Fractions

Of course, also two's complement arithmetic can be extended to fractions. One can interpret a string $a[n-1:0].f[1:p-1]$ as

$$[a[n-1:0].f[1:p-1]] = -a[n-1] \cdot 2^{n-1} + \langle a[n-2:0].f[1:p-1] \rangle.$$

We call string $a.f$ interpreted in this way a *two's complement fraction*. Using

$$[a[n-1:0].f[1:p-1]] = [a[n-1:0]f[1:p-1]] \cdot 2^{-(p-1)}$$

one immediately translates algorithms for two's complement numbers into algorithms for two's complement fractions.

7.1.3 Biased Integer Format

The IEEE floating point standard makes use of a rather particular integer format called the *biased integer format*. In this format, a string

$$e[n-1:0] \notin \{0^n, 1^n\}$$

represents the number

$$[[e[n-1:0]]]_{bias} = \langle e[n-1:0] \rangle - bias_n$$

where

$$bias_n = 2^{n-1} - 1.$$

Strings interpreted in this way will be called *biased integers* Biased integers with n bits lie in a range $[e_{min} : e_{max}]$, where

$$e_{min} = 1 - (2^{n-1} - 1) = -2^{n-1} + 2$$
$$e_{max} = 2^n - 2 - (2^{n-1} - 1) = 2^{n-1} - 1.$$

Instead of designing new adders and subtractors for biased integers, we will convert biased integers to two's complement numbers, perform all arithmetic operations in ordinary two's complement format, and convert the final result back. Recall that for n-bit two's complement numbers, we have

$$[x[n-1 : 0]] = -x_{n-1} \cdot 2^{n-1} + \langle x[n-2 : 0] \rangle$$

and therefore

$$[x[n-1 : 0]] \in \{-2^{n-1}, \ldots, 2^{n-1} - 1\}.$$

Thus, the two numbers excluded in the biased format are at the bottom of the range of representable numbers. Converting a biased integer $x[n-1 : 0]$ to a two's complement number $y[n-1 : 0]$ requires solving the following equation for y

$$\begin{aligned}
[\![x]\!]_{bias} &= [y] \\
\leftrightarrow \quad \langle x \rangle - 2^{n-1} + 1 &= -y_{n-1} \cdot 2^{n-1} + \langle y[n-2 : 0] \rangle \\
\leftrightarrow \quad \langle x \rangle + 1 &= 2^{n-1} \cdot (1 - y_{n-1}) + \langle y[n-2 : 0] \rangle \\
&= \langle \overline{y_{n-1}}, y[n-2 : 0] \rangle.
\end{aligned}$$

This immediately gives the conversion algorithm, namely:

1. Interpret x as a binary number and add 1. No overflow will occur.

2. Invert the leading bit of the result.

Conversely, if we would like to convert a two's complement number $y[n-1 : 0]$ with $[y] \notin \{-2^{n-1}, \ldots, 2^{n-1} + 1\}$ into biased representation, the above equation must be solved for x. This is equivalent to

$$\langle x \rangle = [y] + 2^{n-1} - 1 = [y] + \langle 1^{n-1} \rangle = \langle y \rangle + \langle 1^{n-1} \rangle \bmod 2^n.$$

It suffices to perform the computation modulo 2^n because the result lies between 1 and $2^{n-1} - 2$.

Table 7.1 Components of an IEEE floating point number

	normal	denormal
exponent	$[\![e]\!]_{bias}$	e_{min}
significand	$\langle 1.f' \rangle$	$\langle 0.f' \rangle$
hidden bit	1	0

7.1.4 IEEE Floating Point Numbers

An IEEE floating point number is a triple $(s, e[n-1:0], f[1:p-1])$, where $s \in \{0,1\}$ is called the *sign bit*, $e = e[n-1:0]$ represents the *exponent*, and $f' = f[1:p-1]$ almost represents the *significand* of the number (if it would represent the significand, we would call it f). The most common parameters for n and p are

$$(n,p) = \begin{cases} (8,24) & \text{for single precision} \\ (11,53) & \text{for double precision} \end{cases}$$

Obviously, single precision numbers fit into one machine word and double precision numbers into two words.

IEEE floating point numbers can represent certain rational numbers as well as the symbols $+\infty$, $-\infty$ and *NaN*. The symbol *NaN* represents 'not a number', e.g., the result of computing $0/0$. Let (s, e, f') be a floating point number, then the value represented by (s, e, f') is defined by

$$[\![s,e,f']\!] = \begin{cases} (-1)^s \cdot 2^{[\![e]\!]_{bias}} \cdot \langle 1.f' \rangle & \text{if } e \notin \{0^n, 1^n\} \\ (-1)^s \cdot 2^{e_{min}} \cdot \langle 0.f' \rangle & \text{if } e = 0^n \\ (-1)^s \cdot \infty & \text{if } e = 1^n \quad \text{and} \quad f = 0^{p-1} \\ NaN & \text{if } e = 1^n \quad \text{and} \quad f \neq 0^{p-1}. \end{cases}$$

The IEEE floating point number (s, e, f') is called

- *normal* if $e \notin \{0^n, 1^n\}$ and

- *denormal* (denormalized) if $e = 0^n$.

For normal or denormal IEEE floating point numbers, *exponent*, *significand* and *hidden bit* are defined by table 7.1. Observe that the exponent e_{min} has two representations, namely $e = 0^{n-1}1$ for normal numbers and $e = 0^n$ for denormal numbers. Observe also, that string f' alone does *not* determine the significand, because the exponent is required to determine the hidden bit. If we call the hidden bit $f[0]$, then the significand obviously

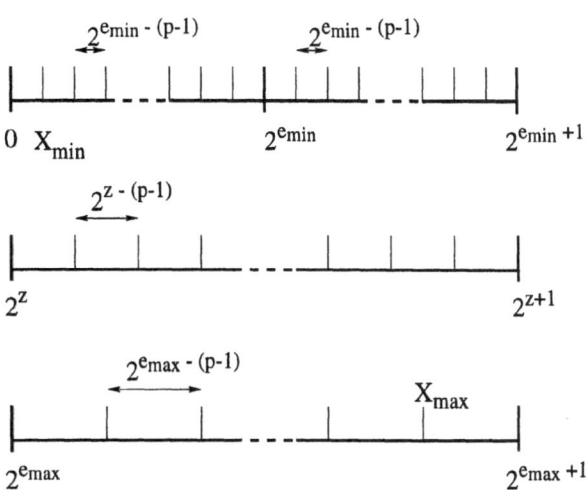

Figure 7.1 Geometry of the non-negative representable numbers

equals $\langle f[0].f[1:p-1]\rangle$. The binary fraction $f = f[0].f[1:p-1]$ then is a proper representation of the significand. It is called normal, if $f[0] = 1$ and denormal if $f[0] = 0$. We have

$$
\begin{aligned}
f[0] \le \langle f \rangle &= f[0] + \langle f[1:p-1]\rangle \cdot 2^{-(p-1)} \\
&\le f[0] + (2^{p-1} - 1) \cdot 2^{-(p-1)} \\
&= f[0] + 1 - 2^{-(p-1)}.
\end{aligned}
$$

Thus, we have

$$
1 \le \langle f \rangle \le 2 - 2^{-(p-1)}
$$

for normal significands and

$$
0 \le \langle f \rangle \le 1 - 2^{-(p-1)}
$$

for denormal significands.

7.1.5 Geometry of Representable Numbers

A rational number x is called *representable* if $x = [\![s,e,f']\!]$ for some IEEE floating point number. The number x is called *normal* if (s,e,f') is normal. It is called *denormal* if (s,e,f') is denormal.

Normal numbers have a significand in the range $[1, 2 - 2^{-(p-1)}] \subset [1,2)$. Denormal numbers have a significand in the range $[0, 1 - 2^{-(p-1)}] \subset [0,1)$.

Figure 7.1 depicts the non-negative representable numbers; the picture for the negative representable numbers is symmetric. The following properties characterize the representable numbers:

1. For every exponent value $z \in \{e_{min}, \ldots, e_{max}\}$, there are two intervals containing normal representable numbers, namely $[2^z, 2^{z+1})$ and $(-2^{z+1}, -2^z]$. Each interval contains exactly 2^{p-1} numbers. The gap between consecutive representable numbers in these intervals is $2^{z-(p-1)}$.

2. As the exponent value increases, the length of the interval doubles.

3. Denormal floating point numbers lie in the two intervals $[0, 2^{e_{min}})$ and $(-2^{-e_{min}}, 0]$. The gap between two consecutive denormal numbers equals $2^{e_{min}-(p-1)}$. This is the same gap as in the intervals $[2^{e_{min}}, 2^{e_{min}+1})$ and $(-2^{e_{min}+1}, -2^{e_{min}}]$. The property, that the gap between the numbers $2^{e_{min}}$ and $-2^{e_{min}}$ is filled with the denormal numbers is called *gradual underflow*.

Note that the smallest and largest positive representable numbers are

$$
\begin{aligned}
X_{min} &= 2^{e_{min}} \cdot 2^{-(p-1)} \\
X_{max} &= 2^{e_{max}} \cdot (2 - 2^{-(p-1)}).
\end{aligned}
$$

The number $x = 0$ has two representations, one for each of the two possible sign bits. All other representable numbers have exactly one representation. A representable number $x = [\![s, e, f']\!]$ is called *even* if $f[p-1] = 0$, and it is called *odd* if $f[p-1] = 1$. Note that even and odd numbers alternate through the whole range of representable numbers. This is trivial to see for numbers with the same exponent. Consecutive numbers with different exponent have significands 0, which is even, and $1 + \langle 1^{p-1} \rangle$, which is odd.

7.1.6 Convention on Notation

One should always work on as high an abstraction level as possible, but not on a higher level. In what follows, we will be able to argue for very long periods about numbers instead of their representations.

So far, we have used the letters e and f for the representations $e = e[n-1:0]$ and $f = f[0].f[1:p-1]$ of the exponent and of the significand. Since there is a constant shortage of letters in mathematical texts, we will use single letters like e and f also for the *values* of exponents and significands, respectively. Obviously, we could use $\langle e \rangle$ and $\langle f[0].f \rangle$ instead, but that would mess up the formulae in later calculations. Using the same notation for two things without proper warning can be the source of very serious confusion. On the other hand, confusion can be avoided, as long as

- we are aware that the letters e and f are used with two meanings depending on context, and

- the context indicates whether we are talking about values or representations.

But what do we do if we want to talk about values and representations in the same context? In such a case, single letters are used exclusively for values. Thus, we would, for instance, write

$$e = [\![e[n-1]]\!]_{bias} \quad \text{and} \quad f = [\![f[0].f[1:p-1]]\!],$$

but we would not write

$$e = [\![e]\!]_{bias} \quad \text{nor} \quad f = [\![f]\!].$$

7.2 Rounding

7.2.1 Rounding Modes

We denote by $\mathcal{R}$ the set of representable numbers and by

$$\mathcal{R}_\infty = \mathcal{R} \cup \{\infty, -\infty\}.$$

Since $\mathcal{R}$ is not closed under the arithmetic operations, one rounds the result of an arithmetic operation to a representable number or to plus infinity or minus infinity. Thus, a rounding is a function

$$r : R \to \mathcal{R}_\infty,$$

mapping real numbers x to rounded values $r(x)$. The IEEE standard defines four *rounding modes*, which are

- r_u round up,

- r_d round down,

- r_z round to zero, and

- r_{ne} round to nearest even.

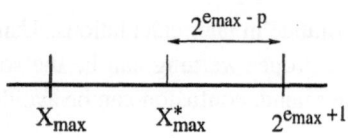

Figure 7.2 Geometry of X^*_{max}

The first three modes have the obvious meaning

$$r_u(x) = \min\{y \in \mathcal{R}_\infty \mid x \leq y\}$$
$$r_d(x) = \max\{y \in \mathcal{R}_\infty \mid x \geq y\}$$
$$r_z(x) = \begin{cases} r_d(x) & \text{if } x \geq 0 \\ r_u(x) & \text{if } x \leq 0 \end{cases}$$

The fourth rounding mode is more complicated to define. For any x with $-X_{max} \leq x \leq X_{max}$, one defines $r_{ne}(x)$ as a representable number y closest to x. If there are two such numbers y, one chooses the number with *even significand*. Let

$$X^*_{max} = 2^{e_{max}}(2 - 2^{-p})$$

(see figure 7.2). This number is odd, and thus, it is the smallest number, that would be rounded by the above rules to $2^{e_{max}+1}$ if that would be a representable number. For $x \notin [-X_{max}, X_{max}]$, one defines

$$r_{ne}(x) = \begin{cases} \infty & \text{if } X^*_{max} \leq x \\ X_{max} & \text{if } X_{max} < x < X^*_{max} \\ -X_{max} & \text{if } -X_{max}* < x < -X_{max} \\ -\infty & \text{if } x \leq -X^*_{max} \end{cases}$$

The above definition can be simplified to

- For $-X^*_{max} < x < X^*_{max}$, one defines $r_{ne}(x)$ as a representable number y closest to x. If there are two such numbers y, one chooses the number with *even significand*.

- For the remaining x, one defines

$$r_{ne}(x) = \begin{cases} \infty & \text{if } X^*_{max} \leq x \\ -\infty & \text{if } x \leq -X^*_{max} \end{cases}$$

7.2.2 Two Central Concepts

Let

$$r : R \to \mathcal{R}_\infty$$

be one of the four rounding functions defined above, and let

$$\circ : R^2 \to R$$

be an arithmetic operation. Then, the corresponding operation

$$\circ_I : \mathcal{R}^2 \to \mathcal{R}_\infty$$

in IEEE arithmetic is – almost – defined by

$$x \circ_I y = r(x \circ y).$$

The result has to be represented in IEEE format. The definition will be completed in the section on exceptions.

If we follow the above rule literally, we first compute an exact result, and then we round. The computation of exact results might require very long intermediate results (imagine the computation of $X_{max} + X_{min}$). In the case of divisions the final result will, in general, not even have a significand of finite length, e.g., think of 1/3. Therefore, one often replaces the two exact operands x and y by appropriate inexact – and in general shorter – operands x' and y' such that the following basic identity holds

$$r(x \circ y) = r(x' \circ y'). \tag{7.1}$$

This means that no harm is done by working with inexact operands, because after rounding the result is the same as if the exact operands had been used. Identities like (7.1) need, of course, proof. Large parts of this section are therefore devoted to the development of an algebra which permits to formulate such proofs in a natural and concise way.

7.2.3 Factorings and Normalization Shifts

Factorings are an abstract version of IEEE floating point numbers. In factorings, the representations of exponents and significands are simply replaced by values. This turns out to be the right level of abstraction for the arguments that follow. Formally, a *factoring* is a triple (s, e, f) where

1. $s \in \{0, 1\}$ is called the *sign bit* ,

2. e is an integer, it is called the *exponent*, and

3. f is a non-negative real number, it is called the *significand*.

We say that f is *normal* if $f \in [1,2)$ and that f is *denormal* if $f \in [0,1)$. We say that a factoring is *normal* if f is normal and that a factoring is *denormal* if $e = e_{min}$ and f is denormal. Note that $f \notin [0,2)$ is possible. In this case, the factoring is neither normal nor denormal. The *value* of a factoring is defined as

$$[\![s,e,f]\!] = (-1)^s \cdot 2^e \cdot f.$$

For real numbers x, we say that (s,e,f) is a *factoring of* x if

$$x = [\![s,e,f]\!]$$

i.e., if the value of the factoring is x. For $x = \infty$ and $x = -\infty$ we provide the special factorings $(s,\infty,0)$ with

$$[\![s,\infty,0]\!] = (-1)^s \cdot \infty.$$

We consider the special factorings both normal and IEEE-normal.

Obviously, there are infinitely many factorings for any number x, but only one of them is normal. The function $\hat{\eta}$ which maps every non-zero $x \in R \cup \{\infty, -\infty\}$ to the unique normal factoring $(s, \hat{e}, \hat{f})$ of x is called *normalization shift*. Note that arbitrary real numbers can only be factored if the exponent range is neither bounded from above nor from below.

A factoring (s,e,f) of x is called *IEEE-normal* if

$$(s,e,f) \quad \text{is} \quad \begin{cases} \text{normal} & \text{if} \quad |x| \geq 2^{e_{min}} \\ \text{denormal} & \text{if} \quad |x| < 2^{e_{min}}. \end{cases}$$

The function η which maps every value $x \in R \cup \{\infty, -\infty\}$ to the unique IEEE-normal factoring of x is called *IEEE normalization shift*. The IEEE-normal factoring of Zero is unique except for the sign. Note that arbitrary real numbers can only be IEEE factored, if the exponent range is not bounded from above. Finally observe, that

$$\hat{\eta}(x) = \eta(x) \quad \text{if} \quad |x| \geq 2^{e_{min}}.$$

7.2.4 Algebra of Rounding and Sticky Bits

We define a family of equivalence relations on the real numbers which will help us identify real numbers that are rounded to the same value.

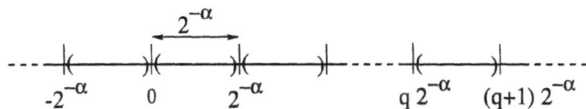

Figure 7.3 Partitioning of the real numbers

Let α be an integer. Let q range over all integers, then the open intervals $(q \cdot 2^{-\alpha}, (q+1) \cdot 2^{-\alpha})$ and the singletons $\{q \cdot 2^{-\alpha}\}$ form a partition of the real numbers (see figure 7.3). Note that 0 is always an endpoint of two intervals.

Two real numbers x and y are called α–*equivalent* if according to this partition they are in the same equivalence class, i.e., if they lie either in the same open interval or if they both coincide with the same endpoint of an interval. We use for this the notation $x =_\alpha y$. Thus, for some integer q we have

$$x =_\alpha y \quad \leftrightarrow \quad x, y \in (q \cdot 2^{-\alpha}, (q+1) \cdot 2^{-\alpha})$$
$$\text{or} \quad x = y = q \cdot 2^{-\alpha}.$$

From each equivalence class, we pick a representative. For singleton sets there is no choice, and from each open interval we pick the midpoint. This defines for each real number x the α–*representative* of x:

$$[x]_\alpha = \begin{cases} (q+0.5) \cdot 2^{-\alpha} & \text{if} \quad x \in (q \cdot 2^{-\alpha}, (q+1) \cdot 2^{-\alpha}) \\ x & \text{if} \quad x = q \cdot 2^{-\alpha}, \end{cases}$$

for some integer q.

Observe that an α-representative is always the value of a binary fraction with $\alpha + 1$ bits after the binary point. We list a few simple rules for computations with α–equivalences and α–representatives.

Let $x =_\alpha x'$. By mirroring intervals at the origin, we see

$$-x =_\alpha -x' \quad \text{and} \quad [-x]_\alpha = -[x]_\alpha.$$

Stretching intervals by a factor of two gives

$$2x =_{\alpha-1} 2x' \quad \text{and} \quad [2x]_{\alpha-1} = 2[x]_\alpha,$$

and shrinking intervals by a factor of two gives

$$x/2 =_{\alpha+1} x'/2 \quad \text{and} \quad [x/2]_{\alpha+1} = [x]_\alpha/2.$$

Induction gives for arbitrary integers e

$$2^e \cdot x =_{\alpha-e} 2^e \cdot x' \quad \text{and} \quad [2^e \cdot x]_{\alpha-e} = 2^e \cdot [x]_\alpha.$$

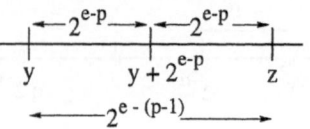

Figure 7.4 Geometry of the values y, $y + 2^{e-p}$, and z

Let y be a multiple of $2^{-\alpha}$. Translation of intervals by y yields

$$x + y =_\alpha x' + y.$$

Let $\beta < \alpha$, then the equivalence classes of $=_\alpha$ are a refinement of the equivalence classes of β, and one can conclude

$$x =_\beta x'.$$

The salient properties of the above definition are, that under certain circumstances rounding x and its representative leads to the same result, and that representatives are very easy to compute. This is made precise in the following lemmas.

Lemma 7.1 ▶ *Let $\eta(x) = (s, e, f)$, and let r be an IEEE rounding mode, then*

1. $r(x) = r([x]_{p-e})$

2. $\eta([x]_{p-e}) = (s, e, [f]_p)$

3. if $x' =_{p-e} x$, then $r(x) = r(x')$.

PROOF   For the absolute value of x, we have

$$|x| \in \begin{cases} [2^e, 2^{e+1}) & \text{if } f \text{ is normal} \\ [0, 2^{e_{min}}) & \text{if } f \text{ is denormal.} \end{cases}$$

In this interval, representable numbers have a distance of

$$d = 2^{e-(p-1)}.$$

Thus, x is sandwiched between two numbers

$$\begin{aligned} y &= q \cdot 2^{e-(p-1)} \\ z &= (q+1) \cdot 2^{e-(p-1)} \end{aligned}$$

as depicted in figure 7.4. Obviously, $x \in [y, z)$ can only be rounded to y, to

$y + 2^{e-p}$, or to z. For any rounding mode it suffices to know $[x]_{p-e}$ in order to make this decision. This proves part one.

Since

$$
\begin{aligned}
[x]_{p-e} &= [(-1)^s \cdot 2^e \cdot f]_{p-e} \\
&= (-1)^s \cdot [2^e \cdot f]_{p-e} \\
&= (-1)^s \cdot 2^e \cdot [f]_p,
\end{aligned}
$$

we know that $(s, e, [f]_p)$ is a factoring of $[x]_{p-e}$. This factoring is IEEE-normal because

- (s, e, f) is IEEE-normal,

- $|x| \geq 2^{e_{min}} \quad \leftrightarrow \quad |[x]_{p-e}| \geq 2^{e_{min}}$, and

- f is normal iff $[f]_p$ is normal.

This proves part 2. Part 3 follows immediately from part 1, because

$$
r(x) = r([x]_{p-e}) = r([x']_{p-e}) = r'(x).
$$

QED

The next lemma states how to get p-representatives of the value of a binary fraction by a so called *sticky bit* computation. Such a computation simply replaces all bits $f[p+1 : v]$ by the OR of these bits.

Let $f = f[-u : 0].f[1 : v]$ be a binary fraction. Let   ◀ Lemma 7.2

$$
g = f[-u : 0].f[1 : p],
$$

and let

$$
s = \bigvee_{i=p+1}^{v} f[i]
$$

be the sticky bit of f for position p (see figure 7.5), then

$$
[\langle f \rangle]_p = \langle gs \rangle.
$$

If $s = 0$ then $\langle f \rangle = \langle gs \rangle$, and there is nothing to show. In the other case,   PROOF
we have

$$
\langle g \rangle < f = \langle g \rangle + \sum_{i=p+1}^{v} f[i] \cdot 2^{-i} < \langle g \rangle + 2^{-p}.
$$

Thus,

$$
[\langle f \rangle]_p = \langle g \rangle + 2^{-(p+1)} = \langle g1 \rangle = \langle gs \rangle.
$$

QED

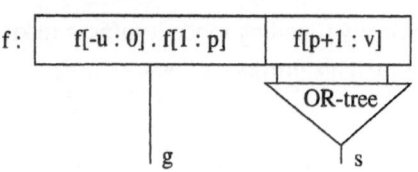

Figure 7.5 Sticky bit s of f for position p

7.2.5 Rounding with Unlimited Exponent Range

We define the set $\hat{\mathcal{R}}$ of real numbers that would be representable if the exponent range would be unlimited. This is simply the set of numbers

$$(-1)^s \cdot 2^e \cdot \langle 1.f[1:p-1] \rangle$$

where e is an arbitrary integer. Moreover, we include $0 \in \hat{\mathcal{R}}$.

For every rounding mode r, we can define a corresponding rounding mode

$$\hat{r} : R \to \hat{\mathcal{R}}.$$

For the rounding modes $\hat{r}_u, \hat{r}_d, \hat{r}_z$ one simply replaces $\mathcal{R}$ by $\hat{\mathcal{R}}$ in the definition of the rounding mode. One defines $\hat{r}_{ne}(x)$ as a number in $\hat{\mathcal{R}}$ closest to x. In case of a tie, the one with an even significand is chosen.

Observe that

$$r(x) = \hat{r}(x) \quad \text{if} \quad 2^{e_{min}} \leq |x| \leq X_{max}.$$

Let $\hat{\eta}(x) = (s, \hat{e}, \hat{f})$. Along the lines of the proof of lemma 7.1, one shows the following lemma:

Lemma 7.3 ▶ *Let $x \neq 0$, let $\hat{\eta}(x) = (s, \hat{e}, \hat{f})$, and let r be an IEEE rounding mode, then*

1. $\hat{r}(x) = \hat{r}([x]_{p-\hat{e}})$

2. $(\hat{\eta}([x]_{p-\hat{e}})) = (s, \hat{e}, [\hat{f}]_p)$

3. *if $x' =_{p-\hat{e}} x$, then $\hat{r}(x) = \hat{r}(x')$.*

7.2.6 Decomposition Theorem for Rounding

Let r be any rounding mode. We would like to break the problem of computing $r(x)$ into the following four steps:

1. IEEE normalization shift. This step computes the IEEE-normal factoring of x

$$\eta(x) = (s, e, f).$$

2. Significand round. This step computes the rounded significand

$$f_1 = sigrd(s, f).$$

The function $sigrd$ will be defined below separately for each rounding mode. It will produce results f_1 in the range $[0, 2]$.

3. Post normalization. This step normalizes the result in the case $f_1 = 2$

$$(e_2, f_2) = post(e, f_1) = \begin{cases} (e_1 + 1, f_2/2) & \text{if } f_1 = 2 \\ (e, f_1) & \text{otherwise} \end{cases}$$

4. Exponent round. This step takes care of cases where the intermediate result $(-1)^s \cdot 2^{e_2} \cdot f_2$ lies outside of $\mathcal{R}$. It computes

$$(e_3, f_3) = exprd(s, e_2, f_2).$$

The function $exprd$ will be defined below separately for each rounding mode.

We will have to define four functions $sgrd$ and four functions $exprd$ such that we can prove

For all rounding modes r holds   ◀ Theorem 7.4

$$(s, e_3, f_3) = \eta(r(x)).$$

This means that the result (s, e_3, f_3) of the rounding algorithm is an IEEE-normal factoring of the correctly rounded result.

Let $\eta(x) = (s, e, f)$, then $f \in [0, 2]$. Significand rounding rounds f to an element in the set

$$\mathcal{F} = \{\langle g[0].g[1:p-1]\rangle \mid g[i] \in \{0, 1\}, \text{ for all } i\} \cup \{2\}.$$

For any f, the binary fractions

$$\begin{aligned} y &= \langle y[-1:0].y[1:p-1]\rangle &= \max\{y \in \mathcal{F} \mid f \geq y\} \\ y' &= \langle y'[-1:0].y'[1:p-1]\rangle &= \min\{y \in \mathcal{F} \mid f \leq y\} \end{aligned}$$

satisfy $y \leq f \leq y'$. The definitions for the four rounding modes are

$$
sigrd_u(s,f) = \begin{cases} y'[-1:p-1] & \text{if} \quad s=0 \\ y[-1:p-1] & \text{if} \quad s=1 \end{cases}
$$

$$
sigrd_d(s,f) = \begin{cases} y[-1:p-1] & \text{if} \quad s=0 \\ y'[-1:p-1] & \text{if} \quad s=1 \end{cases}
$$

$$
sigrd_z(s,f) = y[-1:p-1].
$$

In case of round to nearest even, $sigrd_{ne}(s,f)$ is a binary fraction g closest to f with $g[-1:0].g[1:p-1] \in \mathcal{F}$. In case of a tie one chooses the one with $g[p-1] = 0$. Let $f' = \langle f[0].f[1:p-1]1 \rangle$, then

$$
sigrd_{ne}(s,f) = \begin{cases} y[-1:p-1] & \text{if} \quad f < f' \\ & \text{or} \quad (f=f' \wedge f[p-1]=0) \\ y'[-1:p-1] & \text{if} \quad (f=f' \wedge /f[p-1]=1) \\ & \text{or} \quad f > f' \end{cases} \tag{7.2}
$$

We define

$$
x_1 = [\![s,e,f_1]\!] = (-1)^s \cdot 2^e \cdot f_1.
$$

The following lemma summarizes the properties of the significand rounding:

Lemma 7.5 ▶

$$
x_1 = \begin{cases} r(x) & \text{if} \quad |x| \leq X_{max} \\ \hat{r}(x) & \text{if} \quad |x| > X_{max} \end{cases}
$$

PROOF

For $f \in [1,2)$, x lies in the interval $[2^e, 2^{e+1})$ if $s = 0$, and it lies in $(-2^{e+1}, 2^e]$ if $s = 1$. Mirroring this interval at the origin in case of $s = 1$ and scaling it by 2^{-e} translates exactly from rounding with $\hat{r}$ to significand rounding in the interval $[1,2)$. Mirroring if $s = 1$ and scaling by 2^e translates in the other direction.

If $f \in [0,1)$ then $e = e_{min}$. Mirroring if $s = 1$ and scaling by $2^{-e_{min}}$ translates from rounding with r into significand rounding in the interval $[0,1)$. Mirroring if $s = 1$ and scaling by $2^{e_{min}}$ translates in the other direction.

QED

Finally observe that $r(x) = \hat{r}(x)$ if $|x| \leq X_{max}$ and f is normal.

The following lemma summarizes the properties of the post normalization:

Lemma 7.6 ▶

$$
(s, e_2, f_2) = \eta(x_1).
$$

PROOF

Post normalization obviously preserves value:

$$x_1 = x_2 := [\![s, e_2, f_2]\!] = (-1)^s \cdot 2^{e_2} \cdot f_2.$$

Thus, we only have to show that (s, e_2, f_2) is IEEE-normal. We started out with $\eta(x) = (s, e, f)$ which is IEEE-normal. Thus,

1. f is normal if $|x| \geq 2^{e_{min}}$, and

2. f is denormal and $e = e_{min}$ if $|x| < 2^{e_{min}}$.

If $|x| \geq 2^{e_{min}}$, then $|x_1| \geq 2^{e_{min}}$ and $f_1 \in [1, 2]$. If $f_1 \in [1, 2)$, then $f_2 = f_1$ is normal, and if $f_1 = 2$, then $f_2 = 1$ is normal as well.

If $|x| < 2^{e_{min}}$, then $|x_1| < 2^{e_{min}}$ or $|x_1| = 2^{e_{min}}$, and $e_2 = e = e_{min}$. In the first case, $f_2 = f_1 \in [0, 1)$ is denormal. In the second case, $f_2 = f_1 = 1$ is normal. QED

We proceed to specify the four functions *exprd*.

$$exrd_u(s, e_2, f_2) = \begin{cases} (\infty, 0) & \text{if } e_2 > e_{max} \text{ and } s = 0 \\ (e_{max}, 2 - 2^{-(p-1)}) & \text{if } e_2 > e_{max} \text{ and } s = 1 \\ (e_2, f_2) & \text{if } e_2 \leq e_{max} \end{cases}$$

$$exrd_d(s, e_2, f_2) = \begin{cases} (\infty, 0) & \text{if } e_2 > e_{max} \text{ and } s = 1 \\ (e_{max}, 2 - 2^{-(p-1)}) & \text{if } e_2 > e_{max} \text{ and } s = 0 \\ (e_2, f_2) & \text{if } e_2 \leq e_{max} \end{cases}$$

$$exrd_z(s, e_2, f_2) = \begin{cases} (e_{max}, 2 - 2^{-(p-1)}) & \text{if } e_2 > e_{max} \\ (e_2, f_2) & \text{if } e_2 \leq e_{max} \end{cases}$$

$$exrd_{ne}(s, e_2, f_2) = \begin{cases} (\infty, 0) & \text{if } e_2 > e_{max} \\ (e_2, f_2) & \text{if } e_2 \leq e_{max} \end{cases}$$

Let

$$x_3 = [\![s, e_3, f_3]\!] = (-1)^s \cdot 2^{e_3} \cdot f_3.$$

We can proceed to prove the statement

$$(s, e_3, f_3) = \eta(r(x))$$

of the theorem.

Proof of Theorem 7.4   PROOF

If $(e_3, f_3) = (e_2, f_2)$, then (s, e_3, f_3) is IEEE-normal by lemma 7.6. In all other cases, the factoring (s, e_3, f_3) is obviously IEEE-normal taking into account the convention that the special factorings are IEEE-normal. Thus, it remains to show that

$$x_3 = r(x).$$

If $|x| \leq X_{max}$, then lemma 7.5 implies that

$$x_2 = x1 = r(x).$$

According to lemma 7.6, (s, e_2, f_2) is an IEEE-normal factoring of x_1, and therefore

$$e_2 \leq e_{max}.$$

Thus, we can conclude that

$$(e_3, f_3) = (e_2, f_2) \qquad \text{and} \qquad x_3 = x_2 = r(x).$$

Now let $|x| > X_{max}$. One then easily verifies for all rounding modes r:

$$
\begin{aligned}
& \hat{r}(x) \quad \neq \quad r(x) \\
\leftrightarrow \quad & \hat{r}(|x|) \quad > \quad X_{max} \\
\leftrightarrow \quad & \hat{r}(|x|) \quad \geq \quad 2^{e_{max}+1} \\
\leftrightarrow \quad & \quad\; e_2 \quad > \quad e_{max} \qquad \text{by lemmas 7.5 and 7.6}
\end{aligned}
\tag{7.3}
$$

Recall that in the definition of r_{ne}, the threshold X_{max}^* was chosen such that this holds. We now can complete the proof of the theorem. For $r = r_u$, we have

$$
\begin{aligned}
x_3 &= [\![s, e_3, f_3]\!] \\
&= \begin{cases} \infty & \text{if} \quad e_2 > e_{max} \quad \text{and} \quad s = 0 \\ -X_{max} & \text{if} \quad e_2 > e_{max} \quad \text{and} \quad s = 1 \\ x_2 & \text{if} \quad e_2 \leq e_{max} \end{cases} \\
&= \begin{cases} \infty & \text{if} \quad \hat{r}(x) \neq r(x) \quad \text{and} \quad s = 0 \\ -X_{max} & \text{if} \quad \hat{r}(x) \neq r(x) \quad \text{and} \quad s = 1 \\ x_2 & \text{if} \quad \hat{r}(x) = r(x) \end{cases} \\
&= r(x)
\end{aligned}
$$

because $x_2 = \hat{r}(x)$ by lemma 7.5.

QED

The proof for the other three rounding modes is completely analogous.

We summarize the results of this subsection: Let $\eta(x) = (s, e, f)$, it then holds

$$\eta(r(x)) = (s, exprd(s, post(e, sigrd(s, f)))). \tag{7.4}$$

Exactly along the same lines, one shows for $x \neq 0$ and $\hat{\eta}(x) = (s, \hat{e}, \hat{f})$ that

$$\hat{r}(x) = [\![s, \hat{e}, sigrd(s, \hat{f})]\!],$$

and then

$$\hat{\eta}(\hat{r}(x)) = (s, post(\hat{e}, sigrd(s, \hat{f}))). \tag{7.5}$$

Table 7.2 IEEE floating point exceptions

symbol	meaning
INV	invalid operation
DBZ	division by 0
OVF	overflow
UNF	underflow
INX	inexact result

7.2.7 Rounding Algorithms

By the lemmas 7.1 and 7.2, we can substitute in the above algorithms f and $\hat{f}$ by their p-representatives. This gives the following rounding algorithms:

- For limited exponent range: let $\eta(x) = (s, e, f)$, then

$$\eta(r(x)) = (s, exprd(s, post(e, sigrd(s, [f]_p)))). \qquad (7.6)$$

- For unlimited exponent range: let $x \neq 0$ and $\hat{\eta}(x) = (s, \hat{e}, \hat{f})$, then

$$\hat{\eta}(\hat{r}(x)) = (s, post(\hat{e}, sigrd(s, [\hat{f}]_{p-\hat{e}}))). \qquad (7.7)$$

7.3 Exceptions

THE IEEE floating point standard defines the five exceptions of table 7.2. These exceptions activate event signals of maskable interrupts. The mask bits for these interrupts are also called *enable bits*. Here, we will be concerned with the enable bits *OVFen* and *UNFen* for overflow and underflow.

Implementation of the first two exceptions will turn out to be easy. They can only occur if at least one operand is from the set $\{0, \infty, -\infty, NaN\}$. For each operation, these two exceptions therefore just require a straightforward bookkeeping on the type of the operands (section 7.4).

According to the standard, arithmetic on infinity and NaN is always exact and therefore signals no exceptions, except for invalid operations. Thus, the last three exceptions can only occur if both operands are finite numbers. These exceptions depend on the exact result of the arithmetic operation but not on the operation itself. Therefore, we will now concentrate on situations, where a finite but not necessarily representable number

$x \in R$ is the *exact* result of an operation

$$x = a \circ b \quad \text{where} \quad a, b \in \mathcal{R}.$$

In this section, we will also complete the definition of the result of an arithmetic IEEE operation, given that both operands are finite, non-zero, representable numbers. The arithmetic on infinity, zero, and NaN will be defined in section 7.4.

7.3.1 Overflow

An *overflow* occurs, if the absolute value of $\hat{r}(x)$ exceeds X_{max}, i.e.,

$$OVF(x) \quad \leftrightarrow \quad |\hat{r}(x)| > X_{max}.$$

Let $x' =_{p-\hat{e}} x$. Since $\hat{r}(x) = \hat{r}([x]_{p-\hat{e}})$, it follows that

$$OVF(x) \leftrightarrow OVF([x]_{p-\hat{e}}) \leftrightarrow OVF(x').$$

Only results x with $|x| > X_{max}$ can cause overflows, and for these results, we have $\eta(x) = \hat{\eta}(x)$. Let

$$\eta(x) = \hat{\eta}(x) = (s, e, f).$$

By lemma 7.5, we then have

$$
\begin{aligned}
OVF(x) \quad &\leftrightarrow \quad 2^e \cdot sigrd(s, f) > X_{max} \\
&\leftrightarrow \quad e > e_{max} \quad \text{or} \\
&\quad\quad e = e_{max} \quad \text{and} \quad sigrd(s, f) = 2
\end{aligned}
\tag{7.8}
$$

The first case is called overflow *before rounding*, the second case overflow *after rounding*.

7.3.2 Underflow

Informally speaking, an *underflow* occurs if two conditions are fulfilled, namely

1. *tininess*: the result is below $2^{e_{min}}$ and

2. *loss of accuracy*: accuracy is lost, when the result is represented as a denormalized floating point number.

The IEEE standard gives *two* definitions for each of these conditions. Thus, the standard gives four definitions of underflow. It is, however, required that the same definition of underflow is used for all operations.

Tininess

The two definitions for tininess are *tiny–after–rounding*

$$TINY_a(x) \quad \leftrightarrow \quad 0 < |\hat{r}(x)| < 2^{e_{min}}$$

and *tiny–before–rounding*

$$TINY_b(x) \quad \leftrightarrow \quad 0 < |x| < 2^{e_{min}}.$$

In the four rounding modes, we have

$$TINY_a(x) \quad \leftrightarrow \quad \begin{cases} 0 < |x| < 2^{e_{min}} \cdot (1 - 2^{-(p+1)}) & \text{if } r_{ne} \\ 0 < |x| < 2^{e_{min}} & \text{if } r_z \\ -2^{e_{min}} < x \leq 2^{e_{min}} \cdot (1 - 2^{-p}) \wedge x \neq 0 & \text{if } r_u \\ -2^{e_{min}} \cdot (1 - 2^{-p}) \leq x < 2^{e_{min}} \wedge x \neq 0 & \text{if } r_d \end{cases}$$

For all rounding modes, one easily verifies that tiny-after-rounding implies tiny-before-rounding

$$TINY_a(x) \quad \rightarrow \quad TINY_b(x).$$

Let $x \neq 0$ and $\hat{\eta}(x) = (s, \hat{e}, \hat{f})$, it immediately follows that

$$TINY_b(x) \quad \leftrightarrow \quad TINY_b([x]_{p-\hat{e}})$$

As $\hat{r}(x) = \hat{r}([x]_{p-\hat{e}})$, we can also conclude that

$$TINY_a(x) \quad \leftrightarrow \quad TINY_a([x]_{p-\hat{e}}).$$

Loss of Accuracy

The two definitions for loss of accuracy are *denormalization loss*:

$$LOSS_a(x) \quad \leftrightarrow \quad r(x) \neq \hat{r}(x)$$

and *inexact result*

$$LOSS_b(x) \quad \leftrightarrow \quad r(x) \neq x.$$

An example for denormalization loss is $x = \langle 0.0^p 1 \rangle$ because

$$r_{ne}(x) = 0 \quad \text{and} \quad \hat{r}(x) = x.$$

A denormalization loss implies an inexact result, i.e.,   ◀ Lemma 7.7

$$LOSS_a(x) \quad \rightarrow \quad LOSS_b(x).$$

The lemma is proven by contradiction. Assume $r(x) = x$, then $x \in \mathcal{R} \subset \hat{\mathcal{R}}$,   PROOF
and it follows that

$$\hat{r}(x) = x = r(x).$$

QED

Let $\hat{\eta}(x) = (s, \hat{e}, \hat{f})$ and $\eta(x) = (s, e, f)$. By definition,

$$[x]_{p-\hat{e}} =_{p-\hat{e}} x.$$

Since $\hat{e} \le e$, we have

$$[x]_{p-\hat{e}} =_{p-e} x,$$

and hence,

$$r([x]_{p-\hat{e}}) = r(x).$$

This shows, that

$$LOSS_b(x) \leftrightarrow LOSS_b([x]_{p-\hat{e}}).$$

As $\hat{r}(x) = \hat{r}([x]_{p-\hat{e}})$, we can conclude

$$LOSS_a(x) \leftrightarrow LOSS_a([x]_{p-\hat{e}}).$$

Hence, for any definition of $LOSS$ and $TINY$, we have

$$\begin{aligned} LOSS(x) &\leftrightarrow LOSS([x]_{p-\hat{e}}) \\ TINY(x) &\leftrightarrow TINY([x]_{p-\hat{e}}), \end{aligned}$$

and therefore, the conditions can always be checked with the representative $[x]_{p-\hat{e}}$ instead of with x.

Detecting $LOSS_b(x)$ is particularly simple. If $\eta(x) = (s, e, f)$ and $|x| < X_{max}$, then exponent rounding does not take place and

$$\begin{aligned} \hat{r}(x) \ne x &\leftrightarrow sigrd(s, f) \ne f \\ &\leftrightarrow sigrd(s, [f]_p) \ne [f]_p. \end{aligned}$$

Whether the underflow exception UNF should be signaled at all depends in the following way on the underflow enable flag $UNFen$:

$$UNF \quad \leftrightarrow \quad \begin{cases} TINY \wedge LOSS & \text{if} \quad /UNFen \\ TINY & \text{if} \quad UNFen \end{cases}$$

7.3.3 Wrapped Exponents

In this subsection we complete the definition of the *result* of an IEEE floating point operation. Let

$$\alpha = 3 \cdot 2^{n-2},$$

let $a, b \in \mathcal{R}$ be representable numbers, and for $\circ \in \{+, -, *, ./\}$, let

$$x = a \circ b$$

be the exact result. The proper definition of the result of the IEEE operation is then

$$a \circ_I b = r(y)$$

where

$$y = \begin{cases} x \cdot 2^{-\alpha} & \text{if} \quad OVF(x) \wedge OVFen \\ x \cdot 2^{\alpha} & \text{if} \quad UNF(x) \wedge UNFen \\ x & \text{otherwise.} \end{cases}$$

Thus, whenever non masked overflows or underflows occur, the exponent of the result is adjusted. For some reason, this is called *wrapping* the exponent. The rounded *adjusted* result is then given to the interrupt service routine. In such cases one would of course hope that $r(y)$ itself is a normal representable number. This is asserted in the following lemma:

The adjusted result lies strictly between $2^{e_{min}}$ and X_{max}: ◀ Lemma 7.8

1. $OVF(x) \rightarrow 2^{e_{min}} < x \cdot 2^{-\alpha} < X_{max}$

2. $UNF(x) \rightarrow 2^{e_{min}} < x \cdot 2^{\alpha} < X_{max}$

We only show the lemma for multiplication in the case of overflow. The   PROOF
remaining cases are handled in a completely analogous way.

The largest possible product of two representable numbers is

$$x = X_{max}^2 < (2^{e_{max}+1})^2 = 2^{2e_{max}+2}.$$

For the exponent, it therefore holds

$$\begin{aligned} 2 \cdot e_{max} + 2 - \alpha &= 2 \cdot (2^{n-1} - 1) + 2 - 3 \cdot 2^{n-2} \\ &= 4 \cdot 2^{n-2} - 3 \cdot 2^{n-2} \\ &= 2^{n-2} < e_{max}, \end{aligned}$$

and thus, $|x| < X_{max}$.

There cannot be an overflow unless

$$|x| > X_{max} > 2^{e_{max}}.$$

For the exponents, we conclude that

$$\begin{aligned} e_{max} - \alpha &= 2^{n-1} - 1 - 3 \cdot 2^{n-2} \\ &= -2^{n-2} - 1 \\ &> -2^{n-1} + 2 = e_{min}. \end{aligned}$$

Thus, it also holds that $|x| > 2^{e_{min}}$.   QED

The following lemma shows how to obtain a factoring of $r(y)$ from a factoring of x.

Lemma 7.9 ▶ *Let $\hat{\eta}(\hat{r}(x)) = (s, u, v)$, then*

1. *$OVF(x) \quad \rightarrow \quad \eta(x \cdot 2^{-\alpha}) = (s, u - \alpha, v)$.*

2. *$UNF(x) \quad \rightarrow \quad \eta(x \cdot 2^{\alpha}) = (s, u + \alpha, v)$.*

PROOF

We only show part 1; the proof of part 2 is completely analogous. Let

$$\hat{\eta}(x) = (s, \hat{e}, \hat{f}),$$

then

$$\hat{\eta}(x \cdot 2^{-\alpha}) = (s, \hat{e} - \alpha, \hat{f}).$$

Define f_1 and (u, v) as

$$
\begin{aligned}
f_1 &= sigrd(s, [\hat{f}]_{p-\hat{e}}) \\
(u, v) &= post(\hat{e}, f_1).
\end{aligned}
$$

The definition of post normalization implies

$$(u - \alpha, v) = post(\hat{e} - \alpha, f_1).$$

Applying the rounding algorithm for unlimited exponent range (equation 7.7) gives:

$$\hat{\eta}(\hat{r}(x)) = (s, post(\hat{e}, f_1)) = (s, u, v)$$

and

$$\hat{\eta}(\hat{r}(x \cdot 2^{-\alpha})) = (s, post(\hat{e} - \alpha, f_1)) = (s, u - \alpha, v).$$

Lemma 7.8 implies

$$2^{e_{min}} < |y| = |x| \cdot 2^{-\alpha} < X_{max}.$$

For such numbers, we have

$$2^{e_{min}} \leq r(|y|) = \hat{r}(y) \leq X_{max}.$$

It follows that

$$\eta(r(y)) = \hat{\eta}(\hat{r}(y))$$

QED

and part 1 of the lemma is proven.

7.3.4 Inexact Result

Let

$$y = \begin{cases} x \cdot 2^{-\alpha} & \text{if } OVF(x) \wedge OVFen \\ x \cdot 2^{\alpha} & \text{if } UNF(x) \wedge UNFen \\ x & \text{otherwise.} \end{cases}$$

be the exact result of an IEEE operation, where the exponent is wrapped in case an enabled overflow or underflow occurs. The IEEE standard defines the occurrence of an inexact result by

$$INX(y) \quad \leftrightarrow \quad r(y) \neq y \vee (OVF(y) \wedge /OVFen).$$

So far, we have only considered finite results y. For such results, $OVF(y)$ always implies $r(y) \neq y$ and the second condition is redundant. Hence, we have for finite y

$$INX(y) \quad \leftrightarrow \quad r(y) \neq y.$$

When dealing with special operands ∞, $-\infty$ and NaN, computations like $\infty + \infty = \infty$ with $r(\infty) = \infty$ will be permitted. However, the IEEE standard defines the arithmetic on infinity and NaN to be always exact. Thus, the exceptions INX, OVF and UNF never occur when special operands are involved.

Let $\eta(x) = (s, e, f)$ and $\hat{\eta}(x) = (s, \hat{e}, \hat{f})$. If

$$(OVF(x) \wedge OVFen) \vee (UNF(x) \wedge UNFen)$$

holds, then exponent rounding does not take place, and significand rounding is the only source of inaccuracy. Thus, we have in this case

$$\begin{aligned} INX(y) \quad &\leftrightarrow \quad sigrd(s, \hat{f}) \neq \hat{f} \\ &\leftrightarrow \quad sigrd(s, [\hat{f}]_p) \neq [\hat{f}]_p. \end{aligned}$$

In all other cases we have

$$\begin{aligned} INX(y) \quad &\leftrightarrow \quad sigrd(s, f) \neq f \vee OVF(x) \\ &\leftrightarrow \quad sigrd(s, [f]_p) \neq [f]_p \vee OVF([x]_{p-e}). \end{aligned}$$

7.4 Arithmetic on Special Operands

IN THE IEEE floating point standard [Ins85], the infinity arithmetic and the arithmetic with zeros and NaNs are treated as special cases. This special arithmetic is considered to be *always exact*. Nevertheless, there are situations in which an invalid operation exception INX or a division by zero exception DBZ can occur.

In the following subsections, we specify this special arithmetic and the possible exceptions for any IEEE operation. The factorings of the numbers a and b are denoted by (s_a, e_a, f_a) and (s_b, e_b, f_b) respectively.

7.4.1 Operations with NaNs

There are two different kinds of not a number, signaling NaN and quiet NaN. Let $e = e[n-1:0]$ and $f' = f[1:p-1]$. The value represented by the floating point number (s, e, f') is a NaN if $e = 1^n$ and $f' \neq 0^{p-1}$. We chose $f[1] = 1$ for the quiet and $f[1] = 0$ for the signaling variety of NaN[1].

$$\llbracket s, e, f \rrbracket = \begin{cases} \text{quiet NaN} & \text{if } e = 1^n \wedge f[1] = 1 \\ \text{signaling NaN} & \text{if } e = 1^n \wedge f[1] = 0 \wedge f' \neq 0^{p-1}. \end{cases}$$

A signaling NaN signal an invalid operation exception INV whenever used as an operand. However, copying a signaling NaN without a change of format does not signal INV. This also applies to operations which only modify the sign, e.g., the absolute value and reversed sign[2] operations.

If an arithmetic operation involves one or two input NaNs, none of them signaling, the delivered result must be one of the input NaNs. In the specifications of the arithmetic operations, we therefore distinguish between three types of NaNs:

- qNAN denotes an arbitrary quiet NaN,

- sNAN denotes an arbitrary signaling NaN, and

- qNAN* indicates that the result must be one of the quiet input NaNs.

For the absolute value and reversed sign operations, this restriction does not apply. These two operations modify the sign bit independent of the type of the operand.

---

[1] The IEEE standard only specifies that the exponent $e[n-1:0] = 1^n$ is reserved for infinity and NaN; further details of the coding are left to the implementation. For infinity and the two types of NaNs we therefore chose the coding used in the Intel Pentium Processor [Int95]

[2] $x := -x$

Table 7.3 Result of the addition; x and y denote finite numbers.

$a+b$	b				
a	y	$+\infty$	$-\infty$	qNAN	sNAN
x	$r(x+y)$	$+\infty$	$-\infty$	qNAN*	qNAN
$+\infty$	$+\infty$	$+\infty$	qNAN		
$-\infty$	$-\infty$	qNAN	$-\infty$		
qNAN					
sNAN					

7.4.2 Addition and Subtraction

The subtraction of two representable numbers a and b can be reduced to the addition of the two numbers a and c, where c has the factoring

$$(s_c, e_c, f_c) = (\overline{s_b}, e_b, f_b).$$

In the following, we therefore just focus on the *addition* of two numbers. Table 7.3 lists the result for the different types of operands. There are just a few cases in which floating point exceptions do or might occur:

- An INV exception does occur whenever

  - one of the operands a, b is a signaling NaN, or
  - when performing the operation '$+\infty - \infty$' or '$-\infty + \infty$'.

- The exceptions OVF, UNF and INX can only occur when adding two finite non-zero numbers. However, it depends on the value of the exact result, whether one of these interrupts occurs or not (section 7.3).

Sign
Since zero has two representations, i.e., $+0$ and -0, special attention must be paid to the sign of a zero result $a+b$. In case of a subtraction, the sign of a zero result depends on the rounding mode

$$x - x = -x + x = \begin{cases} +0 & \text{if } r_u, r_{ne}, r_z \\ -0 & \text{if } r_d. \end{cases}$$

When adding two zero numbers with like signs, the sum retains the sign of the first operand, i.e., for $x \in \{+0, -0\}$,

$$x + x = x - (-x) = x.$$

Table 7.4 Result of the multiplication $a \cdot b$; x and y denote finite non-zero numbers.

$a \cdot b$	b				
a	y	0	∞	qNAN	sNAN
x	$r(x \cdot y)$	0	∞		
0	0	0	qNAN		
∞	∞	qNAN	∞		
qNAN				qNAN*	
sNAN					qNAN

7.4.3 Multiplication

Table 7.4 lists the result of the multiplication $a \cdot b$ for the different types of operands. If the result of the multiplication is a NaN, the sign does not matter. In any other case, the sign of the result $c = a \cdot b$ is the exclusive or of the operands' signs:

$$s_c = s_a \oplus s_b.$$

There are just a few cases in which floating point exceptions do or might occur:

- An INV exception does occur whenever

  - one of the operands a, b is a signaling NaN, or
  - when multiplying a zero and an infinity number, i.e., '$0 \cdot \infty$' or '$\infty \cdot 0$'.

- The exceptions OVF, UNF and INX depend on the value of the exact result (section 7.3); they can only occur when both operands are finite non-zero numbers.

7.4.4 Division

Table 7.5 lists the result of the division a/b for the different types of operands. The sign of the result is determined as for the multiplication. This means that except for a NaN, the sign of the result c is the exclusive or of the operands' signs: $s_c = s_a \oplus s_b$.

In the following cases, the division signals a floating point exception:

- An INV exception does occur whenever

Table 7.5 Result of the division a/b; x and y denote finite non-zero numbers.

a/b	b				
a	y	0	∞	qNAN	sNAN
x	$r(x/y)$	∞	0		
0	0	qNAN	0		
∞	∞	∞	qNAN		
qNAN	qNAN*				
sNAN	qNAN				

- one of the operands a, b is a signaling NaN, or

- when performing the operation '0/0' or '∞/∞'.

- An DBZ (division by zero) exception is signaled whenever dividing a finite non-zero number by zero.

- The exceptions OVF, UNF and INX depend on the value of the exact result (section 7.3); they can only occur when both operands are finite non-zero numbers.

7.4.5 Comparison

The comparison operation is based on the four basic relations *greater than*, *less than*, *equal* and *unordered*. These relations are defined over the set $\mathcal{R}_{\infty,NaN}$ consisting of all representable numbers, the two infinities, and NaN:

$$\mathcal{R}_{\infty,NaN} = \mathcal{R} \cup \{+\infty, -\infty, NaN\},$$

Let the binary relation $\circ \in \{<, =, >\}$ be defined over the real numbers R, the corresponding IEEE floating point relation is denoted by $\circ_I$. For any representable number $x \in \mathcal{R}_\infty$, none of the pairs (x, NaN), (NaN, x) and (NaN, NaN) is an element of $\circ_I$. Thus, the relation $\circ_I$ is a subset of $\mathcal{R}_\infty^2$.

- IEEE floating point relations ignore the sign of zero, i.e., $+0 = -0$. Thus, over the set of representable numbers, the relations $\circ$ and $\circ_I$ are the same:

$$\forall x, y \in \mathcal{R} \subset R \quad x \circ_I y \quad \leftrightarrow \quad x \circ y$$

Table 7.6 Floating point predicates. The value 1 (0) denotes that the relation is true (false). Predicates marked with ∗ are not indigenous to the IEEE standard.

predicate		greater	less	equal	unordered	INV if
true	false	>	<	=	?	unordered
F*	T*	0	0	0	0	
UN	OR	0	0	0	1	
EQ	NEQ	0	0	1	0	
UEQ	OGL	0	0	1	1	No
OLT	UGE	0	1	0	0	
ULT	OGE	0	1	0	1	
OLE	UGT	0	1	1	0	
ULE	OGT	0	1	1	1	
SF	ST	0	0	0	0	
NGLE	GLE	0	0	0	1	
SEQ*	SNE*	0	0	1	0	
NGL	GL	0	0	1	1	Yes
LT	NLT	0	1	0	0	
NGE	GE	0	1	0	1	
LE	NLE	0	1	1	0	
NGT*	GT*	0	1	1	1	

- The two infinities ($+\infty$ and $-\infty$) are interpreted in the usual way. For any finite representable $x \in \mathcal{R}$, we have

$$-\infty <_I x <_I +\infty.$$

NaN compares *unordered* with every representable number and with NaN. Thus, for every $x \in \mathcal{R}_{\infty,NaN}$, the pairs (x,NaN) and (NaN,x) are elements of the relation 'unordered', and that are the only elements. Let this relation be denoted by the symbol ?, then

$$? = \{(x,NaN), (NaN,x) \mid x \in \mathcal{R}_{\infty,NaN}\}.$$

The comparison of two operands x and y delivers the value $\circ(x,y)$ of a specific binary predicate

$$\circ : \mathcal{R}_{\infty,NaN} \times \mathcal{R}_{\infty,NaN} \to \{0, 1\}.$$

Table 7.6 lists all the predicates in question and how they can be obtained from the four basic relations. The predicates OLT and UGE, for example, can be expressed as

$$\text{OLT}(x,y) = \overline{\text{UGE}(x,y)} \equiv \overline{(x >_I y)} \vee (x <_I y) \vee \overline{(x =_I y)} \vee (x?y).$$

Note that for every predicate the implementation must also provide its negation.

In addition to the boolean value $\circ(x,y)$, the comparison also signals an invalid operation. With respect to the flag INV, the predicates fall into one of two classes. The first 16 predicates only signal INV when comparing a signaling NaN, whereas the remaining 16 predicates also signal INV when the operands are unordered.

Comparisons are always exact and never overflow or underflow. Thus, INV is the only IEEE floating point exception signaled by a comparison, and the flags of the remaining exceptions are all inactive:

$$INX = OVF = UNF = DBZ = 0.$$

7.4.6 Format Conversions

Conversions have to be possible between the two floating point formats and the integer format. Integers are represented as 32-bit two's complement numbers and lie in the set

$$INT = T_{32} = \{-2^{31}, \ldots, 2^{31} - 1\}.$$

Floating point numbers are represented with an n-bit exponent and a p-bit significand. The range of finite, representable numbers is bounded by $-X_{max}$ and X_{max}, where $X_{max} = (1 - 2^{-p}) \cdot 2^{2^{n-1}}$. For single precision $n = 8$, $p = 24$ and the finite, representable numbers lie in the range

$$\mathcal{R}_s \subset [-(1 - 2^{-24}) \cdot 2^{128}, (1 - 2^{-24}) \cdot 2^{128}],$$

whereas for double precision $n = 11$, $p = 53$ and

$$\mathcal{R}_d \subset [-(1 - 2^{-53}) \cdot 2^{1024}, (1 - 2^{-53}) \cdot 2^{1024}].$$

Table 7.7 lists the floating point exceptions which can be caused by the different format conversions. The result of the conversion is rounded as specified in section 7.2, even if the result is an integer. All four rounding modes must be supported.

Table 7.7 Floating point exceptions which can be caused by format conversions (d: double precision floating point, s: single precision floating point, i: 32-bit two's complement integer)

	INV	DBZ	OVF	UNF	INX
$d \to s$	+		+	+	+
$s \to d$	+				
$i \to s$					+
$i \to d$					
$s \to i$	+				+
$d \to i$	+				+

Floating Point Format Conversions

Double precision covers a wider range of numbers than single precision, and the numbers are represented with a larger precision. Thus, a conversion from single to double precision is always exact and never overflows or underflows, but that is not the case for a conversion from double to single precision.

The conversion signals an invalid operation exception iff the operand is a signaling NaN. Unlike the arithmetical operations, a quiet input NaN cannot pass the conversion unchanged. Thus, in case of an input NaN, the result of the conversion is always an *arbitrary*, quiet NaN.

Integer to Floating Point Conversions

For either floating point format, we have

$$-X_{max} < -2^{31} \quad \text{and} \quad 2^{31} < X_{max}.$$

Thus, any 32-bit integer x can be represented as a single or double precision floating point number. In case of double precision, the conversion is performed without loss of precision, whereas the single precision result might be inexact due to the 24-bit significand. Other floating point exceptions cannot occur.

Floating Point to Integer Conversions

When converting a floating point number into an integer, the result is usually inexact. The conversion signals an invalid operation if the input is a NaN or infinity, or if the finite floating point input x exceeds the integer range, i.e.,

$$x < -2^{31} \quad \text{or} \quad x \geq 2^{31}.$$

In the latter case, a floating point overflow OVF is not signaled because the result of the conversion is an integer.

7.5 Selected References and Further Reading

THE TRANSLATION of the IEEE standard 754 [Ins85] into mathematical language and the theory of rounding presented in this chapter is based on [EP97].

7.6 Exercises

Exercise 7.1 Prove or disprove: For all rounding modes, rounding to single precision can be performed in two steps:

a) round to double precision, then

b) round the double precision result to single precision.

Exercise 7.2 Complete the following proofs:

1. the proof of lemma 7.3

2. the proof of theorem 7.4 for rounding mode r_{ne}

3. the proof of lemma 7.9 part 2

Exercise 7.3 Let x be the unrounded result of the addition of two representable numbers. Show:

1. $TINY_a(x) \leftrightarrow TINY_b(x)$

2. $LOSS_a(x) = LOSS_b(x) = FALSE$

Exercise 7.4 Let $x = 2^e \cdot f$, where e is represented as a 14-bit two's complement number $e = [e[13 : 0]]$ and the significand f is represented as a 57-bit binary fraction $f = \langle f[0].f[1 : 56] \rangle$. Design circuits which compute for double precision:

1. $LOSS_a(x)$

2. $LOSS_b(x)$

Compare the cost and delay of the two circuits.

Chapter 8

Floating Point Algorithms and Data Paths

IN THIS chapter the data paths of an IEEE-compatible floating point unit FPU are developed. The unit is depicted in figure 8.2. It is capable of handling single and double precision numbers under control of signals like $db, dbs, dbr, \ldots$ (double). This requires *embedding conventions* for embedding single precision numbers into 64-bit data.

The data inputs of the the unit are (packed) IEEE floating point numbers with values

$$
\begin{aligned}
a &= [\![s_A, e_A[n-1:0], f_A[1:p-1]]\!] \\
b &= [\![s_B, e_B[n-1:0], f_B[1:p-1]]\!],
\end{aligned}
$$

where

$$
(n, p) = \begin{cases} (53, 11) & \text{if } db = 1 \\ (24, 8) & \text{if } db = 0. \end{cases}
$$

As shown in figure 8.1, single precision inputs are fed into the unit as the *left* subwords of $FA[63:0]$ and $FB[63:0]$. Thus,

$$
\begin{aligned}
&(s_A, e_A[n-1:0], f_A[1:p-1]) \\
&\quad = \begin{cases} (FA2[63], FA2[62:55], FA2[54:32]) & \text{if } /db \\ (FA2[63], FA2[62:52], FA2[51:0]) & \text{if } db. \end{cases}
\end{aligned}
$$

The b operand is embedded in the same way.

The unpacking unit detects special inputs $0, \infty, NaN, sNaN$ and signals them with the flags fl_a and fl_b. For normal or denormal inputs, the hidden

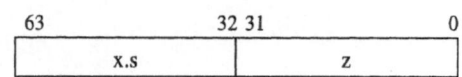

Figure 8.1 Embedding a single precision floating point data $x.s$ into a 64-bit word; z is an arbitrary bit string. In our implementation $z = x.s$.

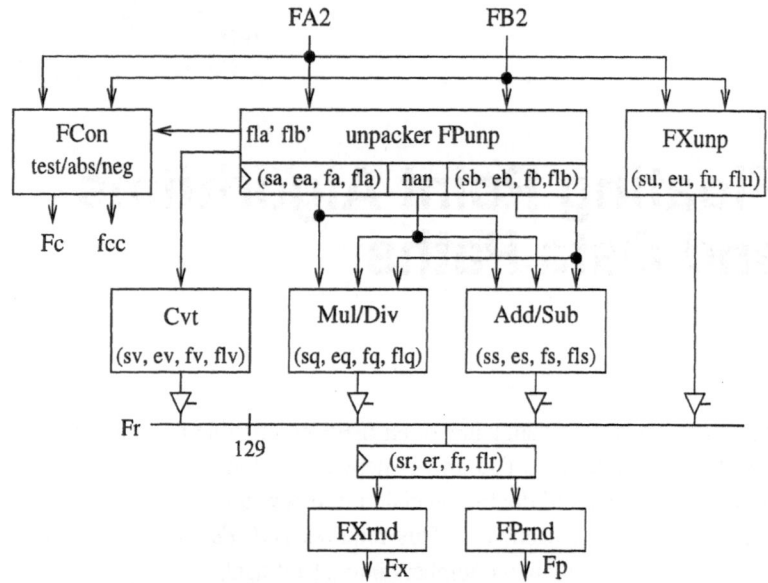

Figure 8.2 Top level schematics of the floating point unit. The outputs Fc, Fx and Fp consist of a 64-bit data and the floating point exception flags.

bit is unpacked, the exponent is converted to two's complement representation, and single precision numbers are internally converted into double precision numbers. Under control of signal *normal*, denormal significands are normalized, and the shift distances $lz_a[5 : 0]$ and $lz_b[5 : 0]$ of this normalization shift are signaled.

Thus, the a-outputs of the unpacker satisfy for *both* single and double precision numbers

$$a = \begin{cases} (-1)^{s_a} \cdot 2^{[e_a[10:0]]} \cdot \langle f_a[0].f_a[1:52]\rangle & \text{if } normal = 0 \\ (-1)^{s_a} \cdot 2^{[e_a[10:0]]-\langle lz_a[5:0]\rangle} \cdot \langle f_a[0].f_a[1:52]\rangle & \text{if } normal = 1 \end{cases}$$

The b-outputs of the unpacker satisfy an analogous equation. The normalization shift activated by *normal* = 1 is performed for multiplications and divisions but not for additions and subtractions.

Table 8.1 Coding of the IEEE rounding modes

RM[1:0]	symbol	rounding mode
00	r_z	round to zero
01	r_{ne}	round to nearest even
10	r_u	round up
11	r_d	round down

Let

$$x = a \circ b$$

be the exact result of an arithmetic operation, and let

$$\hat{\eta}(x) = (s, \hat{e}, \hat{f}).$$

In the absence of special cases the converter, the multiply/divide unit and the add/subtract unit deliver as inputs to the rounder the data $(s_r, e_r[12 : 0], f_r[-1 : 55])$ satisfying

$$x =_{p-\hat{e}} (-1)^{s_r} \cdot 2^{[e_r[12:0]]} \cdot \langle f_r[-1:55] \rangle.$$

and

$$f_r[-1:0] = 00 \quad \rightarrow \quad OVF(x) = 0.$$

Note that $\hat{\eta}(x)$ is undefined for $x = 0$. Thus, a result $x = 0$ is always handled as a special case. Let

$$y = \begin{cases} x \cdot 2^{-\alpha} & \text{if } OVF(x) \wedge OVFen \\ x \cdot 2^{\alpha} & \text{if } UNF(x) \wedge UNFen \\ x & \text{otherwise.} \end{cases}$$

The rounder then has to output $r(y)$ coded as a (packed) IEEE floating point number. The coding of the rounding modes is listed in table 8.1.

Cost and Delay

The cost of the floating point unit depicted in figure 8.2 can be expressed as

$$\begin{aligned} C_{FPU} &= C_{FCon} + C_{FPunp} + C_{FXunp} + C_{Cvt} + C_{MulDiv} \\ &\quad + C_{AddSub} + C_{FXrnd} + C_{FPrnd} + C_{ff}(129) + 4 \cdot C_{driv}(129). \end{aligned}$$

We assume that all inputs of the FPU are taken from registers and therefore have zero delay. The outputs F_x, F_p, F_c and fcc then have the following accumulated delay:

$$A_{FPU} = \max\{A_{FCon}, A_{FXrnd}, A_{FPrnd}\}.$$

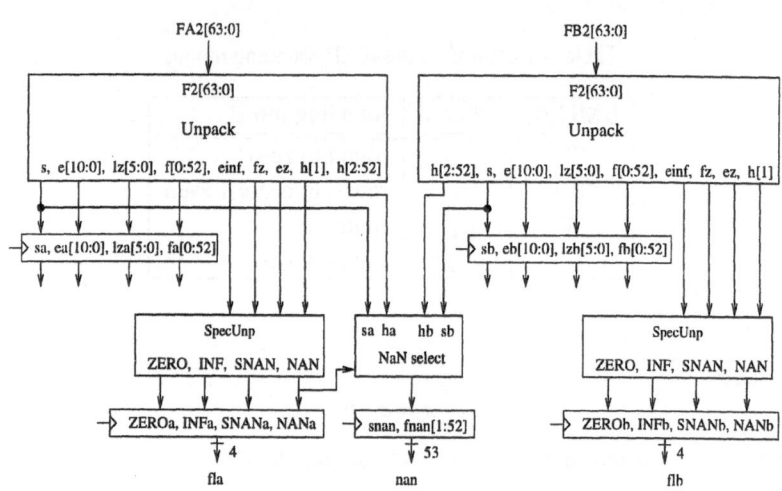

Figure 8.3 Top level schematics of the unpacker FPUNP

Note that A_{FCon} includes the delay of the inputs fla' and flb'. In our implementation, the multiply/divide unit, the add/subtract unit and the two rounders FPRND and FXRND have an additional register stage. Thus, the FPU requires a minimal cycle time of

$$T_{FPU} = \max\{T_{MulDiv}, T_{AddSub}, T_{FPrnd}, T_{FXrnd}, A_{FPU}(Fr) + \Delta\}$$
$$A_{FPU}(Fr) = \max\{A_{FPunp} + D_{Cvt}, A_{FXunp}, A_{MulDiv}, A_{AddSub}\} + D_{driv}.$$

8.1 Unpacking

FIGURE 8.3 depicts the schematics of an unpacking unit FPUNP which unpacks two operands FA2 and FB2. For either operand, the unpack unit comprises some registers (for pipelining), a circuit UNPACK and a circuit SPECUNP. In addition, there is a circuit NANSELECT which determines the coding of an output NaN.

Circuit UNPACK
The circuit UNPACK (figure 8.4) has the following control inputs

- *dbs* which indicates that a double precision source operand is processed,

- and *normal* which requests a normalization of the significand.

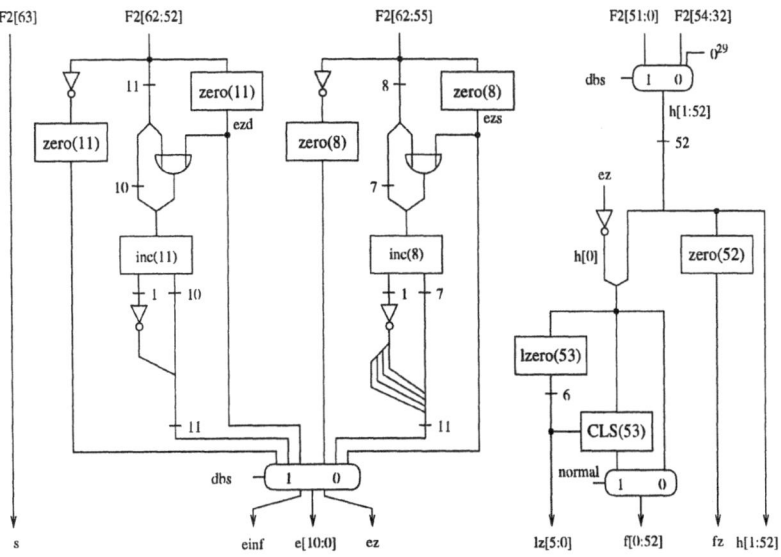

Figure 8.4 Schematics of the circuit UNPACK

The data inputs are $F2[63:0]$. Single precision numbers are fed into the unpacking circuit as the *left* subword of $F2[63:0]$ (figure 8.1). Input data are always interpreted as IEEE floating point numbers, i.e.,

$$(s, e_{in}[n-1:0], f_{in}[1:p-1])$$
$$= \begin{cases} (F2[63], F2[62:52], F2[51:0]) & \text{if} \quad dbs = 1 \\ (F2[63], F2[62:55], F2[54:32]) & \text{if} \quad dbs = 0 \end{cases}$$

We now explain the computation of the outputs. The flag

$$einf = 1 \quad \leftrightarrow \quad e_{in} = 1^n$$

signals that the exponent is that of infinity or *NaN*. The signals ezd and ezs indicate a denormal double or single precision input. The flag

$$ez = 1 \quad \leftrightarrow \quad e_{in} = 0^n$$

signals that the input is denormal.

If the (double or single precision) input is normal, then the corresponding flag ezd or ezs is 0, the bits $e_{in}[n-1:0]$ are fed into an incrementer, and the leading bit of the result is inverted. This converts the exponent from biased to two's complement format. Sign extension produces a 11-bit two's complement number. For normal inputs we therefore have

$$[e[10:0]] = [\![e_{in}]\!]_{bias}.$$

For denormal inputs the last bit of e_{in} is forced to 1, and the biased representation of

$$e_{min} = [\![0^{n-1}1]\!]$$

is fed into the incrementer. We conclude for denormal inputs

$$[e[10:0]] = e_{min}.$$

The inverted flag $h[0] = /ez$ satisfies

$$h[0] = \begin{cases} 1 & \text{for normal inputs} \\ 0 & \text{for denormal inputs.} \end{cases}$$

Thus, $h[0]$ is the hidden bit of the significand. Padding single precision significands by 29 trailing zeros extends them to the length of double precision significands

$$h[1:52] = \begin{cases} F2[51:0] & \text{if } dbs = 1 \\ F2[54:32]0^{29} & \text{if } dbs = 0, \end{cases}$$

and we have

$$\langle .h[1:52]\rangle = \langle .f_{in}[1:p-1]\rangle.$$

Hence, for normal or denormal inputs the binary fraction $h[0].h[1:53]$ represents the significand and

$$[\![s, e_{in}, f_{in}]\!] = (-1)^s \cdot 2^{[e]} \cdot \langle h \rangle.$$

Let lz be the number of leading zeros of the string $h[0:53]$, then

$$lz = \langle lz[5:0]\rangle.$$

In case of *normal* $= 1$ and a non-zero significand, the cyclic left shifter $CLS(53)$ produces a representation $f[0].f[1:53]$ of a *normal* significand satisfying

$$\langle h \rangle = \langle f \rangle \cdot 2^{-lz}.$$

For normal or denormal inputs we can summarize

$$[\![s, e_{in}, f_{in}]\!] = \begin{cases} (-1)^s \cdot 2^{[e]-lz} \cdot \langle f \rangle & \text{if } \quad normal = 1 \\ (-1)^s \cdot 2^{[e]} \cdot \langle f \rangle & \text{if } \quad normal = 0 \end{cases}$$

Flag fz signals that $f_{in}[1:p-1]$ consists of all zeros:

$$fz = 1 \quad \leftrightarrow \quad f_{in}[1:p-1] = 0^{p-1}.$$

Signal $h[1]$ is used to distinguish the two varieties of *NaN*. We chose $h[1] = 0$ for the *signaling* and $h[1] = 1$ for the *quiet* variety of *NaN* (section 7.4.1). Inputs which are signaling NaNs produce an invalid operation exception (INV).

The cost of circuit UNPACK can be expressed as

$$
\begin{aligned}
C_{Unpack} &= 2 \cdot C_{zero}(11) + 2 \cdot C_{zero}(8) + C_{zero}(52) + C_{lz}(53) \\
&\quad C_{inc}(11) + C_{inc}(8) + C_{CLS}(53) + 22 \cdot C_{inv} \\
&\quad C_{mux}(13) + C_{mux}(53) + C_{mux}(52) + 2 \cdot C_{or}
\end{aligned}
$$

With respect to the delay of circuit UNPACK, we distinguish two sets of outputs. The outputs $reg = \{e, lz, f\}$ are directly clocked into a register, whereas the remaining outputs $flag = \{s, einf, fz, ez, h\}$ are fed to circuits SEPCUNP and NANSELECT:

$$
\begin{aligned}
D_{Unpack}(reg) &= D_{zero}(11) + D_{inv} + D_{mux} + \\
&\quad \max\{D_{inc}(11) + D_{or}, D_{lz}(53) + D_{CLS}(53) + D_{mux}\} \\
D_{Unpack}(flag) &= D_{mux} + \max\{D_{zero}(11) + D_{inv}, D_{zero}(52)\}.
\end{aligned}
$$

Special Cases

From the flags $einf$, $h[1]$, fz and ez one detects whether the input codes zero, plus or minus infinity, a quiet or a signaling *NaN* in an obvious way:

$$
\begin{aligned}
ZERO &= ez \wedge fz \\
INF &= einf \wedge fz \\
NAN &= einf \wedge h[1] \\
SNAN &= einf \wedge (/h[1] \wedge /fz) = einf \wedge (h[1] \text{ NOR } fz).
\end{aligned}
$$

This computation is performed by the circuit SPECUNP depicted in figure 8.5. This circuit has the following cost and delay:

$$
\begin{aligned}
C_{SpecUnp} &= 4 \cdot C_{and} + C_{nor} \\
D_{SpecUnp} &= D_{and} + D_{nor}.
\end{aligned}
$$

Circuit NANSELECT

This circuit determines the representation $(s_{nan}, e_{nan}, f_{nan})$ of the output NaN. According to the specifications of section 7.4, the output NaN provided by an arithmetic operation is of the quiet variety. Thus,

$$
e_{nan} = 1^n \quad \text{and} \quad f_{nan}[1] = 1.
$$

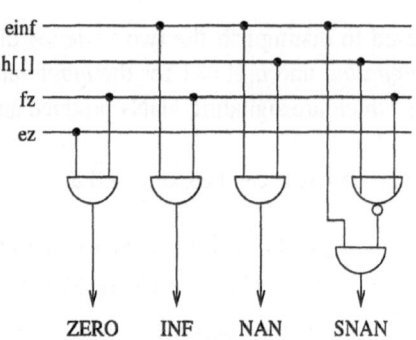

Figure 8.5 Circuit SpecUnp

Quiet NaNs propagate through almost every arithmetic operation, i.e., if one or two input NaNs are involved, none of them signaling, the delivered result must be one of the input NaNs. If both operands are quiet NaNs, the *a* operand is selected. However, in case of an invalid operation ($INV = 1$), an arbitrary quiet NaN can be chosen. Thus, the circuit NANSELECT determines the sign and significand of the output NaN as

$$(s_{nan}, f_{nan}[1:52]) = \begin{cases} (s_a, 1\, h_a[2:52]) & \text{if} \quad NANa = 1 \\ (s_b, 1\, h_b[2:52]) & \text{if} \quad NANa = 0. \end{cases}$$

This just requires a 53-bit multiplexer. Thus,

$$C_{NaNselect} = C_{mux}(53)$$
$$D_{NaNselect} = D_{mux}.$$

Cost and Delay of the Unpacker

The floating point unpacker FPUNP of figure 8.3 has cost

$$C_{FPunp} = 2 \cdot (C_{Unpack} + C_{SpecUnp} + C_{ff}(75)) + C_{NaNselect} + C_{ff}(53)$$

With fl'_a and fl'_b we denote the inputs of the registers buffering the flags fl_a and fl_b. These signals are forwarded to the converter CVT and to circuit FCON; they have delay

$$A_{FPunp}(fla', flb') = D_{Unpack}(flag) + D_{SpecUnp}.$$

Assuming that all inputs of the FPU are provided by registers, the outputs of the unpacker then have an accumulated delay of

$$A_{FPunp} = \max\{D_{Unpack}(reg), D_{FPunp}(fla') + D_{NaNselect}\}.$$

8.2 Addition and Subtraction

8.2.1 Addition Algorithm

Suppose we want to add the representable numbers a and b with IEEE-normal factorings (s_a, e_a, f_a) and (s_b, e_b, f_b). Without loss of generality we can assume that

$$\delta = e_a - e_b \geq 0;$$

otherwise we exchange a and b. The sum S can then be written as

$$
\begin{aligned}
S &= [\![s_a, e_a, f_a]\!] + [\![s_b, e_b, f_b]\!] \\
&= (-1)^{s_a} \cdot 2^{e_a} \cdot f_a + (-1)^{s_b} \cdot 2^{e_b} \cdot f_b \\
&= 2^{e_a} \cdot ((-1)^{s_a} \cdot f_a + (-1)^{s_b} \cdot 2^{-\delta} \cdot f_b).
\end{aligned}
$$

This suggests a so called *alignment shift* of significand f_b by δ positions to the right. As δ can become as large as $e_{max} - e_{min}$ this would require very large shifters. In this situation one replaces the possibly very long aligned significand $2^{-\delta} \cdot f_b$ by its $(p+1)$-representative

$$f' = [2^{-\delta} \cdot f_b]_{p+1},$$

which can be represented as a binary fraction with only $p+2$ bits behind the binary point. Thus, the length of significand f_b is increased by only 3 extra bits. The following theorem implies, that the rounded result of the addition is not affected by this:

For a non-zero sum $S \neq 0$ let $\hat{\eta}(S) = (s, \hat{e}, \hat{f})$, then   ◄ Theorem 8.1

$$S =_{p-\hat{e}} 2^{e_a} \cdot ((-1)^{s_a} \cdot f_a + (-1)^{s_b} \cdot f').$$

If $\delta \leq 3$, then   PROOF

$$f' = 2^{-\delta} \cdot f_b,$$

and there is nothing to prove. If $\delta \geq 2$ then

$$2^{-\delta} \cdot f_b < 2^{-2} \cdot 2 = 1/2.$$

Since (s_a, e_a, f_a) and (s_b, e_b, f_b) are IEEE factorings, neither exponent can be less than e_{min},

$$e_a \geq e_{min} \quad \text{and} \quad e_b \geq e_{min},$$

and a denormal significand implies that the exponent equals e_{min}. Due to the assumption that $e_a \geq e_b$, we have

$$e_a = e_b + \delta \geq e_{min} + \delta.$$

Thus, for $\delta \geq 2$, the f_a and the factoring (s_a, e_a, f_a) are normal, and hence,

$$|(-1)^{s_a} \cdot f_a + (-1)^{s_b} \cdot 2^{-\delta} \cdot f_b| > 1 - 1/2 = 1/2.$$

It follows that

$$\hat{e} \geq e_a - 1 > e_{min} \quad \text{and} \quad p - \hat{e} \leq p + 1 - e_a.$$

Since

$$f' =_{p+1} 2^{-\delta} \cdot f_b$$

and f_a is a multiple of $2^{-(p+1)}$, one concludes

$$
\begin{aligned}
(-1)^{s_a} \cdot f_a + (-1)^{s_b} \cdot 2^{-\delta} \cdot f_b &=_{p+1} & (-1)^{s_a} \cdot f_a + (-1)^{s_b} \cdot f' \\
S &=_{p+1-e_a} & 2^{e_a} \cdot ((-1)^{s_a} \cdot f_a + (-1)^{s_b} \cdot f').
\end{aligned}
$$

QED The theorem follows because $p + 1 - e_a \geq p - \hat{e}$.

Subtraction Algorithm

Let a, b and b' be three representable numbers with factorings (s_a, e_a, f_a), (s_b, e_b, f_b) and $(\overline{s_b}, e_b, f_b)$. The subtraction of the two numbers a and b can then be reduced to the addition of the numbers a and b':

$$
\begin{aligned}
a - b &= a - (-1)^{s_b} \cdot 2^{e_b} \cdot f_b \\
&= a + (-1)^{/s_b} \cdot 2^{e_b} \cdot f_b = a + b'.
\end{aligned}
$$

8.2.2 Adder Circuitry

Figure 8.6 depicts an add/subtract unit which is divided into two pipeline stages. The essential inputs are the following

- the factorings of two operands

$$a = [\![s_a, e_a, f_a]\!], \qquad b = [\![s_b, e_b, f_b]\!]$$

where for $(n, p) = (11, 53)$ the exponents are given as n-bit two's complement numbers

$$e_a = [e_a[n-1:0]], \qquad e_b = [e_b[n-1:0]],$$

and the significands are given as binary fractions

$$f_a = \langle f_a[0].f_a[1:p-1]\rangle, \qquad f_b = \langle f_b[0].f_b[1:p-1]\rangle,$$

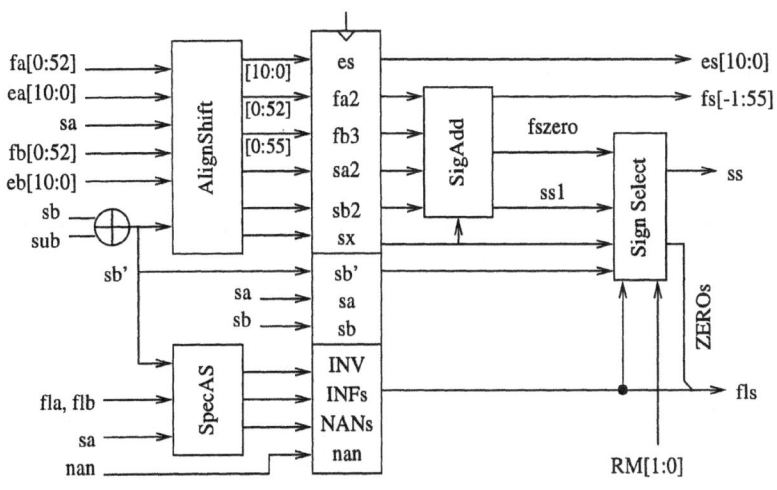

Figure 8.6 Top level schematics of the add/subtract unit

- the flags fl_a and fl_b of the two operands,

- the rounding mode RM, which is needed for the sign computation, and

- the flag sub which indicates that a subtraction is to be performed.

In case of a subtraction $sub = 1$, the second operand is multiplied by -1, i.e., its sign bit gets inverted. Thus, the operand

$$b' = (-1)^{sub} \cdot b$$

has the following factoring

$$(s_b', e_b, f_b) = (s_b \oplus sub, e_b, f_b).$$

The unit produces a factoring (s_s, e_s, f_s) which, in general, is not a representation of the exact sum

$$S = a + b',$$

but if $\hat{\eta}(S) = (s, \hat{e}, \hat{f})$, the output of the unit satisfies

$$S =_{p-\hat{e}} (-1)^{s_s} \cdot 2^{e_s} \cdot f_s.$$

Thus, the output is be rounded to the same result as S. If S is zero, infinite or a NaN, the result of the add/subtract unit is of course exact.

In the first stage special cases are handled, the operands are possibly exchanged such that the a-operand has the larger exponent, and an alignment shift with bounded shift distance is performed. Let

$$\delta = |e_a - e_b|.$$

The first stage outputs sign bits s_{a2}, s_{b2}, an exponent e_s, and significands f_{a2}, f_{b3} satisfying

$$
\begin{aligned}
e_s &= \max\{e_a, e_b\} \\
S &=_{p-\hat{e}} \ 2^{e_s} \cdot ((-1)^{s_{a2}} \cdot f_{a2} + (-1)^{s_{b2}} \cdot f_{b3}).
\end{aligned}
$$

The second stage adds the significands and performs the sign computation. This produces the sign bit s_s and the significand f_s.

Cost and Delay

Let the rounding mode RM be provided with delay A_{RM}. Let the circuit SIGADD delay the significand f_s by $D_{SigAdd}(fs)$ and the flags $fszero$ and s_{s1} by $D_{SigAdd}(flag)$. The cost and cycle time of the add/subtract circuit and the accumulated delay A_{AddSub} of its outputs can then be expressed as

$$
\begin{aligned}
C_{AddSub} &= C_{SpecAS} + C_{AlignShift} + C_{xor} + C_{ff}(182) \\
&\quad + C_{SigAdd} + C_{SignSelect} \\
T_{AddSub} &= D_{xor} + \max\{D_{SpecAS}, D_{AlignShift}\} + \Delta \\
A_{AddSub} &= \max\{D_{SigAdd}(fs), D_{SigAdd}(flag) + D_{SignSelect}, \\
&\quad A_{RM} + D_{SignSelect}\}.
\end{aligned}
$$

Alignment Shift

The circuit ALIGNSHIFT depicted in figure 8.7 is somewhat tricky. Subcircuit EXPSUB depicted in figure 8.8 performs a straightforward subtraction of n-bit two's complement numbers. It delivers an $(n+1)$-bit two's complement number $as[n:0]$. We abbreviate

$$as = [as[n:0]],$$

then

$$
\begin{aligned}
as &= e_a - e_b \\
e_a < e_b &\leftrightarrow as < 0 \leftrightarrow as[n] = 1.
\end{aligned}
$$

This justifies the use of result bit $as[n]$ as the signal 'eb_gt_ea' (e_b greater than e_a), and we have

$$e_s = \max\{e_a, e_b\}.$$

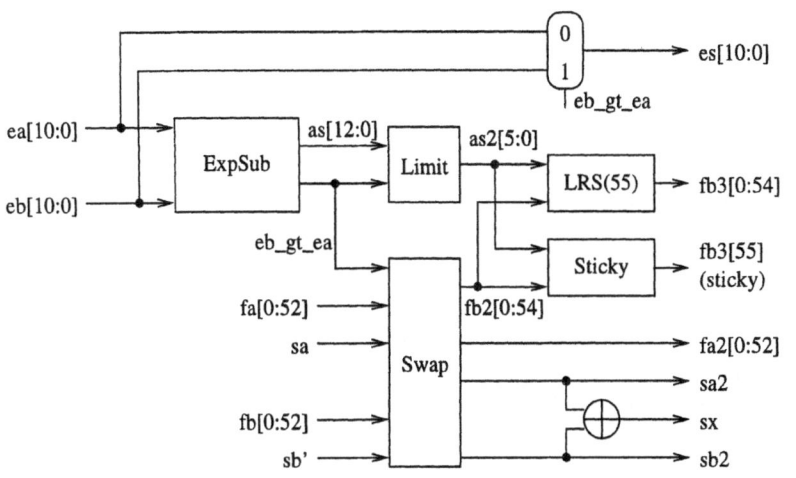

Figure 8.7 Circuit ALIGNSHIFT; circuit LRS is a logical right shifter.

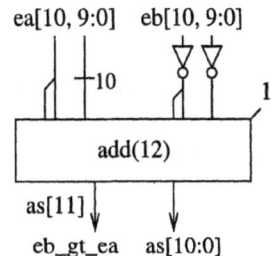

Figure 8.8 Circuit EXPSUB

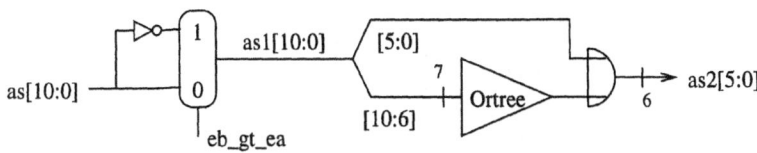

Figure 8.9 Circuit LIMIT which approximates and limits the shift distance

Cost and delay of circuit EXPSUB run at

$$C_{ExpSub} = C_{inv}(11) + C_{add}(12)$$
$$D_{ExpSub} = D_{inv} + D_{add}(12)\}.$$

Approximating the Shift Distance

The shift distance of an unlimited alignment shift would be

$$\delta = |as|.$$

The obvious way to compute this distance is to complement and then increment $as[n:0]$ in case as is negative. Because this computation lies on the critical path of this stage, it makes sense to spend some effort in order to save the incrementer.

Therefore, circuit LIMIT depicted in figure 8.9 first computes an *approximation* $\langle as_1[n-1:0]\rangle$ of this distance by

$$as_1[n-1:0] = \begin{cases} as[n-1:0] & \text{if} \quad as \geq 0 \\ \overline{as[n-1:0]} & \text{if} \quad as < 0 \end{cases}$$

If $as \geq 0$, then $as[n] = 0$ and

$$\langle as_1 \rangle = \langle as[10:0]\rangle = \delta,$$

i.e., no error is made. If $as \leq -1$, then

$$\delta - 1 = -[as[n:0]] - 1 = [\overline{as[n:0]}].$$

Since

$$0 \leq \delta - 1 \leq 2^n - 1,$$

we have

$$\langle as_1[n-1:0]\rangle = [\overline{as[n:0]}] = \delta - 1.$$

Thus,

$$\langle as_1 \rangle = \begin{cases} \delta & \text{if} \quad e_a \geq e_b \\ \delta - 1 & \text{if} \quad e_a < e_b. \end{cases}$$

Circuit LIMIT of figure 8.9 has the following cost and delay

$$C_{Limit} = C_{inv}(11) + C_{mux}(11) + C_{or}(6) + C_{ORtree}(7)$$
$$D_{Limit} = D_{inv} + D_{mux} + D_{or} + D_{ORtree}(7).$$

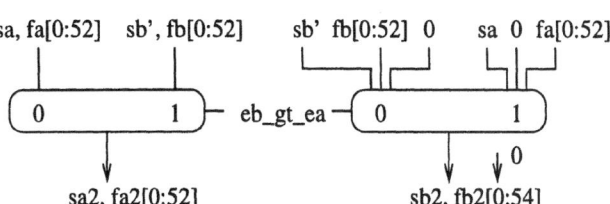

Figure 8.10 Circuit SWAP which swaps the two operands in case of $ea < eb$

Swapping Operands

Circuit SWAP in figure 8.10 swaps the two operands in case $e_a < e_b$. In this case, the representation of significand f_a will be shifted in the alignment shifter by a shift distance $\delta - 1$ which is smaller by 1 than it should be. In this situation, the left mux in figure 8.10 preshifts the representation of f_a by 1 position to the right. Hence,

$$(f_{a2}, f_{b2}) = \begin{cases} (f_a, f_b) & \text{if} \quad e_a \geq e_b \\ (f_b, f_a/2) & \text{if} \quad e_a < e_b. \end{cases}$$

It follows that

$$2^{-\langle as_1 \rangle} \cdot f_{b2} = \begin{cases} 2^{-\delta} \cdot f_b & \text{if} \quad e_a \geq e_b \\ 2^{-\delta} \cdot f_a & \text{if} \quad e_a < e_b. \end{cases}$$

Note that operand f_{b2} is padded by a trailing zero and now has 54 bits after the binary point. The swapping of the operands is done at the following cost and delay

$$\begin{aligned} C_{Swap} &= C_{mux}(54) + C_{mux}(55) \\ D_{Swap} &= D_{mux}. \end{aligned}$$

Limiting the Shift Distance

The right part of circuit LIMIT limits the shift distance of the alignment shift. Motivated by theorem 8.1 (page 359), we replace significand $2^{-\langle as_1 \rangle} \cdot f_{b2}$ by its possibly much shorter $(p+1)$–representative

$$f_{b3} = [2^{-\langle as_1 \rangle} \cdot f_{b2}]_{p+1}.$$

By lemma 7.2, a $(p+1)$–representative is computed by a sticky bit which ORs together all bits starting at position $p+2$ behind the binary point. However, once we have shifted f_{b2} by $p+2$ bits to the right, *all* nonzero bits of f_{b2} already contribute to the sticky bit computation and further shifting changes nothing. Hence, the shift distance can be limited to $p+2 = 55$.

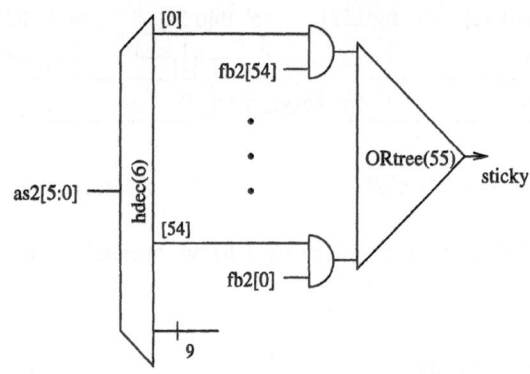

Figure 8.11 Circuit STICKY which performs the sticky bit computation

We limit instead the distance to a power of two minus 1. Thus, let

$$b = \lceil \log(p+3) \rceil = 6$$

and

$$B = 2^b - 1 = \langle 1^b \rangle \geq p+2,$$

then

$$\langle as_1 \rangle \geq B \quad \leftrightarrow \quad \bigvee_{i=b}^{n-1} = 1$$

and

$$\langle as_2 \rangle = \begin{cases} B & \text{if} \quad \langle as_1 \rangle \geq B \\ \langle as_1 \rangle & \text{otherwise.} \end{cases}$$

The alignment shift computation is completed by a 55-bit logical left shifter and the sticky bit computation depicted in figure 8.11.

Sticky Bit Computation

Consider figure 8.12. If $f_{b2}[0 : p+1]$ is shifted by $\langle as_2 \rangle$ bits to the right, then for each position i bit $f_{b2}[i]$ is moved to position $i + \langle as_2 \rangle$. The sticky bit computation must OR together all bits of the shifted operand starting at position $p+2$. The position i such that bit $f_{b2}[i]$ is moved to position $p+2$ is the solution of the equation

$$i + \langle as_2 \rangle = p+2, \quad \text{i.e.,} \quad i = p+2 - \langle as_2 \rangle.$$

The sticky bit then equals

$$sticky = \bigvee_{j=p+2-\langle as_2 \rangle}^{p+1} f_{b2}[j].$$

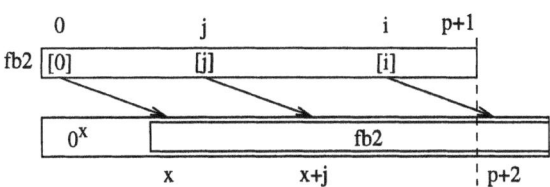

Figure 8.12 Shifting operand $f_{b2}[0 : p+1]$ x bits to the right

This means, that the last $\langle as_2 \rangle$ bits of $f_{b2}[0 : p+1]$ must be ORed together. The last $p+2$ outputs of the half decoder in figure 8.11 produce the mask

$$0^{p+2-\langle as_2 \rangle} 1^{\langle as_2 \rangle}.$$

ANDing the mask bitwise with f_{b2} and ORing the results together produces the desired sticky bit. Cost and delay of circuit STICKY run at

$$
\begin{aligned}
C_{Sticky} &= C_{hdec}(6) + 55 \cdot C_{and} + C_{ORtree}(55) \\
D_{Sticky} &= D_{hdec}(6) + D_{and} + D_{ORtree}(55).
\end{aligned}
$$

Correctness

The correctness of the first stage now follows from the theorem 8.1 because

$$
\begin{aligned}
S =_{p-\hat{e}} & \begin{cases} 2^{e_a} \cdot ((-1)^{s_a} \cdot f_a + (-1)^{s'_b} \cdot [2^{-\delta} \cdot f_b]_{p+1}) & \text{if } e_a \geq e_b \\ 2^{e_b} \cdot ((-1)^{s'_b} \cdot f_b + (-1)^{s_a} \cdot [2^{-\delta} \cdot f_a]_{p+1}) & \text{if } e_a < e_b \end{cases} \\
= & \; 2^{e_s} \cdot ((-1)^{s_{a2}} \cdot f_{a2} + (-1)^{s_{b2}} \cdot [2^{-\delta} \cdot f_{b2}]_{p+1}) \\
= & \; 2^{e_s} \cdot ((-1)^{s_{a2}} \cdot f_{a2} + (-1)^{s_{b2}} \cdot f_{b3}).
\end{aligned}
$$

(8.1)

Cost and Delay of the Alignment Shifter

Figure 8.7 depicts the circuit ALIGNSHIFT of the alignment shifter. Since circuit LIMIT has a much longer delay than circuit SWAP, the cost and the delay of the alignment shifter can be expressed as

$$
\begin{aligned}
C_{AlignShift} &= C_{ExpSub} + C_{Limit} + C_{Swap} + C_{Sticky} \\
& \quad + C_{LRS}(55) + C_{xor} + C_{mux}(11) \\
D_{AlignShift} &= D_{ExpSub} + D_{Limit} + \max\{C_{Sticky}, C_{LRS}(55)\}.
\end{aligned}
$$

Significand Add

Figure 8.13 depicts the addition/subtraction of the significands f_{a2} and f_{b3}. Let

$$s_x = s_a \oplus s'_b = \begin{cases} 0 & \text{if } s_a = s'_b \\ 1 & \text{if } s_a \neq s'_b, \end{cases}$$

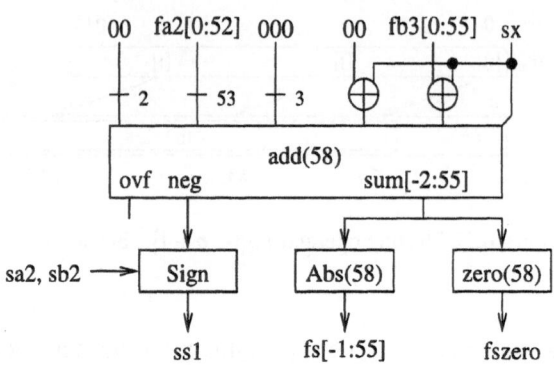

Figure 8.13 Circuit SIGADD which depending on the flag s_x adds or subtracts the significands f_{a2} and f_{b3}

the circuit computes

$$sum = f_{a2} + (-1)^{s_x} \cdot f_{b3}.$$

The absolute value of the result is bounded by

$$|sum| \leq f_{a2} + f_{b3} \leq 2 - 2^{-(p-1)} + 2 - 2^{-(p+2)} < 4.$$

Therefore, both the sum and its absolute value can be represented by a two's complement fraction with 3 bits before and $p + 2$ bits behind the binary point.

Converting binary fractions to two's complement fractions and extending signs, the circuit SIGADD computes

$$
\begin{aligned}
sum &= f_{a2} + (-1)^{s_x} \cdot f_{b3} \\
&= \langle f_{a2}[0].f_{a2}[1:p-1] \rangle + (-1)^{s_x} \cdot \langle f_{b3}[0].f_{b3}[1:p+2] \rangle \\
&= [0f_{a2}[0].f_{a2}[1:p-1]0^3] \\
&\quad + [s_x(f_{b3}[0] \oplus s_x).(f_{b3}[1:p+2] \oplus s_x)] + s_x \cdot 2^{-(p+2)} \\
&= [0^2 f_{a2}[0].f_{a2}[1:p-1]0^3] \\
&\quad + [s_x^2(f_{b3}[0] \oplus s_x).(f_{b3}[1:p+2] \oplus s_x)] + s_x \cdot 2^{-(p+2)} \\
&= [sum[-2:0].sum[1:p+2]]
\end{aligned}
$$

Figure 8.14 depicts a straightforward computation of

$$|sum| = f_s = \langle f_s[-1:0].f_s[1:p+1] \rangle.$$

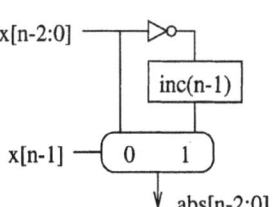

Figure 8.14 Circuit ABS computes the absolute value of an n-bit two's complement number

A zero significand can be detected as

$$fszero = 1 \quad \leftrightarrow \quad f_s[-1:p+1] = 0 \quad \leftrightarrow \quad sum[-2:p+1] = 0.$$

Let

$$neg = sum[-2]$$

be the sign bit of the two's complement fraction $sum[-2:0].sum[1:p+1]$. Table 8.2 lists for the six possible combinations of s_a, s'_b and neg the resulting sign bit s_{s1} such that

$$(-1)^{s_{s1}} \cdot f_s = (-1)^{s_a} \cdot f_{a2} + (-1)^{s'_b} \cdot f_{b3} \qquad (8.2)$$

holds. In a brute force way, the sign bit s_{s1} can be expressed as

$$\begin{aligned}
s_{s1} &= (\overline{s_a} \wedge s'_b \wedge neg) \vee (s_a \wedge s'_b \wedge neg) \vee (s_a \wedge \overline{s'_b} \wedge \overline{neg}) \\
&= (s'_b \wedge neg) \vee (s_a \wedge (s'_b \text{ NAND } neg)).
\end{aligned}$$

For the factoring (s_{s1}, e_s, f_s) it then follows from the Equations 8.1 and 8.2 that

$$\begin{aligned}
S &= [\![s_a, e_a, f_a]\!] + [\![s'_b, e_b, f_b]\!] \\
&=_{p-\hat{e}} 2^{e_s} \cdot ((-1)^{s_{a2}} \cdot f_{a2} + (-1)^{s_{b2}} \cdot f_{b3}) \\
&= 2^{e_s} \cdot (-1)^{s_{s1}} \cdot f_s.
\end{aligned}$$

Cost and Delay

Circuit SIGN generates the sign bit s_{s1} in a straightforward manner at the following cost and delay:

$$\begin{aligned}
C_{Sign} &= 2 \cdot C_{and} + C_{or} + C_{nand} \\
D_{Sign} &= D_{and} + D_{or} + D_{nand}.
\end{aligned}$$

Table 8.2 Possible combinations of the four sign bits s_a, s_b', neg and s_{s1}

result	s_a	s_b'	neg	s_{s1}
$f_{a2} + f_{b3}$	0	0	0	0
impossible	0	0	1	*
$f_{a2} - f_{b3}$	0	1	0	0
$f_{a2} - f_{b3}$	0	1	1	1
$-f_{a2} + f_{b3}$	1	0	0	1
$-f_{a2} + f_{b3}$	1	0	1	0
impossible	1	1	0	*
$-f_{a2} - f_{b3}$	1	1	1	1

Circuit ABS of figure 8.14 computes the absolute value of an n-bit two's complement number. It has cost and delay

$$C_{Abs}(n) = C_{inv}(n-1) + C_{inc}(n-1) + C_{mux}(n-1)$$
$$D_{Abs}(n) = D_{inv} + D_{inc}(n-1) + D_{mux}.$$

For the delay of the significand add circuit SIGADD, we distinguish between the flags and the significand f_s. Thus,

$$C_{SigAdd} = C_{xor}(58) + C_{add}(58) + C_{zero}(58) + C_{Abs}(58) + C_{Sign}$$
$$D_{SigAdd}(flag) = D_{xor} + D_{add}(58) + \max\{D_{zero}(58), D_{Sign}\}$$
$$D_{SigAdd}(fs) = D_{xor} + D_{add}(58) + D_{Abs}(58).$$

Special Cases

The circuit SPECAS checks whether the operation involves special numbers, and checks for an invalid operation. Further floating point exceptions – overflow, underflow and inexact result – will be detected in the rounder. Circuit SPECAS generates the following three flags

- INFs signals an infinite result,

- NANs signals that the result is a quiet NaN, and

- INV signals an invalid addition or subtraction.

The circuit gets 8 input flags, four for either operand. For operand a the inputs comprise the sign bit s_a, the flag INFa indicating that $a \in \{+\infty, -\infty\}$, and the flags NANa and SNANa. The latter two flags indicate that a is a quiet NAN or a signaling NaN, respectively. The flags s_b', INFb, NANb, and SNANb belong to the operand b and have a similar meaning.

According to the specifications of section 7.4.2, an invalid operation must be signaled in one of two cases: if an operand is a signaling NaN, or when adding two infinite values with opposite signs. Thus,

$$INV = (SNANa \lor SNANb) \lor (INFa \land INFb \land (s_a \oplus s'_b))$$

The result is a quiet NaN whenever one of the operands is a NaN, and in case of an invalid operation:

$$NANs = INV \lor (NANa \lor NANb)$$

According to table 7.3 (page 343), an infinite result implies that at least one of the operands is infinite; and in case of an infinite operand, the result is either infinite or a NaN. Thus, an infinite result can be detected as

$$INFs = (INFa \lor INFb) \land \overline{NANs}.$$

Circuit SPECAS generates the three flags along these lines at

$$C_{SpecAS} = 5 \cdot C_{or} + 3 \cdot C_{and} + C_{xor} + C_{inv}$$
$$D_{SpecAS} = D_{xor} + 2 \cdot D_{or} + 2 \cdot D_{and} + D_{inv}.$$

Sign Computation

If the result is a finite non-zero number, circuit SIGADD already provides the correct sign s_{s1}. However, in case of a zero or infinite result, special rules must be applied (section 7.4.2). For NaNs, the sign does not matter.

In case of an infinite result, at least one operand is infinite, and the result retains the same sign. If both operands are infinite, their signs must be alike. Thus, an infinite result has the following sign

$$s_{s3} = \begin{cases} s_a & \text{if} \quad INFa \\ s'_b & \text{if} \quad INFb \land \overline{INFa}. \end{cases}$$

In case of an effective subtraction $(s_x = s_a \oplus s'_b = 1)$, a zero result is always positive, except for the rounding mode r_d (round down) which is coded by $RM[1:0] = 11$. In case of $s_x = 0$, the result retains the same sign as the a operand. Thus, the sign of a zero result equals

$$s_{s2} = \begin{cases} 0 & \text{if} \quad s_x \land (RM[1] \text{ NOR } RM[0]) \\ 1 & \text{if} \quad s_x \land (RM[1] \lor RM[0]) \\ s_a & \text{if} \quad \overline{s_x}. \end{cases}$$

Depending on the type of the result, its sign s_s can be expressed as

$$s_s = \begin{cases} s_{s3} & \text{if} \quad INFs \\ s_{s2} & \text{if} \quad /INFs \land (f_s = 0) \\ s_{s1} & \text{if} \quad /INFs \land (f_s \neq 0). \end{cases}$$

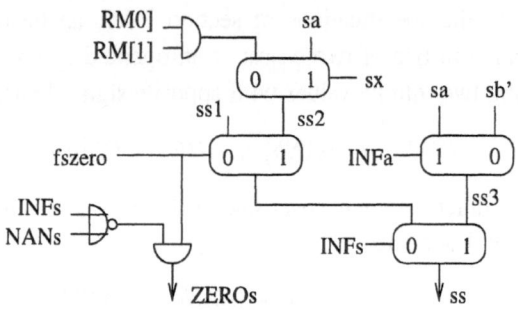

Figure 8.15 Circuit SIGNSELECT selects the appropriate sign s_{s3}

The circuit SIGNSELECT of figure 8.15 implements this selection in a straightforward manner. It also provides a flag *ZEROs* which indicates that the sum is zero. This is the case, if the result is neither infinite nor a NaN, and if its significand is zero ($fszero = 1$). Thus,

$$ZEROs = fszero \wedge (INFs \text{ NOR } NANs).$$

The cost and the maximal delay of circuit SIGNSELECT can be expressed as

$$
\begin{aligned}
C_{SignSelect} &= 4 \cdot C_{mux} + 2 \cdot C_{and} + C_{nor} \\
D_{SignSelect} &= D_{and} + \max\{3 \cdot D_{mux}, D_{nor}\}.
\end{aligned}
$$

8.3 Multiplication and Division

THE UNPACKER delivers unpacked normalized floating point numbers to the multiply/divide unit. The multiplication of normalized numbers is straightforward. Specifying and explaining the corresponding circuits will take very little effort.

Division is more complicated. Let a and b be finite, non-zero, representable floating point numbers with *normal* factorings

$$
\begin{aligned}
\hat{\eta}(a) &= (s_a, e_a - lz_a, f_a) \\
\hat{\eta}(b) &= (s_b, e_b - lz_b, f_b).
\end{aligned}
$$

Thus, $f_a, f_b \in [1,2)$. We will compute the rounded quotient $r(a/b)$ in the following way:

1. Let s_q, e_q and q be defined as

$$
\begin{aligned}
s_q &= s_a \oplus s_b \\
e_q &= e_a - e_b \\
q &= f_a/f_b \in (1/2, 2),
\end{aligned}
$$

then

$$a/b = [\![s_q, e_q, q]\!]$$

and the exponent e' of the rounded result satisfies

$$e' \geq e_q - 1.$$

For $f_d = [q]_{p+1}$, we then have

$$2^{e_q} \cdot f_d =_{p+1-e_q} 2^{e_q} \cdot q,$$

and hence

$$2^{e_q} \cdot f_d =_{p-e'} 2^{e_q} \cdot q.$$

Thus, it suffices to determine f_d and then feed (s_q, e_q, f_d) into the rounding unit.

2. In a lookup table, an initial approximation x_0 of $(1/f_b)$ is determined.

3. With an appropriate number i of iterations of the Newton-Raphson method a much better approximation x_i of $(1/f_b)$ is computed. The analysis will have to take into account that computations can only be performed with finite precision.

4. The value $q' = f_a \cdot x_i$ is an approximation of the quotient f_a/f_b. The correct representative f_d is determined by comparing the product $q' \cdot f_b$ with f_a in a slightly nontrivial way.

8.3.1 Newton-Raphson Iteration

Newton-Raphson iteration is a numerical method for determining a zero of a real valued function $f(x)$. Consider figure 8.16. One starts with an initial approximation x_0 and then determines iteratively for each $i \geq 0$ from x_i a (hopefully) better approximation x_{i+1}. This is repeated until the desired accuracy is obtained.

In the approximation step of the Newton-Raphson method, one constructs the tangent to $f(x)$ through the point $(x_i, f(x_i))$ and one defines

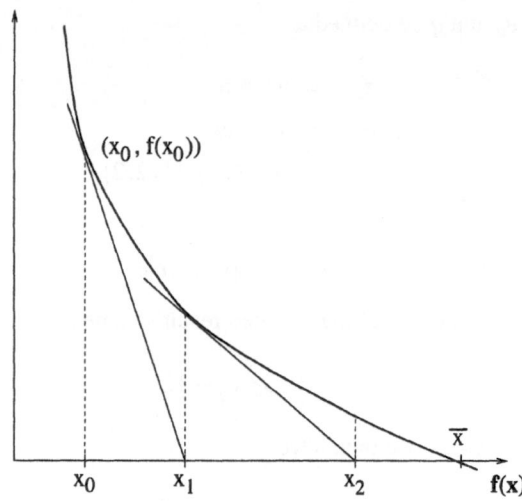

Figure 8.16 Newton iteration for finding the Zero $\bar{x}$ of the mapping $f(x)$, i.e., $f(\bar{x}) = 0$. The figure plots the curve of $f(x)$ and its tangents at $f(x_i)$ for $i = 0, 1, 2$.

x_{i+1} as the zero of the tangent. From figure 8.16 it immediately follows that

$$f'(x_i) = \frac{f(x_i) - 0}{x_i - x_{i+1}}$$

Solving this for x_{i+1} gives

$$x_{i+1} = x_i - f(x_i)/f'(x_i)$$

Determining the inverse of a real number f_b is obviously equivalent to finding the zero of the function

$$f(x) = 1/x - f_b.$$

The iteration step then translates into

$$
\begin{aligned}
x_{i+1} &= x_i + (1/x_i - f_b) \cdot x_i^2 \\
&= x_i(2 - f_b \cdot x_i)
\end{aligned}
$$

Let $\delta_i = 1/f_b - x_i$ be the approximation error after iteration i, then

$$
\begin{aligned}
\delta_{i+1} &= 1/f_b - x_{i+1} \\
&= 1/f_b - 2x_i + f_b \cdot x_i^2 \\
&= f_b \cdot (1/f_b - x_i)^2 \\
&= f_b \cdot \delta_i^2 \leq 2 \cdot \delta_i^2.
\end{aligned}
$$

Observe that $\delta_i \geq 0$ for $i \geq 1$.

For later use we summarize the classical argument above in a somewhat peculiar form:

Let

$$x_{i+1} = x_i \cdot (2 - f_b \cdot x_i),$$
$$\delta_i = 1/f_b - x_i \quad and$$
$$\delta_{i+1} = 1/f_b - x_{i+1},$$

the approximation error is then bounded by

$$\delta_{i+1} \le 2 \cdot \delta_i^2.$$

8.3.2 Initial Approximation

The unpacker delivers a representation $1.f_b[1:p-1]$ of f_b satisfying

$$f_b = \langle 1.f_b[1:p-1] \rangle \in [1,2).$$

The interval $[1,2)$ is partitioned into 2^γ half open intervals of the form

$$[1+t \cdot 2^{-\gamma}, 1 + (t+1) \cdot 2^{-\gamma}).$$

The midpoint of the interval containing f_b is $f_b' = \langle 1.f_b[1:\gamma]1 \rangle$. Let $x' = 1/f_b'$ be the exact inverse of f_b'. The initial approximation x_0 of $1/f_b$ is determined by rounding x' to the nearest multiple of $2^{-\gamma-1}$. In case two multiples are equally near, one rounds up.

Lemma 8.3 below implies, that x_0 lies in the interval $(1/2, 1)$. Hence x_0 can be represented in the form

$$x_0 = \langle 0.x_0[1:\gamma+1] \rangle$$

and the initial approximation can be stored in a $2^\gamma \times \gamma$-ROM. The crucial properties of the initial approximation are summarized in the following lemma:

The approximation error $\delta_0 = 1/f_b - x_0$ of the initial approximation obeys   ◄ Lemma 8.3

$$0 < |\delta_0| = |1/f_b - x_0| \le 1.5 \cdot 2^{-\gamma-1}.$$

We first show the upper bound. Consider the mapping $f(x) = 1/x$ as depicted in figure 8.17. Let $u, v \in [1,2]$ and let $u \le v$, then   PROOF

$$|f(u) - f(v)| \le (v - u) \cdot |f'(u)| \le (v - u).$$

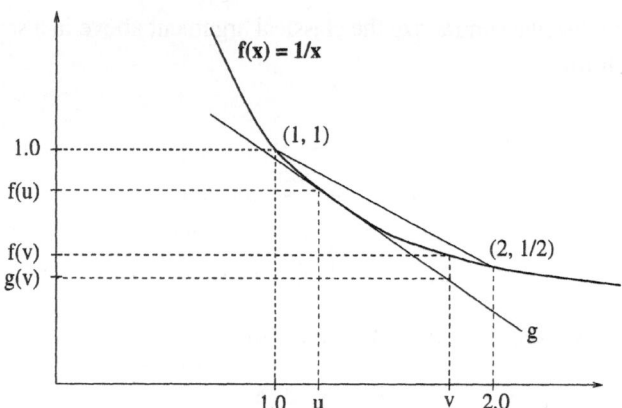

Figure 8.17 The mapping $g(x) = f(u) + f'(u) \cdot (x-u)$ is the tangent to $f(x) = 1/x$ at $x = u$.

Since $|f_b - f_b'| \leq 2^{-\gamma-1}$, we immediately conclude $|1/f_b - x'| \leq 2^{-\gamma-1}$. Rounding changes x' by at most $2^{-\gamma-2}$ and the upper bound follows.

For the lower bound we first show that the product of two representable numbers u and v cannot be 1 unless both numbers are powers of 2. Let u_i and v_j be the least significant nonzero bits of (the representations of) u and v. The product of u and v then has the form

$$u \cdot v = 2^{-(i+j)} + A \cdot 2^{-(i+j)+1}$$

for some integer A. Thus, the product can only be 1 if $A = 0$, in which case the representations of u and v have both an 1 in the single position i or j, respectively.

Thus, for representable $f_b \neq 1$ any finite precision approximation of $1/f_b$ is inexact, and the lower bound follows for all $f_b \neq 1$.

For $f_b = 1$ we have $f_b' = 1 + 2^{-\gamma-1}$. Consider again figure 8.17. The mapping $f(x) = 1/x$ is convex and lies in the interval $(1,2)$ entirely under the line through the points $(1,1)$ and $(2,1/2)$. The line has slope $-1/2$. Thus,

$$\frac{1}{1+t} = f(1+t) < 1 - t/2$$

for all $t \in (0,1)$. For $t = 2^{-\gamma-1}$ we get

$$x' = f(f_b') < 1 - 2^{-\gamma-2}.$$

QED   Thus, x' cannot be rounded to a number x_0 bigger than $1 - 2^{-\gamma-2}$.

8.3.3 Newton-Raphson Iteration with Finite Precision

We establish some notation for arguments about finite precision calculations where rounding is done by chopping all bits after position σ. For real numbers f and nonnegative integers σ we define

$$\lfloor f \rfloor_\sigma = \lfloor f \cdot 2^\sigma \rfloor \cdot 2^\sigma,$$

then

$$\lfloor f \rfloor_0 = \lfloor f \rfloor.$$

Moreover, if $f = \langle f[-i:0].f[1:s] \rangle\rangle$ and $s \geq \sigma$, then

$$\lfloor f \rfloor_\sigma = \langle f[-i:0]f[1:\sigma] \rangle.$$

Newton-Raphson iteration with precision σ can then be formulated by the formula

$$x_{i+1} = \lfloor x_i \cdot \lfloor 2 - f_b \cdot x_i \rfloor_\sigma \rfloor_\sigma.$$

Let

$$z = f_b \cdot x_i.$$

Assume $z \in (1, 2)$ and let $z[0].z[1:s]$ be a representation of z, i.e.,

$$z = \langle z[0].z[1:s] \rangle.$$

The subtraction of z would require the complementation of z and an increment in the last position. As computations are imprecise anyway one would hope that little harm is done – and time is saved – if the increment is omitted. This is confirmed in

Let $z \in (0, 2)$, then   ◀ Lemma 8.4

$$0 < 2 - z \leq \langle \overline{z[0]}.\overline{z[1:\sigma]} \rangle + 2^\sigma.$$

PROOF

$$
\begin{aligned}
2 - z &= \langle 10.0^s \rangle - \langle 0z[0].z[1:s] \rangle \\
&= \langle 10.0^s \rangle + \langle 1\overline{z[0]}.\overline{z[1:s]} \rangle + 2^{-s} \bmod 4) \\
&= \langle \overline{z[0]}.\overline{z[1:s]} \rangle + 2^{-s} \\
&= \langle \overline{z[0]}.\overline{z[1:\sigma]} \rangle + \sum_{i=\sigma+1}^{s} \overline{z[i]} \cdot 2^{-i} + 2^{-s} \\
&\leq \langle \overline{z[0]}.\overline{z[1:\sigma]} \rangle + 2^{-\sigma}.
\end{aligned}
$$

QED ___

The simplified finite precision Newton-Raphson iteration is summarized as

$$
\begin{aligned}
z_i &= f_b \cdot x_i \\
A_i &= \langle \overline{z_i[0:\sigma]} \rangle \\
x_{i+1} &= \lfloor x_i \cdot A_i \rfloor_\sigma \\
\delta_i &= 1/f_b - x_i.
\end{aligned}
$$

For later use we introduce the notation

$$
A_i = appr(2 - f_b \cdot x_i).
$$

The convergence of this method is analyzed in a technical lemma:

Lemma 8.5 ▶ *Let $\sigma \geq 4$, let $x_0 \in (1/2, 1)$ and let $0 < |\delta_0| < 1/8$. Then*

$$
x_{i+1} \in (0,1) \ and
$$

$$
0 < \delta_{i+1} < 2 \cdot \delta_i^2 + 2^{-\sigma+1} < 1/4.
$$

for all $i \geq 0$.

PROOF

$$
\delta_{i+1} = \Delta_1 + \Delta_2 + \Delta_3
$$

where

$$
\begin{aligned}
\Delta_1 &= 1/f_b - x_i \cdot (2 - z_i) \\
\Delta_2 &= x_i \cdot (2 - z_i) - x_i \cdot A_i \\
\Delta_3 &= x_i \cdot A_i - \lfloor x_i \cdot A_i \rfloor_\sigma
\end{aligned}
$$

By the classical analysis in lemma 8.2 we have

$$
0 < \Delta_1 < 2 \cdot \delta_i^2.
$$

Because x_i lies in the interval $(0,1)$, we have

$$
0 < z_i = f_b \cdot x_i < 2.
$$

Lemma 8.4 implies

$$
\begin{aligned}
0 < \Delta_2 &= x_i \cdot (2 - z_i - A_i) \\
&\leq x_i \cdot 2^\sigma < 2^{-\sigma}.
\end{aligned}
$$

Obviously, we have

$$
0 \leq \Delta_3 \leq 2^{-\sigma}
$$

and the first two inequalities of the lemma follow. By induction we get

$$\begin{aligned} \delta_{i+1} \;&<\; 2 \cdot \delta_i^2 + 2^{-\sigma+1} \\ &<\; 1/8 + 1/8 = 1/4 \end{aligned}$$

Finally $0 < \delta_{i+1} = 1/f_b - x_{i+1} < 1/4$ implies

$$1/4 < 1/f_b - 1/4 < x_i < 1/f_b < 1.$$

QED

8.3.4 Table Size versus Number of Iterations

The following lemma bounds the number of iterations necessary to reach $p + 2$ bits of precision if we truncate intermediate results after $\sigma = 57$ bits and if we start with a table, where $\gamma = 8$.

Let $\sigma = 57$, let $\gamma = 8$ and let   ◀ Lemma 8.6

$$i = \begin{cases} 2 & \text{if} \quad p = 24 \\ 3 & \text{if} \quad p = 53 \end{cases} , \quad then \quad \delta_i < 2^{-(p+2)}.$$

By the lemmas 8.3 and 8.5 we have   PROOF

$$\begin{aligned} \delta_0 \;&<\; 1.5 \cdot 2^{-9} \\ \delta_1 \;&<\; 2 \cdot (1.5)^2 \cdot 2^{-18} + 2^{-56} < 4.6 \cdot 2^{-18} \\ \delta_2 \;&<\; 42.32 \cdot 2^{-36} + 2^{-56} \leq 42.33 \cdot 2^{-36} < 2^{-30}. \end{aligned}$$

Thus, $i = 2$ iterations suffice for single precision.

$$\begin{aligned} \delta_3 \;&<\; 3583.7 \cdot 2^{-72} + 2^{-55} \\ &\leq\; 3.5 \cdot 2^{-62} + 2^{-56} < 2^{-55} \end{aligned}$$

Thus, $i = 3$ iterations suffice for double precision.   QED

By similar arguments one shows that one iteration less suffices, if one starts with $\gamma = 15$, and one iteration more is needed if one starts with $\gamma = 5$ (exercise 8.2). The number of iterations and the corresponding table size and cost are summarized in table 8.3 We will later use $\gamma = 8$.

Table 8.3 Size and cost of the $2^\gamma \times \gamma$ lookup ROM depending on the number of iterations i, assuming that the cost of a ROM is one eighth the cost of an equally sized RAM.

i	γ	lookup ROM	
		size [K bit]	gate count
1	15	480	139277
2	8	2	647
3	5	0.16	61

8.3.5 Computing the Representative of the Quotient

By lemma 8.6 we have

$$
\begin{aligned}
0 &< 1/f_b - x_i &< 2^{-(p+2)} \\
x_i &< 1/f_b &< x_i + 2^{-(p+2)} \\
f_a \cdot x_i &< f_a/f_b = q &< f_a \cdot x_i + 2^{-(p+1)}.
\end{aligned}
$$

Thus,

$$
\lfloor f_a \cdot x_i \rfloor_{p+1} < f_a \cdot x_i < q
$$
$$
< f_a \cdot x_i + 2^{-(p+1)} < \lfloor f_a \cdot x_i \rfloor_{p+1} + 2^{-p}.
$$

In other words,

$$
E = \lfloor f_a \cdot x_i \rfloor_{p+1}
$$

is an approximation of q, and the exact quotient lies in the open interval $(E, E + 2^{-p})$. Moreover, we have

$$
[a/b]_{p+1} = \begin{cases} E + 2^{-(p+2)} & \text{if } f_a/f_b < E + 2^{-(p+1)} \\ E + 2^{-(p+1)} & \text{if } f_a/f_b = E + 2^{-(p+1)} \\ E + 3 \cdot 2^{-(p+2)} & \text{if } f_a/f_b > E + 2^{-(p+1)} \end{cases}
$$

In the first case one appends 1 to the representation of E, in the second case one increments E, and in the third case one increments and appends 1.

For any relation $\circ \in \{<, =, >\}$ we have

$$
f_a/f_b \circ E + 2^{-(p+1)} \qquad \leftrightarrow \qquad f_a \circ f_b \cdot (E + 2^{-(p+1)}).
$$

Thus, comparison of f_a with the product

$$
G = f_b \cdot (E + 2^{-(p+1)})
$$

determines which one of the three cases applies, and whether the result is exact.

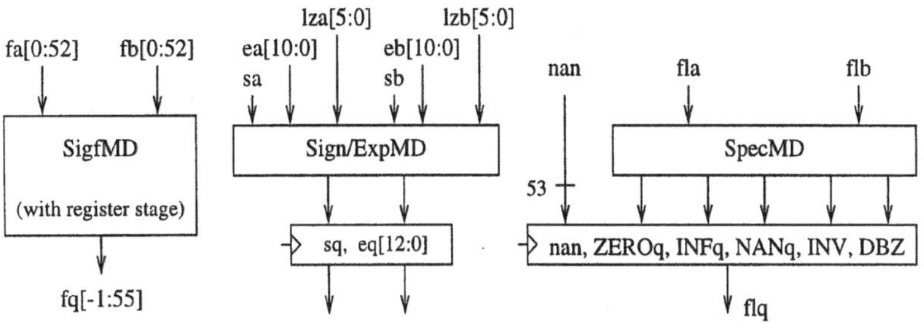

Figure 8.18 Top level schematics of the multiply/divide unit

8.3.6 Multiplier and Divider Circuits

The multiply/divide unit depicted in figure 8.18 is partitioned in a natural way into units

1. SIGN/EXPMD producing the sign s_q and the exponent e_q,

2. SIGFMD producing the significand f_q and

3. SPECMD handling special cases.

The essential inputs for the unit are the sign bit, the exponent, the significand, and the number of leading zeros for two operands a and b satisfying

$$a = (-1)^{s_a} \cdot 2^{e_a - lz_a} \cdot f_a, \qquad b = (-1)^{s_b} \cdot 2^{e_b - lz_b} \cdot f_b,$$

where for $(n, p) = (11, 53)$ the exponents are given as n–bit two's complement numbers

$$e_a = [e_a[n-1:0]], \qquad e_b = [e_b[n-1:0]],$$

the significands are given as binary fractions

$$f_a = \langle f_a[0].f_a[1:p-1]\rangle, \qquad f_b = \langle f_b[0].f_b[1:p-1]\rangle$$

and for

$$r = \lceil \log p \rceil$$

the numbers of leading zeros are given as r–bit binary numbers

$$lz_a = \langle lz_a[r-1:0]\rangle, \qquad lz_b = \langle lz_b[r-1:0]\rangle.$$

In the absence of special cases the factorings are normalized, and thus

$$f_a, f_b \in [1, 2).$$

For operations $\circ \in \{*, /\}$, let

$$x = a \circ b$$

be the exact result of the operation performed, and let

$$\hat{\eta}(x) = (s, \hat{e}, \hat{f}).$$

In the absence of special cases, the unit has to produce a factoring (s_q, e_q, f_q) satisfying

$$[\![s_q, e_q, f_q]\!] =_{p-\hat{e}} a \circ b.$$

Cost and Delay

Circuit SIGFMD which produces the significand f_q has an internal register stage. Thus, the cost and the cycle time of the multiply/divide circuit and the accumulated delay A_{MulDiv} of its outputs can be expressed as

$$
\begin{aligned}
C_{MulDiv} &= C_{SigfMD} + C_{SignExpMD} + C_{SpecMD} + C_{ff}(72) \\
T_{MulDiv} &= \max\{D_{SpecMD} + \Delta, D_{SignExpMD} + \Delta, T_{SigfMD}\} \\
A_{MulDiv} &= A_{SigfMD}.
\end{aligned}
$$

Sign and Exponent Computation

Figure 8.19 depicts the circuit SIGN/EXPMD for the computation of the sign and the exponent. The computation of the sign

$$s_q = s_a \oplus s_b$$

is trivial. The computation of the exponent is controlled by signal $fdiv$ which distinguishes between multiplications and divisions. The exponent is computed as

$$
e_q = \begin{cases}
e_a - lz_a + (e_b - lz_b) & \text{if } /fdiv \quad \text{(multiply)} \\
e_a - lz_a - (e_b - lz_b) & \text{if } fdiv \quad \text{(divide)}.
\end{cases}
$$

We can estimate e_q by

$$2^n - 2 = 2 \cdot e_{max} \geq e_q \geq -2 \cdot e_{min} - p > -2^{n+1}.$$

Therefore, the computation is performed with $(n+2)$–bit two's complement numbers. Circuit SIGN/EXPMD has the following cost and delay:

$$
\begin{aligned}
C_{SignExpMD} &= C_{xor} + 23 \cdot C_{inv} + C_{mux}(11) + C_{mux}(13) \\
&\quad + C_{4/2add}(13) + C_{add}(13) \\
D_{SignExpMD} &= D_{inv} + D_{mux} + D_{4/2add}(13) + D_{add}(13).
\end{aligned}
$$

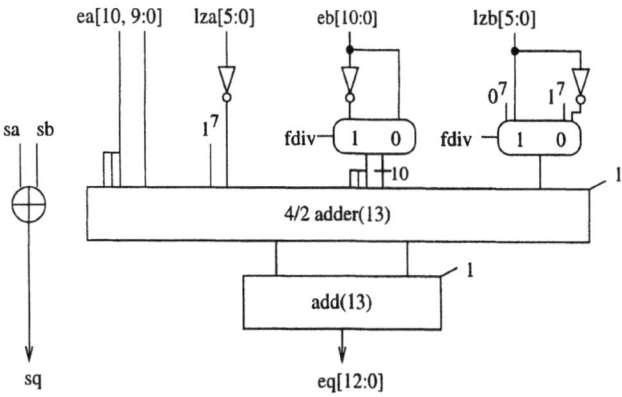

Figure 8.19 Circuit SIGN/EXPMD

Significand Multiplication

Let a and b be the two operands of the floating point multiplication. In case that the operand a is a finite non-zero number, its significand f_a is normalized. The same holds for the significand f_b of operand b. Hence

$$f_a \cdot f_b \in [1,4).$$

Let

$$x = a \cdot b \quad \text{and} \quad \hat{\eta}(x) = (s_q, \hat{e}, \hat{f}),$$

then

$$\hat{e} \geq e_a - lz_a + e_b - lz_b = e_q.$$

Unit SIGFMD depicted in figure 8.20 performs the significand computation of the multiply/divide unit. The multiplication algorithm shares with the division algorithm a 58-bit multiplier. Therefore, the significands are extended by 5 trailing zeros to length 58. Wallace tree, adder and sticky bit computation produce for a 54-representative f_m of the product:

$$\langle f_m[-1:55]\rangle = [\langle f_a[0].f_a[1:52]0^5\rangle \cdot \langle f_b[0].f_b[1:52]0^5\rangle]_{54}.$$

Hence

$$
\begin{aligned}
[\![s_q, e_q, f_m]\!] &= (-1)^{s_q} \cdot 2^{e_q} \cdot [f_a \cdot f_b]_{54} \\
&=_{54-e_q} (-1)^{s_q} \cdot 2^{e_q} \cdot (f_a \cdot f_b) \\
&=_{54-\hat{e}} (-1)^{s_q} \cdot 2^{e_q} \cdot (f_a \cdot f_b).
\end{aligned}
$$

For both single and double precision computations we have $p < 54$ and therefore

$$[\![s_q, e_q, f_m]\!] =_{p-\hat{e}} (-1)^{s_q} \cdot 2^{e_q} \cdot (f_a \cdot f_b).$$

383

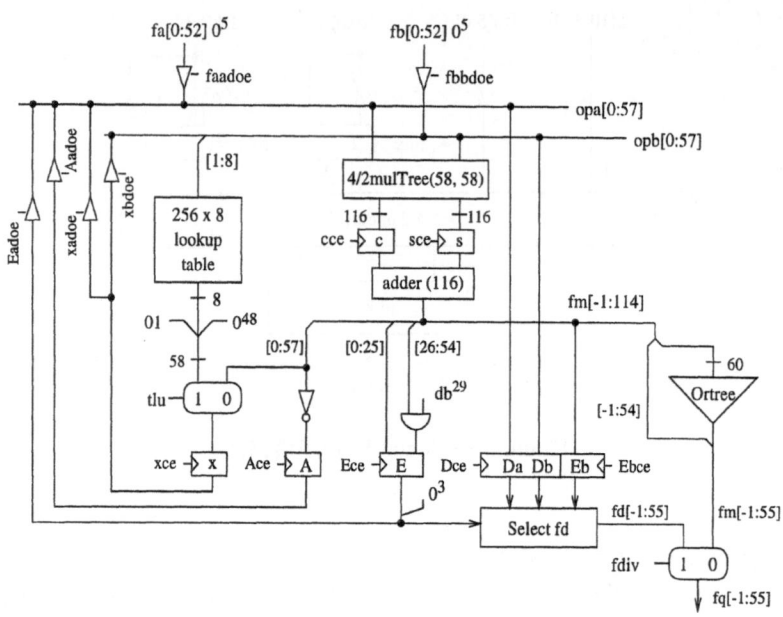

Figure 8.20 Circuit SIGFMD performing the division and multiplication of the significands

Significand Division

Significand division is performed by unit SIGFMD (figure 8.20) under the control of the counter *Dcnt* depicted in figure 8.21 and the FSD of figure 8.22. The corresponding RTL instructions in table 8.4 summarize the steps of the iterative division as it was outlined above. A Newton-Raphson iteration step comprises two multiplications, each of which takes two cycles. Thus, a single iteration takes four cycles; the corresponding states are denoted by Newton 1 to Newton 4. The counter *Dcnt* counts the number of iterations. During the table lookup, the counter is set to the number of iterations required (i.e., 2 for single and 3 for double precision), and during each iteration, *Dcnt* is counted down. After state lookup we have

$$x = x_0 \quad \text{and} \quad Dcnt = dcnt_0 = (db\,?3:2).$$

After the ith execution of state Newton 4 we have

$$
\begin{aligned}
A &= A_{i-1} \\
x &= x_i \\
Dcnt &= dcnt_0 - i.
\end{aligned}
$$

The loop is left after $i = dcnt_0$ iterations. For this i, we have after state

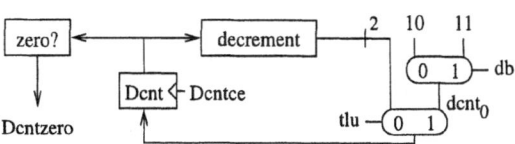

Figure 8.21 Iteration Counter *Dcnt*

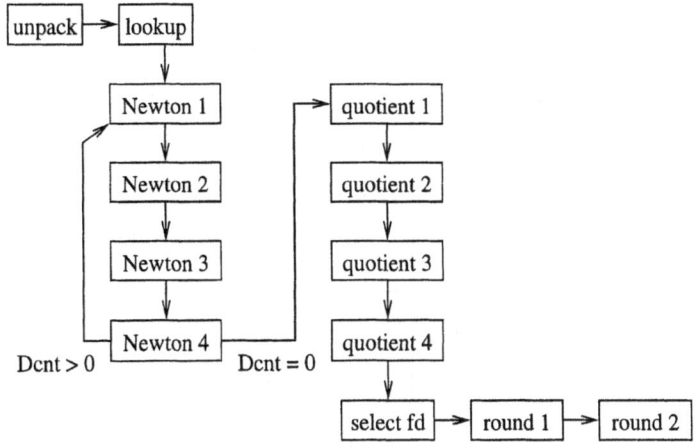

Figure 8.22 FSD underlying the iterative division. The states Newton 1 to Newton 4 represent one Newton-Raphson iteration. *Dcnt* counts the number of iterations; it is counted down.

quotient 4

$$E = \lfloor f_a \cdot x_i \rfloor_{p+1}$$
$$E_b = E \cdot f_b$$

After state quotient 2 we already have

$$f_a = D_a \quad \text{and} \quad f_b = D_b.$$

Note that for single precision, E is truncated after position $p+1 = 25$.

Circuit SELECT FD
Figure 8.23 depicts the circuit selecting the $(p+1)$-representative f_d of the quotient q according to the RTL instructions of state select fd. Since

$$E' = E + 2^{-(p+1)},$$

Table 8.4 RTL instructions of the iterative division (significand only). A multi-plication always takes two cycles.

state	RTL instruction	control signals
unpack	normalize FA, FB	
lookup	$x = \text{table}(f_b)$	xce, tlu, fbbdoe
	$Dcnt = (db?3:2)$	Dcntce,
Newton 1/2	$Dcnt = Dcnt - 1$	Dcntce, xadoe, fbbdoe
	$A = \text{appr}(2 - x \cdot b, 57)$	Ace
Newton 3/4	$x = \lfloor A \cdot x \rfloor_{57}$	Aadoe, xbdoe, sce, cce
		xce
quotient 1/2	$E = \lfloor a \cdot x \rfloor_{p+1}$	faadoe, xbdoe, sce, cce
	$D_a = f_a,\ D_b = f_b$	faadoe, fbbdoe, Dce, Ece
quotient 3/4	$E_b = E \cdot f_b$	Eadoe, fbbdoe, sce, cce
		Ebce
select fd	$E' = E + 2^{-(p+1)},$	
	$\beta = f_a - E_b - 2^{-(p+1)} \cdot f_b$	
	$f_d = \begin{cases} E + 2^{-(p+2)} & ;\text{if } \beta < 0 \\ E' & ;\text{if } \beta = 0 \\ E' + 2^{-(p+2)} & ;\text{if } \beta > 0 \end{cases}$	
Round 1/2	round (s_q, e_q, f_q)	

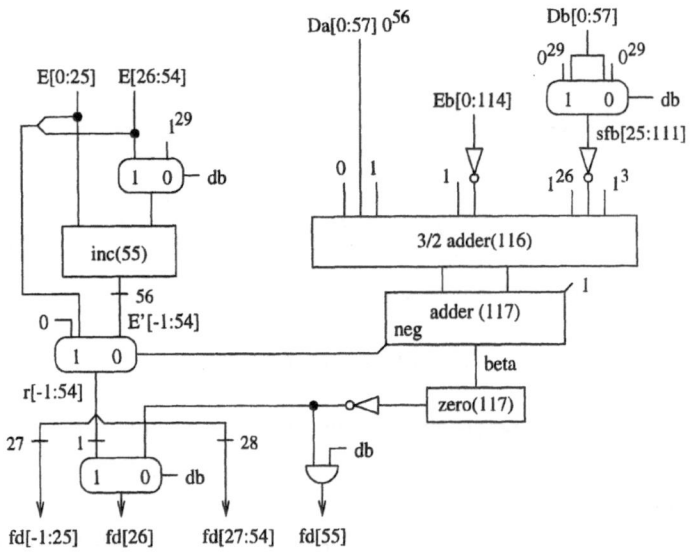

Figure 8.23 Circuit SELECT FD which selects the representative of the exact q

its computation depends on the precision. For double precision $(p = 53)$ holds

$$\langle E'[0].E'[1:54]\rangle = \langle E[0].E[1:54]\rangle + 2^{-54}.$$

For single precision $(p = 24)$, E was truncated after position $p + 1 = 25$. Thus,

$$
\begin{aligned}
\langle E'[0].E'[1:25]\rangle &= \langle E[0].E[1:25]\rangle + 2^{-25} \\
&= \langle E[0].E[1:25]\rangle + \sum_{i=26}^{54} 2^{-i} + 2^{-54} \\
&= \langle E[0].E[1:25]\, 1^{29}\rangle + 2^{-54}.
\end{aligned}
$$

The computation of value β also depends on the precision p. Operand f_b, which is taken from register Db, is first shifted $p + 1$ positions to the right:

$$
\begin{aligned}
\langle 0.0^{24} f_{sb}[25:111]\rangle &= \begin{cases} \langle 0.0^{24}\, 0^{29}\, D_b[0:57]\rangle & ;\text{if}\quad db \\ \langle 0.0^{24}\, D_b[0:57]\, 0^{29}\rangle & ;\text{if}\quad /db \end{cases} \\
&= 2^{-(p+1)} \cdot fb.
\end{aligned}
$$

Now β can be computed as

$$
\begin{aligned}
\beta &= f_a - E_b - 2^{-(p+1)} \cdot f_b \\
&= [0D_a[0].D_a[1:57]\, 0^{57}] - [0E_b[0].E_b[1:114]] \\
&\quad - [00.0^{24} f_{sb}[25:111]\, 0^3] \\
&= [0D_a[0].D_a[1:57]\, 0^{56}\, 1] + [1\, \overline{E_b[0].E_b[1:114]}] \\
&\quad + [11.1^{24}\, \overline{f_{sb}[25:111]}\, 1^3] + 2^{-114}
\end{aligned}
$$

The output significand f_d is computed in the following way: let

$$
r = \begin{cases} E & \text{if}\quad \beta < 0 \\ E' & \text{if}\quad \beta > 0, \end{cases}
$$

then

$$
f_d = \begin{cases} r & \text{if}\quad \beta = 0 \\ r + 2^{-(p+2)} & \text{if}\quad \beta \neq 0. \end{cases}
$$

Thus, in case $\beta \neq 0$ one has to force bit $f_d[p+2]$ to 1.

Cost and Delay

Figure 8.23 depicts circuit SELECT FD which selects the representative of the quotient. The cost and the delay of this circuit run at

$$C_{SelectFd} = C_{inc}(55) + C_{mux}(29) + C_{mux}(56) + C_{mux}$$
$$+ C_{mux}(87) + C_{3/2add}(116) + C_{add}(117)$$
$$+ C_{zero}(117) + 203 \cdot C_{inv} + C_{and}$$
$$D_{SelectFd} = 2 \cdot D_{mux} + \max\{D_{inc}(55) + D_{mux},$$
$$+ 2 \cdot D_{inv} + D_{3/2add}(116) + D_{add}(117) + D_{zero}(117)\}.$$

Circuit SELECT FD is part of the circuit which performs the division and multiplication of the significands. The data paths of circuit SIGFMD have the following cost

$$C_{SigfMD} = 6 \cdot C_{driv}(58) + 5 \cdot C_{ff}(58) + 3 \cdot C_{ff}(116) + C_{ROM}(256,8)$$
$$+ C_{mux}(58) + C_{4/2mulTree}(58,58) + C_{add}(116) + C_{inv}(58)$$
$$+ C_{and}(29) + C_{ORtree}(60) + C_{mux}(57) + C_{SelectFd}.$$

The counter $Dcnt$ and the control automaton modeled by figure 8.22 have been ignored. The accumulated delay of output f_q and the cycle time of circuit SIGFMD can be expressed as:

$$A_{SigfMD} = \max\{D_{SelectFd}, D_{add}(116) + D_{ORtree}(60)\} + D_{mux}$$
$$T_{SigfMD} = \max\{D_{driv} + D_{ROM}(256,8) + D_{mux},$$
$$D_{driv} + D_{4/2mulTree}(58,58), D_{add}(116) + D_{mux}\} + \Delta.$$

Exceptions and Special Cases

The circuit SPECMD checks whether special operands are involved, i.e., whether an operand is zero, infinite or a NaN. In such a case, the result cannot be a finite, non-zero number. The circuit signals the type of such a special result by the three flags ZEROq, INFq and NANq according to the tables 7.4 and 7.5.

The circuit also detects an invalid operation (INV) and a division by zero (DBZ). These two IEEE floating point exceptions can only occur when special operands are involved, whereas for the remaining floating point exceptions – overflow, underflow and inexact result – both operands must be finite, non-zero numbers. Thus, OVF, UNF and INX will be detected by a different circuit during rounding (section 8.4).

For each of the two operands, the circuit SPECMD gets four input flags which indicate its type (ZERO, INF, NAN, and SNAN). Most of the output flags are generated in two steps. First, two sets of flags are generated, one for the multiplication and one for the division. The final set of flags is then selected based on the control signal $fdiv$ which distinguishes between multiplication and division.

Exception Flags

According to section 7.4, the flag DBZ (division by zero) is only activated when a finite, non-zero number is divided by zero. Thus,

$$DBZ = fdiv \land ZEROb \land \overline{(ZEROa \lor INFa \lor NANa \lor SNANa)}.$$

The flag INVm signals an invalid multiplication. According to the specification of section 7.4.3, it is raised when an operand is a signaling NaN or when multiplying a zero with an infinite number:

$$INVm = (INFa \land ZEROb) \lor (ZEROa \land INFb) \lor (SNANa \lor SNANb).$$

The flag INVd which indicates an invalid division is signaled in the following three cases (section 7.4.4): when an operand is a signaling NaN, when both operands are zero, or when both operands are infinite. Thus,

$$INVd = (ZEROa \land ZEROb) \lor (INFa \land INFb) \lor (SNANa \lor SNANb).$$

The IEEE exception flag INV is selected based on the type of the operation

$$INV = \begin{cases} INVm & \text{if} \quad \overline{fdiv} \\ INVd & \text{if} \quad fdiv. \end{cases}$$

Special Result

The flags NANq, INFq and ZEROq which indicate the type of a special result are generated according to the tables 7.4 and 7.5.

The result is a quiet NaN whenever one of the operands is a NaN, and in case of an invalid operation; this is the same for multiplications and divisions. Since signaling NaNs are already covered by INV, the flag NANq can be generated as

$$NANq = INV \lor (NANa \lor NANb)$$

The result of a multiplication can only be infinite if at least one of the operands is infinite. However, if the other operand is a zero or a NaN, the result is a NaN. Thus, the flag $INFm$ signaling an infinite product can be computes as

$$INFm = (INFa \lor INFb) \land \overline{NANq}.$$

The result of a division can only be infinite, when an infinite numerator or a zero denominator is involved. In case of DBZ, the result is always infinite, whereas in case of an infinite numerator, the result can also be a NaN. Thus,

$$INFd = (INFa \land \overline{NANq}) \lor DBZ.$$

The flag $INFq$ is then selected as

$$INFq = \begin{cases} INFm & \text{if} \quad \overline{fdiv} \\ INFd & \text{if} \quad fdiv. \end{cases}$$

The flags ZEROm and ZEROd which indicate a zero product or quotient are derived from the tables 7.4 and 7.5 along the same lines. In case of a zero product, at least one of the operands must be zero. A zero quotient requires a zero numerator or an infinite denominator. Thus,

$$ZEROm = (ZEROa \vee ZEROb) \wedge \overline{NANq}$$

$$ZEROd = (ZEROa \vee INFb) \wedge \overline{NANq}$$

$$ZEROq = \begin{cases} ZEROm & \text{if} \quad \overline{fdiv} \\ ZEROd & \text{if} \quad fdiv. \end{cases}$$

The circuit SPECMD generates all these flags along these lines. It has the following cost and delay:

$$C_{SpecMD} = 10 \cdot C_{and} + 12 \cdot C_{or} + C_{nor} + C_{inv} + 3 \cdot C_{mux}$$
$$D_{SpecMD} = 2 \cdot D_{and} + 4 \cdot D_{or} + D_{inv} + 2 \cdot D_{mux}.$$

8.4 Floating Point Rounder

THE FLOATING point rounder FPRND of figure 8.24 implements 'tiny before rounding' and the 'type b' loss of accuracy (i.e., inexact result). The rounder FPrnd consists of two parts

- circuit RND which performs the rounding of a finite, non-zero result x specified by the input factoring (s, e_r, f_r), and

- circuit SPECRND which handles the special inputs zero, infinity, and NaN. Such an input is signaled by the flags fl_r. This circuit also checks for IEEE floating point exceptions.

Cost and Delay

All the inputs of the floating point rounder have zero delay since they are taken from registers. Thus, the cost and cycle time of the rounder FPRND and the accumulated delay A_{FPrnd} of its outputs run at

$$C_{FPrnd} = C_{NormShift} + C_{REPp} + C_{ff}(140) + C_{SigRnd}$$
$$\qquad\qquad + C_{PostNorm} + C_{AdjustExp} + C_{ExpRnd} + C_{SpecFPrnd}$$
$$T_{FPrnd} = A_{NormShift} + D_{REPp} + \Delta$$
$$A_{FPrnd} = A_{SigRnd} + D_{PostNorm} + D_{AdjustExp} + D_{ExpRnd} + D_{SpecFPrnd}.$$

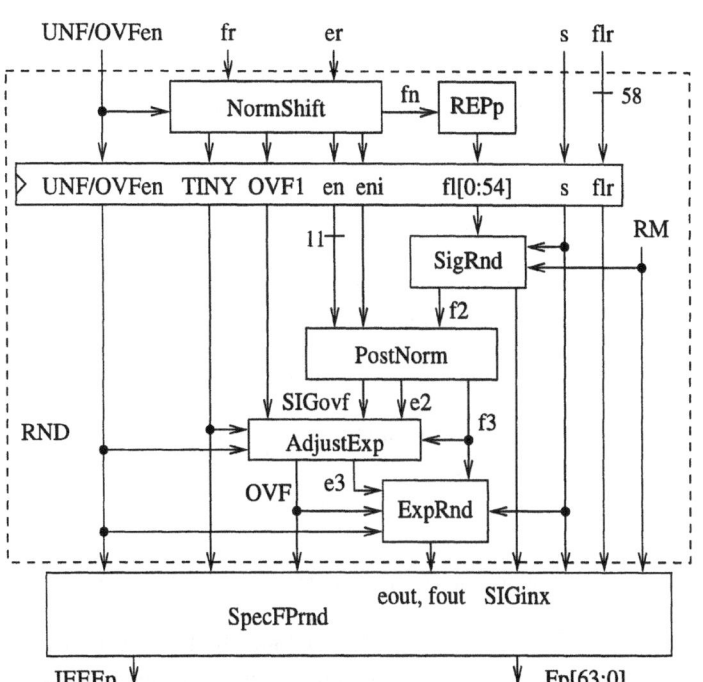

Figure 8.24 Schematics of the floating point rounder FPRND

8.4.1 Specification and Overview

Let $x \in \mathbf{R} \setminus \{0\}$ be the exact, finite result of an operation, and let

$$
y = \begin{cases} 2^{-\alpha} \cdot x & \text{; if } OVF \wedge OVFen \\ 2^{\alpha} x \cdot & \text{; if } UNF \wedge UNFen \\ x & \text{; otherwise} \end{cases}
\tag{8.3}
$$

$$
\hat{\eta}(x) = (s, \hat{e}, \hat{f})
$$
$$
\eta(y) = (s, e, f).
$$

The purpose of circuit RND (figure 8.24) is to compute the normalized, packed output factoring (s, e_{out}, f_{out}) such that $[\![s, e_{out}, f_{out}]\!] = r(y)$, i.e.,

$$
(s, e_{out}, f_{out}) = (s, exprd(s, post(e, sigrd(s, f)))).
\tag{8.4}
$$

Moreover the circuit produces the flags TINY, OVF and SIGinx. The exponent in the output factoring is in *biased* format. The inputs to the circuit are

- the mask bits UNFen and OVFen (underflow / overflow enable)

- the rounding mode $RM[1:0]$

- the signal dbr (double precision result) which defines

$$(n,p) = \begin{cases} (11,53) & \text{; if } dbr = 1 \\ (8,24) & \text{; otherwise} \end{cases}$$

- the factoring s, e_r, f_r, where $e_r[12:0]$ is a 13-bit *two's complement* number and $f_r[-1:55]$ has two bits left of the binary point.

The input factoring has only to satisfy the following two conditions:

- the input factoring approximates x well enough, i.e.,

$$[\![s, e_r, f_r]\!] =_{p-\hat{e}} x. \tag{8.5}$$

- $f_r[-1:0] = 00$ implies $OVF = 0$. Thus, if $|x|$ is large then $f_r \in [1,4)$.

By far the most tricky part of the rounding unit is the normalization shifter NORMSHIFT. It produces an *approximated* overflow signal

$$OVF1 \equiv 2^{e_r} f_r \geq 2^{e_{max}+1}$$

which can be computed before significand rounding takes place. The resulting error is characterized by

Lemma 8.7 ▶ *Let $OVF2 \equiv OVF \wedge /OVF1$, then $OVF2$ implies*

$$\hat{e} = e_{max} \quad \text{and} \quad sigrd(s, \hat{f}) = 2.$$

PROOF   By definition (section 7.3.1), a result x causes an overflow if

$$|\hat{r}(x)| > X_{max}.$$

According to equation 7.8, such an overflow can be classified as an overflow *before* or *after* rounding:

$$OVF(x) \quad \leftrightarrow \quad (\hat{e} > e_{max}) \quad \text{or} \quad (\hat{e} = e_{max} \quad \text{and} \quad sigrd(s, \hat{f}) = 2).$$

Since $/OVF1$ implies

$$|x| =_{p-\hat{e}} 2^{e_r} \cdot f_r < 2^{e_{max}+1},$$

QED   we have $\hat{e} \leq e_{max}$, and the lemma follows.

Thus, the flag $OVF1$ signals an overflow before rounding, whereas the flag $OVF2$ signals an overflow after rounding.

The outputs of the normalization shifter NORMSHIFT will satisfy

$$
e_n = \begin{cases} e + \alpha & \text{; if } OVF2 \wedge OVFen \\ e & \text{; otherwise} \end{cases}
$$

$$
f_n =_p f.
$$

(8.6)

The normalization shifter also produces output $e_{ni} = e_n + 1$. Both exponents will be in biased format.

The effect of the circuits REPP, SIGRND and POSTNORM is specified by the equations:

$$
\begin{aligned}
f_1 &= [f_n]_p \\
f_2 &= sigrd(s, f_1) \\
(e_2, f_3) &= post(e_n, f_2).
\end{aligned}
$$

(8.7)

Circuit SIGRND also provides the flag SIGinx indicating that the rounded significand f_2 is not exact:

$$
SIGinx = 1 \quad \leftrightarrow \quad f_2 \neq f_1.
$$

After post normalization, the correct overflow signal is known and the error produced by the approximated overflow signal $OVF1$ can be corrected in circuit ADJUSTEXP. Finally, the exponent is rounded in circuit EXPRND.

$$
(e_3, f_3) = \begin{cases} (e_{max} + 1 - \alpha, 1) & \text{; if } OVF2 \wedge OVFen \\ (e_2, f_3) & \text{; otherwise} \end{cases}
$$

$$
(e_{out}, f_{out}) = exprd(s, e_3, f_3)
$$

(8.8)

In addition, circuit EXPRND converts the result into the packed IEEE format, i.e., bit $f_{out}[0]$ is hidden, and e_{min} is represented by 0^n in case of a denormal result.

With the above specifications of the subcircuits in place, we can show in a straightforward way:

If the subcircuits satisfy the above specifications, then equation (8.4) holds, i.e., the rounder RND works correctly for a finite, non-zero x. ◄ Theorem 8.8

By equations (8.6) we have PROOF

$$
e_n = \begin{cases} e + \alpha & \text{; if } OVF2 \wedge OVFen \\ e & \text{; otherwise} \end{cases}
$$

$$
f_n =_p f.
$$

Equations (8.7) then imply

$$f_1 = [f]_p$$
$$f_2 = sigrd(s, f)$$

$$(e_2, f_3) = \begin{cases} post(e + \alpha, sigrd(s, f)) & \text{; if } OVF2 \wedge OVFen \\ post(e, sigrd(s, f)) & \text{; otherwise} \end{cases}$$

and equations (8.8) finally yield

$$(e_3, f_3) = post(e, sigrd(s, f))$$
$$(s, e_{out}, f_{out}) = (s, exprd(s, post(e, sigrd(s, f))))$$

QED

8.4.2 Normalization Shift

Overview

Let lz be the number of leading zeros of $f_r[-1 : 55]$. In general, the normalization shifter has to shift the first 1 in f_r to the left of the binary point and to compensate for this in the exponent. If the final result is a denormal number, then $|x|$ must be represented as

$$2^{e_r} f_r = 2^{e_{min}} \cdot 2^{e_r - e_{min}} \cdot f_r.$$

This requires a left shift by $e_r - e_{min}$ which in many cases will be a right shift by $e_{min} - e_r$ (see exercise 8.3). Finally, for a wrapped exponent one might have to add or subtract α in the exponent. The normalization shifter in figure 8.25 works along these lines.

First in circuit FLAGS the signals TINY, OVF1 and the binary representation $lz[5 : 0]$ of the number lz are computed. Then, the exponent e_n and the (left) shift distance σ are computed in circuits EXPNORM and SHIFT-DIST.

We derive formulae for e_n and σ such that equations (8.6) hold. From equations (8.3) and

$$UNF \wedge UNFen \equiv TINY \wedge UNFen$$

we conclude

$$y = \begin{cases} (-1)^s \cdot 2^{\hat{e} - \alpha} \cdot \hat{f} & \text{; if } OVF \wedge OVFen \\ (-1)^s \cdot 2^{\hat{e} + \alpha} \cdot \hat{f} & \text{; if } TINY \wedge UNFen \\ (-1)^s \cdot 2^{\hat{e}} \cdot \hat{f} & \text{; otherwise} \end{cases}$$

$$\hat{\eta}(y) = \begin{cases} (s, \hat{e} - \alpha, \hat{f}) & \text{; if } OVF \wedge OVFen \\ (s, \hat{e} + \alpha, \hat{f}) & \text{; if } TINY \wedge UNFen \\ (s, \hat{e}, \hat{f}) & \text{; otherwise.} \end{cases}$$

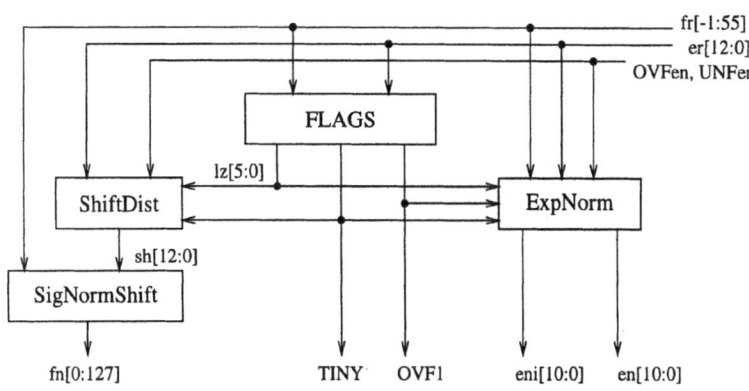

Figure 8.25 Circuit NORMSHIFT of the normalization shift

The two factorings $\hat{\eta}(y)$ and $\eta(y)$ are the same except if y is denormal, i.e., if $(TINY \wedge /UNFen)$. In this case,

$$x = (-1)^s \cdot 2^{\hat{e}} \cdot \hat{f} = (-1)^s \cdot 2^{e_{min}} 2^{\hat{e}-e_{min}} \cdot \hat{f},$$

and

$$\eta(y) = \begin{cases} (s, \hat{e}-\alpha, \hat{f}) & ; \text{if} \quad OVF \wedge OVFen \\ (s, \hat{e}+\alpha, \hat{f}) & ; \text{if} \quad TINY \wedge UNFen \\ (s, e_{min}, 2^{\hat{e}-e_{min}} \cdot \hat{f}) & ; \text{if} \quad TINY \wedge /UNFen \\ (s, \hat{e}, \hat{f}) & ; \text{otherwise} \end{cases}$$

and therefore,

$$e = \begin{cases} \hat{e}-\alpha & ; \text{if} \quad OVF \wedge OVFen \\ \hat{e}+\alpha & ; \text{if} \quad TINY \wedge UNFen \\ e_{min} & ; \text{if} \quad TINY \wedge /UNFen \\ \hat{e} & ; \text{otherwise} \end{cases} \qquad (8.9)$$

$$f = \begin{cases} 2^{\hat{e}-e_{min}} \cdot \hat{f} & ; \text{if} \quad TINY \wedge /UNFen \\ \hat{f} & ; \text{otherwise.} \end{cases}$$

Let $f' = f_r/2$. Thus

$$f'[0:56] = f_r[-1:55],$$

i.e., the representation $f'[0:56]$ is simply obtained by shifting the binary point in representation $f_r[-1:55]$ one bit to the right. In the following we will compute shift distances for $f'[0:56]$.

395

Let lz be the number of leading zeros in $f_r[-1:55]$ or in $f'[0:56]$, respectively. Finally, let

$$\beta = e_r - lz + 1.$$

From equation (8.5), we conclude

$$2^{\hat{e}} \cdot \hat{f} \; = \; |x| \; =_{p-\hat{e}} \; 2^{e_r} \cdot f_r \; = \; 2^{e_r+1} \cdot f' \; = \; 2^{\beta} \cdot 2^{lz} \cdot f'.$$

Since $2^{lz} \cdot f' \in [1,2)$, it follows that

$$\beta = \hat{e} \quad \text{and} \quad 2^{lz} \cdot f' =_p \hat{f}.$$

This immediately gives

$$e = \begin{cases} \beta - \alpha & ; \text{if} \quad OVF \wedge OVFen \\ \beta + \alpha & ; \text{if} \quad TINY \wedge UNFen \\ e_{min} & ; \text{if} \quad TINY \wedge /UNFen \\ \beta & ; \text{otherwise} \end{cases}$$

and

$$\sigma = lz \quad ; \text{unless} \quad TINY \wedge /UNFen.$$

If $(TINY \wedge /UNFen)$ holds, then $x = y$ and $\hat{e} < e_{min}$. From equations (8.9) and (8.5) we know

$$\begin{aligned} f &= 2^{\hat{e}-e_{min}} \cdot \hat{f} \\ 2^{\hat{e}} \cdot \hat{f} &=_{p-\hat{e}} 2^{e_r} \cdot f_r. \end{aligned}$$

Multiplying the second equation by $2^{-e_{min}}$ implies that

$$\begin{aligned} 2^{\hat{e}-e_{min}} \cdot \hat{f} &=_{p-\hat{e}+e_{min}} 2^{e_r-e_{min}} \cdot f_r \\ f &=_{p-\hat{e}+e_{min}} 2^{e_r-e_{min}} \cdot f_r = 2^{e_r-e_{min}+1} \cdot f'. \end{aligned}$$

Since $\hat{e} < e_{min}$, it also holds that

$$f =_p 2^{e_r-e_{min}+1} \cdot f'.$$

Thus, we have

$$\sigma = e_r - e_{min} + 1 \quad ; \text{if} \quad TINY \wedge /UNFen.$$

Up to issues of number format the outputs of circuits SHIFTDIST and EXPNORM are specified by the above calculations. Circuit SIGNORM-SHIFT will *not* produce a representation of $f' \cdot 2^{\sigma}$, because in the case of right shifts such a representation might be very long (exercise 8.4). Instead, it will produce a representation $f_n[0:63]$ such that

$$[[f_n[0:63]]] = f_n =_p f' \cdot 2^\sigma$$

holds.

With the above specifications of the subcircuits of the normalization shifter in place (up to issues of number format), we can immediately conclude

Let ◀ Lemma 8.9

$$e_n = \begin{cases} \beta - \alpha & ; if \quad OVF1 \wedge OVFen \\ \beta + \alpha & ; if \quad TINY \wedge UNFen \\ e_{min} & ; if \quad TINY \wedge /UNFen \\ \beta & ; otherwise \end{cases}$$

$$\sigma = \begin{cases} e_r - e_{min} + 1 & ; if \quad TINY \wedge /UNFen \\ lz & ; otherwise \end{cases}$$

$$(8.10)$$

$$f_n =_p f' \cdot 2^\sigma.$$

Then equations (8.4) hold, i.e., the normalization shifter works correctly.

Flags

Figure 8.26 depicts circuit FLAGS which determines the number lz of leading zeros and the flags TINY and OVF1. The computation of $lz[5:0]$ is completely straightforward. Because no overflow occurs if $f_r[-1:0] = 00$, we have

$$OVF1 \quad \leftrightarrow \quad (e_r > e_{max}) \vee ((e_r = e_{max}) \wedge f_r[-1]).$$

Now recall that $bias = e_{max} = 2^{n-1} - 1 = \langle 1^{n-1} \rangle$ and that n either equals 11 or 8. For the two's complement number e_r we have

$$[e_r[12:0]] > \langle 1^{n-1} \rangle \quad \leftrightarrow \quad /e_r[12] \wedge \bigvee_{i=n-1}^{11} e_r[i].$$

This explains the computation of the OVF1 flag.

Since $f' = f_r/2$, we have to consider two cases for the TINY flag.

$$TINY \quad \leftrightarrow \quad \begin{cases} e_r + 1 < e_{min} & if \quad f' \in [1,2) \\ e_r + 1 - lz < e_{min} & if \quad f' \in [0,1) \end{cases}$$
$$\leftrightarrow \quad e_r + 1 - lz - e_{min} < 0,$$

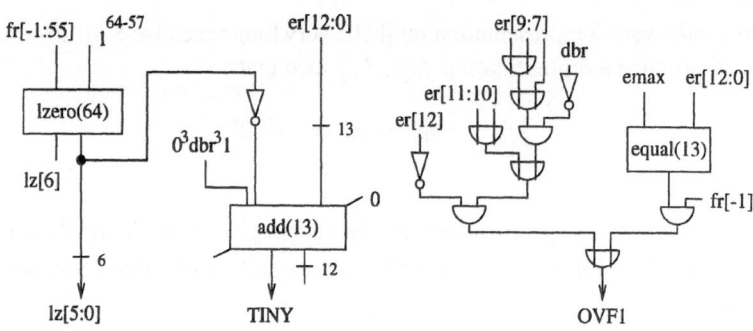

Figure 8.26 Circuit FLAGS. Depending on the precision, the exponent *emax* equals $[0^3 dbr^3 1^7]$.

because $lz = 0$ for an f' in the interval $[1,2)$. Thus, the TINY flag can be computed as the sign bit of the sum of the above 4 operands. Recall that $e_{min} = 1 - bias$. Thus

$$-e_{min} + 1 = bias - 1 + 1 = \langle 1^{n-1} \rangle.$$

$$bias - lz = \langle 1^{n-1} \rangle + 1 + [1\,\overline{lz[5:0]}] = \langle 10^{n-1} \rangle + [1^7\,\overline{lz[5:0]}]$$

$$= \begin{cases} [0^6 1\,\overline{lz[5:0]}] & ; \text{if} \quad n = 8 \\ [0^3 1^4\,\overline{lz[5:0]}] & ; \text{if} \quad n = 11 \end{cases}$$

This explains the computation of the TINY flag.

Circuit FLAGS gets its inputs directly from registers. Thus, its cost and the accumulated delay of its outputs run at

$$C_{FLAGS} = C_{lz}(64) + C_{add}(13) + C_{EQ}(13) + 8 \cdot C_{inv} + 5 \cdot C_{or} + 3 \cdot C_{and}$$

$$A_{FLAGS} = \max\{D_{lz}(64) + D_{inv} + D_{add}(13), D_{EQ}(13) + D_{and} + D_{or},$$

$$4 \cdot D_{or} + 2 \cdot C_{and}\}.$$

Exponent Normalization

The circuit in figure 8.27 implements the exponent e_n of the equations (8.10) in a fairly straightforward way. Along the way it also converts from two's complement to biased representation.

The case $(TINY \wedge /UNFen)$ is handled by two multiplexers which can force the outputs directly to the biased representations $0^{10}1$ and $0^9 10$ of e_{min} or $e_{min} + 1$, respectively. For the remaining three cases, the top portion of the circuit computes biased representations of e_n and $e_n + 1$, or equivalently, the two's complement representations of $e_n + bias$ and $e_n + 1 + bias$.

In particular, let

$$\gamma = \begin{cases} -\alpha & ; \text{if } OVF1 \wedge OVFen \\ \alpha & ; \text{if } TINY \wedge UNFen \\ 0 & ; \text{otherwise,} \end{cases}$$

then the circuit computes the following sums sum and $sum + 1$:

$$\begin{aligned} sum &= e_r - lz + 1 + \gamma + bias \\ &= e_r + 1 + [1\,\overline{lz[5:0]}] + 1 + \gamma + bias \\ &= e_r + 1 + [1\,\overline{lz[5:0]}] + \delta, \end{aligned}$$

where

$$\delta = \begin{cases} bias - \alpha + 1 & ; \text{if } OVF \wedge OVFen \\ bias + \alpha + 1 & ; \text{if } TINY \wedge UNFen \\ bias + 1 & ; \text{otherwise}. \end{cases}$$

Recall that $\alpha = 3 \cdot 2^{n-2} = \langle 110^{n-2} \rangle$ and $bias = 2^{n-1} - 1 = \langle 1^{n-1} \rangle$. Hence

$$\begin{aligned} bias + 1 &= \langle 10^{n-1} \rangle = [00100^{n-2}]. \\ bias + \alpha + 1 &= \langle 110^{n-2} \rangle + \langle 100^{n-2} \rangle \\ &= \langle 1010^{n-2} \rangle = [01010^{n-2}]. \\ -\alpha &= [1001^{n-2}] + 1 = [1010^{n-2}]. \\ bias + 1 - \alpha &= [1110^{n-2}] = [11110^{n-2}]. \end{aligned}$$

In single precision we have $n = 8$ and the above equations define two's complement numbers with only 10 bits. By sign extension they are extended to 13 bits at the last multiplexer above the 3/2–adder. Like in the computation of flag TINY, the value $[\overline{lz[5:0]}]$ can be included in the constant δ', and then, the 3/2-adder in the circuit of figure 8.27 can be dropped (see exercise 8.5).

Without this optimization, circuit EXPNORM provides the two exponents en and eni at the following cost and accumulated delay

$$\begin{aligned} C_{ExpNorm} &= C_{3/2add}(11) + C_{add2}(11) + 2 \cdot C_{mux}(2) + C_{mux}(5) \\ &\quad + C_{inv}(6) + 2 \cdot C_{mux}(11) + 3 \cdot C_{and} + C_{inv} \\ A_{ExpNorm} &= \max\{A_{Flags}, A_{UNF/OVFen}\} + D_{and} \\ &\quad + 4 \cdot D_{mux} + D_{3/2add}(11) + D_{add2}(11). \end{aligned}$$

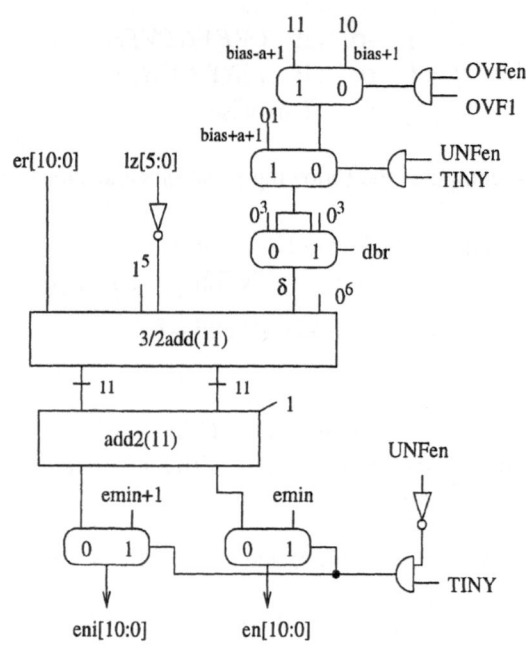

Figure 8.27 Circuit EXPNORM of the exponent normalization shift; the exponents e_{min} and $e_{min} + 1$ are represented as $0^{10}1$ and 0^910. In case of a single precision, only the bits [7:0] of the two exponents *en* and *eni* are used.

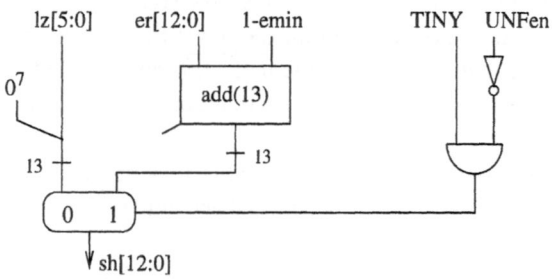

Figure 8.28 Circuit SHIFTDIST provides the shift distance of the normalization shift. Depending on the precision, constant $1 - e_{min}$ equals $0^3\, dbr^3\, 1^7$.

Shift Distance

The circuit in figure 8.28 implements the shift distance σ of the equations (8.10) in a straightforward way. Recall that $e_{min} = 1 - bias = -2^{n-1} + 2$. Thus

$$1 - e_{min} = 1 + 2^{n-1} - 2 = 2^{n-1} - 1 = \langle 1^{n-1} \rangle.$$

It follows that

$$[sh[12:0]] = \sigma.$$

The shift is a right shift if $sh[12] = 1$.

Circuit SHIFTDIST generates the shift distance sh in the obvious way. Since the inputs of the adder have zero delay, the cost and the accumulated delay of the shift distance can be expressed as

$$\begin{aligned}
C_{ShiftDist} &= C_{add}(13) + C_{mux}(13) + C_{and} + C_{inv} \\
A_{ShiftDist} &= \max\{D_{add}(13), A_{FLAGS} + D_{and}, \\
&\quad A_{UNFen} + D_{inv} + D_{and}\} + D_{mux}.
\end{aligned}$$

Significand Normalization Shift

This is slightly more tricky. As shown in figure 8.29 the circuit which performs the normalization shift of the significand has three parts:

1. A cyclic 64 bit left shifter whose shift distance is controlled by the 6 low order bits of sh. This takes the computation of the shift limitation in the MASK circuit off the critical path.

2. A mask circuit producing a 128 bit mask $v[0:63]w[0:63]$

3. Let $fs[0:63]$ be the output of the cyclic left shifter. Then f_n is computed by the bitwise AND of $fs[] fs[]$ and $v[] w[]$.

We begin with the discussion of the cyclic left shifter. For strings $f \in \{0,1\}^N$ and non-negative shift distances d, we denote by $cls(f,d)$ the string obtained by shifting f by d bits cyclically to the left. Similarly, we denote by $crs(f,d)$ the result of shifting f by d bits to the right. Then obviously

$$\begin{aligned}
crs(f,d) &= cls(f, N-d \bmod N) \\
&= cls(f, -d \bmod N).
\end{aligned}$$

Let $\sigma' = \sigma \bmod 64$. For both, positive and negative, shift distances we then have

$$\begin{aligned}
[sh] &= -sh[12] \cdot 2^{12} + \langle sh[11:0] \rangle \\
&\equiv \langle sh[5:0] \rangle \bmod 64 = \sigma'.
\end{aligned}$$

We now can show

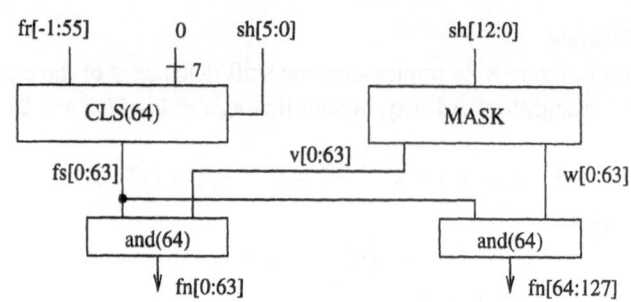

Figure 8.29 Circuit SIGNORMSHIFT

Claim 8.10 ▶ *Let $f' = f_r/2$. The output fs of the cyclic left shifter satisfies*

$$fs = \begin{cases} cls(f', \sigma') & ; \text{if } \sigma \geq 0 \\ crs(f', |\sigma|) & ; \text{otherwise.} \end{cases}$$

PROOF   For non-negative shift distances the claim follows immediately. For negative shift distance σ it follows that

$$crs(f', |\sigma|) = cls(f', \sigma \bmod 64) = cls(f', \langle sh[5:0] \rangle)$$

QED

We proceed to explain the generation of the masks as depicted in figure
8.30. We obviously have

$$\langle t \rangle = \begin{cases} \sigma & ; \text{if } \sigma \geq 0 \\ |\sigma| - 1 & ; \text{otherwise.} \end{cases}$$

Next, the distance in the mask circuit is limited to 63: the output of the
OR-tree equals 1 iff $\langle t \rangle \geq \langle 1^6 \rangle = 63$, hence

$$\langle sh' \rangle = \begin{cases} \langle t \rangle & ; \text{if } \langle t \rangle \leq 63 \\ 63 & ; \text{otherwise} \end{cases} = \begin{cases} \sigma & ; \text{if } 0 \leq \sigma \leq 63 \\ |\sigma| - 1 & ; \text{if } -63 \leq \sigma \leq -1 \\ 63 & ; \text{otherwise} \end{cases}$$

We show that

Claim 8.11 ▶ *The distance of the left shift in the significand normalization shift is bounded by 56, i.e., $\sigma \leq 56$.*

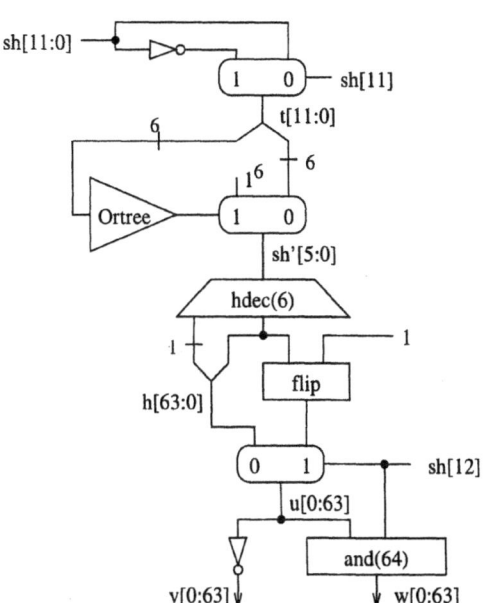

Figure 8.30 The MASK for the significand normalization shift

Left shifts have distance $lz \leq 56$ or $e_r - e_{min} + 1$. The second case only $\quad$ PROOF
occurs if $(TINY \wedge /UNFen)$. In this case we have $e = e_{min}$ and $f_r \neq 0$.
$\quad$ Assume $e_r \geq e_{min} + 55$. Since

$$|x| =_{p-\hat{e}} 2^{e_r} \cdot f_r$$

and since $\hat{e} < e_{min}$, it follows that

$$|x| =_{p-e_{min}} 2^{e_r} \cdot f_r \geq 2^{e_{min}+55} \cdot 2^{-55} > 2^{e_{min}}.$$

This contradicts the tininess of x. $\qquad\qquad$ QED

The half decoder produces from sh' the masks

$$h[63:0] = 0^{64-\langle sh' \rangle} 1^{\langle sh' \rangle}.$$

In case the shift distance is negative a 1 is appended at the right end and
the string is flipped. Thus, for mask u we have

$$u[0:63] = \begin{cases} 0^{64-\sigma} 1^{\sigma} & ; \text{if} \quad 0 \leq \sigma \\ 1^{|\sigma|} 0^{64-|\sigma|} & ; \text{if} \quad -63 \leq \sigma \leq -1 \\ 1^{64} & ; \text{if} \quad \sigma \leq -64 \end{cases}$$

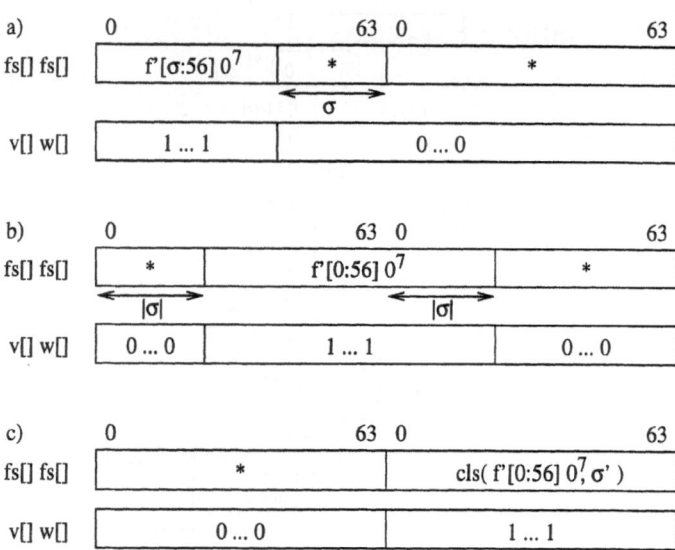

Figure 8.31 Relation between the strings $fs\,fs$ and the masks vw in the three cases
a) $0 \le \sigma$, b) $-63 \le \sigma \le -1$, and c) $\sigma \le -64$.

For the masks $v[]\,w[]$ it follows that

$$
v[0:63]\,w[0:63] = \begin{cases}
1^{64-\sigma}\,0^{64+\sigma} & \text{; if } 0 \le \sigma \\
0^{|\sigma|}\,1^{64}\,0^{64-|\sigma|} & \text{; if } -63 \le \sigma \le -1 \\
0^{64}\,1^{64} & \text{; if } \sigma \le -64.
\end{cases}
$$

The relation between the string $fs[]\,fs[]$ and the masks $v[]\,w[]$ is illustrated in figure 8.31. Let f_l be the result of shifting f' logically by σ bits to the left. From figure 8.31 we immediately read off

$$
f_n[-1:126] = \begin{cases}
f_l\,0^{64} & \text{; if } 0 \le \sigma \\
f_l\,0^{64-\sigma} & \text{; if } -63 \le \sigma \le -1 \\
0^{64}\,cls(f',\sigma') & \text{; if } \sigma \le -64
\end{cases}
$$

In all cases we obviously have

$$
f_n =_p f_l.
$$

Circuit MASK depicted in figure 8.30 generates the masks v and w at the following cost and delay.

$$
\begin{aligned}
C_{MASK} &= C_{inv}(12) + C_{mux}(12) + C_{ORtree}(6) + C_{mux}(6) \\
&\quad C_{hdec}(6) + C_{mux}(64) + C_{inv}(64) + C_{and}(64) \\[6pt]
D_{MASK} &= D_{inv} + 3 \cdot D_{mux} + D_{ORtree}(6) + D_{hdec}(6) + D_{and}.
\end{aligned}
$$

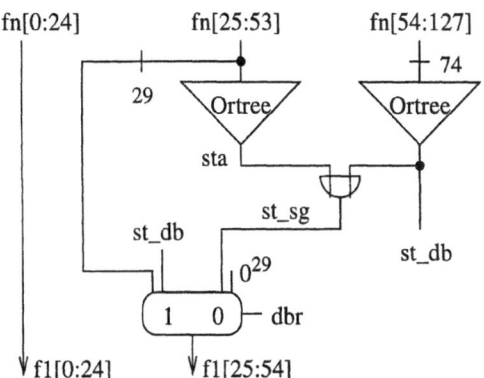

Figure 8.32 Circuit REPP computes the p-representative of fn. The Flag st_{db} (st_{sg}) denotes the sticky bit in case of a double (single) precision result.

Cost and delay of the significand normalization shifter SIGNORMSHIFT run at

$$C_{SigNormShift} = C_{CLS}(64) + C_{MASK} + 2 \cdot C_{and}(64)$$
$$D_{SigNormShift} = \max\{D_{CLS}(64), D_{MASK}\} + D_{and},$$

and the whole normalization shifter NORMSHIFT has cost and delay

$$C_{NormShift} = C_{Flags} + C_{ExpNorm} + C_{ShiftDist} + C_{SigNormShift}$$
$$A_{NormShift} = \max\{A_{ExpNorm}, A_{ShiftDist} + D_{SigNormShift}\}.$$

8.4.3 Selection of the Representative

This is a straightforward sticky bit computation of the form

$$st = \bigvee_{i \geq p+1} f_n[i]$$

where p depends on the precision and is either 24 or 53. Circuit REPP of figure 8.32 selects the p-representative of f_n as

$$f_1[-1 : p+1] = (f_n[-1 : p], st).$$

This circuit has the following cost and delay

$$C_{REPp} = C_{ORtree}(29) + C_{ORtree}(74) + C_{or} + C_{mux}(30)$$
$$D_{REPp} = D_{ORtree}(74) + D_{or} + D_{mux}.$$

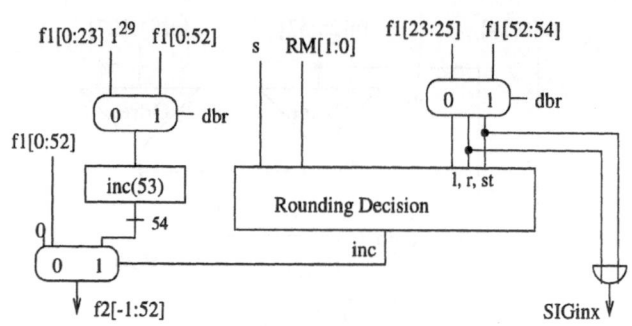

Figure 8.33 Circuit SIGRND

8.4.4 Significand Rounding

In figure 8.33, the least significand bit l, round bit r and sticky bit st are selected depending on the precision and fed into circuit ROUNDINGDECI-SION. The rounded significand is exact iff the bits r and st are both zero:

$$SIGinx = r \lor st.$$

Depending on the rounding decision, $f_1[0:p+1]$ is chopped or incremented at position $p-1$. More formally

$$f_2 = \begin{cases} |f_1[0:p-1]| & ; \text{if} \quad inc = 0 \quad \text{(chop)} \\ |f_1[0:p-1]| + 2^{-(p-1)} & ; \text{if} \quad inc = 1 \quad \text{(increment)}. \end{cases}$$

The rounding decision is made according to table 8.5 which were constructed such that

$$f_2 = sigrd(s, f_1)$$

holds for every rounding mode.

Note that in mode r_{ne} (nearest even), the rounding decision depends on bits l, r and st but not on the sign bit s. In modes r_u, r_d, the decision depends on bits r, st and the sign bit s but not on l. In mode r_z, the significand is always chopped, i.e., $inc = 0$. From table 8.5, one reads off

$$inc = \begin{cases} r \land (l \lor st) & \text{if} \quad r_{ne} \\ \bar{s} \land (r \lor st) & \text{if} \quad r_u \\ s \land (r \lor st) & \text{if} \quad r_d. \end{cases}$$

With the coding of the rounding modes from table 8.1, this is implemented in a straightforward way by the circuit of figure 8.34.

Table 8.5 Rounding decision of the significand rounding. The tables list the value of the flag *inc* which indicates that the significand needs to be incremented. On round to zero (r_z), the flag equals 0.

l	r	st	r_{ne}
0	0	0	0
0	0	1	0
0	1	0	0
0	1	1	1
1	0	0	0
1	0	1	0
1	1	0	1
1	1	1	1

s	r	st	r_u	r_d
0	0	0	0	0
0	0	1	1	0
0	1	0	1	0
0	1	1	1	0
1	0	0	0	0
1	0	1	0	1
1	1	0	0	1
1	1	1	0	1

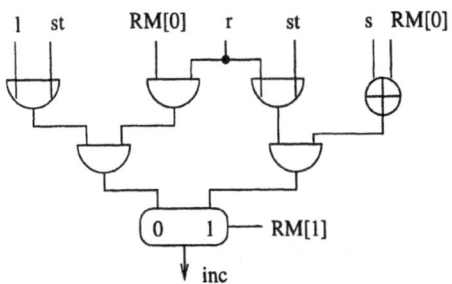

Figure 8.34 Circuit of the rounding decision

The cost and delay of circuit SIGRND which performs the significand rounding can be estimated as

$$
\begin{aligned}
C_{SigRnd} &= C_{mux}(53) + C_{mux}(54) + C_{inc}(53) + C_{or} + C_{mux}(3) \\
&\quad + 3 \cdot C_{and} + 2 \cdot C_{or} + C_{xor} + C_{mux} \\
A_{SigRnd} &= 2 \cdot D_{mux} + \max\{D_{inc}(53), \max\{A_{RM}, D_{mux}\} + D_{xor} + D_{and}\}.
\end{aligned}
$$

8.4.5 Post Normalization

The rounded significand f_2 lies in the interval $[1,2]$. In case of $f_2 = 2$, circuit POSTNORM (figure 8.35) normalizes the factoring and signals an overflow of the significand by $SIGovf = 1$. This overflow flag is generated

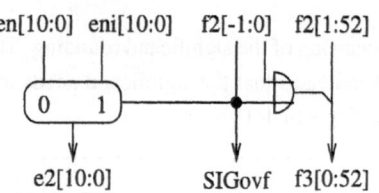

Figure 8.35 Post normalization circuit POSTNORM

as

$$SIGovf = f_2[-1].$$

In addition, circuit POSTNORM has to compute

$$(e_2, f_3) = \begin{cases} (e_n + 1, 1) & ; \text{if } f_2 = 2 \\ (e_n, f_2) & ; \text{otherwise} \end{cases}$$

Since the normalization shifter NORMSHIFT provides e_n and $e_{ni} = e_n + 1$, the exponent e_2 can just be selected based on the flag SIGovf. With a single OR gate, one computes

$$f_3[0].f_3[1:52] = (f_2[1] \lor f_2[0]).f_3[0:52] = \begin{cases} 1.0^{52} & ; \text{if } f_2 = 2 \\ f_2[0:52] & ; \text{otherwise.} \end{cases}$$

Thus, the cost and the delay of the post normalization circuit POSTNORM are

$$C_{PostNorm} = C_{or} + C_{mux}(11)$$
$$D_{PostNorm} = \max\{D_{or}, D_{mux}\}.$$

8.4.6 Exponent Adjustment

The circuit shown in figure 8.36 corrects the error produced by the $OVF1$ signal in the most obvious way. The error situation $OVF2$ is recognized by an active $SIGovf$ signal and $e_2 = [\![e_2[10:0]]\!]_{bias} = e_{max} + 1$. Since $[\![x]\!]_{bias} = \langle x \rangle - bias$, we have

$$e_{max} = \langle 1^{n-1} \rangle - bias$$
$$e_{max} + 1 + bias = \langle 1^n \rangle$$
$$e_{max} + 1 = [\![1^n]\!]_{bias}.$$

Thus, the test whether $e_2 = e_{max} + 1$ holds is simply performed by an AND-tree. If $OVF2 \land OVFen$ holds, exponent e_2 is replaced by the wrapped

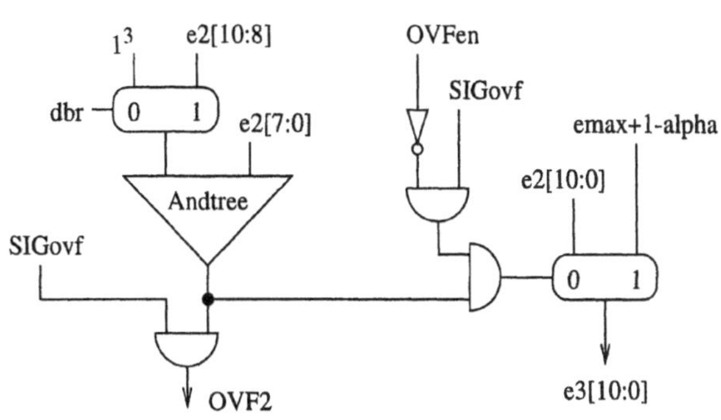

Figure 8.36 Circuit ADJUSTEXP which adjusts the exponent. Depending on the precision, the constant $e_{max} + 1 - \alpha$ equals $0^2 dbr^3 1^3$.

exponent $e_{max} + 1 - \alpha$ in biased format. Note that

$$e_{max} + 1 + bias \ = \ <1^n> \qquad \text{and} \qquad \alpha \ = \ <110^{n-2}>$$

imply

$$
\begin{aligned}
e_{max} + 1 - \alpha + bias &= \ <001^{n-2}> \\
e_{max} + 1 - \alpha &= \ [\![001^{n-2}]\!]_{bias}.
\end{aligned}
$$

Circuit ADJUSTEXP of figure 8.36 adjusts the exponent at the following cost and delay

$$
\begin{aligned}
C_{AdjustExp} &= \ C_{mux}(11) + C_{mux}(3) + C_{ANDtree}(11) + 3 \cdot C_{and} + C_{inv} \\
D_{AdjustExp} &= \ 2 \cdot D_{mux} + D_{ANDtree}(11) + D_{and}.
\end{aligned}
$$

8.4.7 Exponent Rounding

The circuit EXPRND in figure 8.37 computes the function *exprd*. Moreover, it converts the result into packed IEEE format. This involves

- hiding bit $f_{out}[0]$ and

- representing e_{min} by 0^n in case of a denormal result.

In the case $OVF \wedge /OVFen$, the absolute value of the result is rounded to X_{max} or ∞ depending on signal inf. The decision is made according to table 8.6. Circuit *Infinity Decision* implements this in a straightforward way as

$$
inf \ = \ \begin{cases} RM[0] & \text{if} \quad RM[1] = 0 \\ RM[0] \ \text{XNOR} \ s & \text{if} \quad RM[1] = 1. \end{cases}
$$

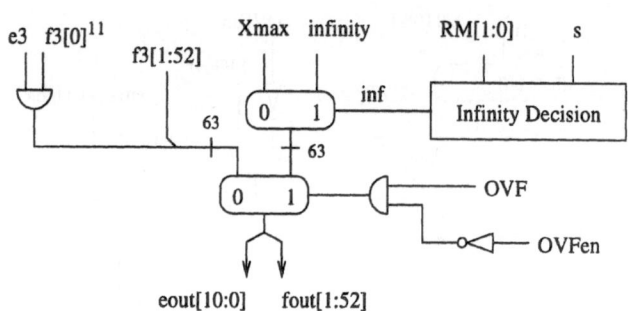

Figure 8.37 Circuit EXPRND. Depending on the precision, the constant X_{max} can be expressed as $(dbr^3\,1^7 0,\ 1^{23}\,dbr^{29})$ and *infinity* can be expressed as $(dbr^3\,1^8,\ 0^{52})$.

Table 8.6 Infinity decision of the exponent rounding. The tables list the value of the flag *inf* which indicates that the exponent must be set to infinity.

RM[1:0]	mode	$s = 0$	$s = 1$
00	r_z	0	0
01	r_{ne}	1	1
10	r_u	1	0
11	r_d	0	1

Denormal significands can only occur in the case $TINY \wedge /UNFen$. In that case, we have $e = e_{min}$ and the result is denormal iff $f_3[0] = 0$, i.e., if the significand f_3 is denormal.

Circuit EXPRND which performs the exponent rounding has the following cost and delay

$$C_{ExpRnd} = 2 \cdot C_{mux}(63) + 2 \cdot C_{and} + C_{inv} + C_{mux} + C_{xnor}$$
$$D_{ExpRnd} = 3 \cdot D_{mux} + D_{xnor}.$$

8.4.8 Circuit SPECFPRND

This circuit (figure 8.38) covers the special cases and detects the IEEE floating point exceptions overflow, underflow and inexact result. In case a is a finite, non-zero number,

$$x = [\![s, e_r, f_r]\!] =_{p-\hat{e}} a$$

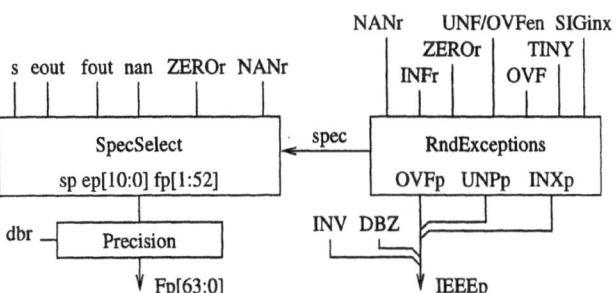

Figure 8.38 Circuit SPECFPRND

and circuit RND already provides the packed IEEE factoring of x

$$(s, e_{out}, f_{out}) = rd(s, e_r, f_r).$$

In case of a special operand a (zero, infinity or NaN) the flags $flr = $ (ZEROr, NANr, INFr, nan, DBZ, INV) code the type of the operand and provide the coding of the NaN

$$nan = (s_{nan}, f_{nan}[1:52]).$$

Thus, circuit SPECSELECT of figure 8.39 computes

$$(s_P, e_P, f_p) = \begin{cases} (s_{nan}, 1^{11}, f_{nan}[1:52]) & \text{if} \quad NANr = 1 \\ (s, 1^{11}, 0^{52}) & \text{if} \quad INFr = 1 \\ (s, 0^{11}, 0^{52}) & \text{if} \quad ZEROr = 1 \\ (s, e_{out}, f_{out}) & \text{if} \quad spec = 0, \end{cases}$$

where signal $spec$ indicates a special operand:

$$spec = NANr \vee INFr \vee ZEROr.$$

Depending on the flag dbr, the output factoring is either in single or double precision. The single precision result is embedded in the 64-bit word Fp according to figure 8.1. Thus,

$$Fp[63:0] = \begin{cases} (s_P, e_P[11:0], f_P[1:52]) & \text{if} \quad dbr \\ (s_P, e_P[7:0], f_P[1:23], s_P, e_P[7:0], f_P[1:23]) & \text{if} \quad /dbr. \end{cases}$$

The circuit PRECISION implements this selection in the obvious way with a single 64-bit multiplexer.

In addition, circuit SPECFPRND detects the floating point exceptions OVF, UNF and INX according to the specifications of section 7.3. These

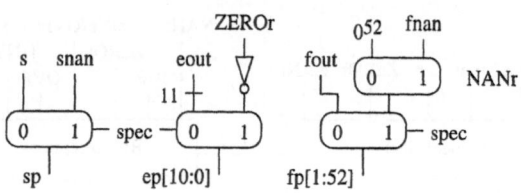

Figure 8.39 Circuit SPECSELECT

exceptions can only occur if a is a finite, non-zero number, i.e., if $spec = 0$. Since the rounder design implements $LOSS_b$, the loss of accuracy equals INX. Thus,

$$
\begin{aligned}
OVF_P &= \overline{spec} \wedge OVF \\
UNF_P &= \overline{spec} \wedge TINY \wedge (UNFen \vee LOSS_b) \\
&= \overline{spec} \wedge TINY \wedge (UNFen \vee INX) \\
INX_P &= \overline{spec} \wedge INX.
\end{aligned}
$$

Since an overflow and an underflow never occur together, signal INX can be expressed as

$$
INX = \begin{cases} SIGinx & \text{if} \quad (OVF \wedge OVFen) \vee (UNF \wedge UNFen) \\ SIGinx \vee OVF & \text{otherwise} \end{cases}
$$

$$
= SIGinx \vee (OVF \wedge \overline{OVFen}).
$$

Circuit RNDEXCEPTIONS generates the exception flags along these equations. In also generates the flag $spec$ indicating a special operand a.

The whole circuit SPECFPRND dealing with special cases and exception flags has the following cost and delay

$$
\begin{aligned}
C_{SpecFPrnd} &= 2 \cdot C_{mux}(52) + C_{mux}(11) + C_{mux} + C_{inv} \\
&\quad + C_{mux}(64) + 5 \cdot C_{and} + 4 \cdot C_{or} + 2 \cdot C_{inv} \\
D_{SpecFPrnd} &= \max\{3 \cdot D_{mux}, 2 \cdot (D_{mux} + D_{or}), D_{inv} + 3 \cdot D_{and} + D_{or}\}.
\end{aligned}
$$

8.5 Circuit FCon

FIGURE 8.40 depicts the schematics of circuit FCON. The left subcircuit compares the two operands FA2 and FB2, whereas the right subcircuit either computes the absolute value of operand FA2 or reverses its sign. Thus, circuit FCON provides the following outputs:

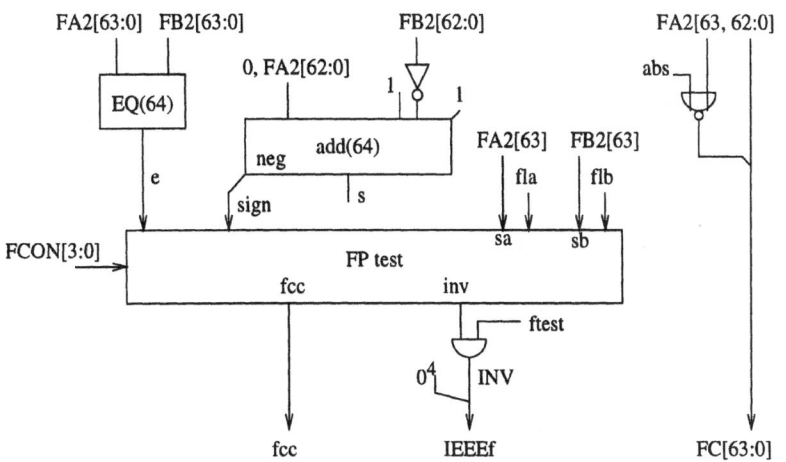

Figure 8.40 Circuit FCON; the left subcircuit performs the condition test, whereas the right subcircuit implements the absolute value and negate operations.

- the condition flag fcc,

- the packed floating point result FC[63:0], and

- the floating point exception flags

$$IEEEf[4:0] = (INX, UNF, OVF, DBZ, INV).$$

Its data inputs are the two packed IEEE floating point operands

$$a = [[s_a, e_A[n-1:0], f_A[1:p-1]]]$$
$$b = [[s_b, e_B[n-1:0], f_B[1:p-1]]]$$

and the flags fl'_a and fl'_b which signal that the corresponding operand has a special value. The circuit is controlled by

- flag $ftest$ which request a floating point condition test,

- the coding $Fcon[3:0]$ of the predicate to be tested, and

- flag abs which distinguishes between the absolute value operation and the sign negation operation.

Except for the flags fl'_a and fl'_b which are provided by the unpacker FPUNP, all inputs have zero delay. Thus, the cost of circuit FCON and the

Table 8.7 Coding of the floating point test condition

predicate		coding	less	equal	unordered	INV if
true	false	Fcon[3:0]	<	=	?	unordered
F	T	0000	0	0	0	
UN	OR	0001	0	0	1	
EQ	NEQ	0010	0	1	0	
UEQ	OGL	0011	0	1	1	No
OLT	UGE	0100	1	0	0	
ULT	OGE	0101	1	0	1	
OLE	UGT	0110	1	1	0	
ULE	OGT	0111	1	1	1	
SF	ST	1000	0	0	0	
NGLE	GLE	1001	0	0	1	
SEQ	SNE	1010	0	1	0	
NGL	GL	1011	0	1	1	Yes
LT	NLT	1100	1	0	0	
NGE	GE	1101	1	0	1	
LE	NLE	1110	1	1	0	
NGT	GT	1111	1	1	1	

accumulated delay of its outputs can be expressed as

$$
\begin{aligned}
C_{FCon} &= C_{EQ}(64) + C_{add}(64) + C_{inv}(63) + C_{FPtest} + C_{and} + C_{nor} \\
A_{FCon} &= \max\{D_{EQ}(64), D_{inv} + D_{add}(64), A_{FPunp}(fla', flb')\} \\
&\quad + D_{FPtest} + D_{and}.
\end{aligned}
$$

8.5.1 Floating Point Condition Test

Table 8.7 lists the coding of the predicates to be tested. The implementation proceeds in two steps. First, the basic predicates *unordered*, *equal* and *less than* are generated according to the specifications of section 7.4.5, and then the condition flag fcc and the invalid operation flag inv are derived as

$$
\begin{aligned}
fcc &= Fcon[0] \wedge unordered \vee Fcon[1] \wedge equal \vee Fcon[2] \wedge less \\
inv &= Fcon[3] \wedge unordered.
\end{aligned}
$$

Predicate Unordered

The operands a and b compare unordered if and only if at least one of them is a NaN. It does not matter whether the NaNs are signaling or not. Thus, the value of the predicate *unordered* equals:

$$unordered \; = \; NANa \vee NANb \; \vee \; SNANa \vee SNANb.$$

Predicate Equal

The flag e indicates that the packed representations of the numbers a and b are identical, i.e.,

$$e = 1 \quad \leftrightarrow \quad FA2[63:0] = FB2[63:0].$$

Note that for the condition test the sign of zero is ignored (i.e., $+0 = -0$), and that NaNs *never* compare equal. Thus, the result of the predicate *equal* can be expressed as

$$equal \;\; = \;\; \begin{cases} 1 & \text{if} \quad a,b \in \{-0,+0\} \\ 0 & \text{if} \quad a \in \{NaN, sNaN\} \\ 0 & \text{if} \quad b \in \{NaN, sNaN\} \\ e & otherwise \end{cases}$$

$$= \;\; (ZEROa \wedge ZEROb) \; \vee \; e \wedge \overline{unordered}$$

Predicate Less

According to section 7.4.5, the relation $<_I$ is a true subset of the $\mathcal{R}_\infty^2$. Thus, the value of the predicate *less* can be expressed as

$$less \; = \; l \wedge \overline{unordered},$$

where for any two numbers $a, b \in \mathcal{R}_\infty$ the auxiliary flag l indicates that

$$l = 1 \quad \leftrightarrow \quad a < b.$$

The following lemma reduces the comparison of packed floating point numbers to the comparison of binary numbers:

Table 8.8 Reducing the test $a < b$ to $|a| < |b|$

s_a	s_b	range	$a < b$ if
0	0	$0 \le a, b$	$[s] < 0 \quad \leftrightarrow \quad sign = 1$
0	1	$b \le 0 \le a$	never
1	0	$a \le 0 \le b$	except for $a = -0 \wedge b = +0$
1	1	$a, b \le 0$	$[s] > 0 \quad \leftrightarrow \quad (sign = 0) \wedge (a \ne b)$

Lemma 8.12 ▶ *For any two numbers $a, b \in \mathcal{R}_\infty$ with the packed representations (s_A, e_A, f_A) and (s_B, e_B, f_B) holds*

$$|a| < |b| \quad \leftrightarrow \quad \langle e_A f_A \rangle < \langle e_B f_B \rangle.$$

Thus, let $sign = s[n + p]$ denote the sign bit of the difference

$$[s[n + p : 0]] = [0 e_A[n - 1 : 0] f_A[1 : p - 1]] - [0 e_B[n - 1 : 0] f_B[1 : p - 1]],$$

we then have

$$|a| < |b| \quad \leftrightarrow \quad [s[n + p : 0]] < 0 \quad \leftrightarrow \quad sign = 1,$$

and according to table 8.8, the auxiliary flag l can be generated as

$$
\begin{aligned}
l \quad = \quad & \overline{s_a} \wedge \overline{s_b} \wedge sign \\
\vee \quad & s_a \wedge \overline{s_b} \wedge (ZEROa \text{ NAND } ZEROb) \\
\vee \quad & s_a \wedge s_b \wedge (sign \text{ NOR } e).
\end{aligned}
$$

PROOF **Proof of Lemma 8.12**
The numbers a and b can be finite normal numbers, finite denormal numbers or infinity. If a is a finite normal number, we have

$$|a| = [\![0, e_A, f_A]\!] = 2^{\langle e_A \rangle - bias} \cdot \langle f_A \rangle$$

with $\langle f_A \rangle \in [1, 2)$ and $0 < \langle e_A \rangle < 2^n$, whereas in case of a denormal significand we have

$$|a| = [\![0, e_A, f_A]\!] = 2^{\langle e_A \rangle + 1 - bias} \cdot \langle f_A \rangle$$

with $\langle f_A \rangle \in [0, 1)$ and $\langle e_A \rangle = 0$.

If both numbers a and b have normal (denormal) significands, the claim can easily be verified. Thus, let a be a denormal number and b be a normal number, then

$$|a| < 2^{e_{min}} \le |b|,$$

and the claim follows because

$$\langle e_A f_A \rangle \leq \langle 0^n 1^{p-1} \rangle < 2^{p-1}$$
$$\leq \langle e_B \rangle \cdot 2^{p-1} = \langle e_B 0^{p-1} \rangle \leq \langle e_B f_B \rangle.$$

Let a be a finite number and let $b = \infty$, then $e_B = 1^n$ and $f_B = 0^{p-1}$. Since $|a| < \infty$ and

$$\langle e_A f_A \rangle \leq \langle 1^{n-1} 0 1^{p-1} \rangle < \langle 1^{n-1} 1 0^{p-1} \rangle = \langle e_B f_B \rangle,$$

the claim also holds for the pairs (a, ∞).   QED

Realization of the Condition Test

In circuit FCON of figure 8.40, a 64-bit equality tester provides the auxiliary flag e, and the output neg of a 64-bit adder provides the bit $sign = s[64]$. These bits are fed into circuit FPTEST which then generates the outputs fcc and inv and the flags of the three basic predicates as described above.

The cost and delay of circuit FPTEST can be expressed as

$$C_{FPtest} = 13 \cdot C_{and} + 8 \cdot C_{or} + 3 \cdot C_{inv} + C_{nor} + C_{nand}$$
$$D_{FPtest} = 3 \cdot D_{and} + 3 \cdot D_{or} + \max\{D_{inv} + D_{and}, D_{nor}, D_{nand}\}.$$

8.5.2 Absolute Value and Negation

For the packed floating point operand $a \in \mathcal{R}_\infty$ with $a = [\![s_A, e_A, f_A]\!]$, the absolute value $|a|$ satisfies

$$|a| = [\![0, e_A, f_A]\!].$$

Thus, the packed representation of the value $|a|$ can simply be obtained by clearing the sign bit of operand FA2. The value $-a$ satisfies

$$-a = [\![\overline{s_A}, e_A, f_A]\!]$$

and just requires the negation of the sign bit.

Thus, both operations only modify the sign bit. Unlike any other arithmetic operation, this modification of the sign bit is also performed for any type of NaN. However, the exponent and the significand of the NaN still pass the unit unchanged. Since

$$s_C = s_A \text{ NOR } abs = \begin{cases} 0 & \text{if } abs = 1 \quad \text{(absolute value)} \\ \overline{s_A} & \text{if } abs = 0 \quad \text{(reversed sign)} \end{cases}$$

the subcircuit at the right hand side of figure 8.40 therefore generates the packed representation of the the value

$$c = [\![s_C, e_C, f_C]\!] = \begin{cases} |a| & \text{if} \quad abs = 1 \\ -a & \text{if} \quad abs = 0. \end{cases}$$

Depending on the flag *abs*, it either implements the absolute value or reversed sign operation.

8.5.3 IEEE Floating Point Exceptions

In the IEEE floating point standard, the two operations absolute value and sign reverse are considered to be special copy operations, and therefore, they never signal a floating point exception.

The floating point condition test is always exact and never overflows nor underflows. Thus, it only signals an invalid operation; the remaining exception flags are always inactive.

Depending on the control signal *ftest* which requests a floating point condition test circuit FCON selects the appropriate set of exception flags:

$$INV = inv \wedge ftest = \begin{cases} inv & \text{if} \quad ftest = 1 \\ 0 & \text{if} \quad ftest = 0 \end{cases}$$

$$(INX, UNF, OVF, DBZ) = (0, 0, 0, 0).$$

8.6 Format Conversion

CONVERSIONS HAVE to be possible between the two packed floating point formats (i.e., single and double precision) and the integer format. For each of the six conversions, the four IEEE rounding modes must be supported.

Integers are represented as 32-bit two's complement number $x[31:0]$ and lie in the set T_{32}:

$$x = [\![x[31:0]]\!] \in T_{32} = \{-2^{31}, \ldots, 2^{31} - 1\}.$$

A floating point number y is represented by a sign bit s, an n-bit exponent e and an p-bit significand. The parameters (n, p) are $(8, 24)$ for single precision and $(11, 53)$ for double precision. The exponent is represented in biased integer format

$$\begin{aligned} e = [\![e[n-1:0]]\!]_{bias} &= \langle e[n-1:0] \rangle - bias_n \\ &= \langle e[n-1:0] \rangle - (2^{n-1} - 1) \end{aligned}$$

and the significand is given as binary fraction

$$f = \langle f[0].f[1:p-1]\rangle.$$

In the packed format, bit $f[0]$ is hidden, i.e., it must be extracted from the exponent. Thus,

$$y = [\![s, e[n-1:0], f[1:p-1]]\!] = (-1)^s \cdot 2^e \cdot f.$$

Each type of conversion is easy but none is completely trivial. In the following, we specify the six conversions in detail. Section 8.6.2 then describes the implementation of the conversions.

8.6.1 Specification of the Conversions

The two parameter sets $(n,p) = (11,53)$ and $(n',p') = (8,24)$ denote the width of the exponent and significand for double and single precision, respectively. As we are dealing with two floating point precisions, we also have to deal with *two rounding functions*, one for single and one for double precision. The same is true for functions like the IEEE normalization shift η and the overflow check OVF. If necessary, the indices 's' and 'd' are used to distinguish between the two versions (e.g., rd_s denotes the single precision rounding function). Since the rounding functions are only defined for a finite, representable operand, the special operands NaN, infinity and zero have to be considered separately.

Double to Single Precision Conversion
Converting a packed, double precision floating point number a with representation

$$\eta_d(a) = (s_A, e_A[n-1:0], f_A[1:p-1])$$

to single precision gives a packed representation $(s_P, e_P[n'-1:0], f_P[1:p'-1])$ which satisfies the following conditions:

- If a is a finite, non-zero number, then

$$(s_P, e_P[n'-1:0], f_P[1:p'-1]) = rd_s(x),$$

  where

$$x = \begin{cases} a \cdot 2^{-\alpha} & \text{if } OVF_s(a) \wedge OVFen \\ a \cdot 2^{\alpha} & \text{if } UNF_s(a) \wedge UNFen \\ a & \text{otherwise.} \end{cases}$$

• If a is a zero, infinity or NaN, then

$$(s_P, e_P, f_P) = \begin{cases} (s_A, 0^{n'}, 0^{p'-1}) & \text{if} \quad a = (-1)^{s_A} \cdot 0 \\ (s_A, 1^{n'}, 0^{p'-1}) & \text{if} \quad a = (-1)^{s_A} \cdot \infty \\ (s_A, 1^{n'}, 10^{p'-2}) & \text{if} \quad a = NaN \end{cases}$$

According to section 7.4.6, the conversion signals an invalid operation exception $INV = 1$ iff a is a signaling NaN.

Single to Double Conversion

Converting a packed, single precision floating point number a with representation

$$\eta_s(a) = (s_A, e_A[n'-1:0], f_A[1:p'-1])$$

to double precision gives a representation $(s_P, e_P[n-1:0], f_P[1:p-1])$ which satisfies the following conditions

• If a is a finite, non-zero number, then

$$(s_P, e_P[n-1:0], f_P[1:p-1]) = \eta_d(rd_d(a)).$$

Due to the larger range of representable numbers, a never overflows nor underflows, i.e., $OVF_d(a) = 0$ and $UNF_d(a) = 0$. In addition, the rounded result is always exact ($INX = 0$).

• If x is a zero, infinity or NaN, then

$$(s_P, e_P, f_P) = \begin{cases} (s_A, 0^n, 0^{p-1}) & \text{if} \quad x = (-1)^{s_A} \cdot 0 \\ (s_A, 1^n, 0^{p-1}) & \text{if} \quad x = (-1)^{s_A} \cdot \infty \\ (s_A, 1^n, 10^{p-2}) & \text{if} \quad x = NaN \end{cases}$$

Although each single precision number is representable in double precision, rounding cannot be avoided because all denormal single precision numbers are normal in double precision. An invalid operation exception $INV = 1$ is signaled iff a is a signaling NaN.

Integer to Floating Point Conversion

Let $x \in T_{32}$ be an non-zero integer coded as 32-bit two's complement number $x[31:0]$. Its absolute value $|x|$, which lies in the set $\{1, \ldots 2^{31}\}$, can be represented as 32-bit binary number $y[31:0]$ which usually has some leading zeros:

$$|x| = \langle y[31:0] \rangle = \langle 0.y[31:0] \rangle \cdot 2^{32} = \langle f[0].f[1:32] \rangle \cdot 2^{32}$$

with $f[0:31] = 0y[31:0]$. The value of the binary fraction f lies in the interval $[0,1)$. Rounding the factoring $(x[31], 32, f)$ gives the desired result. The exceptions overflow, underflow and inexact result cannot occur.

Thus, in case of single precision, the conversion delivers

$$(s_P, e_P, f_P) = \begin{cases} \eta_s(rd_s(\llbracket x[31], 32, f[0:32] \rrbracket)) & \text{if } x \neq 0 \\ (0, 0^{n'}, 0^{p'-1}) & \text{if } x = 0. \end{cases}$$

In case of a double precision result, the rounding can be omitted due to the $p = 53$ bit significand. However, a normalization is still required. Thus, converting a two's complement integer x into a double precision floating point number provides the packed factoring

$$(s_P, e_P, f_P) = \begin{cases} \eta_d(\llbracket x[31], 32, f[1:32] \rrbracket) & \text{if } x \neq 0 \\ (0, 0^n, 0^{p-1}) & \text{if } x = 0. \end{cases}$$

Floating Point to Integer Conversion

Let $(n, p) \in \{(8, 23), (11, 53)\}$ be the length of the exponent and significand in single or double precision format, respectively. When converting a representable number $a = \llbracket s, e, f \rrbracket$ into an integer one has to perform the following three steps:

1. The value a is rounded to an integer value $x = (-1)^s \cdot y$; every one of the four rounding modes is possible.

2. It is checked whether the value x lies in the representable range T_{32} of integers. In the comparison we have to consider the sign bit, because the set T_{32} is not symmetric around zero.

3. If x is representable, its representation is converted from sign magnitude to two's complement, and otherwise, an invalid operation is signaled.

Rounding Let $\mathcal{F}$ be the set of all binary numbers representable with at most $e_{max} + 1$ bits:

$$\mathcal{F} = \{\langle y[e_{max} : 0] \rangle \mid y[i] \in \{0, 1\}, \text{ for all } i\}.$$

For every representable a, there exists an integer $z \in \mathcal{F}$ with

$$z = \max\{y \in \mathcal{F} \mid y \leq |a|\} \quad \text{and} \quad z \leq |a| < z + 1.$$

The rounding of the floating point number a to an integer x is then defined in complete analogy to the significand rounding of a floating point number.

For round to nearest-even, for example, one obtains the rule

$$
rd_{int}(a) = \begin{cases} (s, bin(z)) & \text{if } |a| < z+0.5 \\ & \text{or } |a| = z+0.5 \wedge z[0] = 0 \\ (s, bin(z+1)) & \text{if } |a| > z+0.5 \\ & \text{or } |a| = z+0.5 \wedge z[0] = 1 \end{cases}
$$

Of course, one can obtain this rule by substituting in equation 7.2 (page 332) the number a for f and setting $p = 1$. It follows that

$$
rd_{int}(a) = rd_{int}([a]_1) \quad \text{and} \quad rd_{int}(a) = a \quad \leftrightarrow \quad rd_{int}([a]_1) = a.
$$

The same argument can be made for all four rounding modes.

Range Check   Let $x = (-1)^s \cdot y$ be an integer obtained by rounding a floating point number as described above. Its absolute value $|x| = y$ can be as large as

$$
2 \cdot 2^{e_{max}} = 2 \cdot 2^{2^{10}-1} = 2^{2^{10}}
$$

and thus, an implementation of function rd_{int} would have to provide an 1025-bit binary number y. However,

$$
|a| \geq 2^{32} \quad \rightarrow \quad y \geq 2^{32} \quad \rightarrow \quad x \notin T_{32},
$$

and in this case, the conversion only needs to signal an invalid operation, but the rounding itself can be omitted. Such an overflow is signaled by $Iovf_1$.

In case of $Iovf_1 = 0$, the absolute value y is at most 2^{32}. Thus, y can be represented as 33-bit binary number $y[32:0]$ and $-y$ as 33-bit two's complement number

$$
-y = [z[32:0]] = [\overline{y[32:0]}] + 1.
$$

Let

$$
[x[32:0]] = \begin{cases} \langle y[32:0] \rangle & \text{if } s = 0 \\ [z[32:0]] & \text{if } s = 1 \end{cases} = [y[32:0] \oplus s] + s,
$$

if the integer x lies in the set T_{32} it then has the two's complement representation $x[31:0]$:

$$
x = (-1)^s \cdot y = [x[31:0]].
$$

The conversion overflows if x cannot be represented as a 32-bit two's complement number, i.e.,

$$
Iovf = Iovf_1 \vee Iovf_2 = 1
$$

where due to sign extension

$$Iovf_2 = 1 \quad \leftrightarrow \quad [x[32:0]] \notin T_{32} \quad \leftrightarrow \quad (x[32] \neq x[31]).$$

An invalid operation exception INV is signaled if a is not a finite number or if $Iovf = 1$:

$$INV = 1 \quad \leftrightarrow \quad a \in \{NaN, +\infty, -\infty\} \lor Iovf = 1.$$

8.6.2 Implementation of the Conversions

One could provide a separate circuit for each type of conversion. However, the arithmetic operations already require a general floating point unpacker and a floating point rounder which convert from a packed floating format to an internal floating format and vice versa. In order to reuse this hardware, every conversion is performed in two steps:

- An unpacker converts the input FA2[63:0] into an internal floating point format. Depending on the type of the conversion, the input FA2 is interpreted as 32-bit two's complement integer

$$x = [x[31:0]] \quad \text{with} \quad x[31:0] = FA2[63:32],$$

  or as single of double precision floating point number with packed factoring

$$(s_A, e_A, f_A) = \begin{cases} (FA2[63], FA2[62:52], FA2[51:0] & \text{if} \quad dbs = 1 \\ (FA2[63], FA2[62:55], FA2[54:32] & \text{if} \quad dbs = 0. \end{cases}$$

- A rounder then converts the number (s_r, e_r, f_r, fl_r) represented in an internal floating point format into a 32-bit two's complement integer Fx[31:0] or into a packed floating point representation (s_P, e_P, f_P). In case of double precision $(dbr = 1)$, the floating point output is obtained as

$$Fp[63:0] = (s_P, e_P[10:0], f_P[1:53]),$$

  whereas for single precision $(dbr = 0)$, output Fp is obtained as

$$Fp[63:32] = Fp[31:0] = (s_P, e_P[7:0], f_P[1:24]).$$

In addition to the unpacker FPUNP and the rounder FPRND, the conversions then require a fixed point unpacker FXUNP, a fixed point rounder FXRND, and a circuit CVT which adapts the output of FPUNP to the input format of FPRND (figure 8.2).

The conversion is controlled by the following signals:

- signals *dbs* and *dbr* indicate a double precision floating point source operand and result,

- signal *normal* which is only active in case of a floating point to integer conversion requests the normalization of the source operand, and

- the two enable signals which select between the results of the circuits CVT and FXUNP.

Floating Point Format Conversions

Unpacking The floating point unpacker FPUNP (section 8.1) gets the operand FA2 and provides as output a factoring $(s_a, e_a[10:0], f_a[0:52])$ and the flags fl_a. The exponent e_a is a two's complement number. The flags fl_a comprising the bits ZEROa, INFa, NANa and SNANa signal that FA2 is a special operand.

For a non-zero, finite operand a, the output factoring satisfies

$$a = [\![s_A, e_A, f_A]\!] = (-1)^{s_a} \cdot 2^{[e_a[10:0]]} \cdot \langle f_a[0].f_a[1:52] \rangle.$$

Since *normal* $= 0$, the output factoring is IEEE-normal, i.e., $f_a[0] = 0$ implies $|a| < 2^{e_{min}}$.

Circuit CVT Circuit CVT gets the factoring (s_a, e_a, f_a) and the flags fl_a from the unpacker. It checks for an invalid conversion operation and extends the exponent and significand by some bits:

$$
\begin{aligned}
(s_v, e_v[12:0], f_v[-1:55]) &= (s_a, e_a[10]^3 e_a[9:0], 0 f_a[1:52]0^3) \\
(ZERO, INF, NAN) &= (ZEROa, INFa, NANa \vee SNANa) \\
(INV, DBZ) &= (SNANa, 0) \\
nan &= (s_{nan}, f_{nan}[1:52]) = (s_a, 10^{51}).
\end{aligned}
$$

For a finite, non-zero operand a, we obviously have

$$
\begin{aligned}
a &= (-1)^{s_a} \cdot 2^{[e_a[10:0]]} \cdot \langle f_a[0].f_a[1:52] \rangle \\
&= (-1)^{s_v} \cdot 2^{[e_v[12:0]]} \cdot \langle f_v[-1:0].f_v[1:55] \rangle,
\end{aligned}
\tag{8.11}
$$

and the factoring is still IEEE-normal. The implementation of CVT is straightforward and just requires a single OR gate:

$$C_{Cvt} = C_{or}, \qquad\qquad D_{Cvt} = D_{or}.$$

Rounding   The output (s_v, e_v, f_v, fl_v) of circuit CVT is fed to the floating point rounder FPRND. In order to meet the input specification of FPRND, $f_v \in [0, 1)$ must imply that $OVF = 0$. Since the factoring is IEEE-normal, that is obviously the case:

$$f_v[-1 : 0] = 00 \quad \leftrightarrow \quad f_a[0] = 0 \quad \leftrightarrow \quad |a| < 2^{e_{min}}.$$

Let

$$y = \begin{cases} a \cdot 2^{-\alpha} & \text{if} \quad OVF(a) \wedge OVFen \\ a \cdot 2^{\alpha} & \text{if} \quad UNF(a) \wedge UNFen \\ a & \text{otherwise.} \end{cases}$$

Depending on the flags fl_v, circuit FPRND (section 8.4) then provides the packed factoring

$$(s_P, e_P, f_P) = \begin{cases} (s_v, 0^n, 0^{p-1}) & \text{if} \quad ZERO_v \\ (s_v, 1^n, 0^{p-1}) & \text{if} \quad INF_v \\ (s_{nan}, 1^n, f_{nan}[1 : p-1]) & \text{if} \quad a = NaN_v \\ \eta(rd(y)) & \text{otherwise.} \end{cases}$$

In case of $dbr = 1$, the factoring is given in double precision and otherwise, it is given in single precision. The correctness of the conversion follows immediately from the definition of the flags fl_v.

Integer to Floating Point Conversions

These conversions are also performed in two steps. First, the fixed point unpacker FXUNP converts the two's complement integer $x[31 : 0]$ into the internal floating point format. The floating point rounder FPRND then converts this factoring (s_u, e_u, f_u, fl_u) into the packed floating point format. Depending on the control signal dbr, the output factoring (s_P, e_P, f_P) has either single or double precision.

Unpacking   The unpacker FXUNP converts the two's complement integer $x[31 : 0]$ into the internal floating point format. This representation consists of the flags fl_u and the factoring $(s_u, e_u[13 : 0], f_u[-1 : 55])$ which is determined according to the specification from page 420.

The flags fl_u indicate a special operand (i.e., zero, infinity and NaN) and signal the exceptions INV and DBZ. Since the two's complement integer $x[31 : 0]$ is always a finite number, a zero input is the only possible special case:

$$ZEROu = 1 \quad \leftrightarrow \quad [x[31 : 0]] = 0 \quad \leftrightarrow \quad x[31 : 0] = 0^{32}.$$

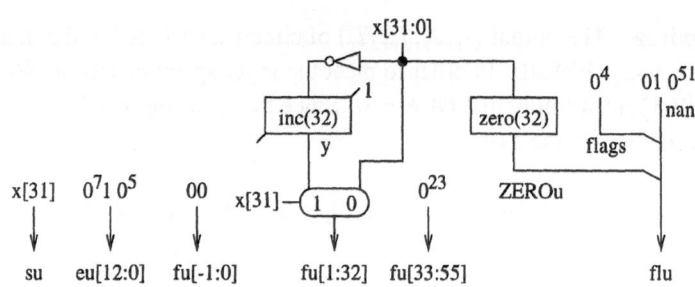

Figure 8.41 Circuit FXUNP converting a 32-bit integer $x[31:0]$ into the internal floating point format; *flags* denotes the bits *INFu*, *NANu*, *INV*, and *DBZ*.

The remaining flags are inactive and *nan* can be chosen arbitrarily:

$$INV = DBZ = INF = NAN = 0$$
$$nan = (s_{nan}, f_{nan}[1:52]) = (0, 10^{51}).$$

Since $|x| \in \{0, \ldots, 2^{31}\}$, the absolute value of x can be represented as 32-bit binary number $y[31:0]$:

$$|x| = \langle y[31:0] \rangle = \begin{cases} \langle x[31:0] \rangle & \text{if } x[31] = 0 \\ \langle \overline{x[31:0]} \rangle + 1 \mod 2^{32} & \text{if } x[31] = 1. \end{cases}$$

Thus, the factoring

$$s_u = x[31] = \begin{cases} 1 & \text{if } x < 0 \\ 0 & \text{if } x \geq 0 \end{cases}$$
$$e_u[13:0] = 0^7 10^5$$
$$f_u[-1:55] = 0^2 y[31:0] 0^{23}.$$

with a 13-bit two's complement exponent satisfies

$$x = (-1)^{s_u} \cdot 2^{32} \cdot \langle 0.y[31:0] \rangle$$
$$= (-1)^{s_u} \cdot 2^{[e_u[13:0]]} \cdot \langle f_u[-1:0].f_u[1:55] \rangle.$$

The circuit of figure 8.41 implements the fixed point unpacker FXUNP in a straightforward manner at the following cost and delay:

$$C_{FXunp} = C_{inv}(32) + C_{inc}(32) + C_{zero}(32) + C_{mux}(32)$$
$$D_{FXunp} = \max\{D_{inv} + D_{inc}(32) + D_{mux}(32), D_{zero}(32)\}.$$

Rounding   Since an integer to floating point conversion never overflows, the representation (s_u, e_u, f_u, fl_u) meets the requirements of the rounder FPRND. Thus, the correctness of the floating point rounder FPRND implies the correctness of this integer to floating point converter.

Floating Point to Integer Conversions

Like any other conversion, this conversion is split into an unpacking and rounding step. The unpacking is performed by the floating point unpacker FPUNP which delivers the flags fl_a indicating a special operand. In case that a is a non-zero, finite number, circuit FPUNP also provides a factoring (s_a, e_a, f_a) of a:

$$a = (-1)^{s_a} \cdot 2^{[e_a[10:0]] - \langle lz_a[5:0]\rangle} \cdot \langle f_a[0].f_a[1:52]\rangle = (-1)^{s_a} \cdot 2^{e'_a} \cdot f_a$$

Due to $normal = 1$, the significand f_a is normal, and for any $|a| \geq 2^{e_{min}}$, the number lz_a is zero.

This representation is provided to the fixed point rounder FXRND which generates the data $Fx[63:32] = Fx[31:0]$ and the floating point exception flag INV. For a finite number a, let $rd_{int}(a) = (s_a, y)$ and

$$x = (-1)^{s_a} \cdot y = (-1)^{s_a} \cdot 2^0 \cdot y.$$

For $x \in T_{32}$, the conversion is valid ($INV = 0$) and x has the two's complement representation Fx[31:0]. If a is not finite or if $x \notin T_{32}$, the conversion is invalid, i.e., $INV = 1$, and Fx[31:0] is chosen arbitrarily.

Fixed Point Rounder FXRD

In section 8.4, the floating point rounder FPRND is described in detail. Instead of developing the fixed point rounder FXRND from scratch, we rather derive it from circuit FPRND.

Implementation Concept   Note that the result of rounder FXRND always has a fixed exponent. For the floating point rounder, that is only the case if the result is denormal. Let (s, e_r, f_r) be a denormal floating point operand, the floating point rounder FPRND then provides the output factoring (s, e_{out}, f_{out}) such that

$$(s, e_{out}, f_{out}) = \eta(rd(s, e_r, f_r)) = (s, exprd(s, post(e_r, sigrd(s, f_r)))).$$

If the result is denormal, the post-normalization and the exponent rounding can be omitted:

$$(s, e_{out}, f_{out}) = \eta(rd(s, e_r, f_r)) = (s, e_r, sigrd(s, f_r)).$$

The major differences between this denormal floating point rounding rd_{dn} and the rounding rd_{int} is the rounding position and the width of the significand. In case of rd_{dn}, the rounding position is p bits to the right of the binary point, whereas in case of rd_{int}, the significand is rounded at the binary point ($p = 1$). However, this is not a problem; let $e'_a = e_a - lz_a$,

$$
\begin{aligned}
a &= (-1)^{s_a} \cdot 2^{e'_a} \cdot f_a \\
&= (-1)^{s_a} \cdot 2^{(p-1)} \cdot (2^{e'_a - (p-1)} \cdot f_a) = (-1)^{s_a} \cdot 2^{(p-1)} \cdot f_r.
\end{aligned}
$$

The equation suggests to make the exponent 1 and shift the significand e'_a positions left, then shift $p - 1$ positions right; this moves the bit with weight 1 into the position $p - 1$ right of the binary point.

The significand f_{out} provided by rd_{dn} has at most two bits to the left of the binary point, whereas y has up to 32 bits to the left of the binary point. However, the rounding rd_{int} is only applied if $f_a \in [0, 2)$ and $e'_a \leq 2^{31}$. For $p = 32$ it then follows that

$$
f_r = 2^{e'_a - (p-1)} \cdot f_a \leq 2^{31-31} \cdot f_a < 2.
$$

Thus, the significand $sigrnd(s_a, f_r)$ has at most 2 bits to the left to the binary point. The significand y can then be obtained by shifting the output significand f_{out} e_{min} positions to the left:

$$
y[32 : 0] = y[p : 0] = f_{out}[-1 : p - 1].
$$

Circuit FXRND   Figure 8.42 depicts the top level schematics of the fixed point rounder FXRND. Circuits NORMSHIFTX, REPPX, and SIGRNDX from the floating point rounder are adapted as follows:

- only denormal results are considered (i.e., $UNF \wedge /UNFen$),

- only one precision $p = 32$ is supported,

- and e_{min} is set to $-(p - 1) = -31$.

Circuit SPECFX is new, it performs the range check, signals exceptions and implements the special case $a = 0$. All the inputs of the rounders have zero delay, thus

$$
\begin{aligned}
C_{FXrnd} &= C_{NormShiftX} + C_{REPpX} + C_{ff}(40) + C_{SigRndX} + C_{SpecFX} \\
T_{FXrnd} &= D_{NormShiftX} + D_{REPpX} + \Delta \\
A_{FXrnd} &= A_{SigRndX} + D_{SpecFX}.
\end{aligned}
$$

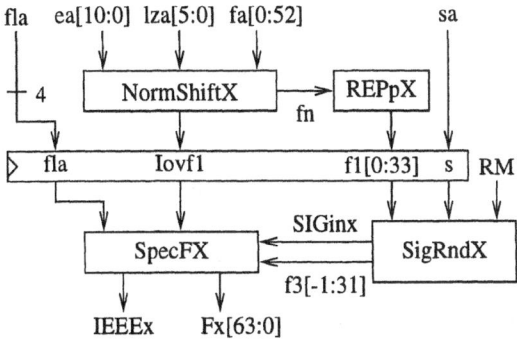

Figure 8.42 Schematics of the fixed point rounder FXRND; IEEEx denote the floating point exceptions flags.

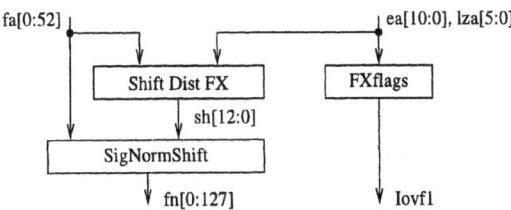

Figure 8.43 Normalization shifter NORMSHIFTX

Circuit NORMSHIFTX   The circuit depicted in figure 8.43 performs the normalization shift. In analogy to the floating point rounder, its outputs satisfy

$$Iovf_1 \equiv 2^{e'_a} \cdot f_a \geq 2^{32}$$
$$e_n = e_{min} = -31$$
$$f_n =_p f = 2^{e'_a - e_{min}} \cdot f_a.$$

Circuit SIGNORMSHIFT which performs the normalization shift is identical to that of the floating point rounder. Since the significand f_a is normal, and since for large operands $lz_a = 0$, we have

$$2^{e'_a} \cdot f_a \geq 2^{32} \quad \leftrightarrow \quad e'_a = e_a - lz_a \geq 32 \quad \leftrightarrow \quad [e_a[10:0]] \geq 32.$$

Thus, circuit FXFLAGS signals the overflow $Iovf_1$ by

$$Iovf_1 = \overline{e_a[10]} \wedge \bigvee_{i=5,\cdots,9} e_a[i].$$

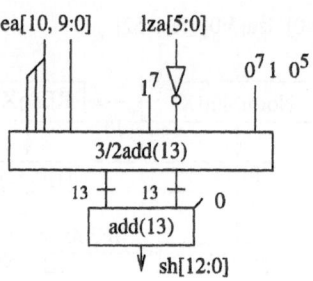

Figure 8.44 Circuit SHIFTDISTFX of the fixed point rounder

Circuit SHIFTDISTFX (figure 8.44) provides the distance σ of the normalization shift as 13-bit two's complement number. Since f is defined as $2^{e'_a - e_{min}} \cdot f_a$, the shift distance equals

$$
\begin{aligned}
\sigma &= [sh[12:0]] = e'_a - e_{min} \\
&= [e_a[10:0]] - \langle lz_a[5:0] \rangle - (-31) \\
&= [e_a[10]^3 \, e_a[9:0]] + [1^7 \, \overline{lz_a[5:0]}] + 32 \mod 2^{13}.
\end{aligned}
$$

The cost and delay of the normalization shifter NORMSHIFTX and of its modified subcircuits can be expressed as

$$
\begin{aligned}
C_{NormShiftX} &= C_{FXflags} + C_{ShiftDistX} + C_{SigNormShift} \\
C_{FXflags} &= C_{ORtree}(5) + C_{and} + C_{inv} \\
C_{ShiftDistX} &= C_{inv}(6) + C_{3/2add}(13) + C_{add}(13) \\[4pt]
D_{NormShiftX} &= \max\{D_{FXflags}, D_{ShiftDistX} + D_{SigNormShift}\} \\
D_{FXflags} &= D_{ORtree}(5) + D_{and} \\
D_{ShiftDistX} &= D_{inv} + D_{3/2add}(13) + D_{add}(13).
\end{aligned}
$$

Circuit REPPX   The circuit of figure 8.45 performs the sticky bit computation in order to provide a p-representative of f_n:

$$
f_1 = [f_n]_p \quad , \quad f_1[0:33] = f_n[0:32]\,st \quad , \quad st = \bigvee_{i>p} f_n[i]
$$

Since we now have only a single precision, this circuit becomes almost trivial:

$$
C_{REPpX} = C_{ORtree}(95), \qquad\qquad D_{REPpX} = D_{ORtree}(95).
$$

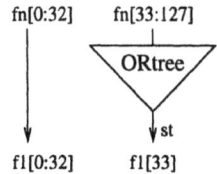

Figure 8.45 Circuit REPpX

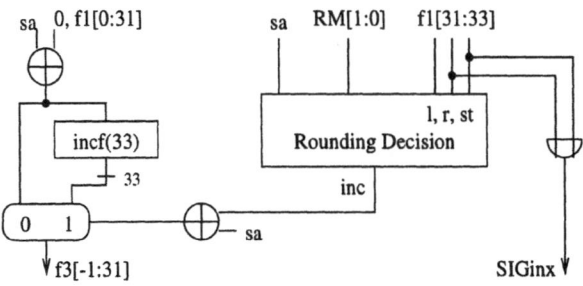

Figure 8.46 Circuit SIGRNDX of the fixed point rounder

Circuit SIGRNDX   Circuit SIGRNDX (figure 8.46) performs the significand rounding and converts the rounded significand $f_2[-1:31]$ into a two's complement fraction $f_3[-1:31]$. Given that the range is not exceeded, we have

$$f_2[-1:31] = sigrnd(s_a, f_1[0:33])$$
$$[f_3[-1:0].f_3[1:31]] = (-1)^{s_a} \cdot \langle f_2[-1:0].f_2[1:31]\rangle.$$

As in the rounder FPRND, the binary fraction f_1 is either chopped or incremented at position $p-1$, depending on the rounding decision:

$$f_2 = \langle f_1[0].f_1[1:p-1]\rangle + inc \cdot 2^{-(p-1)}$$
$$-f_2 = [1\overline{f_1[0].f_1[1:p-1]}] + (1-inc)\cdot 2^{-(p-1)}$$
$$f_3 = [s_a(f_1[0].f_1[1:p-1])\oplus s_a] + (inc\oplus s_a)\cdot 2^{-(p-1)}.$$

The rounded significand is inexact ($SIGinx = 1$) iff $f_1[32:33]\neq 00$.

Like in the floating point rounder, the rounding decision flag inc is generated by the circuit of figure 8.34. Circuit SIGRNDX therefore has cost and delay

$$C_{SigRndX} = C_{mux}(33) + C_{inc}(33) + C_{or} + 2\cdot C_{xor}$$

$$+C_{mux}+3\cdot C_{and}+2\cdot C_{or}+C_{xor}$$
$$A_{SigRndX} = \max\{D_{inc}(33), A_{RM}+D_{xor}+D_{and}+D_{mux}\}$$
$$+D_{mux}+D_{xor}.$$

Circuit SPECFX   This circuit supports the special cases and signals floating point exceptions. If the rounded result x is representable as a 32-bit two's complement number, we have

$$x = 2^{-31}[f_3[-1:0].f_3[1:31]] \quad \text{and} \quad x[32:0] = f_3[-1:31].$$

In case of a zero operand $a = 0$, which is signaled by the flag $ZEROr$, the result Fx must be pulled to zero. Thus:

$$Fx[31:0] = \begin{cases} 0^{32} & \text{if} \quad ZEROr=1 \\ x[31:0] & \text{if} \quad ZEROr=0 \end{cases} = x[31:0] \oplus ZEROr$$
$$Fx[63:32] = Fx[31:0].$$

According to the specifications from page 422, the overflow of the conversion and the invalid operation exception can be detected as

$$Iovf = Iovf_1 \vee x[32]\oplus s_a \vee x[31]\oplus s_a$$
$$INV = Iovf \vee NANr \vee INFr.$$

The conversion is inexact, if the rounded significand is inexact $SIGinx = 1$ and if a is a finite non-zero number:

$$INX = SIGinx \wedge \overline{NANr \vee INFr \vee ZEROr}.$$

Further floating point exceptions cannot occur. Circuit SPECFX implements this in a straightforward way at

$$C_{SpecFX} = C_{xor}(32)+2\cdot C_{xor}+C_{and}+C_{nor}+5\cdot C_{or}$$
$$D_{SpecFX} = \max\{D_{xor}+D_{or}, D_{and}+D_{or}\}+D_{or}.$$

8.7 Evaluation of the FPU Design

IN THE previous subsections, we have designed an IEEE-compliant floating point unit. We now analyze the cost and the delay of the FPU and the accumulated delay of its outputs. We assume that the rounding mode RM and the flags $UNFen$ and $OVFen$ have zero delay.

Table 8.9 Accumulated delay of the units feeding bus FR and cycle time of the FPU and of its units

accumulated delay				
bus FR	ADD/SUB	MUL/DIV	FXUNP	FPUNP/CVT
93	91	64	35	45

cycle time					
FPU	Bus FR	ADD/SUB	MUL/DIV	FPRND	FXRND
98	98	63	69	98	76

Cycle Time of the FPU

In the top level schematics of the FPU (figure 8.2), there are two register stages: The output of the unpacker FPUNP and the intermediate result on bus FR are clocked into registers. Result FR is provided by the unpacker FXUNP, the converter CVT, the add/subtract unit or by the multiply/divide unit, thus,

$$A_{FPU}(Fr) = \max\{A_{FPunp} + D_{Cvt}, A_{FXunp}, A_{MulDiv}, A_{AddSub}\} + D_{driv}$$
$$T_{FPU}(Fr) = A_{FPU}(Fr) + \Delta.$$

According to table 8.9, these results have an accumulated delay of at most 93, and therefore require a minimal cycle time of 98 gate delays. This time is dominated by the add/subtract unit.

In addition, some units of the FPU have an internal register stage and therefore impose a bound on the cycle time of the FPU, as well. These units are the two rounders FPRND and FXRND, the add/subtract unit, and the multiply/divide unit:

$$T_{FPU} = \max\{T_{MulDiv}, T_{AddSub}, T_{FPrnd}, T_{FXrnd}, T_{FPU}(Fr)\}.$$

These units require a minimal cycle time of 98 gate delays like the update of register FR. The floating point rounder FPRND is 30% slower than the other three units.

Accumulated Delay of the Outputs

The outputs of the floating point unit are provided by the two rounders FPRND and FXRND and by unit FCON:

$$A_{FPU} = \max\{A_{FCon}, A_{FXrnd}, A_{FPrnd}\}.$$

Table 8.10 Accumulated delay of the outputs of the FPU. Circuit SIGRND of rounder FPRND uses a standard incrementer (1) or a fast CSI incrementer (2).

version	FPU	FCON	FXRND	FPRND	SIGRND
(1)	91	50	44	91	58
(2)	50	50	44	49	16

According to table 8.10, they have an accumulated delay of 91. Compared to the cycle time of the FPU, a delay of 91 just leaves enough time to select the result and to clock it into a register. However, in a pipelined design (chapter 9), the outputs of the FPU become time critical due to result forwarding.

The floating point rounder FPRND is about 50% slower than the other two units. Its delay is largely due to the 53-bit incrementer of the significand round circuit SIGRND. The delay of a standard n-bit incrementer is linear in n. However, when applying the conditional sum principle recursively, its delay becomes logarithmic in n (see exercise 2.1 of chapter 2). Using such a *CSI* incrementer speeds up the rounder significantly. The outputs of the FPU then have an accumulated delay of 50 gate delays. That now leaves plenty of time for result forwarding.

The FPU receives the underflow enable bit $UNFen$, the overflow enable bit $OVFen$ and the rounding mode at an accumulated delay of $A_{UNF/OVFen}$. The FPU design can tolerate an accumulated delay of $A_{UNF/OVFen} = 40$ before the input signal $UNFen$ and $OVFen$ dominate the cycle time T_{FPU}.

The accumulated delay of the rounding mode RM is more time critical. Already for $A_{RM} = 9$, the rounding mode dominates the delay A_{FPU}, i.e., it slows down the computation of the FPU outputs.

Cost of the FPU

Table 8.11 lists the cost of the floating point unit FPU and of its major components. Circuit SIGRND of the floating point rounder FPRND either uses a standard 53-bit incrementer or a fast 53-bit *CSI* incrementer. Switching to the fast incrementer increases the cost of the rounder FPRND by 3%, but it has virtually no impact on the total cost (0.2%). On the other hand, the CSI incrementer improves the accumulated delay of the FPU considerably. Therefore, we later on only use the FPU design version with CSI incrementer.

The multiply/divide unit is by far the most expensive part of the floating point unit, it accounts for 70% of the total cost. According to table 8.12, the cost of the multiply/divide unit are almost solely caused by cir-

Table 8.11 Cost of the FPU and its sub-units. Circuit SIGRND of rounder FPRND either uses a standard incrementer or a fast CSI incrementer.

ADD/SUB	5975
MUL/DIV	73303
FCON	1982
FPUNP	6411
FXUNP	420
FPRND	7224 / 7422
FXRND	3605
CVT	2
rest	4902
total: FPU	103824 / 104022

Table 8.12 Cost of the significand multiply/divide circuit SIGFMD with a 256×8 lookup ROM. The last column lists the cost relative to the cost of the multiply/divide unit MUL/DIV.

SIGFMD	SELECTFD	4/2mulTree	ROM	CLA(116)	rest
71941	5712	55448	647	2711	8785
98%	7.8%	75.6%	0.9%	3.7%	12%

cuit SIGFMD which processes the significands. Its 58×58-bit multiplier tree accounts for 76% of the cost of the multiply/divide unit and for 53% of the cost of the whole FPU. The table lookup ROM has only a minor impact on the cost.

8.8 Selected References and Further Reading

MORE OR less complete designs of floating point units can be found in [AEGP67] and [WF82]. The designs presented here are based on constructions from [Spa91, EP97, Lei99, Sei00]. Our analysis of the division algorithm uses techniques from [FS89]. A formal correctness proof of IEEE-compliant algorithms for multiplication, division and square root with normal operands and a normal result can be found in [Rus].

8.9 Exercises

Exercise 8.1 A *trivial (n,i)-right shifter* is a circuit with n inputs $a[n-1:0]$, select input $s \in \{0,1\}$ and $n+i$ outputs $r[n-1:-i]$ satisfying

$$r = \begin{cases} 0^i a & \text{if } s+1 \\ a0^i & \text{otherwise.} \end{cases}$$

Thus, in trivial (n,i)-right shifters, the i bits which are shifted out are the last i bits of the result.

One can realize the alignment shift and sticky bit computation of the floating point adder by a stack of trivial shifters. The sticky bit is computed by simply ORing together bits, which are shifted out.

1. Determine the cost and the delay of this construction.

2. In the stack of trivial shifters, perform large shifts first. Then carefully arrange the OR-tree which computes the sticky bit. How much does this improve the delay?

Exercise 8.2 In section 8.3, we have designed a multiply/divide unit which performs a division based on the the Newton-Raphson method. The iteration starts out with an initial approximation x_0 which is obtained from a $2^\gamma \times \gamma$ lookup table. The intermediate results are truncated after $\sigma = 57$ bits. The number i of iterations necessary to reach $p+2$ bits of precision (i.e., $\delta_i < 2^{-p-2}$) is then bounded by

$$i = \begin{cases} 1 & \text{if } p = 24 \wedge \gamma = 16 \\ 2 & \text{if } p = 24 \wedge \gamma = 8 \quad \text{or} \quad p = 53 \wedge \gamma = 16 \\ 3 & \text{if } p = 24 \wedge \gamma = 5 \quad \text{or} \quad p = 53 \wedge \gamma = 8 \\ 4 & \text{if } p = 53 \wedge \gamma = 5 \end{cases}$$

For $\gamma = 8$, this bound was already shown in section 8.3.4. Repeat the arguments for the remaining cases.

Determine the cost of the FPU for $\gamma = 16$ and $\gamma = 5$.

Exercise 8.3 The next three exercises deal with the normalization shifter NORMSHIFT used by the floating point rounder FPRND. The functionality of the shifter is specified by Equation 8.6 (page 393); its implementation is described in section 8.4.2.

The shifter NORMSHIFT gets as input a factoring (s, e_r, f_r); the significand $f_r[-1:55]$ has two bits to the right of the binary point. The final rounded result may be a normal or denormal number, and f_r may have leading zeros or not.

- Determine the maximal shift distance $|\sigma|$ for each of these four cases.

- Which of these cases require a right shift?

Exercise 8.4 The normalization shifter NORMSHIFT (figure 8.25, page 395) computes a shift distance σ, and its subcircuit SIGNORMSHIFT then shifts the significand f'. However, in case of a right shift, the representation of $f' \cdot 2^\sigma$ can be very long. Circuit SIGNORMSHIFT therefore only provides a p-representative f_n:

$$[\![f_n[0:63]]\!] = f_n =_p f' \cdot 2^\sigma.$$

- Determine the maximal length of the representation of $f' \cdot 2^\sigma$.

- Give an example (i.e., f' and σ) for which $f_n \neq f' \cdot 2^\sigma$.

Exercise 8.5 The exponent normalization circuit EXPNORM of the floating point rounder FPRND computes the following sums sum and $sum + 1$

$$sum \quad = \quad e_r + 1 + [1\,\overline{lz[5:0]}] + \delta$$

where δ is a constant.

The implementation of EXPNORM depicted in figure 8.27 (page 400) uses a 3/2-adder and a compound adder ADD2 to perform this task. Like in the computation of flag TINY, the value $[\overline{lz[5:0]}]$ can be included in the constant δ', and then, the 3/2-adder in the circuit EXPNORM can be dropped.

- Derive the new constant δ'.

- How does this modification impact the cost and the delay of the floating point rounder?

Chapter 9

Pipelined DLX Machine with Floating Point Core

IN THIS chapter, the floating point unit from the previous chapter is integrated into the pipelined DLX machine with precise interrupts constructed in chapter 5. Obviously, the existing design has to be modified in several places, but most of the changes are quite straightforward.

In section 9.1, the instruction set is extended by floating point instructions. For the greatest part the extension is straightforward, but two new concepts are introduced.

1. The floating point register file consists of 32 registers for single precision numbers, which can also be addressed as 16 registers for double precision floating point numbers. This aliasing of addressing will mildly complicate both the address computation and the forwarding engine.

2. The IEEE standard requires interrupt event signals to be accumulated in a special purpose register. This will lead to a simple extra construction in the special purpose register environment.

In section 9.2 we construct the data path of a (prepared sequential or pipelined) DLX machine with a floating point unit integrated into the execute environment and a floating point register file integrated into the register file environment. This has some completely obvious and simple consequences: e.g., some parts of the data paths are now 64 bits wide and addresses for the floating point register file must now be buffered as well. There are two more notable consequences:

Table 9.1 Latency of the IEEE floating point instructions; fc denotes a compare and cvt a format conversion.

precision	fneg	fabs	fc	cvt	fadd	fmul	fdiv
single	1	1	1	3	5	5	17
double	1	1	1	3	5	5	21

1. We have to obey throughout the machine an embedding convention which regulates how 32-bit data share 64-bit data paths.

2. Except during divisions, the execute stage can be fully pipelined, but it has variable latency (table 9.1). This makes the use of so called *result shift registers* in the CA-pipe and in the buffers-pipe necessary.

In section 9.3, we construct the control of a prepared sequential machine $FDLX_\Sigma$. The difficulties arise obviously in the execute stage:

1. For instructions which can be fully pipelined, i.e., for all instructions except divisions, two result shift registers in the precomputed control and in the stall engine take care of the variable latencies of instructions.

2. In section 8.3.6, we controlled the 17 or 21 cycles of divisions by a finite state diagram. This FSD has to be combined with the precomputed control. We extend the result shift register of the stall engine (and only this result shift register) to length 21. The full bits of this result shift register then code the state of the FSD.

For the prepared machine $FDLX_\Sigma$ constructed in this way we are able to prove the counter part of the (dateline) lemma 5.9.

In section 9.4, the machine is finally pipelined. As in previous constructions, pipelining is achieved by the introduction of a forwarding engine and by modification of the stall engine alone. Because single precision values are embedded in double precision data paths, one has to forward the 32 low order bits and the 32 high order bits separately. Stalls have to be introduced in two new situations:

1. if an instruction with short latency threatens to overtake an instruction with long latency in the pipeline (see table 9.2); and

2. if pipelining of the execute stage is impossible because a division is in one of its first 13 or 17 cycles, respectively.

Table 9.2 Scheduling of the two data independent instructions fadd and cvt. In the first case, cvt overtakes fadd; the second case depicts an in-order execution.

instruction	cycles of the execution								
fadd	F_1	D_1	E_1	E_1	E_1	E_1	E_1	M_1	W_1
cvt		F_2	D_2	E_2	E_2	E_2	M_2	W_2	
fadd	F_1	D_1	E_1	E_1	E_1	E_1	E_1	M_1	W_1
cvt		F_2	D_2	stall	E_2	E_2	E_2	M_2	W_2

A simple lemma will show for this $FDLX_\Pi$ design, that the execution of instructions stays in order, and that no two instructions are ever simultaneously in the same substage of the execute stage.

9.1 Extended Instruction Set Architecture

B EFORE GOING into the details of the implementation, we first describe the extension of the DLX instruction set architecture. That includes the register set, the exception causes, the instruction format and the instruction set.

9.1.1 FPU Register Set

The FPU provides 32 floating point general purpose registers *FPRs*, each of which is 32 bits wide. In order to store double precision values, the registers can be addressed as 64-bit floating point registers *FDRs*. Each of the 16 FDRs is formed by concatenating two adjacent FPRs (table 9.3). Only even numbers $(0, 2, \ldots, 30)$ are used to address the floating point registers FPR; the least significant address bit is ignored.

Embedding Convention
In the design, it is sometimes necessary to store a single precision value *x.s* in a 64-bit register, i.e., the 32-bit representation must be extended to 64 bits. This embedding will be done according to the convention illustrated in figure 9.1, i.e., the data is duplicated.

FPU Control Registers
In addition, the FPU core also provides some special purpose registers. The *floating point control registers FCR* comprise the registers FCC, RM, and

Table 9.3 Register map of the general purpose floating point registers

floating point general purpose registers	floating point registers	
single precision (32-bit)	double precision (64-bit)	
FPR31[31 : 0] FPR30[31 : 0]	FDR30[63 : 32] FDR30[31 : 0]	} FDR30[63 : 0]
⋮	⋮	
FPR3[31 : 0] FPR2[31 : 0]	FDR2[63 : 32] FDR2[31 : 0]	} FDR2[63 : 0]
FPR1[31 : 0] FPR0[31 : 0]	FDR0[63 : 32] FDR0[31 : 0]	} FDR0[63 : 0]

```
 63            32 31           0
 ┌──────────────┬──────────────┐
 │     X.S      │     X.S      │
 └──────────────┴──────────────┘
```

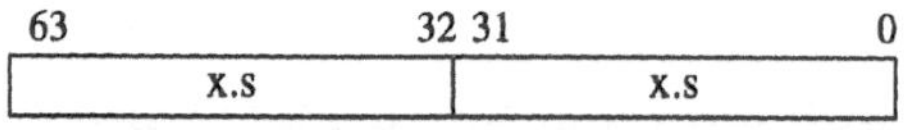

Figure 9.1 Embedding convention of single precision floating point data

IEEEf. The registers can be read and written by special move instructions. Register *FCC* is one bit wide and holds the floating point condition code. FCC is set on a floating point comparison, and it is tested on a floating point branch instruction. Register *RM* specifies which of the four IEEE rounding modes is used (table 9.4).

Register *IEEEf* (table 9.5) holds the IEEE interrupt flags, which are overflow OVF, underflow UNF, inexact result INX, division by zero DBZ, and invalid operation INV. These flags are sticky, i.e., they can only be reset at the user's request. Such a flag is set whenever the corresponding exception is triggered. The IEEE floating point standard 754 only requires that such an interrupt flag is set whenever the corresponding exception is triggered

Table 9.4 Coding of the rounding mode RM

RM[1:0]		rounding mode
00	r_z	round to zero
01	r_{ne}	round to next even
10	r_u	round up
11	r_d	round down

Table 9.5 Coding of the interrupt flags IEEEf

	symbol	meaning
IEEEf[0]	OVF	overflow
IEEEf[1]	UNF	underflow
IEEEf[2]	INX	inexact result
IEEEf[3]	DBZ	division by zero
IEEEf[4]	INV	invalid operation

Table 9.6 Coding of the special purpose registers SPR

	fxSPR						FCR		
	SR	ESR	ECA	EPC	EDPC	Edata	RM	EEEf	FCC
Sad	0	1	2	3	4	5	6	7	8

while being masked (disabled). If the exception is enabled (not masked), the value of the corresponding IEEE interrupt flag is left to the implementation/interrupt handler.

The special purpose registers SPR now comprise the original six special purpose registers *fxSPR* of the fixed point core and the FPU control registers *FCR*. Table 9.6 lists the coding of the registers SPR.

9.1.2 Interrupt Causes

The FPU adds six internal interrupts, namely the five interrupts requested by the IEEE Standard 754 plus the *unimplemented floating point operation* interrupt *uFOP* (table 9.7). In case that the FPU only implements a subset of the DLX floating point operations in hardware, the uFOP interrupt causes the software emulation of an unimplemented floating point operation. The uFOP interrupt is non-maskable and of type continue.

The IEEE Standard 754 strongly recommends that users are allowed to specify an interrupt handler for any of the five standard floating point exceptions overflow, underflow, inexact result, division by zero, and invalid operation. Such a handler can generate a substitute for the result of the exceptional floating point instruction. Thus, the IEEE floating point interrupts are maskable and of type continue. However, in the absence of such an user specific interrupt handler, the execution is usually aborting.

Table 9.7 Interrupts handled by the DLX architecture with FPU

interrupt	symbol	priority	resume	mask	external
reset	reset	0	abort	no	yes
illegal instruction	ill	1	abort	no	no
misaligned access	mal	2			
page fault IM	Ipf	3	repeat		
page fault DM	Dpf	4			
trap	trap	5	continue		
FXU overflow	ovf	6	abort	yes	
FPU overflow	fOVF	7	abort/		
FPU underflow	fUNF	8	continue		
FPU inexact result	fINX	9			
FPU division by zero	fDBZ	10			
FPU invalid operation	fINV	11			
FPU unimplemented	uFOP	12	continue	no	
external I/O	ex_j	$12+j$	continue	yes	yes

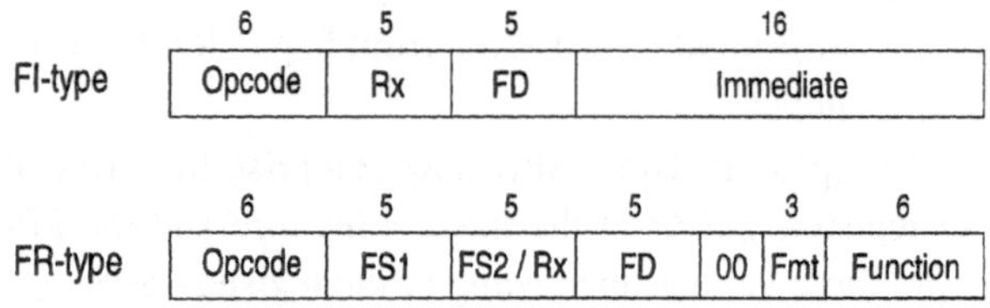

FI-type

6	5	5	16
Opcode	Rx	FD	Immediate

FR-type

6	5	5	5	3	6
Opcode	FS1	FS2 / Rx	FD	00 Fmt	Function

Figure 9.2 Floating point instruction formats of the DLX. Depending on the precision, FS1, FS2 and FD specify 32-bit or 64-bit floating point registers. Rx specifies a general purpose register of the FXU. Function is an additional 6-bit opcode. Fmt specifies a number format.

9.1.3 FPU Instruction Set

The DLX machine uses two formats (figure 9.2) for the floating point instructions; one corresponds to the I-type and the other to the R-type of the fixed point core FXU.

The FI-format is used for moving data between the FPU and the memory. Register Rx of the FXU together with the 16-bit immediate specify the memory address. This format is also used for conditional branches on the condition code flag FCC of the FPU. The immediate then specifies the branch distance. The coding of these instructions is given in table 9.8.

Table 9.8 FI-type instruction layout. All instructions except the branches also increment the PC by four. The effective address of memory accesses equals $ea = \langle GPR[Rx] \rangle + \langle sxt(imm) \rangle$, where $sxt(imm)$ denotes the sign extended version of the 16-bit immediate imm. The width of the memory access in bytes is indicated by d. Thus, the memory operand equals $m = M[ea + d - 1], \cdots, M[ea]$.

IR[31 : 26]	mnemonic	d	effect
Load, Store			
hx31	load.s	4	$FD[31:0] = m$
hx35	load.d	8	$FD[63:0] = m$
hx39	store.s	4	$m = FD[31:0]$
hx3d	store.d	8	$m = FD[63:0]$
Control Operation			
hx06	fbeqz		PC = PC + 4 + (FCC = 0 ? imm: 0)
hx07	fbnez		PC = PC + 4 + (FCC $\neq$ 0 ? imm: 0)

The FR-format is used for the remaining FPU instructions (table 9.9). It specifies a primary and a secondary opcode (Opcode, Function), a number format Fmt, and up to three floating point registers. For instructions which move data between the FPU and the fixed point unit FXU, the field FS2/Rx specifies the address of a general purpose register Rx in the FXU.

Since the FPU of the DLX machine can handle floating point numbers with single or double precision, all floating point operations come in two version; the field Fmt in the instruction word specifies the precision used (table 9.10). In the mnemonics, we identify the precision by adding the corresponding suffix, e.g., suffix '.s' indicates a single precision floating point number.

9.2 Data Paths without Forwarding

IN THIS section we extend the pipelined data paths of the DLX machine by an IEEE floating point unit. The extensions mainly occur within the environments. The top level schematics of the data paths (figure 9.3) remain virtually the same, except for some additional staging registers and the environment *FPemb* which aligns the floating point operands.

The register file environment RFenv now also provides two 64-bit floating point operands FA and FB, and it gets a 64-bit result FC and three additional addresses. The registers Ffl.3 and Ffl.4 buffer the five IEEE ex-

Table 9.9 FR-type instruction layout. All instructions also increment the PC by four. The functions sqrt(), abs() and rem() denote the square root, the absolute value and the remainder of a division according to the IEEE 754 standard. The opcode bits $c[3:0]$ specify the floating point test condition *con* according to table 8.7. Function cvt() converts from one format into another. In our implementation, instructions fsqt and frem are only supported in software.

IR[31:26]	IR[5:0]	Fmt	mnemonic	effect
Arithmetic and compare operations				
hx11	hx00		fadd [.s, .d]	FD = FS1 + FS2
hx11	hx01		fsub [.s, .d]	FD = FS1 - FS2
hx11	hx02		fmul [.s, .d]	FD = FS1 * FS2
hx11	hx03		fdiv [.s, .d]	FD = FS1 / FS2
hx11	hx04		fneg [.s, .d]	FD = - FS1
hx11	hx05		fabs [.s, .d]	FD = abs(FS1)
hx11	hx06		fsqt [.s, .d]	FD = sqrt(FS1)
hx11	hx07		frem [.s, .d]	FD = rem(FS1, FS2)
hx11	$11c[3:0]$		fc.con [.s, .d]	FCC = (FS1 *con* FS2)
Data transfer				
hx11	hx08	000	fmov.s	FD[31:0] = FS1[31:0]
hx11	hx08	001	fmov.d	FD[63:0] = FS1[63:0]
hx11	hx09		mf2i	Rx = FS1[31:0]
hx11	hx0a		mi2f	FD[31:0] = Rx
Format conversion				
hx11	hx20	001	cvt.s.d	FD = cvt(FS1, s, d)
hx11	hx20	100	cvt.s.i	FD = cvt(FS1, s, i)
hx11	hx21	000	cvt.d.s	FD = cvt(FS1, d, s)
hx11	hx21	100	cvt.d.i	FD = cvt(FS1, d, i)
hx11	hx24	000	cvt.i.s	FD = cvt(FS1, i, s)
hx11	hx24	001	cvt.i.d	FD = cvt(FS1, i, d)

Table 9.10 Coding of the number format Fmt.

Fmt[2:0]	suffix	number format
000	.s	single precision floating point
001	.d	double precision floating point
100	.i	32-bit fixed point

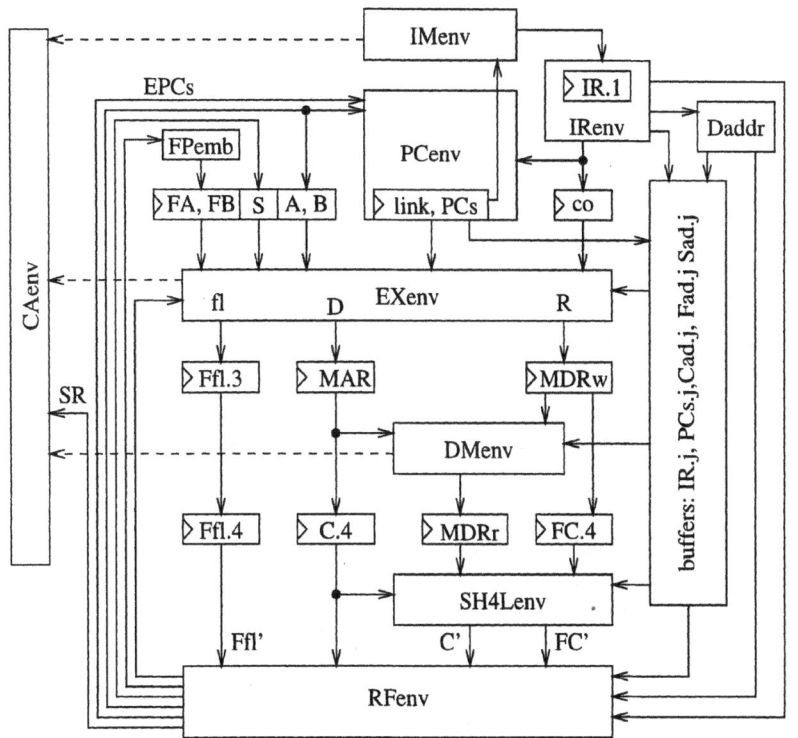

Figure 9.3 Data paths of the DLX design with a floating point core

ception flags. In order to support double precision loads and stores, the data registers MDRw and MDRr associated with the data memory are now 64 bits wide. Thus, the cost of the enhanced DLX data paths can be expressed as

$$
\begin{aligned}
C_{DP} \;=\; & C_{IMenv} + C_{PCenv} + C_{IRenv} + C_{Daddr} + C_{FPemb} + C_{EXenv} \\
& + C_{DMenv} + C_{SH4Lenv} + C_{RFenv} + C_{CAenv} + C_{buffer} \\
& + 6 \cdot C_{ff}(32) + 5 \cdot C_{ff}(64) + 2 \cdot C_{ff}(5).
\end{aligned}
$$

The extended instruction set architecture has no impact on the instruction fetch. Thus, the instruction memory environment IMenv remains the same. The other four pipeline stages undergo more or less extensive changes which are now described stage by stage.

9.2.1 Instruction Decode

The data paths of the decode stage ID comprise the environments IRenv, PCenv, and FPemb and the circuit Daddr which selects the address of the destination register.

Environment IRenv

So far, the environment IRenv of the instruction register selects the immediate operand *imm* being passed to the PC environment and the 32-bit immediate operand *co*. In addition, IRenv provides the addresses of the register operands and two opcodes.

The extension of the instruction set has no impact on the immediate operands or on the source addresses of the register file GPR. However, environment IRenv now also has to provide the addresses of the two floating point operands *FA* and *FB*. These source addresses $FS1$ and $FS2$ can directly be read off the instruction word and equal the source addresses *Aad* and *Bad* of the fixed point register file GPR:

$$\begin{aligned} FS1 &= Aad = IR[25:21] \\ FS2 &= Bad = IR[20:17]. \end{aligned}$$

Thus, the cost and delay of environment IRenv remain unchanged.

Circuit Daddr

Circuit *Daddr* generates the destination addresses *Cad* and *Fad* of the general purpose register files GPR and FPR. In addition, it provides the source address *Sas* and the destination address *Sad* of the special purpose register file SPR.

Address *Cad* of the fixed point destination is generated by circuit *Caddr* as before. The selection of the floating destination *Fad* is controlled by a signal *FRtype* which indicates an FR-type instruction:

$$Fad[4:0] = \begin{cases} IR[15:11] & \text{if} \quad FRtype = 1 \\ IR[20:16] & \text{if} \quad FRtype = 0. \end{cases}$$

The SPR source address *Sas* is generated as in the DLX design. It is usually specified by the bits $SA = IR[10:6]$, but on an RFE instruction it equals the address of register ESR. Except for an RFE instruction or a floating point condition test ($fc = 1$), the SPR destination address *Sad* is specified by *SA*. On RFE, ESR is copied into the status register SPR[0], and on $fc = 1$, the condition flag fcc is saved into register SPR[8]. Thus,

$$Sas = \begin{cases} SA & \text{if} \quad rfe.1 = 0 \\ 00001 & \text{if} \quad rfe.1 = 1 \end{cases} \qquad Sad = \begin{cases} 00000 & \text{if} \quad rfe.1 = 1 \\ 01000 & \text{if} \quad fc.1 = 1 \\ SA & \text{otherwise.} \end{cases}$$

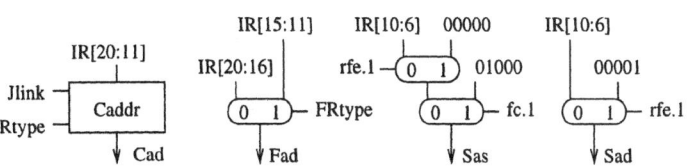

Figure 9.4 Circuit *Daddr* which selects the destination addresses

The circuit of figure 9.4 provides these four addresses at the following cost and delay:

$$C_{Daddr} = C_{Caddr} + 4 \cdot C_{mux}(5)$$
$$D_{Daddr} = \max\{D_{Caddr}, 2 \cdot D_{mux}(5)\}.$$

PC Environment

Due to the extended ISA, the PC environment has to support two additional control instructions, namely the floating point branches fbeqz and fbnez. However, except for the value PC'^{u}_i, the environment PCenv still has the functionality described in chapter 5.

Let signal $bjtaken$, as before, indicate a jump or taken branch. On instruction I_i, the PC environment now computes the value

$$PC'^{u}_i = \begin{cases} EPC_{i-1} & \text{if } I_i = \text{rfe} \\ PC'_{i-1} + imm_i & \text{if } bjtaken_i \wedge I_i \in \{\text{beqz, bnez, j, jal}\} \\ PC'_{i-1} + imm_i & \text{if } bjtaken_i \wedge I_i \in \{\text{fbeqz, fbnez}\} \\ RS1_{i-1} & \text{if } bjtaken_i \wedge I_i \in \{\text{jr, jalr}\} \\ PC'_{i-1} + 4 & \text{otherwise} \end{cases}$$

This extension has a direct impact on the glue logic PCglue, which generates signal $bjtaken$, but the data paths of PCenv including circuit *nextPC* remain unchanged.

Signal $bjtaken$ must now also be activated in case of a taken floating point branch. Let the additional control signal $fbranch$ denote a floating point branch. According to table 9.11, signal $bjtaken$ is now generated as

$$\begin{aligned} bjtaken = \; & branch \wedge (bzero \text{ XNOR } AEQZ) \\ & \vee fbranch \wedge (bzero \text{ XOR } FCC) \\ & \vee jump \end{aligned}$$

This increases the cost of the glue logic by an OR, AND, and XOR gate:

$$\begin{aligned} C_{PCglue} = \; & 2 \cdot C_{or} + C_{and} + C_{xnor} + C_{zero}(32) \\ & + C_{or} + C_{and} + C_{xor}. \end{aligned}$$

Table 9.11 Value of signal *bjtaken* for the different branch instructions

instruction	bzero	AEQZ	FCC	bjtaken
beqz	1	0 1	*	0 1
bnez	0	0 1	*	1 0
fbeqz	1	*	1 0	0 1
fbnez	0	*	1 0	0 1

Both operands A' and FCC are provided by the register file environment, but A' is passed through a zero tester in order to obtain signal $AEQZ$. Thus, FCC has a much shorter delay than $AEQZ$, and the delay of signal $bjtaken$ remains unchanged.

Environment FPemb

Environment FPemb of figure 9.5 selects the two floating point source operands and implements the embedding convention of figure 9.1. It is controlled by three signals,

- the flag $dbs.1$ requesting double precision source operands,

- the least significant address bit $FS1[0]$ of operand FA, and

- the least significant address bit $FS2[0]$ of operand FB.

Circuit FPemb reads the two double words $fA[63:0]$ and $fB[63:0]$ and provides the two operands FA1 and FB1, each of which is 64 bits wide.

Since the selection and data extension of the two source operands go along the same lines, we just focus on operand FA1. Let the high order word and the low order word of input fA be denoted by

$$fAh = fA[63:32] \quad \text{and} \quad fAl = fA[31:0].$$

On a double precision access ($dbs.1 = 1$), the high and the low order word are just concatenated, i.e., $FA1 = fAh, fAl$. On a single precision access, one of the two words is selected and duplicated; the word fAl is chosen on an even address and the word fAh on an odd address. Thus,

$$FA1[63:0] = \begin{cases} fAh, fAl & \text{if} \quad dbs.1 = 1 \\ fAh, fAh & \text{if} \quad dbs.1 = 0 \land FS1[0] = 1 \\ fAl, fAl & \text{if} \quad dbs.1 = 0 \land FS1[0] = 0. \end{cases}$$

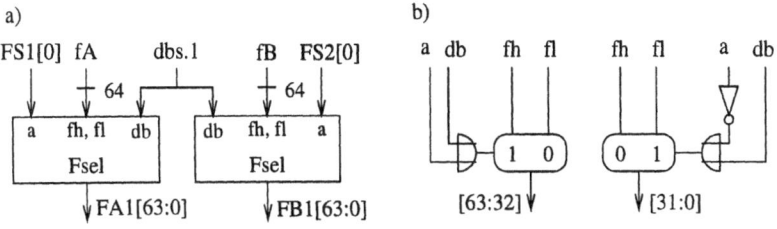

Figure 9.5 Schematics of environment $FPemb$ (a) and of circuit $Fsel$ (b).

Circuit FSel (figure 9.5) implements this selection in a straightforward manner. Environment FPemb comprises two of these circuits. Since the data inputs have a much longer delay than the three control signals, the cost and delay of environment FPemb can be expressed as

$$C_{FPemb} = 2 \cdot C_{Fsel} = 2 \cdot (2 \cdot C_{or} + C_{inv} + 2 \cdot C_{mux}(32))$$
$$D_{FPemb} = D_{mux}(32).$$

9.2.2 Memory Stage

In every cycle, the memory stage passes the address MAR, the 64-bit data MDRw and the floating point flags Ffl.3 to the write back stage:

$$C.4 := MAR$$
$$FC.4 := MDRw$$
$$Ffl.4 := Ffl.3.$$

In case of a load or store instruction, the environment DMenv of the data memory and the memory control perform the data memory access. In order to load and store double precision floating point numbers, the memory access can now be up to 64 bits wide.

Memory Organization
As before, the data memory DM is byte addressable, but in addition to byte, half word and word accesses, it now also supports double word accesses. Therefore, the data memory is organized in 8 memory banks.

In the memory DM, 8-bit, 16-bit and 32-bit data are *aligned* in the same way as before (section 3.1.3). Whereas 64-bit data are aligned at *double word boundaries*, i.e., their byte addresses are divisible by eight. For a double word boundary e we define the *memory double word* of memory DM with address e as

$$DMdword(e) = DM[e+7:e].$$

The bytes within the double word $w[63:0]$ are numbered in little endian order:

$$\begin{aligned}
byte_j(w) &= w[8j+7:8j] \\
byte_{[i:j]}(w) &= byte_i(w)\dots byte_j(w)
\end{aligned}$$

On a read access with address $a[31:0]$, the data memory DM provides the requested double word, assuming that the memory is not busy and that the access causes no page fault. In any other case, the memory DM provides a default value. Thus, for the double word boundary $e = \langle a[31:3]000\rangle$, we get

$$DMout[63:0] = \begin{cases} DMdword(e) & \text{if } Dmr.3 \wedge /dbusy \wedge /dpf \\ DMdefault & \text{otherwise.} \end{cases}$$

A write access only updates the data memory, if the access is perfectly aligned ($dmal = 0$), and if the access causes no page fault ($dpf = 0$). On such an d-byte write access with byte address $a = \langle a[31:0]\rangle$ and offset $o = \langle a[2:0]\rangle$, the data memory performs the update

$$DM[a+d-1:a] := byte_{[o+d-1:o]}(MDin[63:0]).$$

Memory Environment DMenv

Figure 9.6 depicts the new data memory environment DMenv. Like in the pipelined DLX design of section 6.5, the core of DMenv is the data cache interface $D\$if$ with a sectored cache. A cache sector is still $S = 8$ bytes wide.

The cache is connected to the data paths through a 32-bit address port a and the two 64-bit data ports MDin and DMout. The memory interface Mif connects the data cache to the off-chip memory. Even without FPU, the cache and the off-chip memory already operate on 8-byte data. Thus, the interface Mif and D$if remain unchanged.

Without the FPU, the 64-bit data ports of the cache and memory interface had to be patched to the 32-bit ports of the data paths. On the input port MDin, the 32-bit data MDRw was duplicated. On the output port, a multiplexer selected the requested word within the double word.

Since the registers MDRw and MDRr are now 64 bits wide, the patches become obsolete. That saves a 32-bit multiplexer and reduces the cache

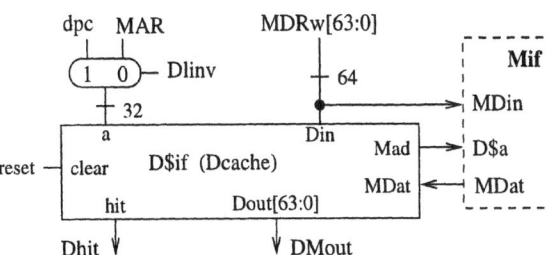

Figure 9.6 Data memory environment of the DLX design with FPU

read time $T_{\$read}$ by the delay D_{mux} and possibly the burst read time $T_{Mrburst}$ as well. However, these two cycle times were not time critical.

$$
\begin{aligned}
T_{\$read} &= A_{\$if}(Dout) + D_{ff} \\
T_{Mrburst} &= D_{driv} + d_{bus} + \delta \\
&\quad + \max\{D_{\$if}(MDat;\$if), D_{\$if}(MDat;Dout) + D_{ff}\} \\
C_{DMenv} &= C_{D\$if} + C_{mux}(32).
\end{aligned}
$$

Data Memory Control

As in the pipelined design of section 6.5, the date cache interface D\$if and the interface Mif to the off-chip memory are governed by the memory interface control $MifC$. Even without FPU, the interfaces D\$if and Mif already supported 8-byte accesses. Thus, the new floating point load instructions (ls, ld, ss, sd) have no impact on the control MifC.

In addition to control MifC, the data memory environment DMenv is governed by the data memory control DMC. As before, circuit DMC generates the bank write signals DMbw[7:0], which on a cache read access $D\$rd = 1$ are clocked into register DMBw. Circuit DMC also checks for a misaligned access, signaled by $dmal = 1$, and masks the memory read and write signal with the flag $dmal$. Since the bank write signals and flag $dmal$ depend on the width of the access, circuit DMC must also account for the new load and store instructions.

The bank write signals DMbw[7:0] are generated along the same lines as before (pages 81 and 201): Feeding address $MAR[2:0]$ into a 3-decoder gives 8 signals $B[7:0]$ satisfying for all j

$$
B[j] = 1 \quad \leftrightarrow \quad \langle MAR[2:0] \rangle = j.
$$

From the the primary opcode $IR.3$, the width of the current access is decoded according to table 9.12 by

$$
B = (IR.3[30] \text{ NOR } IR.3[27]) \wedge \overline{IR.3[26]}
$$

Table 9.12 Coding the width of a data memory access

width		d	IR.3[30,28:26]	instructions
byte	B	1	0*00	lb, lbu, sb
half word	H	2	0*01	lh, lhu, sh
word	W	4	0*11	lw, sw
			1001	load.s, store.s
double word	D	8	1101	load.d, store.d

$$H \;=\; (IR.3[30] \text{ NOR } IR.3[27]) \wedge IR.3[26]$$
$$W \;=\; \overline{IR.3[30]} \wedge (IR.3[27] \wedge IR.3[26]) \;\vee\; IR.3[30] \wedge \overline{IR.3[28]}$$
$$D \;=\; IR.3[30] \wedge IR.3[28].$$

According to table 9.13, the bank write signals are then generated in a brute force way by

$$DMbw[0] \;=\; Dmw.3 \wedge B[0]$$
$$DMbw[1] \;=\; Dmw.3 \wedge ((D \wedge B[0] \vee W \wedge B[0]) \vee (H \wedge B[0] \vee B \wedge B[1]))$$
$$DMbw[2] \;=\; Dmw.3 \wedge ((D \wedge B[0] \vee W \wedge B[0]) \vee (H \wedge B[2] \vee B \wedge B[2]))$$
$$DMbw[3] \;=\; Dmw.3 \wedge ((D \wedge B[0] \vee W \wedge B[0]) \vee (H \wedge B[2] \vee B \wedge B[3]))$$
$$DMbw[4] \;=\; Dmw.3 \wedge ((D \wedge B[0] \vee W \wedge B[4]) \vee (H \wedge B[4] \vee B \wedge B[4]))$$
$$DMbw[5] \;=\; Dmw.3 \wedge ((D \wedge B[0] \vee W \wedge B[4]) \vee (H \wedge B[4] \vee B \wedge B[5]))$$
$$DMbw[6] \;=\; Dmw.3 \wedge ((D \wedge B[0] \vee W \wedge B[4]) \vee (H \wedge B[6] \vee B \wedge B[6]))$$
$$DMbw[7] \;=\; Dmw.3 \wedge ((D \wedge B[0] \vee W \wedge B[4]) \vee (H \wedge B[6] \vee B \wedge B[7]))$$

The memory control DMC also checks for a misaligned access. A byte access is always properly aligned. A double word access is only aligned if it starts at byte 0, i.e., if $B[0] = 1$. A word access is aligned if it starts at byte 0 or 4, and a half word access is aligned if it starts at an even byte. Thus, the misalignment can be detected by

$$malAc \;=\; D \wedge \overline{B[0]} \;\vee\; W \wedge (B[0] \text{ NOR } B[4]) \;\vee\; H \wedge MAR[0].$$

Circuit DMC checks for a misaligned access (signaled by *dmal*) on every load and store instruction. In order to protect the data memory, it masks the memory read and write signal *Dmr* and *Dmw* with flag *dmal*. Thus

$$dmal \;=\; (Dmr.3 \vee Dmw.3) \wedge malAc$$
$$Dmra \;=\; Dmr.3 \wedge \overline{malAc} = \overline{Dmr.3} \text{ NOR } malAc$$
$$Dmwa \;=\; Dmw.3 \wedge \overline{malAc} = \overline{Dmw.3} \text{ NOR } malAc.$$

Table 9.13 Memory bank write signal $DMbw[7:0]$ as a function of the address MAR[2:0] and the width (B, H, W, D) of the access

address	width of the access			
MAR[2:0]	D	W	H	B
000	1111 1111	0000 1111	0000 0011	0000 0001
001	0000 0000	0000 0000	0000 0000	0000 0010
010	0000 0000	0000 0000	0000 1100	0000 0100
011	0000 0000	0000 0000	0000 0000	0000 1000
100	0000 0000	1111 0000	0011 0000	0001 0000
101	0000 0000	0000 0000	0000 0000	0010 0000
110	0000 0000	0000 0000	1100 0000	0100 0000
111	0000 0000	0000 0000	0000 0000	1000 0000

When reusing common subexpressions, the memory control DMC has the cost

$$C_{DMC} = C_{dec}(3) + 6 \cdot C_{inv} + 32 \cdot C_{and} + 20 \cdot C_{or} + 4 \cdot C_{nor} + C_{ff}(8).$$

This includes the 8-bit register DMBw which buffers the bank write signals. Signals DMBw are still provided at zero delay. The accumulated delay A_{DMC} of the remaining outputs and the cycle time of circuit DMC run at

$$A_{DMC} = \max\{A_{CON}(Dmr, Dmw) + D_{or} + D_{and},$$
$$\max\{D_{dec}(3), D_{or} + 2 \cdot D_{and}\} + 2 \cdot D_{and} + 2 \cdot D_{or}\}$$
$$T_{DMC} = A_{DMC} + \Delta.$$

9.2.3 Write Back Stage

The DLX architecture now comprises three register files, one for the fixed point registers GPR, one for the special purpose registers SPR, and one for the floating point registers FPR. These three register files form the environment RFenv

$$C_{RFenv} = C_{GPRenv} + C_{SPRenv} + C_{FPRenv}.$$

The data paths of the write back stage consist of the environment RFenv and of the shifter environment SH4Lenv. Environment GPRenv is the only environment which remains unchanged.

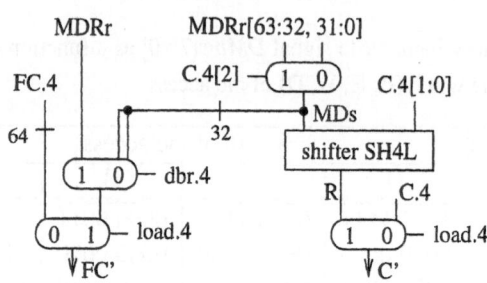

Figure 9.7 Shift for load environment SH4Lenv

Environment SH4Lenv

In addition to the fixed point result C', the environment SH4Lenv now also provides a 64-bit floating point result FC'. The environment is controlled by two signals,

- signal *load*.4 indicating a load instructions and

- signal *dbr*.4 indicating a double precision result.

The fixed point result C' is almost computed as before, but the memory now provides a double word MDRr. The shifter SH4L still requires a 32-bit input data MDs. Depending on the address bit $C.4[2]$, MDs either equals the high or low order word of MDRr:

$$MDs = \begin{cases} MDRr[63:32] & \text{if} \quad C.4[2] = 1 \quad \text{(high order word)} \\ MDRr[31:0] & \text{if} \quad C.4[2] = 0 \quad \text{(low order word)} \end{cases}$$

Let $sh4l(a, dist)$ denote the function computed by the shifter SH4L. The fixed point result C' is then selected as

$$C' = \begin{cases} sh4l(MDs, C.4[1:0]000) & \text{if} \quad load.4 = 1 \\ C.4 & \text{if} \quad load.4 = 0. \end{cases}$$

Depending on the type of the instruction, the output FC' is selected among the two 64-bit inputs FC.4 and MDRr and the 32-bit word MDs which is extended according to the embedding convention. On a load instruction, the environment passes the memory operand, which in case of double precision equals MDRr and MDs, otherwise. On any other instruction, the environment forwards the FPU result FC.4 to the output FC'. Thus,

$$FC'[63:0] = \begin{cases} MDRr & \text{if} \quad load.4 = 1 \wedge dbr.4 = 1 \\ (MDs, MDs) & \text{if} \quad load.4 = 1 \wedge dbr.4 = 0 \\ FC.4 & \text{otherwise} \end{cases}$$

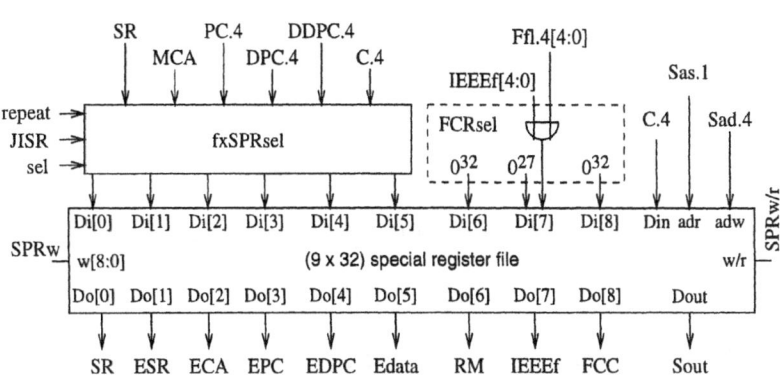

Figure 9.8 Environment SPRenv of the special purpose register file

The circuit of figure 9.7 implements environment SH4Lenv in the obvious way. Its cost and delay can be expressed as

$$C_{SH4Lenv} = C_{SH4L} + 2 \cdot C_{mux}(32) + 2 \cdot C_{mux}(64)$$
$$D_{SH4Lenv} = \max\{D_{SH4L}, D_{mux}\} + 2 \cdot D_{mux}.$$

Environment of the Special Purpose Registers

Figure 9.8 depicts the environment SPRenv of the special purpose register file. Due to the FPU, the register file SPR comprises the original six special purpose registers *fxSPR* of the fixed point core and the FPU control registers *FCR* (table 9.6).

The core of SPRenv is a special register file of size 9×32. The circuits *fxSPRsel* and *FCRsel* provide the inputs $Di[s]$ of the distinct write ports. As before, circuit *SPRcon* generates the write signals $SPRw[8:0]$ and signal *sel* which is used by *fxSPRsel*. The environment is controlled by

- the interrupt signals *JISR* and *repeat*,

- the write signal *SPRw*, and

- signal *fop*.4 denoting an arithmetic floating point instruction, a conversion cvt, or a test fc.

As before, the special purpose registers are held in a register file with an extended access mode. Any register $SPR[s]$ can be accessed through the regular read/write port and through a distinct read port and a distinct write port. In case of a conflict, a special write takes precedence over the write access specified by address Sad. Thus, for any $s = 0, \ldots, 8$, register $SPR[s]$ is updated as

$$SPR[s] := \begin{cases} Di[s] & \text{if} \quad SPRw[s] = 1 \\ C.4 & \text{if} \quad SPRw[s] = 0 \wedge SPRw = 1 \wedge s = Sad. \end{cases}$$

The distinct read port of register $SPR[s]$ provides the data

$$Do[s] = SPR[s],$$

and the standard data output of the register file equals

$$Sout = SPR[Sas].$$

Registers fxSPR   The registers fxSPR still have the original functionality. The write signals of their distinct write ports and signal sel are generated as before:

$$\begin{aligned} sel &= \overline{repeat} \wedge SPRw \wedge (\langle Sad.4 \rangle = 0) \\ SPRw[s] &= JISR. \end{aligned}$$

Circuit $fxSPRsel$ which selects the inputs $Di[s]$ of these write ports can be taken from the DLX design of section 5 (figure 5.6).

Registers FCR   Although the rounding mode RM, the IEEE flags and the condition flag FCC only require a few bits, they are held in 32-bit registers. The data are padded with leading zeros.

   The condition flag FCC can be updated by a special move movi2s or by a floating point condition test. Since in either case, the result is provided by register $C.4$, the distinct write port of register FCC is not used. Thus,

$$Di[8] = 0 \quad \text{and} \quad SPRw[8] = 0.$$

The rounding mode RM can only be updated by a movi2s instruction. Thus,

$$Di[6] = 0 \quad \text{and} \quad SPRw[6] = 0.$$

   Except for the data transfers, any floating point instruction provides flags which signal the five floating point exceptions (overflow, underflow, inexact result, division by zero, and invalid operation). The IEEE standard requires that these exception flags are accumulated, i.e., that the new flags $Ffl.4$ are ORed to the corresponding bits of register IEEEf:

$$Di[7] = 0^{27} \, (Ffl.4[4:0] \vee IEEEf[4:0]) \quad \text{and} \quad SPRw[7] = fop.4.$$

Cost and Delay   The new select circuit FCRsel just requires a 5-bit OR gate. Due to the 4-bit address *Sad*, circuit SPRcon now uses a 4-bit zero tester; SPRcon can provide the additional write signals $SPRw[8:6]$ at no cost. Thus, the cost of the extended environment SPRenv run at

$$
\begin{aligned}
C_{SPRenv} &= C_{SF}(9,32) + C_{fxSPRsel} + C_{FCRsel} + C_{SPRcon} \\
C_{SPRcon} &= 2 \cdot C_{and} + C_{inv} + C_{zero}(4) \\
C_{FCRsel} &= 5 \cdot C_{or}.
\end{aligned}
$$

Except for the width of address *Sad*, the formulae which express the delay of the outputs and the cycle time of environment SPRenv remain unchanged.

Environment of the Floating Point Register File

The extended DLX instruction set requires 32 single precision floating point registers and 16 double precision registers. These two sets of floating point registers have to be mapped into the same register file FPR (section 9.1). In each cycle, the environment FPRenv of the floating point register file performs two double precision read accesses and one write access.

Read Access   The register file environment FPRenv provides the two source operands fA and fB. Since both operands have double precision, they can be specified by 4-bit addresses $FS1[4:1]$ and $FS2[4:1]$:

$$
\begin{aligned}
fA[63:0] &= (FPR[FS1[4:1],1], FPR[FS1[4:1],0]) \\
fB[63:0] &= (FPR[FS2[4:1],1], FPR[FS2[4:1],0]).
\end{aligned}
$$

For the high order word the least significant address bit is set to 1 and for the low order word it is set to 0.

Write Access   The 64-bit input FC' or its low order word $FC'[31:0]$ is written into the register file. The write access is governed by the write signal $FPRw$ and the flag $dbr.4$ which specifies the width of the access.

In case of single precision, the single precision result is kept in the high *and* the low order word of FC', due to the embedding convention. Thus, on $FPRw = 1$ and $dbr.4 = 0$, the register with address $Fad4$ is updated to

$$
FPR[Fad4[4:0]] := FC'[63:32] = FC'[31:0].
$$

On $FPRw = 1$ and $dbr.4 = 1$, the environment FPRenv performs a double precision write access updating two consecutive registers:

$$
\begin{aligned}
FPR[Fad4[4:1]\,1] &:= FC'[63:32] \\
FPR[Fad4[4:0]\,0] &:= FC'[31:0].
\end{aligned}
$$

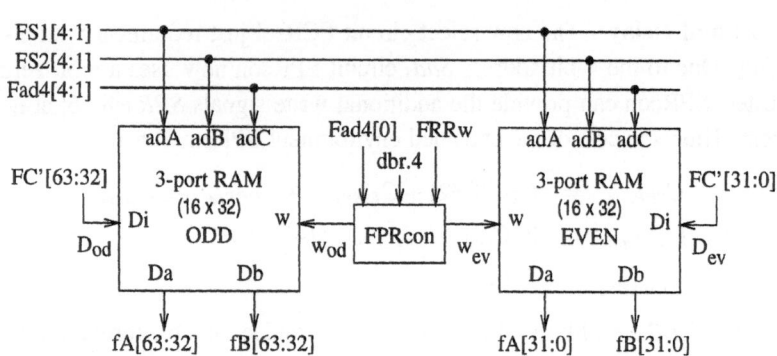

Figure 9.9 Environment FPRenv of the floating point register file

Implementation In order to support single as well as double precision accesses, the floating point register file is split in two banks, each of which provides 16 single precision registers (figure 9.9). One bank holds the registers with even addresses, the other bank holds the registers with odd addresses.

The high order word of a double precision result is written into the odd bank of the register file and its low order word is written into the even bank. In case of single precision, the high and low order word of input FC' are identical. Thus, $FC'[63:32]$ always serves as the input D_{od} of the odd bank, and $FC'[31:0]$ always serves as the input D_{ev} of the even bank (table 9.14).

Each bank of the register file FPR is implemented as a 3-port RAM of size (16×32) addressed by FS1[4:1], FS2[4:1] and Fad4[4:1]. Including circuit FPRcon which generates the two bank write signals w_{ev} and w_{od}, the cost and delay of the register file environment FPRenv run at

$$
\begin{aligned}
C_{FPRenv} &= 2 \cdot C_{ram3}(16,32) + C_{FPRcon} \\
D_{FPR,read} &= D_{ram3}(16,32) \\
D_{FPR,write} &= D_{FPRcon} + D_{ram3}(16,32).
\end{aligned}
$$

In case of a double precision write access ($dbr.4 = 1$), both banks of the register file are updated. Whereas on a single precision access, only one of the banks is updated, namely the one specified by the least significant address bit Fad4[0] (table 9.14). Of course, the register file FPR is only updated if requested by an active write signal $FPRw = 1$. Thus, the two bank write signals are

$$
\begin{aligned}
w_{od} &= FPRw \wedge (dbr.4 \vee Fad4[0]) \\
w_{ev} &= FPRw \wedge (dbr.4 \vee /Fad4[0])
\end{aligned}
$$

Table 9.14 The input data D_{ev} and D_{od} of the two FPR banks and their write signals w_{ev} and w_{od}.

FPRw	dbr.4	Fad4[0]	w_{od}	w_{ev}	D_{od}	D_{ev}
1	0	0	0	1	*	FC'[31:0]
1	0	1	1	0	FC'[63:32]	*
1	1	*	1	1	FC'[63:32]	FC'[31:0]
0	*	*	0	0	*	*

The control FPRcon of the FPR register file can generate these two write signals at the following cost and delay:

$$C_{FPRcon} = 2 \cdot C_{and} + 2 \cdot C_{or} + C_{inv}$$
$$D_{FPRcon} = D_{inv} + D_{or} + D_{and}.$$

9.2.4 Execute Stage

The execute environment EXenv is the core of the execute stage (figure 9.10). Parts of the buffer environment and of the cause environment CAenv also belong to the execute stage. The buffers pass the PCs, the destination addresses and the instruction opcodes down the pipeline. Environment CAenv collects the interrupt causes and then processes them in the memory stage.

Execute Environment
Environment EXenv comprises the 32-bit fixed point unit FXU, the 64-bit floating point unit FPU of chapter 8, and the exchange unit FPXtr. It gets the same fixed point operands as before (A, B, S, co, link) and the two floating point operands FA2 and FB2.

Fixed Point Unit FXU   The FXU equals the execute environment of the DLX architecture from section 5.5.4. The functionality, the cost and delay of this environment remain unchanged. The FXU still provides the two fixed point results D and sh and is controlled by the same signals:

- $bmuxsel$ and $a'muxsel$ which select the operands,

- $AluDdoe$, $SHDdoe$, $linkDdoe$, $ADdoe$, $SDdoe$, and $coDdoe$ which select output D,

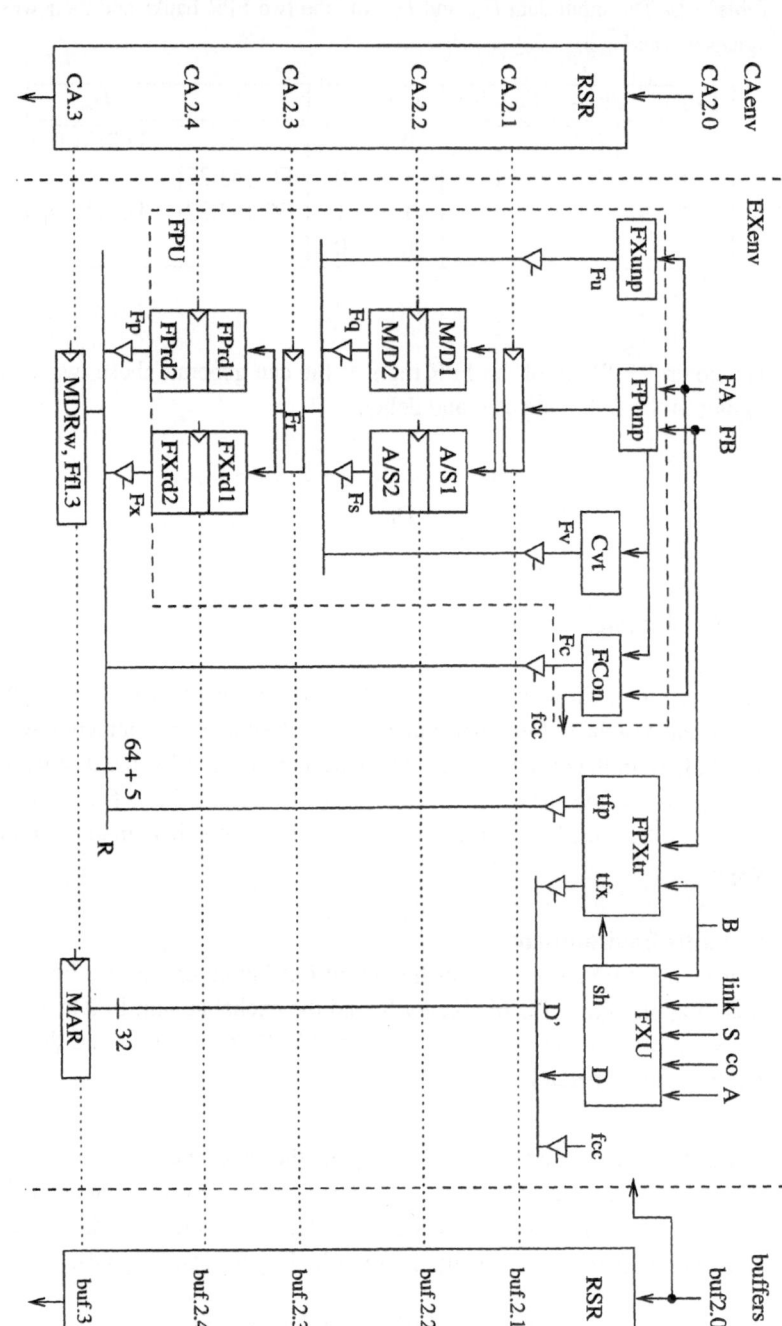

Figure 9.10 Data paths of the execute stage

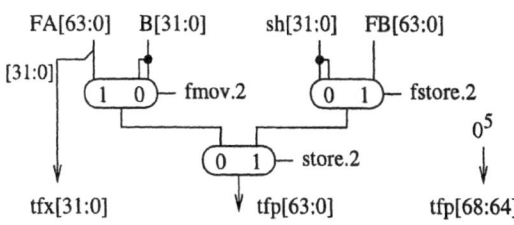

Figure 9.11 Exchange unit FPXtr

- *Rtype*, *add* and *test* which govern the ALU, and

- *shift4s* which governs the shifter SH.

Exchange Unit FPXtr The FPXtr unit transfers data between the fixed point and the floating point core or within the floating point core. It is controlled by

- signal *store*.2 indicating any store instruction,

- signal *fstore*.2 indicating a floating point store instruction, and

- signal *fmov*.2 indicating a floating point move fmov.

The operands $B[31:0]$, $FA[63:0]$ and $FB[63:0]$ are directly taken from registers, operand $sh[31:0]$ is provided by the shifter of the fixed point unit. Circuit FPXtr selects a 69-bit result tfp and a 32-bit result tfx. The bits tfp[63:0] either code a floating point or fixed point value, whereas the bits tfp[68:64] hold the floating point exception flags.

According to the IEEE floating point standard [Ins85], data move instructions never cause a floating point exception. This applies to stores and the special moves mf2i and mi2f. Thus, the exchange unit selects the results as

$$tfx[31:0] = FA[31:0]$$

$$tfp[63:0] = \begin{cases} FB[63:0] & \text{if } fstore.2 \\ sh[31:0]\,sh[31:0] & \text{if } store.2 \wedge /fstore.2 \\ FA[63:0] & \text{if } fmov.2 \\ B[31:0]\,B[31:0] & \text{otherwise} \end{cases}$$

$$tfp[68:64] = 00000.$$

The circuit of figure 9.11 implements the exchange unit in the obvious way. Assuming that the control signals of the execute stage are precom-

463

puted, cost and accumulated delay of environment FPXtr run at

$$C_{FPXtr} = 3 \cdot C_{mux}(64)$$
$$A_{FPXtr} = A_{FXU}(sh) + 2 \cdot D_{mux}(64).$$

Functionality of EXenv   Environment EXenv generates two results, the fixed point value D' and the 69-bit result R. $R[63:0]$ is either a fixed point or a floating point value; the bits $R[68:64]$ provide the floating point exception flags. Circuit EXenv selects output D' among the result D of the FXU, the result tfx of the exchange unit, and the condition flag fcc of the FPU. This selection is governed by the signals $mf2i$ and fc which denote a special move instruction mf2i or a floating point compare instruction, respectively:

$$D'[31:0] = \begin{cases} D[31:0] & \text{if} \quad mf2i = 0 \wedge fc = 0 \\ tfx[31:0] & \text{if} \quad mf2i = 1 \wedge fc = 0 \\ 0^{31}fcc & \text{if} \quad mf2i = 0 \wedge fc = 1. \end{cases}$$

The selection of result R is controlled by the four enable signals $FcRdoe$, $FpRdoe$, $FxRdoe$ and $tfpRdoe$. At most one of these signals is active at a time. Thus,

$$R[68:0] = \begin{cases} Fc[68:0] & \text{if} \quad FcRdoe = 1 \\ Fp[68:0] & \text{if} \quad FpRdoe = 1 \\ Fx[68:0] & \text{if} \quad FxRdoe = 1 \\ tfp[68:0] & \text{if} \quad tfpRdoe = 1. \end{cases}$$

Cost and Cycle Time   Adding an FPU has no impact on the accumulated delay A_{FXU} of the results of the fixed point core FXU. The FPU itself comprises five pipeline stages. Its cycle time is modeled by T_{FPU} and the accumulated delay of its outputs is modeled by A_{FPU} (chapter 8). Thus, cost and cycle time of the whole execute environment EXenv can be estimated as

$$C_{EXenv} = C_{FXU} + C_{FPU} + C_{FPXtr} + 2 \cdot C_{driv}(32) + 4 \cdot C_{driv}(69)$$
$$A_{EXenv} = \max\{A_{FXU}, \max\{A_{FPXtr}, A_{FPU}\} + D_{driv}\}$$
$$T_{EXenv} = \max\{T_{FPU}, A_{EXenv} + \Delta\}.$$

Scheduling of the Execute Stage

In the previous designs, the execute stage always had a single cycle latency, but now, its latency is not even fixed. The FXU and the exchange unit still generate their results within a single cycle. However, the latency of the FPU depends on the operation and precision (table 9.1); it varies between 1 to 21 cycles.

Table 9.15 Cycles required for the actual execution depending on the type of the instruction (i.e., stages EX and M)

stage	fdiv.d	fdiv.s	fmul	fadd fsub	cvt	fc fabs fneg	fmov mi2f mf2i	rest
2.0	unpack					FCon	FPXtr	FXU
2.0.1	lookup							
2.0.2	newton1							
2.0.3	newton2							
2.0.4	newton3							
2.0.5	newton4	lookup						
2.0.6	newton1							
2.0.7	newton2							
2.0.8	newton3							
2.0.9	newton4							
2.0.10	newton1							
2.0.11	newton2							
2.0.12	newton3							
2.0.13	newton4							
2.0.14	quotient1							
2.0.15	quotient2							
2.0.16	quotient3							
2.1	quotient4		mul1	add1				
2.2	select fd		mul2	add2				
2.3	round 1							
2.4	round 2							
3	stage M							

Due to the iterative nature of the Newton-Raphson algorithm, a division passes the multiply/divide unit of the FPU several times. All the other instructions pass the units of the execute stage just once. Since divisions complicate the scheduling of the execute stage considerably, they are handled separately.

Execution Scheme

Except on divisions, the execute stage has a latency of 1 to 5 cycles. Thus, the data paths of environment EXenv are divided into 5 substages, numbered by 2.0 to 2.4. The DLX instructions have different latencies and use these stages as indicated in table 9.15.

Every instruction starts its execution in stage 2.0. Except for divisions, the instructions leave stage 2.0 after a single cycle. They may bypass some of the substages:

- Floating point additions, subtractions and multiplications continue in stage 2.1 and are then processed in stages 2.2 to 3.

- Format conversions cvt continue in stages 2.3, 2.4 and 3.

- All the remaining instructions leave the execute after substage 2.0 and continue in the memory stage 3.

After the unpacking, a division is kept in stage 2.0 for another 12 or 16 cycles, depending on the precision. During these cycles, it is processed in the multiply/divide unit, which is assigned to stages 2.1 and 2.2. Once the division left stage 2.0, it passes through stages 2.1 to 4 almost like a multiplication.

An instruction and its precomputed data must pass through the pipeline stages at the same speed. Thus, a mechanism is needed which lets the interrupt causes, the buffered data and the precomputed control signals fall through some stages, as well. The *Result Shift Register RSR* is such a mechanism.

Result Shift Register

An n-bit shift register *RSR* is a kind of queue with f entries $R_1, \ldots R_f$, each of which is n bits wide. In order to account for the different latency, the RSR can be entered at any stage, not just at the first stage. The RSR (figure 9.12) is controlled by

- a distinct clock signal ce_i for each of the f registers R_i,

- a common clear signal clr, and

- a distinct write signal w_i for each of the f registers R_i.

The whole RSR is cleared on an active clear signal. Let T and $T+1$ denote successive clock cycles. For any $1 \leq i \leq f$, an active signal $clr^T = 1$ implies

$$R_i^{T+1} = 0.$$

On an inactive clear signal $clr^T = 0$, the entries of the RSR are shifted one stage ahead, and the input *Din* is written into the stage i with $w_i^T = 1$, provided the corresponding register is clocked:

$$RSR_i^{T+1} = \begin{cases} Din & \text{if } ce_i^T = 1 \wedge w_i^T = 1 \\ RSR_{i-1}^T & \text{if } ce_i^T = 1 \wedge w_i^T = 0 \wedge i > 1 \\ 0^n & \text{if } ce_i^T = 1 \wedge w_i^T = 0 \wedge i = 1. \end{cases}$$

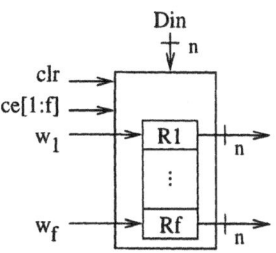

Figure 9.12 Schematics of an n-bit result shift register RSR with f entries

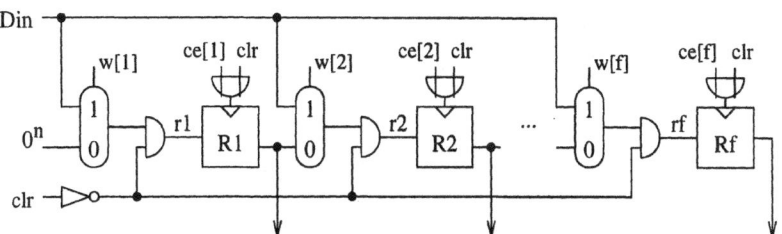

Figure 9.13 Realization of an n-bit result shift register RSR with f entries

The following lemma states that data Din which are clocked into stage i in cycle T are passed down the RSR, provided the clear signal stays inactive, the corresponding registers are clocked at the right time and they are not overwritten.

Let Din enter register R_i at cycle T, i.e., $w_i^T = 1$, $ce_i^T = 1$ and $clr^T = 0$. ◄ Lemma 9.1
For all $t \in \{1, \dots f - i\}$ let

$$w_i^{T+t} = ce_i^{T+t} = 1 \quad and \quad clr^{T+t} = 0,$$

then

$$Din^T = R_i^{T+1} = R_{i+t}^{T+t+1} = R_f^{T+f-i+1}.$$

The result shift register can be operated in a particularly simple way, if all clock enable signals ce_i are tied to a common clock enable signal ce. If the RSR is operated in this way, and if ce-cycles T are considered, then the hypothesis $ce_i^{T+t} = 1$ is automatically fulfilled.

Figure 9.13 depicts an obvious realization of an n-bit RSR with f entries. Its cost can be expressed as

$$C_{RSR}(f,n) = f \cdot (C_{ff}(n) + C_{and}(n) + C_{mux}(n) + C_{or}) + C_{inv}.$$

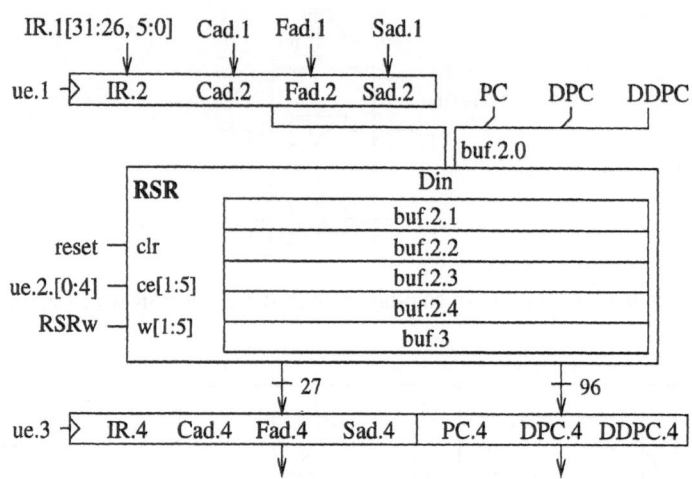

Figure 9.14 Buffer environment of the design with FPU

The outputs R of the RSR have zero delay; the inputs r of its registers are delayed by a multiplexer and an AND gate:

$$D_{RSR}(r) = D_{and} + D_{mux}$$
$$D_{RSR}(R) = 0.$$

The Buffer Environment

The buffer environment (figure 9.14) buffers the opcodes, the PCs, and the destination addresses of the instructions processed in the stages 2.0 to 4.

Due to the FPU, the environment now buffers an additional destination address, namely the address *Fad* for the floating point register file. In order to account for the different latencies of the FPU, a 5-stage RSR is added between the execute substage 2.0 and the write back stage in the obvious way. The RSR is cleared on *reset* and clocked with the update enable signals $ue.2.[0:4]$ provided by the stall engine.

The buffer environment still provides its outputs at zero delay. The cost and cycle time now run at

$$C_{buffers} = C_{RSR}(5,123) + C_{ff}(123) + C_{ff}(27)$$
$$T_{buffers} = \max\{A_{Daddr}, A_{CON}(ue, RSRw) + D_{RSR}(r)\} + \Delta.$$

The Cause Environment

As described in section 5.5.5, the cause environment of figure 9.15 consists of two subcircuits. Circuit *CAcol* collects the interrupt causes, and circuit

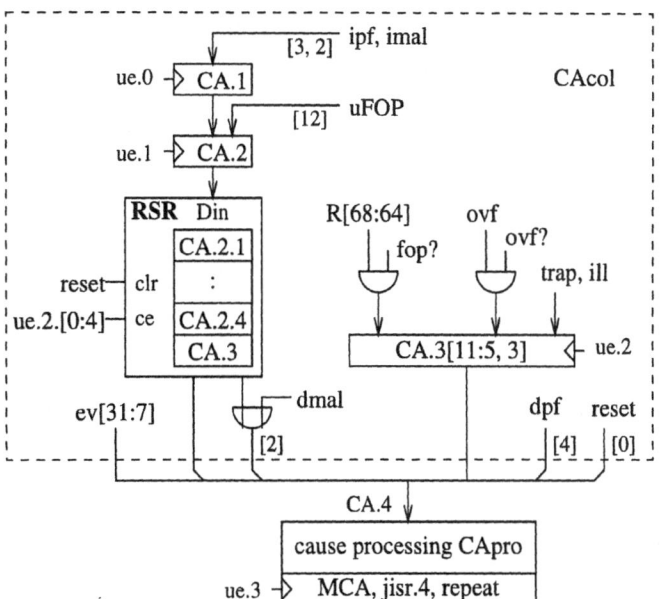

Figure 9.15 Schematics of the cause environment CAenv

CApro processes them. Adding an FPU impacts the cause environment in two ways:

- Due to the different latencies of the execute environment, a 5-stage RSR is added in the collection circuit.

- The floating point unit adds 6 new internal interrupts, which are assigned to the interrupt levels 7 to 12 (table 9.7).

Cause Collection   The interrupt events of the fetch and decode stage are collected in the registers CA.1 and CA.2, as before. These data are then passed through a 5-stage RSR.

An illegal instruction, a trap and a fixed point overflow are still detected in the execute stage and clocked into register CA.3. Since these events cannot be triggered by a legal floating point instruction, the corresponding instruction always passes from stage 2.0 directly to stage 3.

The floating point exceptions are also detected in the execute stage. These events can only be triggered by a floating point instruction which is signaled by $fop? = 1$. Circuit CAcol therefore masks the events with flag $fop?$. The 'unimplemented floating point operation' interrupt $uFOP$

is signaled by the control in stage ID. The remaining floating point events correspond to the IEEE flags provided by the FPU. Environment CAcol gets these flags from the result bus $R[68:64]$.

Let T'_{CAcol} denote the cycle time of circuit CAcol used in the design without FPU. Cost and cycle time of the extended cause collection circuit can then be expressed as

$$
\begin{aligned}
C_{CAcol} &= 6 \cdot C_{and} + C_{or} + 13 \cdot C_{ff} + C_{RSR}(5,3) \\
T_{CAcol} &= \max\{T'_{CAcol}, A_{CON}(uFOP) + \Delta, A_{FPU} + D_{driv} + \Delta\}.
\end{aligned}
$$

Cause Processing Without FPU, the interrupt levels 7 to 12 are assigned to external interrupts which are maskable. Now, these interrupt levels are used for the FPU interrupts. Except for the interrupt $uFOP$, which is assigned to level 12, these interrupts are maskable. Compared to the original circuit of figure 5.10, one just saves the AND gate for masking event CA.4[12]. Thus,

$$
C_{CApro} = C_{and}(25) + C_{tree}(32) \cdot C_{or} + C_{ff}(34) + C_{CAtype}.
$$

9.3 Control of the Prepared Sequential Design

LIKE IN previous DLX designs (chapters 4 and 5), the control of the prepared sequential data paths is derived in two steps. We start out with a sequential control automaton which is then turned into precomputed control.

Figures 9.16 to 9.18 depict the FSD underlying the sequential control automaton. To a large extent, specifying the RTL instructions and active control signals for each state of the FSD is routine. The complete specification can be found in appendix B.

The portion of the FSD modeling the execution of the fixed point instructions remains the same. Thus, it can be copied from the design of chapter 5 (figure 5.12). In section 8.3.6, we have specified an automaton which controls the multiply/divide unit. Depending on the precision, the underlying FSD is unrolled two to three times and is then integrated in the FSD of the sequential DLX control automaton.

Beyond the decode stage, the FSD has an outdegree of one. Thus, the control signals of the execute, memory and write back stage can be precomputed. However, the nonuniform latency of the floating point instructions complicates the precomputed control in two respects:

- The execute stage consists of 5 substages. Fast instructions bypass some of these substages.

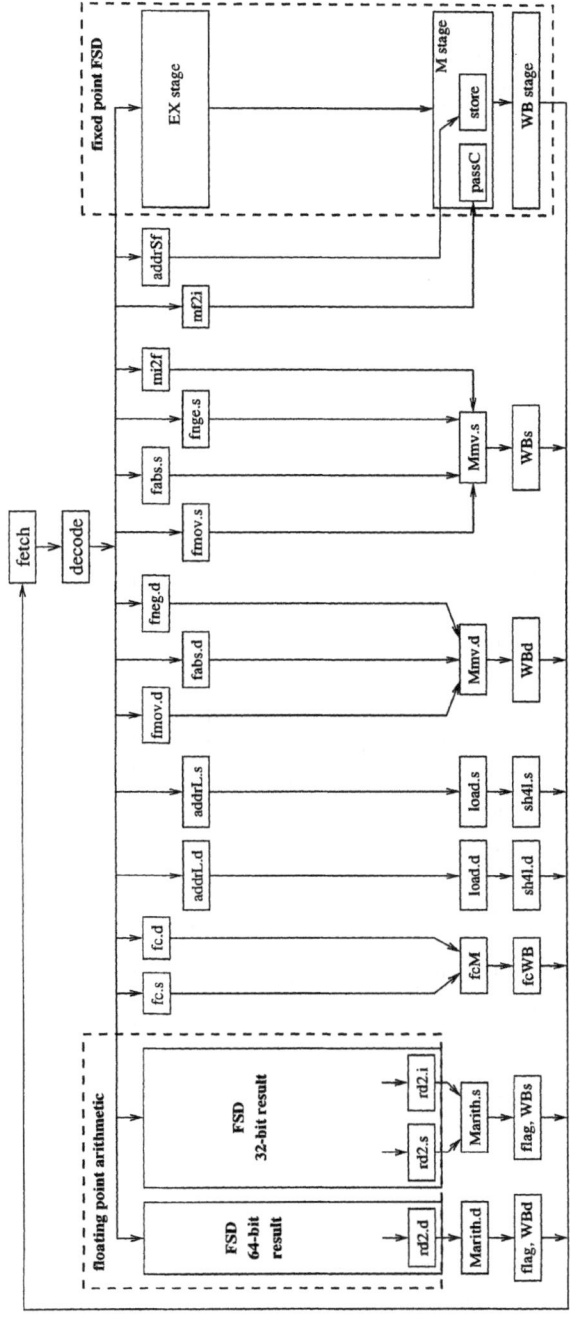

Figure 9.16 FSD underlying the control of the DLX architecture with FPU. The portions modeling the execution of the fixed point instructions and of the floating point arithmetic are depicted in figures 5.12, 9.17 and 9.18.

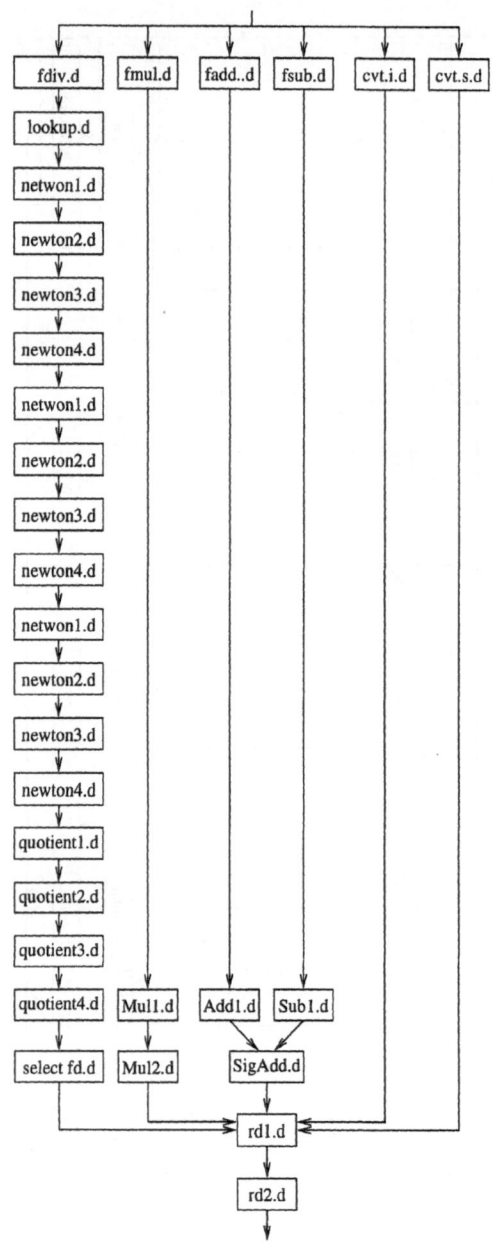

Figure 9.17 FSD modeling the execution of arithmetical floating point operations
with double precision results

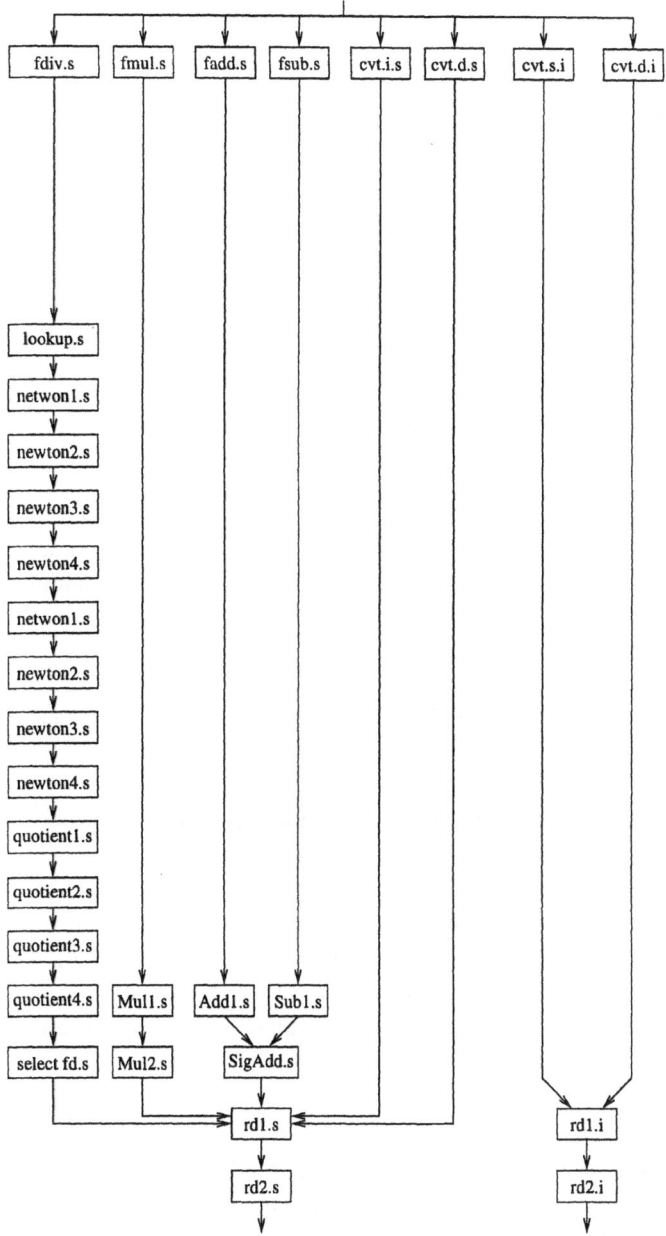

Figure 9.18 FSD modeling the execution of arithmetical floating point operations
with single precision results

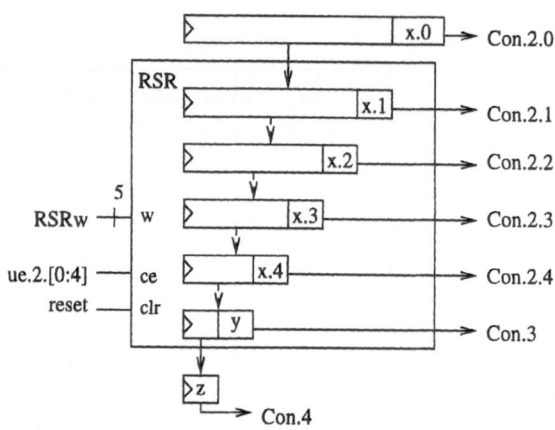

Figure 9.19 Precomputed control of the FDLX design without divider

- Due to the iterative nature of the division algorithm, the execution of divisions is not fully pipelined. A division passes the multiply/divide unit several times. That requires a patch of the precomputed control (section 9.3.2).

Thus, we first construct a precomputed control ignoring divisions.

9.3.1 Precomputed Control without Division

Like in previous designs (e.g., chapter 4), the control signals for the execute, memory and write back stages are precomputed during ID. The signals are then passed down the pipeline together with the instruction. However, fast instructions bypass some of the execute stages. In order to keep up with the instruction, the precomputed control signals are, like the interrupt causes, passed through a 5-stage RSR (figure 9.19).

Controlling the RSR
Depending on the type of the instruction, the latency of the execute stage varies between 1 and 5 cycles. However, the latency is already known in the states of stage 2.0:

- Floating point multiplication, addition and subtraction all have a 5-cycle latency. This is signaled by an active flag $lat5 = 1$. The corresponding states of stage 2.0 are fmul.d, fmul.s, fadd.d, fadd.s, fsub.d and fsub.s.

Table 9.16 Classification of the precomputed control signals

type	x.0	x.1	x.2	x.3	x.4	y	z
number	31	7	3	0	3	3	6

- Format conversions have a 3-cycle latency ($lat3 = 1$). Their execution starts in the states cvt.i.d, cvt.s.d, cvt.i.s, cvt.d.s, cvt.s.i and cvt.d.i.

- The remaining instructions have a single cycle latency, signaled by $lat1 = 1$.

When leaving stage 2.0, an instruction with single cycle latency continues in stage 3. Instructions with a latency of 3 or 5 cycles continue in stage 2.3 or 2.1, respectively. The write signals of the RSRs can therefore be generated as

$$RSRw[1:5] = \begin{cases} 10000 & \text{if} \quad lat5 = 1 \\ 00100 & \text{if} \quad lat3 = 1 \\ 00001 & \text{if} \quad lat1 = 1 \end{cases} = (lat5, 0, lat3, 0, lat1).$$

(9.1)

Structure of the RSR

Without an FPU, there are three types of precomputed control signals:

- type x signals just control the stage EX,

- type y signals control stages EX and M, and

- type z signals control the stages EX, M and WB.

The execute stage now consists of five substages. Thus, the signals of type x are split into five groups $x.0, \ldots, x.4$ with the obvious meaning.

Tables B.12 and B.14 (appendix B) list all the precomputed control signals sorted according to their type. The signals $x.0$ comprise all the x-type signals of the DLX design without FPU. In addition, this type includes the signals specifying the latency of the instruction and the signals controlling the exchange unit FPXtr and the first stage of the FPU.

The stages 2.1 up to 4 are governed by 22 control signals (table 9.16). These signals could be passed through a standard 5-stage RSR which is 22 bits wide. However, signals for type $x.i$ are only needed up to stage 2.i.

We therefore reduce the width of the RSR registers accordingly. The cost of the RSR and of the precomputed control can then be estimated as

$$
\begin{aligned}
C_{ConRSR} &= C_{inv} + 5 * C_{or} + (22 + 15 + 2 \cdot 12 + 9) \cdot (C_{and} + C_{mux} + C_{ff}) \\
C_{preCon} &= C_{ConRSR} + C_{ff}(53) + C_{ff}(6).
\end{aligned}
$$

Thus, the RSR only buffers a total of 70 bits instead of 110 bits. Compared to a standard 22-bit RSR, that cuts the cost by one third.

Stall Engine

The stages k of the pipeline are ordered lexicographically, i.e.,

$$
1 < 2.0 < 2.1 < 2.2 < 2.3 < 2.4 < 3.
$$

Except for the execute stage, the scheduling functions of the designs DLX_Σ and $FDLX_\Sigma$ are alike. One cycle after reset, the execution starts in the write back stage with a jump to the ISR. For $k \in \{0,1,3\}$, instruction I_i passes from stage k to $k+1$:

$$
I_\Sigma(k,T) = i \quad \rightarrow \quad I_\Sigma(k+1,T+1) = i.
$$

Once I_i reaches stage $k = 4$, the execution continues in stage 0 with the next instruction:

$$
I_\Sigma(4,T) = i \quad \rightarrow \quad I_\Sigma(0,T+1) = i+1.
$$

In the $FDLX_\Sigma$ design, the execute stage comprises 5 substages. Fast instructions bypass some of these substages, that complicates the scheduling. For any execute stage 2.k with $k > 0$, the instruction is just passed to the next stage, thus

$$
I_\Sigma(2.k,T) = i \quad \rightarrow \quad i = \begin{cases} I_\Sigma(3,T+1) & \text{if} \quad k = 4 \\ I_\Sigma(2.(k+1),T+1) & \text{if} \quad k \leq 3. \end{cases}
$$

Whereas in case of stage $k = 2.0$, it depends on the latency of instruction I_i whether the execution continues in stage 2.1, 2.3 or 3:

$$
I_\Sigma(2.0,T) = i \quad \rightarrow \quad i = \begin{cases} I_\Sigma(3,T+1) & \text{if} \quad lat1 = 1 \\ I_\Sigma(2.3,T+1) & \text{if} \quad lat3 = 1 \\ I_\Sigma(2.1,T+1) & \text{if} \quad lat5 = 1. \end{cases}
$$

The stall engine of figure 9.20 implements the new schedule in an obvious way. As in the sequential design of section 5.5.6, there is one central clock CE for the whole $FDLX_\Sigma$ design. During reset, all the update enable flags $ue.k$ are inactive, and the full vector is initialized. In order to let an

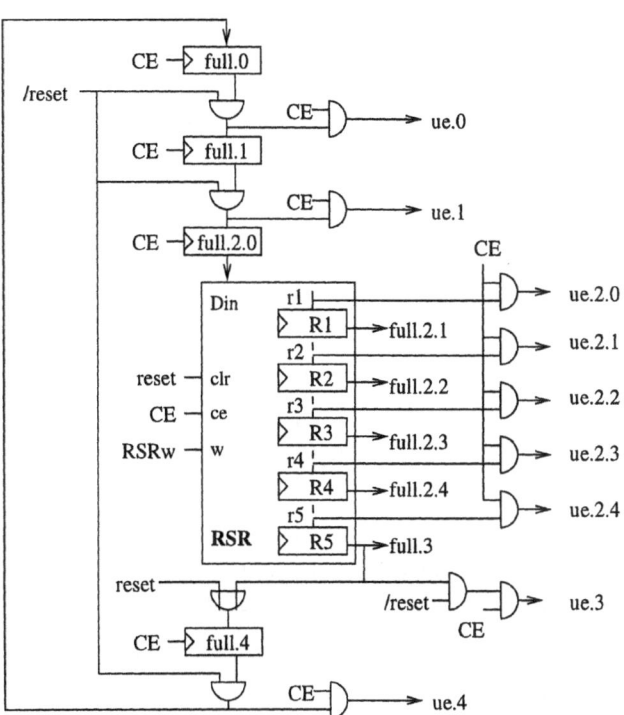

Figure 9.20 Stall engine of the $FDLX_\Sigma$ design without support for divisions

instruction bypass some execute stages, the full flags of stages 2.1 to 2.4 and of the memory stage 3 are held in an RSR. This RSR is, like any other RSR of the sequential DLX design, controlled by the write signals $RSRw$ of equation 9.1. The RSR of the stall engine is operated in a particularly simple way, because all its clock enable signals are all tied to the common clock enable CE.

Figure 9.21 illustrates how the precomputed control, the stall engine and the data paths of the execute environment fit together. As before, the precomputed control provides the clock request signals RCe which are combined (AND) with the appropriate update enable flags to obtain to the actual clock signal RCe'.

However, special attention must be payed to the clock signals of the registers MDRw and Ffl.3. According to the specification in appendix B, these two registers are clocked simultaneously. They either get their data input from stage 2.0 or from stage 2.4, depending on the latency of the instruction. Thus, the clock signal is obtained as

$$MDRwce' = ue.2.4 \land (MDRwce.2.0 \land lat1.2.0 \lor MDRwce.2.4).$$

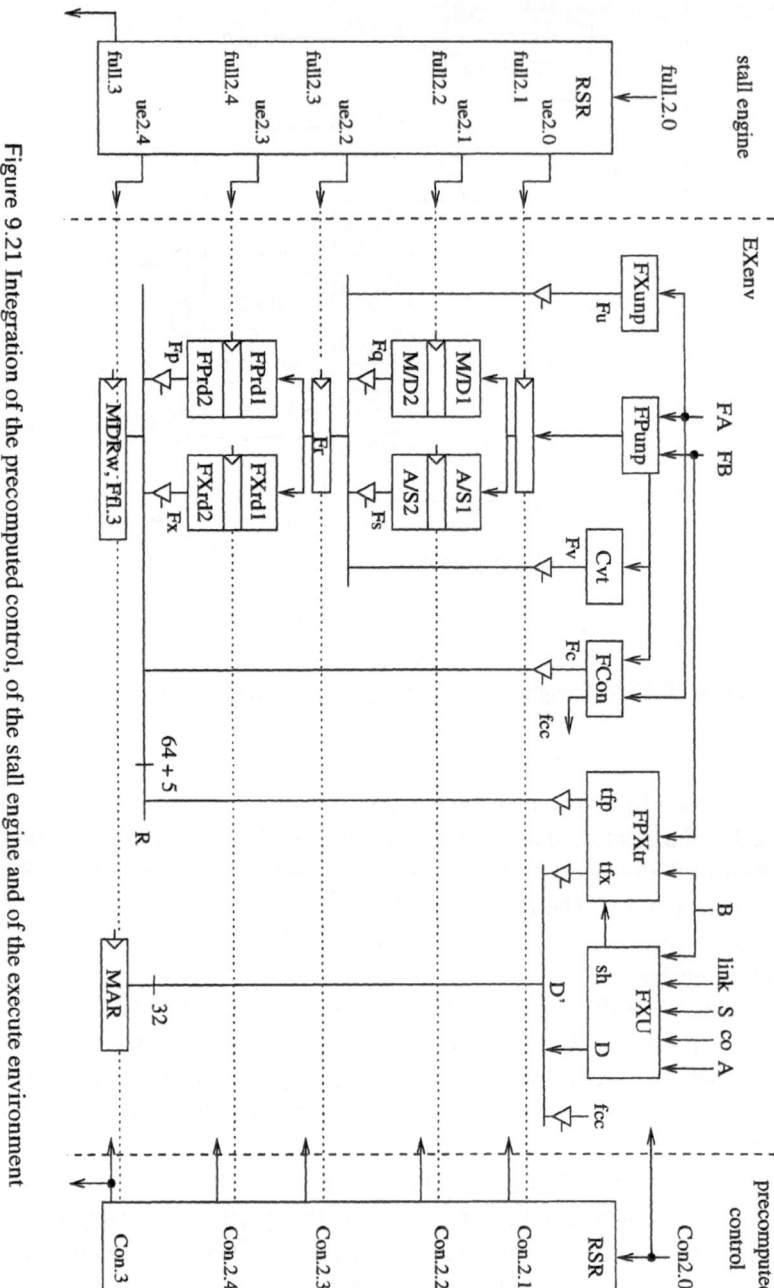

Figure 9.21 Integration of the precomputed control, of the stall engine and of the execute environment

The remaining registers of the FDLX data paths receive their data inputs just from one stage. Register MAR, for example, is only updated by instructions with an 1-cycle execute latency; therefore

$$MARce' = ue.2.4 \wedge MARce.2.0.$$

Correctness of the Design

Along the lines of section 3.4 it can be shown that this $FDLX_\Sigma$ design interprets the extended DLX instruction set of section 9.1 with delayed PC semantics but without floating point divisions. The crucial part is to show that the instruction and its data pass through the pipeline stages at the same speed. More formally:

Let $I_\Sigma(2.0, T) = i$, and let X be a register whose content is passed through ◀ Lemma 9.2
one of the RSRs, i.e., $X \in \{IR, Cad, Fad, Sad, PC, DPC, CA[3:2]\}$. For any stage $k \in \{2.1, \ldots, 3\}$ with $I_\Sigma(k, T') = i$, we have

$$X.2.0^T = X.k^{T'} \quad and \quad full.k^{T'} = 1.$$

This follows from the definition of the write signals $RSRw$ (equation 9.1) and from lemma 9.1. Observe that the hypothesis of lemma 9.1 about the clock enable signals is trivially fulfilled for the RSR in the stall engine. The construction of the stall engine ensures, that the hypothesis about the clock enable signals is also fulfilled for the remaining RSRs in the data paths and in the control.

Outside the stall engine we update the registers of result shift registers with separate update enable signals. Thus, during the sequential execution of a single instruction it is still the case, that no stage $k \in \{0, 1, 3, 4\}$ or substage $2.j$ is clocked twice. Not all instructions enter all substages, but *the dateline lemma 5.9 stays literally the same.*

9.3.2 Supporting Divisions

The execution of a division takes 17 or 21 cycles, depending on the precision. During the unpacking and the four final cycles, a division is processed like any other arithmetical floating point operation. However, in the remaining 12 to 16 cycles, it iterates in circuit SIGFMD of the multiply/divide unit. These steps are numbered with $2.0.1, \ldots, 2.0.16$ (table 9.15). We use the following strategy for handling divisions:

- In the first cycle (stage 2.0), the operands of the division are unpacked. This is governed by the standard precomputed control.

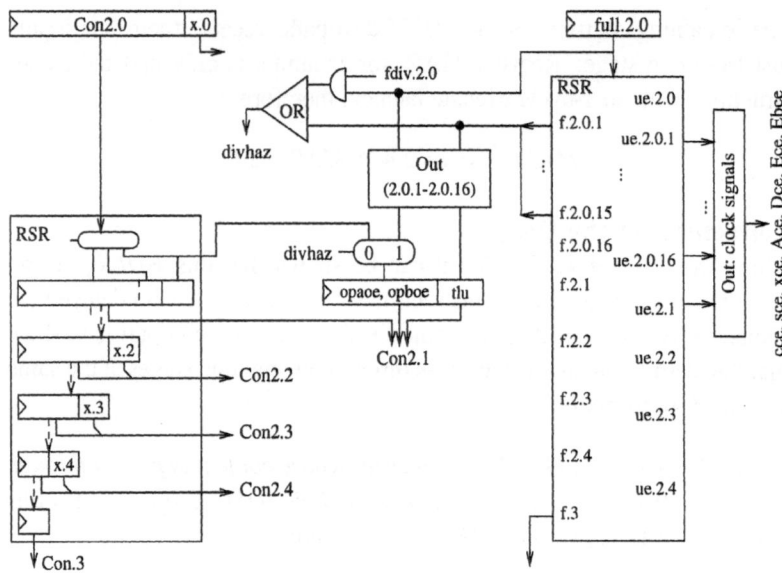

Figure 9.22 Main control for the stages 2.0 to 3 of the full $FDLX_\Sigma$ design

- During the steps lookup to quotient3, the division iterates in the multiply/divide unit. The execution is controlled by the FSD specified in section 8.3.6 (figure 8.22). The data, the cause bits and the precomputed control signals of the division are frozen in the RSRs of stage 2.0.

- In the final four steps (quotient4, select fd, round1, round2), the division passes through the stages 2.1, ..., 2.4. This is again controlled by the precomputed control.

Thus, the main control (figure 9.22) of the floating point DLX design consists of the stall engine, the precomputed control with its 5-stage RSR, and the 'division automaton'. Except for circuit SIGFMD, the data paths are governed by the precomputed control, whereas the stall engine controls the update of the registers and RAMs.

Precomputed Control

The precomputed control of section 9.3.1 is just extended by two signals *lat*21 and *lat*17 of type *x*.0. These signals indicate that the instruction has a latency of 21 or 17 cycles, respectively. They correspond to the states fdiv.d and fdiv.s of the FSD of figure 9.16.

Extended Stall Engine

In order to account for a double precision division, which has a 21-cycle execute latency, the RSR of the stall engine is extended to length 21. Except for the longer RSR, the stall engine remains unchanged. The RSR provides the full flags $full.k$ and the update enable flags $ue.k$ for the stages $k \in \{2.0.1, \ldots, 2.0.16, 2.1, \ldots, 2.4, 3\}$. These 21 full bits code the state of the division FSD in unary as specified in table 9.15.

An instruction, depending on its execute latency, enters the RSR of the stall engine either in stage 2.0.1, 2.0.5, 2.1, 2.3 or 3. The write signals of the RSR are therefore generated as

$$Stallw[1:21] = (lat21, 0^3, lat17, 0^{11}, lat5, 0, lat3, 0, lat1). \quad (9.2)$$

For the scheduling function I_Σ, this implies

$$I_\Sigma(2.0, T) = i \quad \rightarrow \quad i = \begin{cases} I_\Sigma(3, T+1) & \text{if } lat1 = 1 \\ I_\Sigma(2.3, T+1) & \text{if } lat3 = 1 \\ I_\Sigma(2.1, T+1) & \text{if } lat5 = 1 \\ I_\Sigma(2.0.5, T+1) & \text{if } lat17 = 1 \\ I_\Sigma(2.0.1, T+1) & \text{if } lat21 = 1, \end{cases}$$

and for every substage $2.0.j$ with $j \geq 1$ we have

$$I_\Sigma(2.0.j, T) = i \quad \rightarrow \quad i = \begin{cases} I_\Sigma(2.0.(j+1), T+1) & \text{if } 0 < j < 16 \\ I_\Sigma(2.1, T+1) & \text{if } j = 16. \end{cases}$$

In the remaining pipeline stages, the division is processed like any instruction with a 5-cycle execute latency. Thus, the scheduling function requires no further modification.

Unlike the stall engine, the cause environment, the buffer environment and the precomputed control still use a 5-stage RSR. Up to step 2.0.16, a division is frozen in stage 2.0 and then enters the first stage of these RSRs. Thus, the write signals $RSRw[1:5]$ of the RSRs in the data paths and in the precomputed control are generated as

$$\begin{aligned} RSRw[1] &= lat5 \vee (full.2.0.16 \wedge fdiv.2.0) \\ RSRw[3] &= lat3 \\ RSRw[5] &= lat1 \\ RSRw[2] &= RSRw[4] = 0. \end{aligned}$$

Controlling Circuit SIGFMD

Clock Request Signals   The registers A, E, Eb, Da, Db and x of circuit SIGFMD (figure 8.20) are only used by divisions. Thus, they are updated solely under the control of the division automaton.

Table 9.17 Clock request signals of the multiply/divide unit

clocks	stages of the stall engine
xce	2.0.1, 2.0.5, 2.0.9, 2.0.13
sce, cce	2.0.2, 2.0.4, 2.0.6, 2.0.8, 2.0.10, 2.0.12, 2.0.14, 2.0.16, 2.1
Ace	2.0.3, 2.0.7, 2.0.11
Dce, Ece	2.0.15
Ebce	2.1

The output registers s and c of the multiplication tree are also used by multiplications (stage 2.1). A division uses these registers up to stage 2.1. Thus, the registers s and c can be updated at the end of step 2.1 without any harm, even in case of a division.

Table 9.17 lists for each register the stages in which its clock signal must be active. A particular clock request signal is then obtained by ORing the update enable flags of the listed stages, e.g.:

$$cce = ue.2.0.2 \lor ue.2.0.4 \lor ue.2.0.6 \lor ue.2.0.8 \lor ue.2.0.10$$
$$\lor ue.2.0.12 \lor ue.2.0.14 \lor ue.2.0.16 \lor ue.2.1.$$

Control Signals The multiply/divide unit is governed by the following signals

- flag db which signals a double precision operation,

- flag $fdiv$ which distinguishes between division and multiplication

- flag tlu which activates a table lookup, and

- the enable signals for the operand busses opa and opb

$$opaoe[3:0] = (faadoe, Eadoe, Aadoe, xadoe)$$
$$opboe[1:0] = (fbbdoe, xbdoe).$$

The signals $fdiv$ and db are fixed for the whole execution of an instruction. Therefore, they can directly be taken from the RSR of the precomputed control.

The flag tlu selects the input of register x. Since this register is only used by divisions, the flag tlu has no impact on a multiplication or addition. Thus, flag tlu is directly provided by the division automaton.

The operand busses *opa* and *opb* are controlled by both, the precomputed control and the division automaton. Both control units precompute their control signals. The flag *divhaz* selects between the two sets of control signals before they are clocked into the register *Con.2.1*. Let $opaoe'$ and $opboe'$ denote the set of enable signals generated by the division automaton; this set is selected on $divhaz = 1$. The operand busses are then controlled by

$$(opaoe, opboe) := \begin{cases} (opaoe.2.0, opboe.2.0) & \text{if} \quad divhaz = 0 \\ (opaoe', opboe') & \text{if} \quad divhaz = 1. \end{cases}$$

An active signal *divhaz* grants the division automaton access to the operand busses during stages 2.0.1 to 2.0.16. Since the enable signals are precomputed, signal *divhaz* must also be given one cycle ahead:

$$divhaz = \bigvee_{k=1}^{15} full.2.0.k \vee (full.2.0 \wedge fdiv.2.0).$$

The Division Automaton controls the multiply/divide unit according to the FSD of figure 8.22. The full bits provided by the RSR of the stall engine codes the states of the division FSD in unary. Based on these flags, the automaton precomputes the signal *tlu* and the enable signals for the operand busses *opa* and *opb*. For each of these signals, table 9.18 lists the states in which the signal is active and the index of the preceding state. Like in a standard Moore automaton (section 2.6), each control signal is generated by an OR tree which combines the corresponding full flags, e.g.:

$$xbdoe' = \bigvee_{k \in \{3,7,11,13\}} full.2.0.k$$

The 5 clock request signals and the 7 enable signals together have an accumulated frequency of $\nu_{sum} = 30$ and a maximal frequency of $\nu_{max} = 9$. Thus, the control for circuit SIGFMD requires the following cost and cycle time:

$$C_{DivCon} = C_{ff}(7) + C_{mux}(6) + C_{and} + C_{ORtree}(16) + C_{or} \cdot (\nu_{sum} - 11)$$
$$T_{DivCon} = D_{and} + D_{ORtree}(16) + D_{mux} + \Delta.$$

The division automaton delays the clock signals of circuit SIGFMD by the following amount

$$D_{DivCon}(ce) = D_{ORtree}(\nu_{max}).$$

Table 9.18 Control signals for the steps 2.0.1 to 2.0.16 of a division.

FSD state	stall engine previous stage	active signals
lookup	2.0.0	tlu, fbbdoe
newton1	2.0.1, 2.0.5, 2.0.9	xadoe, fbbdoe
newton3	2.0.3, 2.0.7, 2.0.11	Aadoe, xbdoe
quotient1	2.0.13	faadoe, xbdoe
quotient2	2.0.14	faadoe, fbbdoe
quotient3	2.0.15	Eadoe, fbbdoe

Dateline Lemma

With respect to the dateline lemma we are facing two additional problems:

- Some registers are updated by more than one stage. Registers c and s of the circuit SigfMD for instance are updated after stage 2.0.16 during divisions and after stage 2.1 during multiplications. Thus, classifying the registers by *the* stage, which updates them, is not possible any more.

- During the iterations of the division algorithm, some registers are clocked several times. Thus, the dateline lemma cannot possibly hold while the registers have intermediate values.

We coarsely classy the stages into two classes. The class of stages PP which are operated in a pipelined fashion and the class of stages SQ which are operated in a sequential manner:

$$PP = \{0, 1, 2.0, 2.1, \ldots, 2.4, 3, 4\}$$
$$SQ = \{2.0.x \mid 1 \leq x \leq 16\}$$

Different stages in PP update different registers. Thus, for every register R we have $R \in out(t)$ for at most one $t \in PP$, and every stage in PP is updated at most once during the sequential execution of an instruction. The dateline lemma still holds while instructions are in stages PP and for registers R which are output registers of stages PP.

Lemma 9.3 ▶ *Let $k, t \in PP$ and let $I_{\Sigma(k,T)} = i$. For every register and memory cell $R \in out(t)$ the statements of lemma 5.9 apply.*

The value of the output registers of stage 2.0.16 at the end of the iterations for a division operation depend only on the value of the output registers of stage 2.0 before the iterations:

Let I_i be a division operation, let ◀ Lemma 9.4

$$I_\Sigma(2.0, U') = I_\Sigma(2.1, T') = i,$$

and let V be an output register of stage 2.0.16. Then $V^{T'}$ depends only on the values $Q^{U'+1}$ of the output registers Q of stage 2.0 which were updated after cycle U'.

9.4 Pipelined DLX Design with FPU

A S BEFORE, transforming the prepared sequential design into a pipelined design requires extensive forwarding and interlock hardware and modifications in the PC environment and in the stall engine. Figure 9.23 depicts the data paths of the pipelined design $FDLX_\Pi$. Compared to the sequential data paths, its top level schematics just got extended by the forwarding hardware:

$$
\begin{aligned}
C_{DP} = {} & C_{IMenv} + C_{PCenv} + C_{IRenv} + C_{Daddr} + C_{FPemb} + C_{EXenv} \\
& + C_{DMenv} + C_{SH4Lenv} + C_{RFenv} + C_{CAenv} + C_{buffer} \\
& + 5 \cdot C_{ff}(32) + 5 \cdot C_{ff}(64) + 2 \cdot C_{ff}(5) + C_{FORW}.
\end{aligned}
$$

9.4.1 PC Environment

According to section 5.6.1, switching from the prepared sequential design to the pipelined design has only a minor impact on the PC environment. The instruction memory IM is addressed by the input *dpc* of register DPC and not by its output. The circuit *nextPC* which computes the new values of the program counters however remains unchanged.

On the other hand, adding support for floating point impacts the glue logic *PCglue* but not the data paths of environment *PCenv*. Thus, the $FDLX_\Pi$ design uses the PC environment of the pipelined DLX_Π design (figure 5.13) but with the glue logic of the sequential $FDLX_\Sigma$ design.

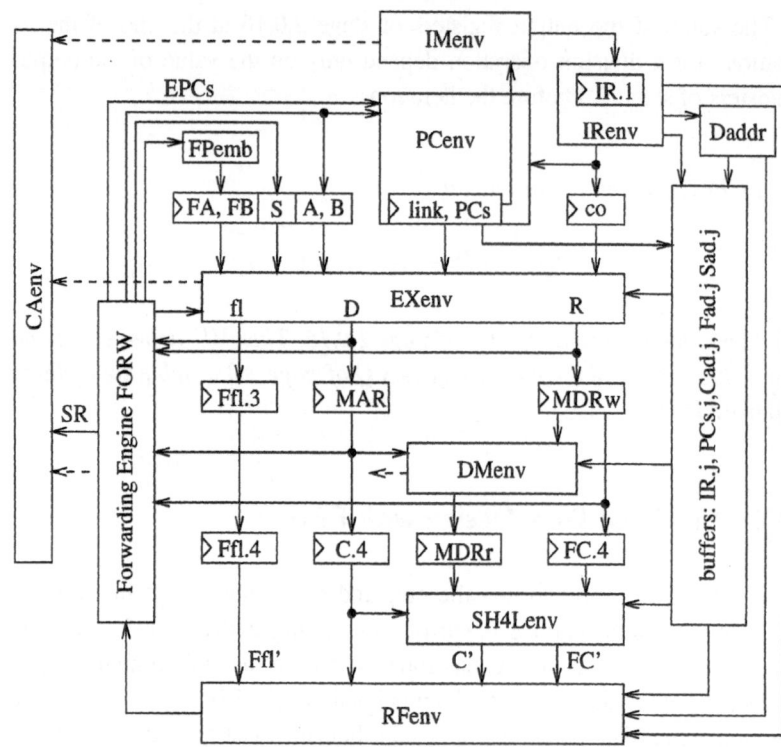

Figure 9.23 Data paths of the pipelined FDLX design with result forwarding

9.4.2 Forwarding and Interlocking

Like in the pipelined designs DLX_π and DLX_Π, the register files GPR, SPR and FPR are updated in the write back stage. Since they are read by earlier stages, the pipelined floating point design $FDLX_\Pi$ also requires result forwarding and interlocking. For the largest part, the extension of the forwarding and interlock engine is straightforward, but there are two notable complications:

- The execute stage has a variable depth, which depending on the instruction varies between one and five stages. Thus, the forwarding and interlock engine has to inspect up to four additional stages.

- Since the floating point operands and results have single or double precision, a 64-bit register of the FPR register file either serves as one double precision register or as two single precision registers. The forwarding hardware has to account for this address aliasing.

General Purpose Registers

The move instruction mf2i is the only floating point instruction which updates the fixed point register file GPR. The move mf2i is processed in the exchange unit FPXtr, which has a single cycle latency like the fixed point unit.

Thus, any instruction which updates the GPR enters the execute stage in stage 2.0 and then directly proceeds to the memory stage 3. Since the additional stages 2.1 to 2.4 never provide a fixed point result, the operands A and B can still be forwarded by circuit $Forw(3)$ of figure 4.16. However, the extended instruction set has an impact on the computation of the valid flags $v[4:2]$ and of the data hazard flag.

Valid Flags The flag $v[j]$ indicates that the result to be written into the GPR register file is already available in the circuitry of stage j, given that the instruction updates the GPR at all. The result of the new move instruction mf2i is already valid after stage 2.0 and can always be forwarded. Thus, the valid flags of instruction I_i are generated as before:

$$v[4] = 1; \quad v[3] = v[2] = /Dmr.$$

Data Hazard Detection The flags $dhazA$ and $dhazB$ signal that the operand specified by the instruction bits $RS1$ and $RS2$ cause a data hazard, i.e., that the forwarding engine cannot deliver the requested operands on time. These flags are generated as before.

In the fixed point DLX design, every instruction I is checked for a data hazard even if I requires no fixed point operands:

$$dhazFX = dhazA \lor dhazB$$

This can cause unnecessary stalls. However, since in the fixed point design almost every instruction requires at least one register operand, there is virtually no performance degradation.

In the FDLX design, this is no longer the case. Except for the move mi2f, the floating point instructions have no fixed point operands and should not signal a fixed point data hazard $dhazFX$. The flags opA and opB therefore indicate whether an instruction requires the fixed point operands A and B. The FDLX design uses these flags to enable the data hazard check

$$dhazFX = (dhazA \land opA) \lor (dhazB \land opB).$$

The data hazard signals $dhazA$ and $dhazB$ are generated along the same lines. Thus, the cost and delay of signal $dhazFX$ can be expressed as

$$
\begin{aligned}
C_{dhazFX} &= 2 \cdot C_{dhazA} + 2 \cdot C_{and} + C_{or} \\
A_{dhazFX} &= A_{dhazA} + D_{and} + D_{or}.
\end{aligned}
$$

Special Purpose Registers

Due to the FPU, the special purpose registers SPR are updated in five situations:

1. All special purpose registers are updated by *JISR*. As in the DLX_Π design, there is no need to forward these values. All instructions which could use forwarded versions of values forced into SPR by *JISR* get evicted from the pipe by the very same occurrence of *JISR*.

2. On a movi2s instruction, value $C.4$ is written into register $SPR[Sad]$.

3. Register *SR* is updated by rfe. In stages 2 to 4, this update is implemented like a regular write into SPR with address $Sad = 0$.

4. Register *FCC* is updated by fc. In stages 2 to 4, this update is implemented like a regular write into SPR with address $Sad = 8$.

5. On an arithmetical floating point instruction, which is signaled by $fop = 1$, the floating point exception flags Ffl.4 are ORed into the Register *IEEEf*.

In case 5, which only applies to register IEEEf, the result is passed down the pipeline in the Ffl.k registers. During write back, the flags Ffl.4 are then ORed to the old value of IEEEf. In the uninterrupted execution of I_i, we have

$$IEEEf_i = IEEEf_{i-1} \lor Ffl_i.$$

That complicates the result forwarding considerably (see exercise 9.9.1). In order to keep the design simple, we omit the forwarding of the flags Ffl. Instead, we generate in appropriate situations a data hazard signal $dhaz(IEEEf)$ and stall the instruction decode until the hazard is resolved.

In case 1, the forwarding does not matter. In the remaining cases 2 to 4, the instruction has a 1-cycle latency. Thus, one only needs to forward data from the stages 2.0, 3 and 4, and the result is already available in stage 2.0. With respect to the update of the SPR register file, the instructions movs2i, rfe and fc are treated alike. Thus, the SPR operands can be forwarded by the standard *SFor* circuit used in the DLX_Π design, and except for an operand IEEEf, no additional data hazard is introduced.

In the FDLX design, data from the SPR registers are used in the following seven places, each of which is treated separately:

1. on a movs2i instruction, register $SPR[Sas]$ is read into S during decode,

2. on an rfe instruction, the two exception PCs are read during decode,

3. the cause environment reads the interrupt masks SR in the memory stage,

4. the rounders of the FPU read SR in the execute stage 2.3,

5. the rounding mode RM is read in stage 2.2 by the floating point adder and in stage 2.3 by the two rounders,

6. on a floating point branch, the condition flag FCC is read during decode,

7. and on an arithmetical floating point operation ($fop = 1$), the IEEE exception flags IEEEf are read during write back.

Forwarding of the Exception PCs   Since the new floating point instructions do not access the two exceptions PCs, the forwarding hardware of EPC and EDPC remains unchanged. EPC is forwarded by the circuit $SFor(3)$ depicted in figure 5.17. The forwarding of EDPC is still omitted, and the data hazard signal $dhaz(EDPC)$ is generated as before.

Forwarding of Operand S   On a special move instruction movs2i, the operand S is fetched during decode. Like in the DLX_Π design, operand S is forwarded by the circuit $SFor(3)$ depicted in figure 5.15. However, in case of an operand IEEEf, one has to check for a data hazard due to the update of an arithmetical floating point instruction (case 5). Such a hazard occurs if

- the decode stage processes a movs2i instruction ($ms2i.1 = 1$),

- the source address $Sas.1$ equals 7,

- a stage $k \geq 2.0$ processes an arithmetical FPU instruction (i.e., $full.k = fop.k = 1$), and

- no stage j between 1 and k processes a movi2s which updates IEEEf (i.e., $hit.j = 0$).

If a special move is in stage 2.0, the remaining execute stages must be empty, due to its single cycle execute latency. Thus,

$$
\begin{aligned}
dhaz(IEEEf) = \ & ms2i.1 \wedge ((\langle Sas.1 \rangle = 7) \wedge \\
& \Big(\bigvee_{2.0 \leq k \leq 2.4} (fop.k \wedge full.k) \vee (\overline{hit.2} \wedge fop.3 \wedge full.3) \\
& \vee ((hit.2 \text{ NOR } hit.3) \wedge fop.4 \wedge full.4) \Big).
\end{aligned}
$$

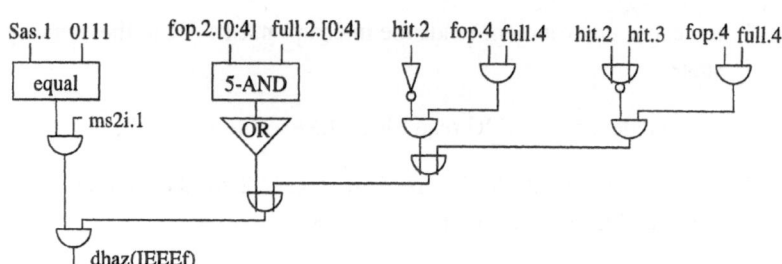

Figure 9.24 Computation of data hazard signal $dhaz(IEEEf)$.

The circuit of figure 9.24 generates the flag in the obvious way. The hit signals are provided by circuit $SFor(3)$. Thus,

$$C_{dhaz}(IEEEf) = C_{EQ}(4) + C_{ORtree}(5) + 11 \cdot C_{and} + 2 \cdot C_{or} + C_{nor} + C_{inv}$$
$$D_{dhaz}(IEEEf) = \max\{D_{EQ}(4), D_{or} + D_{ORtree}(5),$$
$$D_{Sfor}(hit) + 2 \cdot C_{or} + C_{nor}\} + 2 \cdot D_{and}.$$

Forwarding of Register IEEEf   The arithmetical floating point instructions generate IEEE exception flags Ffl which are accumulated in register IEEEf. Such an instruction I_i updates register IEEEf by a read-modify-write access; these special read and write accesses are performed during write. For the uninterrupted execution of I_i with $I_\Pi(4, T) = i$ we have

$$IEEEf_\Pi^{T+1} = IEEEf_{i-1} \vee Ffl.4_\Pi^T.$$

Since the instructions are processed in program order,

$$IEEEf^T = IEEEf_{i-1},$$

and no result forwarding is required.

Forwarding of Register FCC   On a floating point branch, the condition flag FCC is requested by the PC environment during decode. The flag FCC is updated by a special move movi2s and by a floating point compare instruction. Both instructions have a single cycle execute latency and bypass the substages 2.1 to 2.4. Thus, the value of FCC can be forwarded by the 3-stage forwarding circuit $SFor$ of figure 5.16 with $Din = SPR[8] = FCC$ and $ad = 1000$.

The special move and the test instruction update register FCC via the standard write port. Since there result is already available in stage 2.0, the forwarding is always possible and register FCC never causes a data hazard.

Forwarding of Register RM The rounding mode RM is needed in stage 2.2 by the floating point adder and in stage 2.4 by the rounders FPRND and FXRND. Register RM can only be updated by a special move movi2s which has a single cycle execute latency. Since the result of the special move is already valid in stage 2.0, forwarding is always possible; no data hazard is introduced.

A standard 2-stage forwarding circuit $SFor(2)$ can forward RM from stages 3 and 4 to the execute stages. However, the following lemma states that the forwarding of register RM can be omitted if the instructions always remain in program order. The scheduler of the pipelined design $FDLX_\Pi$ ensures such an in-order execution (section 9.4.3). Thus, the SPR register file can directly provide the rounding mode RM to the adder and the rounders at zero delay.

Let instruction I_i read the rounding mode RM in stage 2.2 or 2.4. Furthermore, let I_j be an instruction preceding I_i which updates register RM. Assuming that the instructions pass the pipeline stages strictly in program order, I_j updates register RM before I_i reads RM. ◀ Lemma 9.5

Let the execution of instruction I_i be started in cycle T, PROOF

$$I_\Pi(2.0, T) = i.$$

1) Any instruction which passes the rounder FPRND or FXRND has an execute latency of at least 3 cycles. Thus, the rounder of stage 2.4 processes I_i in cycle $T + 2$, at the earliest:

$$I_\Pi(2.4, T') = i \quad \text{with} \quad T' \geq T + 2.$$

2) If I_i is a floating point addition or subtraction, it already reads the rounding mode RM in stage 2.2. Instruction I_i has a 5-cycle execute latency, thus

$$i = I_\Pi(2.1, T + 1) = I_\Pi(2.2, T + 2).$$

In either case, I_i reads the rounding mode in cycle $T + 2$ at the earliest.

The rounding mode RM is only updated by special moves movi2s which have a single cycle execute latency. For such a move instruction I_j this implies

$$j = I_\Pi(2.0, t) = I_\Pi(3, t + 1) = I_\Pi(4, t + 2).$$

Since the instructions remain in program order, I_j must pass stage 2.0 before instruction I_i. Thus,

$$t < T \quad \leftrightarrow \quad t + 2 < T + 2,$$

and I_j updates register RM at least one cycle before I_i reads RM. QED

Forwarding of Register SR   The status register SR is updated by special moves and by rfe instructions. In either case, register SR is updated by a regular write to SPR with address 0. Since the result is already available in stage 2.0, the forwarding of SR is always feasible.

The cause environment CAenv uses SR for masking the interrupt events in stage 3. As before, a 1-stage forwarding circuit $SFor(1)$ provides the masks SR to the cause environment.

In the FDLX design, register SR also holds the masks for the IEEE floating point exceptions. The rounders FPRND and FXRND require these mask bits during stage 2.3. In analogy to lemma 9.5, one shows

Lemma 9.6 ▶ *Let the instructions pass the pipeline of the $FDLX_\Pi$ design strictly in program order. Let instruction I_i read the status register SR in stage 2.3 during cycle T. Any preceding rfe or movi2s instruction I_j then updates register SR in cycle T or earlier.*

Thus, it suffices to forward the masks SR from the write back stage to the rounders. This forwarding can be performed by the circuit $SFor(1)$ which already provides SR to the cause environment. Like in the DLX design, the masks SR never cause a data hazard.

Forwarding Circuit SFOR   Altogether, the forwarding of the SPR operands can be performed by one circuit $SFor(1)$ for operand SR and by three circuits $SFor(3)$ for the operands EPC, S and FCC. Thus, the forwarding engine $SFOR$ has the cost

$$C_{SFOR} = 3 \cdot C_{SFor}(3) + C_{SFor}(1).$$

The operands S, EPC and SR still have the same accumulated delay as in the DLX_Π design. The accumulated delay of the FCC flag equals that of the S operand

$$A_{SFOR}(FCC) = A_{SFOR}(S).$$

The remaining SPR operands are provided at zero delay.

The flag $dhazS$ signals that a special purpose register causes a data hazard. EDPC and IEEEf are the only SPR register which can cause such a data hazard. Thus, signal $dhazS$ can be obtained as

$$dhazS = dhaz(IEEEf) \vee dhaz(EDPC).$$

The selection of the source address Sas and the forwarding are both governed by control signals of stage ID, therefore

$$
\begin{aligned}
C_{dhazS} &= C_{dhaz}(IEEEf) + C_{dhaz}(EDPC) + C_{or} \\
A_{dhazS} &= A_{CON}(csID) + D_{Daddr} \\
&\quad + \max\{D_{dhaz}(IEEEf), D_{dhaz}(EDPC)\} + D_{or}.
\end{aligned}
$$

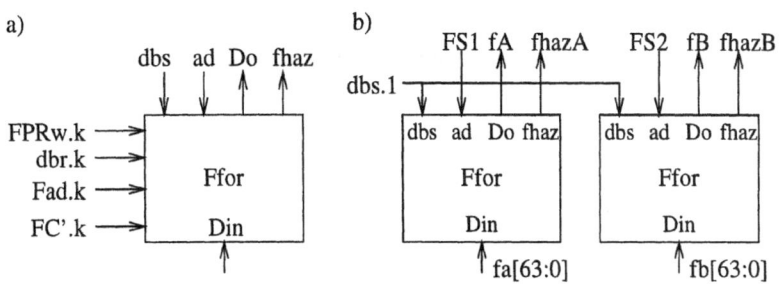

Figure 9.25 Block diagrams of circuit $Ffor$ and forwarding engine $FFOR$

Floating Point Registers

While an instruction (division) is processed in the stages 2.0.0 to 2.0.15, the signal *divhaz* is active. Since the fetch and decode stage are stalled on $divhaz = 1$, it suffices to forward the floating point results from the stages $k \in PP$ with $k \geq 2.0$. In the following, stage 2.0 is considered to be full, if one of its 17 substages 2.0.0 to 2.0.16 is full, i.e.,

$$full.2.0 = \bigvee_{0 \leq j \leq 16} full.2.0.j.$$

Depending on the flag *dbs*, the floating point operands either have single or double precision. Nevertheless, the floating point register file always delivers 64-bit values fa and fb. Circuit *FPemb* of stage ID then selects the requested data and aligns them according to the embedding convention. However, the forwarding engine, which now feeds circuit $FPemb$, takes the width of the operands into account. That avoids unnecessary interlocks.

The floating point forwarding hardware *FFOR* (figure 9.25) consists of two circuits $Ffor$. One forwards operand FA, the other operand FB. In addition, circuit $Ffor$ signals by $fhaz = 1$ that the requested operand cannot be provided in the current cycle. Circuit $Ffor$ gets the following inputs

- the source address *ad* and the precision *dbs*,

- the 64-bit data *Din* from a data port of register file FPR, and

- for each stage $k \in PP$ with $k \geq 2.0$ the destination address *Fad.k*, the precision *dbr*, the write signal $FPRw.k$ and an appropriately defined intermediate result $FC'.k$.

Like in the fixed point core, the forwarding is controlled by valid flags fv which indicate whether a floating point result is already available in one of the stages 2.0, 2.1 to 4. After defining the valid flags fv, we specify the forwarding circuit $Ffor$ and give a simple realization.

The flags $opFA$ and $opFB$ indicate whether an instruction requires the floating point operands FA and FB. These flags are used to enable the check for a floating point data hazard:

$$dhazFP = (fhazA \land opFA) \lor (fhazB \land opFB).$$

Forwarding engine $FFOR$ provides this flag at the following cost and delay

$$
\begin{aligned}
C_{FFOR} &= 2 \cdot C_{Ffor} \\
C_{dhazFP} &= 2 \cdot C_{and} + C_{or} \\
A_{dhazFP} &= A_{CON}(csID) + D_{Ffor}(fhaz) + D_{and} + D_{or}.
\end{aligned}
$$

Valid Flags   Like for the results of the GPR and SPR register files, we introduce valid flags fv for the floating point result FC. Flag $fv[k]$ indicates that the result FC is already available in the circuitry of stage k. The control precomputes these valid flags for the five execute substages $2.0, 2.1, \ldots, 2.4$ and for the stages 3 and 4.

In case of a load instruction ($Dmr = 1$), the result only becomes available during write back. For any other floating point operation with 1-cycle execute latency, the result is already available in stage 2.0. For the remaining floating point operations, the result becomes available in stage 2.4 independent of their latency. The floating point valid flags therefore equal

$$
\begin{aligned}
fv[2.0] &= lat1 \land /Dmr \\
fv[2.1] &= fv[2.2] = fv[2.3] = 0 \\
fv[2.4] &= fv[3] = /Dmr \\
fv[4] &= 1
\end{aligned}
$$

Since the flags $fv[k]$ for stage $k \in \{2.1, \ldots, 2.3, 4\}$ have a fixed value, there is no need to buffer them. The remaining three valid flags are passed through the RSR of the precomputed control together with the write signal $FPRw$.

In any stage $k \geq 2.0$, the write signal $FPRw.k$, the valid flag $fv[k].k$ and the floating point destination address $Fad.k$ are available. For some of these stages, the result $FC'.k$ is available as well:

- $FC'.4$ is the result to be written into register file FPR,

- $FC'.3$ is the input of the staging register FC.4, and

- $FC'.2$ is the result R to be written into register MDRw. Depending on the latency, R is either provided by stage 2.0 or by stage 2.4.

Lemma 4.8, which deals with the forwarding of the fixed point result, can also be applied to the floating point result. However, some modifications are necessary since the result either has single or double precision. Note that in case of single precision, the high and low order word of the results $FC'.k$ are identical, due to the embedding convention (figure 9.1). Thus, we have:

For any instruction I_i, address $r = \langle r[4:0] \rangle$, stage $k \in PP$ with $k \geq 2.0$, and for any cycle T with $I_\Sigma(k,T) = i$ we have: ◀ Lemma 9.7

1. *I_i writes the register $FPR[r]$ iff after the sequential execution of I_i, the address $r[4:1]$ is kept in the register $Fad.k[4:1]$ and the write signal $FPRw.k$ is turned on. In case of a single precision access, the bit $Fad.k[0]$ must equal $r[0]$. Thus, I_i writes register $FPR[r]$ iff*

$$FPRw.k_i = 1 \wedge Fad.k_i[4:1] = r[4:1] \wedge (Fad.k_i[0] = r[0] \vee dbr.k_i = 1)$$

2. *If I_i writes a register, and if after its sequential execution the valid flag $fv[k]$ is turned on, then the value of signal $FC'.k$ during cycle T equals the value written by I_i. Thus, I_i writes $FPR[r]$ and $fv[k]_i = 1$ imply*

$$FPR[r]_i = \begin{cases} FC'.k^T[31:0] & \text{if } r[0]_i = 0 \\ FC'.k^T[63:32] & \text{if } r[0]_i = 1. \end{cases}$$

Floating Point Forwarding Circuit Ffor Circuit Ffor forwards 64-bit floating point data. In order to account for 32-bit operands and results, the high order word $Do[63:32]$ and the low order word $Do[31:0]$ are handled separately.

For any stage $k \geq 2.0$, circuit Ffor provides two hit signals $hitH.k$ and $hitL.k$ and an auxiliary flag $match.k$. Flag $hitH.k$ indicates that the instruction I of stage 1 requests the high order word, and that the instruction of stage k is going to update that data. Flag $hitL.k$ corresponds to the low order word and has a similar meaning. The auxiliary flag $match.k$ signals that the instruction of stage k generates a floating point result, and that its destination address matches the source address ad possibly except for bit 0:

$$match.k = full.k \wedge FPRw.k \wedge (Fad.k[4:1] = ad[4:1]).$$

Lemma 9.7 implies that instruction I requests the high (low) order word if the operand has double precision or an odd (even) address. Due to the embedding convention (figure 9.1), a single precision result is always duplicated, i.e., the high and low order word of a result $FC'.k$ are the same.

Table 9.19 Floating point hit signals for stage $k \in \{2.0, \ldots, 3\}$, assuming that the instruction in stage k produces a floating point result ($FPRw = full.k = 1$) and that the high order address bits match, $Fad.k[4:1] = ad[4:1]$.

destination		source		hitH.k	hitL.k
dbr.k	Fad.k[0]	dbs.1	ad[0]		
		0	0	0	1
0	0	0	1	0	0
		1	*	0	1
		0	0	0	0
0	1	0	1	1	0
		1	*	1	0
		0	0	0	1
1	*	0	1	1	0
		1	*	1	1

The two hit signals of stage k therefore have the values listed in table 9.19; they can be expressed as

$$hitH.k \;=\; match.k \wedge (dbr.k \vee Fad.k[0]) \wedge (dbs.1 \vee ad[0])$$
$$hitL.k \;=\; match.k \wedge (dbr.k \vee /Fad.k[0]) \wedge (dbs.1 \vee /ad[0])$$

Moreover, flag $topH.k$ signals for the high order word that there occurs a hit in stage k but not in the stages above:

$$topH.k \;=\; hitH.k \wedge \bigwedge_{2.0 \le x < k, x \in PP} /hitH.x.$$

The flags $topL.k$ of the low order word have a similar meaning. In case of $topH.k = 1$ and $topL.j = 1$, the instructions in stages k and j generate data to be forwarded to output Do. If these data are not valid, a data hazard $fhaz$ is signaled. Since $fv.4 = 1$, we have

$$fhaz \;=\; \bigvee_{k \in \{2.0, 2.1, \ldots, 3\}} (topH.k \vee topL.k) \wedge /fv.k$$

While an instruction is in the stages 2.1 to 2.3 its result is not valid yet. Furthermore, the execute stages 2.0 and 2.4 share the result bus R which provides value $FC'.2$. Thus, circuit $Ffor$ only has to consider three results for forwarding. The high order word of output Do, for example,

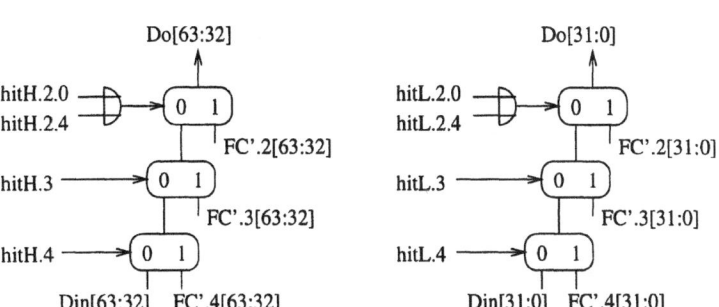

Figure 9.26 A realization of the selection circuit $FforSel$

can therefore be selected as

$$Do[63:32] = \begin{cases} FC'.2 & \text{if} \quad topH.2.0 \vee topH.2.4 \\ FC'.3 & \text{if} \quad topH.3 \\ FC'.4 & \text{if} \quad topH.4 \\ Din & \text{otherwise} \end{cases}$$

Realization of Circuit Ffor Circuit $Ffor$ consists of two subcircuits: $FforC$ controls the forwarding and $FforSel$ selects operand Do.

In the circuit $FforSel$ of figure 9.26, the high and low order word of the operand Do require three multiplexers each. Like in the fixed point forwarding circuit $Forw$, the multiplexers are controlled by the hit signals. Since the stages 2.0 and 2.4 share the result $FC'.2$, the hit signals of the two stages are combined by an OR gate. Thus,

$$C_{FforSel} = 2 \cdot (3 \cdot C_{mux}(32) + C_{or})$$
$$D_{FforSel} = 3 \cdot D_{mux}$$

The control circuit $FforC$ generates the 14 hit and top signals as outlined above and checks for a data hazard $fhaz$. The hit signals can be generated at the following cost and delay:

$$C_{FforHit} = 2 \cdot C_{or} + C_{inv} + 7 \cdot (C_{EQ}(4) + 6 \cdot C_{and} + 2 \cdot C_{or} + C_{inv})$$
$$D_{FforHit} = \max\{D_{EQ}(4), D_{inv} + D_{or}\} + 2 \cdot D_{and}$$

After inverting the hit signals, the signals $topH.k$ and $topL.k$ can be obtained by two parallel prefix AND circuits and some additional AND gates. These signals are then combined using an OR tree. Thus,

$$C_{FforC} = C_{FforHit} + 2 \cdot (7 \cdot C_{and} + 6 \cdot C_{inv} + C_{PP}(6) \cdot C_{and})$$
$$+ 6 \cdot (C_{or} + C_{inv} + C_{and}) + C_{ORtree}(6)$$
$$C_{Ffor} = C_{FforSel} + C_{FforC}.$$

The forwarding circuit $Ffor$ provides the output Do and the flag $fhaz$ at the following delays

$$
\begin{aligned}
D_{Ffor}(Do) &= D_{FforHit} + D_{FforSel} \\
D_{Ffor}(fhaz) &= D_{FforHit} + D_{inv} + (D_{PP}(6) + 2) \cdot D_{and} \\
&\quad + D_{or} + D_{ORtree}(6)
\end{aligned}
$$

The delay of Do is largely due to the address check. The actual data Din and $FC'.j$ are delayed by no more than

$$
D_{Ffor}(Data) = D_{FforSel}.
$$

The data to be forwarded by circuit FFor have the following accumulated delay

$$
A(FC', Din) = \max\{A_{EXenv}, A_{SH4Lenv}, D_{FPR,read}\}.
$$

All the address and control inputs of circuit FFOR are directly taken from registers. FFOR therefore provides the operands $FA1$ and $FB1$ with an accumulated delay of

$$
A_{FFOR}(FA1, FB1) = \max\{A(FC', Din) + D_{Ffor}(Data), D_{Ffor}(Do)\}.
$$

Before the operands are clocked into the registers FA and FB, circuit $FPemb$ aligns them according to the embedding convention. Thus, fetching the two floating point operands requires a minimal cycle time of

$$
T_{Fread} = A_{FFOR}(FA1, FB1) + D_{FPemb} + \Delta.
$$

9.4.3 Stall Engine

Since the divider is only partially pipelined, the division complicates the scheduling considerably. Like for the sequential design, we therefore first ignore divisions. In a second step, we then extend the simplified scheduler in order to support divisions.

Simplified Scheduling

The execute stage still has a nonuniform latency which varies between 1 and 5 cycles. The intermediate results, the precomputed control signals and the full flags must keep up with the instruction. Like in the sequential $FDLX_\Sigma$ design, these data are therefore passed through 5-stage RSRs.

In the pipelined design $FDLX_\Pi$, several instructions are processed at a time. The nonuniform latency cause two additional problems, which are illustrated in table 9.20. When processed at full speed,

Table 9.20 Pipelined schedule for instruction sequence I_1, I_2, I_3, ignoring structural and data hazards

instruction	cycles of the execution
I_1: fadd	IF ID EX.0 EX.1 EX.2 EX.3 EX.4 M WB
I_2: load	IF ID EX.0 M WB
I_3: cvt	IF ID EX.0 EX.3 EX.4 M WB

1. several instructions can reach a stage k at the same time like the instructions I_1 and I_3 do, and

2. instructions can pass one another like the instructions I_1 and I_2.

Every pipeline stage of the $FDLX_\Pi$ design is only capable of processing one instruction at a time. Thus, in the scenario of case 1 the instructions compete for the hardware resources. The scheduler must avoid such a structural hazard, i.e., for any stage k and cycle T it must be guaranteed that

$$I_\Pi(k,T) = i \quad \text{and} \quad I_\Pi(k,T) = i' \quad \rightarrow \quad i = i'. \qquad (9.3)$$

Hardware schedulers like the Tomasulo scheduler [Tom67, KMP99b] and the Scoreboard [Tho70, MP96] allow instructions to overtake one another, but such an *out-of-order* execution complicates the precise processing of interrupts [Lei99, SP88]. In the pipelined execution, instructions are therefore processed strictly in program order (*in-order execution*). Thus, for any two instructions I_i and $I_{i'}$ with $i > i'$ and any stage k which is requested by both instructions, the scheduler must ensure that I_i is processed after $I_{i'}$:

$$i > i' \quad \text{and} \quad I_\Pi(k,T) = i \quad \text{and} \quad I_\Pi(k,T') = i' \quad \rightarrow \quad T > T'. \qquad (9.4)$$

Notation So far, the registers of the RSR are numbered like the pipeline stages, e.g., for entry R we have $R.2.0, \dots, R.2.4, R.3$. The execute latency l of an instruction specifies how long the instruction remains in the RSR. Therefore, it is useful to number the entries also according to their *height*, i.e., according to their distance from the write back stage (table 9.21). An instruction with latency l then enters the RSR at height l.

In the following, we denote by $full'(d)$ the full flag of the stage with height d, e.g.:

$$full.2.1 = full'(5) \qquad full.2.3 = full'(3) \qquad full.3 = full'(1).$$

Table 9.21 Height of the pipeline stages

stage	2.0	2.1	2.2	2.3	2.4	3	4
height	6	5	4	3	2	1	0

Structural Hazards According to lemma 9.1, the entries of the RSR are passed down the pipeline one stage per cycle, if the RSR is not cleared and if the data are not overwritten. Thus, for any stage with height $d \in \{2, \ldots, 5\}$ we have,

$$full'(d)^T = 1 \quad \rightarrow \quad full'(d-1)^{T+1} = 1.$$

This means that an instruction once it has entered the RSR proceeds at full speed. On the other hand, let instruction I_i with latency l_i be processed in stage 2.0 during cycle T. The scheduler then tries to assign I_i to height l_i for cycle $T + 1$. However, this would cause a structural hazard, if the stage with height $l_i + 1$ is occupied during cycle T. In such a situation, the scheduler signals an RSR structural hazard

$$RSRstr^T = full'(l_i + 1)^T = 1,$$

and it stalls instruction I_i in stage 2.0. Thus, structural hazards within the RSR are resolved.

In-order Execution Let instruction I_i and cycle T be chosen as in the previous case. The instructions which in cycle T are processed in the stages 2.1 to 4 precede I_i. This especially holds for an instruction I_j processed during cycle T at height $d > l_i + 1$. Since structural hazards are resolved, lemma 9.1 implies that I_j reaches height l_i in cycle $T + d - l_i$ with

$$T + d - l_i > T + 1.$$

Since $j < i$, the instructions would be not executed in-order (i.e., the condition of equation 9.4 is violated), if I_i leaves stage 2.0 at the end of cycle T.

For $d \leq l_i$, we have $T + d - l_i \leq T$, i.e., instruction I_j reaches height l_i before instruction I_i. Thus, in order to ensure in-order execution, I_i must be stalled in stage 2.0 if

$$RSRorder^T = \bigvee_{d=l_i+2}^{5} full'(d)^T = 1.$$

The flag *RSRhaz* signals a structural hazard or a potential out-of-order execution:

$$RSRhaz = RSRstr \lor RSRorder = \bigvee_{d=l_i+1}^{5} full'(d)^T.$$

Note that an instruction with a latency of $l \geq 5$ never causes an RSR hazard. Thus, depending on the latency of the instruction, the structural hazard *RSRhaz* can be detected as

$$RSRhaz = (lat1.2.0 \land \bigvee_{j=1}^{4} full.2.j) \lor (lat3.2.0 \land \bigvee_{j=1}^{2} full.2.j).$$

at the following cost and delay

$$C_{RSRhaz} = 2 \cdot C_{and} + 4 \cdot C_{or}$$
$$A_{RSRhaz} = D_{and} + 3 \cdot D_{or}.$$

The stall engine of the $FDLX_\Pi$ design stalls the instruction in stage 2.0 if $RSRhaz = 1$. Of course, the preceding stages 0 and 1 are stalled as well.

Hardware Realization Figure 9.27 depicts the stall engine of the design $FDLX_\Pi$. It is an obvious extension of the stall engine from the DLX_Π design (figure 5.19). Like in the sequential design with FPU, the full flags of the stages 2.0 to 3 are kept in a 5-stage RSR.

A more notable modification is the fact that we now use 3 instead of 2 clocks. This is due to the RSR hazards. As before, clock $CE1$ controls the stages fetch and decode. The new clock $CE2$ just controls stage 2.0. Clock $CE3$ controls the remaining stages; it is still generated as

$$CE3 = /busy \lor (/JISR \text{ NOR } Ibusy) \lor reset.$$

Clock $CE2$ is the same as clock $CE3$ except that it is also disabled on an RSR hazard:

$$CE2 = (/RSRhaz \land /busy) \lor (/JISR \text{ NOR } Ibusy) \lor reset.$$

Clock $CE1$ is generated as before, except that it is now disabled in three situations, namely if the memories are busy, on a data hazard and on an RSR hazard:

$$CE1 = (/RSRhaz \land /busy \land /dhaz) \lor (/JISR \text{ NOR } Ibusy).$$

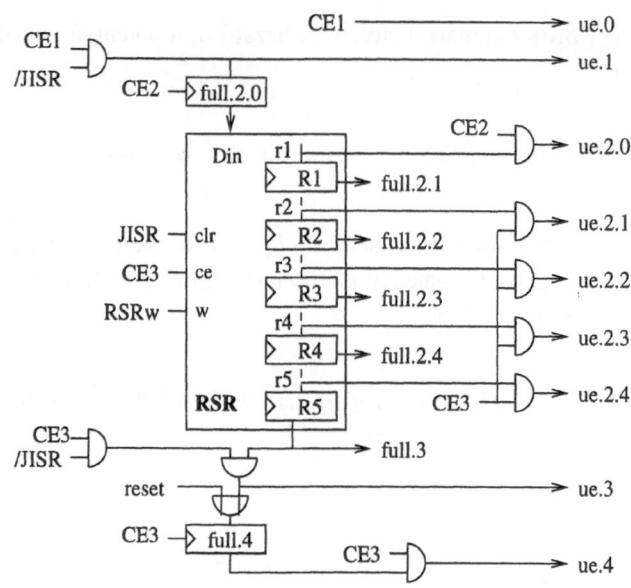

Figure 9.27 Stall engine of the $FDLX_\Pi$ design without support for divisions

Scheduling Function   Except for the execute stages, the FPU has no impact on the scheduling function of the pipelined DLX design. The instructions are still fetched in program order and pass the stages 0 and 1 in lock step mode:

$$I_\Pi(0,T) = i \;\rightarrow\; I_\Pi(0,T+1) = \begin{cases} i & \text{if } ue.0^T = 0 \\ i+1 & \text{if } ue.0^T = 1 \end{cases}$$

$$I_\Pi(1,T) = i \;\rightarrow\; I_\Pi(0,T) = i+1$$

Except for stage 2.0, an instruction makes a progress of at most one stage per cycle, given that no jump to the ISR occurs. Thus, $I_\Pi(k,T) = i$ with $k \neq 2.0$ and $JISR^T = 0$ implies

$$i = \begin{cases} I_\Pi(k,T+1) & \text{if } ue.k^T = 0 \\ I_\Pi(k+1,T+1) & \text{if } ue.k^T = 1 \wedge k \in \{0, 1, 3\} \\ I_\Pi(2.(j+1),T+1) & \text{if } ue.k^T = 1 \wedge k = 2.j \in \{2.1, 2.2, 2.3\} \\ I_\Pi(3,T+1) & \text{if } ue.k^T = 1 \wedge k = 2.4. \end{cases}$$

With respect to stage 2.0, the pipelined and the sequential scheduling function are alike, except that the instruction remains in stage 2.0 in case of an RSR hazard. In case of $JISR = 0$, an active flag $RSRhaz$ disables the update of stage 2.0, i.e., signal $ue.2.0$ is inactive. Thus, for $I_\Pi(2.0,T) = i$ and

$JISR^T = 0$, we have

$$i = \begin{cases} I_\Pi(2.0, T+1) & \text{if} \quad ue.2.0^T = 0 \\ I_\Pi(2.1, T+1) & \text{if} \quad ue.2.0^T = 1 \wedge l_i = 5 \\ I_\Pi(2.3, T+1) & \text{if} \quad ue.2.0^T = 1 \wedge l_i = 3 \\ I_\Pi(3, T+1) & \text{if} \quad ue.2.0^T = 1 \wedge l_i = 1. \end{cases}$$

Integration of Divisions

The division is integrated in the same way as in the $FDLX_\Sigma$ design (section 9.3.2). The RSR of the stall engine is extended to length 21. While a division I_i passes the stages 2.0.1 to 2.0.16 of the stall engine, the data of I_i held in the remaining RSRs are locked in stage 2.0.

During such a division hazard, stage 2.0 is controlled by the division automaton, and otherwise it is controlled by the precomputed control. The division hazard is signaled by flag *divhaz* one cycle ahead of time. While $divhaz = 1$, the stages 0 and 1 are stalled, whereas the instructions in the stages $k \geq 2.2$ do proceed. Thus, only the clock CE1 of stages 0 and 1 must be modified to

$$CE1 = (/divhaz \wedge /RSRhaz \wedge /busy \wedge /dhaz) \vee (/JISR \text{ NOR } Ibusy).$$

Like in the sequential design, the support for divisions only impacts the scheduling function of the execute substages. For $I_\Pi(2.0, T) = i$ and $JISR^T = 0$, we have

$$i = \begin{cases} I_\Pi(2.0, T+1) & \text{if} \quad ue.2.0^T = 0 \\ I_\Pi(2.0.1, T+1) & \text{if} \quad ue.2.0^T = 1 \wedge l_i = 21 \\ I_\Pi(2.0.5, T+1) & \text{if} \quad ue.2.0^T = 1 \wedge l_i = 17 \\ I_\Pi(2.1, T+1) & \text{if} \quad ue.2.0^T = 1 \wedge l_i = 5 \\ I_\Pi(2.3, T+1) & \text{if} \quad ue.2.0^T = 1 \wedge l_i = 3 \\ I_\Pi(3, T+1) & \text{if} \quad ue.2.0^T = 1 \wedge l_i = 1. \end{cases}$$

and for every substage $2.0.j$, $I_\Pi(2.0.j, T) = i$ and $JISR^T = 0$ imply

$$i = \begin{cases} I_\Pi(2.0.(j+1), T+1) & \text{if} \quad ue.2.j^T = 1 \wedge 1 \leq j < 16 \\ I_\Pi(2.1, T+1) & \text{if} \quad ue.2.j^T = 1 \wedge j = 16. \end{cases}$$

9.4.4 Cost and Delay of the Control

Like in the pipelined design without FPU, the control comprises the memory controllers IMC and DMC, the memory interface control MifC, a circuit CE which generates the global clock signals, the stall engine, the precomputed control, a Mealy automaton for stage ID, and a Moore automaton for the stages EX to WB. The parameters of these two automata are

Table 9.22 Classification of the precomputed control signals

type	x.0	x.1	x.2	x.3	x.4	y	z
control signals	31	7	3	0	3	3	6
valid flags	2					2	2

listed in table B.16. Thus, the cost of the whole FDLX control can be expressed as

$$C_{CON} = C_{IMC} + C_{DMC} + C_{MifC} + C_{CE} + C_{stall}$$
$$+ C_{preCon} + C_{CON}(mealy) + C_{CON}(moore).$$

Precomputed Control

The control signals which govern the stages 2.0 to 4 are precomupted in stage ID. Like in the sequential design $FDLX_\Sigma$, they are then passed down the pipeline using a five stage RSR and some registers (figure 9.19). In addition, the control of the pipelined design $FDLX_\Pi$ also buffers some valid flags namely

- the flags $v[4:2]$ for the fixed point result and

- the flags $fv[2.0]$, $fv[2.4]$ and $fv[3]$ for the floating point result.

The valid flags increase the signals of type $x.0$, y and z by two signals each (table 9.22). The RSR of the precomputed control now starts with 26 signals in stage 2.1 and ends with 13 signals in stage 3. The control signals are precomputed by a Moore automaton which already provides the buffering for stage 2.0. This does not include the valid flags; they require 6 buffers in stage 2.0. In addition, an inverter and an AND gate are used to generate the valid flags.

Since divisions iterate in the multiply divide circuit SIGFMD, the precomputed control is extended by circuit $DivCon$, like in the sequential design (figure 9.22). The cost and delay of control $DivCon$ remain the same.

Without the automaton, the cost of the RSR and of the (extended) precomputed control can then be expressed as

$$C_{ConRSR} = C_{inv} + 5 \cdot C_{or} + (26 + 19 + 2 \cdot 16 + 13) \cdot (C_{and} + C_{mux} + C_{ff})$$
$$C_{preCon} = C_{ConRSR} + C_{ff}(8) + C_{ff}(6) + C_{inv} + C_{and} + C_{DivCon}.$$

Computation of the Clocks

The pipelined FDLX design uses three clock signals $CE1$ to $CE3$. These clocks depend on flags $/JISR$, on the hazard flags $/dhaz$ and $RSRhaz$, and on the busy flags $/busy$ and $Ibusy$.

$$CE1 = (/RSRhaz \land /busy \land /dhaz) \lor (/JISR \text{ NOR } Ibusy)$$
$$CE2 = (/RSRhaz \land /busy) \lor (/JISR \text{ NOR } Ibusy) \lor reset$$
$$CE3 = /busy \lor (/JISR \text{ NOR } Ibusy) \lor reset.$$

The forwarding circuitry provides three data hazard flags: flag $dhazFX$ for the GPR operands, flag $dhazS$ for the SPR operands and flag $dhazFP$ for the FPR operands. A data hazard occurs if at least one of these hazard flags is active, thus

$$/dhaz = (dhazFX \lor dhazS) \text{ NOR } dhazFP.$$

Flag $/dhaz$ can be obtained at the following cost and accumulated delay:

$$C_{dhaz} = C_{dhazFX} + C_{dhazS} + C_{dhazFP} + C_{or} + C_{nor}$$
$$A_{dhaz} = \max\{A_{dhazFX}, A_{dhazS}, A_{dhazFP}\} + D_{or} + D_{nor}.$$

The FPU has no impact on the busy flags. They are generated like in the pipelined design DLX_{Π}, at cost C_{busy} and with delay A_{busy}. The JISR flags are obtained as

$$JISR = jisr.4 \land full.4 \qquad /JISR = jisr.4 \text{ NAND } full.4.$$

The three clock signals are then generated at the following cost and delay

$$C_{CE} = C_{dhaz} + C_{RSRhaz} + C_{busy}$$
$$\qquad + 4 \cdot C_{or} + C_{nor} + C_{inv} + C_{nand} + 3 \cdot C_{and}$$
$$A_{CE} = \max\{A_{dhaz}, A_{RSRhaz}, A_{busy}\} + D_{inv} + 2 \cdot D_{and} + D_{or}.$$

Stall Engine

The core of the stall engine is the circuit depicted in figure 9.27 but with an 21-stage RSR. In addition, the stall engine enables the update of the registers and memories based on the update enable vector ue.

According to equation 9.2, the write signals $Stallw$ of the 21-stage RSR are directly taken from the precomputed control of stage 2.0. The core of the stall engine therefore provides the update enable flags at the following cost and delay

$$C_{stall}(core) = C_{RSR}(21, 1) + (21 + 4) \cdot C_{and} + C_{or} + 2 \cdot C_{ff}$$
$$A_{stall}(ue) = A_{CE} + D_{RSR}(r) + D_{and}.$$

The write signals of the register files are generated as before, except that there is now one additional register file.

$$GPRw' = GPRw \wedge ue.4 \wedge (JISR \text{ NAND } repeat)$$
$$FPRw' = FPRw \wedge ue.4 \wedge (JISR \text{ NAND } repeat)$$
$$SPRw' = SPRw \wedge ue.4 \wedge (JISR \text{ NAND } repeat)$$
$$SPRw'[5:0] = SPRw[5:0] \wedge ue.4.$$

The read and write signals of the data memory also remain unchanged. In stage 2.0, the write request signal is disabled in case of page fault during instruction fetch.

$$Dmw.3 := Dmw.2 \wedge \overline{CA.2[2]}$$
$$Dmw'.3 = Dmw.3 \wedge full.3 \wedge (JISR \text{ NOR } reset)$$
$$Dmr'.3 = Dmr.3 \wedge full.3.$$

The same is true for the clock signals of stage ID and of the cause environment.

$$CA4ce = ue.3 \vee reset$$
$$DPCce' = PCce' = ue.1 \vee JISR.$$

However, the output registers of the stages EX and M of the data paths are clocked differently. In the design without FPU, all these registers have a trivial clock request signal which equals one. That is no longer the case. For the registers $R \in \{MDRr, C4, FC4\}$ and for register MAR, the clocks are now obtained as

$$Rce' = ue.3 \wedge Rce.3$$
$$MARce' = ue.2.4 \wedge MARce.2.0.$$

For register MDRw the clocking is a bit more complicated. As already mentioned earlier, MDRw either gets its data from stage 2.0 or from stage 2.4, depending on the latency of the instruction. Thus,

$$MDRwce' = ue.2.4 \wedge (MDRwce.2.0 \wedge lat1.2.0 \vee MDRwce.2.4).$$

The write signals of the RSRs of the data paths are directly taken from the precomputed control $CON2.0$ except for the write signal of the first entry

$$RSRw[1] = lat5.2.0 \vee (full.2.0.16 \wedge fdiv.2.0).$$

The cost and cycle time of the stall engine can then be expressed as

$$C_{stall} = C_{stall}(core) + 14 \cdot C_{and} + 4 \cdot C_{or} + C_{inv} + C_{nand} + C_{nor}$$
$$T_{stall} = \max\{D_{RSR}(r) + D_{and} + D_{or} + \Delta, A_{stall}(ue) + \delta + 2 \cdot D_{and}$$
$$+ \max\{D_{ram3}(32,32), D_{SF}(w,ce;9,32) + D_{ff}, D_{FPR,write}\}\}$$

9.4.5 Simulation Theorem

It suffices to show the simulation theorem for cycles, when instructions are in stages $k \in PP$.

Like theorem 5.11 but with hypothesis ◀ Theorem 9.8

$$I_\Pi(k,T) = I_\Sigma(k,T') = i \quad and \quad ue.k_i^T = 1$$

for $k \in PP$ and statements 1 (a) and (b) for signals S and output registers R of stages $k \in PP$.

The arguments from the induction step of theorems 4.5, 4.7 and 4.11 have to be extended for the execute environment. Two new situations must be treated: PROOF

1. jumping over substages by means of the result shift registers and

2. inputs to stage 2.1 produced by the sequential portion of the division algorithm.

For the first case, let I_i be an instruction which jumps from stage 2.0 to stage x with $x \in \{2.1, \dots, 2.4, 3\}$, and let

$$
\begin{aligned}
i &= I_\Pi(x,T) &= I_\Sigma(x,T') \\
&= I_\Pi(2.0, T-1) &= I_\Sigma(2.0, T'-1).
\end{aligned}
$$

Let $Q \in out(2.0)$ be an output register of stage 2.0 which was updated during cycle $T - 1$. The induction hypothesis and the dateline lemma imply

$$Q_\Pi^T = Q_i = Q_\Sigma^{T'}.$$

Let S be a signal in stage x, which is an input to an output register of stage x which is updated at the end of cycle T. By construction of the machine, the value $S_\Sigma^{T'}$ then depends only on

- the values $Q_\Sigma^{T'}$ of registers Q considered above and

- the values of the special purpose registers RM_{i-1} and SR_{i-1}.

As in the proof of theorem 4.7, one argues that values RM_{i-1} and SR_{i-1} are forwarded to stage x of machine DLX_Π in cycle T. It follows that

$$S_\Pi^T = S_\Sigma^{T'}.$$

For the second case, let I_i be a division instruction and let

$$
\begin{aligned}
i &= I_\Pi(2.1,T) &= I_\Sigma(2.1,T') \\
&= I_\Pi(2.0.16,T-1) &= I_\Sigma(2.0.16,T'-1) \\
&= I_\Pi(2.0,U) &= I_\Sigma(2.0,U').
\end{aligned}
$$

By induction hypothesis we have for all output registers Q of stage 2.0, which were updated after cycle U:

$$
Q_\Pi^{U+1} = Q_\Sigma^{U'+1}.
$$

During the cycles $U'+1,\ldots,T'-1$ of machine DLX_Σ and during the cycles $U+1,\ldots,T-1$ of machine DLX_Π both machines work sequentially. The outputs clocked into the output registers of stage 2.0.16 after cycles $T'-1$ and $T-1$, respectively, depend by lemma 9.4 only on the values of the registers Q considered above. For output registers V of stage 2.0.16 it follows that

$$
V_\Pi^T = V_\Sigma^T = V_i.
$$

From this one concludes for all inputs S of output registers of stage 2.1 which are clocked after cycle T:

$$
S_\Pi^T = S_\Sigma^{T'}
$$

QED   exactly as in the first case.

9.5   Evaluation

IN THIS section, we analyze the impact of the floating point unit on the cost and the performance of the pipelined DLX design. We also analyze how the FPU impacts the optimal cache size (section 9.5.2).

9.5.1   Hardware Cost and Cycle Time

In the following, we compare the cost and the cycle time of the designs DLX_Π and $FDLX_\Pi$. Both designs use a split 4KB cache. The Icache and the Dcache are of equal size, i.e., 2KB each. They are two way set associative with LRU replacement and implement the write allocate, write through policy. With respect to the timing, we assume that the memory interface has a bus delay of $d_{bus} = 15$ and a handshake delay of $d_{Mhsh} = 10$ gate delays.

Table 9.23 Cost of the pipelined DLX data paths. DP\M denotes the data paths without the memory environments.

environment	IR	PC	DAddr	EX	SH4L	RF
DLX_Π	301	2610	60	3795	380	7257
$FDLX_\Pi$	301	2618	90	110093	860	11532
increase		0.3%	50%	2800%	126%	59%

environment	CA	buffer	FORW	IM, DM	DP\M	DP
DLX_Π	471	2064	1624	96088	20610	116698
$FDLX_\Pi$	717	9206	3904	95992	143635	239627
increase	52%	346%	140%	-0.1%	597%	105%

Cost of the Data Paths

Except for the environments IRenv and IMenv, all parts of the data paths and of the control had to be adapted to the floating point instruction set. Significant changes occurred in the execute stage, in the register file environment, in the forwarding hardware, and in the control (table 9.23).

The floating point unit itself is very expensive, its cost run at 104 kilo gates (section 8.7). Compared to the FPU, the FXU is fairly inexpensive. Thus, in the FDLX design, the execute environment is 28 times more expensive than in the DLX design. The FPU accounts for about 95% of the cost of EXenv.

There is also a significant cost increase in the forwarding hardware, in the buffers and in the register file environment. This increase is due to the deeper pipeline and due to the additional floating point operands. The remaining environments contribute at most 1kG (kilo gate) to the cost increase. The memory environments become even slightly cheaper, due to the simpler data memory interface. The data ports of the Dcache and of environment DMenv have now the same width (64 bits); the patch of the data ports therefore becomes obsolete.

In the DLX_Π design, the 4KB split cache is by far the single most expensive unit; it accounts for 82% of cost. The FPU is about 9% more expensive than the 4KB cache. Thus, in the $FDLX_\Pi$ design, the 4KB cache only contributes 40% to the cost of the data paths; environment EXenv contributes another 46%. Adding the FPU roughly doubles the cost of the pipelined data paths (factor 2.05). Without the caches, the FPU has even a stronger cost impact, it increases the cost of the data paths roughly by a factor of 6.

Table 9.24 Cost of the control of the pipelined DLX designs and with FPU.

	MifC	stall, CE	preCon	automata	CON	DLX
DLX_Π	943	165	202	952	2262	118960
$FDLX_\Pi$	1106	623	1440	2829	5898	245514
increase	6.7%	278%	613%	197%	161%	106%

Cost of the Control

Table 9.24 lists the cost of the different control environments and of the whole DLX designs. Adding the FPU increases the cost of the control by 160%. The cost of the memory interface control remains virtually the same. Due to the deeper pipeline, the stall engine becomes about 4 times as expensive.

The control automata become about three times as expensive. This is largely due to the Moore automaton which precomputes the control signals of the stages EX to WB. It now requires 44 instead of 17 states, and it generates 48 instead of 16 control signals. The Moore control signals have a 7 times higher accumulated frequency v_{sum} (342 instead of 48).

The larger number of control signals also impacts the cost of the pre-computed control, which passes these signals down the pipeline. Since the pipeline is also much deeper, the precomputed control is 7 times as expensive as before.

Cycle Time

Table 9.25 lists the cycle time for each stage of the data paths. The cycle time of the write back stage remains the same, despite of the additional register file. The FPR register file consists of two RAM banks, each of which only has half the size of the RAM used in the GPR register file. Thus, time T_{WB} is still dominated by the delay of the shifter SH4L and the GPR register file.

Due to the aliasing of single and double precision registers, each word of a floating point operand must be forwarded separately. Since all the operands are fetched and forwarded in parallel, the floating point extension has only a minor impact on the operand fetch time. The cycle time of stage ID is still dominated by the PC environment.

The FPU is much more complex than the FXU. Thus, the cycle time of the execute stage is increased by about 50%; the execute stage becomes time critical. The cycle time of the control is also increased significantly (16%). This is due to the non-uniform latency of the execute stage, which requires the use of an RSR.

Table 9.25 Cycle times of the data paths of the designs DLX_Π and $FDLX_\Pi$ with 2KB, 2-way Icache and Dcache.

| | ID | | EX | WB | DP | CON / stall | |
	operands	PC					max(,)
DLX_Π	72	89	66	33	89	79	$46 + d_{bus}$
$FDLX_\Pi$	74	89	98	33	98	92	$48 + d_{bus}$

Table 9.26 Memory cycle times of the DLX designs with 2KB, 2-way Icache and Dcache, assuming a bus and handshake delay of $d_{bus} = 15$ and $d_{Mhsh} = 10$.

| | $read | $if | Mreq | Mrburst | Maccess | |
					$\alpha = 4$	$\alpha = 8$
DLX_Π	55	47	42	51	379	707
$FDLX_\Pi$	53	47	42	51	379	707

The memory system remains virtually the same, except for one multi-plexer which is saved in the Dcache interface and a modification of the bank write signals. The latter has no impact on the delay of the memory control. Thus, except for the cache read time $T_{\$read}$, the two DLX designs with and without FPU have identical memory cycle times (table 9.26).

9.5.2 Variation of the Cache Size

Like in sections 6.4.2 and 6.5.3, we now optimize the cache size of the $FDLX_\Pi$ design for performance and for a good performance cost ratio. The optimization is based on a floating point workload.

Cost and Delay

Table 9.27 lists the cost, the cycle time T_{FDLX} of the CPU, and the memory access times for the pipelined FDLX design. The total cache size varies between 0KB and 32KB. The 64MB main memory uses DRAMs which are 4 (8) times slower and denser than SRAM.

As before, doubling the cache size roughly doubles the cost of the memory environment. However, due to the expensive floating point unit, a cache system of 1KB to 4KB only causes a moderate (25 - 65%) increase of the total hardware cost. In combination with small caches, the FPU

Table 9.27 Cost, CPU cycle time and memory access time of the $FDLX_\Pi$ design

total cache	C_M [kG]	C_{FDLX} [kG]	C_{FDLX} [%]	T_{FDLX}	$T_M(4)$	$T_M(8)$
0KB	0	149	100	98	355	683
1KB	30	179	120	98	359	687
2KB	52	201	135	98	367	695
4KB	96	246	165	98	379	707
8KB	184	334	224	98	382	710
16KB	360	510	342	104	385	713
32KB	711	861	578	107	388	716

dominates the CPU cycle time. Beyond a total cache size of 16KB, the detection of a cache hit becomes time critical.

The memory access time grows with the cache size; it is significantly larger than the CPU cycle time. As before, the actual memory access is therefore performed in W cycles with a cycle time of

$$\tau_M = \lceil T_M/W \rceil.$$

The cycle time of the FDLX design then equals

$$\tau = \max\{\tau_M, T_{FDLX}\}.$$

Up to $W = T_M/T_{FDLX}$, increasing the number W of memory cycles reduces the cycle time τ, but it also increases the cycle count. Thus, there is a trade-off between cycle time and cycle count. The optimal parameter W strongly depends on the memory system and on the workload.

Performance

In addition to the integer benchmarks of table 4.20, the SPEC92 suite also comprises 14 floating point benchmarks (for details see [Sta, HP96]). On average, this floating point workload SPECfp92 uses the instruction mix listed in table 9.28; this table is derived from [Del97].

The non-uniform latency of the execute stage makes it very difficult (or even impossible) to derive the CPI ratio of the pipelined FDLX design in an analytic manner. In [Del97], the CPI ratio is therefore determined by a trace based simulation. Assuming an ideal memory which performs every access in a single cycle, the FDLX design achieves on the SPECfp92 workload a CPI ratio of

$$CPI_{ideal}(fp) = 1.759.$$

Table 9.28 Instruction mix of the average SPECfp92 floating point workload

instruction	FXU	load	store	jump	branch
frequency [%]	39.12	20.88	10.22	2.32	10.42

instruction	fadd	fmul	fdiv	cvt	1 cycle
frequency [%]	5.24	5.78	1.17	2.13	2.72

Table 9.29 Memory access time of the FDLX design with cache memory (given in CPU cycles)

read hit	read miss	write hit	write miss
1	$1+S+W$	$2+W$	$2+W+S+W$

The split cache system of the FDLX design has a non-uniform access time which depends on the type of the access (table 9.29). Thus, a read miss takes $1+S+W$ cycles. In the FDLX design each cache line has $S = 4$ sectors. The parameter W depends on the speed of the memory system; in this framework, it varies between 3 and 16 cycles.

The whole pipeline is stalled in case of a slow data memory access. On an instruction fetch miss, only the fetch and decode stage are stalled, the remaining stages still proceed. However, these stages get eventually drained since the decode stage provides no new instructions. Thus, an instruction fetch miss will also cause a CPI penalty.

In order to keep the performance model simple, we assume that the whole pipeline is stalled on every slow memory access. That gives us a lower bound for the performance of the pipelined FDLX design. In analogy to equation 6.5 (page 312), the CPI ratio of the $FDLX_\Pi$ design with cache memory can then be modeled as

$$
\begin{aligned}
CPI(fp) &= CPI_{ideal}(fp) + \nu_{store} \cdot (1+W) \\
&\quad + (\nu_{fetch} \cdot p_{Im} + \nu_{load,store} \cdot p_{Dm}) \cdot W \cdot S \\
&= 1.861 + 0.102 \cdot W + (p_{Im} + 0.311 \cdot p_{Dm}) \cdot W \cdot S,
\end{aligned}
$$

where p_{Im} and p_{Dm} denote the miss ratios of the instruction cache and data cache, respectively. Table 9.30 lists the miss ratios of the instruction and data cache. In addition, it lists the optimal cycle time, CPI and TPI (time per instruction) ratio for the different memory systems.

Doubling the total cache size cuts the miss ratio of the Icache roughly by half, whereas up to 16KB, the miss ratio of the Dcache is only reduced

Table 9.30 Miss ratio, cycle time CPI and TPI ratio of the $FDLX_\Pi$ design. For $\alpha = 4$ (8), a memory access is performed in $W = 4$ (7) cycles.

total	miss ratio [%]		DRAM $\alpha = 4$			DRAM $\alpha = 4$		
cache	I$	D$	τ	CPI	TPI	τ	CPI	TPI
1KB	5.40	10.7	98	2.97	290.8	99	3.54	350.1
2KB	1.98	7.69	98	2.62	256.7	100	3.06	305.6
4KB	1.04	6.08	98	2.50	245.3	101	2.90	292.6
8KB	0.70	5.31	98	2.46	240.8	102	2.83	289.1
16KB	0.46	4.56	104	2.42	251.6	104	2.78	289.3
32KB	0.23	2.33	107	2.35	250.9	107	2.68	286.7

by about 30%. This suggests that the data accesses require a larger working set than the instruction fetches, and that the instruction fetches have a better locality. A larger cache improves the CPI ratio but with diminishing returns. Since a larger cache also increases the cycle time, the 16KB cache system even yields a worse performance than the 8KB system. Thus, with respect to performance, a total of 8KB cache is optimal.

Without caches, every memory access takes $1 + W$ cycles, and the pipelined FDLX design then has a CPI ratio of

$$CPI_{no\$} = 1.759 + W \cdot 1.311.$$

In combination with fast DRAM ($\alpha = 4$), the design runs with $W = 3$ at a cycle time of $\tau = 119$ and achieves a TPI ratio of 677.4. According to table 9.31, the split cache gains a speedup of 2.3 to 2.8 over the design without caches. In combination with slower DRAM ($\alpha = 8$), the FDLX design without caches run with $W = 7$ at $\tau = 98$ and has a TPI ratio of 1071.7. The split cache system then causes even a speedup of 3.1 to 3.7.

Even for the 8KB cache system, the speedup is in either case significantly larger than the cost increase. Thus, the cache is definitely worthwhile.

The diagrams of figure 9.28 depict the quality ratio of the FDLX designs with split cache over that without cache. Note that the quality is the weighted geometric mean of the cost and the TPI ratio: $Q = C^{-q} \cdot TPI^{q-1}$. For a realistic quality measure, the parameter q lies in the range [0.2, 0.5]. Within this range, the design with a total cache size of 4KB is best. The 8KB system only wins, if much more emphasis is put on the performance than on the cost.

Table 9.31 Speedup and cost increase of the $FDLX_\Pi$ with a split 2-way cache over the design without cache

total cache size		1KB	2KB	4KB	8KB
speedup:	$\alpha = 4$	2.33	2.64	2.76	2.81
	$\alpha = 8$	3.06	3.51	3.66	3.71
cost increase factor		1.24	1.39	1.71	2.32

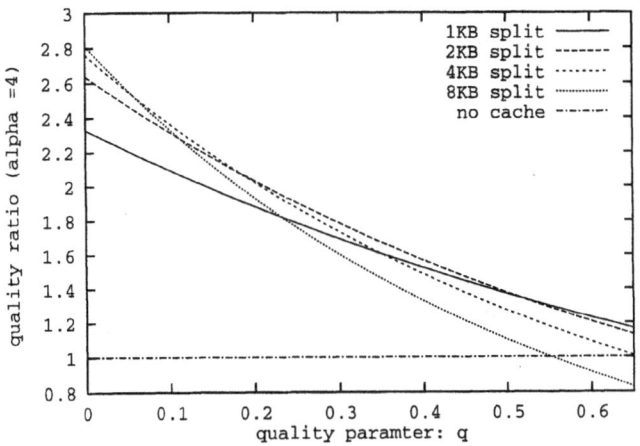

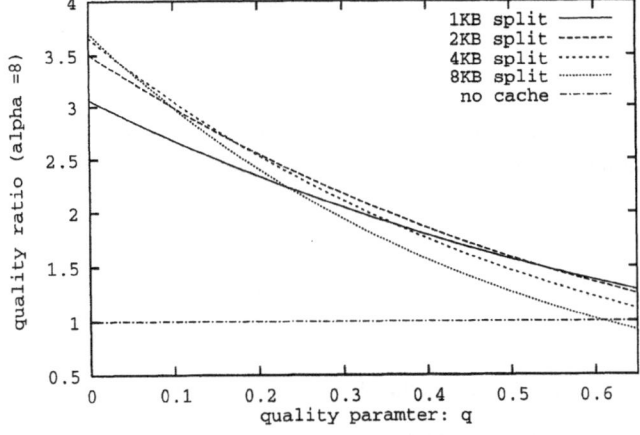

Figure 9.28 Quality ratio of the design with a split 2-way cache relative to the design without cache for two types of off-chip memory.

515

9.6 Exercises

Exercise 9.1 An arithmetical FPU instruction I_i updates the SPR register IEEEf by a read-modify-write access:

$$IEEEf_i = IEEEf_{i-1} \lor Ffl_i.$$

Unlike any other instruction updating the SPR register file, the input of this write access is provided via the special write port $Di[6]$ and not via the standard write port Din. That complicates the forwarding of the SPR operand S. In order to keep the engine forwarding engine (section 9.4.2) lean, the forwarding of the IEEEf flags generated by an arithmetical FPU operation was omitted.

1. The result to be written onto register IEEEf is always available in the circuitry of stage WB. Extend the forwarding engine (and the interlock engine) such that IEEEf is forwarded from stage WB even in case of an arithmetical FPU instruction.

2. Flags Ffl provided by the FPU become available in stage 2.4. When combined with the forwarded IEEEf value from stages 3 and 4, register IEEEf can also be forwarded from the stages 2.4, 3 and 4. Construct a forwarding engine which supports this type of forwarding.

3. How do the modifications of 1) and 2) impact the cost and cycle time?

Exercise 9.2 Construct a sequence of k instructions, such that data from the first $k-1$ instructions have to be forwarded to the k'th instruction. How large can k be?

Exercise 9.3 In many contemporary machines (year 2000) a change of the rounding mode slows programs down much more than an additional floating point instruction (This make interval arithmetic extremely slow). What part of the hardware of the machine constructed here has to be deleted in order to produce this behavior?

Exercise 9.4 Suppose in the division algorithm we use an initial lookup table with $\gamma = 5$ or $\gamma = 16$?.

1. Which parts of the machine have to be changed? Specify the changes.

2. How is the cost of the machine affected?

Exercise 9.5 Sketch the changes of the design required if we want to make division fully pipelined (Conceptually, this makes the machine much simpler). Estimate the extra cost.

Exercise 9.6 Evaluate the quality of the machines from exercises 9.4 and 9.5. Assume, that the cycle time is not affected. For the machine from exercise 9.5 use your estimate for the cost. Compare with the machine constructed in the text.

DLX Instruction Set Architecture

THE DLX is a 32-bit RISC architecture which manages with only three instruction formats. The core of the architecture is the fixed point unit FXU, but there also exists a floating point extension.

A.1 DLX Fixed-Point Core: FXU

THE DLX fixed point unit uses 32 general purpose registers $R0$ to $R31$, each of which is 32 bits wide. Register R0 always has the value 0. The FXU also has a few 32-bit special purpose registers mainly used for handling interrupts. Table A.1 lists these registers as well as a brief description of their usage. For more details see chapter 5. Special move instructions transfer data between general and special purpose registers.

Load and store operations move data between the general purpose registers and the memory. There is a single addressing mode: the effective memory address *ea* is the sum of a register and an immediate constant. Except for shifts, immediate constants are *always* sign-extended to 32-bits.

The memory is byte addressable and performs byte, half-word or word accesses. All instructions are coded in four bytes. In memory, data and instructions must be aligned in the following way: Half words must start at even byte addresses. Words and instructions must start at addresses divisible by 4. These addresses are called word boundaries.

Table A.1 Special purpose registers of the DLX fixed point core

register		usage
PC	program counter	points to the next instruction
SR	status register	holds interrupt masks (among others)
CA	cause register	records pending interrupts
EPC, ESR, ECA, EMAR	exception registers	on a jump to the interrupt service routine they backup the current value of PC, SR, CA respectively the current memory address

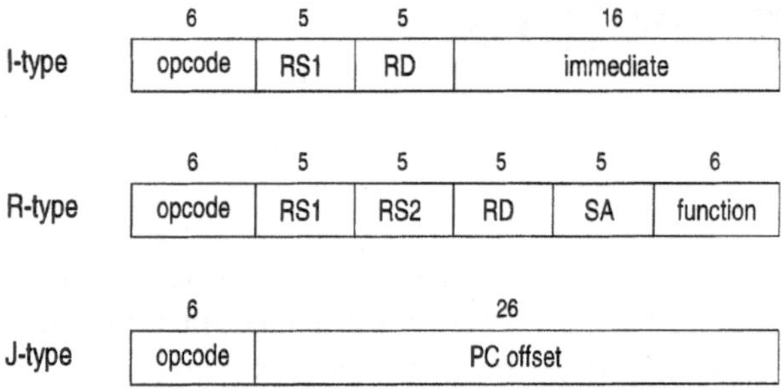

Figure A.1 The three instruction formats of the DLX design. The fields RS1 and RS2 specify the source registers, and the field RD specifies the destination register. Field SA specifies a special purpose register or an immediate shift amount. Function field is an additional 6-bit opcode.

A.1.1 Instruction Formats

All three instruction formats (figure A.1) have a 6-bit primary opcode and specify up to three explicit operands. The I-type (Immediate) format specifies two registers and a 16-bit constant. That is the standard layout for instructions with an immediate operand. The J-type (Jump) format is used for control instructions. They require no explicit register operand and profit from the larger 26-bit immediate operand. The third format, R-type (Register) format, provides an additional 6-bit opcode (*function*). The remaining 20 bits specify three general purpose registers and a field *SA* which specifies a 5-bit constant or a special purpose register. A 5-bit constant, for example, is sufficient as shift amount.

Table A.2 J-type instruction layout; *sxt(imm)* is the sign-extended version of the 26-bit immediate called PC Offset.

IR[31:26]	mnemonic	effect
Control Operation		
hx02	j	PC = PC + 4 + sxt(imm)
hx03	jal	R31 = PC + 4; PC = PC + 4 + sxt(imm)
hx3e	trap	trap = 1; Edata = sxt(imm)
hx3f	rfe	SR = ESR; PC = EPC; DPC = EDPC

A.1.2 Instruction Set Coding

Since the DLX description in [HP90] does not specify the coding of the instruction set, we adapt the coding of the MIPS R2000 machine ([PH94, KH92]) to the DLX instruction set. Tables A.2 through A.4 specify the instruction set and list the coding; the prefix "hx" indicates that the number is represented as hexadecimal. The effects of the instructions are specified in a register transfer language.

A.2 Floating-Point Extension

BESIDES THE fixed point unit, the DLX architecture also comprises a floating point unit FPU, which can handle floating point numbers in single precision (32-bits) or in double precision (64-bits). For both precisions, the FPU fully conforms the requirements of the ANSI/IEEE standard 754 [Ins85].

A.2.1 FPU Register Set

The FPU provides 32 *floating point general purpose registers FPRs*, each of which is 32 bits wide. In order to store double precision values, the registers can be addressed as 64-bit *floating point registers FDRs*. Each of the 16 FDRs is formed by concatenating two adjacent FPRs (table A.5). Only even numbers $(0, 2, \ldots, 30)$ are used to address the floating point registers FPR; the least significant address bit is ignored. In addition, the FPU provides three *floating point control registers*: a 1-bit register *FCC* for the *floating point condition code*, a 5-bit register *IEEEf* for the IEEE *exception flags* and a 2-bit register *RM* specifying the IEEE *rounding mode*.

Table A.3 R-type instruction layout. All instructions increment the PC by four.
SA is a shorthand for the special purpose register *SPR[SA]*; *sa* denotes the 5-bit
immediate shift amount specified by the bits IR[10:6].

IR[31:26]	IR[5:0]	mnemonic	effect
Shift Operation			
hx00	hx00	slli	RD = sll(RS1, sa)
hx00	hx02	srli	RD = srl(RS1, sa)
hx00	hx03	srai	RD = sra(RS1, sa)
hx00	hx04	sll	RD = sll(RS1, RS2[4:0])
hx00	hx06	srl	RD = srl(RS1, RS2[4:0])
hx00	hx07	sra	RD = sra(RS1, RS2[4:0])
Arithmetic, Logical Operation			
hx00	hx20	addo	RD = RS1 + RS2; *ovf* signaled
hx00	hx21	add	RD = RS1 + RS2; no *ovf* signaled
hx00	hx22	subo	RD = RS1 - RS2; *ovf* signaled
hx00	hx23	sub	RD = RS1 - RS2; no *ovf* signaled
hx00	hx24	and	RD = RS1 $\wedge$ RS2
hx00	hx25	or	RD = RS1 $\vee$ RS2
hx00	hx26	xor	RD = RS1 $\oplus$ RS2
hx00	hx27	lhg	RD = RS2[15:0] 0^{16}
Test Set Operation			
hx00	hx28	clr	RD = (false ? 1 : 0);
hx00	hx29	sgr	RD = (RS1 > RS2 ? 1 : 0);
hx00	hx2a	seq	RD = (RS1 = RS2 ? 1 : 0);
hx00	hx2b	sge	RD = (RS1 $\geq$ RS2 ? 1 : 0);
hx00	hx2c	sls	RD = (RS1 < RS2 ? 1 : 0);
hx00	hx2d	sne	RD = (RS1 $\neq$ RS2 ? 1 : 0);
hx00	hx2e	sle	RD = (RS1 $\leq$ RS2 ? 1 : 0);
hx00	hx2f	set	RD = (true ? 1 : 0);
Special Move Instructions			
hx00	hx10	movs2i	RD = SA
hx00	hx11	movi2s	SA = RS1

A.2.2 FPU Instruction Set

The DLX machine uses two formats (figure A.2) for the floating point
instructions; one corresponds to the I-type and the other to the R-type of
the fixed point core. The FI-format is used for loading data from memory

Table A.4 I-type instruction layout. All instructions except the control instructions also increment the PC by four; $sxt(a)$ is the sign-extended version of a. The effective address of memory accesses equals $ea = \langle GPR[RS1]\rangle + \langle sxt(imm)\rangle$, where imm is the 16-bit intermediate. The width of the memory access in bytes is indicated by d. Thus, the memory operand equals $m = M[ea + d - 1], \cdots, M[ea]$.

IR[31:26]	mnemonic	d	effect
Data Transfer			
hx20	lb	1	RD = sxt(m)
hx21	lh	2	RD = sxt(m)
hx23	lw	4	RD = m
hx24	lbu	1	RD = 0^{24}m
hx25	lhu	2	RD = 0^{16}m
hx28	sb	1	m = RD[7:0]
hx29	sh	2	m = RD[15:0]
hx2b	sw	4	m = RD
Arithmetic, Logical Operation			
hx08	addio		RD = RS1 + imm; ovf signaled
hx09	addi		RD = RS1 + imm; no ovf signaled
hx0a	subio		RD = RS1 - imm; ovf signaled
hx0b	subi		RD = RS1 - imm; no ovf signaled
hx0c	andi		RD = RS1 $\wedge$ sxt(imm)
hx0d	ori		RD = RS1 $\vee$ sxt(imm)
hx0e	xori		RD = RS1 $\oplus$ sxt(imm)
hx0f	lhgi		RD = imm 0^{16}
Test Set Operation			
hx18	clri		RD = (false ? 1 : 0);
hx19	sgri		RD = (RS1 > imm ? 1 : 0);
hx1a	seqi		RD = (RS1 = imm ? 1 : 0);
hx1b	sgei		RD = (RS1 $\geq$ imm ? 1 : 0);
hx1c	slsi		RD = (RS1 < imm ? 1 : 0);
hx1d	snei		RD = (RS1 $\neq$ imm ? 1 : 0);
hx1e	slei		RD = (RS1 $\leq$ imm ? 1 : 0);
hx1f	seti		RD = (true ? 1 : 0);
Control Operation			
hx04	beqz		PC = PC + 4 + (RS1 = 0 ? imm: 0)
hx05	bnez		PC = PC + 4 + (RS1 $\neq$ 0 ? imm: 0)
hx16	jr		PC = RS1
hx17	jalr		R31 = PC + 4; PC = RS1

Table A.5 Register map of the general purpose floating point registers

floating point general purpose registers	floating point registers	
single precision (32-bit)	double precision (64-bit)	
FPR31[31 : 0] FPR30[31 : 0]	FDR30[63 : 32] FDR30[31 : 0] $\Big\}$	FDR30[63 : 0]
$\vdots$	$\vdots$	
FPR3[31 : 0] FPR2[31 : 0]	FDR2[63 : 32] FDR2[31 : 0] $\Big\}$	FDR2[63 : 0]
FPR1[31 : 0] FPR0[31 : 0]	FDR0[63 : 32] FDR0[31 : 0] $\Big\}$	FDR0[63 : 0]

	6	5	5	16
FI-type	Opcode	Rx	FD	Immediate

	6	5	5	5	3	6
FR-type	Opcode	FS1	FS2 / Rx	FD	00 Fmt	Function

Figure A.2 Floating point instruction formats of the DLX. Depending on the precision, FS1, FS2 and FD specify 32-bit or 64-bit floating point registers. RS specifies a general purpose register of the FXU. Function is an additional 6-bit opcode. Fmt specifies a number format.

into the FPU respectively for storing data from the FPU into memory. This format is also used for conditional branches on the condition code flag FCC of the FPU. The coding of those instructions is given in table A.6.

The FR-format is used for the remaining FPU instructions (table A.8). It specifies a primary and a secondary opcode (Opcode, Function), a number format Fmt, and up to three floating point (general purpose) registers. For instructions which move data between the floating point unit FPU and the fixed point unit FXU, field FS2 specifies the address of a general purpose register RS in the FXU.

Since the FPU of the DLX machine can handle floating point numbers with single or double precision, all floating point operations come in two version; the field Fmt in the instruction word specifies the precision used. In the mnemonics, we identify the precision by adding the suffix '.s' (single) or '.d' (double).

Table A.6 FI-type instruction layout. All instructions except the branches also increment the PC, $PC \mathrel{+}= 4$; $sxt(a)$ is the sign extended version of a. The effective address of memory accesses equals $ea = RS + sxt(imm)$, where imm is the 16-bit offset. The width of the memory access in bytes is indicated by d. Thus, the memory operand equals $m = M[ea+d-1], \cdots, M[ea]$.

IR[31:26]	mnemonic	d	effect
Load, Store			
hx31	load.s	4	FD[31:0] = m
hx35	load.d	8	FD[63:0] = m
hx39	store.s	4	m = FD[31:0]
hx3d	store.d	8	m = FD[63:0]
Control Operation			
hx06	fbeqz		PC = PC + 4 + (FCC = 0 ? sxt(imm): 0)
hx07	fbnez		PC = PC + 4 + (FCC ≠ 0 ? sxt(imm): 0)

Table A.7 Floating-Point Relational Operators. The value 1 (0) denotes that the relation is true (false).

code	condition		relations				invalid if unordered
	mnemonic		greater	less	equal	unordered	
	true	false	>	<	=	?	
0	F	T	0	0	0	0	
1	UN	OR	0	0	0	1	
2	EQ	NEQ	0	0	1	0	
3	UEQ	OGL	0	0	1	1	no
4	OLT	UGE	0	1	0	0	
5	ULT	OGE	0	1	0	1	
6	OLE	UGT	0	1	1	0	
7	ULE	OGT	0	1	1	1	
8	SF	ST	0	0	0	0	
9	NGLE	GLE	0	0	0	1	
10	SEQ	SNE	0	0	1	0	
11	NGL	GL	0	0	1	1	yes
12	LT	NLT	0	1	0	0	
13	NGE	GE	0	1	0	1	
14	LE	NLE	0	1	1	0	
15	NGT	GT	0	1	1	1	

Table A.8 FR-type instruction layout. All instructions execute *PC += 4*. The format bits Fmt = IR[8:6] specify the number format used. Fmt = 000 denotes single precision and corresponds to the suffix '.s' in the mnemonics; Fmt = 001 denotes double precision and corresponds to the suffix '.d'. FCC denotes the 1-bit register for the floating point condition code. The functions sqrt(), abs() and rem() denote the square root, the absolute value and the remainder of a division according to the IEEE 754 standard. Instructions marked with * will not be implemented in our FPU design. The opcode bits $c[3:0]$ specify a relation "con" according to table A.7. Function cvt() converts the value of a register from one format into another. For that purpose, FMT = 100 (*i*) denotes fixed point format (integer) and corresponds to suffix '.i' .

IR[31:26]	IR[8:0]	Fmt	mnemonic	effect
Arithmetic and Compare Operations				
hx11	hx00		fadd [.s, .d]	FD = FS1 + FS2
hx11	hx01		fsub [.s, .d]	FD = FS1 - FS2
hx11	hx02		fmul [.s, .d]	FD = FS1 * FS2
hx11	hx03		fdiv [.s, .d]	FD = FS1 / FS2
hx11	hx04		fneg [.s, .d]	FD = - FS1
hx11	hx05		fabs [.s, .d]	FD = abs(FS1)
hx11	hx06		fsqt [.s, .d]*	FD = sqrt(FS1)
hx11	hx07		frem [.s, .d]*	FD = rem(FS1, FS2)
hx11	11$c[3:0]$		fc.con [.s, .d]	FCC = (FS1 *con* FS2)
Data Transfer				
hx11	hx08	000	fmov.s	FD[31:0] = FS1[31:0]
hx11	hx08	001	fmov.d	FD[63:0] = FS1[63:0]
hx11	hx09		mf2i	RS = FS1[31:0]
hx11	hx0a		mi2f	FD[31:0] = RS
Conversion				
hx11	hx20	001	cvt.s.d	FD = cvt(FS1, s, d)
hx11	hx20	100	cvt.s.i	FD = cvt(FS1, s, i)
hx11	hx21	000	cvt.d.s	FD = cvt(FS1, d, s)
hx11	hx21	100	cvt.d.i	FD = cvt(FS1, d, i)
hx11	hx24	000	cvt.i.s	FD = cvt(FS1, i, s)
hx11	hx24	001	cvt.i.d	FD = cvt(FS1, i, d)

Specification of the FDLX Design

FIGURES 9.16, 9.17 and 9.18 depict the FSD of the FDLX design. In section B.1, we specify for each state of the FSD the RTL instructions and their active control signals. In section B.2 we then specify the control automata of the FDLX design.

B.1 RTL Instructions of the FDLX

B.1.1 Stage IF

In stage IF, the FDLX design fetches the next instruction I into the instruction register (table B.1). This is done under the control of flag *fetch* and of clock request signal *IRce*. Both signals are always active.

B.1.2 Stage ID

The actions which the FDLX design performs during instruction decode depend on the instruction I held in register IR (table B.2). As for stage IF, the clock request signals are active in every clock cycle. The remaining control signals of stage ID are generated by a Mealy control automaton.

SPECIFICATION OF
THE FDLX DESIGN

Table B.1 RTL instructions of the stage IF

RTL instruction	control signals
$IR.1 = IM(DPC)$	fetch, IRce

Table B.2 RTL instructions of stage ID; farith.d denotes any arithmetical floating point instruction with double precision.

RTL instruction	type of I	control signals
$A = A' = RS1,\ AEQZ = zero(A'),$ $B = RS2,\ PC' = (reset\ ?\ 4 : pc'),$ $DPC = (reset\ ?\ 0 : dpc),$ $link = PC' + 4,\ DDPC = DPC,$ $IR.2 = IR.1,\ Sad.2 = Sad$		Ace, Bce, PC'ce, DPCce, PCce
$(FA, FB) = FPemb(fa, fb)$	farith.d, fc.d, cvt.d, load.d	dbs.1
	otherwise	
$co = constant(IR.1)$	j, jal, trap	Jimm
	slli, srli, srai	shiftI
	otherwise	
$(pc', dpc) =$ $nextPC(PC', A', co, EPCs)$	rfe	rfe.1
	jr, jalr	jumpR, jump
	beqz	branch, bzero
	bnez	branch
	fbeqz	fbranch, bzero
	fbnez	fbranch
	otherwise	
$Cad = CAddr(IR.1)$	jalr, jal	Jlink
	R-type	Rtype
	otherwise	
$(Sas, Sad, Fad) = DAddr(IR.1)$	rfe	rfe.1
	fc	fc.1, FRtype
	FR-type (no fc)	FRtype
	otherwise	
$CA.2[12] = 1$	fsqt, frem	uFOP

B.1.3   Stage EX

The execute stage has a non-uniform latency which varies between 1 and 21 cycles. The execute stage consists of the five substages 2.0, 2.1 to 2.4. For the iterative execution of divisions stage 2.0 itself consists of 17 substages 2.0.0 to 2.0.16. In the following, we describe the RTL instructions for each substage of the execute stage.

Update of the Buffers

In stage 2.0, the update of the buffers depends on the latency of the instruction I. Let

$$k = \begin{cases} 3 & \text{if} \quad I \text{ has latency of } l = 1 \\ 2.3 & \text{if} \quad I \text{ has latency of } l = 3 \\ 2.1 & \text{if} \quad I \text{ has latency of } l \geq 5, \end{cases}$$

stage 2.0 then updates the buffers as

$$
\begin{aligned}
(IR.k, Cad.k, Sad.k, Fad.k) &:= (IR.2, Cad.2, Sad.2, Fad.2) \\
(PC.k, DPC.k, DDPC.k) &:= (PC', DPC, DDPC).
\end{aligned}
$$

If I is a division, this update is postponed to stage 2.0.16.

For any stage $k \in \{2.1, \ldots, 2.4\}$, let k' be defined as

$$k' = \begin{cases} 3 & \text{if} \quad k = 2.4 \\ 2.(j+1) & \text{if} \quad k = 2.j < 2.4. \end{cases}$$

In stage k the buffers are then updated as

$$
\begin{aligned}
(IR.k', Cad.k', Sad.k', Fad.k') &:= (IR.k, Cad.k, Sad.k, Fad.k) \\
(PC.k', DPC.k', DDPC.k') &:= (PC.k, DPC.k, DDPC.k).
\end{aligned}
$$

Substage 2.0

Tables B.3 and B.4 list the RTL instructions for the fixed point instructions and for the floating point instructions with 1-cycle execute latency. From stage 2.0, these instructions directly proceed to stage 3.

The operand FB is only needed in case of a floating point test operation fc. By fcc and Fc we denote the results of the floating point condition test circuit FCON as defined in section 8.5

$$(fcc, Fc[68:0]) = FCon(FA, FB)$$

Tables B.5 and B.6 list the RTL instructions which stage 2.0 performs for instructions with an execute latency of more than one cycle.

Table B.3 RTL instructions of the execute stages for the fixed point instructions.

state	RTL instruction	control signals
alu	$MAR = A$ op B	ALUDdoe, Rtype, bmuxsel opA, opB, MARce, lat1
aluo	$MAR = A$ op B, *overflow?*	*like alu*, ovf?
aluI	$MAR = A$ op co	ALUDdoe, opA, MARce, lat1
aluIo	$MAR = A$ op co, *overflow?*	*like aluI*, ovf?
testI	$MAR = (A$ rel $co\,?\,1:0)$	ALUDdoe, test, opA, MARce, lat1
test	$MAR = (A$ rel $B\,?\,1:0)$	*like testI*, Rtype, bmuxsel, opB
shiftI	$MAR = \text{shift}(A, co[4:0])$	SHDdoe, shiftI, Rtype, opA, MARce, lat1
shift	$MAR = \text{shift}(A, B[4:0])$	*like shiftI*, bmuxsel, opB
savePC	$MAR = link$	linkDdoe, MARce, lat1
trap	$MAR = co, trap = 1$	coDdoe, trap, MARce, lat1
Ill	$MAR = A, ill = 1$	ADdoe, ill, opA, MARce, lat1
ms2i rfe	$MAR = S$	SDdoe, MARce, lat1
mi2s noEX	$MAR = A$	ADdoe, opA, MARce, lat1
addrL	$MAR = A + co$	ALUDdoe, add, opA, MARce, lat1
addrS	$MAR = A + co, F\,fl.3 = 0,$ $MDRw =$ $\text{cls}(B, MAR[1:0]000)$	ALUDdoe, add, amuxsel, opA, opB, store.2, MARce, MDRce, Ffl3ce, lat1, tfpRdoe

Substages 2.1 and 2.2

The execute substages 2.1 and 2.2 are only used by the arithmetic instructions fadd, fsub, fmul and fdiv. The RTL instructions for the divisions are listed in table B.6 and for the other three types of operations they are listed in table B.7.

Substages 2.3 and 2.4

In these two stages the FPU performs the rounding and packing of the result (table B.8). In order to keep the description simple, we introduce the following abbreviations: By FPrdR and FXrdR, we denote the output registers of the first stage of the rounders FPRD and FXRD, respectively. The two stages of the floating point rounder FPRD compute the

Table B.4 RTL instructions of the execute stages for floating point instructions with a single cycle latency.

state	RTL instruction	control signals
addrL.s addrL.d	$MAR = A + co$,	ALUDdoe, add, opA, MARce, lat1
addrSf	$MAR = A + co$, $MDRw = FB$, $Ffl.3 = 0$	ALUDdoe, add, opA, MARce, store.2, fstore.2, tfpRdoe, MDRwce, Ffl3ce, lat1, (amuxsel)
mf2i	$MAR = FA[31:0]$	opFA, tfxDdoe, MARce, lat1
mi2f	$MDRw = (B, B)$, $Ffl.3 = 0$	opB, tfpRdoe, MDRwce, Ffl3ce, lat1
fmov.s fmov.d	$MDRw = FA$, $Ffl.3 = 0$	opFA, fmov, tfpRdoe, MDRwce, Ffl3ce, lat1
fneg.s fneg.d	$MDRw = Fc[63:0]$, $Ffl.3 = Fc[68:64]$	opFA, FcRdoe, MDRwce, Ffl3ce, lat1
fabs.s fabs.d	$MDRw = Fc[63:0]$, $Ffl.3 = Fc[68:64]$	opFA, FcRdoe, MDRwce, abs Ffl3ce, lat1
fc.s, fc.d	$MAR = 0^{31} fcc$, $(Ffl.3, MDRw) = Fc$	opFA, opFB, ftest, fccDdoe, MARce FcRdoe, MDRwce, Ffl3ce, lat1

Table B.5 RTL instructions of the execute substage 2.0 for instructions with a latency of at least 3 cycles.

state	RTL instruction	control signals
fdiv.s	$(Fa2.1, Fb2.1, nan2.1)$	lat17, normal
fdiv.d	$= FPunp(FA, FB)$	lat21, normal, dbs
fmul.s		lat5, normal
fmul.d		lat5, normal, dbs
fadd.s		lat5
fadd.d		lat5, dbs
fsub.s		lat5, sub
fsub.d		lat5, sub, dbs
cvt.s.d	$Fr =$	lat3, FvFrdoe, Frce
cvt.s.i	$Cvt(FPunp(FA, FB))$	lat3, FvFrdoe, Frce, normal
cvt.d.s		lat3, FvFrdoe, Frce, dbs
cvt.d.i		lat3, FvFrdoe, Frce, dbs, normal
cvt.i.s	$Fr = FXunp(FA, FB)$	lat3, FuFrdoe, Frce
cvt.i.d		lat3, FuFrdoe, Frce

Table B.6 RTL instructions of the iterative division for stages 2.0.1 to 2.2 (single precision). In case of double precision (suffix '.d'), an additional control signal *dbr* is required in each state. A multiplication always takes two cycles. Since the intermediate result is always held in registers s and c, we only list the effect of the multiplication as a whole.

state	RTL instruction	control signals
lookup	$x = \text{table}(f_b)$	xce, tlu, fbbdoe
newton1.s	$A = \text{appr}(2 - x \cdot b, 57)$	xadoe, fbbdoe
newton2.s		Ace
newton3.s	$x = \lfloor A \cdot x \rfloor_{57}$	Aadoe, xbdoe, sce, cce
newton4.s		xce
quotient1.s	$E = \lfloor a \cdot x \rfloor_{p+1}$	faadoe, xbdoe, sce, cce
quotient2.s	$D_a = f_a,\ D_b = f_b$	Dce, faadoe, fbbdoe, Ece
quotient3.s	$E_b = E \cdot f_b$	Eadoe, fbbdoe, sce, cce
quotient4.s	$(s_q, e_q) = SigExpMD(Fa2.1, Fb2.1)$, $fl_q = SpecMD(Fa2.1, Fb2.1, nan2.1)$	sqce, eqce, ebce, flqce
select fd.s	$E' = E + 2^{-(p+1)}$, $\beta = f_a - E_b - 2^{-(p+1)} \cdot f_b$ $f_d = \begin{cases} E + 2^{-(p+2)} & ; \text{if } \beta < 0 \\ E' & ; \text{if } \beta = 0 \\ E' + 2^{-(p+2)} & ; \text{if } \beta > 0 \end{cases}$ $Fr = (fl_q, s_q, e_q, f_d)$	fdiv, FqFrdoe, Frce

functions $FPrd1()$ and $FPrd2()$ as specified in section 8.4. The the fixed point rounder FXRD (page 427) also consists of two stages. They compute the functions denoted by $FXrd1()$ and $FXrd2()$.

B.1.4 Stage M

Table B.9 lists the RTL instructions which the FDLX design performs in stage M. In addition, stage M updates the buffers as follows:

$$(IR.4, Cad.4, Sad.4, Fad.4) := (IR.3, Cad.3, Sad.3, Fad.3)$$
$$(PC.4, DPC.4, DDPC.4) := (PC.3, DPC.3, DDPC.3)$$

Table B.7 RTL instructions of the substages 2.1 and 2.2, except for the divisions.

state	RTL instruction	control signals
Mul1.s Mul1.d	$(sq, eq) = SigExpMD(Fa2.1, Fb2.1)$, $flq = SpecMD(Fa2.1, Fb2.1, nan2.1)$, $(s, c) = mul1(Fa2.1, Fb2.1)$	sqce, eqce, flqce, sce, cce, faadoe, fbbdoe
Add1.s Add1.d	$ASr = AS1(Fa2.1, Fb2.1, nan2.1)$	ASrce
Sub1.s Sub1.d	$ASr = AS1(Fa2.1, Fb2.1, nan2.1)$	ASrce, sub
Mul2.s Mul2.d	$fq = mul2(s, c)$, $Fr = (flq, sq, eq, fq)$	FqFrdoe, Frce
SigAdd.s SigAdd.d	$Fr = AS2(ASr)$	FsFrdoe, Frce

Table B.8 RTL instructions of the substages 2.3 and 2.4

state	RTL instruction	control signals
rd1.s	$FPrdR = FPrd1(Fr)$	FPrdRce
rd1.d		FPrdRce, dbr
rd1.i	$FXrdR = FXrd1(Fr)$	FXrdRce
rd2.s	$(Ffl.3, MDRw) = FRrd2(FPrdR)$	FpRdoe, MDRwce, Ffl3ce
rd2.d		*like rd2.s*, dbr
rd2.i	$(Ffl.3, MDRw) = FXrd2(FXrdR)$	FxRdoe, MDRwce, Ffl3ce

Table B.9 RTL instructions of the memory stage M.

state	RTL instruction	control signals
load, load.s load.d	$MDRr = DMdword[\langle MAR[31:3]000\rangle]$ $C.4 = MAR$	Dmr, DMRrce C4ce
store	$m = bytes(MDRw), C.4 = MAR$	Dmw, C4ce
ms2iM, noM, mi2iM, passC	$C.4 = MAR$	C4ce
Marith.[s, d], Mmv.[s, d]	$FC.4 = MDRw$ $Ffl.4 = Ffl.3$	FC4ce, Ffl4ce
fcM	$FC.4 = MDRw, C.4 = MAR$ $Ffl.4 = Ffl.3$	FC4ce, C4ce, Ffl4ce

Table B.10 RTL instructions of the write back stage WB

state	RTL instruction	control signals
sh4l	$GPR[Cad.4] =$ $sh4l(MDs, MAR[1:0]000)$	GPRw, load.4
sh4l.s	$FPR[Fad.4] = MDs$	FPRw, load.4
sh4l.d	$FDR[Fad.4] = MDRr$	FPRw, load.4, dbr.4
wb	$GPR[Cad.4] = C.4$	GPRw
mi2sW	$SPR[Sad.4] = C.4$	SPRw
fcWB	like mi2sW, $IEEEf = IEEEf \vee Ffl.4$	SPRw, fop.4
WBs	$FPR(Fad.4) = FC'[31:0]$	FPRw
flagWBs	like WBs, $IEEEf = IEEEf \vee Ffl.4$	FPRw, fop.4
WBd	$FDR(Fad.4) = FC'$	FPRw, dbr.4
flagWBd	like WBd, $IEEEf = IEEEf \vee Ffl.4$	FPRw, fop.4
noWB	(no update)	

B.1.5 Stage WB

Table B.10 lists the RTL instructions which the FDLX design processes in stage WB, given that no unmasked interrupt occurred. In case of a JISR, the FDLX design performs the same actions as the the DLX_Π design (chapter 5).

B.2 Control Automata of the FDLX Design

THE CONTROL automaton is constructed as in the fixed point DLX designs. The control is modeled by an FSD which is then turned into precomputed control.

- The control signals of stage IF are always active.

- The control signals of stage ID are generated in every cycle, they only depend on the current instruction word.

- The control signals of the remaining stages are precomputed during ID by a Moore automaton.

Table B.11 Disjunctive normal forms of the Mealy automaton of stage ID

signal	IR[31 : 26]	IR[5 : 0]	Fmt	length	comment
Rtype	000000	******	***	6	
shiftI	000000	0000*0	***	11	
	000000	00001*	***	11	
Jlink	010111	******	***	6	
	000011	******	***	6	
jumpR	01011*	******	***	5	
jump	00001*	******	***	5	
	01011*	******	***	5	
rfe.1	111111	******	***	6	
Jimm	00001*	******	***	5	
	111110	******	***	6	
branch	00010*	******	***	5	
bzero	*****0	******	***	1	
fbranch	00011*	******	***	5	
fc	010001	11****	***	8	
FRtype	010001	11****	001	11	fc.d
	010001	000***	001	12	farith.d
	010001	001000	001	15	fmov.d
	010001	100001	***	12	cvt.d
	111101	******	***	6	store.d
uFOP	010001	00011*	***	11	fsqt, frem
accumulated length of the monomials				147	

B.2.1 Automaton Controlling Stage ID

According to table B.2, the clock request signals of stage ID are independent of the instruction. Like in stage IF, they are always active. Thus, the control automaton of stage ID only needs to generate the remaining 13 control signals. Since they depend on the current instruction word, a Mealy automaton is used.

Table B.11 lists the disjunctive normal form for each of these signals. The parameters of the ID control automaton are listed in table B.16 on page 539.

Table B.12 Type $x.0$ control signals to be precomputed during stage ID (part 1)

signals	states of stage 2.0
lat1	alu, aluo, aluI, aluIo, test, testI, shift, shiftI, savePC, trap, mi2s, noEX, ill, ms2i, rfe, addrL, addrS, addrL.s, addrL.d, addrSf, mf2i, mi2f, fmov.s, fmov.d, fneg.s, fneg.d, fabs.s, fabs.d, fc.s, fc.d
lat3	cvt.s.d, cvt.s.i, cvt.d.s, cvt.d.i, cvt.i.s, cvt.i.d
lat5	fmul.s, fmul.d, fadd.s, fadd.d, fsub.s, fsub.d
lat17	fdiv.s
lat21	fdiv.d
opA	alu, aluo, aluI, aluIo, test, testI, shift, shiftI, mi2s, noEX, ill, addrL, addrS, addrL.s, addrL.d, addrSf
opB	alu, aluo, test, shift, addrS, mi2f
opFA	fmov.s, fmov.d, fneg.s, fneg.d, fabs.s, fabs.d, fc.s, fc.d, cvt.s.d, cvt.s.i, cvt.d.s, cvt.d.i, cvt.i.s, cvt.i.d, fmul.s, fmul.d, fadd.s, fadd.d, fsub.s, fsub.d, fdiv.s, fdiv.d
opFB	addrSf, fc.s, fc.d, fmul.s, fmul.d, fadd.s, fadd.d, fsub.s, fsub.d, fdiv.s, fdiv.d

B.2.2 Precomputed Control

As in the previous designs, only state decode has an outdegree greater than one. Thus, the control signals of all the stages that follow can be precomputed during decode using a Moore control automaton. The signals are then buffered in an RSR; the RSR passes the signals down the pipeline together with the instruction. Each stage consumes some of these control signals. Therefore, the signals are classified according to the last stage in which they are used. A signal of type $x.3$, for example, is only used up to stage 2.3, whereas a signal of type z is needed up to stage 4.

The tables B.12 to B.14 list for each control signal the states of stage 2.0 in which the signal must be active. There are some signals which are always activated together, e.g., the signals *Dmw*, *amuxsel* and *store*. The automaton only needs to generate one signal for each such group of signals. According to table B.15, the majority of the precomputed control signals is of type $x.0$.

In circuit SIGFMD of the multiply divide unit, there is a total of six tristate drivers connected to the operand busses *opa* and *opb*. The access

Table B.13 Type $x.0$ control signals to be precomputed during stage ID (part 2)

signals	states of stage 2.0
ALUDdoe	alu, aluo, aluI, aluIo, test, testI, addrL, addrS, addrL.s, addrL.d, addrSf
ADdoe	mi2s, noEX, ill
SDdoe	ms2i, rfe
SHDdoe	shift, shiftI
linkDdoe	savePC
coDdoe, trap	trap
ftest, fccDdoe	fc.s, c.d
tfxDdoe	mf2i
FcRdoe	fabs.s, fabs.d, fneg.s, fneg.d, fc.s, fc.d
FuFrdoe	cvt.s.i, cvt.s.d, cvt.d.s, cvt.s.i
FvFrdoe	cvt.i.s, cvt.i.d
test	test, testI
ovf?	aluo, aluIo
add	addrL, addrS, addrL.s, addrL.d, addrSf
bmuxsel	alu, aluo, test, shift
Rtype	alu, aluo, test, shift, shiftI
Ill	ill
fstore	addrSf
fmov	fmov.s, fmov.d
abs	fabs.s, fabs.d
normal	fmul.s, fmul.d, fdiv.s, fdiv.d, cvt.s.i, cvt.d.i
dbs	fmov.d, fneg.d, fabs.d, fc.d, cvt.d.s, cvt.d.i, fmul.d, fadd.d, fsub.d, fdiv.d

to these busses is granted by the control signals

$$opaoe[3:0] \ = \ (faadoe, Eadoe, Aadoe, xadoe)$$
$$opboe[1:0] \ = \ (fbbdoe, xbdoe).$$

Although multiplications only use two of these tristate drivers, the precomputed control provides six enable signals

$$faadoe = fbbdoe \ = \ \begin{cases} 1 & \text{if } I \in \{ \text{fmul.s, fmul.d} \} \\ 0 & \text{otherwise} \end{cases}$$
$$Eadoe = Aadoe \ = \ xadoe = xbdoe = 0.$$

Table B.14 Control signals of type $x.1$ to z to be precomputed during stage ID

	signals	states of stage 2.0
x.1	sub	fsub.s, fsub.d
	faadoe, fbbdoe	fmul.s, fmul.d
x.2	fdiv	fdiv.s, fdiv.d
	FqFrdoe	fmul.s, fmul.d, fdiv.s, fdiv.d
	FsFrdoe	fadd.s, fadd.d, fsub.s, fsub.d
x.4	Ffl3ce, MDRwce	addrS, addrSf, mi2f, fmov.s, fmov.d, fneg.s, fneg.d, fabs.s, fabs.d, fc.s, fc.d, cvt.s.d, cvt.s.i, cvt.d.s, cvt.d.i, cvt.i.s, cvt.i.d, fmul.s, fmul.d, fadd.s, fadd.d, fsub.s, fsub.d, fdiv.s, fdiv.d
	FpRdoe	cvt.d.s, cvt.i.s, cvt.s.d, cvt.i.d, fadd.s, fadd.d, fsub.s, fsub.d, fmul.s, fmul.d, fdiv.s, fdiv.d
	FxRdoe	cvt.s.i, cvt.d.i
y	amuxsel, Dmw, store	addrS, addrSf
	MARce, C4ce	alu, aluo, aluI, aluIo, test, testI, shift, shiftI, savePC, trap, mi2s, noEX, ill, ms2i, rfe, addrL, addrS, addrL.s, addrL.d, addrSf, mf2i
	FC4ce, Ffl4ce	mi2f, fmov.s, fmov.d, fneg.s, fneg.d, fabs.s, fabs.d, fc.s, fc.d, cvt.s.d, cvt.s.i, cvt.d.s, cvt.d.i, cvt.i.s, cvt.i.d, fmul.s, fmul.d, fadd.s, fadd.d, fsub.s, fsub.d, fdiv.s, fdiv.d
z	DMRrce, Dmr, load	addrL, addrL.s, addrL.d
	fop	fc.s, fc.d, cvt.s.d, cvt.s.i, cvt.d.s, cvt.d.i, cvt.i.s, cvt.i.d, fmul.s, fmul.d, fadd.s, fadd.d, fsub.s, fsub.d, fdiv.s, fdiv.d
	dbr	fmov.d, fneg.d, fabs.d, cvt.s.d, cvt.i.d, fmul.d, fadd.d, fsub.d, fdiv.d
	SPRw	mi2s, rfe, fc.s, fc.d
	GPRw	alu, aluo, aluI, aluIo, test, testI, shift, shiftI, savePC, ms2i, addrL, addrL.s, addrL.d, mf2i
	FPRw	addrL.s, addrL.d, mi2f, fmov.s, fmov.d, fneg.s, fneg.d, fabs.s, fabs.d, cvt.s.d, cvt.s.i, cvt.d.s, cvt.d.i, cvt.i.s, cvt.i.d, fmul.s, fmul.d, fadd.s, fadd.d, fsub.s, fsub.d, fdiv.s, fdiv.d

Table B.15 Types of the precomputed control signals

type	x.0	x.1	x.2	x.3	x.4	y	z
number	31	7	3	0	3	3	6

Table B.16 Parameters of the two control automata which govern the $FDLX_\Pi$ design. Automaton *id* generates the Mealy signals for stage ID; automaton *ex* precomputes the Moore signals of the stages EX to WB.

	# states	# inputs	# and frequency of outputs		
	k	σ	γ	v_{sum}	v_{max}
id	1	15	13	21	5
ex	44	15	48	342	30

	fanin of the states		# and length of monomials		
	fan_{sum}	fan_{max}	#M	l_{sum}	l_{max}
id	–	–	21	147	15
ex	53	3	53	374	15

Except on divisions, the busses *opa* and *opb* are only used in stage 2.1. Thus, together with signal *sub* (floating point subtraction), the FDLX design requires 7 type *x*.1 control signals.

Tables B.17 and B.18 lists the disjunctive normal forms for the automaton which controls the stages EX to WB. The parameters of this Moore automaton are summarized in table B.16.

SPECIFICATION OF
THE FDLX DESIGN

Table B.17 Disjunctive normal forms of the precomputed control which governs stages EX to WB (part 1)

state	IR[31 : 26]	IR[5 : 0]	Fmt	length
alu	000000	1001**	***	10
	000000	100**1	***	10
aluo	000000	1000*0	***	11
aluI	0011**	******	***	4
	001**1	******	***	4
aluIo	0010*0	******	***	5
shift	000000	0001*0	***	11
	000000	00011*	***	11
shiftI	000000	0000*0	***	11
	000000	00001*	***	11
test	000000	101***	***	9
testI	011***	******	***	3
savePC	010111	******	***	6
	000011	******	***	6
addrS	10100*	******	***	5
	1010*1	******	***	5
addrL	100*0*	******	***	4
	1000*1	******	***	5
	10000*	******	***	5
mi2s	000000	010001	***	12
ms2i	000000	010000	***	12
trap	111110	******	***	6
rfe	111111	******	***	6
noEX	0001**	******	***	4
	000010	******	***	6
	010110	******	***	6
accumulated length of the monomials				178

Table B.18 Disjunctive normal forms used by the precomputed control (part 2)

state	IR[31 : 26]	IR[5 : 0]	Fmt	length
addrL.s	110001	******	***	6
addrL.d	110101	******	***	6
addrSf	111*01	******	***	5
fc.s	010001	11****	000	11
fc.d	010001	11****	001	11
mf2i	010001	001001	***	12
mi2f	010001	001010	***	12
fmov.s	010001	001000	000	15
fmov.d	010001	001000	001	15
fadd.s	010001	000000	000	15
fadd.d	010001	000000	001	15
fsub.s	010001	000001	000	15
fsub.d	010001	000001	001	15
fmul.s	010001	000010	000	15
fmul.d	010001	000010	001	15
fdiv.s	010001	000011	000	15
fdiv.d	010001	000011	001	15
fneg.s	010001	000100	000	15
fneg.d	010001	000100	001	15
fabs.s	010001	000101	000	15
fabs.d	010001	000101	001	15
cvt.s.d	010001	010000	001	15
cvt.s.i	010001	010000	100	15
cvt.d.s	010001	010001	000	15
cvt.d.i	010001	010001	100	15
cvt.i.s	010001	010100	000	15
cvt.i.d	010001	010100	001	15
accumulated length of the monomials				196

Bibliography

[AA93]   D. Alpert and D. Avnon. Architecture of the Pentium microarchitecture. *IEEE Micro*, 13(3):11–21, 1993.

[AEGP67]   S.F. Anderson, J.G. Earle, R.E. Goldschmitt, and D.M. Powers. The IBM system 360 model 91: Floating-point unit. *IBM Journal of Research and Developement*, 11:34–53, January 1967.

[AT97]   H. Al-Twaijry. *Area and Performance Optimized CMOS Multipliers*. PhD thesis, Stanford University, August 1997.

[BD94]   J.R. Burch and D.L. Dill. Automatic verification of pipelined microprocessor control. In *Proc. International Conference on Computer Aided Verification*, 1994.

[BM96]   E. Börger and S. Mazzanti. A practical method for rigorously controllable hardware design. In J.P. Bowen, Hinchey M.B., and D. Till, editors, *ZUM'97: The Z Formal Specification Notation*, volume 1212 of *LNCS*, pages 151–187. Springer, 1996.

[BS90]   M. Bickford and M. Srivas. Verification of a pipelined microprocessor using Clio. In M. Leeser and G. Brown, editors, *Proc. Mathematical Sciences Institute Workshop on Hardware Specification, Verification and Synthesis: Mathematical Aspects*, volume 408 of *LNCS*, pages 307–332. Springer, 1990.

[CO76]   W. Chu and H. Opderbeck. Program behaviour and the page-fault-frequency replacement algorithm. *Computer*, 9, 1976.

[CRSS94]   D. Cyrluk, S. Rajan, N. Shankar, and M. K. Srivas. Effective theorem proving for hardware verification. In *2nd International Conference on Theorem Provers in Circuit Design*, 1994.

Bibliography

[Del97] P. Dell. Run time simulation of a DLX processor with stall engine. Laboratory Project, University of Saarland, Computer Science Department, Germany, 1997.

[Den68] P.J. Denning. The working set model for program behavior. *Communications of the ACM*, 11(5):323–333, 1968.

[Den80] P.J. Denning. Working sets past and present. *IEEE Transactions on Software Engineering*, 6(1):64–84, 1980.

[EP97] G. Even and W.J. Paul. On the design of IEEE compliant floating point units. In *Proc. 13th IEEE Symposium on Computer Arithmetic*, pages 54–63. IEEE Computer Society, 1997.

[ERP95] J.H. Edmondson, P. Rubinfeld, and R. Preston. Superscalar instruction execution in the 21164 Alpha microprocessor. *IEEE Micro*, 15(2):33–43, 1995.

[FS89] D.L. Fowler and J.E. Smith. An accurate, high speed implementation of division by reciprocal approximation. In *Proc. 9th Symposium on Computer Arithmetic*, pages 60–67, 1989.

[GHPS93] J.D. Gee, M.D. Hill, D.N Pnevmatikatos, and A.J. Smith. Cache performance of the SPEC92 benchmark suite. *MICRO*, 13(4):17–27, 1993.

[Han93] J. Handy. *The Cache Memory Book*. Academic Press, Inc., 1993.

[Hew94] Hewlett Packard. *PA-RISC 1.1 Architecture Reference Manual*, 1994.

[Hil87] M.D. Hill. *Aspects of Cache Memory and Instruction Buffer Performance*. PhD thesis, Computer Science Devision (EECS), UC Berkeley, CA 94720, 1987.

[Hil95] M. Hill. *SPEC92 Traces for MIPS R2000/3000*. University of Wisconsin, ftp://ftp.cs.newcastle.edu.au/pub/r3000-traces/din, 1995.

[HP90] J.L. Hennessy and D.A. Patterson. *Computer Architecture: A Quantitative Approach*. Morgan Kaufmann Publishers, INC., San Mateo, CA, 1990.

[HP96] J.L. Hennessy and D.A. Patterson. *Computer Architecture: A Quantitative Approach*. Morgan Kaufmann Publishers, INC., San Mateo, CA, 2nd edition, 1996.

[HQR98] T.A. Henzinger, S. Qadeer, and S.K. Rajamani. You assume, we guarantee: Methodology and case studies. In *Proc. 10th International Conference on Computer-aided Verification (CAV)*, 1998.

[Ins85] Institute of Electrical and Electronics Engineers. *ANSI/IEEE standard 754–1985, IEEE Standard for Binary Floating-Point Arithmetic*, 1985. for a readable account see the article by W.J. Cody et al. in the IEEE MICRO Journal, Aug. 1984, 84–100.

[Int95] Intel Corporation. *Pentium Processor Family Developer's Manual, Vol. 1-3*, 1995.

[Int96]   Integrated Device Technology, Inc. *IDT71B74: BiCMOS Static RAM 64K (8K x 8-Bit) Cache-Tag RAM, Data Sheet*, August 1996.

[KH92]   G. Kane and J. Heinrich. *MIPS RISC Architecture*. Prentice Hall, 1992.

[KMP99a]   D. Kroening, S.M. Mueller, and W.J. Paul. Proving the correctness of processors with delayed branch using delayed PC. In *Numbers, Information and Complexity*. Kluwer, 1999.

[KMP99b]   D. Kroening, S.M. Mueller, and W.J. Paul. A rigorous correctness proof of the tomasulo scheduling algorithm with precise interrupts. In *Proc. SCI'99/ISAS'99 International Conference*, 1999.

[Knu96]   R. Knuth. *Quantitative Analysis of Pipelined DLX Architectures (in German)*. PhD thesis, University of Saarland, Computer Science Department, Germany, 1996.

[Kor93]   I. Koren. *Computer Arithmetic Algorithms*. Prentice-Hall International, 1993.

[KP95]   J. Keller and W.J. Paul. *Hardware Design*, volume 15 of *Teubner-Texte zur Informatik*. Teubner, 1995.

[KPM00]   Daniel Kroening, Wolfgang J. Paul, and Silvia M. Mueller. Proving the correctness of pipelined micro-architectures. In *ITG/GI/GMM-Workshop Methoden und Beschreibungssprachen zur Modellierung und Verifikation von Schaltungen und Systemen, to appear*, 2000.

[Kro97]   D. Kroening. Cache simulation for a 32-bit DLX processor on a SPEC workload. Laboratory Project, University of Saarland, Computer Science Department, Germany, 1997.

[Lei99]   H. Leister. *Quantitative Analysis of Precise Interrupt Mechnisms for Processors with Out-Of-Order Execution*. PhD thesis, University of Saarland, Computer Science Department, Germany, 1999.

[LMW86]   J. Loeckx, K. Mehlhorn, and R. Wilhelm. *Grundlagen der Programmiersprachen*. Teubner Verlag, 1986.

[LO96]   J. Levitt and K. Olukotun. A scalable formal verification methodology for pipelined microprocessors. In *33rd Design Automation Conference (DAC'96)*, pages 558–563. Association for Computing Machinery, 1996.

[MP95]   S.M. Mueller and W.J. Paul. *The Complexity of Simple Computer Architectures*. Lecture Notes in Computer Science 995. Springer, 1995.

[MP96]   S.M. Mueller and W.J. Paul. Making the original scoreboard mechanism deadlock free. In *Proc. 4th Israel Symposium on Theory of Computing and Systems (ISTCS)*, pages 92–99. IEEE Computer Society, 1996.

[Ng92]   R. Ng. Fast computer memories. *IEEE Spectrum*, pages 36–39, Oct 1992.

Bibliography

[Omo94] A.R. Omondi. *Computer Arithmetic Systems; Algorithms, Architecture and Implementations.* Series in Computer Science. Prentice-Hall International, 1994.

[PH94] D.A. Patterson and J.L. Hennessy. *The Hardware/Software Interface.* Morgan Kaufmann Publishers, INC., San Mateo, CA, 1994.

[Prz90] S.A. Przbylski. *Cache and Memory Hierarchy Design.* Morgan Kaufman Publishers, Inc., 1990.

[PS98] W.J. Paul and P.-M. Seidel. On the complexity of Booth recoding. In *Proc. 3rd Conference on Real Numbers and Computers (RNC3)*, pages 199–218, 1998.

[Rus] D. Russinoff. A mechanically checked proof of IEEE compliance of a register-transfer-level specification of the AMD K7 floating-point division and square root instructions. Available at http://www.onr.com/user/russ/david/k7-div-sqrt.html.

[Sei00] P.-M. Seidel. *The Design of IEEE Compliant Floating-point Units and their Quantitative Analysis.* PhD thesis, University of Saarland, Computer Science Department, Germany, 2000.

[SGGH91] J.B. Saxe, S.J. Garland, J.V. Guttag, and J.J. Horning. Using transformations and verification in circuit design. Technical report, Digital Systems Research Center, 1991.

[SP88] J.E. Smith and A.R. Pleszkun. Implementing precise interrupts in pipelined processors. *IEEE Transactions on Computers*, 37(5):562–573, 1988.

[Spa76] 0. Spaniol. *Arithmetik in Rechenanlagen.* Teubner, 1976.

[Spa91] U. Sparmann. *Structure Based Test Methods for Arithmetic Circuits (in German).* PhD thesis, University of Saarland, Computer Science Department, 1991.

[SPA92] SPARC International Inc. *The SPARC Architecture Manual.* Prentice Hall, 1992.

[Sta] Standard Performance Evaluation Corporation. SPEC Benchmark Suite. http://www.specbench.org/.

[Sun92] Sun Microsystems Computer Corporation, Mountain View, CA. *The SuperSPARC Microprocessor: Technical White Paper*, 1992.

[Tho70] J.E. Thornton. *Design of a Computer: The Control Data 6600.* Scott Foresman, Glenview, Ill, 1970.

[Tom67] R.M. Tomasulo. An efficient algorithm for exploiting multiple arithmetic units. In *IBM Journal of Research and Developement*, volume 11 (1), pages 25–33. IBM, 1967.

[Weg87] I. Wegener. *The Complexity of Boolean Functions.* John Wiley & Sons, 1987.

[WF82] S. Waser and M.J. Flynn. *Introduction to Arithmetic for Digital Systems Designers*. CBS College Publishing, 1982.

[Win93] G. Winskel. *The Formal Semantics of Programming Languages; An Introduction*. Foundations of Computing Series. MIT Press, 1993.

[Win95] P.J. Windley. Formal modeling and verification of microprocessors. *IEEE Transactions on Computers*, 44(1):54–72, 1995.

[WS94] S. Weiss and J.E. Smith. *Power and PowerPC*. Morgan Kaufmann Publishers, Inc., 1994.

Index

Index